The Delos Symposia
and Doxiadis

Edited by Mantha Zarmakoupi
and Simon Richards

The Delos Symposia and Doxiadis

Evangelos Pistiolis Foundation
Lars Müller Publishers

6   Preface
9   Introduction
    Simon Richards and Mantha Zarmakoupi

Section I
40 Foundations and Ideals

43 **History as a Framework**
    Mantha Zarmakoupi

73 **The Past as a Stage Set for C. A. Doxiadis**
    Dimitris Philippides

89 **Some Rhetorical Aspects of the Delos Symposia**
    Kostas Tsiambaos

114 **East–West: The Delos Dialogue with Japanese Urbanism**
    Ellen Shoshkes

142 **Delos and "The Human Factor"**
    Simon Richards

Section II
166 Practices and Implementations

169 **Ecology, Ekistics and the "Texture of Settlements"**
    Ioanna Theocharopoulou

191 **Infrastructuring Development**
    Filippo De Dominicis

217 **Basic Democracy and Doxiadis Associates' School-Reformation Project in East Pakistan**
    Farhan Karim

249 **Shaping Ekistics**
    Lefteris Theodosis

285 **The Visionary in the Marsh**
    Harrison Blackman

Section III
Futures and Legacies

310

313 **Metacriticisms of Ekistics' Environmental Design**
Panayiota Pyla

337 **Urban Ecosystems and Global Ecological Balance**
Ahmed Z. Khan

383 **Bio-systemic Thinking for Holistic Design**
Yannis Zavoleas

407 **Japanese Delos in 27 Points**
Tilemachos Andrianopoulos

439 **Doxiadis Associates' Master Plan for Skopje and the Global Ecological Balance**
Thomas Doxiadis

465 **Afterword**
The Three Antiquities of C. A. Doxiadis and the Road to Eutopia
Panayotis Tournikiotis

482 **Acknowledgments**

485 **Appendix**
486 About the Authors
489 Bibliography
494 Image Credits
498 Index

Preface

This book maps out the intellectual agenda of the Delos Symposia in relation to the dominant political and intellectual "geographies" of the 1960s–1970s, tracing the ways in which urban-design solutions were sought in vernacular and ancient cultures. It explores how the conceptual underpinnings of the Delos Symposia were channeled into practical planning tools and subsequently applied in urban projects, as exemplified by Doxiadis Associates' worldwide planning-and-consultancy business in the 1960s and 1970s. Finally, the book appraises the potential value and legacy of the Delos Symposia for contemporary discussions on sustainable and resilient urban planning. In doing so, it addresses the ways in which the preoccupations, themes and environmental solutions explored at the Delos Symposia relate to current discourses and practices on sustainable urban design and landscape urbanism.

As an avid student of history, I am interested in supporting innovative conversations that shed light on the multivalent character of our historical past. Even though the Delos Symposia featured the leading scholars and practitioners of the times, were widely reported and feted in the international mass media, and led to planning and infrastructural projects of international significance, they are not well known and certainly not well researched today. This book corrects that oversight by bringing together scholars who are currently looking into this fascinating period of intellectual history.

Constantinos A. Doxiadis's choice of Delos for the meeting place of the Symposia was not accidental. During the nascent stages of the Roman Empire, Delos became an important trading point between Rome and the Hellenistic East. Despite its importance for geopolitical developments in the Mediterranean, there is a tendency to overlook this aspect of its history and focus on the classical and early Hellenistic phases of the sanctuary of Apollo on the island. In developing the Ancient Greek Cities Project, Doxiadis was aware of the lasting influence that the Roman Empire had on urban culture throughout its territory and in Greece, and he chose Delos – this nodal point in the Aegean – to host these international discussions.

The Evangelos Pistiolis Foundation supports research that clarifies the enduring impact that imperial Rome had on urban culture across the empire and in Greece, where this influence has been long overlooked – as it has been in the case of Delos. I have developed a cultural and charitable institution dedicated to the study, investigation and promotion of the legacy of the Roman Empire through archaeological research and the financing of archaeological excavations and educational seminars, scholarships and sponsorships in Greece, Switzerland and further afield. The initiatives of the Foundation support individuals who further our understanding of Roman economic, technological and architectural innovations and the ways in which these innovations have resonated in contemporary practices and thinking. The Foundation aims to shed light on the pioneering ideas behind the organization, management and sustainability of imperial Rome and its provinces, as well as on architectural design innovations, construction quality and speed, and city planning and design in the Roman Empire. The establishment of the Foundation was spurred by my passion for Roman history with a focus on the Think Big Revolution of the Roman Empire vis-à-vis economic, technological and architectural innovations. Like Doxiadis, I am a practitioner with a strong interest in studying the past and utilizing what we can learn from it in planning for the future. This book therefore bridges my passion for Roman urban culture and sustainability and the need to think afresh about our cities today.

Evangelos Pistiolis
Evangelos Pistiolis Foundation

Introduction

Simon Richards and Mantha Zarmakoupi

This book represents the first comprehensive analysis, mapping and appraisal of the history and legacy of the Delos Symposia, which constituted a highly ambitious but relatively little-known project that attempted to raise ecological concerns in twentieth-century architecture and planning discourses and relate the study of ancient Greek and Roman cities to such discourses. Representing arguably the first attempt to frame a joined-up approach to dealing with planetary urbanism, population growth and environmental destruction, the Delos Symposia exerted global significance – and generated media fascination – during their time, and they also hold some compelling lessons for the present day. Running from 1963 to 1975, the Symposia were a wide-ranging, interdisciplinary series of events that were initiated and choreographed by the Greek architect–planner Constantinos A. Doxiadis along with his colleague, the South African-born urban planner Jaqueline Tyrwhitt, and took place at the archaeological site of Delos [Fig. 1].[1] The Delos Symposia were aligned with numerous truly colossal urban-planning projects that Doxiadis was rolling out across the developed and developing world, and were informed by his systematic study of "Ancient Greek Cities," the title of a research project led by Doxiadis that produced twenty-four volumes "in order to prove the ways in which the ancient city can provide information for the city of the present."[2] But who were Doxiadis and Tyrwhitt, and how did they come together over the Symposia?

Doxiadis had been the chief town planner of Greater Athens prior to Greece's entry into World War II in 1940 and he continued to have a prominent role in the reconstruction of Greece after 1945, holding several ministerial positions. His international reputation grew after he left government to establish his private firm, Doxiadis Associates (DA), in 1953, and over the next quarter century their design and consultancy work spread to cover dozens of countries, administered from their state-of-the-art headquarters in Athens – one of the first architectural and urban-design studios in the world to integrate computing as the cornerstone of their operations.[3] But, as well as running his private firm, from 1958 onwards he had also been running two non-profit privately sponsored research and educational institutions for technology and science: the Athens Technological Organization (ATO) and the Athens Technological Institute (ATI). These served for the development and dissemination of Ekistics, a term first coined by Doxiadis in the 1940s to refer to his new syncretic "science" of human settlements and planning. In addition, 1963 saw Doxiadis founding the Athens Center of Ekistics (ACE) as an offshoot of ATI, in order to "serve as the principal setting for education and exchange of ideas in all aspects of theory and practice related to human settlements and ekistic development."[4] Predictably he was much in demand in these years as an adviser to governments, the United Nations (UN) and the World Health Organization (WHO) on matters of planning and infrastructural development in the developing world, and it was in this connection that he met Jaqueline Tyrwhitt. They had much in common, not least their professional experiences during World War II.[5]

During this time, Tyrwhitt had worked both as Director of Research and Director of Studies at the School of Planning and Research for Regional Development (SPRRD), which had been established as an adjunct of the Architectural Association (AA) in London in 1935 to provide evening courses in town planning. By 1941, she had set up the Association for Planning and Regional Reconstruction (APRR), a research group that specialized in gathering statistics and drafting plans for post-war reconstruction, and during the later war years she designed and delivered a well-subscribed correspondence course in town planning for British servicemen. Like Doxiadis, Tyrwhitt was frequently consulted – and traveled widely – under the auspices of the UN and WHO, and by 1951 she had relocated to the University of Toronto and thence to the Graduate School of Design (GSD) in Harvard by 1955 – in both of which roles she established and delivered courses in city and regional planning. All the while, she was an influential presence and organizer within the International Congresses of Modern Architecture (Congrès Internationaux d'Architecture Moderne – CIAM) and especially its British wing, the Modern Architecture Research Group (MARS).

Fig. 1 View of the ancient theater of Delos during the 1963 Delos Symposion.

It was in January 1954 that Tyrwhitt first met Doxiadis at the inaugural UN Seminar on Housing and Community Planning, which was held in New Delhi. Tyrwhitt was there as overall director of the seminar as well as UN technical adviser to the Indian government – clear markers of her international prestige. And from that initial meeting they launched, in 1955, the *Tropical Housing & Planning Monthly Bulletin*. Edited by Tyrwhitt, this was an in-house bulletin intended for the staff of Doxiadis Associates as well as sections of UN staff, focused on gathering statistics, case studies and the analysis of planning in the developing world. Shortly thereafter the bulletin was renamed *Ekistics* and its remit expanded, becoming dedicated

Introduction

to exploring and distributing this fledgling science for a worldwide, multidisciplinary audience.[6]

The Delos Symposia were instituted by Doxiadis in tandem with the networker supreme Tyrwhitt in 1963, and they massively amplified the development and dissemination – but also the critical interrogation – of Ekistics as a new urban proposition. The participants in the Symposia were wide-ranging indeed. They included world-renowned architects and planners as well as archaeologists, classicists, historians, sociologists, geographers, anthropologists, psychologists, civil-rights activists, inventors, media theorists, artists and many others, who came together to rethink the global built environment and devise ways of reshaping it to solve all the planet's environmental and demographic problems.[7] The papers, reports, arguments and commentaries from the Symposia were published each year in the *Ekistics* journal, of course, but always under the iron grip of Tyrwhitt's editorial hand.

Principally, the Symposia were conceived as an urgently needed reboot of the groundbreaking fourth conference of CIAM, which had been held in 1933.[8] The CIAM congresses were the primary forum at the time for modernist architects and planners to thrash out what effectively amounted to an international design policy, which they successfully implemented in their various national schools and governments between the late 1920s and the late 1950s. It is largely for this reason that we see the spread of modernist ideals – such as inner-city "slum" clearance, segregation by "zoning" and functionalist architectural aesthetics – all over the world in these years. Given the destruction caused to established communities and the historical fabric of cities over these decades, architect–planners would increasingly come to be treated with distrust.[9]

But CIAM 4 had been noteworthy as the first orchestrated international discussion about the "globalized city," and it was published in various abridged and expanded formats – notably by Josep Lluís Sert as *Can Our Cities Survive?* in 1942 and then, most famously, by Le Corbusier as *The Charter of Athens* in 1943.[10] The intention of Doxiadis was to try to reclaim and re-energize the legacy of CIAM 4, and the Delos Symposia were indeed remarkable not only in the range and content of the discussions they generated but also in terms of their format. They were run according to ancient Greek practices of the *sympósion*, which implied a tightly choreographed social gathering in which participants drank together, conversed and enjoyed themselves in a convivial and cultured atmosphere. Doxiadis was very par-

ticular in the use of this term, insisting on it rather than *symposium* with its dreary implications of conventional academic or professional conferences. Much of the activity, then, took place in a most engaging atmosphere on board a ship called *New Hellas*, or *New Greece*, in the Aegean Sea. Significantly, CIAM 4 had also taken place on a chartered boat in the Mediterranean, named *Patris II* (meaning *Homeland II*), albeit a less well-appointed and much less lively one. The analogy with the fourth CIAM conference was clear, and the intention of Doxiadis was to improve upon the earlier meeting.[11] Predictably, the extravagance of the Symposia and the antics of their world-famous guests became something of a cause célèbre in the international media, and the Delians – as they came to be known – seemed to relish the attention [Fig. 2].

Each Symposion concluded not in modern Athens, which in its crush and pollution represented only the failure of existing cities that the Delians sought to address, but at the deserted island and archaeological site of Delos, once a pivotal player in an ancient regional network of culture and trade and a prototype for their globally networked city of the future [Fig. 3].[12] Delos was the mythical birthplace of Apollo and Artemis, and had been the home of the sanctuary of Apollo since the archaic period. The island was used as an arena of competitive displays of piety and power since the archaic period; during the third and second centuries BCE, the sanctuary was monumentalized with a series of porticoes by the Hellenistic monarchs and became an important trading point in the late Hellenistic period, when the city and its harbor infrastructure expanded to accommodate the needs of the emporium.[13] The port-city was presumably abandoned after the first century BCE, when the geopolitical developments of the nascent Roman Empire shifted the trading networks of the Mediterranean.[14]

Fig. 2 "First press comments," October 1963.

Here on Delos, world-famous figures as diverse as Margaret Mead, Arnold Toynbee, Sigfried Giedion, Richard Buckminster Fuller, Jean Gottmann, Kenzo Tange, Barbara Ward and Marshall McLuhan, among many dozens of other Delians, would process across the island, weaving snake-like through its ruins towards the ancient theater [Figs. 4 and 5]. Once there, they would participate in torchlit ceremonial declarations on global planning issues and signings that confirmed their joint commitments and undertakings for the year to come before they gathered again [Figs. 6 and 7]. This extraordinary, almost ritualistic spectacle was repeated each year and became an iconic part of the imagery that the Delians projected to the world [Fig. 8].

Doxiadis and Tyrwhitt's ambition to bring international actors together to solve urban, demographic and ecological problems on a global scale was remarkable, and the Symposia had real presence and indeed impact in their time – both "on the ground," with real planning schemes, and also across the popular and specialist media. But there was a problem. CIAM had been formally dissolved in 1959, never having recovered from the internal sabotage of the Team 10 group. Led by younger members such as Jacob Bakema, Alison and Peter Smithson, and Giancarlo de Carlo, Team 10 had hijacked the 1956 meeting in Dubrovnik and declared the CIAM old guard out of touch and even dead to the modern world.[15]

The Delos Symposia, however, sought to keep the ambitions of CIAM alive, while also recognizing the need to revitalize them with a fresh focus on environmental and demographic issues and a new kind of scientific ambition to replace the machine-based rhetoric of the 1920s and 1930s. But this meant they were going against the grain, as the emerging mainstream of architecture and planning in the 1960s was heading towards increasingly modest and small-scale urban interventions. Iconic examples include the grassroots community work of Jane Jacobs, the advocacy planning of Robert Davidoff, the new historicist tendencies of Aldo Rossi and the Venice School, and the playful pop commercialism of Denise Scott Brown and Robert Venturi – all of which suggested a new, democratic take on the relationship between the built-environment professional and the people they were designing for.[16] Against this, the Delos Symposia represented the last concerted push for a totally designed, expert-led "solution" for the built environment on a global

Fig. 3 Plan of the central area of Delos. Yellow indicates large commercial buildings; red indicates shops, workshops and multifunctional spaces; and blue indicates house-workshops.

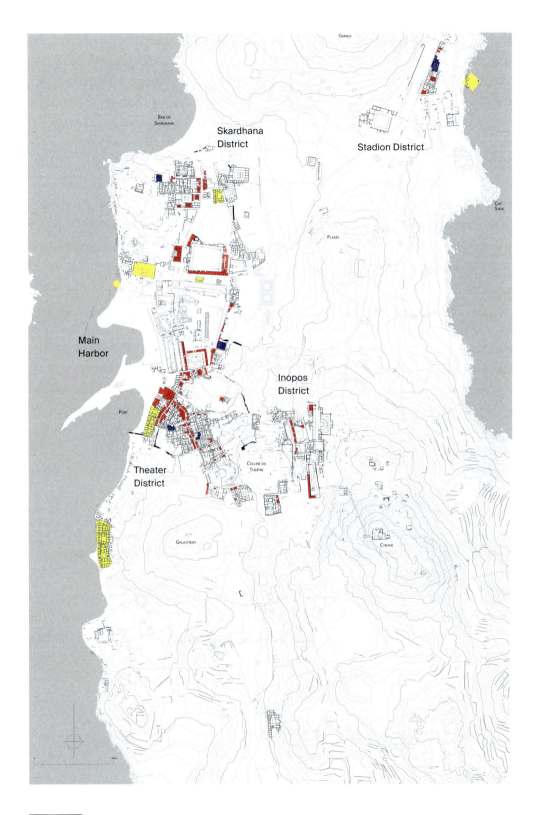

Introduction

scale – an endeavor that was finally brought to a halt by the global oil crisis and financial crash of 1973–1974. The Symposia themselves were wrapped up one year later, in 1975, the year of Doxiadis's death. The whole enterprise seemed to be caught, curiously, between the overt utopianism of modernism and the neoliberalist tendencies that were just beginning to emerge.

These late-modernist ambitions of the Delos Symposia might have seemed misaligned with the emerging trends of their day, then, especially as these coalesced into the dominant orthodoxies of the 1970s and 1980s: respect for urban context, community empowerment, the architect–planner recast into "advocacy" guise as friendly collaborator rather than domineering expert, and so on. And this is probably the main reason they are relatively little known among scholars and practitioners today. But this situation is undeserved. Many of the things the Delos Symposia explored were extremely progressive for their day and clearly prescient of subsequent approaches and values – including some of our contemporary ones. As the chapters in this book will demonstrate, they included:

- a willingness to work on the adaptation of the built environment rather than demolition and new build;

- a commitment towards contemporary regional values, typologies and vernaculars rather than an "international style" of urban and architectural design;

- serious research into deep historical precedent, leading to the incorporation of tried-and-tested building and planning typologies from the distant past;

- a willingness not only to acknowledge the centrality of "the user" as a factor in design decision-making but also to base this on investigations into the philosophy and psychology of human nature, to try to understand what people truly are and need;

- finally, an engaged and innovative approach to what nowadays we call sustainability that went beyond blending urban development with a simple respect for nature, instead seeking to learn from natural systems and incorporate them into design processes.

Despite these remarkable commitments, the grandiose ambitions of the Delos Symposia, mixed with the pervasive rhetoric of science and expertise – a paternalistic "techno-optimism" in the eyes of some detractors – have clearly cast a shadow over their subsequent reputation.

This book offers the first comprehensive reappraisal of the history and legacy of the Delos Symposia not only as a groundbreaking global humanitarian network but also as intellectual theater and a publicity machine full of strong yet divergent personalities. It explores their ideals, commitments and fights; the way they fed into the colossal urban-planning projects

Fig. 4 View of the Theater District as the Delos Symposion participants reach the ancient theater of Delos, July 12, 1963.

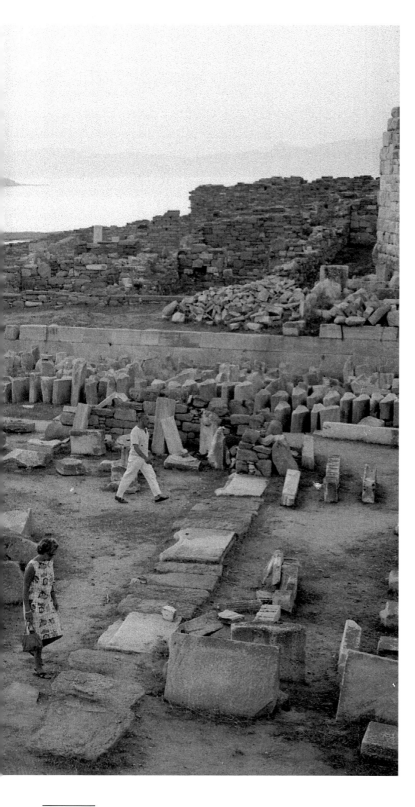

Fig. 5 View of the ancient theater of Delos as the Delos Symposion participants arrive, July 12, 1963.

that Doxiadis was implementing across the world; and the lessons they might offer for contemporary thinking on sustainable development. This is tackled in three distinct but interrelated sections, entitled "Foundations and Ideals," "Practices and Implementations," and "Futures and Legacies." Each section focuses on a particular set of thematic concerns or activities emerging from the Delos Symposia as well from the urban-planning and consultancy work of Doxiadis Associates, which informed and was informed by the Symposia agenda. Indeed, one of the themes running throughout the volume is the frequent shift in register between humanitarian idealism and commercial business. So, although each section will offer appreciative assessments of the potential relevance and value of what the Symposia achieved for future urban discourse – particularly Section III – the authors also offer some critique. These critiques tend to focus on how Symposia ideals came to be applied in practical masterplanning and infrastructure projects, on how different rhetoric and techniques of persuasion were sometimes deployed strategically to win favor and

Fig. 6 C. A. Doxiadis addressing the participants of the fifth Delos Symposion, ancient theater of Delos, July 1966.

Fig. 7 Arnold Toynbee addressing the participants of the fifth Delos Symposion, ancient theater of Delos, July 1966.

Fig. 8 Cover of *Ekistics* (October 1971).

contracts, on the interfacing with some highly problematic national politics and also on some of the philosophical arguments that were given the floor in Symposia debates. The section themes and individual chapters are elaborated below.

Section I, "Foundations and Ideals," maps out the conceptual underpinnings and communicative practices of the Delos Symposia in relation to the dominant political and intellectual geographies of the 1960s–1970s. Its chapters trace the ways in which urban-design solutions were sought in contrary directions, taking in the latest scientific technologies, wide-ranging investigations into human psychology, philosophies of the self and environmental determinism, as well as lessons from the vernacular and classical pasts – for example, by studying ancient Greek cities as prototypes. They also explore how the Symposia operated by cultivating international networks of influence and expertise, as well as the overarching imaginative and rhetorical aspects of the Symposia that worked so successfully to capture the attention of the world's media.

Mantha Zarmakoupi, in "History as a Framework: The Appropriation of the Classical Past in the Delos Symposia," looks into the ways in which the classical past was represented and redeployed in Delos discourse. The archaeological site of Delos, as well as other sites visited by the participants of the Symposia, were the physical stage against which the discussions took place. But it was not merely the archaeological context that operated as a backdrop, as history itself was perceived and conceptualized as a framework for the future of the city – a framework that participants attempted to integrate into their conceptualization of the present urban environment and its future. In discussing the ways in which history and the past operated in the Delos Symposia, this chapter tackles more broadly the axiological approach of the Delos group vis-à-vis historiography and historic urban environments.

Thematically following with "The Past as a Stage Set for C. A. Doxiadis," Dimitris Philippides looks at how Doxiadis employed targeted and extensive references to the past in Greek culture, from pre-Christian antiquity to the more recent so-called traditional period under Ottoman rule. For Doxiadis, the past was considered reliable, free from the mutability of the present and from the ambiguities hidden in the future. The past could, then, be used to legitimize projections into the future and make them seem more credible. This chapter analyzes the ways in which Doxiadis went on to sanction his planning tools and techniques, including density ratios and the hierarchical arrangement of communities, according to their ostensible rootedness in esteemed historical precedents. Doxiadis's approach also played with the relationship of high to low culture, and this is demonstrated to be crucial in understanding how the notion of tradition was used as a legitimizing construct in the wider Delos Symposia.

Kostas Tsiambaos, in "Some Rhetorical Aspects of the Delos Symposia," builds upon the previous chapters to explore the well-oiled communication machine that sustained this new urban venture. The Delos Symposia, he argues, were a sophisticated rhetorical endeavor choreographed by Doxiadis, the strategies of which were deployed in two directions: from Doxiadis to the other Delians, and from the Delians to an international audience. Doxiadis had to persuade the Delians about his theories and ideas, and the Delians had to persuade everyone about the authority and significance of their Symposia. A kind of theatrical play, with Doxiadis at center stage, was cultivated on the cruise boats that served both as heterotopia and panopticon at the same time. The target, as everyone in Doxiadis Associates admitted, was the commercial promotion of Ekistics as the new, interdisciplinary science of human settlements. Casting a light back on the history-mobilizing themes of the previous chapters, Tsiambaos maintains that Delos ultimately represented a rhetorical invention of a mythical land of the past, one designed to inspire a novel view and direction to the brave new world of the future.

In "East–West: The Delos Dialogue with Japanese Urbanism," Ellen Shoshkes explains how international networks were more than merely a communicative or publicizing feature of Delos, serving also as a means of forging a global consensus of urban ideals. Shoshkes situates the Delian discourse in the larger context of the creative dialogue between Eastern and Western civilization. It is widely acknowledged that the opening of Japan to the West in 1868 served as the "midwife" of modernism before World War I. Less widely known is that Japan went on to play a vital role in the increasingly interactive exchanges that inspired the co-evolution of modern social and aesthetic ideals in Japan and the West, which by the mid-twentieth century had generated an ecological worldview envisioning an ideal, decentralized community based on human cooperation and harmony with nature. The formation of this dynamic synthesis of Eastern and Western ideals coincided with the rise of planning as a profession worldwide, and the formation of transnational scholarly networks of exchange, coming together in a global East–West consensus around a biologically informed and regionally inflected urban model with a common root in the theories of Patrick Geddes. These ideas were a palpable current in the new field of urban design, which was established as an academic discipline at Harvard in the 1950s, and the closely related discourse on Ekistics. Doxiadis's relationship with Jaqueline Tyrwhitt, Kenzo Tange, Fumihiko Maki and others illuminates how these dynamics played out – sometimes by chance, sometimes by plan – in transnational academic communities based primarily at Harvard University, the Athens Center of Ekistics and Tokyo University.

The final chapter of Section I, Simon Richards's "Delos and 'The Human Factor'," examines the Delos Symposia in relation to one of the perennial themes of architectural and planning discourse: how the well-designed environment can have an improving effect upon how people think, feel and act. This theme is often founded upon a deeper sense – sometimes intuitive and impressionistic, sometimes explicit and deeply researched – of what human beings *are* in their most essential processes and natures. Given the import of such implications, and the fact that most architect–planners are not specialist philosophers or psychologists, the link between design, environment, behavior and human nature is usually assumed but seldom gone into in much depth. In Richards's account, however, the Delos Symposia seem to have been truly remarkable for the amount of attention they dedicated to what one contributor called "the human factor." Indeed, it was often given center stage, the assumption being that if one were designing for what Doxiadis called "Anthopocosmos: The World of Man" (1966), then one should have a clear idea of what "man" truly is. This chapter explores how this debate was carried and evolved across Delos Symposia 1 through 7 (1963–69) and reported in the *Ekistics* journal, which brought a wide variety of competing interpretations about the human factor into play. It also contrasts the richness of this discourse with the rather vague assumptions and formulas around "wellbeing" that characterize discussion of the issue in the present day.

To sum up, the first section explores the historical framework and diverse principles upon which the contributors to the Symposia sought to ground the Delos project of stewarding the planet to a better future. Given the great variety of contributors and disciplines, these principles came from numerous sources – including the building types and urban paradigms of the ancient past, the local wisdom inscribed into indigenous communities and vernacular technologies, the legitimizing power of agreement among networked international communities and the assumed philosophical bedrock of human nature and conduct. This section also explores how the Symposia and their publications were carefully orchestrated to create an aura – or "rhetoric" – of antiquarian and scientific legitimacy around their subsequent proposals for action.

Section II, "Practices and Implementations," explores the ways in which the ideals and science of the Delos Symposia were channeled into practical design and analytical tools and applied across many urban projects, as exemplified in Doxiadis Associates' worldwide planning and consultancy business in the 1960s and 1970s. Individual chapters focus on their Islamabad masterplan for the new capital of Pakistan and on residential and infrastructural plans for Philadelphia and Detroit, as well as on their vast transport projects across Asia and Africa.

Ioanna Theocharopoulou's "Ecology, Ekistics and the 'Texture of Settlements'" delves into the way that Doxiadis and his colleagues at Doxiadis Associates probed alternative visions of global human settlements based on an anthropological interest in "reading" existing structures as a prerequisite for any new proposals to be made. This chapter argues that this pioneering approach represented a fruitful, creative tension between Doxiadis's belief in "pure" science as a tool for planning human settlements and a kind of "thick description" attempted by his associates in every project they undertook throughout different regions and cultures. This tension was eventually fed into their syncretic science of Ekistics. For Doxiadis, the reading of existing settlements represented a search for pre-existent order while also serving as a signal of an emerging ecological awareness that had to do with connecting and integrating *anthropos* – the "world of man" – with wild, vulnerable nature in new and more balanced ways. By focusing on Doxiadis's work in Lebanon from the late 1950s, this chapter tackles the ways in which Doxiadis and his team of architects and engineers engaged in complex and densely textured field research to try to "read" human settlements and redeploy their lessons, no matter how humble they might originally have seemed. A key argument of Theocharopoulou is that the attention given by Doxiadis Associates to listening to and recording local voices in thousands of pages of reports and photographs represented a genuine respect for regional context and values – a significant departure from the dominant, top-down model of Western development at this time.

Introducing the loaded term "social science entrepreneurs," Filippo De Dominicis's "Infrastructuring Development: Doxiadis's Continental Plans at the End of Ideologies" explores the controversial narrative of two continent-wide transport schemes for Africa and Asia issued by Doxiadis in the 1960s under the patronage of the United Nations. This involved the formulation of a global planning and infrastructure consensus that sought to deal with – and in many ways to capitalize upon – the tensions of the Cold War as well as fractious post-colonial situations. Formulated in leading universities, non-governmental organizations and research foundations in the United States, the provision of planning and infrastructure became a way to instill a pro-Western, capitalist development agenda on nations in the developing world recently freed from the imperial yoke – which, of course, were susceptible to Soviet influence as well. This chapter shows how Doxiadis maneuvered himself deftly into these circles, providing them with a design theory and spatial vocabulary as well as an educational program tied to several regional headquarters. The key projects emerging from his office at this time included the African Transport Plan (1962) and the Trans-Asian Highway (1963–64), which possibly remain the largest design projects ever undertaken by a private practice. Picking up themes introduced in Section I, the chapter further explores how Doxiadis appealed to both sides of his audience by rhetorically framing these projects as a kind of political capital – a pushback against the West by recently post-colonial nations.

Farhan Karim's chapter on "Basic Democracy and Doxiadis Associates' School-Reformation Project in East Pakistan" deepens the political theme with an exploration of the activities of Doxiadis Associates in the midst of the complex regional and international politics of post-independence Pakistan. This politics was dominated by the authoritarian regime of President and ex-General Muhammad Ayub Khan, who came to power via a military coup in 1958 and who wished to improve educational provision but always with an eye, it seemed, on educating the populace just enough to maintain his power. At the same time, however, the United States, the United Nations and influential funding bodies like the Ford Foundation were keen to provide funding and expertise to increase education as a global humanitarian aim – but always with the ulterior motive, at the feverish height of the Cold War, of holding back the tide of communism. Doxiadis

Associates took advantage of the opportunities offered by this tense situation to conduct a nationwide survey of school infrastructure and building typologies in Pakistan, focusing exclusively upon the colonial period and neglecting traditional school typologies, and concluded with the proposition of a comprehensive set of new, modular prototypes. This chapter argues that Doxiadis's research and proposals, while rooted in the science of Ekistics, sidestepped the sensitive political and historical reasons for poor educational attainment in the country; instead, they offered a spatio-geographical diagnosis of the problem that was unlikely to be seen as controversial by the Pakistan government.

Lefteris Theodosis's "Shaping Ekistics: From Baghdad to Detroit" takes an in-depth look at two of the most ambitious projects of Doxiadis's career: the national housing project and master plan for Baghdad of the mid-1950s, and the multi-city Urban Detroit Area planning and infrastructure project from the mid-1960s. Both sought to revitalize their city centers, combat population loss and propose new urban and regional patterns for future growth. Despite their distinctive historical, social and economic circumstances, Doxiadis Associates approached both projects through core Ekistics concepts – in particular, those of the "Dynapolis" and the "Human Sector." Theodosis makes the argument that, in Doxiadis's reckoning, this approach allowed for the fusion of international techniques and pressures while preserving some elements of distinctive local culture, ultimately allowing the cities in each region to assume a unique place in the upcoming world city or "Ecumenopolis." But this approach – based as it was on the abstracts of technique, space and scale, all number-crunched through thousands of potential design solutions in Doxiadis's pioneering computer labs – played another role as well that comes back round to the difficult business of negotiating urbanism into different political contexts. In short, Theodosis argues, it allowed Doxiadis Associates to work around the politically sensitive particularities of Detroit and Baghdad with a universalizing solution to planning, one that was ostensibly immune to the polarizing discourses of East versus West, and operating – as is eloquently described in the first Delos Symposion invitation letter – "between East and West and North and South."

The final chapter of Section II is "The Visionary in the Marsh: Doxiadis and the Dream of Eastwick" by Harrison Blackman, and it explores another poignant example of urban idealism clashing against sociopolitical or, in this case, racial realities. In the late 1950s, the Philadelphia neighborhood of Eastwick was in a state of appalling decay – abandoned houses, illegal dumps and rodent infestations marked the swampy terrain, revealing a society in trouble. To address the situation, city-planning director Edmund Bacon made a logical and consequential choice: he hired the world-famous architect and planner Constantinos A. Doxiadis. The Athenian was no stranger to working in less-than-ideal conditions: in wartime Greece, he had led a resistance group against the German occupation; in Iraq, his team of architects had survived a coup d'état; in Pakistan, he had realized an entire city from the ground up. Doxiadis's efforts in Eastwick were no less ambitious – at the time, many considered them the largest urban-renewal effort in American history. But despite the praise of its initial residents the redeveloped Eastwick never took off, and today, to the untrained eye, it appears an unremarkable, low-income suburb on the fringes of the Philadelphia airport. Blackman's chapter traces the causes of Eastwick's failure vis-à-vis its original vision, finding the answer not in the overly idealistic dream of its international master planner but in what his dream ran up against. At the heart of Eastwick's disappointment was a deep-seated American phenomenon that Doxiadis's development model had failed to take account of – the racial prejudices of its prospective inhabitants.

The second section, to pull the above threads together, contains chapters that explore how the ideals explored in the Delos Symposia fed into the many master plans and consultancy projects conducted by Doxiadis Associates during these years as well as their dealings with various political regimes, when DA was one of the most influential and powerful practices in the world. Sometimes, the ideals of Ekistics appear to have been respected and applied faithfully; at others, they were adapted and possibly compromised under the weight of practical pressures and political realities. These projects included urban master plans in Iraq and Iran, a new schools program in Pakistan and infrastructural development across Africa and Asia, as well as extensive community and transport plans for Philadelphia and Detroit. The section also investigates the fieldwork techniques deployed by Doxiadis and his colleagues to try to draw out the inherent socio-environmental wisdom within existing regional settlements. All these examples highlight the intense difficulties and frustrations of realizing the most ambitious urban schemes as practical realities.

Section III, "Futures and Legacies," appraises the potential lessons of the Delos Symposia for contemporary discourses and practices in architecture and urban planning. There is a strong focus in this section on assessing the Delians' faith in technological solutions towards sustainability and mitigating the effects of environmental destruction, and in this they were incontrovertibly pioneers. Individual chapters offer case studies on urban master plans from North Macedonia to Pakistan, and the new opportunities they opened up for combining urban and ecological interventions. Doxiadis Associates' visionary incorporation of natural and biomimetic systems as paradigms for design is explored in relation to contemporary design methods, and some of the tropes of contemporary urban-historical scholarship are also reinterrogated in light of the importance of the Delian project.

As scholarship on Doxiadis, Ekistics and the Delos Symposia has grown, so too have the critiques of it: historiographic critiques of modernism, Foucauldian critiques of power and governmentality, Marxist critiques of development and critiques of planning politics imposed unsympathetically into specific locales, to name just a few. Many have uncovered problematic aspects of the visions professed by the members of the Delos Symposia. The purpose of Panayiota Pyla's chapter, "Metacriticisms of Ekistics' Environmental Design," is to interrogate how these critiques throw light on our alternative contemporary values, which evince concerns against "techno-optimism" in planning, against the lucrative conflation of design and ecology with profit and diversionary public-relations exercises, and against Western-led international development models in general. Analyzing how recent scholarship has critiqued these three aspects of Delian discourse, Pyla's chapter argues that a better understanding of the motives of these very critiques themselves can enrich development and collaborative practices today. The chapter also explores how, even though the alarming effects of climate change make today's global environmental problems seem unprecedented, many of our current realities and anxieties are rooted in the discussions of the 1950s and 1960s. Moreover, Ekistics-based solutions to climate issues seem to preempt and resonate with many current concepts and strategies on environmentally conscious development.

Urban-sustainability issues have triggered a tremendous interest in reconceptualizing nature–city relations as well as calls for "renaturing" cities, and this is the theme of Ahmed Z. Khan's chapter on "Urban Ecosystems and Global Ecological Balance: Rethinking Doxiadis's Legacy as Nature–Settlement Dialectics." Over the last two decades, this shift has led to a proliferation of new disciplinary realignments and discourses, such as landscape urbanism, ecological urbanism, resilience, transitions, sustainable urban design and nature-based solutions. In this commitment to develop a broader framework of environmentalism in architectural culture, several historical figures of twentieth-century modernism have been revisited and their ideas rediscovered. Despite significant contributions to both the theory and practice of environmentalism, however, Doxiadis and the Delos Symposia remain substantially overlooked. Khan's chapter traces the key environmental concepts of Doxiadis in both his practice and his theory, including his master plan for Islamabad and the methodology of "diagrammatic reasoning," and resituates them in the context of the 1950s–1960s while also articulating their contemporary relevance for urban-sustainability theory and practice under a new concept of "nature–settlement dialectics." The main argument of nature–settlement dialectics builds upon a double thought structure in the practice and theory of Doxiadis when dealing with nature: first, nature as a literal element within a settlement; second, nature conceived as a system, contributing to design thinking at various scales. This dialectic serves to supplement previous practices of introducing nature into the city (gardens, parks, green belts, etc.) by incorporating nature as an organizing framework within specific design processes.

Picking up Khan's theme is Yannis Zavoleas's chapter on "Bio-systemic Thinking for Holistic Design: On the Legacy of the Delos Symposia in Contemporary Environmental Thinking and Environmentally Conscious Design." Zavoleas argues that the discourse on ecological matters in the Delos Symposia may be understood as the desire to achieve pervasive sustainability at a global scale. But nature featured in a very different way within Delos as well. Beyond the pioneering exploration of transdisciplinary scientific methods and solutions that the Symposia represented, scientific models were also explored to elaborate on nature's dynamic functions such as adaptation, mutation and evolution – invoking recursive operations and trial-and-error iterations – which could then be applied in spatial design. Zavoleas's chapter explores the deep fascination among Doxiadis Associates and the Delians for scientific discourse, ecology and natural systems generally, but in particular the application of these in their pioneering approaches to computationally driven architectural and urban design. Looking at more recent deployments of computation in architectural design and communication platforms – and, in particular, the constraints these place upon intuition, creativity and craft – Zavoleas argues that the Delians' "bio-systemic thinking" and transdisciplinary approaches can be considered prototypes, or indeed correctives, for a more holistic vision of computationally driven spatial design in the present day.

Returning us to a theme explored by Shoshkes in Section I, Tilemachos Andrianopoulos's "Japanese Delos in 27 Points" adopts a suggestive photo-essayistic approach to its scholarship. Inspired by Jean-Luc Godard's characteristically provocative film *On the Origin of the 21st Century* (2000), which spliced footage of World War II and Nazi atrocities with Hollywood and avant-garde cinema, Andrianopoulos presents twenty-seven short texts. Abandoning chronology to make the relevant connections as impactful as possible, the chapter draws on material from the Doxiadis archives to highlight the network of ideas moving between Japan and the Delos Symposia, amplified with reference to other major cultural figures such as architect Ioannis Despotopoulos, surrealist philosopher Georges Bataille and filmmaker Max Ophüls. Taken together, these episodes contribute to a vivid, multifaceted portrayal of the Delos Symposia – not least as occupying a transitional phase between high-modernist utopian planning and the neo-liberal approaches that were to dominate later.

With the push for more sustainable urban design during the twenty-first century, contemporary practitioners have turned increasingly to evaluating earlier approaches to the problem. This is the topic of the final chapter by Thomas Doxiadis, "Doxiadis Associates' Master Plan for Skopje and the Global Ecological Balance: The Element of Nature." Since 1999, Thomas Doxiadis has led the Athens-based practice doxiadis+, a design team creating landscapes and architecture with a focus on people, nature and sustainability, and with a keen sense of the legacy inherited from Doxiadis Associates in the 1960s. This chapter tackles an important DA project, the 1964 Outline Plan for the City of Skopje, which was a United Nations-backed initiative to redesign the Balkan capital following the 1963 earthquake that devastated it. Doxiadis examines the DA master plan through the contemporary lens of landscape ecology, overlaying it onto the Google Earth model of the existing city and region so that proposed and present-day relationships to the local and surrounding ecological context can be compared and investigated. The DA master plan is analyzed with respect to the following factors: topography, hydrology, soils, biodiversity, connectivity, green infrastructure and static versus dynamic systems. The retrospective appraisal that this chapter offers shows that contemporary ecological-design approaches are well aligned with the thinking and strategies of the urban-planning initiatives of the 1960s, and that there is still much to be learned from the latter.

The final section, to summarize, explores the legacy of the Delos Symposia in relation to contemporary attitudes and approaches towards architecture, urban planning and the environment, but also to urban scholarship itself, assessing its lessons – positive, negative and cautionary – for now and the future. The theme of sustainability is of central importance in these chapters, involving a return to Islamabad and speculative extrapolations from Doxiadis Associates' urban master plan for Skopje, as well as more theoretical explorations of the origins of urban environmental thinking. Relatedly on the theme of nature, this section introduces the Delians' fascination with natural systems and biomimicry, and traces how these were incorporated into the design process of Doxiadis's practice as clear precursors to contemporary algorithmic or parametric urban and architectural design. And we are also introduced, rather playfully, to the proposition that an acknowledgment of the importance of the Delos network disrupts many aspects of established urban-historical scholarship and criticism.

In the Afterword, entitled "The Three Antiquities of C. A. Doxiadis and the Road to Eutopia," Panayotis Tournikiotis offers a richly intriguing way to reflect back on Doxiadis's ideals and *modus operandi* – one which takes us back almost to the beginning. The themes that came to characterize the Delos Symposia, Tournikiotis argues, and which seemed to erupt there spontaneously in the coming together of so many voices, were already inscribed into the Ph.D. thesis that Doxiadis completed in Germany in 1937 as "Raumordnung im griechischen Städtebau" – published in 1972 as *Architectural Space in Ancient Greece*. Strangely, however, the island of Delos was barely acknowledged in the first of these works, and is absent entirely from the later translation. But Tournikitios shows us how Doxiadis had situated himself very self-consciously within a long tradition of utopian thinkers, from Plato and Thomas More through to Edward Bellamy, Aldous Huxley and others. And just like the ambivalent play of "idealism, pragmatism and positivism" that characterizes utopian discourse – the *Utopia* of More, after all, is famously translated as the "non-place" or "impossible place" – Delos itself had to be discovered, or recuperated, or conjured into discursive existence, along with a strange new "tribal" population to inhabit it: the Delians. Returning us to some of the earlier discussions on the importance of rhetoric in the Delos Symposia, Tournikiotis shows how Delos served as a real, historical place – an expansive thought experiment – as well as a pragmatic symbol of future potential, around which the "three antiquities" of Doxiadis – the architectural, utopian and archaeological – could be set into motion.

The authors included in this volume include academic historians and theorists, creative writers, and architectural and urban practitioners, as well as former colleagues of Doxiadis. The nature of the contributions is accordingly diverse, ranking from provocative discursive pieces though to more theoretical discussions, as well as work heavily dependent on archival research. All of them, to varying degrees, seek to contextualize Doxiadis's contribution within the ever-changing contours of the Symposia, and all of them are aware of the complex ways in which the Delos machine operated as ideology and practice, communication and performance. As with the Delos Symposia themselves, however, not every voice here is necessarily in agreement, but we present this variety and challenge as a strength. It is an open invitation to the reader to thread their own path through this fascinating network of ideas.

The chapters will immerse the reader straight into the flow of arguments and personalities in the Delos Symposia, although we are careful to provide sufficient background detail to hold the many threads together. We should stress, however, that the book does not provide a systematic biographical account of Doxiadis or the other key player in the story of the Delos Symposia, Tyrwhitt. Readers wishing to obtain such detail would be well advised to consult Alexandros-Andreas Kyrtsis's *Constantinos A. Doxiadis: Texts, Design Drawings, Settlements* (2006) and Dimitris Philippides's *Κωνσταντίνος Δοξιάδης (1913–1975): Αναφορά στον Ιππόδαμο* [*Constantinos Doxiadis (1913–1975): Reference to Hippodamus*] (2015), which offer an encyclopedic exploration of Doxiadis's life across all his activities and also include well-chosen selections from many of his key writings. Ellen Shoshkes's *Jaqueline Tyrwhitt: A Transnational Life in Urban Planning and Design* (2013) is also required reading, exploring as it does the Delos Symposia and Ekistics as just one aspect of the extraordinary life and activities of this pioneering British planner, educator and networker. For the background of international modernist architecture and planning against which the Delians were trying to establish their new eco-friendly, regionally inflected yet high-tech visions, readers should consult Eric Mumford's meticulously researched *The*

Fig. 9 View of the ancient theater of Delos during the May 2024 Alpha Mission ΔELOS meeting, organized by the World Human Forum.

CIAM Discourse on Urbanism, 1928–1960 (2002). A more lively read for those wishing to get a flavor of the cut-and-thrust debate within the Delos Symposia would be Mark Wigley's "Network Fever" (2001), which enjoyably lays bare the almost comical rivalry and one-upmanship between the inventor–poet–engineer Buckminster Fuller and the media theorist Marshall McLuhan across several raucous meetings. Finally, for readers wishing to understand at first hand some of the key positions argued among the Delians in these years, the best single resource is *Human Identity in the Urban Environment* (1972), edited by Gwen Bell and Jaqueline Tyrwhitt.[17] This collection brings together numerous articles, reports and essays that were published in *Ekistics* right across the Symposia years, focusing on one of their largest scales of urban deliberation – the "megalopolis." For more detailed reading on and around the Delos Symposia and its many personalities, readers are encouraged to consult the works listed in the author biographies in this volume and the notes provided to their individual chapters, as well as the bibliography.

The discussions of the 1960s and the 1970s were very much part of their era, and some might consider the Delos Symposia to represent the last gasp of modernist urban utopianism before the discipline took a more modest, low-key and pragmatic turn. The recent reconsideration of these discussions in view of the current discourse on ecology and design, however, suggests that if we focus on their utopianism alone we have missed the point and missed their value. The boundless energy and boldness of the Delians – as well as their incredible diversity in terms of background, ethnicity, outlook and expertise – was symptomatic of a willingness to recognize the built environment not only as the cause but also potentially as the cure for many global issues. Such approaches still permeate contemporary thinking vis-à-vis ecology and the future. For instance, the Alpha Mission ΔELOS meetings that have taken place on Delos since 2021 and are organized by the World Human Forum mobilize the paradigm of the Delos Symposia and invite astrophysicists, archaeologists and artists to reflect on art, space and technology as we are assessing climate change [Fig. 9].[18]

Contemporary discourses on landscape urbanism, urban design, ecology and sustainability revisit the discussions of the 1960s and 1970s. They attempt to rescript the historical narrative of architectural modernism to include environmental concerns as a central aspect of architectural culture and the building industry over the course of the twentieth century, and to dissolve the humanist distinction between natural history and human history – as, for instance, in Daniel Barber's *Modern Architecture and Climate: Design before Air Conditioning* (2020).[19] They also adopt an ecocritical approach to architecture and landscape, which prioritizes perceptions of ecology, environment and human–nature relationships over canonical systematizations of architecture and culture, and points to the relationship of architecture and landscape beyond aesthetic understandings of urban design. The Delos Symposia, among their many other contributions, are an important historical reference for this urgent contemporary discourse.

1 Documentation on the Delos Symposia can be found in Doxiadis Archives, File 2761. Doxiadis Archives, File 2761, August 5, 1958. See also Simon Richards, "'Halfway between the Electron and the Universe': Doxiadis and the Delos Symposia," in Gerald Adler, Timothy Brittain-Catlin and Gordana Fontana-Giusti (eds), *Scale: Imagination, Perception and Practice in Architecture* (London: Routledge, 2012), 170–81; Mark Wigley, "Network Fever," *Grey Room*, no. 4 (Summer 2001), 82–122; Dimitris Philippides, Κωνσταντίνος Δοξιάδης (1913-1975): Αναφορά στον Ιππόδαμο [*Constantinos Doxiadis (1913–1975): Reference to Hippodamus*] (Athens: Melissa Books, 2015), 164–68; Mantha Zarmakoupi, "Balancing Acts between Ancient and Modern Cities: The Ancient Greek Cities Project of C. A. Doxiadis," *Architectural Histories* 3, no. 1: 19 (December 2015), 1–22.

2 "για να αποδείξωμε πως μπορούμε να πάρωμε απ' την αρχαία πόλη στοιχεία για την σημερινή." Doxiadis Archives, File 22075, S-D 7082, Μελέτες Αρχαίων Ελληνικών Πόλεων [*Studies of Ancient Greek Cities*], (January 1, 1964), 2. Volumes 1–24 of the AGC program are: vol. 1, *An Ekistical Study of the Hellenic City–State* (A. Toynbee 1971); vol. 2, *Method for the Research of Ancient Greek Settlements* (C. A. Doxiadis 1972); vol. 3, *Corinthia – Cleonaea* (M. Sakellariou and N. Faraklas 1971); vol. 4, *Cassopaia and the Elean Colonies* (S. Dakaris 1971); vol. 5, *Thasos and Peraia* (D. Lazaridis 1971); vol. 6, *Non-sense and Legitimacy* (D. Lazaridis 1971); vol. 7, *Samothrace and Its Peraia* (D. Lazaridis 1971); vol. 8, *Sikiyonia* (N. Faraklas 1971); vol. 9, *Prehistory of Eastern Macedonia and Thrace* (D. Theocharis 1971); vol. 10, *Trizinia, Kalavria, Methana* (N. Faraklas 1972); vol. 11, *Floesia* (N. Faraklas 1972); vol. 12, *Epidavria* (N. Faraklas 1972); vol. 13, *Amphipolis and Argilos* (D. Lazaridis 1972); vol. 14, *Megaris, Aegosthena, Erenaea* (M. Sakellariou and N. Faraklas 1972); vol. 15, *Thesprotia* (S. Dakaris 1972); vol. 16, *Maronoea and Orthagoria* (D. Lazaridis 1972); vol. 17, *Athens: Ekistic Data – Initial Report* (I. Travlos, M. Petroulakos and E. Pentazos 1972); vol. 18, *Crete – Stone Age* (A. Zois 1973); vol. 19, *Hermionis – Alias* (N. Faraklas 1973); vol. 20, *Plilippoi – A Roman Colony* (D. Lazaridis 1974); vol. 21, *Attica: Ekistic Data – Initial Report* (M. Petropoulakos and E. Pentazos 1973); vol. 22, *Thera and Therasia* (J. W. Sperling 1973); vol. 23, *The Grand City of Arcadia* (Arg. Petronotis 1973); vol. 24, *Lesbos and the Asia Minor Region* (I. D. Kontis 1978). The twelve unpublished monographs are: *Crete – Early Minoan Age* (A. Zois 1975–1978); *The Inland of Aegean Thrace* (D. Lazaridis 1974); *Ilis* (N. Gialouris 1971–1977); *Argaea – Asinaea* (M. Sakellariou and N. Faraklas, 1974–1975); *Aegina* (N. Faraklas 1975); *Western Likris* (N. Faraklas); *Eastern Likris* (N. Faraklas 1976); *Akarnania* (N. Faraklas [1977]); *The Spercheios Valley: Malis – Oetaea – Aenis* (N. Faraklas 1977); *Delphi* (Angelou 1970–1971); *Greek Cities in Southern France* (A. Tseklenis 1972); *The Neolithic Age in Greece* (Shivaji Singh 1970–1971). See discussion in Mantha Zarmakoupi, "Balancing Acts between Ancient and Modern Cities," 6–15.

3 Doxiadis had been planning his office since 1951, while still in Australia. For the early career of Doxiadis, see Philippides, *Constantinos Doxiadis*, 11–19, 213–28.

4 "Athens Center of Ekistics," *DA Newsletter* 3, no. 11 (November 1963), 38–48, quotation 38.

5 Sources for the following introductory account of the personal and professional backgrounds of Constantinos A. Doxiadis and Jaqueline Tyrwhitt, the circumstances leading to their collaboration and the general agenda and conduct of the Delos Symposia are spread throughout the chapters of this volume. But, for a concise overview of these matters, see Philippides, *Constantinos Doxiadis*; Richards, "'Halfway between the Electron and the Universe'"; Ellen Shoshkes, "Jaqueline Tyrwhitt: a founding mother of modern urban design," *Planning Perspectives* 21, no. 2 (April 2006), 179–97; Ellen Shoshkes, *Jaqueline Tyrwhitt: A Transnational Life in Urban Planning and Design* (Farnham, Surrey: Ashgate, 2013).

6 Constantinos A. Doxiadis, *Ekistics: An Introduction to the Science of Human Settlements* (London: Hutchinson, 1968).

Introduction

7   For instance, the participants in the first Symposion were: Charles Abrams (USA), Edmund N. Bacon (USA), Stewart Bates (Canada), Pedro Bidagor Lasarte (Spain), A. K. Brohi (Pakistan), C. S. Chandrasekhara (India), Walter Christaller (Germany), Jacob L. Crane (USA), C. A. Doxiadis (Greece), Leonard Duhl (USA), O. E. Fischnich (UN), Lyle C. Fitch (USA), R. Buckminster Fuller (USA), Clifford Furnas (USA), S. Giedion (Switzerland), J. Gorynski (Poland), Eiichi Isomura (Japan), Sture Linner (UN), Richard Llewelyn-Davies (Great Britain), Mohamed S. Makiya (Iraq), Edward S. Mason (USA), Sir Robert Matthew (Great Britain), Marshall McLuhan (Canada), Margaret Mead (USA), Waclaw Ostrowski (Poland), Alfred R. Otoo (Ghana), David Owen (UN), Charles H. Page (USA), E. Papanoutsos (Greece), Shafic H. El-Sadr (UAR), Carl Schweyer (Germany), C. H. Waddington (Great Britain), Barbara Ward (Lady Jackson) (Great Britain) and Sir Robert Watson-Watt (Great Britain). The participants in the Symposia of Delos were presented in the journal *Ekistics* (for the first Symposion, see vol. 16, no. 95, October 1963, 218–34). See also Richards, "'Halfway between the Electron and the Universe'."

8   See discussion in Panayiota I. Pyla, "Ekistics, Architecture and Environmental Politics, 1945–1976: A Prehistory of Sustainable Development," Ph.D. dissertation, Massachusetts Institute of Technology, 2002, http://dspace.mit.edu/handle/1721.1/32715#files-area, 114–21 (accessed March 18, 2024); Zarmakoupi, "Balancing Acts between Ancient and Modern Cities," 4–6.

9   The literature on architectural and urban modernism is extensive and highly specialized, often focusing on particular national contexts or influential individuals. But, for a wider overview of how architectural and urban modernism was formulated into a broad international consensus and then adapted and applied to different regional contexts, as well as the upheavals that were felt as these orthodoxies began to crumble, see Hilde Heynen and Hubert-Jan Henket (eds), *Back from Utopia: The Challenge of the Modern Movement* (Rotterdam: 010 Publishers, 2002); Sarah Williams Goldhagen and Réjean Legault (eds), *Anxious Modernisms* (Cambridge, MA: MIT Press, 2002).

10 E. Mumford, "CIAM Urbanism after the Athens Charter," *Planning Perspectives* 7 (1992), 391–417, in particular 392–94.

11 Zarmakoupi, "Balancing Acts between Ancient and Modern Cities," 4–6.

12 For the choice of Delos, see Zarmakoupi, "Balancing Acts between Ancient and Modern Cities," 4–6; Mantha Zarmakoupi, "Τόπος και εντοπία: τα Συμπόσια της Δήλου [Topos and Entopia: The Symposia of Delos]," in D. I. Kyrtatas, I. Konstantopoulos and C. Boulotis (eds), *Τόπος Τοπίο, Τιμητικός Τόμος για τον Δημήτρη Φιλιππίδη* [*Topos Topio, Honorary Volume for Dimitris Philippides*] (Athens: Melissa Books, 2018), 63–70; Mantha Zarmakoupi, "The Blue Marble of Greek Architectural History: Delos and the Delos Symposia," in M. Zarmakoupi (ed.), *Looking at the City: Architectural and Archaeological Perspectives* (Athens: Melissa Books, 2023); and Zarmakoupi in this volume.

13 Jean-Charles Moretti, "L'architecture publique à Délos au iiie s. a.C.," in J. de Courtiles (ed.), *L'architecture monumentale grecque au IIIe siècle a.C.* (Bordeaux: Ausonius, 2015), 83–115. On the urban growth of the port-city of Delos, see Mantha Zarmakoupi, "Die Hafenstadt Delos," in F. Pirson, S. Ladstätter and T. Schmidt (eds), *Häfen und Hafenstädte im östlichen Mittelmeerraum von der Antike bis in byzantinische Zeit. Aktuelle Entdeckungen und neue Forschungsansätze*, Byzas 14 (Istanbul: Zero Books, 2015), 553–70; Mantha Zarmakoupi, "Hellenistic & Roman Delos: The City & Its Emporion," *Archaeological Reports* 61 (2015), 115–32; Mantha Zarmakoupi, "The Urban Development of Late Hellenistic Delos," in Daniel Millette and Samantha Martin-McAuliffe (eds), *Ancient Urban Planning in the Mediterranean: New Research Directions* (London: Ashgate, 2018), 28–49; Mantha Zarmakoupi, "Shaping the City of Late Hellenistic Delos," *Journal of Ancient Architecture* 1 (2022), 65–85. On the harbor infrastructures, see Hervé Duchêne and Philippe Fraisse, *Le paysage portuaire de la Délos antique: recherches sur les installations maritimes, commerciales et urbaines du littoral délien*, Exploration archéologique de Délos 39 (Athens and Paris: École française d'Athènes, 2001); Mantha Zarmakoupi and Magdalini Athanasoula. "Υποβρύχια αρχαιολογική έρευνα στη βορειοανατολική πλευρά της Δήλου (Συνοικία του Σταδίου) [Underwater Archaeological Investigation of the Northeast Side of Delos (Stadion District)]," in A. Simosi and A. Sotiriou (eds), *Βουτιά στα περασμένα: Η υποβρύχια αρχαιολογική έρευνα, 1976–2014* [*Diving in the Past: The Underwater Archaeological Research, 1976–2014*] (Athens: Ministry of Culture and Sports, 2018), 91–102; Mantha Zarmakoupi, Aggeliki Simosi and Magdalini Athanasoula, "The Delos Underwater Survey Project (2014–2016)," forthcoming.

14 Zarmakoupi, "Hellenistic & Roman Delos," 126–28.

15 For a vivid firsthand insight into the collective agenda of Team 10, presented in the aggressive manifesto style typical of the times, see Alison Smithson (ed.), "Team 10 Primer," *Architectural Design*, 32, no. 2 (1962), 559–602. For a historical analysis of the diverse personalities and projects of Team 10, see Max Risselada and Dirk Van den Heuvel (eds), *Team 10: 1953–1981: In Search of a Utopia of the Present* (Rotterdam: Nai Publishers, 2005).

16 Jane Jacobs, *The Death and Life of Great American Cities* (1961) (London: Penguin Books, 1994); Aldo Rossi, *The Architecture of the City* (1966), translated

by Diane Ghirardo and Joan Ockman (Cambridge, MA: MIT Press, 1997); Steve Izenour, Denise Scott Brown and Robert Venturi, *Learning from Las Vegas* (1972) (Cambridge, MA: MIT Press, 1997).

17 Alexandros-Andreas Kyrtsis (ed.), *Constantinos A. Doxiadis: Texts, Design Drawings, Settlements* (Athens: Ikaros, 2006); Shoshkes, *Jaqueline Tyrwhitt: A Transnational Life in Urban Planning and Design*; Eric Mumford, *The CIAM Discourse on Urbanism, 1928–1960* (Cambridge, MA: MIT Press, 2002); Mark Wigley, "Network Fever," *Grey Room*, no. 4 (Summer 2001), 82–122; Gwen Bell and Jaqueline Tyrwhitt (eds), *Human Identity in the Urban Environment* (Harmondsworth: Penguin Books, 1972).

18 Alpha Mission ΔELOS: https://alphamission.delos.earth, organized by the World Human Forum: https://worldhumanforum.earth (both accessed June 8, 2024).

19 Daniel A. Barber, *Modern Architecture and Climate: Design before Air Conditioning* (Princeton, NJ: Princeton University Press, 2020).

Foundations and Ideals

Section I

43 **History as a Framework**
The Appropriation of the Classical Past
in the Delos Symposia
Mantha Zarmakoupi

73 **The Past as a Stage Set for C. A. Doxiadis**
Dimitris Philippides

89 **Some Rhetorical Aspects of the Delos Symposia**
Kostas Tsiambaos

114 **East–West: The Delos Dialogue with Japanese Urbanism**
Ellen Shoshkes

142 **Delos and "The Human Factor"**
Simon Richards

History as a Framework
The Appropriation of the Classical Past in the Delos Symposia
Mantha Zarmakoupi

Introduction

Organized by Constantinos A. Doxiadis, the Symposia of Delos (1963–1975) attempted to revitalize urban-planning approaches through the study of ancient cities and the revival of their urban-planning principles.[1] When Constantinos Doxiadis started the organization of the Delos Symposia in the 1960s, he was already established as an expert on housing and urban development and was well known in American and international urban-planning and development circles. The private firm (Doxiadis Associates) of the Greek architect and planner was founded in 1953, and by 1963 it had been engaged in important international development projects beyond Greece: housing projects in Iraq (1955–1958), the restructuring of the plan of Homs in Syria (1959) and the planning of the new capital in Pakistan (1960) – among others.[2]

The first Symposion of Delos took place in 1963, and eleven more were held from 1964 to 1975, each preceded by an intensive workshop in Athens – the Athens Ekistics Month [Fig. 1].[3] With the Symposia of Delos, Doxiadis attempted to launch an international interdisciplinary discussion on the current state of human settlements, a condition that was deteriorating rapidly as noted in the first "Declaration of Delos" – the manifesto that was yearly signed by the Delians, as the participants were called [Fig. 2].[4] The Symposia brought together architects, planners, historians, economists, sociologists, geographers and philosophers to exchange new ideas about urban crises around the world – including anthropologist Margaret Mead, economist Barbara Ward, developmental biologist and philosopher Conrad Waddington, historian Arnold Toynbee, philosopher of communication

theory Marshall McLuhan, geographer Jean Gottmann and architect Richard Buckminster Fuller.[5]

The Symposia had been conceived as a continuation of the fourth CIAM (Congrès Internationaux d'Architecture Moderne) conference in 1933 – the first organized discussion of the modern movement about the city and urban planning, the results of which were codified by Le Corbusier in the historic "Charter of Athens."[6] Doxiadis must have been present at the fourth CIAM conference and, during the same period, translated Le Corbusier's *Précisions*.[7] The conceptualization of the Symposion of Delos as a continuity of the fourth CIAM conference in 1933 and Le Corbusier's "Charter of Athens" can be seen in the first documented correspondence (May 8, 1958) of Doxiadis with his colleagues Jaqueline Tyrwhitt and John Piperoglou, where he talks about a conference for architects and planners along with other scientists on Delos during which "the Charter of Delos on the science of Ekistics" will be formulated and signed.[8] The analogy with

Fig. 1 View of the Theater District as the new Delians reach the ancient theater of Delos on July 12, 1963, for the first Delos Symposion.

the fourth CIAM conference was clear and Doxiadis's intention was to make things better: a meeting adhering to the ancient standards of a Greek banquet (symposion) – rather than a simple conference – to be held aboard a ship called *New Hellas* – not *Patris II* (*Homeland II*) – and to conclude at the deserted ancient city of Delos – not in modern Athens, which exemplified the failure of existing cities that the meeting aimed to address.[9]

While the fourth CIAM conference focused on the modern city, however, the Delos Symposia placed the relationship of the ancient with the current city at the center of the discussion. This relationship was further underlined by the selection of the site where the final discussion of the meetings took place, the island of Delos – that is, the archaeological site of Delos [Fig. 3]. Delos is an island in the center of the Cyclades, and had been home to the sanctuary of Apollo since the seventh century BCE. The island became an important commercial port in the second and first centuries BCE, a trading point during Rome's conquest of the Greek East. During this

Fig. 2 Final preparation before signing the first "Declaration of Delos" in July 1963; from left: Edmund Bacon, Jaqueline Tyrwhitt and Constantinos A. Doxiadis.

period, Delos underwent a rapid urban development. The small settlement that clustered around the area of the sanctuary of Apollo expanded significantly and new neighborhoods were created, centered around the island's natural harbors to accommodate the growing emporium of the port-city.[10] The fact that Delos – as a place (or *topos*) – had played an important geopolitical role in the late Hellenistic period, uniting the East and West, appealed to Doxiadis. For Doxiadis, Delos was the ideal place because it "was [the] seat of the ancient Athenian confederation which united the Hellenized settlements of the East with those of the mainland of Greece and the Western Mediterranean in Sicily, Marseilles and Spain […] The Charter of Delos would represent the community of interest, resource and talent among all nations of East and West, North and South, developed and less developed."[11]

In the 1960s and 70s, the island was deserted – as it remains today – and only guards and archaeologists lived there when the Symposia took place [Fig. 4]. The abandonment of Delos (a literary *topos*) toyed with the relative solitude of the island in the first and second centuries CE – for example, allusions to the Sibylline prophecy "Δῆλος ἄδηλος" (Delos, meaning visible, to *adelos*, meaning invisible), which had already been picked up by Callimachus in his "Hymn to Delos" and later in the epigrams of Antipater and Alpheus.[12] The choice of a rapidly urbanized ancient port-city, which is today abandoned, as the site of the meetings is telling about the ways in which Doxiadis and his circle conceptualized history and the past. Ten years after the first Symposion, Doxiadis explained the reasons behind this choice in the following way: "We had to go to places without problems in order not to be influenced by any local problem and be really objective and we had to finish in the quietest possible one. Quietest meant with no inhabitants either enjoying or suffering from anything and this was the island of Delos, right in the middle of the Aegean Sea without any single inhabitant, only with ruins."[13] Indeed, the participants walked among these ruins like new "Delians" – as Doxiadis himself referred to the participants in the Symposia – in search of new concepts and approaches for the design of the city of the present in July 1963, as well as in the following Symposia that, until 1972, concluded on Delos.

The reasons, however, were more intricate and profound than the comments by Doxiadis might suggest. The choice of Delos as the place where the meetings ended is indicative of the ways in which Doxiadis and his

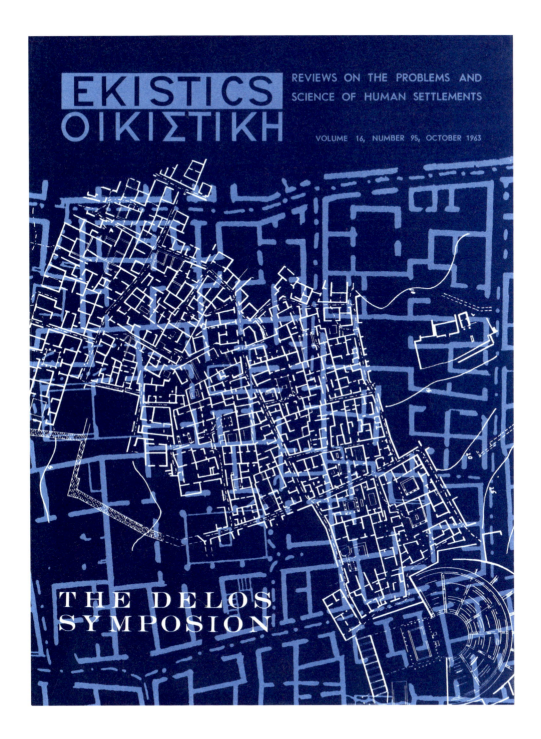

Fig. 3 Cover of the journal *Ekistics/ΟΙΚΙΣΤΙΚΗ: Reviews on the Problems and Science of Human Settlements* (October 1963). The cover features an overlay of maps of Delos at different scales. Every year, the September or October issue of the DA Review was dedicated to presenting an account of that year's Symposion.

History as a Framework

Fig. 4 View of the sanctuary of Apollo on Delos from the northwest.

entourage employed historical information to craft their very own approach to contemporary architecture and urbanism. This approach was permeated by an affective connection with the historical past, whose principles of design were lost and "whose revival was now being sought."

Ancient Greek Cities Project

The relationship of the ancient with the contemporary city lay at the center of the discussions that occurred during the Delos Symposia, as these discussions were also informed by a research project on ancient Greek cities that Doxiadis had initiated at the same time. When Doxiadis launched the Delos Symposia in the 1960s, he was running not only his private firm but also, since 1958, two non-profit privately sponsored research-and-educational institutions for technology and science – the Athens Technological Organization (ATO) and Athens Technological Institute (ATI) – where he was teaching the science of Ekistics. In 1963, Doxiadis founded the Athens Center of Ekistics (ACE) as part of ATI in order to "serve as the principal setting for education and [the] exchange of ideas in all aspects of theory and practice related to human settlements and ekistic development."[14] Doxiadis had coined the term "Ekistics" – deriving from the Greek noun οἶκος, "home, habitat," and the verbs οἰκῶ (οἰκέω), "to live in" and οἰκίζω, "to settle in" – to signify the science of human settlements as a new field of study.[15] By conceptualizing the study of human settlements as a science, Doxiadis aimed, on the one hand, to engage in the ongoing post-Renaissance discourse of "architecture as a scientific discipline" and, on the other, to respond to the totality of human needs across cultural, geographic and socioeconomic differences in a holistic manner.[16] For Doxiadis, the natural and human-made arenas were interdependent and needed to be conceptualized as a whole in order to develop a balanced coexistence between the two.[17] Doxiadis and his entourage intended to respond to the totality of human needs through the study of the settlements of the past – and one of the first research projects that he launched in this period was the Ancient Greek Cities (AGC) Project in order to "create a collection [...] of designs from the ancient city, in an appropriate scale and with the proper presentation [...] in order to prove the ways in which the ancient city can provide information for the city of the present."[18]

This project produced twenty-four published volumes, as well as a series of international conferences and ensuing publications organized in conjunction with the project [Fig. 5].[19] By pursuing the Ancient Greek Cities research project, Doxiadis and his team were not merely interested in understanding a distant past. The starting point of their interest was the challenge that the problems of contemporary cities posed. Doxiadis believed that the study of the ancient Greek city could provide modern architects and urban planners with the means to deal with these problems. In his book on the science of human settlements (i.e. Ekistics), Doxiadis assessed the evolution of human settlements – from their most primitive phase to the present-day Megalopolis – in order to identify their pathology and, through an interdisciplinary approach that he deemed necessary for solving their problems, propose their "ekistic therapy." By studying ancient settlements, Doxiadis and his team wanted to identify the parameters by which city and nature coexisted harmoniously in the past, so as to reintroduce such principles of design in the modern metropolis.

The idea that related the ancient with the present-day city was the concept of human scale, which had been lost in modern cities: "[…] in the ancient city size, and in general the concept of scale, was in a human scale. […] The dimensions were such that man could easily walk from one end of the city to the other and could thus feel that the city was made in dimensions relative to him […] The city of the present has overcome and lost the human dimensions."[20] In the case of the Symposia of Delos, the ancient city (of Delos) offered for Doxiadis the necessary distance from the problems of the present city to discover the crucial methodological means to address them.[21] In the case of the research project on the ancient Greek city, the ancient city presented an exemplary paradigm for the relationship between human scale and urban scale, the study of which would not only lead to an understanding of the problems of the city of the present but also help to address them.

Doxiadis conceptualized "human scale" in relation to walking distances. A city has a "human scale" when its size allows its accessibility on foot; thus, the scale of the city is limited by walking distances. Therefore, the spatial experience of its citizens should define the design of the city. Understanding the ancient city and its proportionate design vis-à-vis human scale would in turn lead to the understanding that the human scale has been overtaken in the present-day city. For Doxiadis, data analysis of the ancient city would be conducted toward not statistical but conceptual ends: the analysis of statistical information would lead to the conceptualization of

ARNOLD TOYNBEE
An Ekistical Study of the Hellenic City - State

C. A. DOXIADIS
The Method for the Study of the Ancient Greek Settlements

M. SAKELLARIOU - N. FARAKLAS
Corinthia - Cleonaea

Σ. ΛΑΖΑΡΙΔΗΣ
Σαμοθράκη καὶ ἡ Περαία της

Ν. ΦΑΡΑΚΛΑΣ
Σικυωνία

D. THEOCHARIS
Prehistory of Eastern Macedonia and Thrace

Δ. ΛΑΖΑΡΙΔΗΣ
Ἀμφίπολις καὶ Ἄργιλος

Μ. ΣΑΚΕΛΛΑΡΙΟΥ - Ν. ΦΑΡΑΚΛΑΣ
Μεγαρίς, Αἰγόσθενα, Ἐρένεια

Σ. ΔΑΚΑΡΗΣ
Θεσπρωτία

Ν. ΦΑΡΑΚΛΑΣ
Ἑρμιονίς - Ἁλιάς

Δ. ΛΑΖΑΡΙΔΗΣ
Φίλιπποι - Ρωμαϊκή ἀποικία

Μ. ΠΕΤΡΟΠΟΥΛΑΚΟΥ - Ε. ΠΕΝΤΑΖΟΣ
ΑΤΤΙΚΗ Οἰκιστικὰ στοιχεῖα - πρώτη ἔκθεση

Fig. 5 Covers of the twenty-four published volumes of the Ancient Greek Cities Project.

Θ. LAZARIDIS
Thasos and Its Peraia

Ν. ΠΑΠΑΧΑΤΖΗΣ
Cassopaia and the Elean Colonies

Δ. ΛΑΖΑΡΙΔΗΣ
Ἄβδηρα καὶ Δίκαια

Ν. ΦΑΡΑΚΛΑΣ
Τροιζηνία, Καλαύρεια, Μέθανα

Ν. ΦΑΡΑΚΛΑΣ
Φλειασία

Ν. ΦΑΡΑΚΛΑΣ
Ἐπιδαυρία

Δ. ΛΑΖΑΡΙΔΗΣ
Μαρώνεια καὶ Ὀρθαγορία

Ι. ΤΡΑΥΛΟΣ Μ. ΠΕΤΡΟΠΟΥΛΑΚΟΥ Ε. ΠΕΝΤΑΖΟΣ
Α Θ Η Ν Α Ι
Οἰκιστικὰ στοιχεῖα - πρώτη ἔκθεση

Α. ΖΩΗΣ
Κρήτη - Ἐποχὴ τοῦ Λίθου

J. W. SPERLING
Thera and Therasia

ΑΡΓ. ΠΕΤΡΟΝΩΤΗΣ
Ἡ Μεγάλη Πόλις τῆς Ἀρκαδίας

Ι. Δ. ΚΟΝΤΗΣ
Λέσβος καὶ ἡ Μικρασιατική της περιοχή

> Fig. 6 Islamabad, master plan of metropolitan area.

History as a Framework

Each of the three parts defined by the alignment of the main axes of the Metropolitan Area is sub-divided into Sectors. The approved Master Plan for the Metropolitan Area, as shown on these pages, covers the whole area of Islamabad, Rawalpindi, and the National Park. Details of land uses are given in the legend of the illustration.

Islamabad being constructed.
In the background the Margala hills

the information itself. The statistical analysis would provide not merely an average in statistics but also a range of conceptual approaches (e.g. "conceptual average size") – or, to paraphrase, a means of understanding the ancient city. The analysis of the rules governing the ancient city would then give the conceptual tools to intervene in the present-day city.[22] As he himself indicates in an intra-office communication to Alexandros Tombazis, "(ii) It is necessary to find a way to restore this scale in small sizes that will lead in a city of small-scale areas that are encircled by major roadways-like in [our plans for] ISLAMABAD" – that is, the plans that Doxiadis Associates had created for the new capital of Pakistan (1960).[23]

And here it becomes clear how Doxiadis and his team intended to resolve the problems of the modern city: through a kind of collage of urban grids and infrastructures, in which ideal "scaled to humans" urban clusters, modeled after small-scale ancient settlements, would be surrounded by highways. Doxiadis's office had implemented such urban-planning schemes in its proposals for Islamabad in 1960 [Fig. 6] – to which he explicitly refers in the aforementioned communication – as well as for the town of Aspra Spitia (1961–1965), situated on the coast of the Corinthian Gulf (Greece) about one hour's drive from Delphi.[24]

For both these projects, direct analogies to ancient Greek cities were drawn – for example, in Doxiadis's presentation "The Ancient Greek City

Fig. 7 Perspectival view of a pedestrian road in Islamabad's Community Class III (right) compared with a perspectival view of a road in Priene (350 BCE) (left), which featured in the presentation and accompanying exhibition entitled "The Ancient Greek City and the City of the Present" for the sixth International Congress of the European Cultural Foundation in Athens, May 1964.

and the City of the Present" and the accompanying exhibition for the sixth International Congress of the European Cultural Foundation in May 1964.[25] The plan of Islamabad's Community Class V was juxtaposed with the plan of ancient Athens, presented at the same scale.[26] A perspective view of a pedestrian road in Islamabad's Community Class III was compared with a perspective view of a road in Priene (350 BCE) [Fig. 7].[27] Equally, plans of Aspra Spitia, Olynthus (400 BCE) and Priene (350 BCE) were presented together at the same scale.[28] Diagrams paralleled the average size of the population and area of the ancient Greek city with that of cities of other ages, while plans juxtaposed the traffic of contemporary Athens (1964) with that of ancient Priene (350 BCE) and the public spaces of ancient Greek cities with those cities of other ages.[29]

Such comparisons were used to evaluate the high densities in contemporary public and private spaces and highlight the fact that the present-day city has lost its human dimensions.[30] Embracing both the human scale and the larger-than-human scale imposed by industrialization, Doxiadis concluded that contemporary cities must be an amalgamation of the two scales – the human scale as exemplified in ancient Greek cities and the scale of the machine age.[31] The analysis and presentation of ancient Greek cities offered a streamlined analysis of ancient settlements, while the proposed projects concretized the paradigmatic relationship between the ancient and the modern city.

Doxiadis's approach and commitment to urban industrialization, as expressed in these projects, was hardly innovative, as it was influenced by post-war trends in regional planning with their critique of the simplistic application of the pre-war ideas of CIAM. He was inspired by CIAM's post-war debate on the Habitat and Gropius's (1955) notion of total architecture.[32] His theory of Ekistics embraced contemporary environmental concerns and drew on the philosophical and methodological structure of human ecology, defined in the early 1920s. As Panayiota Pyla has shown, Doxiadis was also influenced by Patrick Geddes's attempts to associate urban and social analyses in a comprehensive research model, and he engaged, in his overall formulation of Ekistics, in the contemporary discourse on biological analogies in architecture.[33] He extended Geddes's theories, however, to propose that human settlements are complex biological systems, whose growth is dependent on the multiple patterns of mobility made available by numerous overlapping networks, and whose complexity can be resolved if we integrate the principles of past cities in urban-planning projects.[34] Doxiadis's approach differs in that it shows a deep engagement with ancient cities, showcased by the streamlined analysis of their urban-planning principles, densities and complex datasets aiming to employ them as blueprints in designing the city of the future.

Some of the ideas that Doxiadis put forth in his projects – for example, the concept of the city as a nodal point of a supra-regional network and the refined notion of human scale that included the six sensory modalities (visual, auditory, kinaesthetic, olfactory, thermal and tactile) of humans' interaction with space (conceptualized in Edward T. Hall's visualization of the human bubble) – foreshadowed later developments in the field of archaeology.[35] These kinds of analyses highlight the importance of trade routes and systems of communication, as well as the subjectivity of human experience, in the study of ancient settlements – results of the influence of the "sensory turn" in the social sciences in the 1990s and the application of network approaches in archaeology since the 2000s. The field of archaeology, which was undergoing a major transformation in the 1960s and 1970s, tackled such issues only after the advent of post-processual archaeology – otherwise known as interpretative archaeology – in the 1980s.[36]

His streamlining approach to ancient cities through statistical analysis, indeed, points toward more recent developments in the field of classical archaeology. The employment of statistical information as a means of understanding the ancient city has gained momentum over the past two decades, with large-scale projects pursuing big datasets that enable us to quantify the available information on Greek and Roman cities.[37] These projects are of extreme importance, admirable in their efforts and invaluable for further research. Yet, in providing a rationalized analysis of ancient settlements they might be seen as offering an aestheticized view of the past. I would, in fact, say that if the nineteenth century was the era of the "big digs," the twenty-first century is the era of "big data" – and we really ought to equally resist the sensationalism associated with it. Doxiadis resisted the oversimplification that the streamlined analysis of ancient datasets by an architect and planner might lead to, and invited archaeologists and historians to work on the AGC project so as to ensure an in-depth study of ancient settlements that he could then use for the city of the future.[38]

The Delos Symposia

While the Ancient Greek Cities Project directly fed into urban-planning projects, the Delos Symposia employed the archaeological sites as stages and history and the past as a framework for the discussion. They offered both a streamlining approach to and an affective connection with the historical past.

Lawrence Halprin, a pioneer practitioner of landscape architecture, for instance, stated in his talk on "landscape as matrix" and macro- and micro-infrastructures in the 1971 Athens Ekistics Month [Fig. 8]:

> It is interesting for me here amongst the ancient and very beautiful Greek cities AND the equally existing villages to see the essential quality of the Micro-infrastructure (that is the spaces between buildings). What remains to us of the ancient Greek cities – of Delphi, Olympia, Mistra, the Acropolis and others we have seen are the magnificent spaces, the outdoor amphitheatres, the great stadia, the experience of walking up steps around boulders, among the beautiful pines and figs and Italian cypress – the oleander and mint fragranting the air... The actual cities are long gone, the structures have tumbled into a mud of man-made talus slope but the infrastructure remains hauntingly – it peoples the landscape with echoes of past events, of people long gone, of fantasies half imagined.
>
> (When our own cities lie in ruins will they ever show beautiful infrastructures to future Delos symposium participants?).[39]

For Halprin, the experience of visiting the ancient cities as well as existing villages provided an affective connection with their material culture and ecosystems.

The Delians themselves were almost staged in the archaeological sites they visited in the ensuing publications of the deliberations of the Athens Month of Ekistics and the Delos Symposia in the October issue of *Ekistics*. See, for instance, Richard Buckminster Fuller as seen in 1972 in Mycenae writing down his thoughts – an image that accompanied his presentation in the 1972 Athens Month of Ekistics, entitled "Energy Past and Future" in the October issue of *Ekistics* that year [Fig. 9].[40] The presentations of the speakers and the ways in which these are portrayed in the issues of *Ekistics* are telling

ATHENS TECHNOLOGICAL ORGANIZATION — ATHENS CENTER OF EKISTICS
24, Strat. Syndesmou, Athens 136, Greece

The 1971 Athens Ekistics Month

Delos Symposion (Delos Nine)
Document B No. 54
15 July 1971

THE LANDSCAPE AS MATRIX
macro & micro infrastructures

by Lawerence Halprin

Much mention has been made of infrastructure and the increasing realization of its importance in housing urban and suburban populations.

What has emerged however in the discussion increasingly makes infrastructure sound like boring CONDUITS - ways only of transferring things or people from one place to another.....

> sewerage: away from
> power: toward
> transportation: to and fro. etc.

always however as though infrastructure was a means toward an end, not an end in itself.

I wish to point out that infrastructure is <u>IN FACT</u> the very core of a culture and of a civilization. It is infrastructure which sets the tone of cities, which establishes life styles, which is where the life of cities goes on, which - in fact - more importantly than shells establishes the quality of our Environment.....

<u>Micro-infrastructure</u>

It is interesting for me here amongst the ancient and very beautiful greek cities AND the equally beautiful existing villages to **see** the essential quality of the <u>Micro</u>-infrastructure (that is the spaces between buildings). What remains to us of the ancient greek cities - of Delphi, Olympia, Mistra, the Acropolis and others we have seen are the magnificent spaces, the outdoor amphitheatres, the great stadia, the experience of walking up steps around boulders, among the beautiful pines and figs and Italian cypress - the oleander and mint fragranting the air.....The actual cities are long gone, the structures have tumbled into a mud of man-made talus slope but the infrastructure remains hauntingly - it peoples the landscape with echoes of past events, of people long gone, of fantasies half imagined.

(When our own cities lie in ruins will they ever show beautiful **infrastructures to future Delos symposium participans?**)

Fig. 8 The 1971 Athens Ekistics Month, Delos Symposion (Delos Nine): "The Landscape as Matrix: Macro & Micro Infrastructures," by Lawrence Halprin.

Engineering efficiency related to the amount of energy realized as work by a machine, compared to the amount of energy put into the machine to do that work. You are all familiar with automobile engines and know that they have pistons. If you have an explosion on the top of a piston it sends the piston downward. But there is a connecting rod to the crank shaft. The crank shaft turns around and sends it right back, contradicting you. This is called 180° restraint of momentum. A reciprocating engine is inherently only about 15% efficient. By the time we transmit that energy through 3 or 4 right angles of gears the energy is reduced some more and a great deal of it goes into just starting our automobile tires.

If I have a connecting rod and explosion on the side instead of the top and I do not have a crank shaft, just a fixed shaft which goes around, we call it a turbine. This has 90% restraint instead of 180° restraint, and the turbine is twice as efficient as a reciprocating engine. We then get into the gas turbine and the jet engine which has no connecting rod at all. It is just thrust, displacement action, reaction, and we have got up to 65% efficiency: doubled again! Now we have fuel cells, in which hydrogen and oxygen come together electrolytically, thus reducing energy, and they get up to 85% efficiencies. If we turn to a water wheel, we are 90% efficient.

We are operating in North America (with 9% of all humanity) at an overall 4% efficiency. In North America through 24 hours a day there are over two million cars standing at red lights with their engines going, each using well over 100 hp. This means we have 200,000,000 horses jumping up and down going nowhere. We are taking the savings account of millions of years and burning them up in this very ignorant manner. There are oil ships coming from Arabia, often running onto rocks and causing pollution for that kind of nonsense.

It is not feasible to think about 100% efficiency but the 85% of the fuel cell level is realizable. This means that by 1985 we could get to an overall efficiency of 12% which would mean that instead of 40% of humanity enjoying a high standard of living, 100% of humanity would have a higher standard of living than anybody has ever known. This is technically feasible.

We are still expending an enormous potential in warfaring. The nation with the greatest hitting power over the longest distance, in the shortest time, with the greatest accuracy, with the least effort is the one who wins. Over 200 billion dollars is spent by United States, NATO, Russia and China annually for this war project.

In the 10 years that I have been involved in the Ekistics meetings and the Delos Symposia I have seen a change regarding this kind of knowledge. There is a realization by the young world but the older world is still tied up with its conditioned reflexes. Once we have a conception that we can make it, this eliminates the need for heroism, for the feeling that you have to

Buckminster Fuller at Mycenae

fight the other guy in order to help the people who are depending on you. Heroism was just fundamental: "I like you and I'd like to spend some time with you, but my people need this and so do yours. So we might as well have it out and whoever gets killed, his people have to go away." The conception that we can make it is relevant to our conception of energy and how energy behaves.

Energy in structures. Through structuring, nature has a push and a pull; a compression and a tension: cohesion and relative crushability. The ultimate compressibility of masonry is the point at which it fails. Masonry can take an average of 50,000 lbs. per square inch ultimate load. But masonry has only about 50 lbs. per square inch tensile strength. It is a thousand times stronger in compression than in tension. So stone was not very good at holding things together. Building walls, placing a stone block on top of another stone block, had gravity pulling them and holding them together. So this is why we have all kinds of vertical stone walls from antiquity still standing. But when it comes to the horizontal we have beams. The beam has supporting columns and the load instead of compressing the center of the beam tends to split it. The bottom of the beam is trying to come apart and the top is trying to come together. Wood had the best tensile strength. With the best trees you could get up around 5,000 lbs./sq. inch tensile strength as against 50 lbs./sq. inch for stone. This means they were 100 times stronger. But they rotted and only lasted a little while.

Dr. Leake thinks that man has been on earth for twenty million years and throughout that time we have used stone with a very high compressibility capability

Fig. 9 Richard Buckminster Fuller, "Energy Past and Future."

about the ways in which history and the past are integrated in developing new design ideas. Each one of the Delians selects an aspect of the past that relates to their own interests. In the discussions between the Delos participants, the historical place becomes a framework in which their ideas are developed.

In fact, the past, present and future are collated in this streamlined view and become a continuous thread enabling them to understand cities, humanity and metaphysics. We see this in a poem-manifesto entitled "Metaphysical Mosaic" that Buckminster Fuller presented during the eighth Delos Symposion in 1970:

> Of all the humans now aboard
> Or about to come aboard
> Our Spaceship Earth
> Which witnessed a condition
> Only two-thirds of a century ago
> When less than one percent
> Of its human passengers
> Enjoyed an, in anyway, comparable standard of living.[41]

Later on, in the same poem, it is evident that Fuller is profoundly shaken by the consequences of war; he expresses his hope:

> To help tip the scales
> In favor of
> World society's becoming preoccupied
> With the design revolution
> And its inherently required
> Educational process revolution.
> [...]
> Of whatever my unique role may be
> In the consummation
> Of those evolutionary options
> Leading to the continuable success
> Of all humanity aboard our planet.

It was thus that intuition
Suggested the Sloop intuition.
For ships, sailors and the sea
Have been my greatest
Teachers and conditioners.

And it is not the least
Of such lessons
That Dinos Doxiadis
Finds it logical and propicious [*sic*]
To convene world around
Exploratory thinkers
To consider human settlements
From abroad a ship –
A mobile organic city –
Plying swiftly the Aegean Sea
Therefrom to inspect
The city states of its islands and shores
Regenerated for five milleniums [*sic*]
By history's most rugged, yet artistic
And intellectually inspired sailors
The Greeks [...]⁴²

The language used by Buckminster Fuller – we are all human passengers on "Spaceship Earth," "aboard our planet" – is highly indicative of the conceptualization of the very historical moment in which the Symposia took place, and finds parallels in many other presentations during the Athens Month of Ekistics.

The Symposia took place in the period of the emergence of an environmental movement in the Western world that called for an immediate and radical cutback of the industrial and economic mode of the so-called developed world and for action to limit its detrimental environmental effects.⁴³ Environmental concerns were expressed about the future – in particular, that of Earth and its future management. The figure of Spaceship Earth framed and structured the narrative of this environmental discourse.⁴⁴ The astronauts of the US Apollo missions of the 1960s and 1970s provided photographs of Earth as a whole. Their pictures, displaying the dynamic blue and green colors attributed to three billion years of transforming sunlight into the processes of life, nurtured the view of Earth and its human settlements as an organic whole. Such ideas seem to be crystallized in the Blue Marble photographs, the iconic view of Earth from space taken by Apollo astronauts starting in 1968.[45] Fuller presented on July 6, 1970, after the first landing on the Moon on July 20 the previous year, his *Operating Manual for Spaceship Earth* – already published in 1969 – summoning the engineering elite to take control of an environment in bad repair [Fig. 10].[46] His poem-manifesto relates the Delos discussions to contemporary developments of the time. Fuller invites his fellow Delians to explore the history of human settlements in their navigation of "the city-states of the islands and shores of the Aegean Sea" and to decipher the "Metaphysical Mosaic" or, better yet, the "Blue Marble of Greek Architectural History" that these settlements represented for the Delos symposiasts.[47]

History thus becomes a framework for the discussion as much as the present becomes a backdrop, a blue marble, for the future. For the Delians, while all humans are aboard the spaceship called Earth, the mobile organic city of the ship aboard which the Delos participants were traveling goes around the city-states of the islands and shores of the Aegean Sea that have been regenerated for five millennia.

What we see in the Delos meetings is not merely history as a framework but chiefly the conceptualization of the present in a continuum between past, present and future. This becomes apparent in a document compiled by John Papaioannou, outlining the chronology of the sites visited by the Delians. In this document, entitled "Outline of Chronology of Sites in the Area of the Tour," the last chronological section in the tour is the *future*. The timeline begins from prehistory and the first farming settlements of the Neolithic period, moves on to ancient sites (meaning archaic, classical, Hellenistic and Roman), then Byzantine sites, then modern (Ottoman period and the creation of modern Greece); next come contemporary sites, to conclude with the future: Megalopolis and Ecumenopolis [Figs. 11–12]:

Megalopolis	2010–2040 AD	Athens–Thessaloniki–Ptolemais
Ecumenopolis	2080–2150 AD	Athens–Thessaloniki–Central Europe, Epirus–Thessaloniki–Thrace, Patras–Athens–S.W. Turkey[48]

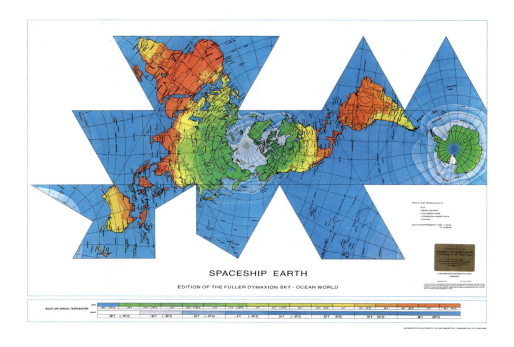

And although such conceptualizations might seem very much of their time, we only need to turn to current equivalents to see their continuing relevance. These include the concept of the Anthropocene, coined by the Anthropocene Working Group (AWG) to formally designate the current epoch dating from the commencement of significant human impact on Earth's geology and ecosystems – including, but not limited to, anthropogenic climate change; and more recent initiatives in the art world place present inquiries in an aestheticized view of the past and the present, such as the 2017 exhibition of Hauser and Wirth entitled *Bronze Age: c. 3500 BC– AD 2018* or even Damien Hirst's 2017 exhibition at Palazzo Grassi in Venice, *Treasures from the Wreck of the Unbelievable*.[49] Similarly to the Delos Symposia project, in these efforts history becomes a framework for the discussion as much as the present becomes a backdrop, a blue marble, for the future. In these approaches, the artists, scholars or curators employ the historical past to bring a historical perspective to, and an endorsement of, the present. In the case of the Delians, the streamlined analysis of and affective

Fig. 10 Spaceship Earth: 1982 edition of the Dymaxion map by Buckminster Fuller and cartographer Shoji Sadao. Fuller had been developing this map since the 1940s. It is a projection of a world map onto the surface of an icosahedron, which can be unfolded and flattened to two dimensions.

ATHENS TECHNOLOGICAL ORGANIZATION — ATHENS CENTER OF EKISTICS
24 Strat. Syndesmou St., Athens 136, Greece

The 1970 Athens Ekistics Month | Greek Settlements through the Ages
Document O No. 4
1 July 1970

OUTLINE OF CHRONOLOGY
of Sites in the Area of the Tour
by J. Papaioannou

The following tabulation groups the main sites to be visited, visible from the itinerary, or otherwise in the area of the Tour by main periods:

LEGEND:

CAPITALS	Sites to be visited during Tour; important remains from period considered.
CAPITALS	" " " " " " ; less important remains from period considered.
(CAPITALS)	" " " traversed non-stop (or with very short stop).
Small letters	" clearly visible from itinerary.
Small letters	" faintly " " "
(Small letters)	" invisible from itinerary, but in the general area of the Tour.

Period	Approx. Dates	Sites
Prehistory		
Lower Palaeolithic	ca. 500,000 BC	(Chalkidiki, skull)
Acheullean	ca. 70,000 BC	(Thessaly), (Chalkidiki), (Epirus)
Upper Palaeolithic	ca. 10 to 20,000 BC	Thessaly, (Chalkidiki)
Mesolithic	ca. 7 to 10,000 BC	Thessaly
Neolithic		
First Farming Settlements	ca. 6,000 BC	SESKLO, Nea Nikomedia, Orchomenos
Bronze Age	ca. 2 to 3,000 BC	SESKLO, DIMINI, Kastoria, Pherai, Orchomenos
Mycenean	1600 to 1100 BC	Olg, Orchomenos, Iolkos, Pagasai, Pherai, Verghina, Thebes, (Thessaly), (Macedonia)

Figs. 11–12 The 1970 Athens Ekistics Month, Delos Symposion (Delos Eight), "Greek Settlements through the Ages."

ATHENS TECHNOLOGICAL ORGANIZATION — ATHENS CENTER OF EKISTICS

Greek Settlements through the Ages
Document C No. 4
Page 2

Period	Approx. Dates	Sites
Ancient		
Archaic	700 to 480 BC	DELOS, Edessa, Pherai
Classic	480 to 300 BC	DELOS, DEMETRIAS, PELLA, TEMPE VALLEY, Thermopylae, Amphiaraeion, Thebes, Verria, Orchomenos, Dion, Pagasai, Pherai, Sounion, (Marathon), (Halkis)
Hellenistic	300 BC to 4th C.AD	PELLA, DEMETRIAS, DELOS, THESSALONIKI, Pagasai, Pherai, Dion, Verria, Herakleion (Platamon)
Roman	2nd C.BC to 4th C.AD	THESSALONIKI, PELLA, DELOS, Dion, Verria
Byzantine (Medieval)		
Early Christian	4th to 7th C. AD	THESSALONIKI, Edessa, Demetrias, Dion, Verria, Orchomenos
Middle and Late Byzantine	7th to 15th C. AD	THESSALONIKI, KASTORIA, Orchomenos, Verria, Edessa, (Hosios Loukas), (Daphni)
Modern		
Turkish Occupation	15th C.AD to 1830	KASTORIA, SIATISTA, VERRIA, MAKRYNITSA, PORTARIA, THESSALONIKI, (KOZANI), Platamon, (Florina)
Modern Greece	1830-1950	MAKRYNITSA, PORTARIA, AND VOLOS, MYKONOS, (VOLOS), (LAMIA), (KATERINI), Larissa, Syros, Tinos
Contemporary	1950-1970	VOLOS, THESSALONIKI, KASTORIA, MYKONOS, ARNITSA, (ARGOS ORESTIKON), Syros, Tinos, Stylis, Almyros, Larissa, Vogatsiko, Kamena Tourla, (Ptolemais)
Future		
Megalopolis	2010-2040 AD	Athens-Thessaloniki-Ptolemais
Ecumenopolis	2080-2150 AD	Athens-Thessaloniki-Central Europe, Epirus-Thessaloniki-Thrace, Patras-Athens-S.W.Turkey

History as a Framework

connection with the historical and archaeological context inform their proposals for the future of human settlements.

The choice of Delos as the place where the meetings ended sheds further light on the ways in which Doxiadis and, by consequence, other Delians employed historical information to craft their very own approach to contemporary architecture and urbanism. Delos is an example of a city that was rapidly urbanized during the late Hellenistic period, and this rapid urbanization must have surely fed into the discussions of the participants of the Delos Symposia on modern urbanization phenomena and the desired proportionate design vis-à-vis human scale. Doxiadis's conceptualization of Delos, and ancient Greek cities more broadly, in this context is perhaps best showcased on the cover of the October 1963 *Ekistics* magazine, which presented the proceedings of the first Delos Symposium [Fig. 3]. It features two superimposed plans, at different scales, of the urban fabric of Delos and, more specifically, of the Theater District – the district through which the Delians had walked to sign the "Declaration of Delos" in July 1963 [Fig. 1] and to which they would return in their yearly peregrination to the site. These two superimposed plans point to Doxiadis's interest in understanding the ideal "human-scaled" urban fabric of rapidly urbanized Delos and its conceptual average scale, a scale that he and the other Delians experienced yearly, so as to implement it in the design of the present-day city.

Delos was indeed so important that its name was reserved for the final two Symposia (1974–1975) – the last one after Doxiadis's death on June 28, 1975 – which were held at Apollonio in Porto Rafti, a model settlement designed by the Doxiadis office at the human scale: on the one hand, Delos, the birthplace of Apollo; on the other, Apollonio, which was designed according to the standards of Apollo's harmony. We could say that, for Doxiadis, Delos symbolized Entopia, meaning "in place" – the *topos* that he conceived of between utopia and reality, and that he realized at Apollonio – and perhaps functioned in such a way in his conceptual horizon of ancient and modern cities.[50]

1 The first discussions for the Delos Symposia began in 1958. Doxiadis Archives, File 2761, "Discussion between D[oxiadis], J. Tyrwhitt and Piperoglou on the subject of a conference in Delos" (August 5, 1958). For a general discussion on the Delos Symposia, see Simon Richards, "'Halfway between the Electron and the Universe': Doxiadis and the Delos Symposia," in G. Adler, T. Brittain-Catlin and G. Fontana-Giusti (eds), *Scale: Imagination, Perception and Practice in Architecture* (London: Routledge, 2012), 170–81; Mark Wigley, "Network Fever," *Grey Room*, no. 4 (2001), 82–122; Dimitris Philippides, Κωνσταντίνος Δοξιάδης (1913–1975): Αναφορά στον Ιππόδαμο [*Constantinos Doxiadis (1913–1975): Reference to Hippodamus*] (Athens: Melissa Books, 2015), 164–68; Mantha Zarmakoupi, "Balancing Acts between Ancient and

2. Modern Cities: The Ancient Greek Cities Project of C. A. Doxiadis," *Architectural Histories* 3, no. 1 (2015), 1–22.

2. On the creation of the firm, see Panayiota I. Pyla, "Ekistics, Architecture and Environmental Politics, 1945–1976: A Prehistory of Sustainable Development," Ph.D. dissertation, Massachusetts Institute of Technology, 2002, http://dspace.mit.edu/handle/1721.1/32715#files-area, 36 (accessed March 18, 2024); Philippides, *Constantinos Doxiadis*, 11–19, 213–28. On the housing projects in Iraq, see Panayiota I. Pyla, "Back to the Future: Doxiadis's Plans for Baghdad," *Journal of Planning History* 7, no. 1 (2008), 3–19; Panayiota I. Pyla, "Baghdad's Urban Restructuring, 1958: Aesthetics and Politics of Nation Building," in S. Isenstadt and K. Rizvi (eds), *Modernism and the Middle East: Architecture and Politics in the Twentieth Century* (Seattle: University of Washington Press, 2008), 97–115; Lefteris Theodosis, "'Containing' Baghdad: Constantinos Doxiadis' Program for a Developing Nation," in P. Azara (ed.), *Ciudad del espejismo: Bagdad, de Wright a Venturi* [*City of Mirages: Baghdad, from Wright to Venturi*] (Barcelona: Universitat Politecnica de Catalunya – Departament de Composicio Arquitectonica, 2008), 167–72. For the restructuring of the plan of Homs in Syria (1959), see Pyla, "Ekistics, Architecture and Environmental Politics, 1945–1976," 67–70. For the planning of the new capital in Pakistan (1960), see Ahmed Z. Khan, "Representing the State: Symbolism and Ideology in Doxiadis's Plan of Islamabad," in M. Swenarton, I. Troiani and H. Webster (eds), *The Politics of Making* (London and New York: Routledge, 2007), 61–75; Ahmed Z. Khan, "Constantinos A. Doxiadis' Plan for Islamabad: The Making of a 'City of the Future' 1959–1963," unpublished Ph.D. thesis, University of Leuven, Department of Architecture, Urbanism and Planning, 2008; Markus Daechsel, "Misplaced Ekistics: Islamabad and the Politics of Urban Development in Pakistan," *South Asian History and Culture* 4 (2013), 87–106, 87–99; Markus Daechsel, *Islamabad and the Politics of International Development in Pakistan* (Cambridge: Cambridge University Press, 2015), 106–47; Philippides, *Constantinos Doxiadis*, 244–73. Generally, see Pyla, "Ekistics, Architecture and Environmental Politics, 1945–1976," 55–74.

3. Documentation of the Delos Symposia can be found in Doxiadis Archives, File 2761. August 5, 1958.

4. Doxiadis Archives, File 32298, "Η Διακήρυξης της Δήλου [The Declaration of Delos One]" (1963). See also Pyla, "Ekistics, Architecture and Environmental Politics, 1945–1976," 114–21; Wigley, "Network Fever," 89–92; Richards, "'Halfway between the Electron and the Universe': Doxiadis and the Delos Symposia," 172–73; Philippides, *Constantinos Doxiadis*, 164–68; Zarmakoupi, "Balancing Acts," 4–6.

5. For example, the participants in the first Symposion were: Charles Abrams (USA), Edmund N. Bacon (USA), Stewart Bates (Canada), Pedro Bidagor Lasarte (Spain), A. K. Brohi (Pakistan), C. S. Chandrasekhara (India), Walter Christaller (Germany), Jacob L. Crane (USA), C. A. Doxiadis (Greece), Leonard Duhl (USA), O. E. Fischnich (UN), Lyle C. Fitch (USA), R. Buckminster Fuller (USA), Clifford Furnas (USA), S. Giedion (Switzerland), J. Gorynski (Poland), Eiichi Isomura (Japan), Sture Linner (UN), Richard Llewelyn-Davies (Great Britain), Mohamed S. Makiya (Iraq), Edward S. Mason (USA), Sir Robert Matthew (Great Britain), Marshall McLuhan (Canada), Margaret Mead (USA), Waclaw Ostrowski (Poland), Alfred R. Otoo (Ghana), David Owen (UN), Charles H. Page (USA), E. Papanoutsos (Greece), Shafic H. El-Sadr (UAR), Carl Schweyer (Germany), C. H. Waddington (Great Britain), Barbara Ward (Lady Jackson; Great Britain) and Sir Robert Watson-Watt (Great Britain). The participants in the first Symposion of Delos were presented in the journal *Ekistics* (vol. 16, no. 95, October 1963, 218–34).

6. Pyla, "Ekistics, Architecture and Environmental Politics, 1945–1976," 114–21. On the "Charter of Athens," see Mumford, "CIAM Urbanism after the Athens Charter," *Planning Perspectives* 7 (1992), 391–417, 392–94.

7. Doxiadis Archives, File 18645, "C. A. Doxiadis Greek translation from Le Corbusier's 'Précisions'" (1931–1935).

8. Doxiadis Archives, File 2761, "AEM Organization 1958–1968 (Folder I), 1958–1963 (1964), 1–222 (1)," 1. Subject: Discussion between D, J. Tyrwhitt and Piperoglou on the subject of a conference in Delos. Date: August 5, 1958. The analogy between the "Charter of Athens" and the "Declaration of Delos" was clearly spelled out by Doxiadis in a letter written on April 22, 1963, to Jaqueline Tyrwhitt, asking her to draft a text for the first Symposion of Delos: "As we are going to refer often to the Charter of Athens and to the Meeting of Athens in 1933, I beg you to prepare an objective statement of no more than 5 or 6 pages on the Athens meeting, incorporating at the end the Charter of Athens with a few words on its inception and preparation, how the meeting took place, on whose initiative, on the attendance, on the discussions, on its importance and on its effects. I imagine you would like to speak about CIAM, too." Doxiadis Archives, File 2761, "AEM Organization 1958–1968 (Folder I), 1958–1963 (1964), 1–222 (1)," 75. This text was published in the proceedings of the first Symposion of Delos, which presents the fourth CIAM congress as a comparable effort of a previous generation. Jaqueline Tyrwhitt, "Appendix. The CIAM Charter of Athens, 1933: Outcome of a Similar Effort," *Ekistics / Οικιστική. Reviews on the Problems and Science of Human Settlements* 16, no. 95 (1963), 263–67, quotation 263.

9. Zarmakoupi, "Balancing Acts."

10. For a brief introduction to the history of Delos, see Philippe Bruneau and Jean Ducat, *Guide de Délos*

(4th revised ed.) (Athens: École française d'Athènes, 2005), 31–48. On the rapid urbanization of Delos, see Mantha Zarmakoupi, "Shaping the City of Late Hellenistic Delos," *Journal of Ancient Architecture* 1 (2022), 65–85.

11 Doxiadis Archives, File 2761, "AEM Organization 1958–1968 (Folder I), 1958–1963 (1964), 1–222 (1)," 7–9, "A proposal for a conference of planners on the island of Delos for the formulation and declaration of the Charter of Delos," 8. See also discussion in Mantha Zarmakoupi, "Τόπος και εντοπία: τα Συμπόσια της Δήλου [Topos and Entopia: The Symposia of Delos]," in D. I. Kyrtatas, I. Konstantopoulos, and C. Boulotis (eds), *Τόπος Τοπίο, Τιμητικός Τόμος για τον Δημήτρη Φιλιππίδη* [*Topos Topio, Honorary Volume for Dimitris Philippides*] (Athens: Melissa Books, 2018), 63–70.

12 Maria Ypsilanti, "Deserted Delos: A Motif of the Anthology and Its Poetic and Historical Background," *Greek, Roman, and Byzantine Studies* 50 (2010), 63–85. The literary *topos* was a constant point of reference for the authors, who dealt not only with the mythological figure of Delos but also with her historical fate, explained through mythology. See also discussion in Mantha Zarmakoupi, "The Blue Marble of Greek Architectural History: Delos and the Delos Symposia," in M. Zarmakoupi (ed.), *Looking at the City: Architectural and Archaeological Perspectives* (Athens: Melissa Books, 2023), 202–34, 208–11.

13 Doxiadis Archives, File 22831, "Book on Delos Symposia (working file)," 3–4. Such ideas were echoed in the introduction by Gwen Bell and Jaqueline Tyrwhitt to their edited book *Human Identity in the Urban Environment* (Harmondsworth: Penguin Books, 1972), 15. See discussion in Richards, "'Halfway between the Electron and the Universe': Doxiadis and the Delos Symposia," 175.

14 Constantinos A. Doxiadis, "Athens Center of Ekistics," *DA Newsletter* 3, no. 11 (1963), 38–48, quotation 38.

15 Doxiadis Archives, File 19087, S-D 2120, April 3, 1960.

16 Philippides, *Constantinos Doxiadis*, 111–37.

17 Pyla, "Ekistics, Architecture and Environmental Politics, 1945–1976," 32–51, 111–14, 121–30; Panayiota Pyla, "Planetary Home and Garden: Ekistics and Environmental-Developmental Politics," *Grey Room*, no. 36 (2009), 6–35, 7–11, 17–21; Ahmed Z. Khan, "Nature and the City: The Legacy of Doxiadis' Plan for Islamabad," in *Proceedings of the WSSD Workshop on Human Settlements and Environment, Islamabad, December 14–15, 2004* (Islamabad: Ministry of Environment, Government of Pakistan, 2004), 86–98; Ahmed Z. Khan, "Rethinking Doxiadis' Ekistical Urbanism," *Positions* 1 (2010), 6–39, 8–10).

18 "[…] να δημιουργηθή μια συλλογή […] με σχέδια απ' την αρχαία πόλη, σε σωστή κλίμακα, με σωστή παρουσίαση, […] για να αποδείξωμε πως μπορούμε να πάρωμε απ' την αρχαία πόλη στοιχεία για την σημερινή." Doxiadis Archives, File 22075, S-D 7082, "Μελέτες Αρχαίων Ελληνικών Πόλεων [Studies of Ancient Greek Cities]" (January 7, 1964), 2.

19 Volumes 1–24 of the AGC program are: vol. 1, *An Ekistical Study of the Hellenic City-State* (A. Toynbee 1971); vol. 2, *Method for the Research of Ancient Greek Settlements* (C. A. Doxiadis 1972); vol. 3, *Corinthia – Cleonaea* (M. Sakellariou and N. Faraklas 1971); vol. 4. *Cassopaia and the Elean Colonies* (S. Dakaris 1971); vol. 5, *Thasos and Peraia* (D. Lazaridis 1971); vol. 6. *Non-sense and Legitimacy* (D. Lazaridis 1971); vol. 7, *Samothrace and its Peraia* (D. Lazaridis 1971); vol. 8. *Sikiyonia* (N. Faraklas 1971); vol. 9, *Prehistory of Eastern Macedonia and Thrace* (D. Theocharis 1971); vol. 10, *Trizinia, Kalavria, Methana* (N. Faraklas 1972); vol. 11, *Floesia* (N. Faraklas 1972); vol. 12. *Epidavria* (N. Faraklas 1972); vol. 13. *Amphipolis and Argilos* (D. Lazaridis 1972); vol. 14, *Megaris, Aegosthena, Erenaea* (M. Sakellariou and N. Faraklas 1972); vol. 15, *Thesprotia* (S. Dakaris 1972); vol. 16, *Maronoea and Orthagoria* (D. Lazaridis 1972); vol. 17. *Athens: Ekistic Data – Initial Report* (I. Travlos, M. Petroulakos and E. Pentazos 1972); vol. 18, *Crete – Stone Age* (A. Zois 1973); vol. 19, *Hermionis – Alias* (N. Faraklas 1973); vol. 20, *Pilippoi: Roman Colony* (D. Lazaridis 1974); vol. 21, *Attica: Ekistic Data – Initial Report* (M. Petropoulakos and E. Pentazos 1973); vol. 22, *Thera and Therasia* (J. W. Sperling 1973); vol. 23, *The Grand City of Arcadia* (Arg. Petronotis 1973); vol. 24, *Lesbos and the Asia Minor Region* (I. D. Kontis 1978). Twelve completed monographs remained unpublished and can be consulted in manuscript form in the Doxiadis Archives: *Crete – Early Minoan Age* (A. Zois 1975–1978); *The Inland of Aegean Thrace* (D. Lazaridis 1974); *Ilis* (N. Gialouris 1971–1977); *Argaea – Asinaea* (M. Sakellariou and N. Faraklas, 1974–1975); *Aegina* (N. Faraklas 1975); *Western Likris* (N. Faraklas); *Eastern Likris* (N. Faraklas 1976); *Akarnania* (N. Faraklas [1977]); *The Spercheios Valley: Malis – Oetaea – Aenis* (N. Faraklas 1977); *Delphi* (Angelou 1970–1971); *Greek Cities in Southern France* (A. Tseklenis 1972); and *The Neolithic Age in Greece* (Shivaji Singh 1970–1971).

20 Doxiadis Archives, File 22075, S-D 7082, "Μελέτες Αρχαίων Ελληνικών Πόλεων [Studies of Ancient Greek Cities]" (January 7, 1964), 2.

21 Zarmakoupi, "Τόπος και εντοπία [Topos and Entopia]," 63–70.

22 Zarmakoupi, "Balancing Acts," 6–7.

23 "Πρέπει να βρούμε έναν τρόπο να την αναβιώσωμε αυτή την κλίμακα στα μεγέθη τα μικρά που οδηγεί στην πόλη κατά τομείς τους οποίους περιβάλλουν μεγάλοι αυτοκινητόδρομοι—σαν στο ISLAMABAD," Doxiadis Archives, File 22075, S-D 7154, 2.

24 On Islamabad, see Constantinos A. Doxiadis, "Islamabad: The Creation of a New Capital," *Town Planning Review* 36, no. 1 (1965), 1–28; Khan, "Representing the state," 61–75; Khan, "Constantinos A. Doxiadis' Plan for Islamabad"; Christos Costis, "Το Ισλαμαμπάντ ως

το κατεξοχήν πεδίο εφαρμογής της Οικιστικής [Islamabad as the Case Study par excellence of Ekistics]," in G. Kazazi and N. Gounari (eds), *Ο Κωνσταντίνος Δοξιάδης και το έργο του, δεύτερος τόμος* [*Constantinos Doxiadis and His Work*] (Athens: Technical Chamber of Greece, 2009), vol. 2, 126–32; Daechsel, "Misplaced Ekistics," 87–99; Daechsel, *Islamabad and the Politics of International Development*, 106–47; Philippides, *Constantinos Doxiadis*, 244–73.

On Aspra Spitia, see Andreas Simeon, "Aspra Spitia: A Feeling of Tradition in a Modern Community Plan Concept," *DA Review* 1, no. 4 (1964), 8–11; Panayiotis Tournikiotis, "Η αρχαία και η μοντέρνα πόλη στο έργο του Κωνσταντίνου Δοξιάδη [The Ancient and the Modern City in the Work of Constantinos Doxiadis]," in A. Defner, F. Loikissa, M. Marmaras, S. Tsilenis and V. Chastaoglou (eds), *Η πολεοδομία στην Ελλάδα από το 1949 έως το 1974: Πρακτικά του 2ου Συνεδρίου Εταιρείας Ιστορίας της Πόλης και της Πολεοδομίας* [*Urban Planning in Greece from 1949 to 1979: Proceedings of the 2nd Conference of the Society of the History of the City and Urban Planning*] (Volos: University Press of Thessaly, 2000), 85–98; Panayiotis Tournikiotis, "Ancient and Modern Cities in the Work of Constantinos Doxiadis," in *The Modern City Facing the Future: Conference Proceedings: Sixth International Docomomo Conference. Brasilia, September 1920-22, 2000* (São Carlos: Docomomo International, 2004), 97–112; Panayiotis Tournikiotis, "Ο Οικισμός 'Άσπρα Σπίτια': Η κληρονομιά του Κ. Α. Δοξιάδη [The Settlement of Aspra Spitia: The Heritage of C. A. Doxiadis]," in G. Kazazi and N. Gounari (eds), *Ο Κωνσταντίνος Δοξιάδης και το έργο του, δεύτερος τόμος* [*Constantinos Doxiadis and His Work*] (Athens: Technical Chamber of Greece, 2009), vol. 2, 209–28; Eleni Kalafati, "Άσπρα Σπίτια Βοιωτίας: Ζητήματα σχεδιασμού μιας νέας πόλης [Aspra Spitia of Boeotia: Issues of Designing a New City]," in V. Petridou, P. Pangalos and N. Kyrkitsou (eds), *Εργάζομαι άρα κατοικώ: Η περίπτωση του συγκροτήματος κατοικιών των Μεταλλείων Μπάρλου στο Δίστομο Βοιωτίας, των Δ. & Σ. Αντωνακάκη* [*I Work Therefore I Live: The Case of the Complex of Houses of the Mines at Distomo of Boeotia, of D. & S. Antonakakis*] (Patras: University of Patras, 2012), 17–24; Pyla, "Ekistics, Architecture and Environmental Politics, 1945–1976," 130–32; Alexander Tzonis and Alcestis P. Rodi, *Greece* (London: Reaktion Books, 2013), 175; Philippides, *Constantinos Doxiadis*, 321–30. See also Doxiadis Archives, File 36580, "Aspra Spitia: A new Greek city" (undated) and http://www.doxiadis.org/Downloads/aspra_spitia.pdf (accessed March 18, 2024).

25 See Constantinos A. Doxiadis, "The Ancient Greek City and the City of the Present," *DA Newsletter* 4, no. 5 (1964), 3–5. The revised text was published in English in the proceedings of the conference: Constantinos A. Doxiadis, "The Ancient Greek City and the City of the Present," in *The Living Heritage of Greek Antiquity* [*L'héritage vivant de l'antiquité grecque*] (The Hague: Mouton, 1967), 192–211. A synopsis of this text was also published in English and Greek: Constantinos A. Doxiadis, "The Ancient Greek City and the City of the Present," *Ekistics* 18, no. 108 (1964), 346–64; Constantinos A. Doxiadis, "Η αρχαία ελληνική και η σημερινή πόλη [The Ancient Greek City and the City of the Present]," *Αρχιτεκτονική* [*Architecture*], July–August (1964), 2–15. The full text is accessible at Doxiadis Archives, File 2681 (Greek), File 2701 (English).

26 Doxiadis Archives, File 2701, "The Ancient Greek City and the City of the Present," 66.
27 Ibid., 67.
28 Ibid., 74.
29 Ibid., 46–47.
30 Ibid., 59.
31 Ibid., 69–77.
32 On CIAM's post-war debate on the Habitat, see Eric Mumford, *The CIAM Discourse on Urbanism, 1928–1960* (Cambridge, MA: MIT Press, 2002), 225–38. On the ways in which Doxiadis's approach related to this debate, see Pyla, "Ekistics, Architecture and Environmental Politics, 1945–1976," 46–50; and Khan, "Rethinking Doxiadis' Ekistical Urbanism," 10–12.
33 Pyla, "Ekistics, Architecture and Environmental Politics," 1945–1976," 85–88.
34 On Doxiadis's use of networks, see Wigley, "Network Fever," 87–88, 104–111; Yannis Zavoleas, *Η μηχανή και το δίκτυο ως δομικά πρότυπα στην αρχιτεκτονική* [*Machine and Network as Structural Models in Architecture*] (Athens: Futura, 2013), 181–90.
35 Zarmakoupi, "Balancing Acts," 7.
36 On post-processual archaeology, see Ian Hodder and Scott Hutson, *Reading the Past: Current Approaches to Interpretation in Archaeology* (3rd ed.) (Cambridge: Cambridge University Press, 2003), 206–35 (ch. 9, "Post-processual Archaeology").
37 Alan K. Bowman and Andrew I. Wilson, *Quantifying the Roman Economy: Methods and Problems*, Oxford Studies on the Roman Economy (Oxford: Oxford University Press, 2009); Alan K. Bowman and Andrew I. Wilson (eds), *Settlement, Urbanization, and Population*, Oxford Studies on the Roman Economy (Oxford: Oxford University Press, 2011); John W. Hanson, *An Urban Geography of the Roman World, 100 B.C. to A.D. 300* (Oxford: Archaeopress, 2016); Alan K. Bowman and Andrew I. Wilson (eds), *Trade, Commerce, and the State in the Roman World*, Oxford Studies on the Roman Economy (Oxford: Oxford University Press, 2017); Alan K. Bowman and Andrew I. Wilson (eds), *The Roman Agricultural Economy: Organisation, Investment, and Production*, Oxford Studies on the Roman Economy (Oxford: Oxford University Press, 2018). See also other publications and projects of the Oxford Roman Economy Project: http://oxrep.classics.ox.ac.uk (accessed June 29, 2024).

38 Doxiadis Archives, File 19181; Doxiadis Archives, File 22144, SD-ACE 1379, "Αρχαίες Ελληνικές Πόλεις [Ancient Greek Cities]," August 5, 1971.
39 Doxiadis Archives, DELOS AEM Box 21, ATO/ACE AEM 1971, The 1971 Athens Ekistics Month, Delos Symposion (Delos Nine), Document B No. 54, July 15, 1971, "The Landscape as Matrix: Macro & Micro Infrastructures," by Lawrence Halprin.
40 R. Buckminster Fuller, "Energy Past and Future," *Ekistics* 34, no. 203 (October 1972), 241–45, image 243.
41 Doxiadis Archives, File 2532, ATO/ACE AEM 1970, The 1970 Athens Ekistics Month, Delos Symposion (Delos Eight), Document B No. 26, July 6, 1970, "Intuition: Metaphysical Mosaic," by R. Buckminster Fuller, 13.
42 Ibid., 22.
43 Daniel Barber, *Modern Architecture and Climate: Design Before Air Conditioning* (Princeton, NJ: Princeton University Press, 2020), 219–45.
44 Kenneth Boulding, "The Economics of the Coming Spaceship Earth," in H. Jarrett (ed.), *Environmental Quality in a Growing Economy* (Baltimore, MD: Johns Hopkins University Press, 1966), 3–14; Barbara Ward, *Spaceship Earth* (New York: Columbia University Press, 1966); R. Buckminster Fuller, *Operating Manual for Spaceship Earth* (New York: E. P. Dutton, 1969); Sabine Höhler, *Spaceship Earth in the Environmental Age, 1960–1990* (New York: Routledge), 1–25. See also discussion in Ioanna Laliotou, *Ιστορία του μέλλοντος: πως ο εικοστός αιώνας φαντάστηκε έναν "άλλο κόσμο"? [History of the Future History: How Did the Twentieth Century Imagine an "Other World"?]* (Athens: Historein, 2015).
45 These images were published from the *Whole Earth Catalogue* to *Time* magazine. See Robin Kelsey, "Reverse Shot: Earthrise and Blue Marble in the American Imagination," *New Geographies* 4 (2011), 1016; Sheila Jasanoff, "Image and Imagination: The Formation of Global Environmental Consciousness," in C. E. Miller and P. N. Edwards (eds), *Changing the Atmosphere: Expert Knowledge and Environmental Governance* (Cambridge, MA: MIT Press, 2001), 309–37.
46 Fuller, *Operating Manual*.
47 See discussion in Zarmakoupi, "The Blue Marble of Greek Architectural History."
48 Doxiadis Archives, File 2532, ATO/ACE AEM 1970, The 1970 Athens Ekistics Month, Delos Symposion (Delos Eight), "Greek Settlements through the ages," Document C, no. 4, July 1, 1970, "OUTLINE OF CHRONOLOGY of Sites in the Area of the Tour," by J. Papaioannou.
49 *Bronze Age: c. 3500 BC–AD 2018*: https://thewirthbronzegallery.com (accessed March 18, 2024); *Treasures from the Wreck of the Unbelievable*, presented at the Punta della Dogana and Palazzo Grassi in Venice from April 9 to December 3, 2017; see documentary on the show: https://www.youtube.com/watch?v=13ShK2UAeP0 (accessed July 2, 2024). For a critique of the latter, see discussion in Elizabeth S. Greene and Justin Leidwagner, "Damien Hirst's Tale of Shipwreck and Salvaged Treasure," *American Journal of Archaeology* 122, no. 1 (January 2018), published online at https://www.ajaonline.org/online-museum-review/3581 (accessed March 18, 2024).
50 "In the vast space penetrated by man's projections into the future, somewhere between dreams and reality, between utopias and topias, we have to conceive entopia – the place which satisfies the dreamer and is accepted by the scientist, the place where the projections of the artist and the builder meet." Constantinos A. Doxiadis, "Need of Entopia," in Constantinos A. Doxiadis, *Between Dystopia and Utopia* (London: Faber and Faber, 1968), 49–65, quotation 50–51; C. A. Doxiadis, *Building Entopia* (New York: Norton, 1975). See also discussion in Zarmakoupi, "Τόπος και εντοπία [Topos and Entopia]." On Apollonio, see Harrison Blackman, "The Demolition at Porto Rafti: Retracing Doxiadis' Remarkable Life and Contested Legacy," special issue: "Ekistics-Related Research – A Critical Approach to the Ekistics Legacy," *Ekistics and the New Habitat* 82, no. 1 (2022), 91–94, https://doi.org/10.53910/26531313-E2022821464 (accessed June 29, 2024).

The Past as a Stage Set for C. A. Doxiadis
Dimitris Philippides

The Past as a Stage

One can justifiably claim that C. A. Doxiadis was a product of his time. Therefore, his usage of historical precedents and his orchestrated performance before an audience in support of his planning theory and projects could both be understood as theatrical props connected to major intellectual currents in inter-war Greece, the period and place of his upbringing. One such notion was that there might be a hidden connection between Greek antiquity and vernacular tradition, as visualized in modern Greek ideology; Doxiadis accepted this notion as a basis for his pragmatism and promotional tactics.

Such traits could be traced in a few prominent inter-war Greek intellectuals such as the architect D. Pikionis, the author N. Kazantzakis, the music composer M. Kalomoiris, the entrepreneur K. Bastias and the philologist M. Triantafyllides. Doxiadis displayed similar ideological traits in his everyday conduct and theoretical treatises. In this manner, he proved to be an adherent to the inter-war group of Greek intellectuals called the Generation of the '30s.

As far as we know, C. A. Doxiadis persistently strove to dominate the stage in whichever activity he participated – be it a prestigious presentation, an invited lecture or any of the more demanding Delos Symposia.[1] Those who had a chance to see him perform in public would testify that he absolutely relished such carefully staged moments [Fig. 1]. Furthermore, Doxiadis injected a similar "theatrical" flair into his more private interviews, as well into his writings – be they books, articles or even sketchy handwritten internal memos at the DA (Doxiadis Associates) office. He absolutely mesmerized audiences or readers by artfully dramatizing the issues he dealt with, by turning them into elaborate, fully organized theatrical acts with him always as the protagonist. In view of this exceptional talent of his, one could interpret Doxiadis's position on any conceivable issue according to its merit as a theatrical prop. One such case would be his targeted, extensive referencing of the past.

Why appeal to the past in the first place? In broader terms, the world in the early post-war period was dominated by notions of progress and development based on continual economic growth for the masses supported by incessant technological leaps. Modernism heralded and reflected the optimism inherent in this upward movement. Taking advantage of this upsurge, Doxiadis excelled in a worldwide competitive field by supporting a radical vanguard position in contemporary planning and design issues. Why, then, would someone like Doxiadis, a visionary primarily concerned with taming the future, relate to the past?

Such a strategy has certain advantages. The past is usually free of the ambiguities hidden in the future or even in the mutability of the present. It can legitimize projections into the future and make them seem credible. Furthermore, planning tools, such as density ratios or the hierarchy of communities, would not be affected by the passage of time; due to their connection to historical precedents, they seemed scientifically validated and beyond any doubt.

In a broader perspective essential to our discussion, modern Greek national ideology was firmly founded on two historical abstractions: antiquity and the Byzantine Empire legacy. Irrespective of their conflicting aspects, these two poles – symbolized by the Acropolis in Athens and Hagia Sophia in Istanbul (Byzantine-era Constantinople) – constituted the bedrock of national identity. Whereas antiquity bridged the gap between the modern Greek state and its glorious forefathers, Byzantium provided a secular counterpart to the Greek Orthodox Church, the official creed of the new state. Moreover, during the long period under Ottoman rule, which lasted until the War of Independence (1821–1827), the Church also supplied a common cultural background, based on tradition, to dispersed Greek communities in the Balkans. This very tradition was initially, when the Greek state was formed, despised and discarded as a burden of Europeanization. Towards the end of the nineteenth century, however, it was reinstated as a legitimate part of the Greek national identity. The interplay of such

ideological undercurrents was also related to shifts in cultural patterns in Greek society, which favored either high- or low-culture affinities such as the appreciation of either Neoclassical or vernacular architecture, respectively. These interrelations are crucial in understanding Doxiadis's usage of generalized notions such as tradition, as will be presently demonstrated.

If we examine the contribution of recent Greek researchers to the role of the past in Doxiadis's worldview – such as Panayotis Tournikiotis, Mantha Zarmakoupi, Kostas Tsiambaos and Costandis Kizis – we find that, while Doxiadis's reference to antiquity has been extensively studied, his connection to tradition is still kept in relative obscurity. In more general terms, whenever the issue of tradition is mentioned in interviews related to Doxiadis,[2] it follows a rather circumstantial course, as if it were unimportant – perhaps even a subject that would potentially damage the vanguard "image" of Doxiadis. This uneven treatment is based on a viewpoint popular among proponents of modernism,[3] that antiquity can be deservedly connected to international modernism while tradition is a retrograde regional force opposed to the progressive context of modernism. Tradition is thus perceived as merely a product of sentimental excess or as an escapist tendency that is related to old-fashioned ethnocentricity. In this sense, tradition

Fig. 1 C. A. Doxiadis at a lecture, Harvard Graduate School of Design, February 1967.

complies with its general perception by critics in Greece as a hindrance to progress and development. This is a paradox because the same argument could be easily reversed or, better still, both these facets of the past could be summoned as supportive evidence for modernity.

Such a conceptual ambiguity recalls the atmosphere of deceit and artifice connected to the art of theater. By omitting unfit or embarrassing details, the reduction of the past to a bipartite ideological model, like the one discussed above, is convincing because it seems impregnable to doubt, a property much appreciated by the pragmatist Doxiadis. In fact, prominent in Doxiadis's value system was the fact that he never faltered; doubting to him was unthinkable, a betrayal of a set mission.[4] Therefore, one can maintain that the past, as exemplified by both ancient and vernacular precedents in Greece, served as a fitting stage set for his performances.

The Bipartite Model of Antiquity and Tradition

The bipartite model of antiquity and tradition ideally fits Doxiadis's spectrum of the past as a paradigm. In view of his multiple references to the past, our first task is to find how the past was allotted such a variety of roles. At the outset, he seems to have treated antiquity and tradition unevenly as sources of inspiration. Antiquity to him was a goldmine of figures and ratios to be applied directly to physical planning practice, whereas tradition was a subtler reference to contemporary issues of identity and contextualization. The former seemed cerebrally processed and was related to the ultimate scientific tool, mathematics, while the latter seemed emotionally perceived and helped define his attachment to place and society.

He was either unaware of contrasting aspects in accepted notions of the past, as outlined above, or he may have had a hunch, based on strong ideological grounds, that such apparent discrepancies were illusory – namely, that there might be some deeper, unsuspected connection between Greek antiquity and tradition that enabled their convergence. Our task is to expose this hidden link in Doxiadis and his milieu. To clarify things, we will resort to the method previously suggested by following two intertwining yet distinct directions. The first refers to Doxiadis's cultural milieu, which encouraged and nurtured his stance, whereas the second focuses on Doxiadis's character and mentality.

In relation to the first direction, we will single out two prominent cases: Dimitris Pikionis and Nikos Kazantzakis, both of whom were one

generation older than Doxiadis. Aside from generally being grouped, with these two plus several others, in the local intellectual circle called Generation of the '30s,[5] Doxiadis seems to have had certain close affinities particularly with Pikionis and Kazantzakis. As we shall see shortly, he was deeply influenced in his conduct by the subtleties of the former and the heroics of the latter.

Dimitris Pikionis (1887–1968) [Fig. 2], Doxiadis's much-revered university teacher and mentor, twenty-six years his senior, strove throughout his life to attain a synthesis of antiquity and tradition within an all-inclusive (pan-Hellenic) cultural construct. In this context, Pikionis strove to merge high with low cultures, a mix that we claim Doxiadis extensively exploited in his performances.

The renowned author Nikos Kazantzakis (1883–1957), thirty years his senior, also exerted a strong influence on Doxiadis. Friedrich Nietzsche's ideas permeated Kazantzakis's books [Fig. 3].[6] Although he never acknowledged it, Nietzsche was the main source of the image cultivated by Doxiadis, of a planner-philosopher with a noble mission to save world by treating its ailing settlements.

Fig. 2 Dimitris Pikionis, self-portrait.

Fig. 3 Nikos Kazantzakis.

Pikionis's infatuation with the mystic properties of numbers has been exhaustively documented by K. Tsiambaos, who also suggested that Pikionis provided Doxiadis with a subject for his dissertation. We additionally know that, aside from reviewing it in the vanguard periodical *to 30 mati*, Pikionis subsequently used Doxiadis's theory on polar angles in ancient monumental complexes in a number of his projects. Thus, we need no further proof of this connection.

As noted above, by promoting a cultural syncretism model, Pikionis also justified Doxiadis's exploitation of the past as a form of high drama. Since this aspect illuminates a lesser-known side of him, we will now discuss at some length Pikionis's historical exhibition of folk art in Athens in 1938. The 1938 exhibition was officially organized by the Society of Greek Folk Art. It bypassed Greek antiquity and focused on specimens dating from the Ottoman occupation period. As described in a magazine announcement at the time, the exhibition included "illustrations in popular pamphlets, woodcuts, calligraphy and sculpture of the Greek Folk," together with architectural drawings and "decorative paintings of 18th century mansions." More specifically, it also showed "measured drawings and photographs" by three architects, paintings of house architecture by a number of artists, a separate section with paintings by two folk artists and "shadow theater advertisements and folk toys."[7]

Pikionis was the uncontested mastermind behind this original mix, which was favorably received by the public. He had brought together on the one hand architects and artists as representatives of high culture, and on the other contemporary folk-art products and, if possible, their creators, as representatives of low culture. We can have a fairly good idea of the drawings and paintings of traditional houses exhibited because some of those surfaced later in various publications, including monographs on painters and collected editions on traditional architecture.[8] Shadow-theater figures remained popular long after the theater form itself declined and died off.[9] Folk toys had already risen in status when Pikionis devoted an article to them in 1935, praising their value in connection to the "new art" (i.e. the modern movement) which illuminated the ties, in his words, between "the art of the past, the primitive and the folk."[10] The Pikionis Archive at the Archive of Modern Greek Architecture (ANA) of Benaki Museum in Athens has preserved a number of metal plates from the catalog's illustrations.

This exhibition was ingenious yet not preposterous. Pikionis was justified in claiming that the "new art" had helped us see things in a different light. One year earlier, in 1937, Kazantzakis had published several newspaper articles about his travels in the Peloponnese, later collected in the book *Journey to the Morea*. The ideological ambiguity in the air at the time was expressed in one such article of his on the archaeological site of Olympia, where he describes a roaring peasant feast with its tumultuous disorder by the river and then compares it to a conventionally idealized image of ancient Greece.[11]

Doxiadis was twenty-four years old in 1937, and one can surmise that at this tender age he was conscious of the existence of contrasts such as those described by Kazantzakis. In later life, he would exhibit a genuine interest toward ordinary people he met by chance or in his employment.

Two such cases can be cited. In the first instance, Doxiadis describes his meeting with a workman in 1969: "While crossing over to Aegina Island yesterday, […] I sat next to a man whom I liked; he was a workman with his tools. […] He operates with a small group of one or two persons and he undertakes constructing and plastering. I liked him and asked him if he could perform similar tasks in our projects. […] He said that he accepts wholeheartedly and will call me."[12]

In the second instance, the recently deceased Marika Zagorisiou, an old colleague of Doxiadis's, described a typical scene at the DA office:

> Let us say that we headed toward the elevator. It so happened that at this very moment a cleaning woman was inside the cabin descending from higher up, with her pail and mop. He would immediately rush to open the door for her, to help her out.[13]

Doxiadis's influential book titled *Architecture in Transition* (1963), a manifesto urging contemporary architects to assume a challenging new role, is a notable source for his interest in the potential value hidden in ordinary people and the significance of vernacular architecture. In the first case, Doxiadis asks about today's architect: "Is he going to mingle with the common man, even if he has to be an anonymous worker, in order to emerge some day, remolded as by fire?"[14] Further on, he argues, "we shall have to turn our attention much more to the traditional solutions, for they have a lot to teach us not only about the locality we are working for, but also about the ecumenic architecture which is developing throughout the world."[15]

We can next trace the influence of Kazantzakis on Doxiadis as a decisive factor that formulated a role imbued with tradition in Doxiadis's imagination. The young Kazantzakis submitted a tragedy to the Lassaneios Literary Contest in 1909 called *O Protomastoras* [*The Master Mason*], based on the renowned Greek folk song "The Bridge of Arta." This recounted the story of the master mason's wife, sacrificed and interred in the foundations of the bridge in order to stabilize it because it had repeatedly fallen apart.[16] The drama was published the following year (1910) and Manolis Kalomoiris (1883–1962), the Greek national music composer [Fig. 4], turned it into a cantata performed in 1916.[17] Kalomoiris reworked his cantata in 1929 and stated that this was a "symbol of my life and Destiny." Doxiadis was just thirteen years old when the revised cantata was performed.

The term *protomastoras* was officially used by Doxiadis in the title of an internal conference held exclusively for his employees at Mount Parnis in 1962.[18] In 1963, we find him using the term at the third Architects' Conference at Nauplion (on the contribution of the Greek architect and planner to the country's development), where he states that architects should be restricted to their main task and, following tradition, an architect should "once more become an architect, master mason and constructor."[19] Eight years later, we find him commenting on two verses by the poet Elytis: "The use of the term God as Protomastoras is appropriate. He is the genuine Protomastoras and the only thing we can accomplish is to rearrange elements and put the basic elements in a new order."[20] The term *protomastoras* was still in his mind in 1971, nine years after its initial use, when he chose it as the title for an internal meeting with five of his top employees.[21]

The Protomastoras concept plays a dominant role in Doxiadis's book *Architecture in Transition*, to which we have already referred. One such instance can be cited, when Doxiadis spells out the four recommended directions of action for current architects. The first one (fig. 24 in the book) is to "(a) Resume his traditional role of master builder, as coordinator of all forces leading to the creation of the building, without limiting himself to the designing aspect of the creation."[22]

Doxiadis in contrast used the humbler term "mason" in reference to himself: "A mason thinks at night and builds during the day. […] If he has built enough, he knows that in the morning he *has* to pour the concrete."[23] He seems to prefer being called simply a mason because he wanted to profit from the natural gift of the anonymous folk mason to create and find solutions to technical problems, in response to Pikionis's model of the folk mason.[24]

So far, we have discussed Pikionis and Kazantzakis as two distinct influences on the young Doxiadis.. Although there is no record of any type of communication between the two of them, we discern some prominent similarities. Whereas Kazantzakis dramatized the master mason of Arta in 1909, Pikionis had deified an anonymous mason on Aegina Island; when Kazantzakis praised ordinary people's earthy feasting in 1937, Pikionis raised the folk creator to artistic excellence status in 1938. An additional common trait is that both were received with suspicion or even persecuted in their country; Doxiadis was no exception, since he also was a victim of slander throughout his career in Greece.

Let us now follow our second lead, exploring Doxiadis's character and mentality. At an initial, more intimate level, there is enough evidence to show that Doxiadis purposely and systematically hid his personal sensitivity and generosity behind a theatrical mask of strictness and discipline in order to control his vast "empire." His resort to sacred "laws" derived from antiquity easily fitted into such a strategy.

Strict discipline belies another side of Doxiadis's character. Those who knew him well testify that he was a fervent patriot with a strong belief in his mission to house the needy of this world. His adherence to the notion of place is also well documented: it underlies, regardless of any obviously economic advantage, his choice of Greece as his headquarters location and the consistent exploitation of his Greek identity when hosting prominent foreigners, as in the case of the Delos Symposia.

One also notices that Doxiadis fluctuated between a set of roles based on chosen ancient philosophers. Once, he mused to a correspondent that he felt like Protagoras, who sailed on a small boat from island to island peddling his wares.[25] On other occasions, he similarly suggested that he

Fig. 4 Manolis Kalomoiris.

considered himself a follower of the planner–philosopher Hippodamus, and he repeatedly identified himself with Aristotle on his quest for happiness in the ideal human community (Entopia).

Although Doxiadis's mind rushed forward in anticipation of the oncoming future, he was consciously attached to an idealized antique past, rendered harmless by omitting its social context. Indeed, the three ancient models mentioned above belong to an antiquity carefully cleansed of political context. Yet none of these philosophers had failed to recognize the social context within which they had developed their theories. Protagoras was a revolutionary sophist, who rocked the foundations of the Athenian society of his time; Hippodamus had in mind a clearly hierarchical model of society for the settlements he planned; Aristotle, in his *Politics*, was measuring the pros and cons of existing political systems in his time.

The ambitious research project undertaken by the Athens Center of Ekistics (ACE) on ancient Greek cities was typical of this approach. According to the testimony of Marika Zagorisiou, an architect and project manager for the project, she once debated with Doxiadis on the purpose of studying ancient cities that sported a theater, an Odeon or a stadium as manifestations of a civilized life. When she expressed her doubts whether such ancient parameters could apply to any modern case, in her words, "within this social organization, the present social system," his answer was typical: "Listen, Marika, I have made [up] my mind and I do not deviate from it. I will do whatever I consider right for myself; to satisfy what I want."[26]

However, Doxiadis's infatuation with antiquity was an interim step toward advanced abstraction as expressed in numerical relationships. He had already demonstrated this shift in his dissertation (Berlin, 1936). The use of such numerical values by Doxiadis culminated in the formulation of the Ekistic Scale, as an all-inclusive icon of quantitative and qualitative values. To cite just one such instance, Doxiadis had an image of the Ekistic Scale precede each article in the magazine *Ekistics*, thus enabling the reader to surmise the content of the article at a glance – more quickly, even, than by looking at its title. Perhaps one could discover some parallels there with Peter Greenaway's film *Drowning by Numbers* (1988), namely, the obsessive use of numerical repetitions which denote the underlying structure of interpretation in each case.

In addition, his explicit instructions on, as he termed it, "methodology" for research projects by the ACE personnel clearly show his concern with reaching preset goals. Research was thus closely monitored to verify Ekistic theory. Doxiadis's documented secretiveness concerning research projects and his reluctance to share the ACE experience with other research agencies may be attributed to his need to keep his supposedly "suspect" scientific approach under wraps.

Conclusion

Our discussion so far has dealt with Doxiadis's infatuation with antiquity as a source of planning principles and philosophical concepts. In this context, we conclude that connecting to antiquity automatically led to abstraction and, hence, to the replacement of language by numerical ratios as a medium of communication.

As previously suggested, Doxiadis's alternate use of tradition relates to a sentimental attachment to place and people as experiential, lived history.[27] We therefore have to shift from Doxiadis's character to his cultural background. The earliest evidence of Doxiadis's interest in Greek vernacular architecture is recorded in the 1930s. This is testified by his summer trips to Skyros Island to sketch local traditional houses, a customary habit with architectural students then and later, together with his future wife, Emma, and her brother Arthur Skepers. Projects from his pre-war architectural office in the Doxiadis Archives also indicate that he followed current trends in Greek architecture, alternating between moderate modernism and simplified classicism, but also, in some cases, by applying vernacular "motifs."[28]

Typical of the last-named case was the use of insular motifs in the Kostis Bastias house project. Bastias (1901–1972) [Fig. 5] became a major cultural agent

Fig. 5 Kostas Bastias.

in Greece in the late 1930s by being appointed Director of Letters and Fine Arts in the government. Taking advantage of his influential position, he assigned promising youngsters to key posts and managed to rejuvenate the troubled Royal Theater organization by pulling it out of its isolation and initiating a daring performance policy, foreign and domestic. Bastias commissioned three prestigious projects from Doxiadis: a theater on the Thessaloniki waterfront; a 1,000-seat mobile theater transported by sixteen trucks [Fig. 6];[29] and an open-air theater on Philopappou Hill in Athens, which remained incomplete.[30] Although these commissions show that Bastias encouraged innovation, his house was a typically retrogressive neo-vernacular specimen.

At the end of the German occupation of Greece, Doxiadis was assigned the coordination of reconstruction of the war-devastated country by the Ministry of Reconstruction (1945–1950). In this connection, he published a set of manuals to record the activities of his department. One such book concerned house models (*Types of Agricultural Cores*, 1949). In order to help restore the displaced rural population to their former homeland, he proposed that house types adopted forms already familiar to peasant farmers. A phrase in the book's preface attests to Pikionis's early involvement in Doxiadis's projects.[31] Additional such opportunities would arise later, after

Fig. 6 C. A. Doxiadis, Arma Thespidos, a 1,000-seat mobile theater transported by sixteen trucks.

the Doxiadis Associates office was founded in 1953. In sum, Pikionis allegedly acted as a consultant to certain Doxiadis Associates projects;[32] was invited to give lectures to office employees; and had an exhibition of his work, his very first, organized at the DA office in 1962.[33]

Another aspect of Doxiadis's mentality, intimately connected to his adherence to vernacular architecture, was his steadfast support for a "genuine" Demotic language as opposed to the official language, the "artificial" Katharevousa. This could be considered yet another sign of Doxiadis's progressiveness, since the followers of Demotic were frequently stigmatized as politically suspect. In his aforementioned government-assigned position, Doxiadis created a scandal by urging his employees to use the Demotic language in their reports and even invited the renowned philologist Manolis Triantafyllides (1883–1959) to teach them its correct usage [Fig. 7].[34]

In attempting to understand the role played by theatricality in Doxiadis's performance and personality, we have exposed a mesh of aspects that connected him to antiquity and tradition. The mere examination of data has, however, revealed a number of controversial sides to his conduct, sometimes based on prejudices. Such issues are deeply contaminated due to their ideological saturation.

One such case is Doxiadis's intimate relationship with his revered professor Dimitris Pikionis. Their relationship may be well documented, yet their differences, although hinted at by Doxiadis, have never been adequately explored. To what extent were their notions of tradition identical? Doxiadis's multiple references to tradition in his book *Architecture in Transition* are equally well known, but did his emphasis on universally applied typologies contradict the role of contextual creativity? The design of workers' housing sectors in Aspra Spitia is presented as a rational approach to the

Fig. 7 Manolis Triantafyllidis.

needs of users with a rural origin, but is that sufficient to justify the iconography of traditional settlements? This author has suggested a link between Pikionis's Karamanos House (1925), based on a Hellenistic model,[35] and Doxiadis's house at Porto Rafti (early 1970s). Is this connection irrelevant or does it imply that Doxiadis was, after all, closer in mentality to a stripped-down classicism as interpreted by modernism?

We believe that Doxiadis was too sophisticated to allow such obvious discrepancies to go unnoticed. Therefore, his theatrical performance was an automatic defense mechanism in order to provide the essential illusionary atmosphere that would lead to conviction. It was not just a smoke screen but a conscious strategy to use the past as a practical tool towards action, which was always his goal. We here emphasize the practical side of his conduct because one is easily led astray by the atmosphere of mystical nostalgia that underlies the master-mason literature or by a holistic notion of universal unity in architectural expression, thus forgetting that we are dealing with Doxiadis's ultimate strategy: to formulate a practical tool for everyday usage.

In this sense, the so-called inherent discrepancies we have traced show a need for abstraction and transference as readily provided by the theater. The intensely theatrical character of Doxiadis's approach to the past thus reaches the necessary state of illusion incorporated as *mimesis* (imitation) in the theater. Aristotle's definition of ancient drama could be useful at this point: "We have established, then, that tragedy is an imitation of an action which is complete and whole and has some magnitude."[36]

The internal logic of Doxiadis's theatrical performance connects *mimesis* to scenography: to a false, unreal construction meant to provide an illusory image of reality. Theater is, after all, an artful deceit. We can now better understand a phrase used at the beginning of this chapter. As we suggested then, by being such a gifted actor Doxiadis made use of the historical setting as an artful backdrop to soften an otherwise cold-blooded, technocratic procedure – called either physical planning or architectural design – meant to serve today's urbanized masses.

1   This faculty of Doxiadis's is amply attested by many of his employees and friends in interviews now found at the Doxiadis Archives at the Benaki Museum in Athens.
2   Unpublished recordings of interviews with Doxiadis's former colleagues and friends, made on different occasions after his death in 1975, can be found in the Doxiadis Archives.
3   Doxiadis operated within the context of triumphant post-war modernism; therefore, his contribution will be always measured against the accomplishments of the international spread of this powerful unifying agent.
4   There is adequate testimony included in interviews with former aides of Doxiadis to prove that, despite his willingness to discuss issues with his colleagues, he always followed his own decision in the end.

5. Well established as a term that defines a group of Greek intellectuals who were active in the interwar period, the Generation of the '30s is ideally represented in the permanent exhibition of the Hadjikyriakos-Ghika Museum in Athens, curated by Angelos Delivorrias, Director of the Benaki Museum.
6. Kazantzakis recounted his "encounter" with Nietzsche in Paris in chapter 23 of his book *Report to Greco*; moreover, his dissertation (1909) was related to Nietzsche and he also translated two of the latter's works into Greek.
7. All quotes from *Neoellinika Grammata* 61 (1938), back cover.
8. Coincidentally, in 1960, when Doxiadis was attempting to secure the commission for public buildings in the central area of Islamabad, he asked Spyros Vassiliou, also a participant in the exhibition in 1938 and a well-known painter and instructor teaching at the Doxiadis Technical Schools, to create renderings of his proposed buildings.
9. Incidentally, a shadow-theater performance was given each Christmas at the celebration offered at the Doxiadis office for the benefit of the families of employees in the 1960s.
10. D. Pikionis, "The Toys of Aiolou Street," *to 3o mati*, 1 (1935), 12–13.
11. N. Kazantzakis, "Το τοπίο της Ολυμπίας [The Landscape of Olympia]," *I Kathimerini*, November 15, 1937.
12. Doxiadis Archives, SD-DC 698/2.8.1969, File 19025, Subfile 2.
13. Doxiadis Archives, M. Zagorisiou, undated interview, c. 1982.
14. C. A. Doxiadis, *Architecture in Transition* (London: Hutchinson, 1963), 86.
15. Ibid., 186.
16. In this tragedy, N. Kazantzakis had mixed ancient Greek drama with Nietzschean notions.
17. The term was later used by the architect Aris Konstantinidis in 1942 (Lecture, "Circle of Technicians"), and by the poet Odysseas Elytis (*To Axion Esti*, song D, Athens, 1959).
18. Doxiadis Archives, File 28559, Internal conference of DA employees held at Mount Parnis. Doxiadis consistently tried to always use terms or to devise new ones of Greek origin. In inventing new terms, he was imitating Kazantzakis, who, in his lengthy epic *Odyssey*, had concocted 5,500 new words.
19. C. K. Bousbourelis, "The Third Greek Architectural Conference," *Oikonomikos Tachydromos*, December 21, 1963.
20. Doxiadis Archives, S-D 10060, October 29, 1965, File 18961, Subfile 4, "Study of Entopia (for the file)."
21. Doxiadis Archives, S-D 14349a, October 22, 1971, File 19008, Subfile 3.
22. Doxiadis, *Architecture in Transition*, 95.
23. C. A. Doxiadis, *Between Dystopia and Utopia* (Hartford, CT: Trinity College Press, 1966), 84. See also his manuscript "Talking to the winds," File Entopia: Draft I, First version of chapter organization, ch. 7. He retained this role till the end of his life (see the concluding sentences in the introduction to his book *Building Entopia*, Athens: Athens Publishing Center, 1975).
24. D. Pikionis, "Our Folk Art and Us," *Filiki Etairia* 4 (1925), 145–58.
25. Doxiadis Archives, File 28554, Letter to W. A. Nielsen, August 4, 1965.
26. M. Zagorisiou, interview with the author, 2010. Doxiadis Archives.
27. In the memorandum for his election to the Athens Academy (1974), Doxiadis lists his respect for traditional architecture among his four main beliefs. Doxiadis Archives, File 19197.
28. Some pre-war house projects demonstrating vernacular "motifs" are included in the Doxiadis Archives. Despite his pre-war courtship of the vernacular, Doxiadis seems to have mostly adhered to a vaguely classicizing tendency later in life.
29. The mobile unit of the Royal Theater, based on similar units in Italy and Germany, performed in the Greek countryside for almost a year before it was dismantled in anticipation of the forthcoming war.
30. Construction on the Bastias Theater at Koile started in 1939 but was halted in 1940 as a result of objections by archaeologists.
31. Professor Pikionis "has directed the formulation of certain elevations of the cores" (*Types of Agricultural Cores*, Athens: Ministry of Reconstruction, 1949, preface).
32. An anecdote places Pikionis at least as a consultant on exterior colors used for the experimental community of Agios Georgios in Piraeus (1947). He was also officially named a partner of Doxiadis for the design of the National Research Foundation building in Athens (1964–1968).
33. Pikionis gave a number of lectures to DA employees and was honored with the first exhibition of his work at the DA office premises. Doxiadis tried, but failed, to invite him to the Delos Symposia as the only exception to his rule to keep Greeks off the invitees' list.
34. G. G. Papaioannou interview, Doxiadis Archives. As a member of a group of experts, Manolis Triantafyllidis had prepared a book on the grammar of the Demotic language (1941), which took an additional twenty years to be officially accepted. Due to that higher-level reaction, Doxiadis was also forced to abandon the use of the Demotic language in his ministry.
35. Kostas Tsiambaos mentions a house for Elsa Lambrakis as another prewar project by Doxiadis: K. Tsiambaos, *From Doxiadis' Theory to Pikionis' Work: Reflections of Antiquity in Modern Architecture* (London: Routledge, 2018), 102.
36. In Greek: "Εστιν ουν τραγωδία μίμησις πράξεως σπουδαίας και τελείας."

Some Rhetorical Aspects of the Delos Symposia

Kostas Tsiambaos

Rhetoric may be defined as the faculty of observing in any given case the available means of persuasion.[1]

The Conference before the Symposion

Thoughts about organizing an international event on the future of human settlements on the uninhabited island of Delos had been in the mind of Constantinos A. Doxiadis since at least 1958. As "D" (Doxiadis's code name used in his Doxiadis Associates office) had written in a report addressed to his assistants Jaqueline Tyrwhitt, Demetrius Iatridis and John Piperoglou in January 1961, the idea of having a conference in Greece in order to discuss the global problems of human settlements had been in his mind for over three years.[2] Doxiadis wanted the participants in the conference to "be representatives of as wider classes [sic] as possible even if, in order to get this representation, we have in some cases to go to lower level [sic] than others";[3] that is why he thought that it was extremely important to ensure the participation of architects, planners, policy makers and other representatives from countries of the Global South and the Far East (Central Africa, India, Pakistan, Japan and Indonesia).[4] There was also no doubt that the location of the conference would be Delos, as reports from as early as 1958 affirmed: "A plan to convene some time in 1959 a conference of senior architects and planners as well as other scientists in Delos in order to frame and sign the Charter of Delos on the science of Ekistics."[5]

In a letter that Doxiadis sent to Jaqueline Tyrwhitt on January 19, 1959, he suggested that she postpone the conference for the next year as he already had many other commitments (new urban projects, books under contract, invitations for lectures, etc.).⁶ However, the conference at Delos – it was not called a symposion yet – would not take place in 1959 nor in 1960. The year 1961 seemed more appropriate for such an international event, as Doxiadis believed that it would suit well the J. F. Kennedy administration's plans to "form a Ministry or Department of Urban Affairs."⁷ Moreover, 1961 was suitable for another important reason; it was exactly thirty years ago that a similar conference had taken place:⁸

> In the history of recent architecture, the year 1931 is one of the most important landmarks. In that year, a group of architects convened in the Aula of Athens University to promulgate the Charter of Athens, which officially sanctioned and established Contemporary Architecture [...] The most important conceptual change for Architecture in the last generation has been a shift in objectives [...] attention is shifting more and more away from "The Building" and more towards "The Settlement" where the architect must join efforts with the engineer, the economist, and the social scientist and become the planner of the whole.⁹

Doxiadis was obviously referring to the famous fourth CIAM congress, which took place on board ship, from Marseille to Athens and back, as well as in front of the monumental Neoclassical portico of the National Technical University of Athens (NTUA). However, it was not in 1931 but in 1933 that this legendary conference took place. How could it be possible that Doxiadis, who was a student at NTUA's School of Architecture from 1930 to 1935, had misremembered the exact year of such an exceptional event? In any case, Doxiadis believed that the heritage of CIAM was not significant and influential any more, and that the infamous "Athens Charter" should be replaced by a new "Delos Charter."¹⁰ Nevertheless, as many of the main protagonists of that conference were still active, Doxiadis expressed his intention of inviting some of those modern, "heroic" figures like Le Corbusier, Alvar Aalto, Josep Lluís Sert, Sigfried Giedion and Walter Gropius (although the last-named had not participated in the 1933 conference).¹¹ Replying to one of D's letters, Tyrwhitt wrote, "I think the last two (Corbusier and Gropius) are rather out of place."¹² But Le Corbusier was too important for D to ignore; this is proven by the fact that Doxiadis himself sent two letters to Le Corbusier, trying to persuade him. Le Corbusier's first reply, by cable, on March 3, 1963 was, "MILLE REGRETS IMPOSSIBLE

AMITIES – LE CORBUSIER." The second letter was sent by Doxiadis on March 12, 1963. Le Corbusier declined again in his letter of March 21, 1963, concluding, "Vous devez comprendre que je suis l'objet des demandes analogues presque chaque jour. Soyez gentil et ne m'en voulez pas"[13] [Fig. 1]. Although undervalued by Doxiadis, the 1933 CIAM conference was still considered as the definite ancestor – albeit a decidedly dead one – as, according to Doxiadis, it marked "a similar effort undertaken by architects one generation back."[14] That older "similar effort" would have to officially acknowledge the new effort; for this reason, Doxiadis asked Tyrwhitt to prepare a translation of the "Athens Charter" into English since he wanted to make the Delos conference an event where the two generations would meet in order to endorse their "family ties":

> It is also time and a good opportunity now to bring together the older generation of the Charter of Athens and the architecture that was represented in it to meet the younger and rising generation of planners who are working in terms of Settlements and to declare the Charter of Delos for the creation of better human settlements through a new scientific approach.[15]

It goes without saying that it was no coincidence that Doxiadis suggested that the Delos conference take place afloat, not only because of its broader symbolic links to the 1933 cruise but also because of its definite attractiveness: "the ideal solution is certainly to have a boat [...] this will be a big attraction."[16]

As the archival material indicates, there was a greater mobilization in January 1961 in regard to the conference's organization. It was then that the first contacts were made in order to secure the financial support needed. Both the Ford Foundation and the Rockefeller Foundation had been contacted by Doxiadis, and Charles Burton Fahs, Director for the Humanities at the Rockefeller Foundation, had already promised that body's support; he had told Doxiadis in a private discussion they had during their meeting at the Doxiadis Associates (DA) office in Athens, "Definitely go ahead, prepare your plans, submit an application to us, we will finance it."[17] Following this off-the-record discussion, a standard letter asking for support was sent by Doxiadis to Fahs in April 1961. The estimated cost of $30,000 (approx. $248,000 in current money) was certainly not a small one.[18] Unfortunately, and despite Fahs's initial promise, Chadbourne Gilpatric wrote to Doxiadis on behalf of Fahs, replying that it was not the Rockefeller Foundation's practice to finance international meetings.[19] The response by Shepard Stone, Director of International Affairs at the Ford Foundation, was also negative; the Ford Foundation could not support the project either.[20] It would take a few months of negotiations before Doxiadis accepted, in early 1962, that none of the US foundations he had contacts with would eventually give any money to his project.[21] He had to look for funding elsewhere.

Communication Strategies

The probable lack of financial resources was certainly disappointing, but it did not make Doxiadis any less determined. On the contrary, he sounded even more motivated judging by the correspondence that followed. His main concern was not money but time; as he was explaining to his assistants, they should definitely launch the announcement of an international conference in 1962 and before someone else did so, thereby "taking the job we have already done."[22] What was urgently needed was a communication boost: "Publicity is extremely important as it will help IN TRIGGERING OFF ACTION at the neglected sector of settlements and because it is a fine means of promotion."[23] Without losing precious time, Doxiadis decided to write to one of his old wartime comrades. Philip Deane, a journalist and Director of the UN's Information Center in Washington, DC, agreed that the idea of an international conference at Delos was promising, and that it would make for an appealing event that the press would love to follow since a "trip in the Aegean with a score of captive geniuses seems fine and a good news story" [Fig. 2].[24] As Deane stressed the importance of establishing a strong communication strategy, he suggested that Doxiadis contact David Brinkley, a well-known American newscaster who "has the most prestigious public affairs program on American and Canadian Television," a show that was "extremely influential."[25]

The idea was to invite Brinkley on board to film the conference – the "Delos Symposion," as it was then identified. However, having a journalist continuously on board covering the daily discussions of the famous scientists or interviewing them was not such an easy task. Doxiadis noted that too much publicity was not desirable as there was always the danger of all this turning into "a kind of a SPECTACLE."[26] Although he considered the filming of the Symposion by Brinkley to be crucial, he wrote to Deane

LE CORBUSIER

Paris, le 21 Mars 1963

Monsieur C.A. DOXIADIS
Président
Athens Technological Institute
24, Strat. Syndesmou
<u>A T H E N S</u>

Cher Monsieur,

    J'ai votre nouvelle lettre du 12 mars 1963. Mille regrets une fois encore; je serai absent à cette époque. Ne nous désolons pas de cette impossibilité; j'ai écrit suffisamment de papiers imprimés pour que mes idées puissent être discutées, combattues ou approuvées. Vous devez comprendre que je suis l'objet de demandes analogues presque chaque jour. Soyez gentil et ne m'en voulez pas.

    Veuillez agréer, cher Monsieur, l'expression de mes meilleurs sentiments.

LE CORBUSIER

35, RUE DE SÈVRES : PARIS (6e)
TÉL. : LITTRÉ 99-62

Fig. 1 Letter from Le Corbusier to C. A. Doxiadis, March 21, 1963.

emphasizing that "there is one important condition: the filming must in no way disturb the conference; we want the conference to work in an atmosphere completely free of any disturbance."[27] The goal was to cover the conference but without disturbing its setting, which was that of a more sociable and less formal event, with people in light, summer clothes engaged in discussion around a table, over lunch or dinner.[28] As an announcement of the 1963 Symposion published in the UK *Sunday Times* would affirm, "There will be no papers, no agenda and no minutes. 'We do not want it to be the one of the usual congresses strangled by formalities,' Mr. Doxiadis said."[29] In contrast to the glamor of a public, cosmopolitan event, the rewards for the participants in this unique forum on board would be informality, isolation and many opportunities to visit famous Greek archaeological sites.[30]

Deane approved, adding that in order "to make the program artistically successful, he [Brinkley] will want to film not only the symposium itself but some scenes from the islands."[31] So, it was not just the theme of the conference and the glamor of its participants but also its context and setting that were important for Doxiadis, who discussed with his assistants the option of taking some attractive shots of this selected group of "wise" scientists walking and discussing on the famed Greek island. Agreeing with Deane's suggestion that "the magazines will think in terms not only of a good story, but of how many newsworthy names are there,"[32] Doxiadis started working with his colleagues on a kind of script for the story to be told through Brinkley's shooting. As Asteris Stangos noted on the subject,

> The "special cases" he [Brinkley] can film – besides the three main activities of the Symposion and scenes from the islands – are instances of social activity of the conferees: outings on the islands, visits to archaeological places, a conferee strolling [a]lone on deck, one of our "sages" ascending a hill and using a Greek "glitsa," etc.[33]

Unfortunately, Brinkley was not destined to cover the Symposion. In a letter that he sent to Doxiadis in June 1963, Philip Deane announced that Brinkley's show would not go on air the following year. Although the show was rather successful, having recently won an Emmy Award, its sponsors had decided to withdraw. Deane admitted that in this way "we are losing an excellent chance of publicizing your great work," but he had nothing better to suggest.[34]

UNITED NATIONS NATIONS UNIES

United Nations Information Centre, Washington 6, D.C.

1028 Connecticut Avenue, N.W.

EXecutive 3-4272
296-5370

4 April, 1963

My dear Dino:

I have been asked to give up my leave this summer and I am fighting against this, because I have given up every leave since 1956. I think I will win, but I do not know at this time, when precisely I will manage to come this summer; much depends on Congress.

Your trip in the Aegean with a score of captive geniuses seems fine and a good news story. Can you let me have some names; then, if you agree, I could suggest to some magazines and newspapers that it would be a good story to cover. Would you be able to give passage to one or two correspondents, or even more? The Washington Post - Los Angeles Times Syndicate are already interested.

Yours sincerely,

Philip Deane
Director

Mr. C. A. Doxiadis
Doxiadis Associates
24, Strat.Syndesmou
Athens 136, Greece

Fig. 2 Letter from Philip Deane to
C. A. Doxiadis, April 4, 1963.

All this effort to produce imposing broadcasting material proves that the design of a comprehensive communication strategy was a priority for Doxiadis from the very start. An intelligent rhetoric was not something peripheral or secondary, something that could just complete or follow the preparation of the conference itself, but the main factor to guarantee its future success. The well-designed invitation card publicizing the press conference was just a hint of DA's approach. From the layout of the card to the arrangement of the room hosting the press conference, nothing was left to chance. At the conference hall located on the eighth floor of the DA building in Athens, everything was planned, prepared and arranged meticulously in order to serve its purpose as a rhetorical verbal and visual act:

> According to D's original instructions, the Press Conference will take place in the D.A. 8th floor conference room [...] The big map of Greece with the itinerary of the cruise, on which Mr. Savakis is presently working, should be also placed in the conference room. If there is any other exhibit material, like photographs of participants, that you feel should be posted, please do so in consultation with Dr. Doxiadis.[35]

Everything related to the cruise, the boat and its crew had also been coordinated with extreme care. Doxiadis had already traveled with the MV *New Hellas* a few weeks before the Symposion, checking everything and taking notes in order to secure the best possible conditions. As the fine-tuning of this floating performance could easily be affected by external circumstances, one had to be sure that everything and everyone was under control: from the food menus on board, the arrangements for the dinners on the coast and the choice of refreshments and alcoholic drinks to the quality of the towels; the proper functioning of the plumbing; the type, program and volume of music; even down to the crew, who should know how to offer their service without being noticed and when to "remain silent while on board."[36]

As James E. Clayton wrote in his article published in the *AIA Journal* and titled "The Remarkable Cruise of the NEW HELLAS," it was "during the second week of July, that the *New Hellas* sailed from Piraeus with what was undoubtedly the strangest – and certainly the most distinguished – passenger list it had ever carried."[37] The itinerary, which was not the most typical either, included a visit to the Aesculapium in Epidaurus and the mythical "stronghold of Agamemnon"; a dinner at Mykonos, which included "all the variations of preparation of sea food which centuries of experience [have] taught the island folk"; a visit to the ruins of Priene, "the first planned city" [*sic*]; and, finally, the arrival at Delos, "the birthplace of Apollo, the ancient trading center of the Aegean, the island on which nobody was born and no one was permitted to die."[38] There, Clayton wrote,

> in the ruins of an ancient amphitheater at Delos one day last July, a handful of spectators, including some bemused Greek boatmen, several goats and one mule, looked on as thirty men and two women solemnly signed a document calling for a basic change in the profession we call "city planning."[39]

Nonetheless, the image of a handful of strange foreigners on a deserted island was exactly the environment that Doxiadis needed in order for his "Floating Symposion" to succeed:[40]

> We saw Mycenae and Epidaurus, Hydra and Mykonos, Rhodes and Lindos, Priene and Miletus. It was no wonder that the participants found something wrong with modern cities and their sterile, artless, sprawling form, after they looked over the pastoral countryside and at the ruins of these once great civilizations.[41]

For Doxiadis, the journey to Delos was not at all about a romantic adventure. The contrast between the ancient utopian cities and the modern dystopian settlements had to be vivid and powerful.

After this educational experience, there was no excuse. The ancients themselves were not romantics either; they knew very well how to deal with reality, developing a philosophy that was daring and visionary but also exact, positive and scientific. According to Doxiadis, urban planning, at least in its ancient Greek version, was nothing but a practical science: "The first scientific town planners were Greeks and a long tradition has been built up in dealing with problems of human settlements."[42] Delos, as a paradigm, proved the "scientific" status of ancient planning on the one hand and pointed towards the new science of the human settlements, called Ekistics, on the other. Past and future were rhetorically linked to the present, showing what Chaïm Perelman had described as the power of the orator to make distant things appear present:

> Things present, things near to us in space and time, act directly on our sensibility. The orator's endeavors often consist, however, in bringing to mind things that are not immediately present [...] To make "things future and remote appear as present," that is, to create presence, calls for special efforts of presentation.[43]

Doxiadis insisted that they had to call it a Symposion, a transliteration of the original Greek word, and not Symposium, as in English.[44] And, as Stangos noticed while reflecting on the outcome of the first Delos Symposion, the event could provide the ideal opportunity to advance DA's networking and publicity – two fields of their practice that needed to be strengthened:

> The Symposion will prove of great value to Public Relations and Publicity [...] Our efforts in the field of P.R. and Publicity begun [sic] late [...]
> This is a job – especially when concerning the foreign press – that needs a long-range and systematic effort and should never be done hurriedly [...] We did not exploit to the proper extent the historical period and the environment. Reactions of participants show that this historical and geographical environment contributed greatly to the creation of an atmosphere of exaltation and community of purpose, that proved so important for the success finally achieved [...] It is imperative that P.R. and publicity be handled in a continuous manner and never spasmodically.[45]

Effectively working on public relations and publicity was seen as a "job," if not a science by itself, that had to follow exact methods and needed proper management. As one of the Symposion's most famous participants, Marshall McLuhan had been suggesting that the world of the future cannot exist without publicity and communication. Humans, their cities and their future could not but be woven together by invisible digital threads and networks. In James Clayton's words,[46]

> Marshall McLuhan, perhaps more than any other participant, set off new trains of thought with his comments on communication and transportation [...] Radio and television are but electric extensions of man's own senses. For ages past, man could see and hear only what went on in his own community; now he sees and hears and participates vicariously in events all over the world. What effects does this have on the political

processes involved in urban planning and on the needs of individuals that planners must consider?[47]

In that sense, the cruise ship *New Hellas* was not just a heterotopia floating in the Aegean Sea. It was also a moving hub with a transmitter broadcasting its message to the world.

Mapping the Emotions

The thirty-four distinguished "Delians" could not have imagined that, by accepting Doxiadis's invitation to spend a week in July 1963 on board a ship, they were agreeing at the same time to participate in a socio-psychological experiment that attributed roles and evaluated behaviors according to a precise "sociometric scale."[48] Neither did they know that each one of them was classified in categories, along a linear scale, according to their participation [Fig. 3] and contribution, their number of times "holding the floor" [Fig. 4], their seating position and their overall "sociometric flavor."[49] Obviously, the academic hierarchy of the speakers and the scientific impact of their contributions was not the only thing that mattered; at another level, a distinction was made according to the personality, preference or status of each one so that the feedback gathered from one Delos Symposion informed the possible members' list of the next one.[50] As cool and informal as it may have seemed, the assembly of the "sages" had been reconstructed by Doxiadis into a virtual Foucauldian panopticon on the foundations of the group psychology (it is no coincidence that Doxiadis had suggested inviting Cyril Sofer, an expert on "group process" at London's Tavistock Institute, to the 1964 Symposion).[51] Doxiadis, with the aid of his assistants, had the authority to "scan" his guests, analyze their roles and reactions, and choose those who were to "survive" in the quest for the precious title of the "Delian": Mr. X is a "prima donna," who "leaves no one in peace"; Mr. Y "wants to bring his son with him"; Mr. Z is "very old and bitter"; etc.[52]

On the stage of the cruise ship [Fig. 5], everyone had a function, a mission, a role to play – even if they did not know it – from Doxiadis and his assistants to the guides, the crew, the conferees and their relatives: "Relatives of participants should also be 'cultivated' and influenced during the conference by relatives of DA, ATI participants. They play a more important role than it appears on the surface."[53] That was an important but silent role indeed, as the "Song of the Wives," written by Ruth Bacon, revealed:

TABLE I

Extent of participation in Symposion

Serial No.	Name	1		2		3		4		5		6		7		8		Total participation		
		Less than 5 mts	More than 5mts															Less than 5 mts	More than 5mts	Total
(1)	(2)	(3)	(4)	(5)	(6)	(7)	(8)	(9)	(10)	(11)	(12)	(13)	(14)	(15)	(16)	(17)	(18)	(19)	(20)	(21)
1.	Charles Abrams	-	2	-	2	-	1	1	1	2	-	2	-	5	-	1	-	11	6	17
2.	Edmund Bacon	6	-	1	-	1	1	-	1	2	-	7	-	13	-	5	-	35	2	37
3.	Stewart Bates	2	-	1	1	-	-	-	-	-	-	-	-	2	-	2	-	7	1	8
4.	A.K. Brohi	-	1	1	-	-	1	-	1	2	-	3	-	6	-	4	-	16	3	19
5.	W. Christaller	-	-	1	-	-	-	-	-	-	-	-	-	-	-	-	-	1	-	1
6.	Jacob Crane	-	1	-	-	-	-	-	-	-	-	-	-	3	-	-	-	3	1	4
7.	R.L. Davies	3	-	3	-	A	A	A	A	9	-	4	-	32_C	-	6	-	57	-	57
8.	C.A. Doxiadis	4	1	-	3	-	1	-	1	4	1	3	-	17	-	9	1	37	8	45
9.	L. Duhl	3	1	5	-	3	1	2	1	6	-	19_C	-	-	-	7	1	46	3	49
10.	Shafik H. El Sadr	1	-	-	-	1	-	1	-	-	-	-	-	-	-	1	-	4	-	4
11.	O.E. Fischnich	A	A	1	-	-	-	-	-	-	-	-	-	1	-	-	-	2	-	2
12.	Lyle C. Fitch	-	2	-	1	-	1	-	-	-	1	2	-	4	-	2	-	8	5	13
13.	R.B. Fuller	2	1	2	1	-	-	1	-	-	1	3	-	5	-	2	-	15	3	18
14.	C. Furnas	-	1	2	1	-	1	A	A	A	A	A	A	A	A	A	A	2	3	5
15.	S. Giedion	1	1	-	1	-	-	-	-	-	-	1	1	5	-	-	-	6	3	9
16.	J. Gorynski	-	-	-	2	-	-	-	1	-	-	-	-	3	-	-	-	3	3	6
17.	E. Isomura	1	-	-	1	-	-	-	-	1	-	-	-	8	-	3_C	-	13	1	14
18.	Koh. Makiya	1	1	-	1	-	1	-	-	-	-	2	-	2	-	2_C	-	7	3	10
19.	Barbara Jackson	4	-	3	-	1	1	1	-	19_C	-	4	-	8	-	13	-	53	1	54
20.	P.B. Lasarte	-	-	-	-	-	-	1	-	-	-	-	-	-	-	1	-	1	1	2
21.	Edward Mason	1	2	20	2_C	-	-	-	-	2	2	-	-	4	-	4	-	31	6	37
22.	Robert Matthew	28_C	-	3	-	2	-	3	1	3	-	4	-	A	A	A	A	43	1	44
23.	Margaret Mead	1	1	4	-	1	-	1	-	1	-	4	-	17	-	6	-	35	1	36
24.	Herbert McLuhan	1	-	5	1	1	-	-	-	-	-	2	-	4	-	1	-	14	2	16
25.	W. Ostrowski	-	-	-	1	1	-	-	-	-	-	-	-	2	-	-	-	3	1	4

TABLE IV

RANK ORDER: FIRST FIVE IN TERMS OF TIMES HOLDING THE FLOOR (EXCLUDING CHAIRMANSHIP)*

Serial No.	Rank	Name	No. of times holding the floor
(1)	(2)	(3)	(4)
1	1	C. A. Doxiadis	45
2	2	(Edmund Bacon	37
		(R. L. Davies	57-20 = 37
3	3	Margaret Mead	36
4	4	Barbara Jackson	54-20 = 34
5	5	C. H. Waddington	33

* This rank order has been established by deducting 20 from the total number of times the Chairmen spoke - 20 being the average of the number of times the chairmen held the floor on the eight occasions.

Fig. 3 "Sociometric Data on Delos Symposion – Table I: Extent of participation in Symposion."

Fig. 4 "Sociometric Data on Delos Symposion – Table IV: Rank order: First five in terms of times holding the floor (excluding chairmanship)."

> The wives of ekistical planners
> Live surely a life of delight
> We abandon our hearthside conjunctures
> To listen in to your plight.
> We leave complex settlements human
> To sail round the islands of Greece
> Hearing superior IQ semantics
> Having never to speak our own piece.
> From chair-moving to closing we've loved it
> Admiring your powers of debate
> Whether tuned to the roll of the anchor
> Or with waves lapping into your face.
> As time and space now approach zero.
> Our affections always will be
> With Delians Emma and Dino,
> Olive trees, jasmine and sea.[54]

Nevertheless, an effort was made for this staging not to be noticeable by the conferees, who could otherwise react mechanically if they realized they were being watched (as if they didn't) or feel restricted and oppressed. As Stangos reported, "Unity does not mean uniformity. It includes theses and antitheses, disagreements, intra-stimulants […] the Delians must be free to say and do whatever they like among themselves."[55] But the organizers were responsible for achieving the right balance between overexposure and understimulation; as an example, even if visits to archaeological and other sights were important, seeing too many of them could be overwhelming – even tiring. According to Doxiadis, "It is the consensus of everybody that we have overworked them this year with sights. Nobody wants to see so many places even if they are wonderful, as they said. It is the consensus of everybody that we should not visit more than 3–4 places."[56]

It was important that, at the end of the day, Delians felt calm and free, content and gratified, since the success of the Delos Symposia, as Stangos was noticing, depended on the Delians themselves: "They must think of themselves as Delos, as parts, members, units, which, together, form an organic unity, not a structural unity but DELOS. C.I.A.M. succeeded in doing this. And C.I.A.M. was more limited in scope."[57] And, as expected, this effort to find the correct balance of independence and control through emotional engagement bore fruit: "Everyone extremely pleased [...] Definite success in terms of results; more than expected [...] Emotional environment and dramatization of circumstances helped a lot."[58]

Corresponding to the strategy developed when working on his urban projects worldwide, the first thing that Doxiadis wanted to prepare was the "battleground" of the project itself, since, as in the case of Aristotelian rhetoric, "[e]xisting potentially, existing as potentiality, rhetoric begins before its first (practical) move, a beginning that begins with the question of its contingent ground."[59] If this collection and analysis of "sociometric data" was something like the foundation stone of Delos's rhetorical construction, the prediction of movements, reactions and behaviors was also a matter of concern:

> Precisely because there are no formal means of influencing the behavior of members a heavy burden falls upon the "flow of communication" which constrains membership behavior and therefore produces group structure and spirit [...] the flow of communication (Roles and norms) must be a continuous process or without it the group ceases to exist. The particular messages which are transmitted, the informal allocation of functions (resulting in development of certain roles, right and duties), and the consequent development of norms (group-wide acceptance) exert a powerful cohesive effect upon members and reaffirm the group process. The consequent ordering of behavior (through sanctions) makes possible the attainment of group objectives. Thus the functional interdependence of a given aggregate of individuals, giving rise to a flow of communication, results in sanctions which serve to order behavior. When this occurs, we have an ongoing social group; when one of the above three necessary conditions is not met the group will be in trouble.[60]

But, what was the final aim of all this effort? Why did everything have to be so masterfully calculated, down to the last detail? What ought this experiment to produce at the end? According to Stangos, this effort was a part of a broader "war" plan: "When you are in a battle-field you do not ask: 'Why shall I attack?' Ultimate questions are of no use in the midst of action, when we only have time to think of our next move."[61] At least for those in the higher "ranks" inside DA, the targets of the Delos mission were clear: to promote Ekistics as a science, to increase business for DA, to promote

Doxiadis's theoretical prestige, to "create a better world through applied ekistics" but also "to have fun once every year":[62]

> "Delos" promotes Ekistics, we should not kid ourselves [...] We have "Delos" because we want people to hear and learn about Ekistics [...] Delos should be projected, then, as vividly as possible on to the outer circle of the greater public, capturing their imagination which goes into their daily acts, the building of their houses, of their towns etc. This is the objective of Delos [...] We want them to become convinced and do, buy, construct.[63]

Fig. 5 The 1964 Delos Symposion on board the *New Hellas*.

This ambition was clearly part of a power game for the benefit of DA and Doxiadis himself. Even the "organic unity" that Stangos was talking about was in practice a camouflaged structure with Doxiadis at its center. As Stangos explained, Doxiadis was the center of the core formed by the Delos Secretariat and the Delians; around them, in growing homocentric circles, were the participants in the conference; other interested people; scientific journals; the press; the electronic mass media; and, finally, the general public.[64] As CIAM's "worldwide publicity was due to the personal writings of Le Corbusier and S. Giedion," publicity for the Delos Symposia was expected to arise from Doxiadis's presence and command.[65] This is precisely what Jaqueline Tyrwhitt was explaining to Miloš Perović in the late 1970s:

> Both the CIAM and the Delos gatherings were dominated by a central figure [...] The dynamism and provocative views of Le Corbusier and of Doxiadis, undoubtedly focused the discussions of CIAM and Delos, but a reluctance to follow their leadership wholeheartedly weakened the official utterances of both groups. It was easier to criticize the strong, if sometimes too dogmatic, views held so strongly by the dominant figure than to come up with equally firm alternatives in the limited time available.[66]

Similarly, as Margaret Mead recounted, reflecting on her experience from the Delos Symposia, using the common nickname for Doxiadis:

> When I look back over the last twelve years since the first Delos Symposium, and realize all that it has meant to the world and to all of us who were fortunate enough to share in it, I wonder to myself what made it possible. Dinos's vision of Ecumenopolis? Dinos's vision of the way in which different talents and temperaments in ekistics could be orchestrated into a vast symphony? Dinos's reception of all of us into his family? Or simply Dinos [Constantinos Doxiadis] himself? This I cannot answer. I can only acknowledge the wonder of it.[67]

Hence, the final "show" at Delos's ancient theater was just the outcome of a concealed "theatrical play" that was unfolding long before and after Delos. In this play, many actors had contributed but Doxiadis was the only person at the center of the stage.

Delos, or the Power of Emptiness

There is no doubt that the first Delos Symposion made a strong impression, as the newspaper titles and magazine articles of the epoch affirm. An article published in the *Weekly People* described the declared war between the Delians and capitalism,[68] while a *Sunday Times* article explained how, in the words of its headline, "World Experts Hunt Way to End Threat of Chaos in Urban Living" [Fig. 6]:

> Hunted by the fear that a rapid deterioration in urban conditions throughout the world is leading to disaster, 33 experts from 12 countries sailed today on a week's Aegean cruise to discuss the situation and decide if anything can be done to avert chaos […] "If we continue along the present course, chaos will prevail" the conference organizers said.[69]

References to Doxiadis and his Delos Symposia were made often – and Ekistics, "[t]he science of human settlements, as invented and developed by Constantinos Doxiadis, a Greek who is probably the world's leading urbanologist [sic]," now appeared as a new word in journals around the world.[70]

In a handwritten draft of a text titled "The Ten Delos Symposia," Doxiadis recorded his own view on when and how everything started: "When I was a student, when I was walking with my professor Demetrios Pikionis in the early 1930s around Athens, we could see the problems created by expanding Athens. When I turned [sic] around Europe in the late 1930s I could see the same problems everywhere"[71] [Fig. 7]. It is interesting that Doxiadis compared Athens to other European cities, arguing that all cities in the 1930s shared the same problems. However, the idea of 1930s Athens as a modern capital sounds oxymoronic, as, at that time the Greek capital, although in a process of modernization, was not comparable with other European capitals in terms of its scale, economy, production, industries, infrastructures, etc. Certainly, Athens in the 1930s did not face the problems and challenges that other capitals around the world did. Was this narrative a part of Doxiadis's rhetoric too? Further into his text, one also reads about the choice of Delos as the ideal environment for the conference:[72]

> Then I thought for its [the conference's] location and I went to [the site of] Plato's Academy but the olive-groves were covered by 3-storey houses and then for [sic] Aristotle's Lyceum but the 8-storey buildings

World Experts Hunt Way to End Threat of Chaos in Urban Living

Fuller and Abrams on Panel on Vessel in the Aegean— 12 Nations Represented

Special to The New York Times

ATHENS, July 6—Haunted by the fear that a rapid deterioration in urban conditions throughout the world is leading to disaster, 33 experts from 12 countries sailed today on a week's Aegean cruise to discuss the situation and decide if anything can be done to avert chaos.

This unusual meeting, called by a Greek town planner, Constantine A. Doxiadis, is attended by experts on every aspect of ekistics, the science of human settlement in a changing world.

The guests include planners, housing experts, sociologists, economists, geographers, ethnologists, psychiatrists, art historians, philosophers and public administrators.

The United States panel is composed of Prof. R. Buckminster Fuller of Southern Illinois University; Edward S. Mason of Harvard, Charles Abrams of the Massachusetts Institute of Technology; Margaret Mead, anthropologist; Edmund Bacon, Philadelphia town planner; Jacob L. Crane, town planning consultant; Leonard J. Fuhl, who developed a mental-health program for the United States Peach Corps, and Lyle C. Fitch, president of the Institute of Public Administration in New York.

'More Insecure Than Ever'

Mr. Doxiadis, speaking of the problem facing the conference, said: 'Big cities grow rapidly and completely uncontrolled; the motor car conquers the streets and pushes man to the side, leaving him more insecure than ever; conditions of life become more and more unfavorable, with dramatic repercussions on our economic and social life, as well as on the inner equilibrium and physical health of man."

The first task of the weeklong meeting, he said, is to establish the elements of the problem and then to see what can be done about it.

"We may decide it is a hopeless situation," he said.

As he spoke he waved his hand toward the mountains surrounding the growing city of Athens, whose slopes were dotted with encroaching settlements. "These houses are too high up," he said, "they will never have running water. It would be cheaper to resettle the inhabitants somewhere else than to pump water up to them. This is the kind of problem we are up against."

Present conditions are viewed by the conferees as deplorable, but the problems in store for the future are of terrifying magnitude, the organizers asserted.

They cited two estimates: the present outlook for the world population in 100 years is between 18,000,000,000 and 26,000,000,000; the value of buildings to be erected within the next 40 years is estimated to equal $10,000,000,000,000.

'Chaos Will Prevail'

"If we continue along the present course, chaos will prevail," the conference organizers said. "What we think of as a jungle today will be insignificant in magnitude and complexity when compared with settlements of the future."

The Delos Symposium—so named because the final session will be held on Delos, an island sacred to the ancient Greeks —is described as an informal gathering of intellectuals where freedom will be the keynote. There will be no papers, no agenda and no minutes. "We do not want it to be one of the usual congresses strangled by formalities," Mr. Doxiadis said.

The ship will take the participants on a tour of ancient sites girdling the Aegean, where they will see human settlement from its birth.

Dr. Constantine A. Doxiadis

Fig. 6 "World Experts Hunt Way to End Threat of Chaos in Urban Living," *Sunday Times*, July 7, 1963.

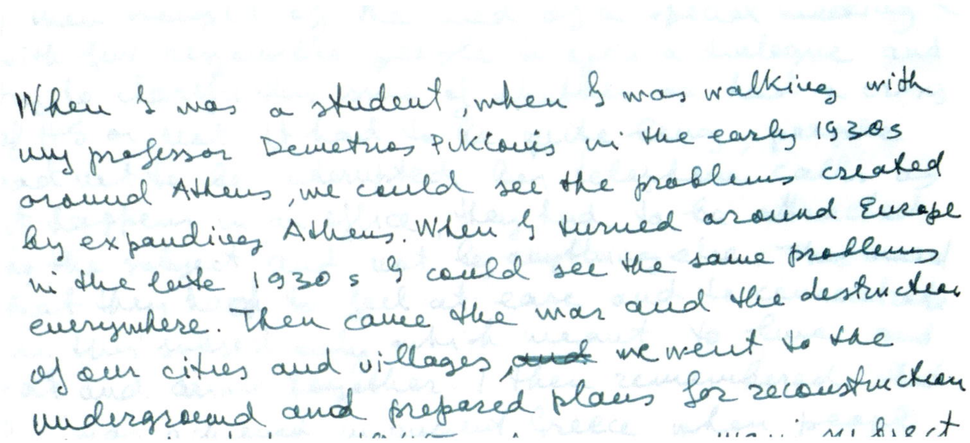

> When I was a student, when I was walking with my professor Demetrios Pikionis in the early 1930s around Athens, we could see the problems created by expanding Athens. When I turned around Europe in the late 1930s I could see the same problems everywhere. Then came the war and the destruction of our cities and villages, and we went to the underground and prepared plans for reconstruction...

> at it did not allow me to feel anything but pressures from concrete and danger from cars [...] The answer was simple; we had to go to places without problems in order not to be influenced by any local problem [...] this was the island of Delos, right in the middle of the Aegean sea without any single inhabitants [*sic*], only with ruins.[73]

According to Doxiadis, the sites of neither Plato's Academy nor Aristotle's Lyceum were appropriate as places of contemplation; only "the aloofness and loneliness of Delos, with its wonderfully preserved ruins, constitutes a perfect retreat for the calm deliberation necessary to promulgate the Charter of Delos."[74] It was not only the fact that Delos was, symbolically, the island of Apollo or a place located between East and West, at the center of the Aegean Sea.[75] Even more important was the fact that Delos "remains a non-inhabited settlement, really a kind of no-man's land."[76] What was the rhetorical use of such a deserted land? As journalists confirmed, chaos was Doxiadis's main enemy. Against chaos – the original, void state that had existed before all other things, according to ancient Greek cosmogony – Doxiadis proposed another void: Delos – the void island, the island of emptiness – was the place from which to counter modern chaos. In his search for a method, a science or a "medium" through which to fight chaos, Doxiadis sent a message. The deserted island of the god Apollo was the place that would amplify this message, the place that would make his words more powerful and influential. The more silent the island was, the louder Doxiadis's voice would be.

Fig. 7 Extract from "The Ten Delos Symposia," handwritten text by Doxiadis.

It is no coincidence that Apollo, the ancient Greek god of Delos, was also the name of the famous US space mission unfolding over roughly the same years as the Symposia took place, from 1961 to 1972. In a July 1969 documentary by CBS, titled *The Heritage of Apollo*, these links between traveling to Delos and traveling to the Moon were made manifest in the most expressive way.[77] The image of the capsule landing on the Moon's emptiness had its analog in the image of the ship docking at Delos's emptiness, and the footage of the astronauts walking on the Moon's "dead" geological surface had its analog in the footage of the Delians walking on the "dead" archaeological site [Fig. 8]. In both cases, the medium was more important than the fact, and the rhetoric more influential than the actual event.

Both endeavors were full of symbolism, and the Delians themselves felt like sharing their duty towards humanity with the scientists of the contemporary space missions:

> The recent successes of the space programs of the US and the USSR highlight how high our capacity is for organization, assembly of resources and application of technical skill, and how woefully low our use of this capacity is for the general betterment of mankind. We believe that concentrated programs of this sort should be organized to solve the pressing problems of world order, urbanization, population policies, housing, food supply, education and health, equality and justice, and the interpretations in action of science and technology in the political process.[78]

Today, nobody can be certain of what exactly the actual outcome of the Delos Symposia was – and, similarly, very few can describe the actual benefits of the Apollo space mission. But most would argue that both were exceptional events whose protagonists were brilliant, heroic figures whose endeavors were directed at the benefit and advancement of all humankind.[79] In the case of the Apollo mission, it is well known how the reactivation of typical American myths such as adventure, exploration, individualism and the new frontier were used by the Kennedy administration to sell Apollo to the press and to Congress.[80] The Apollo program was not only a triumph of science but also "a triumph of spectacle" addressed to the public, a scientific mission that had also "been as much theatrical effect."[81] As it is often argued, this is the main reason why, by the time Neil Armstrong walked on the Moon, funding for the Apollo program was being severely cut. The

rhetorical goal was accomplished the moment the US image of commitment to space exploration and to the benefit of all humanity had been broadcast.[82]

I would argue that the aftermaths of both the Delos Symposia and the Apollo missions were alike, since their most important legacy is perhaps their rhetorical aspect itself. As Chaïm Perelman argued about modern rhetoric, it is not only the ideas and their clarification that are important but also the way ideas and definitions are used and circulated as rhetorical figures in order to accentuate those aspects of meaning that will have "the desired persuasive effect."[83]

We are in an era in which, while some of the world's wealthier private companies compete in a post-ideological space race and new utopian architectural projects like SOM's "Moon Village"[84] propose yet another model for "life beyond earth," the global discussion is focusing on climate change and our determination to secure a sustainable future on Earth for

Fig. 8 Collage by the author of stills from *The Heritage of Apollo*, CBS News Division, July 1969.

the generations to come. Through this prism, the rhetoric of the Delos Symposia can be seen as something developed in parallel to the space-age rhetoric but against the plans of establishing settlements outside Earth. Similarly to current efforts in the field of environmental humanities, DA's aim was the establishment of Entopia on Earth via the reformation of existing settlements, the repair of the negative impact of what we now call the Anthropocene and the redirection of the future onto a more controllable path. As bold, ambitious and futuristic as it may retrospectively seem, the rhetoric of the Delos Symposia was more socially, culturally and environmentally conscious than it first appears: responsible, realistic, inclusive and empathetic at a level that very few global projects of this scale were at that time. Rather than setting a view from Earth to outer space, the Delos Symposia set a novel view from outer space to what Richard Buckminster Fuller called "Spaceship Earth."

On the night of July 20, 1969, a waxing Moon was dimly lighting the empty island of Delos. The seventh Delos Symposion had just ended the day before. The god Apollo had already left his island for a voyage into space and was now walking on the surface of the Moon: on this parallel desert and silent "island" on which nobody had ever been before. This time Apollo was not naked, though. He was wearing his new, bright-white spacesuit, smiling behind his glossy fishbowl helmet. The twenty-first century was approaching fast, and he was ready for it.

1. Aristotle, *Rhetoric*, 350 BCE, trans. W. Rhys Roberts, https://classics.mit.edu/Aristotle/rhetoric.1.i.html (accessed August 23, 2024).
2. D to Tyrwhitt, Iatridis and Piperoglou, subject: "Delos Conference," S-D 2830, January 19, 1961, File 18931, Doxiadis Archives.
3. Ibid., 3.
4. Ibid.
5. Report by BD, subject: "Discussion between D, Tyrwhitt and Piperoglou on the subject of the Conference in Delos," S-BD 181, August 5, 1958, File 2761, Doxiadis Archives.
6. File 2761, Doxiadis Archives.
7. D to Tyrwhitt, Iatridis, Piperoglou, subject: "Delos Conference," S-D 2830, January 19, 1961, 1, File 18931, Doxiadis Archives.
8. D to Tsitsis, Iatridis, subject: "Delos Case (Υπόθεσις Δήλου)," S-D 3760, February 12, 1962, File 18931, Doxiadis Archives.
9. "A proposal for a conference of planners on the island of Delos for the formulation and declaration of the Charter of Delos," File 2761, Doxiadis Archives.
10. Report by D to Tsitsis, Iatridis, subject: "Delos Case (Υπόθεσις Δήλου)," S-D 3760, February 12, 1962, File 18931, Doxiadis Archives.
11. See also File 6977, Doxiadis Archives.
12. Tyrwhitt to D, February 22, 1962, File 2761, Folder II, Doxiadis Archives.
13. File 6977, Folder I, Doxiadis Archives.
14. D to BD, S-D 6388, June 16, 1963, 1, File 2761, Doxiadis Archives.
15. "A proposal for a conference of planners on the island of Delos for the formulation and declaration of the Charter of Delos," File 2761, Folder II, Doxiadis Archives. Lost somewhere between J. L. Sert's and Le Corbusier's diverse versions, Tyrwhitt decided to follow Le Corbusier's version.
16. D to Tyrwhitt, Iatridis, Piperoglou, subject: "Delos Conference," S-D 2830, January 19, 1961, 3, File 18931, Doxiadis Archives.
17. Ibid., 1. Charles Burton Fahs (1908–1980) received a B.Sc., an M.A. and a Ph.D. in Political Science from

Northwestern University, Illinois. Fahs specialized in international studies, with a focus on the Far East. Upon graduating in 1933, he accepted a fellowship that allowed him to study Japanese abroad. At the end of his fellowship years, Fahs took up a teaching position at Pomona College, California, but left during World War II in order to lend his expertise to the Far Eastern Division of the Office of Military Strategic Services. By 1945, he had become chief of the division. In 1946, Fahs accepted the position of Assistant Director of the Humanities Division at the Rockefeller Foundation (RF); by 1950, he had been promoted to Director. Fahs resigned from the RF in 1961. He later served as the Minister-Counselor for Cultural and Pacific Affairs at the US Embassy in Tokyo. In 1967, he was appointed Director of International Studies at Miami University. His papers were donated to the Rockefeller Archive Center (RAC) and they are available for use by researchers. His officer's diaries are digitized and can be accessed through the RAC's online collections: https://rockfound.rockarch.org/biographical/-/asset_publisher/6ygcKECNI1nb/content/charles-fahs? (accessed December 11, 2019).
18 File 2761, Doxiadis Archives.
19 Ibid.
20 File 2761, Folder II, Doxiadis Archives. Shepard Stone (1908–1990) was an American journalist and foundation administrator. He joined the *New York Times* in 1933, but in 1942 enlisted in the US army and was active in wartime intelligence work. He served in military government in 1945, establishing a press in the American Occupation Zone in liberated Germany. He rejoined the *Times* in 1946 but in 1949 returned to Berlin, having been recruited as Assistant Director of Public Affairs for Occupied Germany. He was subsequently promoted to Director. Stone returned to the United States as Director of International Affairs at the Ford Foundation, serving from 1952 to 1967. From 1967 to 1974, he was President of the International Association for Cultural Freedom. In 1974, Stone went again to Berlin as the first director there of Aspen, a partner institute to the American Aspen Institute. He remained there until his retirement in 1988. He was a participant in many of the Bilderberg and Pugwash conferences and a member of the Steering Committee of the Bilderberg Group. In 1957, the first US conference of the Bilderberg Group – held on St. Simons Island, Georgia – was funded with $30,000 from the Ford Foundation. The foundation also supplied funding for the 1959 and 1963 conferences.
21 D to Tsitsis, Iatridis, subject: "Delos Case (Υπόθεσις Δήλου)," S-D 3760, February 12, 1962, File 18931, Doxiadis Archives.
22 Ibid.
23 BD to D, Subject: "Delos Symposium – publicity," S-BD 89, April 16, 1963, 1, File 2677, Doxiadis Archives.
24 Philip Deane to Doxiadis, April 4, 1963, File 2677, Doxiadis Archives. Philip Deane Gigantès (1923–2004) served in the British Royal Navy during World War II. After the war, he worked as a journalist for the London *Observer* in Greece, North Africa and South Asia from 1946 to 1961. While covering the Korean War, he was taken prisoner. After his release, he wrote a book titled *I Was a Captive in Korea* and returned to his career in journalism. He also worked as a UN official and then as Secretary-General to King Constantine II of Greece. In 1964, he was appointed to the post of Associate Greek Minister of Culture but left before the 1967 coup. During the 1970s, he was a speech writer and top aide to Canadian Prime Minister Pierre Trudeau.
25 Ibid. *The Huntley–Brinkley Report* was NBC's flagship evening-news program from October 29, 1956 to July 31, 1970. It was anchored by Chet Huntley in New York City and David Brinkley in Washington, DC.
26 BD to D, subject: "Delos Symposium – publicity," S-BD 89, 1, File 2677, Doxiadis Archives.
27 D to Philip Deane, May 8, 1963, File 2677, Doxiadis Archives.
28 Report by D to BD, subject: "Delos," S-D 5516, January 30, 1963, 2, File 18931, Doxiadis Archives.
29 "World Experts Hunt Way to End Threat of Chaos in Urban Living," *Sunday Times*, July 7, 1963 (File 2677, Doxiadis Archives).
30 Report by D to BD, subject: "Delos," S-D 5516, January 30, 1963, 2, File 18931, Doxiadis Archives.
31 Philip Deane to D, April 8, 1963, File 2677, Doxiadis Archives.
32 Philip Deane to Asteris Stangos, May 16, 1963, File A2677, Doxiadis Archives.
33 Asteris Stangos to Deane, May 11, 1963, File 2677, Doxiadis Archives. *Glitsa* is the Greek word describing a long wooden stick used by shepherds.
34 Deane to D, June 7, 1963, File 2677, Doxiadis Archives.
35 Report by O-GA 001 to Stangos, subject: "Delos Symposion," May 24, 1963, File 2677, Doxiadis Archives.
36 Report by D to BD, subject: "Delos," S-D 6446, June 29, 1963, File 18931, Doxiadis Archives.
37 James E. Clayton, "The Remarkable Cruise of the NEW HELLAS," *AIA Journal* (December 1963), 27 (File 2677, Doxiadis Archives).
38 D to BD, S-D 6388, June 16, 1963, 1, File 2761, Doxiadis Archives.
39 Clayton, "The Remarkable Cruise."
40 Demetrius Iatridis to the *New York Times*, Reuter's [sic] and Associated Press, June 18, 1964, File 2677, Doxiadis Archives.
41 Clayton, "The Remarkable Cruise," 29.
42 File 2761, Doxiadis Archives.
43 Chaïm Perelman, *The New Rhetoric and the Humanities* (Dordrecht and Boston, MA: D. Reidel, 1979), 17.

44 D to BD, subject: "Delos," S-D 5516, January 30, 1963, 2, File 18931, Doxiadis Archives.
45 Report by Stangos, subject: "Exploitation of Delos Symposion," August 8, 1963, 3, File 2677, Doxiadis Archives.
46 McLuhan's doctoral dissertation at Cambridge (1943) had been on the Elizabethan writer Thomas Nashe and the influence on him of the classical *trivium* and especially rhetoric, its tropes and techniques. Apart from the last chapter, which was dedicated to Nashe's work, McLuhan's dissertation, which was not published until 2006, was in effect a concise history of rhetoric and dialectic that can be seen as the basis of his interest in media as the global technological extension of a world of verbal acts. See: Marshall McLuhan, *The Classical Trivium: The Place of Nashe in the Learning of His Time* (Corte Madera, CA: Gingko Press, 2006).
47 Clayton, "The Remarkable Cruise," 32 (File 2677, Doxiadis Archives).
48 H-EGSE to D, CC-ACE 5, August 7, 1963, subject: "Sociometric Data on Delos Symposion," File 6977, Folder I, Doxiadis Archives. Doxiadis noted on top of the report, "Very good, thanks. Useful for who to call next year and how we will sit."
49 Ibid.
50 Tyrwhitt and Stangos to D, subject: "Sociometric Data on Delos Symposion," August 16, 1963, File 2761, Folder I, Doxiadis Archives.
51 D to BD, S-D 6522, July 26, 1963, File 6977, Folder II, Doxiadis Archives. Sofer was the author of *The Organization from Within: A Comparative Study of Social Institutions based on a Sociotherapeutic Approach* (London: Tavistock Publications, 1961). Erich Fromm was another famous social psychologist included in the list of potential Delians.
52 D to AKO 3, subject: "Delos VI," SD-ACE 620, August 8, 1967, 1, File 2761, Folder III, Doxiadis Archives.
53 H-EGSE (signed by D. Iatridis) to N. Avronidakis, subject: "Personal Impressions on Delos Symposion," CC-DI 111, July 22, 1963, File 2761, Doxiadis Archives.
54 Published in *Delos Newsletter* 2, 1 (August 1964), 8 (File 32283, Doxiadis Archives).
55 Stangos to Vice-President ACE, subject: "The Future of the Delos Symposion," S-IPD 5, October 15, 1963, 3, File 2761, Folder II, Doxiadis Archives.
56 D to Tyrwhitt, Tsompanopoulos, subject: "Points on Delos," S-D 8023, August 5, 1965, 1, File 18931, Doxiadis Archives.
57 Stangos to Vice-President ACE, subject: "The Future of the Delos Symposion," S-IPD 5, October 15, 1963, 1, File 2761, Folder II, Doxiadis Archives.
58 H-EGSE (signed by D. Iatridis) to N. Avronidakis, subject: "Personal Impressions on Delos Symposion," CC-DI 111, July 22, 1963, File 2761, Doxiadis Archives.
59 Erik Doxtader, "In the Name of a Becoming Rhetoric: Critical Reflections on the Potential of Aristotle's Rhetoric 1355b," *Philosophy & Rhetoric* 46, 2 (May 2013), 232.
60 Report CC-DI 114, 3–4, File 2761, Doxiadis Archives.
61 Stangos to Vice-President ACE, subject: "THE DELOS PROJECT – Policy ii," S-IPD 6, October 19, 1963, 1, File 2761, Folder II, Doxiadis Archives.
62 Ibid., 2.
63 Stangos to Vice-President ACE, subject: "The Future of the Delos Symposion," S-IPD 5, October 15, 1963, 3–4, File 2761, Folder II, Doxiadis Archives.
64 Ibid., 2.
65 D to BD, S-D 6388, June 16, 1963, 1, File 2761, Doxiadis Archives.
66 Miloš R. Perović, *Dialogues with the Delians* (Ljubljana: Revija Sinteza, 1978), 131 (File 7870, Doxiadis Archives).
67 Quote by Margaret Mead published at https://www.doxiadis.org/Default1.aspx (accessed December 11, 2019).
68 "City Planners vs. Capitalist Jungle," *Weekly People*, August 17, 1963 (File 2677, Doxiadis Archives).
69 "World Experts Hunt Way to End Threat of Chaos in Urban Living," *Sunday Times*, July 7, 1963 (File 2677, Doxiadis Archives).
70 Sarah Montoya, "Word Wise, More New Words," *The Secretary*, October 1969. A clipping of this magazine article was sent to Doxiadis by Patricia Del Villan, secretary to G. J. Tarkensley of the East Ohio Gaz Company. Doxiadis sent a letter on October 24 to thank her for letting him know. See Library of Congress (LOC), Kōnstantinos Apostolou Doxiadēs Papers, Box 1, Folder: Ekistics.
71 Constantinos Doxiadis, "The Ten Delos Symposia" (handwritten text), 1, File 2761, Folder I, Doxiadis Archives.
72 Mantha Zarmakoupi, "Τόπος και εντοπία: τα Συμπόσια της Δήλου [Topos and Entopia: The Symposia of Delos]," in D. I. Kyrtatas, I. Konstantopoulos, and C. Boulotis (eds), *Τόπος Τοπίο: Τιμητικός Τόμος για τον Δημήτρη Φιλιππίδη* [*Topos Topio: Honorary Volume for Dimitris Philippides*] (Athens: Melissa Books, 2018), 63–70.
73 Doxiadis, "The Ten Delos Symposia," 2.
74 File 2761, Doxiadis Archives.
75 In his letter to Doxiadis on June 7, 1963, Emmanuel Papageorgiou, a dentist from Samos, suggested that "it would be of greater value and importance if this symposium would take place in the island where the one who was, is and would be the creator of harmony […] the island that bore and raised Pythagoras." Doxiadis replied to Papageorgiou (on June 14, 1963), telling him that Samos should certainly be among the places to visit during a future Delos Symposion (File 2761, Doxiadis Archives).
76 D to Tyrwhitt, Iatridis, Piperoglou, subject: "Delos Conference," S-D 2830, January 19, 1961, 2, File 18931, Doxiadis Archives.
77 *The Heritage of Apollo* was a production by the CBS News Division. The documentary included clips

78 from the Apollo 11 mission; clips from the conference on board SS *Orpheus*; interviews by Mike Wallace with Constantinos A. Doxiadis, Margaret Mead, Karl Deutsch, Thomas Lambo and Richard Buckminster Fuller; views of the islands of Delos, Kos and Mykonos; and a statement by the astronaut Neil Armstrong (File 29147, Doxiadis Archives).
78 Delos Seven Report, File 2677, Doxiadis Archives.
79 Box 1, Folder: "Delos symposium," Kōnstantinos Apostolou Doxiadēs papers, Library of Congress, Washington, DC. Persons involved in the US space program were invited to the Delos Symposia. In 1972, Doxiadis invited Herman Kahn of the Hudson Institute, who would arrive in Athens on July 11, traveling through Osaka. Herman Kahn (1922–1983) was a physicist, military strategist and "futurist" employed at the RAND Corporation since 1948. In 1961, he founded the Hudson Institute, a global policy-strategy think tank, together with Max Singer and Oscar Ruebhausen. He used systems theory and game theory in order to envision the global future in a geopolitical perspective. His books include *On Thermonuclear War* (1960), *Thinking about the Unthinkable* (1962), *The Emerging Japanese Superstate* (1970), *The Next 200 Years* (with W. Brown and L. Martel, 1976) and *The Coming Boom* (1982).
80 David A. Mindell, *Digital Apollo* (Cambridge, MA: MIT Press, 2008), 12.
81 As asserted in "Men of the Year," *Time*, December 31, 1968. On the visual rhetoric of the Apollo missions, see Denis Cosgrove, "Contested Global Visions: One-World, Whole-Earth, and the Apollo Space Photographs," *Annals of the Association of American Geographers* 84, no. 2 (June 1994), 284–85.
82 Joan Johnson-Freese, *Space as a Strategic Asset* (New York: Columbia University Press, 2007), 51.
83 Perelman, *The New Rhetoric*, 20.
84 Presented at the 2021 Venice Biennale: https://www.som.com/research/moon-village/ (accessed August 24, 2024).

East–West: The Delos Dialogue with Japanese Urbanism

Ellen Shoshkes

Introduction

This chapter examines the contribution of Japanese urbanists to the Delos Symposia and related events that, by 1972, pictured the Megalopolis centered on Tokyo – Tokaido – as a step towards the ideal urban future that Constantinos Doxiadis (1913–1975) termed Ecumenopolis: "an interlocking global urban system within which each individual can achieve his own identity."[1] This shared image evolved interactively through exchanges within transnational scholarly communities of urbanists based primarily in Cambridge, Massachusetts; Tokyo; and Athens. I highlight the role of the urban planner Jaqueline Tyrwhitt (1905–1983) in facilitating exchanges that engaged participants in the Delos Symposia (the "Delians") with Japanese urbanists, notably Kenzo Tange (1913–2005) and Fumihiko Maki (1928–2024), both associated with the Metabolist Group.[2] The cross-fertilization of urban-design ideas discussed at Delos was amplified by the participation of key Delians, notably geographer Jean Gottmann (1915–1994) and sociologist Eiichi Isomura (1903–1997), in a series of concurrent conferences on regional planning in Japan sponsored in part by the United Nations (UN) and the Ford Foundation that dovetailed with City of the Future (COF) research underway at Doxiadis's Athens Center of Ekistics (ACE). This chapter begins by situating the Delians' utopian ideals in creative dialogue between Eastern and Western civilization and introduces utopian realism as the analytical framework that supports this argument. Utopian realism refers to the transformative power of an image of the ideal community that appears realizable, once grounded in a particular place.[3]

Utopian Realism: An Analytic Framework

Ecumenopolis epitomizes a particular type of utopian vision: an image of the ideal community as decentralized, based on cooperation and in harmony with nature. This ideal originated in the West in fifth-century BCE Greece, and was typified by the Athenian Acropolis. A similar humanistic ideal – based on a mixture of Buddhist, Confucian and Taoist thought – crystallized in Zen Buddhism, which flourished in Japanese culture and permeated daily life, embodied in the traditional house and garden.[4] These ideals evolved as comparable traditions of utopian realism along separate paths – emphasizing opposing tendencies, Western individualism and Eastern collectivism – that became increasingly interactive during the rise of a global system. Utopian realism was a vital current in the creative East–West dialogue spurred by the opening of Japan to the West in 1853, which inspired utopian modernism – progressive efforts to use design to lever social change – before World War I. An important conduit for these exchanges was the formation of transnational progressive networks, which soon consolidated as academic communities. During the inter-war years, utopian modernism coevolved in both the West and Japan, most actively in cities where these academic communities were based, such as Tokyo in Japan and Cambridge, Massachusetts in the United States.

The cross-fertilization of Eastern and Western social–aesthetic ideals in utopian realism coincided with the emergence of planning as a profession, notably in the line of thought pioneered by Scottish biologist and sociologist Patrick Geddes (1854–1932). He explained the new *urban planning ideal* in this way: "Eutopia, then, lies in the city around us; and it must be planned and realized, here or nowhere, by us as its citizens – each a citizen of both the actual and the ideal city seen increasingly as one."[5] Geddes had a small but significant impact on planning thought in Japan in the inter-war years. His ideas exerted an influence on three key figures who inspired members of the Metabolist Group: leading city planner Hideaki Ishikawa (1893–1955), architect Wajiro Kon (1888–1973) and prominent philosopher and cultural historian Tetsuro Watsuji (1889–1960).

Geddes's ideas inspired Ishikawa to develop his own influential theory of planning and civic art based on the concept of *kaiwai* ("liveliness"). Ishikawa conceived of the design of the *sakariba* ("thriving place") – the entertainment and shopping districts that were becoming the realm of modern life[6] – as the Japanese equivalent of the Western urban plaza. *Sakariba* became plaza-like by virtue of *kaiwai* – an atmosphere that encouraged free exchange and public gatherings. As Director of Urban Planning for Tokyo (1933–1955), Ishikawa created a Geddessian plan anchoring development around such subcenters of activity at planned transit hubs.[7] In the early postwar years, he sponsored design competitions to realize this vision, notably for Shinjuku Station;[8] this was the focus of Maki's collaboration with Masato Otaka (1923–2010) and their contribution to the 1960 Metabolist Manifesto.

Secondly, Kon adapted Geddes's survey techniques in formulating his own methodology – so-called Modernologie – to systematically study the new patterns of everyday life emerging in Tokyo after the Great Earthquake of 1923.[9] Like Geddes, he inspired his followers to conceive of the everyday as the site of utopian aspiration.[10] Kon taught housing and town planning at Waseda University (1920–1954), where his disciples included two core members of the Metabolist Group: critic Noboru Kawazoe (1926–2015) and architect Kiyonori Kikutake (1928–2011). Architect Takamasa Yoshizaka (1917–1980) was also affiliated with them and taught at Waseda (1955–1964).

The third key figure, Watsuji, published *Fudo* in 1935, which presented a theory of the interaction between environmental factors and human culture based on his observations of settlements in Asia, the Middle East and Europe (the three major world climatic regions).[11] Watsuji conceived of *fudo* (literally, "climate") broadly, as the character of a place, comprising both objective factors and subjective human experience.[12] His *fudo* corresponded to Geddes's cultural regionalism, and echoed Geddes's synoptic approach in calling for a new holistic discipline (*fudu gaku*) combining philosophy, ontology, geography, history and ethnography.

While Watsuji presented *fudo* as a universal construct, his narrative focused on defining Japan's unique identity. This was determined, he argued, by its distinctive monsoon climatic space: a primordial ideal embodied in the traditional house and garden. He theorized that over centuries of survival in their monsoon milieu, the Japanese had cultivated the ability to assimilate external influences and "layer" them over their traditional cultural foundation, enabling perseverance beneath change. Japan's hybrid civilization was thus a source of its cultural creativity. Watsuji thought this was a distinctively Japanese trait, however, which explained the uniqueness and the *superiority* of the Japanese spirit.[13]

Significantly, Watsuji viewed Japan as the "Greece of the East." As early as 1918, he connected ancient Greek and Japanese aesthetic sensibilities, seeing in them "a shared commonality of climate, terrain and human sentiment,"[14] and speculated about cross-cultural fertilization along the Silk Road. That image of Japan reverberated in transnational modernist networks. The shared-origins argument bolstered claims being made by pioneering Japanese modernists, notably CIAM (Congrès Internationaux d'Architecture Moderne) member Kunio Maekawa (1905–1986), and their disciples, including Tange, for the latent modernity in Japanese tradition, and the potential for the evolution of a *cosmopolitan*, modern, national cultural identity from these origins. *Fudo* also thus represents an expression of utopian realism.

Watsuji inspired many philosophically minded young Japanese, including both Tange and Maki, at Tokyo Imperial University. After working briefly for Maekawa, Tange re-enrolled there in 1942 to earn a Ph.D. in regional planning, devoting much of his time to researching the ancient Greek agora and Roman forum, which in turn led him to study traditional Japanese spatial order.[15] Tange recalled, "this was the time when I began considering the importance of urban design."[16] But the rise of militant nationalism in Japan and Germany, and outbreak of war in 1939, stifled this East–West dialogue among progressive architects and planners.

Regional Planning, Tange and CIAM 8

After the war, it was through regional planning and urban design that Tange engaged in the renewal of exchange with Western architects and planners. Geddessian bioregional planning, which had become suspect in Japan during the war years, was reintroduced in 1946 by Edward Ackerman, a professor of geography in the new regional-planning program at Harvard, who served as technical adviser (1946–1948) in the General Headquarters of the Supreme Command of Allied Powers (SCAP) in charge of the American occupation of Japan (1945–1952). These ideas, epitomized by the Tennessee Valley Authority, inspired a group of Japanese progressives working with SCAP – notably, economist Saburo Okita (1914–1993), who later championed regional planning as chief of the Resources Research Council (*Shigen Chosakai*).[17] In 1950, this group published Tange's report "Theory of Regional Planning," based on his Ph.D. research about the regional structure and architectural form of contemporary large cities. Tange, then teaching at Tokyo University, was also designing the Hiroshima Peace Memorial Park, a component of his master plan to revitalize that city's center. His design distilled the Greek agora in terms of a spatial configuration derived from traditional Japanese forms that he reinvented using a modern architectural vocabulary, ostensibly appropriate for Japan's new democratic national identity.[18]

Maekawa invited Tange to present his Hiroshima Peace Park project at the CIAM 8 congress in England in June 1951 – which is where Tange met Tyrwhitt, along with Maekawa's old friends Josep Lluís Sert (1902–1983), now CIAM president, and Ernest Weissmann (1903–1985), now Assistant Director of the new Town and Country Planning Section of the UN Division of Social Affairs. By then, Tyrwhitt had forged an influential synthesis of Geddes's bioregionalism and CIAM utopian modernism while planning for the physical reconstruction of post-war Britain, and was engaged in a range of activities – notably for CIAM and the UN – that helped revive post-war exchange through transnational networks. With Tange's participation, the East–West dialogue at CIAM 8 marked the beginning of the next phase in the evolution of Tyrwhitt's synthesis of Geddessian modernism.

Tyrwhitt helped organize CIAM 8 on the theme of the Core of the City, conceived as a Greek agora: "the gathering place of the people." At the congress and in the accompanying book, *Heart of the City* (1952), she presented her notion of the *urban constellation*, "a further development of Geddes' concept of the conurbation," as an organizing principle for the discussion of cores at five "scale levels" within a city region.[19] Maekawa and Tange recognized the similarities between Tyrwhitt's urban constellation and Tange's polycentric master plan for Hiroshima, as well as with Ishikawa's plan for Tokyo. In the discussion at CIAM 8, Maekawa explained that Japan lacked such agora-type open spaces, "but in the Hiroshima Peace project one is being built."[20] Tange suggested the obstacle was perhaps less cultural than political: getting "various governmental jurisdictions […] to organize into a single body so that a civic scheme can in fact be realized."[21]

Through the personal connections established at CIAM 8 (many participants became Delians or active in Ekistics or UN initiatives), East–West dialogue on the urban core and urban constellation intensified and became more collaborative, initially at Harvard's Graduate School of Design (GSD), when Sert became dean in 1953. Maki entered this scene when he spent his senior year at Tokyo University in Tange's lab (1951–1952) and then studied at the GSD under Sert (1953–1954). Sert was then beginning to reorganize the regional-planning program to focus on urban design, *based on CIAM 8 discourse*. He hired Sigfried Giedion (1888–1968) to introduce the new curriculum in 1954 with a seminar on the history of urban design; Tyrwhitt joined the faculty in 1955 as Sert's key ally in establishing the new program. Maki was studying part-time at Harvard then, and attended the historic conference that Tyrwhitt helped organize in April 1956 to build support for *the design section of the planning process* as a basis for collaboration between architects, planners and landscape architects on urban-scale projects. Maki remained engaged with the Harvard program over the next decade, and served as a vital liaison with Tange and the circle of young designers associated with his lab in Tokyo.

Japan's Economic Recovery and the Culture Debate

Meanwhile in Japan, Tange engaged in a revival of the long-standing debate about Japan's cultural identity, now framed in terms of Watsuji's *fudo*. Due to his wartime support for fascistic nationalism, Watsuji's reputation had suffered in the early post-war era, when many Japanese wanted to break with their past. His book *Fudo* enjoyed renewed popularity after 1952 as Japan reasserted its political autonomy and rebuilt its economy, and there was renewed appreciation for continuity and Watsuji's brand of cultural nationalism.[22] Concurrently, Watsuji elaborated on *fudo* as an ecological ethos based on a dynamic social process of constant reconciliation of the dualities of individual/collective, subjective/objective, body/mind and self/nature.[23]

In 1953, Tange and Maekawa participated in this debate at a symposium titled "Kokusei-sei, Fudo-sei, Kokumin-sei [Nationalism versus Internationalism]"[24] which re-examined what was distinctly Japanese about Japanese architecture. Kawazoe expanded this conversation in 1955, famously inviting Tange and others to write on this topic in the journal *New Architecture*. Tange's essay celebrated the Katsura Imperial Villa as the essence of Japanese traditional design, and an inspiration for his uniquely Japanese form of international modernism.[25] Watsuji's writing about Katsura's significance at this time bolstered Tange's argument that this Historic Villa merited preservation as a cultural resource for Japan that also had global relevance.[26] Kawazoe, a key theorist for the Metabolists, reported that these debates, grounded in the concept of *fudo*, served as a framework for the development of their ideas, over the next five years, for a uniquely Japanese form of *urban bioregionalism*.[27]

Habitat, CIAM 10 and the Human Scale Urban Design Seminar

Concurrently, parallels between Watsuji's ethos of *fudo* and the Zen-infused philosophy of Martin Buber indicated that a convergence was emerging by mid-century in both East and West on an ecological concept of self: a holistic worldview that emphasized the potential of the individual, their interaction with the environment, the importance of a spiritual connection to the world *and* the need for cooperation.[28] This hybrid ideal – which I call postmodern utopian realism – was manifest in the concept of the Habitat, the theme for CIAM 10 in Dubrovnik in 1956. CIAM General Secretary Sigfried Giedion alluded there to Buber's philosophy in explaining the metaphor of the Habitat: "The city is above all a matter of interrelations, encounters, the confrontation of you and me, the interaction of the habitat of the individual and that of society."[29]

The Human Scale urban-design seminar at the GSD (1957–1959) picked up the examination of Habitat where CIAM 10 had left off. Led by Giedion with support from Tyrwhitt and Sert, the seminar aimed to derive universal principles for the future Habitat based on analyses of historical settlement patterns in both East and West. In a discussion on Japanese principles of spatial organization, Giedion observed that Western influences had penetrated Japan for twenty years and it was time for a more reciprocal relationship. Tyrwhitt agreed there was much to learn from Japan regarding "our contemporary urban planning problem: how to find the key to an intellectual system that will help us to organize buildings, color and movement in space."[30] Tyrwhitt also introduced to the seminar Doxiadis's analysis of an ancient Greek system of architectural spacing that had been similarly designed for sequential perception (which she referred to as "the moving eye") [Fig. 1].[31] This parallel evokes Watsuji's recognition of affinities between ancient Greek and Japanese aesthetic sensibilities.

Tyrwhitt had met Doxiadis in 1954, while based in India to direct the UN's first Seminar on Housing and Community Improvement in Asia. One outcome of this seminar – attended by many future Delians – was that Tyrwhitt agreed to publish a newsletter that later evolved into the journal *Ekistics*, Doxiadis's term for a new "science of human settlements." Another outcome was that the UN hosted a subsequent conference on regional planning in Asia in Tokyo in 1958, which fostered further UN-supported initiatives in Japan involving connections to both the Harvard urban-design program and the Delians. Tyrwhitt used Ekistics as a medium for sustaining

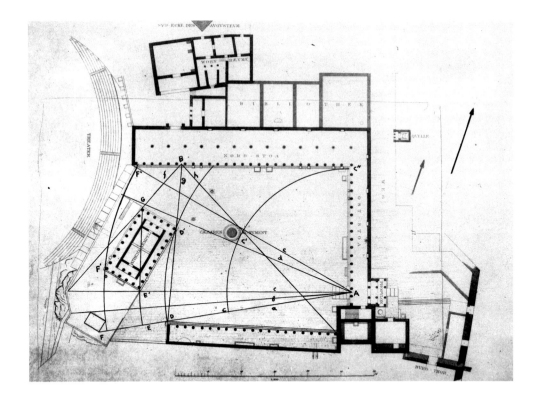

such exchanges through these overlapping networks. In 1956, she published the first article in *Ekistics* about Japan. This was an excerpt of a UN report on Japanese urbanization by the sociologist Eiichi Isomura, whose thinking, influenced by the ecological approach of the Chicago School, also aligned with that of Geddes.[32] As a further link in the chain, Isomura had been a close friend and colleague of Ishikawa and had served as chief liaison between the Tokyo Metropolitan Government and SCAP.[33]

Maki, *Fudo*, Habitat and Group Form

The convergence inherent in the concepts of *fudo* and Habitat came to the fore in 1957, when Giedion and Sert used their role as advisers to the Graham Foundation's new Traveling Fellowship Program to enthusiastically support Maki's proposal to retrace Watsuji's journey as recounted in *Fudo* to study traditional patterns of urbanism in Asia, the Middle East and Europe. Giedion helped Maki clarify the questions to investigate. Tyrwhitt advised

Fig. 1 Drawing of the Temple of Athena, Pergamon, from Doxiadis's doctoral thesis, illustrating his analysis of an ancient Greek system of architectural spacing designed to enhance sequential perception – which Tyrwhitt referred to as "the moving eye."

him to visit Doxiadis in Athens, perhaps noting the affinity between *fudo* and her view of Ekistics as "the inter-relation of man and environment."[34] She likely also gave Maki a copy of "The Shape of the City," co-authored with Sert as a background paper for the 1958 UN Seminar on Regional Planning in Tokyo, which aimed to illuminate shared aspects of urban culture globally. Martin Meyerson, who had recently joined the GSD Urban Design Faculty, was on the UN Team of Experts to the Seminar, which drew interest and contributions from Okita, Isomura and Tange among others.

Maki met with Tange soon after he arrived in Tokyo to prepare for his study tour. The latter introduced him to the group of young designers, later known as the Metabolists, who were planning the program for the World Design Conference (WoDeCo) in Tokyo in May 1960. Tange had to delegate much of this responsibility as he would be at the Massachusetts Institute of Technology (MIT) in the fall of 1959. Kawazoe organized this group to present their own, uniquely (*fudo*-informed) Japanese visions for how to structure explosive urban growth, positing "a theory [of bioregional urbanism] originating from Japan but applicable to the world in general."[35] Maki would later join them when he accepted the invitation of Otaka, then a lead designer in Maekawa's office, to collaborate on a design for Shinjuku Station, which had been designated an official subcenter in the new (Geddessian) National Capital Regional Plan. But first, Maki embarked on the first leg of his trip.

Maki was impressed while visiting Greece – where he visited the offices of Doxiadis Associates in Athens – by the clustered forms of Greek hill villages. Primed by his reading of *Fudo*, he viewed these as an "expression of regional culture [...] a body of native wisdom accumulated over many years"[36] that was comparable with the form of traditional Japanese villages. Maki cited this impression as his inspiration for Group Form: "an approach to seek a unified form on top of relations between a constantly changing whole and individual parts."[37] Otaka had proposed a similar concept in 1949 while developing a proposal for Shinjuku, a *sakariba* as envisioned by Ishikawa: "group architecture" was a method for arranging buildings on the small and fragmented sites typical of Tokyo real estate, so they could aggregate into a single form.[38] In its initial conception, therefore, Group Form as a spatial organizational system had both Eastern and Western origins.

Meanwhile, the Japanese government invited the UN Team of Experts, which included Meyerson and several others who later become key Delians, to the Seminar on Regional Planning in Tokyo to advise Japanese colleagues on planning for the Hanshin region. Related to that, Isomura visited the new Harvard–MIT Joint Center for Urban Studies during the fall of 1959, where he met Tyrwhitt. Isomura likely attended Tange's presentation that term to the Human Scale seminar at Harvard, which in its second year broadened its focus to include studies of recent large-scale projects. Tange spoke there on Japanese regionalism and the connection between Japan's premodern culture and Japanese modernism. He had just presented Kikutake's work at the post-CIAM meeting in Otterloo in September 1959 and was exploring similar mega-structural ideas in his architectural studio at MIT, testing modular principles derived from Katsura villa in a proposal for Boston Harbor.[39] Tyrwhitt had also attended the Otterloo conference. Before returning to Harvard, she went to work with Doxiadis in Athens, advising on the establishment of the Graduate School of Ekistics (GSE), which he saw as strategically situated "midway between east and west."[40] At Harvard, she likely encouraged Isomura, who, on his way back to Japan, stopped in Athens to meet Doxiadis. Isomura soon became an enthusiastic supporter and later founded the Japan Society of Ekistics.

Both Tange and Maki returned to Japan in January 1960 and joined the Metabolists' weekly gatherings. The group's shared ideas coalesced during these informal discussions, which mingled many threads circulating in international discourse from Buddhism, Marxism, systems theory, and ecology and hybrid concepts such as *fudo*, *kaiwai* and *modernology*. Otaka and Maki's concept of Group Form represented a distinctive expression of Metabolism, a system for the *decentralized* cumulative growth of forms through the addition of dynamic, singular elements as opposed to a hierarchical mega-structure that allowed individual elements to grow freely.[41] Maki's transnational experience uniquely qualified him to interpret the Metabolists' ideas in English for an international audience at the 1960 WoDeCo. This conference propelled the group onto the world stage as the most significant Japanese architectural movement of that era.

East–West Dialogue on Urban Design and Ekistics

Maki's association with Tyrwhitt at Harvard in the early 1960s greatly enhanced his theorization of Group Form, its applications to pedagogy and its dissemination as a foundational thread of urban-design ideology and practice. In turn, Maki's work on Group Form spurred the cross-fertilization of Eastern and Western utopian realism within the discourse on urban design at Harvard and in Tokyo, which now evolved interactively with Doxiadis's COF project in Athens.

Tyrwhitt's primary role at Harvard, then, was to implement the new urban-design program, which operated at the macro and the micro scales and which explored issues through a series of studios and conferences on Designing for Intercity Growth. Maki was a guest critic for Intercity I in spring 1962, which focused on the macro scale. Students analyzed historical and contemporary projects for large urban areas, including work by Doxiadis and Tange's 1960 plan for Tokyo Bay, which Tyrwhitt had published in the July 1961 edition of *Ekistics* as comparable with Doxiadis's concept of the dynamic city or Dynapolis [Fig. 2]. In the June 1961 *Ekistics*, she had excerpted Tange's article on the future city showing the Boston Harbor project from the MIT studio. Tyrwhitt was concurrently involved with Doxiadis's COF project, which was then broadening its focus to include assessment of traditional settlements as one basis for desirable future alternatives, based on the assumption of the inevitable development of human settlements on a global scale – the Ecumenopolis.[42] Tyrwhitt ensured cross-fertilization between COF research and the Intercity program; both were infused with Metabolist ideas, notably introduced by Maki and Tange.

Maki applied the Harvard approach to urban design in his continued investigation of Group Form at Washington University. Tyrwhitt highlighted this connection when she published an excerpt of his report, "Linkage in Collective Form," with her discussion of Intercity I in the same *Ekistics* issue. She considered Group Form to be a compelling method for urban design at the micro scale: an attempt to "find a system of establishing coherence" that emphasized "continuity and repetition of forms to give shape and meaning to the community."[43] Maki had based his further exploration of these ideas on an analysis of traditional Japanese residential districts, among other patterns, and his ongoing work with Otaka in Tokyo. He was also in touch with a group of young architects and planners in Tange's lab who were close to the Metabolists and had been inspired by the Harvard urban-design program to conduct similar historical analyses of urban form as the basis for their own approach to this new profession. They presented their work in a special issue of the Japanese architectural journal *Kenchiku Bunka* titled "City Design" (November 1961). Tyrwhitt included this issue, which provided English titles and abstracts, in her May 1962 Bibliography

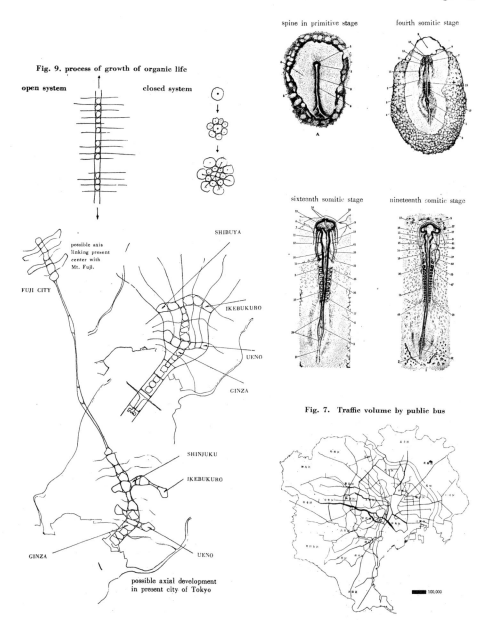

Fig. 2 Studies of the process of growth of organic life prepared by Kenzo Tange's team for their Plan for Tokyo, 1960. Tyrwhitt presented this work in *Ekistics* as comparable with Doxiadis's concept of the dynamic city, or Dynapolis.

for the Harvard urban-design program. That same year, Tange co-founded the first academic program in city planning in Japan at Tokyo University, institutionalizing the foundation for this growing transnational academic community and facilitating yet further exchanges.

Learning from Japan

The growing involvement of the UN in urban and regional development fostered both the internationalization of planning education and interest in learning from Japan. The UN Team of Experts collaborating on the Hanshin regional plan, which was issued in June 1962, commended it and other Japanese regional planning initiatives as "comprehensive and new approaches to problems of rapid urbanization that were highly desirable of study."[44] Japan's high economic growth rate sparked particularly intense interest in its unique corporate form of capitalism and collective culture. This fascination was further promoted by the Japanese government's commissioning of an English translation of *Fudo*, published in 1961 as *A Climate*, as part of its contribution to UNESCO's (United Nations Educational, Scientific and Cultural Organization) lengthy campaign to promote East–West mutual understanding (1957–1966).

In March 1963, UNESCO co-sponsored a meeting on reciprocal Eastern and Western influences in architecture and urbanism[45] at Doxiadis's new Athens Center of Ekistics, which consolidated his educational and research programs in "a true melting pot of East and West."[46] Maekawa was among the participants who agreed on the need to channel urban growth and change "to the proper directions" [Fig. 3]. This was to be the first of a series of meetings convening experts from various nations and disciplines "for a more systematic study of the existing problems [of rapid urbanization] and for the attainment of practical conclusions."[47] Tyrwhitt helped Doxiadis orchestrate the next ACE event that July on board the ship *New Hellas*, which came to represent the very first official Delos Symposion, encouraging him to invite Tange among other "Ekistic minded" young architects from Japan.[48]

It was in this spirit of East–West exchange that for her own "indirect contribution" to Delos 1, Tyrwhitt commissioned Sunichi Watanabe – one of her students who had graduated from Tange's lab at Tokyo University – to translate an excerpt of "City Design" for the June 1963 *Ekistics*. She paired this article – which "indicates what the authors believe to be the most fruit-

ful directives for the future" – with two others on "Urban Form," praising the contribution of "the young Japanese group" as "by far the most adventurous of the three." Tyrwhitt further praised the group as "steeped in [...] ekistic studies," whose work aligned with Doxiadis's idea of "a more or less anonymous or 'international' framework with 'local-traditional' characteristics in its micro-space" [Fig. 4].[49] Tyrwhitt's paper for Delos I underscored the connection to the Intercity program at Harvard, asserting that global urbanization called for a new urban ideal at the macro scale variously called "the conurbation (by Patrick Geddes) [...] megalopolis (by Jean Gottmann) [...] and Dynapolis (by Doxiadis)."[50] (She might have added her own term "urban constellation" to that list). Tange's Tokyo Bay plan, Tyrwhitt argued, showed that this ideal was not simply utopian but also realistic: it could be realized through public investment in transportation infrastructure.

Fig. 3 Photograph from the meeting of experts on "Reciprocal Influence on Urban and Architectural Forms and Structures on the Orient and the Occident" at ACE in the Athens Technological Institute on March 5–6, 1963. From left to right: C. Doxiadis, P. Vigo, M. de Silva, E. Albert and K. Maekawa.

scatterd plan / まき散らす

五 pattern plan / 五の字をつくる

grid plan / 格子に割る

thunder plan / 稲妻型にする

linear plan / 帯状にする

cluster plan / 房をつける

unit plan / 単位をつなげる

satellite plan / 衛星都市をつくる

focal-plan / 焦点をつくる

multi-focal plan / 焦点をつなぐ

excentric plan / 偏心させる

finger plan / 手のひら型にする

twin plan / 二つの都市をつなぐ

conurbation plan / 連担都市を計画する

Fig. 4 Analysis of urban form by a group of Japanese students who were "steeped in Ekistics studies." Tyrwhitt praised their work as aligned with Doxiadis's idea of a relatively anonymous or "international" macro urban structure that can accommodate "local-traditional" characteristics at the micro scale.

Ellen Shoshkes

Reciprocal Eastern and Western Influences in Bioregional Urbanism: Convergence at Delos

The next phase in the evolving East–West synthesis in bioregional urbanism began in the Inter-City II urban design studio that Tyrwhitt co-taught with Maki, then on the Harvard faculty, in the fall of 1963. They used the studio to apply regional urbanism at the micro scale, studying how to leverage public investments in transportation infrastructure to enhance pedestrian spaces to enliven Boston's core. In the course of this work, Maki now envisioned Group Form as "regionalism at the collective scale" – a strategy for creating local character in the micro spaces of an "international" framework. This studio provided fertile ground for the hybridization of urban ideals, in part because a new generation of international students was prepared by their training and background to engage the disparate threads from East and West that were now available as shared cultural resources. Koichi Nagashima (1936–2022) was particularly receptive to the teachings of Maki and Tyrwhitt. Nagashima trained under a Kon disciple, Yoshizaka, at Waseda, then became interested in studying urban design at Harvard and learning more about Doxiadis after hearing a talk by Maki. Maki and Tyrwhitt enabled Nagashima to spend a postgraduate year at GSE (1964–1965), where he continued to work with Tyrwhitt.

Shortly afterwards, Tyrwhitt took leave from Harvard to work full time at ACE, which was hosting the Delos Symposia annually and expanding related international programs funded by the Ford Foundation. In her capacity as sole rapporteur of the Delos Symposia and editor of the "official report" in *Ekistics*, Tyrwhitt played an influential role in shaping the narrative of creative East–West dialogue that inspired the evolution of the new hybrid ideal of bioregional urbanism. The focus on the significance of Japanese urbanism was a result of leadership by Isomura, who attended five Delos Symposia, and Martin Meyerson; in 1963, they helped mobilize UN support for Tange and Okita, former head of Japan's Economic Planning Agency, to establish the Japan Center for Area Development Research (JCADR) to guide national land planning. The formation of the World Society of Ekistics (WSE) – as proposed by Meyerson at Delos 2 in 1964 – facilitated deeper collaboration among Delians and in their connection with the JCADR, which hosted a concurrent series of international seminars on regional development also funded by the Ford Foundation and involving Delians and participants in other UN-supported regional-planning initiatives in Japan. Isomura, who met Jean Gottmann at Delos 2 and became an early promoter of Gottmann's Megalopolis concept in Japan,[51] fostered their reciprocal influence in his capacity as JCADR executive director and, later, WSE president (1973–1975), succeeding Gottmann's own directorship (1971–1973).

Tange presented his paper "Tokaido-Megalopolis: The Japanese Archipelago in the Future" at a small JCADR seminar in 1965, attended by Delians including Doxiadis, Gottmann, Richard Meier and Paul Ylvisaker of the Ford Foundation (part of the UN team that collaborated on the Hanshin plan), along with Weissmann (who had brokered Tange's new collaboration with Doxiadis on the reconstruction plan for Skopje in present-day North Macedonia). Tange was invited to but was, however, unable to attend Delos 3 in 1965, where problems of living at high densities were discussed. In this meeting, Giedion championed Tange's Tokyo Bay project as a promising solution to the need for a new urban spatial organization with variable density, and hailed the "younger generation" – notably Tange and Maki – that was experimenting with the mega-structure and Group Form. Underscoring the sense of almost mythically shared values, he also noted that archaeologists now considered the Athenian Acropolis to be a Group Form – as, indeed, Doxiadis's thesis had argued.[52]

At Delos 3, it was reported that COF research would now focus on how the Megalopolis represented one stage in the evolution toward Ecumenopolis. As explained in the July 1965 edition of *Ekistics*, the concept of Ecumenopolis assumes the inevitability of the global spread of an urban system; the question was how to guide the evolution of the components of this system toward a desirable form [Fig. 5].[53] COF research now began to dovetail explicitly with Tange's work for the JCADR in a way that directly involved Tyrwhitt and her niece, Catharine Huws, a Welsh geographer who worked on the COF research team. In September 1965, when Tange and Maki visited Tyrwhitt at her home outside Athens, they discovered that Nagashima was about to marry Catharine. Maki was on his way to Tokyo to open his own office and offered Nagashima a job, and Catharine continued her COF research from her new home in Japan, analyzing the Tokaido Megalopolis.

Tyrwhitt now had a personal connection to Japan, and paid closer attention to the quality of life in Tokaido. Her first visit to the Nagashimas coincided with the twenty-eighth International Federation of Housing and

Planning Congress (IFHP), on "Urban Transportation and Housing," in Tokyo in May 1966, which she featured in the August 1966 issue of *Ekistics*. Tyrwhitt acknowledged that Japanese "ideas regarding urban improvement mainly consist in providing better means of transportation," but she was cautiously optimistic about the country's "exhilarating vision" of an urban future blending West and East.[54] At Delos 4 in July 1966, Isomura encouraged Tyrwhitt to undertake research through the JCADR to study this further, and she published her proposal to survey pedestrian behavior in old Tokyo neighborhoods, where narrow winding streets discouraged through traffic, the very next month in the August 1966 issue of *Ekistics*.[55]

At Delos 4, Tange had presented his JCADR report "Image of the Future Japanese Archipelago," arguing that Japan was advancing toward "a higher level of organic composition" and that strengthening the transportation and communication linkages in the Tokaido Megalopolis – acting as a central "nervous system" – could be a vital factor in that transformation.[56] Catharine Nagashima's COF research on Tokaido and the discourse at Delos now became interconnected with Tange's work and the JCADR's International Symposia on Regional Development. The first symposium, in Hakone in April 1967, on "Future Images of the Urban Environment, with Emphasis on the Future of the Japanese Archipelago," discussed the visions of Tange, Isomura, Gottmann and Doxiadis. Tyrwhitt abstracted four reports, including Gottmann's and Tange's, in the May 1968 issue of *Ekistics* on "Urban Systems and Urban Form." Cover art derived in part from Kisho Kurokawa's 1959 diagram for the restructuring of Tokyo illustrated the issue's theme – "the notion of open-ended urban forms, able to interconnect within a more or less hierarchical regional structure" – and reflected the influence of Metabolist visions of this ideal.[57]

East–West Synthesis: Tokaido Megalopolis

The narrative Tyrwhitt curated across the *Ekistics* journal now focused on evidence of this *conscious* evolution of Megalopolis that was ostensibly surfacing in and around Tokyo. In May 1967 *Ekistics* published Richard Meier (a contributor to COF research) on "The Foundation for a New Urbanism," which explored the "sophisticated systems design lying behind the good life in the megalopolis" centered on Tokyo. Attributing more potential for guided evolution of this urbanization process than its drivers in private real estate ever allowed for, Meier asserted "that the major contribution the

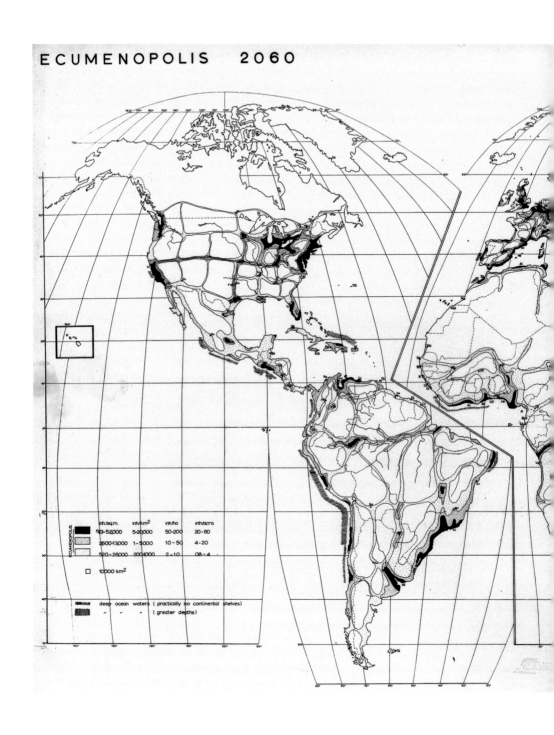

Fig. 5 Ecumenopolis in 2060. The concept of Ecumenopolis assumes the inevitability of the global spread of an urban system; the question was how to guide the evolution of the components of this system toward a desirable form.

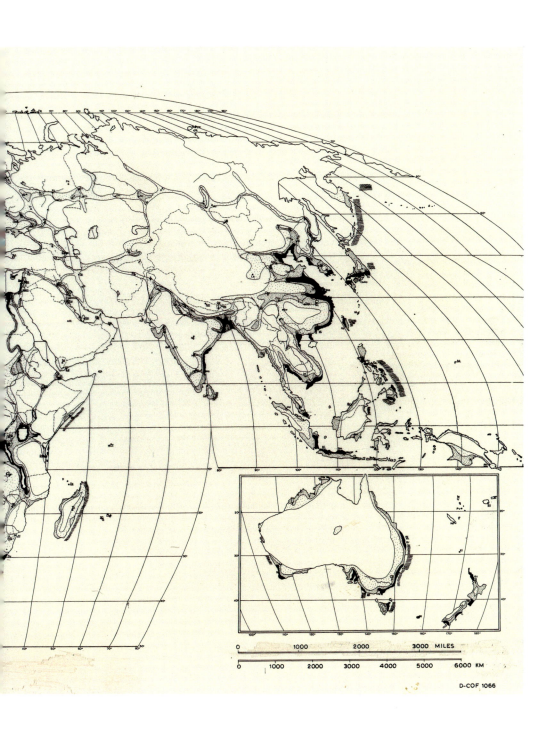

Japanese can make to megalopolitan concepts lies in the experience they are accumulating from the construction and the tuning of the developmental engine that provides the motive power in the progress toward megalopolis [...] [with] its enhanced capacity to innovate, improvise and organize."[58] The first of a series of articles on Catharine Nagashima's analysis of the Tokaido Megalopolis appeared in the July 1967 issue of *Ekistics*, to coincide with Delos 5.[59] In the February 1968 *Ekistics*, Tyrwhitt reported on her study of the pedestrian in Megalopolis, viewing traditional Tokyo residential districts as a collective form that could be used as human-scale building blocks ("pedestrian islands") in a large urban complex [Fig. 6].

The second part of Catharine's research on Tokaido appeared in the July 1968 issue of *Ekistics*, coinciding with Delos 6, while at a concurrent seminar at ACE Meier reported on the widespread adoption of new lifestyles that accompanied Japan's sudden entrance into the megalopolitan era, as manifested in inner Tokyo from 1951 onward. Echoing Watsuji, he concluded, "The most striking feature about Japanese cultural growth during a period of accelerated development is the extent to which it drew upon alien images [...] [using a] selective, highly sophisticated borrowing system."[60]

Cultural factors in urban development were also discussed at the second JCADR International Symposium in Hakone in September 1968 – attended by both the Nagashimas and Watanabe – where Christopher Alexander explained his theory of a "pattern language": physical forms aligned with specific, culturally shaped behavioral patterns. Alexander was on Tange's panel on Environmental Development, along with Kurokowa, who presented "A Theory of Metabolism in Planning." Tyrwhitt excerpted Alexander's paper in the August 1969 issue of *Ekistics*[61] – perhaps to elucidate the lead article by J. M. Richards, which admired the apparent chaos of the Japanese city as satisfying a popular need for a sense of participation.[62] Tyrwhitt offered another cultural explanation for Tokyo's vitality in the September 1969 issue of *Ekistics*, with Koji Taira's article contending that the regeneration of a ragpickers' settlement depended "as greatly on a psychological uplift within the area itself – 'love energy' – as on the necessary social institutions set up to counteract" its problems.[63]

Doxiadis intended Delos 10 in 1972 to be the final Symposion, and Tyrwhitt retired as editor of *Ekistics* in September of the same year. In preparation, Tyrwhitt and Gwen Bell – her co-editor and successor – produced *Human Identity in the Built Environment* (1972), a compilation of *Ekistics*

articles that highlighted themes discussed at Delos with a particular focus on the megalopolitan scale. Fittingly, their introduction began by reiterating Ekistics' connection both to Geddes's "essentially ekistic" approach to urban analysis and CIAM's comparative methodology. They organized the compilation according to the five Ekistical categories, concluding with the Synthesis exemplified by the Tokaido Megalopolis, which presented "a unique image of man (human identity) and megalopolis, illustrating [their] synergistic interrelations." The editors explained, "[T]he Tokaido megalopolis provides a unique bridge between the developed and the developing worlds, rural and urban economies, and the Oriental and Occidental ways of life. [...] [I]t may be symbolic of a more distant urban future of ecumenopolis, when all parts of the globe will become linked to a single interlocking urban system, within which each individual can achieve his own identity" [Fig. 7].[64]

Fig. 6 Children playing in the street in a traditional Tokyo neighborhood. Tyrwhitt viewed such residential districts as a collective form that could be used as human-scale building blocks ("pedestrian islands") in a large urban complex.

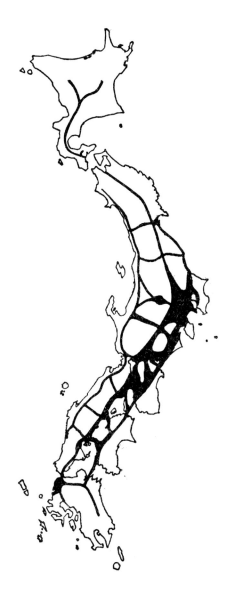

Grounding Group Form in the Japanese Megalopolis

In some ways, *Human Identity in the Built Environment* represented the swansong for the Delos Symposia, even though they continued for another couple of years without Doxiadis at the helm and were still nourished by the East–West discourse of a global yet regionally inflected urban system and the narrative of Tokaido as the emergent urban ideal. This was largely thanks to Tyrwhitt and other Asian urbanists. Through her continuing role as consulting editor of *Ekistics*, involvement in WSE, contacts with the JCADR and efforts to broker ties between Maki and Koichi Nagashima, Tyrwhitt had been applying Group Form in practice. Notably, she supported the group of WSE members who in 1970 had formed APAC (Asian Planning and Architecture Consultants), including Maki, Nagashima, William Lim from Singapore (an Ekistics correspondent who attended Delos 11), Tao Ho from Hong Kong (who attended Delos 11 and 12) and Sumet Jumsai from Thailand.

Involvement in APAC stimulated Nagashima, then teaching urban design at the University of Singapore, to theorize about urban space and revive Ishikawa's concepts of *sakariba* and *kaiwai* as principles to guide the design of post-industrial Japanese cities. Tyrwhitt published his paper on

Fig. 7 Tokyo as a Megalopolis (Tokaido) in the context of the Japanese archipelago, seen in terms of the Megalopolis concept.

The editors of *Ekistics* presented the Tokaido Megalopolis as symbolic of an emergent Ecumenopolis.

Ellen Shoshkes

the evolution of these concepts in the September 1970 issue of *Ekistics*. Nagashima interpreted *kaiwai* as "the space for spontaneous human contacts," comparable with the Greek agora but uniquely Japanese, and he envisioned an urban future pervaded by such spaces.[65] Maki also began theorizing about *kaiwai* as a feature of Japanese urban space after joining the faculty of Tokyo University in 1971. Tyrwhitt presented Maki's observations on urbanization and communication in Japan as the lead article in the September 1974 *Ekistics*, which focused on "Japan and China: Different Approaches to Mechanization." In this article, Maki drew on Watsuji and Alexander in examining connections between behavioral patterns that mark Japanese urban society and physical aspects of urban life considered "particularly Japanese." The large Japanese city, he said, was "a great gathering place comprising many small places" (the insular districts Tyrwhitt had characterized as "pedestrian islands") distinguished by their *kaiwai*: the atmosphere found in the micro-infrastructure of public and semi-public spaces, where people create community through spontaneous interactions. Maki concluded that this manifestation of collective form, despite its uniquely Japanese features, had global relevance as "one ideal form of a metropolis for the emerging information age."[66]

Conclusion: Moving toward Entopia

In compiling the September 1974 issue of *Ekistics* on Japan and China, Tyrwhitt sought to ground Delian discourse on the Japanese Megalopolis more firmly in the realities of everyday life in that region. This issue can be seen as a contribution to the document WSE would produce at Delos 12 in 1975 – the *actual* final Symposion – that sought to influence the agenda of the UN's 1976 Conference on Habitat. The issue directly addressed Isomura's cautionary comment at Delos 11: "In Japan, […] the term 'megalopolis' is not well understood […] [it is] now a symbol of the overconcentration of people, a not-so-ideal type of human settlement."[67] Tyrwhitt included two articles prepared for the JCADR's Seminar on the International Comparative Study of Megalopolises in Tokyo in June 1973: one by Watanabe called for further study of the problems of the Japanese Megalopolis, including the severe deterioration of the environment, which had "extremely practical implications" for other industrializing countries, especially in Asia; the other, by Catharine Nagashima, attempted to classify the numerous definitions of Megalopolis that had emerged in Japan since the mid-1960s, including

Fig. 8 The July/August 1981 issue of *Ekistics* was focused on the significance of Japan's organization of its national space in response to the rapid evolution of its economy and society in the twentieth century.

those by ACE, Kurokawa and Tange. Enthusiasm for the Japanese Megalopolis was tempered temporarily.

The image of Japanese urbanism as an ideal – which co-evolved in Japan and the West from a complex web of utopian pioneers of modern planning, through CIAM urbanism, the establishment of the new field of urban design and COF research projects – culminated in and was claimed as the legacy of the Delos Symposia with the publication of the July/August 1981 issue of *Ekistics* dedicated to "Japan's Organization of Space." This issue featured articles by Isomura – who had established the Japan Society of Ekistics (JSE) in 1975 – and the Nagashimas, as well as a semiotic reading of Maki's theory of uniquely Japanese placemaking processes. Jean Gottmann served as guest editor, "due to his long involvement in Japan,"[68] after meeting Isomura at Delos 2. Gottmann wrote that he had gradually realized that "the immense scope and importance in this century of the Japanese experiment […] was organizing and re-organizing national space to fit the rapid evolution of its economy and society." Amid its "metamorphosis," he argued – echoing Maki and Watsuji – Japan preserved its traditions, notably the "special and essential" value attached to the "inner core of spatial as well as social organization," which helped explain the spirit in which the Japanese accept continual change and the renewal of aspects of their habitat and environment [Fig. 8].

In his editor's note, Panayis Psumoupolous, Doxiadis's right-hand man throughout the Delos Symposia, acknowledged, "The final product of the effort reflected in this issue was made possible also by Jaqueline Tyrwhitt's involvement, and whose knowledge of Japan and continuous contact with the country proved very valuable."[69]

---

1. Gwen Bell and Jaqueline Tyrwhitt, "Introduction," in G. Bell and J. Tyrwhitt (eds), *Human Identity in the Urban Environment* (Harmondsworth: Penguin Books, 1972), 36.
2. Ellen Shoshkes, *Jaqueline Tyrwhitt: Transnational Life in Urban Planning and Design* (Burlington, VT: Ashgate, 2013).
3. Ellen Shoshkes, "East-West: Interactions between the United States and Japan and Their Effect on Utopian Realism," *Journal of Planning History* 3, no. 3 (August 2004), 215–40.
4. J. W. Hall and R. K. Beardsley, *Twelve Doors to Japan* (New York: McGraw-Hill, 1965), 158.
5. Patrick Geddes, *Cities in Evolution* (New York: Howard Fertig, 1915/1968), xxvi–xxvii.
6. Henry Smith, "Tokyo as an Idea," *Journal of Japanese Studies* 4, no. 1 (Winter 1978), 45–80.
7. Naoto Nakajima, "Biographical Study of Japanese 'Civic Artists' before the W.W. II," in *IPHS Conference Proceedings*, July 2004, https://www.etsav.upc.es/personals/iphs2004/pdf/151_p.pdf (accessed August 25, 2020).
8. Carola Hein, "Visionary Plans and Planners: Japanese Traditions and Western Influences," in N. Fieve and P. Waley (eds), *Japanese Capitals in Historical Perspective: Place, Power and Memory in Kyoto, Edo and Tokyo* (Abingdon: Routledge Curzon, 2003), 309–46.
9. Izumi Kuroishi, "Urban Survey and Planning in Twentieth-Century Japan," *Journal of Urban History* 42, no. 3 (2016), 557–81.

10 Harry Hartoonian, *Overcome by Modernity* (Princeton, NJ: Princeton University Press, 2000), 96.
11 Tetsuro Watsuji, *A Climate: A Philosophical Study*, trans. G. Bownas (Tokyo: Japanese Government Printing Bureau, 1961), https://monoskop.org/images/9/90/Tetsuro_Watsuji_A_Climate_A_Philosophical_Study.pdf (accessed August 2, 2017).
12 Robert Carter and Erin McCarthy, "Watsuji Tetsurō," in Edward N. Zalta (ed.), *The Stanford Encyclopedia of Philosophy* (Winter 2019), https://plato.stanford.edu/entries/watsuji-tetsuro/ (accessed April 22, 2024).
13 Robert Bellah, "Japan's Cultural Identity: Some Reflections on the Work of Watsuji Tetsuro," *Journal of Asian Studies* 24, no. 4 (August 1965), 573–94.
14 Hartoonian, *Overcome by Modernity*, 252.
15 Zongjie Lin, "City as Process: Tange Kenzo and the Japanese Urban Utopias, 1959–1970," dissertation, University of Pennsylvania, 2006, 84, https://www.proquest.com/docview/305258252 (accessed August 25, 2020).
16 Agnes Nyilas, *Beyond Utopia* (New York: Routledge, 2018), 174.
17 J. Sato, "The Resources Committee Experiment," Proceedings of Environmental Policy Conference, University of Maryland, June 2009, http://www.umdcipe.org/conferences/epckdi/35.PDF (accessed August 25, 2020).
18 Lin, "City as Process," 69–70.
19 Jaqueline Tyrwhitt, "Cores within the Urban Constellation," in J. Tyrwhitt, J. L. Sert and E. N. Rogers (eds), *CIAM 8: The Heart of the City* (New York: Pellegrini and Cudahy, 1952), 103–4.
20 "Conversation at CIAM 8," in Tyrwhitt et al. (eds), *CIAM 8: The Heart of the City*, 39–40.
21 K. Tange, "Japan: Hiroshima," in Tyrwhitt et al. (eds), *CIAM 8: The Heart of the City*, 137.
22 Naoki Sakai, *Translation and Subjectivity: On Japan and Cultural Nationalism* (Minneapolis: University of Minnesota Press, 2008).
23 Jonathan Reynolds, *Maekawa Kunio and the Emergence of Japanese Modernist Architecture* (Berkeley: University of California Press, 2001), 214–15.
24 Ibid., 285.
25 Kajiya Kenji, "Post-historical Traditions in Art, Design, and Architecture in 1950s Japan," *World Art* 5, no. 1, (2015), 21–38.
26 Dana Buntrock, "Katsura Imperial Villa: A Brief Descriptive Bibliography, with Illustrations," *Cross-Currents: East Asia History and Culture Review*, no. 3 (June 2012), https://escholarship.org/uc/item/6z4060zx (accessed April 22, 2024).
27 Cherie Wendelkin, "Putting Metabolism Back in Place," in Sarah W. Goldhagen and Rejean Légault (eds), *Anxious Modernisms* (Cambridge, MA: MIT Press, 2000), 279–99.
28 Steve Odin, "The Social Self in Japanese Philosophy and American Pragmatism: A Comparative Study of Wasuji Tetsuro and George Herbert Mead," *Philosophy East and West* 42, no. 3 (1992), 475–501.
29 Meeting of Delegates at Sarraz, December 15, 1955, C017, CIAM Collections, Frances Loeb Library, Harvard University, Cambridge, MA.
30 J. Tyrwhitt, "Fatehpur Sikri," *Architectural Review* 123, no. 733 (1958), 124–28, quotation 128.
31 J. Tyrwhitt, "The Moving Eye," *Explorations* 4 (1955), 90–95.
32 E. Isomura, "United Nations ECAFE Seminar: Urbanization in Japan," *Ekistics* 2, no. 14/15 (November/December 1956), 39.
33 Y. Matsumoto, "Japanese Urban Sociology: Development and Current Trends," *American Sociologist* (Fall 2000), 58–71.
34 J. Tyrwhitt, "Editorial," *Ekistics* 4, no. 25 (1957), iii.
35 Lin, "City as Process," 20.
36 Fumihiko Maki, "Formative Years," in M. Mulligan (ed.), *Nurturing Dreams* (Cambridge, MA: MIT Press, 2008), 16–27, quotation 26–27.
37 H. Yatsuke, "The Structure of the Exhibition," *Metabolism: The City of the Future* (Tokyo: Mori Art Museum, 2012), 54.
38 R. Koolhaas and H. Obrist, *Project Japan: Metabolism Talks* (Cologne: Taschen, 2011), 294, 647.
39 Ibid., 185.
40 "The Athens Center of Ekistics," *Ekistics* 16, no. 94 (September 1963), 142.
41 G. Nitschke, "The Metabolists of Japan," *Architectural Design* (October 1964), 509–24.
42 "City of the Future," *Ekistics* 20, no. 116 (July 1965), 4.
43 J. Tyrwhitt, "Editorial," *Ekistics* 14, no. 82 (August–September 1962), 72–73, quotation 73.
44 Resolution 418 (Category II) Workshop on Urban Development (Fall of 1964), Social Matters Correspondence/SO 117 Weissmann E., 3, United Nations Archive, New York.
45 "East and West – Reciprocal Influences," *Ekistics* 15, no. 89 (April 1963), 204.
46 Lefteris Theodosis, "Victory over Chaos? Constantinos Doxiadis and Ekistics 1945–1975," dissertation, Universitat Politècnica de Catalunya, Barcelona, 2015, 215.
47 "East and West."
48 Theodosis, "Victory over Chaos?," 227.
49 J. Tyrwhitt, "Editorial: Studies of Urban Form," *Ekistics* 15, no. 91 (June 1963), 342–43.
50 J. Tyrwhitt, "Shapes of Cities that Can Grow and Change," *Architectural Association Journal* 90, no. 876 (1963), 87–102, quotation 88.
51 Jeffery Hanes, "From Megalopolis to Megaroposisu," *Journal of Urban History* 19, no. 2 (February 1993), 56–94.
52 Sigfried Giedion, "Density and Urbanism," *Ekistics* 20, no. 119 (October 1965), 208–9.
53 "The City of the Future," *Ekistics* 20, no. 116 (July 1965), 51.

54 J. Tyrwhitt, "Editorial," *Ekistics* 22, no. 129 (August 1966), 103–4.
55 J. Tyrwhitt, "Outline for a Research Study in Tokyo," *Ekistics* 22, no. 129 (August 1966), 124.
56 "Papers from Participants," *Ekistics* 22, no. 31 (October 1966), 248–50.
57 J. Tyrwhitt, "Editorial," *Ekistics* 25, no. 150 (May 1968), 277–79, quotation 278.
58 Richard Meier, "Notes on the Creation of an Efficient Megalopolis," *Ekistics* 23, no. 138 (May 1967), 294–307.
59 Catharine Nagashima, "Megalopolis in Japan," *Ekistics* 124, no. 140 (July 1967), 6–14.
60 R. Meier and Ikumi Hoshino, "Cultural Growth and Urban Development: Inner Tokyo 1951–1968," *Ekistics* 26, no. 155 (October 1968), 390–94, quotation 391.
61 C. Alexander, "Major Changes in Environmental Form Required by Social and Psychological Demands," *Ekistics* 28, no. 165 (August 1969), 78–85.
62 J. M. Richards, "Lessons from the Japanese Jungle," *Ekistics* 28, no. 165 (August 1969), 75–77.
63 Koji Taira, "Urban Poverty, Ragpickers, and the 'Ants Villa' in Tokyo," *Ekistics* 28 no. 166 (September 1969), 163–67.
64 Bell and Tyrwhitt, "Introduction," 15–37, quotations 33, 36.
65 Koichi Nagashima, "Future Urban Environment: Evolution of Social and Leisure Space with Reference to Japan," *Ekistics* 30, no. 178 (September 1970), 218–22.
66 Fumihiko Maki, "Some Observations on Urbanization and Communication in Japan," *Ekistics* 38, no. 226 (September 1974), 156–60.
67 "World Society of Ekistics," *Ekistics* 38, no. 229 (December 1974), 404.
68 Panayis Psomopoulos, "The Editor's Page," *Ekistics*, 48, no. 289 (July/August 1981), 255.
69 Ibid.

Delos and "The Human Factor"
Simon Richards

Introduction

The Delos Symposia were a great and oftentimes unruly clamor of voices, each one seeking to pinpoint the developmental priorities for the future of the planet. Whether concerning agriculture or education, work or leisure, manufacture or infrastructure, or the natural ecosystem – these priorities were always wrapped up into the primary problem of urbanization. And the solution always involved a new version of the architect–planner as the catalyst for what needed to be done: the revitalized "Ekistician" as opposed to the beleaguered old guard of the International Congresses of Modern Architecture (Congrès Internationaux d'Architecture Moderne – CIAM), defunct since 1959. But, despite the best efforts of Jaqueline Tyrwhitt, editor of the *Ekistics* journal and – in the absence of official recordings or minutes that might hamper spontaneous discussion – shorthand documenter of everything that went on in the Symposia, the message that came out each year was never completely clean and unified.[1]

The purpose of this chapter is to recapture some of the priorities of the seven Delos Symposia of the 1960s, using the published deliberations and associated articles in *Ekistics* to do so, some of which also reflect satellite activities across the "Ekistics Month" during which the Symposia took place. But we will tease out a particular thread of ideas that runs beneath and around all the others, which the liberal philosopher Karl Popper, in his critique of utopian thinking, called "the human factor."[2] By this we refer to the ways that proposals for ideal societies, cities and buildings often presuppose some idea of the person that is meant to slot neatly into them. And this is more than just the obvious matter of assessing user or client needs.

It often involves much deeper ideas about human nature and interaction taken from diverse fields of inquiry – philosophy, sociology, psychology, neuroscience, even poetry.

This is a long-standing trope within built-environment discourses but one which usually hides deep beneath the surface, and in previous research I have worked to unearth and interrogate this across much of twentieth-century architecture and planning.[3] The remarkable thing about the Delos Symposia and indeed the wider adventure of Ekistics, however, is how readily they invited these discussions into the open, acknowledging them as a core theme and problematic across environmental thinking and design that needed to be grappled with. One can see this from the "Ekistic Grid" that was published and revised constantly during these years as a way of visualizing the range of remedial activities required across all scales and population densities of the built environment [Fig. 1]. One vector of the grid points to interventions at the largest scale, cross-referencing "Function" (sometimes referred to as "Networks") and "Ecumenopolis" to indicate the need to deal with the infrastructure of a totally urbanized planet. At the other end of the scale, however, "Nature" and "Man" are cross-referenced to point out the need to consider the fullness of human nature. Indeed, the primary position of this vector (column 1, line 1, at top left of the grid) perhaps operates as a tacit acknowledgment that it is fundamental to all the rest.[4]

Doxiadis's own views on this matter were very well developed over these years. He believed that human nature required close human contact and intimacy – bodily, familial and community contact. He also believed that town planning that displayed design sensitivity towards local or regional conditions, such as by using vernacular planning typologies and architectural styles, was more nourishing for people than more generic townscapes. This focus on regional vernaculars and human intimacy might seem to contradict the headline image of Ekistics as being an enterprise committed to coordinating global networking, infrastructure and populations into a single Ecumenopolis. For Doxiadis, however, and also for Tyrwhitt, these measures were not the end goal but merely the steps necessary to preserve the local and the intimate for people. To let urban development run amok would only end in hyper-stimulation of the mind; exhaustion of the body; and, ultimately, the ineradicable deformation of human nature.[5]

But there was no shortage of opinion on this matter in the Delos Symposia, and despite their own views Tyrwhitt and Doxiadis let it run freely.

This chapter will offer a series of brief vignettes that try to encapsulate these discussions at the main Delos touchpoints of 1963 to 1969 – discussions which grew increasingly wild across the years despite Tyrwhitt's efforts to shape a publicly facing consensus around Ekistics in many other areas. To do this, our focus will need to be narrow and will shut out much of the rest of the extraordinarily wide-ranging Delos deliberations, as we try to identify the core "human factor" thematic of each Delos event. The chapter concludes with a brief assessment of how the Delos explorations into this topic compare with discussions that are had among architect–planners and urbanists nowadays.

Delos 1, July 1963: Man or Men?

The first Delos Symposion – the Greek term being favored by the Delians over the Latin *symposium* because it was more suggestive of an informal gathering – was concerned with setting out the broad agenda of dealing with urbanization at a planetary scale. But in his *Washington Post* report on Delos 1, James Clayton offered a pointed – if unacknowledged – echo of Popper's phrase when noting the prevalence of discussions on "The Human Factor." This had been prompted somewhat testily by the anthropologist Margaret Mead, who was one of the intellectual heavyweights of Delos and often positioned in the thick of debate there. Clayton's report focused in part on the disagreement in this Symposion over whether the architect–planner should take a preemptive or a responsive approach to the issue – that is, should designs for the physical environment seek to actively shape people and their behaviors? Or should the approach be one that first tries to understand what fundamental human nature consists of, *before* going on to formulate a plan for the built environment that suits it? Put simply: should the built environment shape people or should it be *shaped by* people?[6]

This division is fundamental and recurring within discussions of the relationship between built environment and behavior, and it is the active, operational component of a deeper philosophical question about human nature: is human nature a constant and perhaps even universal quality (a position which suggests it is "self-sufficient" and not conditioned by environmental factors), or is it a malleable quality that changes through time and influence into a multiplicity of possible alternatives (a position which suggests a "self/other" dynamic as well as considerable influence from socioenvironmental factors)?[7] It is noteworthy, then, that this very first

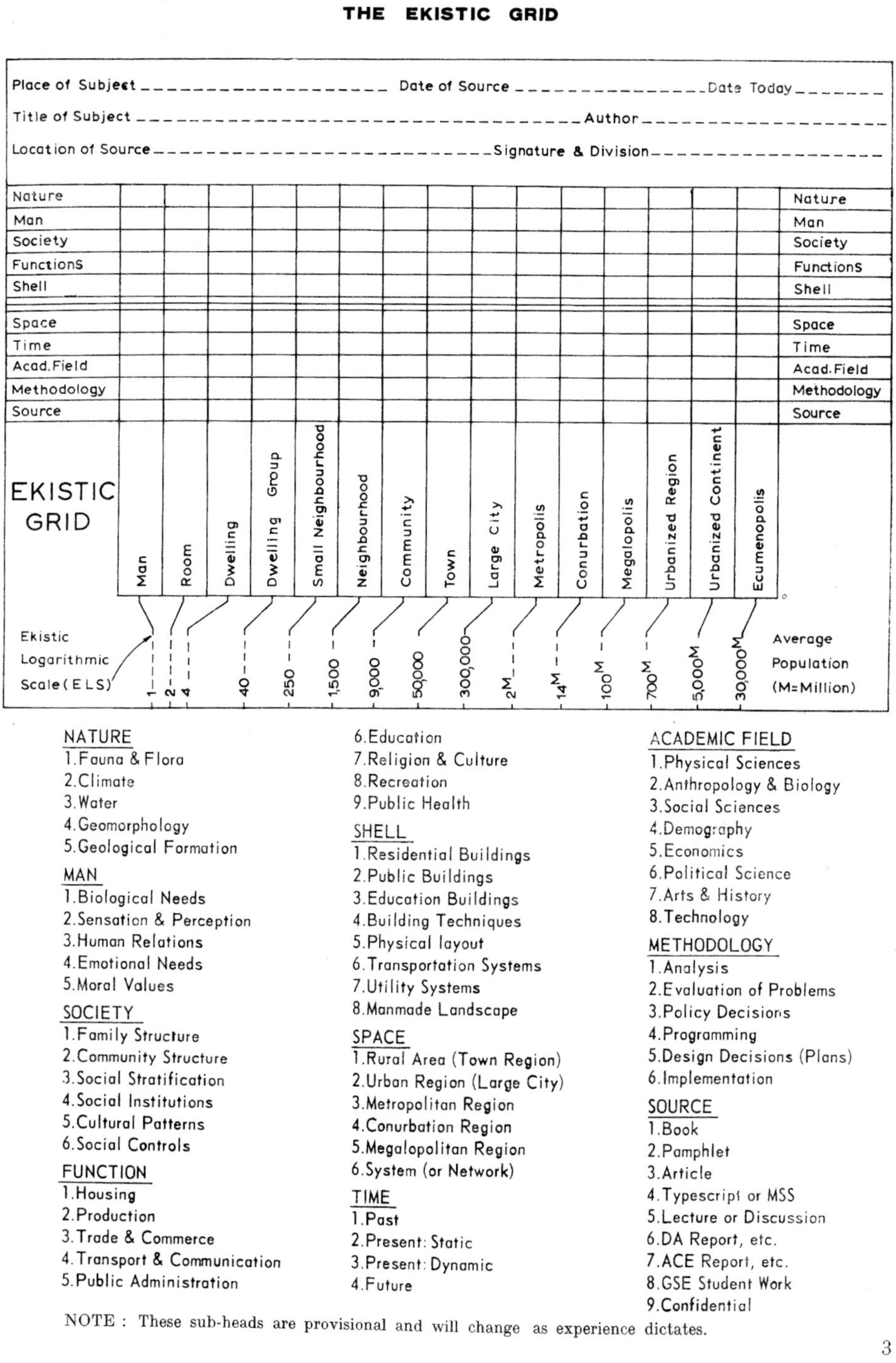

THE EKISTIC GRID

	Man	Room	Dwelling	Dwelling Group	Small Neighbourhood	Neighbourhood	Community	Town	Large City	Metropolis	Conurbation	Megalopolis	Urbanized Region	Urbanized Continent	Ecumenopolis	
Nature																Nature
Man																Man
Society																Society
Functions																Functions
Shell																Shell
Space																Space
Time																Time
Acad. Field																Acad. Field
Methodology																Methodology
Source																Source

Place of Subject _____ Date of Source _____ Date Today _____
Title of Subject _____ Author _____
Location of Source _____ Signature & Division _____

EKISTIC GRID

Ekistic Logarithmic Scale (ELS): 1, 2, 4, 40, 250, 1,500, 9,000, 50,000, 300,000, 2M, 14M, 100M, 700M, 5,000M, 30,000M — Average Population (M=Million)

NATURE
1. Fauna & Flora
2. Climate
3. Water
4. Geomorphology
5. Geological Formation

MAN
1. Biological Needs
2. Sensation & Perception
3. Human Relations
4. Emotional Needs
5. Moral Values

SOCIETY
1. Family Structure
2. Community Structure
3. Social Stratification
4. Social Institutions
5. Cultural Patterns
6. Social Controls

FUNCTION
1. Housing
2. Production
3. Trade & Commerce
4. Transport & Communication
5. Public Administration

6. Education
7. Religion & Culture
8. Recreation
9. Public Health

SHELL
1. Residential Buildings
2. Public Buildings
3. Education Buildings
4. Building Techniques
5. Physical layout
6. Transportation Systems
7. Utility Systems
8. Manmade Landscape

SPACE
1. Rural Area (Town Region)
2. Urban Region (Large City)
3. Metropolitan Region
4. Conurbation Region
5. Megapolitan Region
6. System (or Network)

TIME
1. Past
2. Present: Static
3. Present: Dynamic
4. Future

ACADEMIC FIELD
1. Physical Sciences
2. Anthropology & Biology
3. Social Sciences
4. Demography
5. Economics
6. Political Science
7. Arts & History
8. Technology

METHODOLOGY
1. Analysis
2. Evaluation of Problems
3. Policy Decisions
4. Programming
5. Design Decisions (Plans)
6. Implementation

SOURCE
1. Book
2. Pamphlet
3. Article
4. Typescript or MSS
5. Lecture or Discussion
6. DA Report, etc.
7. ACE Report, etc.
8. GSE Student Work
9. Confidential

NOTE: These sub-heads are provisional and will change as experience dictates.

Fig. 1 "The Ekistic Grid."

Symposion grappled with this idea of "man" as universal constant versus "men" as malleable pluralities, with the terms and their connotations frequently slipping over each other.

Media theorist Marshall McLuhan pushed hard on the idea that information technology, networks and cybernetics pointed the way towards a more fluid, open-ended future environment in which human nature itself would be made fluid and endlessly redrawn – not least by being cybernetically brain-plugged into this network. This represented an imminent and "enormous upgrading of man" that the planner must be ready to deal with: cities and people would no longer be "zoned" apart but enmeshed into one continuity. Mead, given her research into tribal cultures, responded with a commitment to cultural relativism, but argued also that there is a stable core of universal human spirit that must be respected and from which variations emerge. Conrad Waddington, the evolutionary biologist, focused similarly on the idea that there are certain biological constants that required a stable environmental situation – at least at key stages of life, such as early childhood and old age. And the lawyer and politician A. K. Brohi observed that, in order to work effectively, "a doctor has before him the image of a healthy man to aid him in diagnosing the ailment of his patient." It is important to note in this connection that the Delos 1 edition of *Ekistics* included a reprint of the 1933 "Athens Charter" from CIAM, which likewise foregrounded the need to consider the "[p]sychological and biological constants [...] of the basic human being." Predictably, perhaps, the heavily symbolic invitation to this initial meeting of CIAM founder Sigfried Giedion resulted in his own reconfirmation of the "Athens Charter" position: the need to look for constancy and a fixed point of reference when discussing the human factor.[8]

The first Symposion laid out the classic dichotomies on environmental psychology and its philosophical underpinnings, with representatives spread equally over the conventional arguments of both sides: change versus constancy; environmental preemptiveness versus environmental responsiveness. It felt perfectly responsible and respectable. The next year, however, the human factor took a turn for the weird.

Delos 2, July 1964: Cautions, Mutations and Eternal Children

After the broad mapping of the agenda at Delos 1, Delos 2 focused down on the question of how the architectural and planning professions might be reformulated to deal with global problems, with much of the attention devoted to new approaches to professional education. The human factor continued to run through the discussions, however, driven in large part by the introduction of the hyper-energetic presence of inventor, futurist and techno-poet Richard Buckminster Fuller. It was central also to the announcement of a new Doxiadis Associates research program featuring twelve interrelated parts, five of which would focus on getting to grips with various facets of human nature: parts two, four and eight would try to determine which elements within us are constant, part nine would explore the development differences caused by upbringing and milieu, and part ten would speculate on how humankind might change in the future. In Doxiadis's words, Ekistics must commit itself to the goal of "human happiness, leading to the evolution of [a] better human species by the formation of appropriate Human Settlements."9

Again, a diversity of voices made themselves heard: Brohi returned to argue that planning must broaden its remit to aim to satisfy all of "man's" faculties and senses, not just "his" rational and utilitarian needs, while sociologist John W. Riley argued for the incorporation of "behavioural science knowledge" for the "future well-being on man on this earth" [Fig. 2]. A rather cautious note was sounded by political scientist R. G. Tugwell, who, conceding to some of the points raised by McLuhan on how technology will infiltrate human life and consciousness, suggested the need for safeguards to prevent technology from utterly conditioning behavior and compromising freedoms. And a yet stronger caution came from psychiatrist Leonard Duhl, who sought to mitigate the influence of the architect–planner by arguing the need to listen to communities and empower people to shape their own neighborhoods and identities – the grassroots advocacy positions that were being pioneered in that decade by Jane Jacobs and Robert Davidoff.10

But, despite these fairly moderate positions, the notion of the imminent change of human beings as a result of environmental factors got a greater airing this time around than at Delos 1. The urbanist Jean Gottmann, for example, anticipated that prolonged exposure to greater population densities across megalopolitan regions – his region of specialty – would provoke a "mutation of the way of life" towards a new "age of neo-nomadism."11 Fuller took this notion to its extreme. Presenting ideas from his paper "The Prospects of Humanity: 1965–1985," he argued that imminent extraterrestrial contact would confirm that humans had evolved from aliens mating with monkeys. The next phase of human evolution would be precipitated by medical science, which – through interchangeable limbs and organs increasingly blending organics with synthetics – "may be about to develop the continuous or deathless man." Space would ultimately have to be made for this new species through tensegrity domes and lighter-than-air floating cities in which they could live their eternal lives. The man–machine cybernetic interfaces that McLuhan was committed to would also happen, Fuller said, acknowledging "the computer catalyzed reorientation of man," but artificial intelligence was unlikely to reach true brain-level complexity for another one million years – after which point, however, another stage of machine-enabled human evolution might happen. But there were dangers before the species got that far, Fuller went on, as it was exhibiting a tendency towards narrow specialization, ego-fulfillment and – with them – nationalist belligerence. This left humanity dangerously ill-equipped to deal with the planet's challenges in a joined-up way. To compensate, the entire military–industrial complex would need to be dismantled, including nuclear disarmament, and retooled for the great build-out required, with all efforts refocused to allow people to rediscover the creativity, joy and curiosity of children: "to permit the integrated being of the child to remain unfractionated throughout the total lifespan." Coming round to the claims of deathlessness, this meant humanity – or some android version of it – would no longer be specialists but "comprehensivists" living endless lives with the joyfulness of children.[12]

Few things were more extreme than Fuller's interventions at Delos, which recurred every year after this, although McLuhan rose to the challenge; indeed, it seemed that they enjoyed sparring with each other and one-upping on the outrageousness of their futurist propositions.[13] The Delos audience often did not know how to take them. But if it was a performance intended to amuse and entertain, as some suspected, Fuller always played it straight.

Delos 3, July 1965: Conflict, Constancy and Classicism – Enter Plato

Themed to questions of urban densities, regional planning and historical precedents for good practice, Delos 3 seemed to dial back a little on the imaginative speculations of the previous year. This is not to say it was without its debates on the human factor, however, which centered around themes of the reformability of human nature and the role of the expert over

this, whether the tendency towards sociability and community was innate, and the relationship between urban scale and civic-mindedness.

The headline debate occurred between Margaret Mead and Lester Granger, a sociologist with a background in social work and civil-rights activism, and former president of the National Urban League [Fig. 3]. Again tying into the theme of community planning and the socio-psychological and political benefits of urban propinquity, Mead questioned whether this "toleration of close contact is an invariant for each living species." Inclining to the view that the knack for propinquity was learned and fragile, she argued that care must be taken to understand the individual's hopes, tolerances, stresses and breaking points, as well as the likelihood of the outbreak of conflict – which occurred even in the smallest, most tight-knit tribes.[14] Granger set out the position that human nature and civilization was all about "living together well and efficiently," but that people were clearly not fulfilling that promise. In a twist that recalled the hardline early Plato of *The Republic*, which was somewhat surprising given his work at the urban grassroots, Granger argued for strong, enlightened leadership to take charge of the unruly "bottom layer" – "apt to be thickest of all [and] composed of 'uncivilized'" people unable to control their appetites – as well as to eradicate the urban predators (speculative capitalists and real-estate developers) that preyed upon them. Comprehensive reeducation through popular media like TV would also help bring the masses round to the urbane community-mindedness that they would already be enjoying if they had

Fig. 2 "Allah Bukhsh K. Brohi (seated right), Pakistani lawyer and statesman, draws attention." Meeting at the Athens Technological Institute.

not been perverted from their natural state.[15] The parallel with the Platonic "Guardians," restoring a "Third Class" at the mercy of their own passions to the proper socio-psychological balance, could hardly be clearer – although this was not referenced explicitly by Granger.[16]

The historicizing turn of Delos 3 surfaced again in a discussion involving Sigfried Giedion and the historian Arnold Toynbee. Giedion argued that there was no question of a return to the actual urban typologies and styles of the past, whether the ancient Greek *polis* or the medieval city, "[b]ut the human values inherent in both of these have an immutable constancy that is deeply anchored in human nature."[17] But there was a danger in the loss of historic buildings, Toynbee argued, picking up on the increasingly neohistoricist tendencies of architectural discourse of the 1960s, which – along with the shift to community values – represented another great pushback against the legacy of CIAM. Without this recognition of the past in our built environments, he stated simply, we "cease to be human."[18] Responding to these prompts, Doxiadis observed that the default urban unit in the global Ecumenopolis would have no more than a ten-minute walk from residential periphery to the amenities at its center, a human scale that was historically proven to work best for face-to-face community- and civic-mindedness to develop.[19]

Delos 4, July 1966: Eruption and Reset

The fourth Delos event was themed to transport, telecommunications and infrastructure and to exploring the way planning interventions were frequently blocked by bureaucracy and vested interests. Despite this packed agenda, however, the human factor loomed large and was debated with a vociferousness not encountered before.

Architecture journalist Diana Rowntree led the reporting this year, noting a particularly energetic and excitable event that reflected the fact that twenty-three out of the thirty-six delegates were attending for the first time. The arguments hinged on the perennial question of whether human nature was a constant or whether it was changeable, a question that was felt particularly acutely in the context of the Symposion's main theme. "In short," Rowntree said, "we do not yet know how the measure of stability essential to human being will be combined with the mobility and flux experienced throughout reality." The Symposion divided into two clear camps, she observed: on the one side was Doxiadis himself, supported by the likes of

pediatrician Robert Aldrich, who argued for the need for concentrated, stable, small-scale settlements that maintained face-to-face contact as the basis of community and psychological wellbeing; on the other, represented by architect Richard Llewelyn-Davies as well as Conrad Waddington, were those who argued that dispersal, mobility and the new speed of life were perfectly in keeping with what people needed in order to flourish. This division also figured on the level of urban aesthetics: Toynbee argued in favor of the beauty of traditional townscapes once again, while planner Robert Mitchell argued in favor of the new kind of beauty of the American suburb and highway – it was just a matter of adapting the eye to see it, he maintained, as had happened with the appreciation of abstract painting in the early twentieth century. Pointedly and perceptively, however, Rowntree noted a stalemate at the root of these claims and counterclaims: "Both schools claim to meet the needs of Man, and a whole Man at that."[20]

The proceedings, as recorded by Tyrwhitt, painted a picture of unresolvable tension from the start, even though she clearly did her best to

Fig. 3 "Dr. S. Giedion tries to convince Dr. Margaret Mead during a discussion."

Between them and gazing directly to camera is Lester Granger.

smooth the clashing anonymized voices into a coherent narrative. Utopian schemes were being thrown around with increasing abandon, she cautioned, which "means architects playing God without first taking the measurement of man." "Anthropics," however, which was the hoped-for "science of man," demanded that "his" nature must first be determined before one could "find its physical expression" in architectural and urban designs.[21]

Much of the debate centered around determining the correct level of community engagement. Fundamental to this was a dynamic psycho-social model whereby the insularity and cohesion required for a sense of community identity and safety were in interplay with a more expansive model, where connectivity – physical and technological – offered the invitation to test, transcend and redraw group boundaries in a flexible way. Hard physical boundaries in the urban fabric were to be avoided. This was a model of psycho-social development that seemed to be indebted to the sociology of Georg Simmel, as was much of the community-planning ideology of the 1960s and indeed subsequently.[22]

Even so, huge uncertainty remained over the nature of "man," especially "man" in the modern city. Indeed, the very fact that the subject of the problem was located in cities that were *themselves* acknowledged as problems made it methodologically tricky to determine "his" nature. "You cannot study the behaviour and actions of a prisoner and draw normative conclusions," said one of Tyrwhitt's anonymous voices: "Man is not becoming different, but he is becoming dehumanized. We must return him to the human scale of the age-old city before the advent of machines." This adaptability of "man" to different circumstances and urban conditions, particularly when these were corrupting in their influence, made the study of "his" essential essence extremely difficult: "the city adapts him only to destroy him." Against an objection that "[t]his is a very male-oriented series of remarks," the proceedings moved to a demand that "man's" nature must first be determined before one can act confidently on the design of cities: "Where is the science of man – Anthropics? We have professions that represent parts of him, but until he is fully represented how can we build his shells?" The proceedings end with a flurry of dissenting voices asking how this might be possible when "man" is only studied "when he is sick." And what of the different types of "man" throughout history: the tough but ignorant primitive, the well-balanced ancient Greek, the intellectually brilliant but physically atrophied modern scientist? "Is the model Doxiadis has placed before us of universal application? If not, what are his variables?" A diagram was presented, illustrating in the blandest way possible the research pathways available to determine the nature of "man" [Fig. 4]. Interestingly, and this is probably down to there being so many new Delians at this event, there was even now some incredulity at and questioning of the most basic premise: exactly *why* must one "comprehend the grammar of human existence" before embarking upon an urban design?[23] Was consideration of the human factor needed at all?

Evidently this was quite a fiery Delos when it came to the human factor, featuring forthright challenges to Doxiadis's established position. However, the concluding ceremony at the ancient theater on the island Delos ended in more urbane, conciliatory fashion. Toynbee delivered the evocative final words, stating that the Symposion had identified two key priorities. One was to look more intensively at the problems faced by the developing world. The other was "the need for a study of 'Anthropics': man, the most important even if the second in the historical time of the five elements – nature, man, society, shell, networks. The gap between our knowledge of unhuman nature and of human nature is constantly increasing. We now have power to move mountains but not our own stubborn wills and hearts."[24]

Delos 5, July 1967: Where to Stick the Needle?

After the heated arguments of Delos 4 that architect–planners must not act in the world without properly understanding the human beings on whose behalf they claim to be acting, Delos 5 ploughed ahead and prioritized action. A new cadre of Delians dominated the proceedings, including lawyers, economists, bankers and property developers, with prominent contributions from F. K. A. Jiagge, Managing Director of the Tema Development Corporation of Ghana, and Felipe Herrera, President of the Inter-American Development Bank. The theme was the implementation of physical solutions on the ground, including the investigation of legal blockages and capital funding arrangements – particularly in the developing worlds of Africa and Latin America, and with a focus on regional development as the expanded urban scale.[25]

The philosophical wranglings that had dominated Delos 4 were reduced to occasional comments within the torrent of practical measures. One anonymous voice in the discussion commented as follows:

> We have assumed that man is a constant and that physical variables are dynamic, but man living in the midst of change is himself a rapidly changing creature. Who is going to make decisions about what kind of people we should develop? We know that personalities can be adjusted. Who sets the criteria as to what they are to be adjusted to?

Although this was an isolated intervention it was an important one, especially so that it should arise with clarity and force in a Delos event committed to practical action. The question cut right to the ethics of the issue: making pronouncements on how the built environment might affect behavior is one thing, but who gets to decide what are the right and wrong behaviors, the right and wrong *people*? Ultimately, though, it was the practical focus that dominated Delos 5. When seeking to influence things it was best, we are told, "to take advantage of moments when man is out of balance – when he is uncomfortable. It is then that he is interested in change." For the men and women of action of Delos 5, then, the behavioral sciences were not to be plundered for ontological questions about the nature of humankind but instead to be used strategically to reorient people when they were at their most susceptible and vulnerable in order to get the desired results from them. A "SPICE Formula" introduced a handy equation of humankind, offering several variables that might be worked on [Fig. 5]. The key question was simple: "Where do you needle to get a response?"[26]

Delos 6, July 1968: Stalemate

If the practical focus of Delos 5 managed to suppress the human factor, it returned with a vengeance the following year. Delos 6 represented a concerted attempt to resolve the issue and bring on the science of Anthropics as a complement – or, rather, a foundation – to the science of Ekistics. And to inform this, there was an increase in experts from the fields of biology and medicine. The theme of the Symposion was "Man and His Settlements."

The challenge was broken down meticulously by sociologist Suzanne Keller, who observed that the discussion had "oscillated between" biological, psychiatric and sociological modes of analysis without a common terminology or "satisfactory modus vivendi": the first field of knowledge focused on the species and genetics, the second focused on the individual psyche and the third focused on the social aggregate and systems. And "[t]his is why discussions of MAN in the abstract obscures rather than

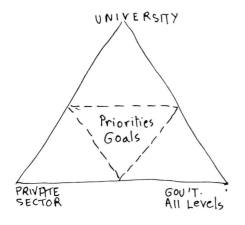

$$\frac{S}{P}(I+C+E)$$

S = survival needs, self-preservation pressures.
P = pleasurable needs.
I = identity, the individual's self image.
C = cultural patterns built into the individual.
E = energy level of the individual aggressiveness.

clarifies." In order to find common ground, Keller proposed that the genetic and biological strata of human being should be understood in relation to social interaction and related psychological phenomenon, which, she said, endlessly reshaped human physiology and its future potentials. The purpose of the Symposion should be to identify key questions in need of urgent resolution that delegates could take back to their "professional nests," setting their colleagues and research students to work, and reporting back in the subsequent year.[27] Edmund Bacon of the Philadelphia City Planning Commission offered a parallel suggestion with his proposal that experts from behavioral research, education, private enterprise and government pool their brainpower for the development of a "total quality of life" "machine": in essence, a measuring instrument that could be used to accurately record a person's psychology as the basis for policy decisions.[28] Responding was Reginald Lourie, a specialist in pediatric psychology, who argued that the things that can be said for certain about the psychology of children in particular "do not lend themselves to precise measurement," and that he was therefore skeptical of the idea that "hard data" could be used in such a way. Even so, the "soft facts cannot be ignored in the building of our cities." For the healthy development of the child's psyche, these included: the benefits of sensory stimulation and variety; the careful restriction of cultural imagery that might destabilize the mind, especially images of violence; and the provision of attractive environmental amenities to make up for anxieties caused by rapid changes in the modern city. The artist and

Fig. 4 "Principal resources in society for the study of man."

Fig. 5 "SPICE formula."

educator György Kepes likewise focused on the qualitative, immeasurable aspects of human beings – in particular, the benefits of environmental beauty and total sensual immersion in nature and art: a phenomenological wholeness of a "total quality of life, a life worth living." These were precisely the things, for Kepes, that contemporary cities failed to provide.[29]

Doxiadis restated his broadly Simmelian position on the need for a careful gradation of socio-spatial spheres and opportunities that allowed for social development while also protecting the individual's sense of personal integrity, which – he said – had been deranged by the hyper-stimulation of modern urban living, causing withdrawal and alienation.[30] Other old battle lines were reestablished, too: Waddington ingeniously substituted verse and prose on the contemporary "wasteland" – from T. S. Eliot, George Benello and C. P. Cavafy – as surrogates for his own view that too much technology was damaging to the psychological constants of humanity and the ecological constants of the world; Toynbee concurred, arguing that the technology-driven reduction of "persons [to] things, serial numbers, ciphers" was one of the drivers for the widespread social uprisings of that year and "an affront to human nature." The solution, once again, lay in the intimate micro-communities of the coming Ecumenopolis – respecting the lessons of classical cities.[31] And equally predictably, perhaps, Fuller reasserted his counterpoint that the answers lay not in the "old world" with its assumption of individuality, intimacy and propinquity, but instead in the networked future collective.[32]

The intention of Delos 6 had been to move the conversation on the human factor forwards and find some practical solutions. Although it seems to have been less heated than Delos 4, the demarcation lines around the various positions were perhaps even more entrenched than before – reproducing the old lines of change versus constancy, virtual networks versus place-bound communities – and the methodological proposals for a way out were likewise at loggerheads. The concluding declaration acknowledged this: "Confrontation and communication between those concerned with physical structure and those concerned with man is at the core of the problem." Ultimately, though, it offered a clarion call reminiscent of the one at Delos 4, for "research on human behaviour that is as vigorous as research on the physical environment." Only this would provide the foundation to develop new models of open, responsive, collaborative planning that would "embody and generate the human values we seek."[33]

Delos 7, July 1969: Grounded

Scheduled for the same month as the Apollo 11 Moon landing, Delos 7 restated the priorities of the group with a greater urgency than ever before. Far from being a cause for celebration, however, the success of the US – in its ongoing space race with the USSR – was seen by both sides at Delos as an unconscionable waste of economic and technological resources, which could be better deployed in dealing with the pressures of population growth and migration, natural-resource depletion and food shortages. The Symposion theme, then, was for better cooperation among international governments on targeted humanitarian goals, rather than competition over technological vanity projects that led only to a wastage of resources. But the human factor figured prominently as well, with calls to respect regional diversity in terms of culture, value and identity, while also being mindful of the emergence of a new type of global citizen that was increasingly shaped by mass media. There was a proposal to use media more positively for "constructive intervention," at the childhood level especially, as well as a proposal for the scientific management of population growth.[34]

But Tyrwhitt's collective overview of the research discussions presented a chillingly bleak diagnosis of the current situation and the kind of interventions required [Fig. 6]. Humankind was to remain blighted as a result of its congenital and environmentally determined defects for the next three to five generations, but once the requisite "genetic manipulation" technologies had been developed there would be "a decontamination of the gene pool by reducing the propagation of demonstrably deleterious genes in the population." This was "the only realistic prospect" for humanity's survival, and this manipulation of fundamental physiology would over time be supplemented by a more advantageous environment, both physical and social, involving careful regulation of stimuli to prevent the early development of "defects or personality disorders that cannot afterwards be overcome," and indeed perhaps extending to the state-rearing of children rather than leaving them to the vagaries of family life. "The ethical aspects of this," it is stated rather coyly, "were not discussed."[35] Discussions followed pathways that by now were firmly entrenched at Delos – theories of change versus constancy in human nature, when and how much to apply the levers of correctional influence and so on – but all coalesced around the "first policy [...] that society must see that only optimally functional individuals populate its cities." But holding them back from the ethical brink was a consensually

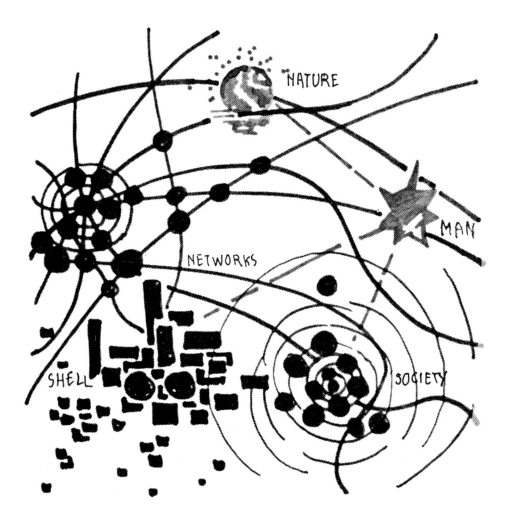

agreed statement, that "[w]e cannot be god-like in deciding how we can engineer our children." And of course, this being Delos, strongly countervailing voices could always be heard. "We should not strive," said one, "consciously or unconsciously, to create the ideal or uniform man."[36] Despite these cautions and criticisms, however, it is clear that the Plato of the "real pedigree herd [whose] defective offspring […] will be quietly and secretly disposed of" – in other words, the idealistic young Plato of *The Republic* – had made his return at Delos 7.[37]

It is significant that Doxiadis tempered this mood with reference to another classical philosopher, one who challenged so many of the

Fig. 6 "The five elements of Human Settlements are now out of balance." "Nature," "Man," "Society," "Shell" and "Networks" (by now officially adopted instead of the "Functions" of Fig. 1) presented as a disjointed mess.

uncompromising stances of his teacher Plato. Acknowledging the difficulty in balancing the elements of human settlements – emerging from the craving for contact, privacy and protection, all delivered and regulated within a finite pool of human energy – Doxiadis concluded with a more fundamental question: "We must ask ourselves, what is the goal which we lost, could we not re-establish it? I do not know a better definition than the one given by Aristotle: that the goal of the city is to make man happy and safe."[38]

Delos Redacted

The human factor was only one thread in the complicated tapestry of Delos deliberations, but it was one that participants collectively deemed important enough to return to year after year. One might legitimately ask, however, what it was that they achieved through all these speculations? For all their many fascinating insights and proposals, some of their ideas on human nature were so extreme they appeared unhinged and even comical – and, occasionally, they were commonplace to the point of seeming almost trite. And indeed, in moments of tension, some of their ideas came through in so heavy-handed and paternalistic a form that the Delians balked at their ethical implications even as they themselves gave them voice. Moreover, these discussions never ended in consensus but instead tied the Delians in knots, exposing deeply embedded values among them about what people are and what people need – and all this before they could even get to the practical implications of those values for the design of the built environment. Stalemates ensued, followed by pledges to revisit the issue and find an answer next year, which would duly be attempted before ending in another stalemate. And so it went on.

An uncharitable view might be that none of it really mattered. While this was going on, after all, Doxiadis Associates continued to work unabated across the world on the vast infrastructural projects, master plans and consultations that are discussed elsewhere in this volume. This view would be short-sighted, however. It was an admirable achievement for Doxiadis and Tyrwhitt to have helped forge a commitment among the Delians that a sincere engagement with the human factor was the necessary precursor for any responsible action on the design of buildings and cities. Indeed, the bold and disruptive inclusion of so many specialists from beyond the fields of architecture and planning practically forced the issue.

The remarkableness of this Delos moment is evident in the simple fact that nothing comparable can be found in the history of architecture and planning, save for isolated glimmers by individual practitioner–theorists with the courage to stick their necks out. Robert Lamb Hart's *A New Look at Humanism* (2015) is one such example: a book rich in philosophical, psychological and ecological sources that explores the evolution of the human mind in response to the natural and built environments. It calmly argues for an architecture that finds a balance between giving people a sense of protection, peace and security and stimulating the mind and senses with fresh decorative incident, spatial vistas, and opportunities for exploration, learning and growth.[39] A much more assertive example is *Humanise: A Maker's Guide to Building Our World* by the British designer Thomas Heatherwick. Published in 2023 to coincide with the launch of the "Humanise" campaign, Heatherwick's book deploys all the rhetorical and visual tricks of the architectural manifesto to successful effect, including heroes and villains, rampant sloganeering, absurdist contrasts, calculated oversimplifications or indeed misrepresentations, and schizophrenic typography. Although enjoying huge international success as an architectural designer, Heatherwick – in his calls for the public to nominate buildings for quasi-scientific testing against the "Boringometer" – is clearly seeking to provoke the architectural mainstream. With Le Corbusier deemed "the paradoxical God of Boring," the central argument is that bland buildings lead to "psychological deprivation" and "starvation of the mind," with ostensibly causal links to cancer, diabetes, stroke and heart disease, as well as psychological disorders such as depression, anxiety, addiction and gambling, not to mention antisocial and violent behavior. Hinging his remedy on the assertion that "necessary visual complexity [is] a fundamental part of human nature," Heatherwick argues that architects must provide "emotionally nutritious" designs full of eclectic visual incident in a diversity of materials and surface textures.[40]

Despite its limited focus upon the visual impact of façades on passers-by rather than on buildings as a full spatial experience, and despite also its narrower range of philosophical and psychological sources, Heatherwick's thesis is superficially reminiscent of Hart's. Where they differ is in the circumspect approach of Hart, which is reminiscent of the Delians, in contrast to the conviction of Heatherwick and his team that they have many of the answers already and it is now primarily a matter of persuasion and implementation. That said, the Humanise initiative – with its ten-year global campaign to reform architectural culture, practice and education – certainly echoes the feel of the Delos adventure. As does the demand to "take the human factor seriously" and commission cutting-edge new research into it, despite Doxiadis and Delos not being mentioned in Heatherwick's book.[41]

For the most part, however, the human factor tends to run beneath the surface of architectural and urban discourse, whether as an unconscious motivator or as a consciously suppressed prejudice about how people should be and should behave in the built environment. On the one hand, this is not altogether surprising: if the Delos deliberations proved one thing conclusively, it was that trying to drill deep into this issue is difficult indeed, let alone finding a consensus on it. But, on the other hand, it is extremely surprising. I have never met with, or read the words of, any architect or planner who did not believe that the built environment shapes human life and influences human behavior in some way. Almost none, unfortunately, are willing to scrutinize these beliefs or question the kinds of human life and behavior they presume to value, even while they design environments for us to live in. It has been argued that architects engage with this topic only when they need to differentiate their product in a competitive marketplace – and then out come the nebulous claims that their design will improve "quality of life" more than those of their competitors.[42] If the environmental-determinist premise is true, and if buildings and cities do indeed shape us, then this represents an evasion of professional care and ethics.

The Delians should be commended for placing the issue center stage, despite – or perhaps because – of the arguments and divisions that resulted. Doing so stopped them rushing headlong into easy solutions for the built environment. It made them genuinely uneasy and gave them pause. It made them think.

Contrast this with the current state of the discourse, which can be summed up in one all-encompassing concept: wellbeing. This has much to recommend it, with valuable research having been done into therapeutic communities, for example. A highly specialized field, this investigates the spatial layouts, environmental qualities, material detailing, color and overall ambience that might best support and inspire people who are suffering in some way, such as from dementia or terminal illness. A related branch of this research, and one that is particularly popular with governments, is nudge theory. This asks what subtle cues can be placed in an environment to effect micro-behavioral changes in people, such as raising a child's attentiveness at a school crossing or defusing flashpoints of potential antagonism in a prison. And another important driver in these initiatives has been the emergence of "neuroarchitecture," which represents the attempt to systematically incorporate the lessons of pure neuroscience into architectural design. This was given impetus and legitimacy by the establishment of the Academy of Neuroscience for Architecture (ANFA) in 2002, an initiative sponsored by the American Institute of Architects (AIA).[43] But the rapid uptake of wellbeing in built-environment discourse has led to the concept now becoming as nebulous as it is ubiquitous, and consequently adaptable to almost any discursive usage or practical application. It is perhaps most frequently taken to denote the state of "happiness" achieved when a person is working as an effective and productive economic unit and is deemed to be well adapted to society. With this formulation we have witnessed the efflorescence of consultancy courses for architects and planners by organizations such as the UK's Building Research Establishment (BRE), where wellbeing and happiness in the workplace – often combined with "biophilia," or the technique of incorporating plants and nature-inspired forms into buildings – is measured in direct proportion to statistics for reducing absenteeism and increasing worker productivity.[44] This peculiar equivalence makes one wonder whether, if Frederick Winslow Taylor were alive to promote scientific management in the present day, he would call it wellbeing – or, indeed, whether the whipmaster on a slave galley might do the same. It is important to note, however, that there are studies that question these environmental behaviorist claims, not least on the grounds that their range of research methodologies is so divergent and inconsistent that it is currently not possible to say anything conclusive on the matter.[45]

Nonetheless, in terms of its relation to Delos, current discourse on the human factor has apparently skipped ahead to practical measures that can be selected, applied or bought in. It no longer engages with fundamental psychological, social or philosophical questions about the nature of human being or the purview of human potential. And it neglects entirely to address the trickier questions about the kinds of normative behaviors that the built environment is supposed to promote and condition. Who decides on these behaviors? What or whose socioeconomic values do they serve? What behaviors are excluded because they are unacceptable, and *why* are they unacceptable? Ultimately, what are the ethics of using the built environment to meddle in behavior? When you are in the business of selling built environment "solutions" to human behavioral problems, questions like these only muddy the water and get in the way. Consequently, contemporary discourse prefers to avoid them when it can or redact them when it cannot.

In 2017, the Design Commission section of the Policy Connect think tank published its report into "People and Places: Design of the Built Environment and Behaviour." This report was sponsored by the BRE Trust and chaired by Baroness Janet Whitaker and Professor Alan Penn, then Dean of the Bartlett School of Architecture and founder of Space Syntax Ltd, a hugely successful technology and consultancy firm specializing in the analysis and control of movement patterns in buildings and cities.

I was invited to the House of Lords along with two other specialists to give testimony to an evidence session on "History, Theory, Policy – Where Do We Stand on This Debate?" Naturally, I raised the questions listed above and others besides, and was pleased to see them featured in a preparatory draft of the report. They were eliminated for the final published report, however, as indeed – amusingly – was any acknowledgment of my own presence in the Evidence Session. So this was less a debate and more a ratification. As far as the official historical record is concerned, no one present at this consultation raised any questions about its fundamental assumptions about human nature and functioning, let alone its self-appointed remit to design human behavior.[46]

For all the difficulties these kinds of question cause, the Delians cracked their heads against them again and again, year after year, never put off by the intractability of the positions that emerged – and never retreating, despite Tyrwhitt's heavy editorial hand. They embraced the issue for the ethical imperative that it is. And, although this led them occasionally to some questionable zones of inquiry, the Delos debates and documents from the 1960s represent the high-water mark for rigorous, sustained engagement with the human factor in architecture and planning.

---

1   Ellen Shoshkes, "Jaqueline Tyrwhitt: A Founding Mother of Modern Urban Design," *Planning Perspectives* 21, no. 2 (April 2006), 179–97; Mark Wigley, "Network Fever," *Grey Room*, no. 4 (Summer 2001), 82–122.

2   Karl Popper, "Piecemeal Social Engineering" (1944), in D. Miller (ed.), *A Pocket Popper* (Oxford: Oxford University Press, 1983), 304–18, quotation 311.

3   Simon Richards, *Le Corbusier and the Concept of Self* (New Haven, CT and London: Yale University Press, 2003); Simon Richards, *Architect Knows Best: Environmental Determinism in Architecture Culture from 1956 to the Present* (London: Ashgate, 2012).

4   On the history and evolution of the Ekistic Grid, see Sharmila Jagadisan and Tom Fookes, "Antecedents for the Ekistic Grid and the Anthropocosmos Model: A Critical View of Ekistic Methodology," *Ekistics* 73, no. 436/441 (January/December 2006), 265–76.

5   Simon Richards, "'Halfway between the Electron and the Universe': Doxiadis and the Delos Symposia," in Gerald Adler, Timothy Brittain-Catlin and Gordana Fontana-Giusti (eds), *Scale: Imagination, Perception*

and Practice in Architecture (London: Routledge, 2012), 170–81.

6   James E. Clayton, "A Cruise Party Ponders the Menace of the City," *Washington Post*, July 23, 1963, reprinted in *Ekistics* 16, no. 95 (October 1963), 237–39.

7   Richards, *Le Corbusier*, 188–202.

8   All of the following references are taken from *Ekistics* 16, no. 95 (October 1963). Jaqueline Tyrwhitt, "The Delos Symposion," 205–10, quotation/paraphrase of A. K. Brohi, 207; Jaqueline Tyrwhitt et al., "Meetings of the Delos Symposion," 243–54, especially 246–47; Jaqueline Tyrwhitt et al., "Contributory Papers," 254–62, especially 254–55 (Margaret Mead) and 257 (Marshall McLuhan), quotation 257; Jaqueline Tyrwhitt et al., "The CIAM Charter of 1933: Outcome of a Similar Effort," 263–67, quotation 264 (items 2 and 3); see also 266 item 71.

9   C. A. Doxiadis, "Framework for a New Discipline of Human Settlements: Introductory Paper," *Ekistics* 18, no. 107 (October 1964), 188–89, quotation 189; and Jaqueline Tywhitt et al., "Summary of Discussions," ibid., 190–91.

10 Jaqueline Tyrwhitt et al., "Words Spoken at Delos," *Ekistics* 18, no. 107 (October 1964), 180–85, quotation 184; Leonard Duhl, "Some Added Comments on Planning, and Its Implementation," ibid., 193–94.

11 A. Stangos, "A Real 'Symposion'," *Ekistics* 18, no. 107 (October 1964), 185–88, esp. 187–88.

12 Richard Buckminster Fuller, "The Prospects of Humanity: 1965–1985," *Ekistics* 18, no. 107 (October 1964), 232–42, quotations 233, 238, 242. See also his contribution to Delos 3, "Why I Am Interested in Ekistics," *Ekistics* 20, no. 119 (October 1965), 180–81, in which he revisits the theme of how world military–industrial capacity must be reoriented towards Ekistics-led environmental concerns.

13 For a brilliant account of this extraordinary rivalry and the techno-futurist agenda at Delos, see Wigley, "Network Fever," 82–122.

14 Margaret Mead, "Social Aspects of Density: A Real Life Situation," *Ekistics* 20, no. 119 (October 1965), 214.

15 L. B. Granger, "Social Aspects of Density: Urban Living," *Ekistics* 20, no. 119 (October 1965), 215.

16 Plato, *The Republic*, trans. D. Lee (London: Penguin Books, 1987), 177–224.

17 Sigfried Giedion, "The Historical Approach: The Planner and Human Values," *Ekistics* 20, no. 119 (October 1965), 247–48.

18 Arnold Toynbee, "The Historical Approach: How to Learn from History," *Ekistics* 20, no. 119 (October 1965), 247.

19 C. A. Doxiadis, "The Historical Approach: Delos One Hundred," *Ekistics* 20, no. 119 (October 1965), 249.

20 Diana Rowntree, "The Fourth Delos Symposium," *Ekistics* 22, no. 131 (October 1966), 235–43, quotations 236, 242.

21 Jaqueline Tyrwhitt et al., "Urban Life: Its Values and the Problems It Faces," *Ekistics* 22, no. 131 (October 1966), 244–53, quotation 244.

22 Ibid., 244–46. For an account of Georg Simmel's theory and its influence on community planning from 1960s grassroots and advocacy planning through to New Urbanism, see Richards, *Architect Knows Best*, 29–91, esp. 33–34.

23 Jaqueline Tyrwhitt et al., "Urban Life," 247. The first half of these proceedings are anonymized – but see pp. 250–53, where landscape architect Garrett Eckbo, ecologist and pediatrician Robert Aldrich and child psychiatrist Reginald Lourie discuss the question of how to determine fundamental human nature when the subject of study is always changing and especially when acknowledged to be already sick.

24 Jaqueline Tyrwhitt et al., "Words at Delos," *Ekistics* 22, no. 131 (October 1966), 308.

25 Jaqueline Tyrwhitt, "Report of the Fifth Symposion," and Jaqueline Tyrwhitt et al., "Words at Delos," *Ekistics* 24, no. 143 (October 1967), 299–303, 304–9. For more on this highly pragmatic focus, see C. A. Doxiadis, "The Process of Development," ibid., 322–24.

26 Jaqueline Tyrwhitt et al., "Points Made in Discussion," *Ekistics* 24, no. 143 (October 1967), 325–30.

27 Suzanne Keller, "A Modest Proposal," *Ekistics* 26, no. 155 (October 1968), 347–48, quotations 347.

28 Edmund N. Bacon, "Response to Delos Statement 1968: Man and His Settlements," *Ekistics* 26, no. 155 (October 1968), 319–20.

29 Jaqueline Tyrwhitt et al., "Words at Delos," *Ekistics* 26, no. 155 (October 1968), 320–23, quotations 320, 322.

30 C. A. Doxiadis, "Some Introductory Notes," *Ekistics* 26, no. 155 (October 1968), 325.

31 C. H. Waddington, "Three Relevant Quotations," *Ekistics* 26, no. 155 (October 1968), 324; Arnold Toynbee, "Personality versus Technology," *Ekistics* 26, no. 155 (October 1968), 376–77, quotations 376.

32 Buckminster Fuller, "What Is the Purpose of Man's Life?," *Ekistics* 26, no. 155 (October 1968), 344–46.

33 Jaqueline Tyrwhitt et al., "Delos Six: Delos Declaration 1968: Man and His Settlements," *Ekistics* 26, no. 155 (October 1968), 314–15, quotations 315.

34 C. A. Doxiadis and Richard Buckminster Fuller, "Introduction: Report of Delos 7," *Ekistics* 28, no. 167 (October 1969), 215–22, quotation 216.

35 Jaqueline Tyrwhitt et al., "Excerpts from Report of Research Discussions: The Individual and the Family," *Ekistics* 28, no. 167 (October 1969), 223.

36 Jaqueline Tyrwhitt et al., "The Individual and the Family: The Individual and the Family," *Ekistics* 28, no. 167 (October 1969), 225–27, quotations 225–26; see also Spyros Doxiadis, "Early Influences Shaping the Individual," ibid., 230–31; and Robert Aldrich and Ralph Wedgwood, "Changes in the United States Which Affect the Health of Children," ibid., 227–30.

37 Plato, *The Republic*, 240–41.
38 C. A. Doxiadis, "Five Principles for the Creation of Human Settlements: The Individual and the Family," *Ekistics* 28, no. 167 (October 1969), 223–25, quotation 225.
39 Robert Lamb Hart, *A New Look at Humanism: In Architecture, Landscapes and Urban Design* (Middletown, CA: Meadowlark Publishing, 2015).
40 Thomas Heatherwick, *Humanise: A Maker's Guide to Building Our World* (London: Penguin Random House, 2023), quotations 40, 112, 406–9, 429, 440; see also 463–65 on the "Boringometer."
41 Ibid., 458; see also https://humanise.org/ (accessed February 5, 2024).
42 Duncan Philip, "The Practical Failure of Architectural Psychology," *Journal of Environmental Psychology* 16, no. 3 (September 1996), 277–84.
43 For an overview of these fast-growing fields, see the following. On wellbeing, including workplace and therapeutic applications: *Wellbeing: A Complete Reference Guide*, especially vol. II: Rachel Cooper, Elizabeth Burton and Cary L. Cooper (eds), *Wellbeing and the Environment*, and vol. III: Peter Y. Chen and Cary L. Cooper (eds), *Work and Wellbeing* (Chichester: Wiley, 2014); Lily Bernheimer, *The Shaping of Us: How Everyday Spaces Structure Our Lives, Behaviour, and Well-Being* (London: Robinson, 2017); Ann Sloan Devlin (ed.), *Environmental Psychology and Human Well-Being: Effects of Built and Natural Settings* (London: Academic Press, 2018); Esther M. Sternberg, *Healing Spaces: The Science of Place and Well-Being* (Cambridge, MA: Harvard University Press, 2009). On neuroarchitecture: John P. Eberhard, *Architecture and the Brain: A New Knowledge Base from Neuroscience* (Atlanta, GA: Greenway Communications, 2007); Harry Francis Mallgrave, *The Architect's Brain: Neuroscience, Creativity, and Architecture* (Hoboken, NJ: Wiley-Blackwell, 2009); Sarah Robinson and Juhani Pallasmaa (eds), *Mind in Architecture: Neuroscience, Embodiment, and the Future of Design* (Cambridge, MA: MIT Press, 2017); Ian Ritchie (ed.), *Architectural Design* special issue on "Neuroarchitecture," 90, no. 6 (November/December 2020), 1–136; and Academy of Neuroscience for Architecture: https://anfarch.org/ (accessed February 5, 2024).
44 BRE Group, "The Biophilic Office," https://bregroup.com/services/research/the-biophilic-office/ (accessed February 5, 2024); Yannick Joye, "Architectural Lessons from Environmental Psychology: The Case of Biophilic Architecture," *Review of General Psychology* 11, no. 4 (2007), 305–28.
45 Isabella Bower, Richard Tucker and Peter G. Enticott, "Impact of Built Environment Design on Emotion Measured via Neurophysiological Correlates and Subjective Indicators: A Systematic Review," *Journal of Environmental Psychology* 66 (December 2019), 1–11.
46 Jack Tindale and Naomi Turner, *People and Places: Design of the Built Environment and Behaviour* (London: Policy Connect, 2017), https://www.policy-connect.org.uk/research/design-commission-people-and-places-design-built-environment-and-behaviour/ (accessed April 16, 2024).

Practices and Implementations

Section II

169 **Ecology, Ekistics and the "Texture of Settlements"**
Ioanna Theocharopoulou

191 **Infrastructuring Development**
Doxiadis's Continental Plans at the End of Ideologies
Filippo De Dominicis

217 **Basic Democracy and Doxiadis Associates' School-Reformation Project in East Pakistan**
Farhan Karim

249 **Shaping Ekistics**
From Baghdad to Detroit
Lefteris Theodosis

285 **The Visionary in the Marsh**
Doxiadis and the Dream of Eastwick
Harrison Blackman

Ecology, Ekistics and the "Texture of Settlements"

Ioanna Theocharopoulou

> We are in the middle of a major ecological crisis on a global scale. [...] It is the first crisis of such seriousness and magnitude in historical times.[1]

In his posthumously published book *Ecology and Ekistics* (1977), Constantinos A. Doxiadis advanced an expansive form of ecologically engaged architecture and planning. Critical of what he considered continual human aggression against Earth, Doxiadis argued that the closest discipline to Ekistics, "the science of human settlements," is ecology. To better understand how we can live together on a finite planet, we need to imagine how to bring the two – ecology and Ekistics – into greater balance. Settlements both construct and are constructed by the environments around them. If ecology could merge with Ekistics, this new, expanded discipline would encompass history, economics, social life and, crucially, the study of the world's climate in relation to the built environment. The goal of this new discipline would be to "develop the globe scientifically" whereby there would be a "proper and realistic" distribution of resources and obligations – and, ultimately, "human happiness."[2]

This mostly unknown book shares several themes with the first Delos Symposion (1963): a mandatory education in ecology for all those working with human settlements; a concern regarding the potentially devastating consequences of population expansion and wasteful overuse of vital resources, especially water; and the "inexcusable waste" of "overdeveloped" countries.[3]

One of the ways in which Doxiadis approached the notion of an ecologically engaged practice in his own work was by employing the concept of the survey as a way of collecting extensive knowledge about a site before drafting any proposals, making every effort to consider local climate, customs and ways of life. We sense that Ekistics was conceived as a lens through which to gather and make sense of complete ecological systems, where humans are one among a dizzying number of categories for analysis, including plants, animals, geography and weather. While in the 1940s Doxiadis had utilized the survey widely as a tool to build up knowledge about Greece, and especially regarding damages caused by World War II, in the 1950s he extended this practice outside Greece.

It was in 1954 that he met Jaqueline Tyrwhitt, an extraordinarily talented and accomplished planner and educator who also believed in the usefulness of the survey, having edited and brought to publication the work of Patrick Geddes, one of its earliest proponents. This chapter considers the role of the survey in Doxiadis's practice in the 1950s, as a way of embracing the uniqueness of different cultures, geographies and ways of thinking about the built environment. It argues that striving for a reconsideration of what an *ecologically engaged architecture* in the broadest sense might mean today is still a relevant question, perhaps even more than it was in Doxiadis's time.

Modes of Noticing, Modes of Collecting

Born out of war, Ekistics had as its primary focus rebuilding and repair with the goal of improving people's lives. In his book *Ekistics: An Introduction to the Science of Human Settlements*, Doxiadis recounted that, as he crossed Greece on foot from its northern border with Albania, where he fought with the Greek army against the Axis powers, all the way south to Athens, he was struck by the realization that the study of single buildings could never be enough to help entire areas that had been destroyed by war. It was then that he began envisioning a new, more wide-ranging discipline that he named Ekistics:

> [...] in passing through the devastated cities and villages I realized that I was unable to help give them a new life, on the basis of my studies in architecture, engineering and planning. Twenty-six years have gone by since I started working, lecturing, and writing in a systematic way towards a comprehensive approach to the problems of cities and villages that is, since I began developing Ekistics as the science of human settlements.[4]

Upon returning to Athens, and during the German occupation, Doxiadis worked in the Office for Reconstruction in the Ministry of Public Works.[5] There, he became determined to gauge the scope of human and material damage brought by the violence of war and occupation in Greece's cities, countryside and infrastructure using extensive surveys. To make the aims and the method of a survey as clear as possible, Doxiadis began publishing a series of booklets that articulated in great detail the need for extensive information gathering.[6] The very first booklet published was called *Ekistic Analysis*, written in 1945 and published in 1946. It set out to utilize the survey as a tool in the context of a country that had lacked current data even before the war. In fact, up to the 1940s, Greece was mostly "unknown" to itself.

In contrast to the abundant expertise regarding ancient Greek art and culture among many educated elites, there was hardly any official data available regarding the character of the country since the founding of the modern Greek state (1832). During war and occupation, Doxiadis started to assemble an extensive archive. Working through the data with a team of "scientific collaborators" – architects, engineers, social scientists and other intellectuals – the ministry under Doxiadis produced a number of publications, the most remarkable of which was *Sacrifices of Greece* (1946), a large-format book in four languages (Greek, English, French and Russian) with powerful graphics that was also used as the material for a traveling exhibition to persuade the Allies to give reconstruction aid.[7] To produce these publications, the ministry employees collected data on multiple scales, systematically documenting not only buildings and settlements but also agricultural production, fisheries, infrastructure, birth rates, mortality rates, family structure, religion and much more. *Ekistic Analysis* laid out the kind of work that was necessary for the country to get back on its feet:

> From October 1945 to January 1947, about 70 engineers ["architects" were included under "engineers"] were sent to the same number of the most destroyed areas of the country, where they undertook a detailed *ekistic* analysis of all settlements. The collected data was then turned into reports, on the basis of a questionnaire, [...] and were classified in the archives of *ekistic* research.[8]

The method, purpose and scope of the survey were described in minute detail. Ministry employees were to gather cartographic data; demographic data;

data on history, natural and political geography, building and town planning development, transportation, large and small-scale infrastructural works and aspects of everyday life. They were expected to draw maps, make sketches, take photographs and write extensive reports for each Ekistic area, and to make lists of all buildings and structures. In order to obtain homogeneous data, they were given a series of wide-ranging questionnaires organized around hundreds of categories on a long list of topics, aiming to illuminate local ways of life, ranging from hygiene practices and gender disparities to customs, dialects, building traditions and deeply rooted social and religious beliefs.

Those working on the survey were to visit *all settlements* in the area they were assigned, without exception. They were to cover cities; villages; institutional compounds such as prisons, sanatoria and monasteries; and even groups of two or three houses, if they constituted a stand-alone settlement. Importantly, the teams of technical staff were directed to listen to what the local people had to say, and to carefully note their views and opinions regarding their settlements. Getting as close as possible to each community under review to identify what he called its unique "texture," Doxiadis encouraged and guided his associates in terms of the value of what we today might call *situatedness*: a deep knowledge of place that he believed would help shape how best to rebuild.

After founding his private practice in the post-war years, Doxiadis Associates (DA), Doxiadis began to apply this method of analysis to gradually build up a distinct spatial knowledge about contexts outside of Greece, some of which had been similarly depleted by war and occupation. In fact, the work of formulating and developing the concept of the survey as a key part of the rationale for Ekistics helped Doxiadis to gradually turn the trauma of war and occupation into valuable professional know-how and expertise. In many respects, the "lessons" Doxiadis gained during wartime, particularly in utilizing empirical research, became the foundation of DA's professional practice in the post-war period.

Over time, Doxiadis and his associates gathered an enormous amount of closely noted and precisely articulated contextual data and reports from multiple areas around the world where they worked. Explicitly in contrast to the modern movement and to other well-known architects and planners from the first post-war decades, Doxiadis never assumed his projects were to be built on a *tabula rasa* but was instead interested to find out who lived there, rendering visible those who did not normally feature in such plans. The sur-

veys demonstrate an engagement and an effort to listen to what local communities needed most. Since in the 1950s, Doxiadis mostly practiced in the Global South, studying these surveys today we gain an insight into another history – one that is focused on the lives of the world's neediest inhabitants.

A Manifesto

Toward the end of the first year of his private practice, Doxiadis was invited to present a paper at a UN Seminar in Delhi, from January 21 to February 17, 1954. This was an important turning point for Doxiadis, who presented the ways he was going to utilize his Ekistic research method to an international group of his peers. It was particularly significant because this is where he met Jaqueline Tyrwhitt, who was to become one of his closest collaborators. The seminar was convened and directed by Tyrwhitt, who at that time led the graduate program in city and regional planning at the University of Toronto [Fig. 1]. It was accompanied by an international exhibition on

Fig. 1 "Community Development Workers and Members of the Housing Team." UN seminar participants, Delhi, India, 1954. This photograph was taken on an afternoon following talks and meetings perhaps just before the well-dressed group boarded a small bus to see Chandigarh, at that time under construction. Doxiadis stands in the middle of the semicircle of delegates, smiling for the camera. Jaqueline Tyrwhitt, the seminar director and convener, was uncomfortable with being at the center of attention: she appears standing fifth to the left of Doxiadis in the photo, while Jacob Crane is the fifth person to the right of Doxiadis.

"Low-Cost Housing and Community Improvement" organized by the Indian government with her assistance.[9] As Ines Tolić has noted, "the presentations, exhibitions and workshops organized in New Delhi were intended to be part of a growing number of actions to promote ideals contained in the Universal Declaration of Human Rights, namely higher standards of living, social progress and economic development."[10] A sole woman among male architects and planners of her time, Tyrwhitt had studied in London and in Berlin. She had worked as a landscape architect, planner and educator, first in England and later in Canada; in Indonesia, where she established a new school of planning; and in the US, where she taught at the city-planning department of Harvard's Graduate School of Design.

Tyrwhitt's interest in the survey as a planning tool had begun during the war, when she had organized a highly successful correspondence course in planning for servicemen and later for ex-servicemen from her base in London, where, in lieu of a textbook on planning that did not yet exist, she compiled readings for her students by Patrick Geddes, Lewis Mumford and Leslie Patrick Abercrombie, among others.[11] She was particularly interested in Patrick Geddes (1854–1932), the Scottish botanist, sociologist, geographer, town planner and conservationist. Working with Geddes's son, Arthur, Tyrwhitt managed to collect a great deal of his dispersed writings, which she edited and published. Geddes's ideas about conserving and improving the built environment, especially for the poor, were likely key in Doxiadis's thinking.[12] It was Tyrwhitt who "translated" Geddes for post-war planning, as Ellen Shoshkes has shown. Tyrwhitt's edited edition of his writings, *Patrick Geddes in India*, with an introduction by Lewis Mumford, was read widely, including by India's first prime minister after independence, Jawaharlal Nehru.[13] The Prime Minister must have been impressed by this book and its editor, because he went to visit the UN exhibition on "Low-Cost Housing and Community Improvement" and was shown around by Tyrwhitt, who was seen discussing the work with him [Fig. 2].

In his discussion of the Delos conferences, Mark Wigley began to reveal the complex and fascinating relationship between Tyrwhitt and Doxiadis, exposing how the very private, almost self-effacing Tyrwhitt played a key role in many of Doxiadis's projects and ideas.[14] Both Wigley and Shoshkes note that Tyrwhitt was the link between CIAM (the Congrès Internationaux d'Architecture Moderne) and the Delos Symposia. It was the reserved but brilliant Tyrwhitt who actually brought people together, made important

connections, organized hundreds of meetings, initiated new contacts and produced multiple publications. According to Wigley, when Tyrwhitt and Doxiadis met in Delhi, "the sense of a shared venture was immediate."[15] In his talk in Delhi, Doxiadis emphasized that before making any proposals, planners need to understand the local context and that technological solutions are far from appropriate to apply everywhere in the same way. He cautioned that because "technological civilization spreads outwards from wealthier countries," we must take greater care about how we introduce this technical civilization to traditional societies:

> [...] if we are dealing with an area where settlement has already taken place, [we have] to survey it and investigate and understand the systems locally in use, that is, the densities and the patterns of accumulation of houses and their different types. We have much to learn from an observation of local practice, if we look at the solutions applied with an understanding and critical eye.[16]

Unlike other experts, and perhaps because of his own background in a country that was still developing, Doxiadis elaborated on an important difference between the West and the so-called developing world: in the latter, people built their own homes. There was no separation between "builders" and "owners." Instead, most architects and planners from the West believed that mass housing could be designed by meeting pragmatic needs as they

Fig. 2 Jawaharlal Nehru, Prime Minister of India, visiting the international exhibition on "Low-Cost Housing and Community Improvement," discussing the "model village" with UN technical assistance expert Jaqueline Tyrwhitt. The United Nations Regional Seminar on Housing and Community Improvement opened in New Delhi on January 2 and ended on February 17, 1954.

saw them, away from their context. The intended owners of these new buildings were to have no say in any part of their design or construction. For Doxiadis, embracing ideas based on traditional knowledge and communicating with those who were to inhabit his proposed projects was essential, and we know that he appreciated vernacular ways of thinking about housing. These included the gradual expansion of a house according to a family's needs, which is common around the world; helping people build their own homes; and providing only key parts of buildings that are difficult for an ordinary person to build alone – an approach that has since become much more common and one that some architects have recently begun to employ with great success.[17]

Doxiadis proposed coalitions with local governance and administrators, and an open conversation and exchange with those for whom the projects were designed. We see evidence of this participatory process in DA's preparatory surveys. This material, largely unpublished, advances a different kind of architectural history, one that predominantly pays attention to the lives of the poor. At a moment when we are readjusting our attitude toward the role

Fig. 3 A handwritten caption by Doxiadis, "The builders and the buildings," highlights the striking contrast between the workers' settlement in the foreground and the buildings for Chandigarh, which are seen rising in the background. Photograph taken on a trip organized for the Delhi UN seminar participants by Jaqueline Tyrwhitt.

Ioanna Theocharopoulou

Figs. 4–5 A page with two photographs taken by Doxiadis of a village well (top) and of local children standing in front of a building neatly plastered with mud (bottom). Note the drawings around the door made by village women.

Ecology, Ekistics and the "Texture of Settlements"

of "monuments" and "masterpieces" in the histories of art and architecture, the relevance of the Ekistic survey has to do with the attention paid to the fragile everyday lives of those who lived with very little [Figs. 3–5]. These early surveys help us piece together a more complex image of life in the first decades of the post-war era in a developing world on the cusp of major changes.

In documenting the everyday lives of the poor, Ekistic surveys amount to more than a collection of neutral data. They indicate a spectacularly rich method of studying a site as a "living organism, not static but kinetic."[18] Conceptually, we might think of Ekistics as a lens, a periscope, a camera, a notebook for understanding the world and its cultures. The surveys uncover and afford agency to those who do not usually appear in architectural drawings, studies or histories. They tell *spatial stories* in empathetic ways. One of the first places the DA office began to test the value of the survey outside Greece was Lebanon.

Listening: From North to South

In part due to his highly successful and productive working relationships with foreign experts coming to Greece in the aftermath of World War II, and particularly with the American civil engineer and planner Jacob L. Crane (1892–1988), in 1957 DA secured an important commission for the National Housing Program of Lebanon from the Lebanese government and the United States Operations Mission in Lebanon.[19] Crucially (as seen in Figure 1), Crane had been present at the Delhi seminar in 1954, where he had also presented a paper and served as an adviser.[20] He was also a great admirer of Geddes's ideas on planning, which he had come across through Tyrwhitt's editions. For Lebanon, the DA office began with a careful reading of an existing UN Technical Assistance Administration report on "Low-Cost Housing in Beirut" from 1951.[21] They then set out to construct their own Lebanon Reports by soliciting contributions from a number of architectural historians and other academics from Greece and Lebanon as well as from Jaqueline Tyrwhitt, who had begun to collaborate with Doxiadis as a consultant soon after the Delhi seminar.

In parallel, Doxiadis established a small office in Beirut and assigned two young associates from that office to "scout" the country conducting surveys: Panagis Psomopoulos, an architect, and Emmanuel Theocharopoulos, a civil engineer. They were to gather data from the entire country, starting from Tripoli in the north and ending in the Hasbaya area, south of

Beirut. Doxiadis instructed Andreas Simeon, a civil engineer who was to lead the Beirut office for this project:

> Mr Simeòn is kindly asked to arrange the program of visits throughout the country [...]. We need to begin by a reading of the country through similar geographical and ekistic sectors and take a decision in terms of which routes through these sectors our team should stop. I think that they should see the center of each sector, and also during their route, see whatever points they will deem "typical." This cannot be decided ahead of time, but the centers can already be defined.[22]

Psomopoulos and Theocharopoulos crisscrossed the entire country in six months of constant travel to visit "*all but twelve* of Lebanon's 1,692 villages and towns."[23] Accompanied by an officer from the Lebanese Ministry of Social Affairs, Elias Khoury, who also facilitated their communication (neither of them spoke Arabic), they began the Lebanon Survey in July 1957. This was an incredible feat, conducted, one senses, with a great deal of enthusiasm by the young scouts, who were driven from village to village in a station wagon lent to them by the ministry. Their dedication was reciprocated by the warm reception offered to them by local people at every stop – visible in the hundreds of photographs in the Doxiadis Archives, many of which are images of local people in their daily lives.

On the road for five days each week, the scouts carried with them a detailed questionnaire prepared by the Doxiadis office.[24] They had to find ways to communicate beyond the level of an official exchange. Their interactions were vastly different from the stereotype of the "Western expert" who looks down on the local people. They visited people's homes [Figs. 6-9], spoke with them, asked questions and spent time listening to what it was that they needed most. They documented people's occupations, visited mosques [Fig. 10-11] and churches, saw important infrastructure under construction and learned about local building materials and techniques. They were particularly interested in masonry walls as well as dry-stone construction, and documented many kinds of such examples from different areas [Figs. 12-14]. They collected all this information in hundreds of pages of exquisitely well-organized and detailed reports that were later processed as part of the Final Country Reports produced by the DA office in Athens.

The two colleagues would first visit the governor of each area, the *Caimakam*, to obtain basic data such as maps, demographic information, housing and a long list of other categories.[25] They would pose questions to the *Caimakam*, to other officials and to ordinary inhabitants. In Figure 15, a photograph taken by Panagis Psomopoulos, we see Emmanuel Theocharopoulos sitting in the middle of a circle of men who seem engaged in thought, presumably answering questions and discussing the reasons for the questionnaire, in the Akkar region in Lebanon. The questionnaires covered data on education; religion; prevailing winds; soil quality; jobs or professions; and infrastructure such as water supply, wells, communal fountains, the provision of sewage and the percentage of houses with electricity. There were also detailed questions on "building activity," such as "complete types of houses, facilities, ways of construction, price, ways of making them available, etc."; how many houses were built by private initiative per year by

Fig. 6 A man standing in the courtyard of his stone house, Akkar area, Lebanon.

Fig. 7 Akkar area, Lebanon. A woman making butter in a semi-outdoor room. Behind her are stacked bundles of bedding that leave the area free for housework during the day. At night, the bedding would be unrolled for use.

number, volume, price; and whether building cooperatives or other organizations were involved.

The small selection of photographs presented here starts to demonstrate the breadth of interest and curiosity shared by the young employees, who sought to document what Doxiadis termed the "texture of settlements."[26] The urge to find similarities and to connect with people from other parts of the world, no matter where Ekisticians surveyed, was an important component of DA's methodology. First elaborated in *Ekistic Analysis*, Doxiadis expanded upon the notion of "texture" in terms of Lebanon's similarities to Greece: "The closest country to Lebanon from the point of view of the configuration of settlements is Greece. Only in Greece have I seen villages and urban settlements developed on mountain slopes in a manner as close to those in Lebanon."[27]

As mentioned above, Doxiadis believed that not all development could or should be the same everywhere. The emphasis on listening to what local people wanted set the office of Doxiadis Associates apart from other firms working in the post-war era. Instead of the usual hurry to propose projects, produce buildings and then move on – being ever mindful of "the bottom line" – DA continued to give time to surveys and to learn about each local context in remarkable detail. The fact that Doxiadis treated each associate as a colleague, and made sure their input was heard and utilized in the final reports, made the DA office an attractive place for young professionals – including a number of remarkable young women graduates in architecture

Fig. 8 Caza of Akkar, Lebanon. A handwritten caption on the side of this image notes "old house, walls made of dry-wall masonry construction."

Fig. 9 Home interior showing a beautifully sculptural kitchen area made by the women of a family in Tripoli, Lebanon.

and civil engineering.²⁸ In addition, the office was organized around a horizontal hierarchy, a fact that becomes apparent when one reads even a sample of the hundreds of memos, letters and reports: all data were immediately accessible to all via a sophisticated duplication-and-archival system.

The country surveys were a way to almost literally absorb the kinds of changes and issues that were important to their inhabitants, trying to capture what was unique in each region. This work was slow and methodical. Hashim Sarkis has noted that "invariably, the data-gathering phase of every one of Doxiadis's commissions sometimes exhausted the resources of the project."²⁹ Below is a short segment from the first paragraph of the scouts' preparatory survey report from Jbail, which describes the city and some of its pressing needs:

Figs. 10–11 Two humble mosque interiors, Akkar area, Lebanon.

R-LB 70, p 21,
Date: 17. 10. 1957
Information from:
1. Caimakam of Caza JBAIL (Byblos)
2. President of the MUNICIPALITY
3. Secretary of the MUNICIPALITY
4. Residents.

Jbail is ancient Byblos (according to tradition the most ancient city in the world) is [sic] the capital city of the eponymous Caza, its administrative, trade and educational center. Today JBAIL with its antiquities, welcomes a significant number of tourists which gives it a special character. There are caravans of tourists that visit the city every day to see the

Figs. 12–14 Tripoli, Lebanon. Examples of traditional masonry building. The photograph on the left shows the insertion of a layer of reinforced concrete to strengthen the buildings at the ceiling level. A caption for this photo reads: "Old [masonry] houses with mud as binding agent. The wooden roof was replaced by a reinforced concrete slab (with mud applied on top). Note a mosaic above the door." Top right: "Small windows high up." Bottom right: "Fences."

Ecology, Ekistics and the "Texture of Settlements"

antiquities. [...] According to the Caimakam and the other officials, the city needs: a. An internal road network, b. Sewers, c. A hotel and a museum, d. An abattoir (the existing is too old), e. They want to move the cemetery away from the center of the town where it is today, f. They need trucks for trash collection, street maintenance [...] g. A medical clinic under the jurisdiction of the Municipality. The Municipality wants a small loan in order to begin building the clinic.[30]

The emphasis on history as a critical part of Ekistics, and the idea of viewing architecture and settlements as part of a specific context, were constantly reinforced at the DA office. Prior to visiting Lebanon, Panayis Psomopoulos produced a fascinating annotated bibliography about the country for those colleagues who were about to study it. Once in Lebanon, and in spite of their full schedule, the scouts were encouraged to visit important archaeological and cultural sites and to write about them in the reports

Fig. 15 Emmanuel Theocharopoulos sitting among local inhabitants gathering information for the survey, Akkar area, Lebanon.

that accompanied their surveys. For example, Psomopoulos, Emmanuel Theocharopoulos and Anastasia Tzakou (one of the few young female architects at Doxiadis Associates in Lebanon) visited multiple archaeological sites including those in Byblos and Baalbek [Fig. 16].

As the scouts collected material, they were also being trained in Ekistics. A great many of them went on to have distinguished careers both within the Doxiadis circle and beyond.[31] Ekistics surveys gave voice to the people DA hoped to build for, not simply as token representation but instead as a key component of the practice of architecture and planning in the post-war era. The survey was used as a tool for a sophisticated socio-ecological data gathering to show us ways to bring the disciplines of ecology and Ekistics together, and to slow down the process of development so as to produce a more thoughtful contextual response.

The vignettes presented here help us visualize the material worlds of ordinary people and their histories, and speak to the power of architecture and material culture to impact our lives as inhabitants. The relevance of this work today has to do with the surveys' ability to give voice to those who are so often ignored in the construction of their own worlds. Ekistics became the literal practice of transcribing and learning from their communal methods of survival. By reading these surveys today, we are starting to listen to them once more.

The National Housing Project for Lebanon was never realized due to the political crisis of 1958 (which included a United States military intervention). All the same, the ways in which Doxiadis and his associates

Fig. 16 Baalbek, "Antiquities,"
September 6, 1957.

produced these field surveys in the late 1950s was important in furthering Ekistics, the science of human settlements. Kept in well-organized office archives and accessible to all who worked there, these surveys were critical for the advancement of DA's work and provide a record of Doxiadis's lasting contribution to our thinking about settlements. During the 1950s, Ekistics was a tool for repair, regeneration and adjustment wherein the emphasis on context worked as a critique of "progress" understood only in Western techno-utopian terms. Today, we might appreciate one more aspect of this work: probing the preparatory Surveys of Lebanon at the Doxiadis Archives in Athens is akin to a rescue mission. The hundreds of photographs and densely packed volumes of text help us to appreciate how people lived in a country that was on the cusp of major changes and extended periods of war.

It has often been remarked that Doxiadis was a "Cold Warrior" who saw development simply as "containment" of communism. As a result, he has been demonized particularly by the Left in Greece, and by scholars who consider his projects and ideas as just another Western intervention in non-Western contexts. Besides being extremely reductive assessments, these purely ideological interpretations of complex historical figures such as Doxiadis fail to properly acknowledge the richness and diversity of their contributions. Even as Doxiadis allied himself primarily with the US in the post-war period and collaborated closely with important American intellectuals such as Jacob Crane and others such as Jaqueline Tyrwhitt – both of whom had links with the Ford Foundation, which in turn helped finance a great deal of DA research – as these surveys start to show, not all "containment" was the same.

Many scholars from the Global North fail to consider that far from being a typical Westerner, Doxiadis came from a country that had been under Eastern imperialist rule for centuries and had only recently gained its independence.[32] This surely complicates his origins and ways of understanding the world, and starts to explain the warmth with which the Greek "experts" were received by locals in Lebanon as well as in many other areas in the "developing world" – such as Iraq, Pakistan and India in particular – who saw themselves as having had a shared history with Greece since ancient times and, as was the case in Lebanon, having lived under similar Eastern rulers for centuries. Further, during the Cold War, Greece may have been claimed as "Western," a label the country was eager to accept for complex historical reasons, but unlike other Western countries, it was impoverished and in dire need of support – especially following the end of World War II and the German occupation.

Doxiadis believed in talking with and listening to local people, and was fascinated with what he called "folk art." He valued close relationships and personal bonds – such as with Jacob Crane and Jaqueline Tyrwhitt – and he cultivated these throughout his life. The Delos Symposia were yet another way to increase and extend these bonds. Those who came to Delos were not invited for their politics but for their intellectual and personal contributions – for instance, Walter Rostow, author of *The Stages of Economic Growth: A Non-Communist Manifesto* (1960), a keystone of US policies in the post-war era, came to Delos once, and Doxiadis made sure he never returned.[33]

Besides Lebanon, the Doxiadis Archives contain many more surveys, diaries and preparatory reports from the 1950s, in relation to Jordan, Syria, Iraq, India, Pakistan and Bangladesh. Doxiadis's many books – including his last, *Ecology and Ekistics* – and the Delos Symposia raise the issue of growth as a question, and interrogate the appropriateness of rapid processes of development and industrialization as the answer to all problems. Already by the 1970s, in his *Ecology and Ekistics*, Doxiadis had critiqued the dire ecological consequences of industrial technology. His multiple writings and projects, and the work of his colleagues and associates, deserve closer attention. They are an important component of an ecologically engaged architectural history.

The author wishes to thank Giota Pavlidou, Archivist at the Doxiadis Archives in Athens, for her essential help in identifying research material and her professional and welcoming attitude to scholars.

1 C. A. Doxiadis, "Introduction," in *Ecology and Ekistics* (London: Paul Elek; Boulder, CO: Westview Press, 1977), 3.

2 Doxiadis, *Ecology and Ekistics*, 13. Under the subheading "Human Satisfaction," Doxiadis writes, "In our consideration of environmental quality, we must always remember that our goal is human happiness and safety for human development" (ibid., 67–68).

3 "[…] we must introduce coordinated education programs. All those who are studying architecture, planning, economics, and other subjects concerned with humans and their settlements should also be required to study basic ecology. Similarly, those studying ecology, geography and related disciplines should be required to learn about the elements of ekistics. In this way we will help to establish firm connections between disciplines and attract to this area of activity those few young minds interested in inter-disciplinary innovation" (ibid., 74). Quotation regarding these concerns from "The Delos Symposion," *Ekistics* 16, no. 95 (October 1963), 206.

4 C. A. Doxiadis, *Ekistics: An Introduction to the Science of Human Settlements* (New York: Oxford University Press, 1968), 2.

5 Doxiadis held public-sector posts from 1937, upon his return to Greece from his doctoral studies in Berlin, to the end of 1950. The names of his posts changed frequently. He worked in the Office for Reconstruction in the Ministry for Public Works and, when the Ministry of Reconstruction became autonomous in 1947, Doxiadis maintained the position of General Director. In May 1948, he became head of

the Greek Recovery Program Coordinating Office at the Ministry for Coordination – a position he held until the end of 1950, when the government abruptly canceled the post and Doxiadis fled to Australia, where he remained for two years before returning to Greece to set up a private practice.

6   I have written about this period of Doxiadis's career in my book *Builders, Housewives and the Construction of Modern Athens*, first published in London by Artifice in 2017, and in Athens by the Onassis Foundation, 2022. See especially the discussion of the "Circle of Technical Experts" and the journal *Chorotaxia* (1942) in chapter 4.

7   Ibid., chapter 4.

8   *Oekistic Geography*, section "2. Typescript," Doxiadis Archives, File 17409. Doxiadis and his team devised elaborate questionnaires and collected as much data as they could, sometimes risking their lives as they operated behind enemy lines.

9   See Ellen Shoshkes, "Jaqueline Tyrwhitt Translates Patrick Geddes for Post-World War Two Planning," *Landscape and Urban Planning* 166 (2017), 15–24.

10 Ines Tolić, "News from the Modern Front: Constantinos A. Doxiadis's *Ekistics*, the United Nations, and the Post-war Discourse on Housing, Building and Planning," *Planning Perspectives* 37, no. 5 (2022), 974.

11 See Shoshkes on this in "Jaqueline Tyrwhitt Translates Patrick Geddes," 16.

12 Like Doxiadis and Tyrwhitt, Geddes had traveled widely. He lived in India from 1917 to 1924, where he made detailed and careful suggestions for the replanning of a considerable number of Indian cities. He also held the Chair of Sociology and Civics at Bombay University from 1919 to 1924. In 1919, Geddes was also commissioned to suggest improvements to the city of Jerusalem and to plan the new Hebrew University there, and in 1920 he went to Ceylon to report on the replanning of Colombo. Tyrwhitt was responsible for making Geddes's work widely available by collecting his writings. His work in India (see *Patrick Geddes in India*, London: Lund Humphries, 1947) was particularly influential, as we will see below.

13 See all the material and information exhibited in the seminar and exhibition on "Low-Cost Housing and Community Improvement" here: https://architexturez.net/doc/az-cf-177948 (accessed March 21, 2024).

14 Mark Wigley, "Network Fever," *Grey Room*, no. 4 (2001): 82–122.

15 Characteristically, Wigley notes that in the Delos Symposia, Tyrwhitt "typically sat to one side of the lead speaker but rarely spoke. While all heads are up in animated debate, hers is usually down" and "the ever-public Doxiadis is unthinkable outside the ever-private Tyrwhitt" (ibid., 95, 96).

16 From "Types and Densities of Housing Accommodation. Section II, Methods of Preparing Housing and Community Improvement Programmes," in India Report and Photographs, January–February 1954, Doxiadis Archives, File 24965, 17.

17 See, for instance, Prizker-winner Alejandro Aravena's Quinta Monroy housing development in Chile in 2004, among other projects. See also Paul Oliver's "Rebirth of a Rajput Village," *Traditional Dwellings and Settlements Review* 3, no. 2 (Spring 1992), 15, where the author makes the same point about people building their own houses in the developing world, and that "when western experts start to advise local governments, they are not aware or have little time or interest in exploring local ways of doing things and assigning housing the cultural significance that it deserves."

18 Doxiadis, *Jordan Report*, vol. 1, 1955, Doxiadis Archives, File 24956, 2. Doxiadis made the same point in *Ecology and Ekistics*: "the greatest mistake that one can make about settlements is to consider them as if they were static, whereas in reality they are complex and dynamic" (Doxiadis, *Ecology and Ekistics*, 66).

19 For an extensive discussion of Doxiadis's relationship with some of the "key actors in promoting housing policy" with whom he saw eye-to-eye in terms of his own views on Ekistics in the post-war period – such as Jacob L. Crane, head of the International Housing Office of the Housing and Home Finance Agency; Ernest Weissmann, a longtime CIAM delegate who directed the Housing, Building and Planning Branch of the UN – see Lefteris Theodosis, "Victory over Chaos? Constantinos A. Doxiadis and Ekistics 1945–1975," Ph.D. dissertation, Department de Composicio Arquitectonica Escola Tecnica Superior d'Arquitectura de Barcelona, Universitat Politecnica de Catalunya, Barcelona, 2015, 92–94.

20 Ellen Shoshkes writes that Jacob Crane included an extensive excerpt from Tyrwhitt's *Geddes in India* book as an appendix in a 1951 report (Shoshkes, "Jaqueline Tyrwhitt Translates Patrick Geddes," 21).

21 The full title of the report was "Final Report on the Study in Connection with Low-Cost Housing in Beirut," written by Stephen Ronart, Social Welfare Expert for the UN Technical Assistance Administration. Lebanon Reports, November 1956–June 1957, Doxiadis Archives, File 24871.

22 "Scientific Work for Lebanon" [in Greek], R-LA 4, November 1956–June 1957_3, Doxiadis Archives, File 24871.

23 Hashim Sarkis, *Circa 1958: Lebanon in the Pictures and Plans of Constantinos Doxiadis* (Beirut: Editions Dar An-Nahar, 2003), 32. Sarkis also noted that DA's fieldwork "just for Lebanon was illustrated by some 15,000 photographs and 500 sketches of the most representative cases" (ibid., 31).

24 "Questionnaire for the team who will travel in Lebanon to collect data," 10, 118, R-LA 12, November 1956–June 1957, Doxiadis Archives, File 24871.

25 The *Qaim Maqam*, or *Kaymakam* (also spelled *Kaimakam* and *Caimacam*), was the title used for the governor of a provincial district. It had been used as a title for roughly the same official position in the Ottoman Empire.
26 C. A. Doxiadis, R-LA 1–14, November 1956–June 1957_3, Doxiadis Archives, File 24871.
27 Ibid.
28 Doxiadis also made sure female associates were treated equitably with men. Some of the most prominent women architects from the post-war period had long working relationships with DA. Besides Anastasia Tzakou (1928–2016), other notable figures were Marika Zagorisiou (1921–2013), who produced remarkable surveys of Iraq, and Effi Kaliga (1931–2020).
29 Sarkis, *Circa 1958*, 25.
30 Theocharopoulos and Psomopoulos, "Lebanon Reports," [in Greek], R-LB 26–80, September–December 1957, Doxiadis Archives, File 24898.
31 Panayis Psomopoulos eventually became a key collaborator of Doxiadis's and continued the latter's legacy by publishing the journal *Ekistics* well after his death. Importantly, Psomopoulos also helped establish the Doxiadis Archives, an invaluable resource for scholars.
32 In fact, Doxiadis was born in an ethnically Greek enclave in Bulgaria just before World War I, and had arrived in Greece at a young age as a refugee.
33 As Rosemary Wakeman has shown in her book *Practicing Utopia: An Intellectual History of the New Town Movement* (Chicago: University of Chicago Press, 2016), for "policy makers who avidly followed [Rostow's] ideas, progress was hampered in the so-called Third World by indigenous obstacles such as traditionalism, endemic poverty, a lack of skills and education, and the absence of infrastructure" (Wakeman, *Practicing Utopia*, 103). Rostow considered traditional non-Western societies as somehow inferior to the West. Instead, Doxiadis did not see "traditionalism" as an "obstacle." As we see in the surveys explored here, he admired the communal work of ordinary people and respected their struggle to survive. His openness to learning from traditional societies could not be further from Rostow's and other Western planners' approaches. At the same time, even if he was not invited back to Delos, Rostow remained fond of Doxiadis, as is evident from his contribution to a collection in honor of Doxiadis's sixtieth birthday.

Infrastructuring Development
Doxiadis's Continental Plans at the End of Ideologies
Filippo De Dominicis

Introduction

Between 1962 and 1964, Doxiadis Associates were committed to preparing two continent-wide transportation schemes for Africa and Asia, most likely the two biggest plans ever produced by a single professional firm. Witnessing the need to embrace the largest possible scale of planning, these two plans brought full evidence of the new auspices under which the Atlantic bloc attempted to remodel the world at its post-colonial turn. With the breakdown of colonial rule, in fact, the Western hemisphere in general and the United States in particular looked at new strategies based on a non-political hegemony, with the twofold aim of countering Soviet influence and exerting control over natural resources. Economic growth and development arose as the federating agents of a new global order built upon technical advancements and the increasing circulation of money and people. Under the unceasing action of the Atlantic intellectual elite – the "social science entrepreneurs,"[1] called to meet old and new global challenges – the so-called periphery of the world started to become a crucial asset for the fate of the East–West contraposition. Therefore, planning in the newly independent countries of Asia and Africa gradually emerged as a form of soft power enabling social and spatial control.

The opening up and the making of the post-colonial world offered professionals and experts from the Western hemisphere an unexpected perspective. After the dissolution of CIAM (the Congrès Internationaux d'Architecture Moderne) in 1959 after several years of bitter challenge to its guiding principles, modern architects and planners were in search of alternative strategies – and most of them felt called to reinvent their professional profile. They started traveling, working and networking throughout the world, taking advantage of the evolving political framework. The need to address technical deficiencies in underdeveloped Asian and African nations required the increasing presence of professionals in urban design and planning for the elaboration of long-term and large-scale schemes. Beyond fostering genuine transnational professionalism, consultancies provided to young independent governments and corporations enabled practitioners to connect design with fields such as politics, economics and the social sciences – and thus to expand their expertise. Such a professional shift implied the rise of new approaches and directions, no longer aimed at modeling formally defined structures but instead intended to develop generative systems of control for directing economic growth and technical progress.

Against this background, Constantinos Doxiadis was perhaps the only person capable of turning this shifting practice into a comprehensive theoretical perspective. Although not fully aligned with the Atlantic intelligentsia, the Greek architect–planner was able to translate into spatial terms the global developmental discourse set by the Western establishment, leading to the reformulation of the very tenets of the planning discipline. The largest scale became the inevitable frame in which to inscribe the post-ideological logic of growth and modernization, and countries entering the era of development would be the prime terrain for testing out and embedding this new world system. Doxiadis's innovative program resulted from a prodigious skill in networking associated with an inextricable faith in global growth, with the latter considered a driver for new planning directions. He became the man whom international institutions and charities sought out to provide the new political order with an appropriate global spatial layout. At the same time, he regarded them as the agents allowing the implementation of his own theoretical discourse through design practice.

The projects for the African and the Asian transportation systems sit at the intersection of all these aspects: closely connected with the ambitions of the international establishment, they played a substantial role in Doxiadis's approach to human settlements and his theoretical advancement. On the one hand, both the African Transport Plan and the study for the Asian Highway represent the effort toward a global interconnectedness, being preludes of a post-political and no longer nation-based scenario ultimately federated under the auspices of global technical guidance. On the other hand, they demonstrate how crucial developing countries and infrastructure were on the path toward the conceptualization of the human settlement of the future. In this sense, they fully mirror the controversial relationship between the fall of ideology in the name of technical modernization and the rise of a new and contradictory ideology – that of development for a new world order under the aegis of capital growth. Not coincidentally, they both stand at the convergence of Doxiadis's theoretical and professional achievements.

Doxiadis's Maneuverings and the US-Led Developmental Agenda

In the aftermath of World War II, the rising East–West contraposition required the Atlantic powers, and the US in particular, to set alternative strategies for exerting their control over the rest of the world. The outcome of the Korean War had demonstrated the risks related to military operations, but it also showed that the heart of the Cold War was drifting toward the world periphery. The shift materialized immediately after 1953, when the making of the post-colonial world offered the US an unexpected terrain on which to experiment with new forms of hegemony. In 1954, during a conference sponsored by the Massachusetts Institute of Technology's (MIT) Center for International Studies (CIS), one of the participants drew attention to the need to look to Asia and Africa as the places where the bases of a new global order were being placed. The US needed to counter the possibility that a communist model could prevail by backing instead the establishment of a framework in which nations could freely develop. The upheaval that formerly colonized territories were undergoing was the starting point for this mission.[2] Most of these newborn countries were, in fact, suffering from a substantial technological gap, and political freedom alone could not supply all of the economic, social and technical tools needed for survival. Therefore, according to a later CIS report titled "Objectives of the United States Economic Assistance Programs," the broader goal of American foreign policy became to create a "prosperous, expanding world economy, in which trade would become increasingly free," in accordance with the Truman Point Four program.[3] However, the question of how to implement this world-scale Marshall Plan was not obvious, as this required the building of new capacities and prospects: "it is one thing to set out in Europe to restore what once was […] it is another thing to build in Asia what never was, and under the handicap of scant technological know-how."[4]

This implementation was to be based on an "order-peaceful coexistence in condition[s] of scarcity," a notion borrowed from structural functionalism that was to become the keystone of American foreign policy as one of the imperatives for the stability of social systems.[5] Consensus, harmony and individualism would be the values and factors ensuring the survival of a stable equilibrium, recalling mechanical and biological laws. The aim was to extend worldwide the American social and economic system, whose structure was not exempt from risks. What happened in the aftermath of World War II, in fact, demonstrated that the structure of American liberalism was far from being merely conservative and self-regulating. Instead, to effectively maintain its stability, it had to be regularly fueled by new investments. Such an assumption implied the necessity of continual expansion, beyond the idea of closed boundaries posited by classical theories in economics. In other words, the US system needed to trade, while the leaders of the newly independent countries called for foreign investments to strengthen their political sovereignty.[6] This background was the driver that pushed US foreign policy to seek development and modernization in underdeveloped and non-aligned countries, often with the help of private charity foundations and under the auspices of international institutions.[7] A network of intellectuals in the social sciences, economics and planning supported the attempt to provide a theoretical framework for the world-wide expansion of American values and capital. Therefore, to create a genuine demand for growth and progress, the deep cultural structure of post-colonial territories was to be investigated and, if needed, manipulated to prepare the ground for action. This led to a set of multilateral initiatives that preceded or replaced political intrusions, especially in the field of social studies. In 1953, on behalf of UNESCO (the United Nations Educational, Scientific and Cultural Organization), the anthropologist Margaret Mead curated a volume entitled *Cultural Patterns and Technical Change*, a bold investigation of how the introduction of technical knowledge by means of multilateral development programs might affect local cultural elements in view of their gradual modernization.[8]

Within a few years, development and modernization became the key concepts to foster new discourses on the goals of this political ideology and the rise of a new global order. In such a scenario, no room was left for traditional societies, whose structures would be definitively wiped out in the name of economic growth, progress and free trade.[9]

The root of a similar narrative, which was likewise aimed at legitimizing American hegemony, resided in the efforts of academic bodies and non-governmental organizations like the CIS and the Congress of Cultural Freedom (CCF) – the latter born as a sort of intellectual equivalent of the Marshall Plan.[10] The CCF comprised a circle of American and foreign activists established in 1950 whose aim was to challenge communist ideology and spread worldwide consensus in favor of the Atlantic bloc. From its launch, it was able to count on the affiliation of major personalities – journalists, writers, philosophers but also CIA agents such as Sidney Hook, Michael Josselson, Arthur Koestler, Nicolas Nabokov and Ignazio Silone.[11] After Joseph Stalin's death in 1953, the CCF had lost its anti-communist focus in favor of an alternative, more constructive and comprehensive approach based on a "burgeoning international membership."[12] With the support of donors like the Rockefeller and Ford Foundations, it became one of the leading agents in the debate's advancement, positioned at the intersection of culture and power and emerging as one of the most active agents of US foreign policy. Its 1955 conference, held in Milan and titled "The Future of Freedom," set an important milestone in the debate. The meeting aimed to prove that freedom could not be questioned since the values it was associated with – progress and wealth – were themselves no longer in question. However, the scholars of the CCF said that this assumption was true only for the Western industrialized world, as the rising states of Asia and Africa were turning to new and controversial ideologies because of their economic and political weakness. Scientists and scholars attending the conference were called to respond to the anxieties that were mounting in the developing world, to help explain how development and modernization could pave the way for its political emancipation through free markets and trade. For most of them, however, political emancipation implied not only the end of ideologies but also and especially the rise of a global technocratic society under the rule of American values. In underdeveloped countries, the Atlantic world would appease revolutionary claims with the injection of foreign capital, knowledge and techniques. However, social scientists had already proved how sensitive traditional societies were to technical progress and economic growth, and what their effects would be.

    The panels at the 1955 CCF conference mostly involved sociologists, economists and anthropologists. The only scholar dealing with spatial planning was Constantinos Doxiadis, whose speech addressed the problem of economic progress in underdeveloped countries with a specific focus on the rivalry between democratic and communist methods.[13] Although not explicitly mentioned in its title, urban and regional planning were at the heart of his contribution. In this way, they entered the debate on development for the first time. Doxiadis had already got a foothold in underdeveloped countries since 1953 as a consultant to the Harvard Advisory Group (HAG), one of the leading non-governmental organizations involved in development and modernization programs.[14] Consultancy granted to the Pakistani government with HAG was the circumstance under which he renewed and intensified the old bonds with the transnational network he had known when he was involved in post-war Greek reconstruction, and with whom he had kept up a regular correspondence.[15] Hence, he was more than familiar – not to say aligned – with the topics addressed at the conference: as he wrote to his nephew Dimitris Iatridis in 1956, "we have to deal with people who sometimes come even from a pre-historic age and have to be adjusted in a modern technological society."[16] Like other scholars, Doxiadis did not fail to emphasize the global perspective offered by progress and growth, underlining how crucial they were in the path to political freedom. However, he was among the few who tried to go deeper, translating this discourse into spatial terms. While the narrative of development as a measure for bridging technological gaps had been largely acknowledged, the reason this gap was so apparent was still under question. To answer this, Doxiadis turned to the new geospatial scenario emerging from the ashes of World War II: even the most remote areas of the globe, he argued, had gradually lost their state of isolation, being connected to the rest of the world by an increasing number of roads and communication lines.[17] This global interconnectedness, moreover, involved both the Atlantic and the developing world, with the former seeing the possibility of exploiting all sorts of raw materials throughout the world and the latter appreciating the benefits of the technologically driven model established by the Western societies. This shortcut, according to Doxiadis, would make development a non-reversible process that was to be pursued "at all costs": as geographical isolation was no longer possible, he said, "progress would have found its way across frontiers" anyhow, regardless of political action.[18] In this sense, Doxiadis was the first to link the appearance of progress with the rise of a globally interconnected world. The perspective of the Greek planner implied an idea of development inherently grounded not only in the social sciences but also in spatial geographies, and this was the reason progress and growth were to be designed and planned spatially. Indeed, translating development into spatial terms enabled the discourse on the end of ideology to materialize – namely, the new global order that social scientists aimed for was also ready to be physically implemented. However, questions remained on the form that development could take and where it would be located. These questions were complicated by the geographical roots of the discourse and its ineluctable post-political dimension.

Partially shifting from contemporary developmental politics, Doxiadis was persuaded that crucial factors such as workforce and capital must be mobilized in the places most likely to attract foreign entrepreneurship, where the rates of demographic growth and population transfer were the highest: cities. Under this assumption, he offered the congress a new and innovative perspective, emphasizing three essential aspects: the role of individual and private initiatives in meeting the need for investments claimed by the leaders of the developing world; a focus on the city and its immediate productive surroundings as the most effective places where development should start; and the responsibility of technical experts in activating and implementing these strategies, in place of political action. The last two aspects, in particular, played a crucial role: in Doxiadis's perspective, experts were entrusted with theoretically limitless power in both management and control. They were the ones who would decide how to put development politics into practice and to transfer techniques across borders. At the same time, human settlements in general and the city in particular were identified as having a new and outstanding function. Sitting at the intersection of forces guiding that developmental scenario, they were to become the beating heart of a global transfer process that had found in infrastructure and physical interconnectedness the necessary precondition.

Such a belief was already underway in Doxiadis's plea to the UN San Francisco conference ten years before, where he had claimed that human settlements were the tool for veritable world-scale reconstruction, with new forms of international cooperation through the exchange of resources and knowledge. In the wake of these convictions, which matured over the subsequent decade, Doxiadis would further model both his professional agenda and theoretical discourse with the aim of providing the narrative of modernization with a proper spatial layout. This happened by merging skills in networking with a quasi-ideological trust in growth and progress: combined together, these two drivers enabled Doxiadis to develop a thorough theoretical reflection and, at the same time, expand his professional practice throughout the world. In the years that followed the CCF conference, he emerged as a veritable coalition builder: far from being the mere agent of transnational agencies – which did not look kindly on his oscillation between pragmatism and theoretical speculation – Doxiadis dived into continual multilateral action looking at the ambitions of the Atlantic world and the requests of underdeveloped countries on equal terms.[19] On the one hand, because of his obsession with organization and management, he turned planning into a kind of entrepreneurial activity. On the other, however engrossing his commercial activity was, he would always leave room for theoretical speculations toward new conceptualizations for human settlements.

Ruling Freedoms: Dynapolis, Indoctrination and the COF Project

Underdeveloped countries had been Doxiadis's main professional target since the launch of his Athens-based office. After the 1953 consultancy for the Pakistani government on behalf of the Harvard Advisory Group, he had turned so resolutely to the Middle East that Jacob Crane, in 1957, would claim that in the region "D." stood equally for development and Doxiadis.[20] The first studies for Syria and Jordan, carried out for the World Bank in 1955, were followed by the Five-Year National Plan commissioned by the Iraqi government. Quite deliberately, Doxiadis used to feature himself and his office as an "organization specializing in the development of future towns […] especially in the Middle East," committed to housing and urban problems but also community development.[21] As an office with a strong entrepreneurial imprint, Doxiadis Associates expanded their action beyond the region, providing planning services not only to the Middle East but also to Asian and African cities like Khartoum, Islamabad and Tema (Ghana). However, while coping with a huge variety of contexts and places, Doxiadis kept his theoretical concerns focused on how to give a unique form to future towns. Indeed, all achievements and findings in his urban-design practice were fed into a general theoretical model specifically conceived to support growth and development. "Dynapolis" – which was the name of the model – appeared for the first time toward the end of 1959 in the title of talks that Doxiadis gave in Warsaw and Oslo.[22] Dynapolis was nothing less than the city of the future – a structure responding to issues like demographic growth, technological progress and the expansion of the world's limits in the form of an iterative and incremental diagram [Fig. 1]. In this sense, Dynapolis was

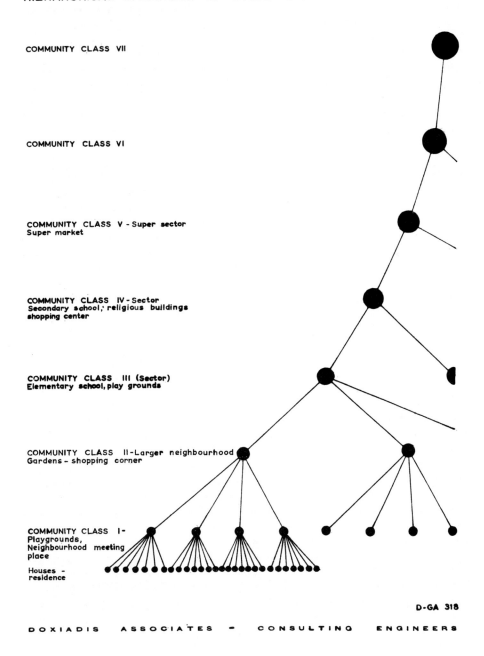

Fig. 1 Doxiadis Associates "Hierarchical Structure of Dynapolis," 1960.

deeply rooted in the position Doxiadis had expressed five years before, in Milan. Indeed, it was explicitly conceived for and addressed to those newly independent countries that needed to tackle these issues first.[23] Fundamentally, Dynapolis came to be the model with which the governments of underdeveloped countries would interact and which would rein in their own ideological impetus. At the same time, it epitomized a new vision for planning at large scale, materializing the required social conditions so that humankind and the city "could develop freely and naturally along a predetermined course."[24] Needless to say, the goal of this pre-established course was growth, the condition to which all local behaviors had to adapt in the name of a future global alignment. Hence, the deep structure of Dynapolis was paradoxically modeled on a mix of proscriptions and freedoms. The spatial rules to achieve future of wealth and prosperity were based on a strict sequence of human communities, each provided with a certain degree of independence according to its level – with the aim of absorbing demographic increases over time and space, and fostering growth through the free circulation of money, goods and people.[25] This deep structure resulted in a layout growing dynamically and incrementally toward a hypothetical optimum configuration, in which economic and spatial factors would finally be balanced. Dynapolis was the demonstration of how the city could perform the developmental role Doxiadis had been carefully tailoring over the previous fifteen years. Both in its deep structure and its apparent layout, Dynapolis mirrored the need for a continual creation of matter, in line with the rules of liberalism posited by classical theories on political economy.[26] Inherently provided with the laws enabling its growth, its sectorized structure was meant to be the perfect frame within which to attract private initiatives and maximize the mobilization of workforce and capital. However, the potential limitlessness of its layout evidenced a substantial indifference to local and regional political constraints: as a developmental and incrementally growing body, Dynapolis was ready to physically expand across and beyond the limits imposed by national or administrative borders.

To verify and understand how to apply these assumptions globally, Doxiadis Associates turned to the Ford Foundation. On January 19, 1960, when the idea of Dynapolis had been formally elaborated, the office sent a grant application to Waldemar Nielsen, Associate Director of an American charitable institution called the International Affairs Program.[27] Officially, the application was submitted by the Athens Technological Institute (ATI),

Doxiadis Associates's research branch created for educational purposes. Educational programs in underdeveloped countries had been among the Ford Foundation's focus areas since 1952, when the increase of "American capacities in understanding and dealing with the non-Western world" started ranking high on the domestic US agenda.[28] Doxiadis requested funds to disseminate the results and findings emerging from the planning of Islamabad, the most relevant testing ground for Dynapolis at that time.[29] Designed and built from scratch, Islamabad fully epitomized how the city of the future was to be built according to this model. Nevertheless, the aim of the research program was far more ambitious than its initial scope, since "the fostering of capitals for the new nations [had] not been a passion that stirred the Ford Foundation."[30] After consultations with Ford, which approved the grant in mid-March, the idea underlying the research evolved into the production of an open-ended manual of planning recommendations, to be updated on a continuing basis. The aim was to develop "methods and techniques for planning the optimum urban settlement within the next three or four generations," gathering and selecting all relevant materials and making them available to all "those from all over the world concerned in the city of the future."[31] Despite its open and progressive character, however, Doxiadis did not intend the planning manual to be a do-it-yourself tool: the city of the future first had to be developed as an abstract and theoretical model.[32] Then its tenets and principles would be conveyed worldwide through an extensive educational program, with significant outposts in Greece, Indonesia, Venezuela, Colombia and Ghana.[33] This would be instrumental not only in reconceptualizing and disseminating the results and findings on human settlements but also in training a new class of experts entrusted with an innovative and restricted form of knowledge.

Doxiadis Associates' educational program was fundamental to the whole venture, aiming to shape the technical elite that would provide development aid to developing countries. Students and professionals coming from all over the world were called to focus on human settlements and adopt the new systemic approach that Doxiadis called "Ekistics" – literally, the "science of human settlements" – which embraced disciplines like sociology, demography, economics, geography, history, transportation, housing, administration, architecture and landscape architecture.[34] Ekisticians, those engaged with the development of this new approach, would eventually serve as consultants to the emerging administrations suffering from a lack of technical services, with the further aim of replacing or complementing governmental action in all development-related matters. Beyond theoretical conceptualizations, therefore, the city of the future required a new lingua franca and a network of people committed to its implementation throughout the world. Both aspects were necessary to drive and control development through the planned and pre-determined path Doxiadis had developed in his work on Dynapolis.

The research project, officially named "The City of the Future" (COF), was launched in June 1960.[35] The first step consisted in assembling a group of multidisciplinary consultants to establish connections and collect materials about world cities. While the information obtained was being processed in order to understand how each city could fit with and develop according to the Dynapolis model, experts would persuade local administrators to aim for Dynapolis as the best way to attain development and growth. The function Doxiadis had assigned to experts and human settlements in 1955 was to come to pass: as the COF project took shape, Doxiadis gradually fine-tuned its scope, turning planning into a veritable soft power at the crossroads of knowledge and control. Against this background, technical expertise was intended to play an increasingly influential role, equal to if not higher than that played by the young governments. This was particularly true for the developing countries of Asia and Africa.

Continental Infrastructures: Asia and Africa

The Egyptian architect Hassan Fathy, who had been carving out a niche for his vernacular expertise within the more explicitly technocratic currents of Doxiadis Associates since the mid-1950s, was the first COF consultant to leave Athens for the African continent.[36] The choice to start with Africa was a conscious one. Indeed, since the late 1950s, African countries had begun ranking high among the Ford Foundation's priorities.[37] The rising Pan-African enthusiasm and the increasing number of intra-territorial meetings encouraged Ford to establish programs on a continent-wide scale and to challenge the balkanized geography characterizing those areas. Seen from Athens, Africa seemed an attractive testing ground. The continent's absence of large cities and its terrific rate of demographic growth had led Doxiadis to emphasize Africa's importance from the earliest phases of the research.[38] Thus, Fathy's trip across the continent was expected to yield new findings, particularly about the role of planning in underdeveloped countries.³⁹ He visited some twenty cities throughout North and sub-Saharan Africa, taking photographs, conducting surveys, drafting maps and meeting with local people. Although differing profoundly from Doxiadis's developmental approach, the conclusions drawn by Fathy were substantially aligned with the role the COF research had assigned to the continent. However, the feelings and impressions Fathy brought back from Africa provided the COF research with a significant added value, questioning the very nature of Dynapolis and offering the research a new field of investigation. The state of apartness characterizing the African city – one of the main issues raised by Fathy during the survey – urged the Egyptian architect to search for an alternative, quality-oriented approach. In the eyes of Fathy, African cities appeared as an inconsistent conglomerate of parts that had to be investigated in terms of their most recondite aspects. Against this background, planning could not be treated as a problem-solving process addressing no more than practical issues such as traffic flow or housing construction. Contrarily, it should persuade planners and architects to consider what the city was for and the purpose for which people tended to come together into larger and larger towns – in other words, how African urbanization could contribute to the trajectory of human evolution.⁴⁰ In this sense, growth was not necessarily the only or the most appropriate solution for the continent and the role its people would play in the future.⁴¹ The path each city should undertake, Fathy said, was not to seek to encourage growth but rather to evolve toward new forms of urbanization. Nevertheless, he still considered Dynapolis the model for reference. Dynapolis, he said, was flexible enough to trigger evolution rather than growth and to enable urban organisms to establish broader and more harmonious relationships, especially within an extended and more comprehensive frame [Fig. 2]. For this reason, he claimed that Dynapolis's principles ought to be expanded regionally, beyond the limits of the city, to embrace the concepts of Dynaregion and Dynacountry.⁴² To do so, and particularly to avoid any further divergence between the city and the countryside of the future, the model should operate as a large-scale system – first on the regional scale and then expanding to the entire continent through an extended infrastructural pattern.⁴³

Fathy's approach was quite controversial within Doxiadis Associates. While his observations on the evolutionary and harmonic nature of Dynapolis were substantially neglected, conclusions referring to the regional scale and infrastructure-related aspects were largely appreciated by the

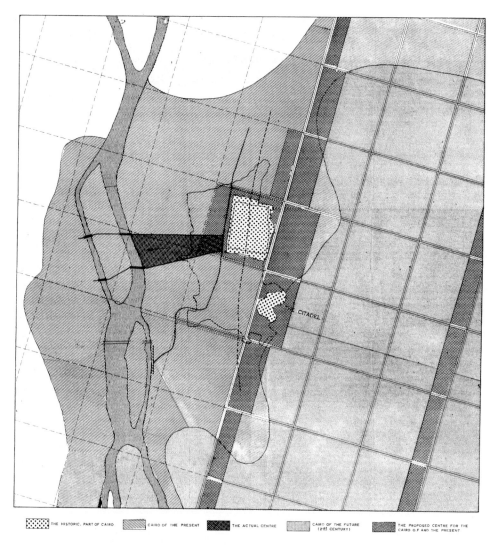

research team, as they constituted the basis of a new design perspective. In October 1961, one month before Fathy was to end his collaboration with the COF project, Doxiadis Associates produced a document entitled "Regional Development through Transport in Africa."[44] Initially included in the COF project and inspired mainly by the Egyptian architect, this short report was later converted into a more extensive independent initiative known as the Africa Transport Plan (ATP).

Fig. 2 Hassan Fathy, Dynapolis for Cairo, 1961.

This plan represented the first attempt to inscribe the COF research into a design-oriented frame. Therefore, infrastructure was one of the key issues developed by the intra-territorial institutions involved in the making of post-colonial Africa: in the same year that the plan was published, the United Nations Economic Commission for Africa (UNECA) had met in Monrovia with West African transport ministries to understand how integrated infrastructure could support growth and fill the gaps in economic and industrial development [Fig. 3].[45] Ambitions expressed by African leaders in Monrovia became the key to outline a new scenario aimed at assigning Africa a new role. In this sense, Doxiadis's discourse was profoundly indebted to Fathy's contribution. At the same time, Doxiadis proved extremely responsive to solicitations from transnational institutions and was keenly aware of the political mood. Combining cunning entrepreneurial skills and theoretical ambitions, he then framed the plan as a genuine political manifesto: beyond meeting economic gaps through the interstate circulation of money and products, the plan would also encourage young countries to erase the imprint of former colonial rule. The ultimate purpose of an extended infrastructural network, Doxiadis said, was to reverse the outward-looking layout that had been linking Africa to European powers during the last five centuries [Fig. 4]. Instead of transport being linked ideologically to the colonial-era mandate of removing resources and capital from the continent, it would now look to regional growth, empowerment and self-governance.

With the implementation of a continental transport scheme, African nations would be stimulated to go beyond the post-colonial balkanization observed by the UN and the Ford Foundation's officers, each country partially suspending its sovereignty to share knowledge, money and goods in a frame of mutual and transnational cooperation. In such a scenario – which winked at the resurgent Pan-Africanist ambitions of Kwame Nkrumah and Jomo Kenyatta – political ideologies would fall apart in the name of a common and increasing wealth.[46] Infrastructure meant increasing energy demand, new foreign investments and the possibility of larger industrial establishments. In other words, infrastructure meant that technical empowerment would convert political instability into peaceful coexistence. Therefore, the Africa Transport Plan enabled Doxiadis to put his post-political vision into practice for the first time: progress would definitely find its way across frontiers, he believed, making Africa the largest world platform where domestic borders would have lost their significance. The plan showed how

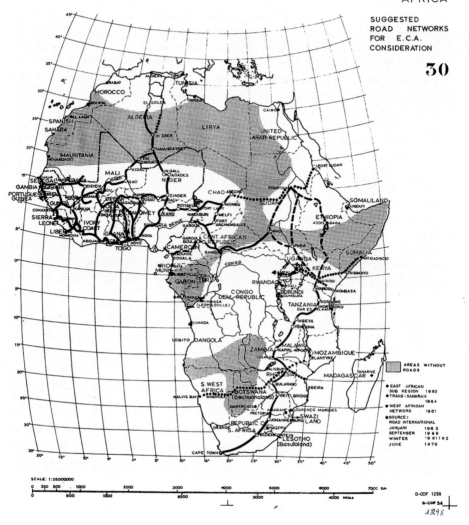

Doxiadis could act as a reliable coalition builder, leveraging both the aims of transnational institutions and the needs of national governments. As independently promoted research, however, there were very few possibilities to implement the plan; nonetheless, Doxiadis strove to make it real, capitalizing on the efforts of his multilateral activity as much as possible. While approaching national governments to stimulate demand for and to encourage the adoption of the plan, he mobilized his network overseas, with the aim of obtaining the patronage of the Ford Foundation and

Fig. 3 Doxiadis Associates, "Suggested Road Networks for E.C.A. Consideration," n.d.

Filippo De Dominicis

TOWARD AN AFRICAN TRANSPORT PLAN
A FIRST APPROACH TO ITS PREPARATION

THE ORIGINS OF THE PROBLEM

Africa's current political, economic and ekistic structure is largely the result of developments over the last few centuries which linked large parts of the continent to overseas metropolises. Through the understanding of the origins of existing conditions, the transport problems and requirements facing Africa today can be formulated. The existing conditions of the continent's development and their origins can be summed up as follows:

Concentration of development on the coastline, initially on the North African Mediterranean coast, which was more accessible, and later extending to the Eastern, Western, and Southern coastlines. Transport links were initially possible only by sea; however, at a later stage, overland routes were further developed and linked the inland productive areas with the existing coastal settlements, thus giving additional importance to the latter. The existing development pattern of the continent is that a great number of African economies are dominated by a single export crop cultivated in a specific area while elsewhere the population lives at a close to subsistence economic level.

The result of these two phenomena, namely, concentration of development on the coastline and single export crop economies, is that Africa evolved as an outward-looking continent with an outward-looking transport system, with a multiplicity of land strips having a narrow front on the seashore and extending inland. The whole pattern of Africa's development covers a relatively narrow belt on the outer rim of the continent.

The conception of a transport plan in such a way as to bring an equilibrium between the continent's population, space, and resources is the best means of remedying this situation.

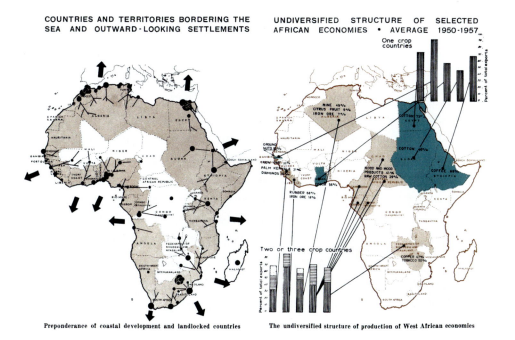

Fig. 4 Doxiadis Associates,
"Toward an African Transport Plan," 1964.

the UN Special Funds.[47] However, despite raising significant interest, especially within UNECA and UNESCO circles, the overall plan remained a dead letter.[48]

In the meantime, the scope of the COF research had changed drastically [Fig. 5]. Theoretical inputs from Fathy were already outdated when, in January 1961, Doxiadis resolved to move in a new direction. Defining all aspects of the city of the future through Dynapolis turned out, in retrospect, to be mostly ineffective, prompting an alternative approach. Dynapolis, in fact, did nothing but forecast future patterns through present trends. While this model seemed appropriate for the near future, and then for designing the city of the present, it proved to be too rigid to outline the effects of long-term global development – as had been the research group's ambition.

With the arrival of Jaqueline Tyrwhitt, the COF project acquired a truly global dimension. Now the world was no longer simply the methodological frame to translate growth into spatial terms but also – and particularly – the geographical and conceptual field on which to explore new forms of physical and relational structures, as if the city of the future had already developed and reached its widest possible configuration.[49] Unlike Dynapolis, which projected present trends forward, the new model attempted to forecast and apply future factors of growth with the aim of understanding the extent to which the city of the future could expand. The challenge, therefore, was to predict not only patterns but also factors of growth by conceiving the ultimate destiny of the city of the future, and then working backwards to drive all future actions. This conceptualization implied going through all the areas where the world's population could settle in order to create the ideal conditions to make those areas habitable and productive.[50] The scope of such reasoning was inevitably extended to the whole Earth, and its result, "Ecumenopolis," was nothing less than a settlement covering the entire planet within the next 150 years. This body, which was to appear like an octopus, would create a massive infrastructural network with its tentacles reaching into every area of the world [Fig. 6].[51]

Again, the opportunity to put such a theoretical ambition into practice came from an international institution, the Economic Commission for Asia and the Far East (ECAFE), which entrusted Doxiadis with the planning of a continental transportation system cutting east–west across the Asian continent.[52] The feasibility study for the Asian Highway, a 6,600-kilometer system of roads connecting Istanbul to Singapore, enabled Doxiadis Associates

C O N F I D E N T I A L

ATO – GSE – RESEARCH PROJECT "THE CITY OF THE FUTURE" – 26, FOKYLIDOU ST. – ATHENS

To :	"THE CITY OF THE FUTURE" RESEARCH STAFF	No :	R-ERES 6
		By :	D
For :	COMMENTS	Date :	25. 1. 61
Copy to :	H-GAP, H-GAR, H-GAI, H-PI	File No:	
		Atts :	

Subject : TOWARDS ECUMENOPOLIS: A DIFFERENT APPROACH TO THE PROBLEM OF "THE CITY OF THE FUTURE"

1. In two meetings of the COF staff, including Prof. J. Tyrwhitt, held on Jauary 14th and 17th, 1961, D proposed a different approach to the problem of the "COF", as outlined hereinbelow.

2. This text is to be considered as STRICTLY CONFIDENTIAL, and no announcement or release, of its contents to third parties should be made; comments on it, on the other hand, to be addressed to H-ERES, are warmly invited.

A. INTRODUCTORY CONCEPTS

3. Up to now all our attempts towards the "City of the Future" (which we described as the possible city of 100 years from now) have been based on the evolution of the human settlement up to now, and on reasonable projections for the next hundred or two hundred years, with an attempt to foresee what is going to happen in about a century from now.

4. This is the most sound approach definitely, but it is not the only one. There is another approach which is exactly the opposite. It is the approach of going farther into the future and working backwards in order to see what kind of a city we should have in a hundred years from now in order to foresee in the proper way the city of the farthest future, and in order not to connect only the city of a century from now with the present one, but also to consider it as a good foundation for the city of several centuries from now or perhaps theoretically speaking thousands of years from now.

Fig. 5 Constantinos A. Doxiadis, "Toward Ecumenopolis: A Different Approach to the Problem of 'The City of the Future'," 1961.

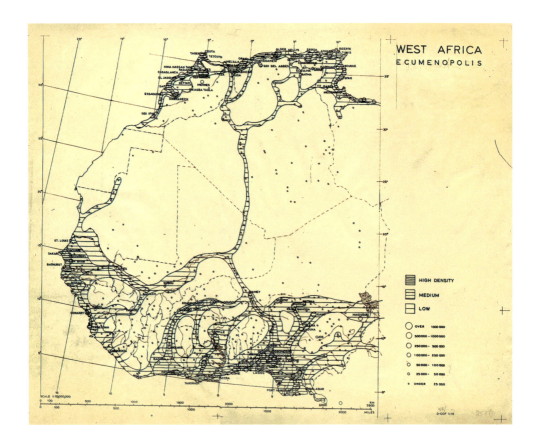

to test the design principles they had envisioned while conceptualizing Ecumenopolis.[53] Hence, before proceeding with the actual road design, the office developed a toolkit to define a hypothetical, thoroughly modern scenario free of any political or physical interference. While it was widely acknowledged that modernization would increase economic and social wealth on a transnational basis, leading to a post-political scenario, the way in which technical progress would physically reshape the planet was still under investigation. In this respect, Doxiadis's position was relatively simple: being persuaded that a parkway across the mountains would potentially be far more expensive than a straight tunnel passing underneath, he claimed that future technical advancements would allow designers and planners to disregard physical obstacles. Therefore, if the challenge was to define the settlement of the future and its backbone, by implication this would require forecasting in order to use all the devices that future progress could provide.

Fig. 6 Doxiadis Associates, Ecumenopolis in West Africa, n.d.

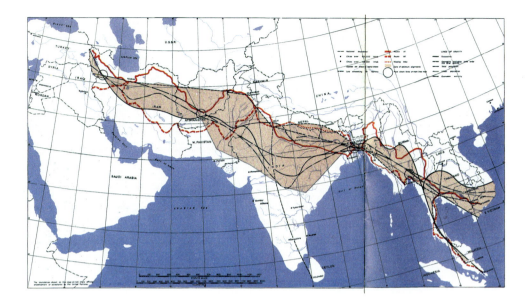

With the study for the Asian Highway, Doxiadis put this theoretical assumption into practice, looking at land as an ideal platform where progress had already been accomplished.

After identifying and sidestepping all the obstacles that could hamper transport and development, the study defined the key elements affecting the design of the highway. Aspects like population density and distribution, production typology, average revenue, traditional trade routes and significant tourist attractions were all weighted and investigated separately to understand their influence on the location of the route. Each analysis resulted in the design of a gravity line, the best theoretical alignment serving one particular aspect. Finally, the study pondered all impacts comparatively, shaping a zone of theoretically optimum alignment [Fig. 7].[54] Practically, this exercise aimed to identify existing trunk roads falling in the zone of optimum alignment to include them in the highway, whose actual design was developed in the second part of the study. On a theoretical level, however, the aims were much broader: the challenge was to understand which existing conditions to manipulate and how, in order to reduce the gap between the reality and the one best way as much as possible. In this sense, the study for the Asian Highway was conceived as a dynamic project that was meant

Fig. 7 Doxiadis Associates, The Asian Highway, "Zone of Optimum Alignment as Defined by Gravity Lines," 1964.

Infrastructuring Development

to evolve according to the development of Asian countries and changing transportation technology. Like Ecumenopolis, it projected forward the best possible scenario. Then it worked backwards to figure out interventions in the proximal future. Not incidentally, the zone of optimum alignment – a sort of spindle-shaped network of fibers where development would first start to flourish – did not differ from the image of Ecumenopolis provided by Tyrwhitt: "an infinite extensibility of urbanized regions, each consisting of recognizable finite components," linked together through a massive infrastructural network.[55]

Present conditions confirm the veracity of Doxiadis and Tyrwhitt's prefiguration. Today, planetary urbanization and the exploration of extreme territories for the purpose of settlement have been widely acknowledged as global issues, while infrastructure and supply chain play an increasingly decisive role for the destiny of the planet.[56] However, paraphrasing Arnold Toynbee, we still do not know if humankind is going to be the master or the victim of a system that shares many similarities with the one Doxiadis had forecast on the eve of the 1960s.[57] Whatever the truth is, both the African and the Asian projects are still far from complete – although they rank high on the agenda of transnational and regional organizations. In this respect, both actual and theoretical perspectives on planning seem to validate Doxiadis's pioneering attitude. At the same time, however, they seriously call into question his methodology and the validity of the motto he had used in the opening pages of Ecumenopolis to support his progressive approach. Although the inevitable planetary settlement is real, something has gone wrong in the meantime and little has changed – at least, in the agenda of transnational institutions. Uncertainties over future factors and trends persist and, contrary to what Doxiadis assumed, today the future is still what it used to be in the early 1960s: a look into the darkness.[58]

1   The expression is ascribed to Max Millikan (1913–1969), Professor of Economics at Yale and MIT and a founding member of the Center for International Studies. See http://cis.mit.edu/history (accessed March 6, 2024).

2   Michael. E. Latham, *The Right Kind of Revolution: Modernization, Development and US Foreign Policy from the Cold War to the Present* (Ithaca, NY and London: Cornell University Press, 2010), 65–92.

3   Nils Gilman, *Mandarins of the Future: Modernization Theory in Cold War America* (Baltimore, MD and London: Johns Hopkins University Press, 2006), 176.

4   David Ekbladh, *The Great American Mission: Modernization and the Construction of an American World Order* (Princeton, NJ and Oxford: Princeton University Press, 2010), 156. The quotation is from Harold Stassen, Director of US Foreign Operations Administration in the Eisenhower administration.

5   For the dualism between developmentalism, evolutionism and structuralism in economics and politics, with a special focus on Cold War America, see Anthony Wilden, *System and Structure: Essays in Communication and Exchange* (New York: Tavistock Publications, 1972), 332.

6   For the action of the Commission on Foreign Economic Policy, also known as the Randall Commission, established under the Eisenhower administration in 1953, see Ekbladh, *The Great American Mission*, 157.
7   On the role of charity foundations, see Barry D. Karl and Stanley N. Katz, "Foundations and Ruling Class Elites," *Daedalus* 116, no. 1 (Winter 1987), 1–40; Kathleen D. McCarthy, "From Cold War to Cultural Development: The International Cultural Activities of the Ford Foundation, 1950–1980," *Daedalus* 116, no. 1 (Winter 1987), 93–117.
8   Margaret Mead, *Cultural Patterns and Technical Change* (Paris: UNESCO, 1953). For a brief overview, see also Walter H. C. Laves, "*Cultural Patterns and Technical Change*. Edited by Margaret Mead," *American Political Science Review* 48, no. 3 (1954), 854–56.
9   In this regard, see Daniel Lerner, *The Passing of Traditional Society: Modernizing the Middle East* (New York: Free Press, 1958). Lerner's book was based on a field study conducted within the Bureau of Applied Social Research at Columbia University, New York, investigating the impact of foreign broadcasting, newspapers and movies on Middle Eastern people.
10 Giles Scott-Smith, "The Congress for Cultural Freedom, the End of Ideology and the 1955 Milan Conference: 'Defining the Parameters of Discourse'," *Journal of Contemporary History* 3, no. 37 (2002), 437–55.
11 Ibid., 438.
12 Ibid.
13 Doxiadis had been invited to the Milan conference by the musician Nicolas Nabokov; see Lefteris Theodosis, "Victory over Chaos? Constantinos A. Doxiadis and Ekistics, 1945–1975," Ph.D. dissertation, ETSAB, Universitat Politécnica de Catalunya, Barcelona, 2015, 78. On his speech, see Constantinos A. Doxiadis, "Economic Progress in Underdeveloped Countries and the Rivalry of Democratic and Communist Methods," in "The Future of Freedom, An International Conference Sponsored by the ongress of Cultural Freedom," unpublished conference proceedings, Milan, 1955, 227–40, File 6872, Doxiadis Archives.
14 "Planning Board: The First Five-Year Plan," *Tropical Housing and Planning Monthly Bulletin* 10, no. 1 (1956), 9–15.
15 Between 1952 and 1956, Doxiadis corresponded with managers and officials from international and charitable institutions like the International Bank for Development and Reconstruction, the UN and the Ford Foundation. Moreover, he had close contact with a number of US academics – among them Jacob Crane, Paul Hofmann and Jaqueline Tyrwhitt. See General Correspondence 56/57 (C-G), File 19248, Doxiadis Archives.
16 Constantinos A. Doxiadis to Dimitris Iatridis, November 26, 1956, C-G 40, General Correspondence 56/57 (C-G), File 19248, Doxiadis Archives. Dimitris Iatridis was a sociologist educated in the US.
17 Doxiadis, "Economic Progress in Underdeveloped Countries," 228–29.
18 Ibid., 234.
19 Ray Bromley, "Towards Global Human Settlements: Constantinos Doxiadis as Entrepreneur, Coalition-Builder and Visionary," in Mercedes Volait and Joe Nasr (eds), *Urbanism: Imported or Exported?* (Hoboken, NJ: John Wiley and Sons, 2003), 316–40. For the relationship with transnational agencies, see Constantinos A. Doxiadis to Jaqueline Tyrwhitt, February 16, 1957, C-G 102, General Correspondence 56/57 (C-G), File 19248, Doxiadis Archives.
20 Theodosis, "Victory over Chaos?," 98.
21 Constantinos A. Doxiadis to G. E. von Grunenbaum, January 3, 1957, C-G 58, General Correspondence 56/57 (C-G), File 19248, Doxiadis Archives.
22 Constantinos A. Doxiadis, "Dynapolis, the City of the Future," *Ekistics* 9, no. 51 (January 1960), 5–20; Constantinos A. Doxiadis, "Dynapolis, the City of the Future," unpublished paper, 1960, R-GA 185, File 2529, Doxiadis Archives.
23 Doxiadis, "Dynapolis, the City of the Future," unpublished paper, 17.
24 Ibid., 27.
25 Ibid., 49.
26 See the theory of Wilfredo Pareto, quoted in Wilden, *System and Structure*, 332.
27 For the project application, see E. Papanoustos to W. Nielsen, January 19, 1960, Request for a Ford Foundation Grant for an Educational Project Related to the Federal Capital of Pakistan, C-EATI 499, C-EATI 318–794, 1959–1961, File 17722, Doxiadis Archives.
28 Francis X. Sutton, "The Ford Foundation's Urban Programs Overseas: Changes and Continuities," in *Philanthropy and the City: An Historical Overview*, conference proceedings (New York: Rockefeller Archive Center Publications, 2002), 1.
29 Doxiadis Associates, "The Spirit of Islamabad," *Ekistics* 12, no. 73 (November 1961), 315–35; Doxiadis Associates, "Islamabad: The New Capital of Pakistan," *DA Monthly Bulletin* 65 (March 1964), 1–18.
30 Sutton, "The Ford Foundation's Urban Programs Overseas," 5.
31 Ibid.
32 Constantinos A. Doxiadis, ATO-GSE – Research Project "The City of the Future," Subject: "Questions by Team Members and Answers by D on the Project and its Contents," note to staff, December 6, 1960, R-ERES 2, File 18403, Doxiadis Archives.
33 "New Schools on Ekistics," *Ekistics* 2, no. 68 (June 1961), 459–68.
34 Viviana d'Auria, "Taming an 'Undisciplined Discipline': Constantinos Doxiadis and the Science of Human Settlements," *OASE* 95 (2016), 8–21.

35 Constantinos Doxiadis, ATO-GSE – Research Project "The City of the Future," Subject: "An Analysis of the Scope and the Design of the Project," note to staff, October 5, 1960, R-ERES 1, File 18403, Doxiadis Archives.

36 Panayiota Pyla, "Hassan Fathy Revisited: Postwar Discourses on Science, Development and Vernacular Architecture," *Journal of Architectural Education* 3, no. 60 (2007), 28–39.

37 Francis X. Sutton, "The Ford Foundation's Development Program in Africa," *African Studies Bulletin* 3, no. 4 (December 1960), 1–7.

38 Constantinos Doxiadis, ATO-GSE – Research Project "The City of the Future," Subject: "An Analysis of the Scope and the Design of the Project," note to staff, October 5, 1960, R-ERES 1, File 18403, Doxiadis Archives.

39 Hassan Fathy, ATO-GSE – Research Project "The City of the Future," Subject: "Report on Towns Visited in North and West Africa – Introduction," Internal Report, April 20, 1961, R-ERES 15 (14), File 18604, Doxiadis Archives.

40 Filippo De Dominicis, "To Survey, Control, and Design: Doxiadis and Fathy on Africa's Future and Identity (1959–1963)," in Carlos Nunes Silva (ed.), *Routledge Handbook of Urban Planning in Africa* (New York: Routledge, 2020).

41 Hassan Fathy, ATO-GSE – Research Project "The City of the Future," Internal Reports, R-ERES 15 (1–10), File 18604, Doxiadis Archives.

42 Fathy made explicit reference to the Dynaregion and Dynacountry in the report he wrote for Togoland. See Hassan Fathy, ATO-GSE – Research Project "The City of the Future," Subject: "Togoland and Dahomey," Internal Report, June 28, 1961, R-ERES 15 (9), File 19866, Doxiadis Archives.

43 Hassan Fathy, ATO-GSE – Research Project "The City of the Future," Subject: "Africa – Case-Studies of Cities Visited – Some Conclusions," Internal Report, July 2, 1961, R-ERES 15 (15), File 18604, Doxiadis Archives; Hassan Fathy, "Dynapolis in Africa," *Ekistics* 12, no. 71 (September 1961), 206–8.

44 Doxiadis Associates, Subject: "Regional Development through Transport in Africa," Internal Report, November 11, 1961, DOX-GA 2, ATO-ACE Working File 1961–1962, File 18731, Doxiadis Archives; Doxiadis Associates, "Toward an African Transport Plan," *DA Monthly Bulletin* 63 (February 1964).

45 Economic Commission for Africa, "Transport Problems in Relation to Economic Development in West Africa," *Ekistics* 11, no. 68 (June 1961), 506–10.

46 Kwame Nkrumah (1909–1972) and Jomo Kenyatta (1889–1978), first presidents of independent Ghana and Kenya respectively, were among the most prominent anti-colonial activists and active promoters of Pan-African ideals in the years of African independence. See David J. Francis, *Uniting Africa: Building Regional Peace and Security Systems* (Aldershot: Ashgate, 2006). Doxiadis came in contact with Nkrumah during the preparation of the ATP (see n. 47).

47 According to the correspondence Doxiadis had with the UN Special Fund, the Africa Transport Plan was prepared after consultations Doxiadis had had with President Nkrumah (see ATO-ACE Working File 1961–1962, File 18731, Doxiadis Archives). Contacts for promoting the study were active from December 1962: through Paul-Marc Henri, Associate Director at the Bureau of Operations in New York and Director General of the Special United Nations Fund for Development, Doxiadis obtained important information on countries to mobilize and people to contact. Among the latter were David Lilienthal, former director of the Tennessee Valley Authority, and Waldemar Nielsen from the Ford Foundation.

48 W. H. Owens, "New Patterns of Transport for Africa," *The UNESCO Courier* 19 (January 1966), 11–15.

49 Constantinos A. Doxiadis and Jaqueline Tyrwhitt, ATO-GSE – Research Project "The City of the Future," Subject: "Toward Ecumenopolis: A Different Approach to the Problem of 'The City of the Future'," note to the staff, January 25, 1961, R-ERES 6, File 18607, Doxiadis Archives; Constantinos A. Doxiadis and Jaqueline Tyrwhitt, ATO-GSE – Research Project "The City of the Future," Subject: "Trying to Define Ecumenopolis," note to staff, January 27, 1961, R-ERES 7, File 18607, Doxiadis Archives.

50 Constantinos A. Doxiadis, ATO-GSE – Research Project "The City of the Future," Subject: "Ecumenopolis, 'The Settlement of the Future'," Internal Report, June 23, 1961, R-ERES 18, File 2650, Doxiadis Archives. See also Constantinos A. Doxiadis, Subject: "Ecumenopolis, 'The Settlement of the Future'," Working Files, 1958–1961, working papers, bulk dates, File 17391, Doxiadis Archives.

51 Constantinos A. Doxiadis, "Ekistics and Regional Science," *Ekistics* 14, no. 84 (November 1962), 193–200.

52 Doxiadis Associates, Subject: "The Asian Highway," Internal Report, December 31, 1963, DOX-ASA 1, File 23292, Doxiadis Archives; Leonidas Stylianopoulos, "The Asian Highway," in G. Kazazi and N. Gounari (eds), *Ο Κωνσταντίνος Δοξιάδης και το έργο του, δεύτερος τόμος* [*Constantinos Doxiadis and His Work*] (Athens: Technical Chamber of Greece, 2009), 334–41. Leonidas Stylianopoulos was the engineer in charge of the project.

53 M. S. Ahmad, "The Great Asian Highway," *The UNESCO Courier* 16 (June 1965), 12–17.

54 Doxiadis Associates, "The Asian Highway," *DA Monthly Bulletin* 63 (February 1964).

55 ATO-GSE – Research Project "The City of the Future," Jaqueline Tyrwhitt, Subject: "Points which might be included under headings of final report," Internal Report, S-ERES 44, January 18, 1961, File 18616, Doxiadis Archives.

56 Neil Brenner (ed.), *Implosions/Explosions: Towards a Study of Planetary Urbanization* (Berlin: Jovis, 2014). On the history of planetary design, see also Hashim Sarkis, Roi Salgueiro Barrio with Gabriel Kozlowski, *The World as an Architectural Project* (Cambridge, MA: MIT Press, 2019).

57 See Arnold J. Toynbee, *Cities on the Move* (New York: Oxford University Press, 1970), 195–96. Toynbee writes, "The open question is not whether Ecumenopolis is going to come into existence; it is whether its maker, mankind, is going to be its master or to be its victim. Are we going to succeed in making the inevitable Ecumenopolis a tolerable habitat for human being?"

58 See Constantinos A. Doxiadis and J. Papaioannou, *Ecumenopolis, the Inevitable City of the Future* (Athens: Athens Center of Ekistics, 1974), 16. Doxiadis erroneously ascribed the quotation "The future is not what it is used to be" to Mark Twain. See also Constantinos A. Doxiadis, ATO-GSE – Research Project "The City of the Future," Subject: "Ecumenopolis, 'The Settlement of the Future'," Internal Report, June 23, 1961, R-ERES 18, File 2650, Doxiadis Archives, 157.

Basic Democracy and Doxiadis Associates' School-Reformation Project in East Pakistan

Farhan Karim

Introduction

The cultural and political leaders of the Pakistan movement imagined the new nation as more than a collection of citizens governed by the state.[1] The popular understanding of Pakistan was as both a new sovereign state and a cathartic space that would ensure the unhindered political expression of the Muslim minorities across the subcontinent. A fruitful realization of the idea of Pakistan, the political elites believed, would not come naturally to its new citizens but needed rather to be learned and practiced.[2] Naveeda Khan discusses how the political and cultural leaders held that, owing to the decline of general educational levels in the Indian Muslim community, the overall political consciousness and moral strength of Muslims had been significantly diminished.[3] To awaken the Muslim consciousness in Pakistan, the political elites held, public education would have to be modernized.[4] The notion of Pakistan as a transcendental idea thus triggered a didactic mission among the political elites of Pakistan who believed that the nation must be trained to understand and practice its modern Islamic identity. In many instances, this didactic mission was revisionist in nature, encouraging a retelling of the history of the Muslim past of the subcontinent, but also idealistic in that it propagated an ideal form of becoming a post-colonial subject and an ideal Pakistani citizen. The post-independence establishment of massive educational infrastructures in West and East Pakistan – which included several new universities, polytechnics and vocational institutes for essential public education – should be in the context of this political drive to develop the human resources of the new country in a particular line of education.

In this chapter, I will discuss the Ford Foundation-funded national school-building project in East Pakistan, for which Doxiadis Associates (DA) developed several prototype school buildings of different scales and for different geographic and economic contexts. DA did not design any specific buildings, their task being to lead a national survey to study the current conditions of the educational infrastructure and to make a judgment on the economic and physical resources needed to develop a replicable school prototype. Although DA's suggested design strategy and prototype was never fully adopted by the East Pakistan government, this chapter contends that the intensive research that DA undertook for this project, and the conclusion they came to in regard to the solution of educational problems in East Pakistan, provide us with a new and productive avenue for discussing how education was instrumentalized to sustain political discrimination between East and West Pakistan. The Ministry of Education briefed Doxiadis to consider the issue of declining educational infrastructure in East Pakistan as a physical design problem; in this chapter, I will term this a formal problem. I will argue that the resulting formalist approach to a political problem led to a design solution that advocated for a technological fix to a political challenge. This formalization of political problems complemented the ruling authoritarian military government of General Muhammad Ayub Khan, who also used the language of technological development and education to suppress political dissent and to sustain his repressive style of governance.

What is important to note here is that Doxiadis maintained an uncritically professional relationship with Ayub Khan and the military bureaucracy for which he designed significant projects in both West and East Pakistan. As Markus Daechsel has discussed, the application of Doxiadis's theory of Ekistics to Pakistan's authoritarian governance revealed obvious fissures between Ekistics theory and its application, for its practical implication contradicts the politically inclusive principles that Doxiadis had laid out in the theory.[5] Doxiadis's successful collaboration with the military rulers of Pakistan was facilitated by a US foreign policy that supported Ayub Khan on the condescending grounds that Pakistan was not ready for full democracy, as well as by the Cold War interest in playing off Pakistan against the USSR, which was the main motive for US intervention in the country.[6] Doxiadis himself came from an elite political family and was raised in an environment that was sympathetic to authoritarian governance as a pragmatic solution to complex political problems.[7] His father, Apostolos Doxiadis, was a minister for the Venizelos Liberal Party, which rebelled against the king, Constantine I, and formed a provisional government in the north of Greece. Doxiadis's partnership with the authoritarian state establishment began early in his career, when Ioannis Metaxas, the autocratic president, commissioned him to design the Royal Theater on Philopappu Hill. Metaxas was a former military officer turned politician and a great admirer of the governments of Hitler, Mussolini and other mid-1930s authoritarian regimes. Metaxas appointed Konstantinos Kotzias as the Minister Governor of the Capital, and Doxiadis's second major project for them was the establishment of an industrial zone for Athens that was subsequently accused of destroying the Ilissos river, one of the most significant cultural-heritage sites in Athens.

The Crisis in Education during the Cold War

At the Pakistan Educational Conference held in 1947, the Education Minister Fazlur Rehman stated that the general aim of education should be the "training of citizenship":

> The possession of a vote by a person ignorant of the privileges and responsibilities of citizenship […] is responsible for endless corruption and political instability. Our education must [… teach] the fundamental maxim of democracy, that the price of liberty is eternal vigilance and it must aim at cultivating the civil virtues of discipline, integrity, and unselfish public service.[8]

After independence, Pakistan relied on the US for direction on issues related to economic planning and development. A group of Harvard University faculties, named the Harvard Advisory Group (HAG), was formed to offer expert advice to world governments, including Pakistan's.[9] When, in 1954, the famous economist Gustav Papanek assumed the role of the chief economic adviser to the HAG, he strongly suggested that the Pakistan government advance large-scale development projects for a growth-centered economy by mobilizing large-scale capital accumulation to fast-track industrialization and infrastructure.[10] Papanek's scheme was not directly concerned with the physical and spatial planning of Pakistan. He considered investing in housing and physical infrastructure to be the "least remunerative" way to achieve "development." Nevertheless, upon the recommendation of planner Jacob Crane,[11] the HAG referred to Doxiadis in their recommendations as the physical planner and architect best able to provide guidelines to the Pakistani government about building new institutions to mobilize such an extensive development plan. As soon as Ayub Khan assumed power in 1958, he quickly initiated construction of the educational institutes prescribed by the HAG.[12] The group emphasized in their report that educating the new generation of Pakistanis along the lines of free thinking ought to be one of the prime concerns of Pakistan.[13] The HAG's suggestions intersected with a popular view that cultivating a liberal sense of citizenship that was aligned with the modern would be the precondition for nurturing both a sense of citizenship and the development projects in Pakistan.[14]

In December 1958, during a period of martial law, the government of Ayub Khan appointed a commission to develop a national education system. The commission identified two limitations in society which education should address: the lack of national unity as evidenced by passivity and non-cooperation in public affairs, and the failure to make "technological progress."[15] Although the HAG was discontinued during the Ayub era, the basic principle that framed the overall development goal of the general's authoritarian governance was based on the premise that, due to an underdeveloped economic condition and lack of political consciousness among its people, Pakistan was not yet ready for Western-style liberal democracy. It was strongly suggested that its people needed to be properly educated to achieve the intellectual levels of their Western peers.[16] Ayub Khan used education in this respect as an alibi for his authoritarian government. Education was also considered as a political and economic tactic to define a new form of citizenship.[17] In Pakistan during the 1950s, creating a visual and spatial manifestation of citizenship and nationalism was of vital importance because these aspects were still unclear in the public imagination – especially to the large number of displaced populations. Something was needed to project a unified and coherent national identity and solidarity.[18]

Continuing the argument for educating the Pakistani people, Ayub Khan introduced the concept of "Basic Democracy" on June 12, 1959, eight months after he assumed power. Basic Democracy was a theory that, for most of the illiterate and politically disenfranchised rural population, parliamentary democracy would not be effective in Pakistan.[19] Ayub Khan asked how rural voters, who had no knowledge about the broader issues of the country and were familiar only with the people and problems in their own village, could contribute to the structure of an effective parliamentary democracy.[20] Basic Democracy therefore justifies a political theory that people can reasonably apply their voting rights only to matters with which they are most familiar; for example, a villager should only vote to select the Thana, or chairperson.[21] Basic Democracy is therefore Pakistan's own version of modernization theory, in which the people of Pakistan are imagined as being stuck in a limbo between premodern rural agricultural society and modern industrialized society. Basic Democracy enabled Ayub Khan to envision a striated and neatly ordered society in the image of a military administration, in which the members' participation in governance and decision-making would be determined by a newly formed social rank and monitored through a systematic chain of command of local administration.[22] Basic Democracy allowed for a shift in government policy to restructure public administration, which strengthened Ayub Khan's authoritarian governance by reducing citizens' political agency while – paradoxically – appearing to enable this in relation to local matters only.

The central tenet of Ayub Khan's Basic Democracy intersected with the United Nations' various initiatives of self-help and community-development projects across the emerging decolonized world.[23] The didactic theory of self-help holds that "traditional" societies lack a strong sense of community or, in other words, adequate political consciousness to form a modern sociopolitical collective, which the theory identified as one of the root causes not only of underdevelopment but also of the so-called developing world's susceptibility to communism. In order to tackle this problem, the UN experts on community development determined that Indigenous people must receive a proper education in order to build a productive and politically conscious community.[24] The self-help theory displaced the issue of poverty from its economic and political core to a new social and cultural ground. This depoliticization of underdevelopment, which interprets economic drawbacks as a result of mass illiteracy or low levels of education, was an appropriate fit for Ayub's concept of Basic Democracy, as both theories' main objective was to move the public discourse of inequity away from politics.[25] A variety of institutions – such as village development, agricultural development and teacher-training institutes – were created to support community-development projects in rural and urban areas in East and West Pakistan. The architectural expression of these institutes has taken a nuanced form, projecting a romantic, idealized vision of communal harmony, brotherhood and cooperation.

Concurrently, to support the theory of Basic Democracy and also to address the practical needs of developing human resources, Ayub Khan's government undertook massive educational projects such as establishing "Ideal" and "Laboratory" schools, universities, vocational institutes, the country's first professional architectural schools and the first Home Economics college for women. These were established with technical help from Texas Agricultural and Mechanical University and Oklahoma State University. The first professors of these newly founded institutes came from various American universities. Most of their buildings were designed by Western architects, commissioned through the United States Agency for International Development (USAID) or the Ford Foundation's Technical Assistance Program. While these Western "expert" architects translated the instrumentalized form of education into architectural rhetoric, Ayub Khan promoted these new educational buildings as evidence of the efficiency of his government, marshalling architecture as tangible proof of the country's development.

While American architects and educators were working to reform the educational infrastructure of Pakistan, in the US the question of education was also occupying a central position in political debates. It is important to contextualize Ayub Khan's education-reformation programs and American interest in them against the broader US debate regarding education in the global Cold War. Hannah Arendt's 1954 essay "The Crisis in Education" captures the broader role of education in US domestic politics. Quoting from Arendt:

> Technically, of course, the explanation lies in the fact that America has always been a land of immigrants; it is obvious that the enormously difficult melting together of the most diverse ethnic groups – never fully successful but continuously succeeding beyond expectation – can only be accomplished through the schooling, education, and Americanization of the immigrants' children.[26]

From the 1950s through the 1970s, the issue of education was central to the United States' domestic and international policy for training the population at home and across the world in an exportable line of liberal democracy; Arendt identified this phenomenon as "Americanization" – the process of discovering commonalities and forging a new shared identity among diverse people from different ethnic groups. As a result, Matthew Levin argues, the American approach to education underwent a fundamental shift during 1960s and 1970s.[27]

While the question of educating the new generation remained a highly contested ground at home in the US, American engagement – both governmental and non-governmental – in overseas educational projects was directly instrumentalized as a Cold War strategy. For instance, Matthew K. Shannon discusses the period between the 1950s and the 1970s, when an American–Iranian partnership allowed Iranian youths to stay and study in the US and fostered an intellectual alliance between these Iranians and the American progressive political view.[28] Working with non-governmental US organizations and operating through various scholarship programs, American policy banked on creating a new generation of bureaucrats for the Pahlavi regime that was empathetic to US causes.[29] In parallel, US international policy also tapped into the already existing educational infrastructures of the recently decolonized worlds to raise awareness against communism.[30] In Nigeria, where universities were seen as hotspots for generating emancipatory, post-colonial political views – and in response, British colonial policy aimed to restrict university education – US interest was exclusively focused on incorporating progressive American political and social values into Nigerian university curricula.[31] US interest in foreign countries operated at the time through various ostensibly non-governmental organizations such as the Carnegie Foundation, the Rockefeller Foundation and the Ford Foundation, as well as USAID.[32] Inderjeet Parmar reveals the complex inter-relations, shared mindsets and collaborative efforts of influential public and private organizations in the building of American hegemony.[33] Focusing on the involvement of the Ford, Rockefeller and Carnegie Foundations in US foreign affairs, Parmar traces the transformation of the United States from an "isolationist" nation into the world's first superpower – all in the name of benevolent stewardship.

The Education Crisis: Spatio-geographical Diagnoses Leading to Architectural and Urban Solutions

Doxiadis Associates were commissioned by the Ford Foundation to work on five different educational building projects in East Pakistan: the Home Economics College, the National Educational Management Center, the Rural Development Center, Dhaka University Teachers and Students Center and the National School Building. These five schemes, along with three other major educational projects (Maymensingh Agricultural University, designed by Paul Rudolph; Rajsahai University, designed by Australian architect and planning consultant G. Svayne Thomas; and the five Polytechnic Institutes designed by Muzharul Islam and Stanley Tigerman), were envisioned as the new, integrated educational infrastructure for East Pakistan. The foundational stage of making this infrastructure was intended to reform and modernize the existing school system and to build a new national public-school system. During colonial times, the public-school system had been virtually absent in East Bengal, but with independence the government inherited an under-resourced and extremely limited infrastructure to begin to support this.[34] In order to get an expert's view on how to develop – qualitatively and quantitatively – the building stocks of primary- and secondary-level schools, Pakistan's central government commissioned (with financial assistance from the Ford Foundation) Doxiadis Associates (DA) to assist with a long-term (1962–1990) education-reformation program.[35] DA's proposals were part of the broader changes in educational planning in the so-called East Wing of Pakistan, which aimed to create a new generation of liberal and progressive citizens.[36] To initiate this educational planning, the HAG and later the Ford Foundation played a major role, reflecting the aforementioned American interest in promoting liberal education in the developing countries to contain radical, left-leaning pedagogic practices. This began by providing "modern" schooling in the newly established "ideal schools" and continued through higher-level education either in liberal universities or in vocational/technical institutes. To support this new system, several new teacher-training programs and institutes were also established to train a new generation of progressive schoolteachers.

Doxiadis investigated the issue of illiteracy and underdevelopment from a different perspective. Rather than considering education simply as a problem of technicality and lack of resources, he presented a spatio-geographical thesis that the issue of under-education emerged from the hostile landscape and unique climatic context of the Bengal Delta – an ever-changing and vulnerable landscape affected by the unpredictable shift of the courses of rivers and periodic flooding during the monsoon. Doxiadis presented his observation:

> Rivers change their course continuously. There are no landmarks of any permanent value. Everything is destroyed and recreated and this characteristic of the landscape has influenced the character of the people. It has given them insularity, self-centerness [sic], self-sufficiency, lack of hospitality: they are unsociable and shy due to the very big difficulty of communication.[37]

Doxiadis traveled through East Bengal on an amphibious plane and observed the landscape from above. He meticulously documented his journey with aerial photographs of rivers and villages. By studying these aerial photographs, Doxiadis arrived at a conclusion of how the rural settlements took shape in responding to the landscape and how the settlements' "insular" nature also impeded the political development of the inhabitants [Fig. 1].[38] Historian Markus Daechsel shows that aerial photography was a strong tool used by development officers to create a hypothetical structural framework for development theory.[39] Aerial travel inscribed a deep sense of authority, independence and heroic zeal in the minds of the development officers, transforming them into the winged heroes of modernization – a calculated rhetorical flourish that linked the adventure back to Le Corbusier's aerial surveys of Latin America in the 1930s. Daechsel further explained that Doxiadis considered "seeing" and photographic documentation as key research methods, for he believed photographs recorded reality in minute detail. But "seeing," and especially seeing as a consultant's research method, was not a purely objective scientific observation in this case. It was a very conscious, carefully choreographed and rather subjective investigation of the environment. Doxiadis's diaries present an astonishingly detailed account of his purposeful traveling through an unknown and unexplored land of infinite potential for future growth, with the photographs also playing their part in this personal take on the history of a foreign land.

Informed by his selective reading on the history of India, supplied to him by the USAID area experts, and his firsthand observation of the East Bengal landscape, Doxiadis was convinced that the problem of education in East Bengal resulted mainly from the insular, unstable and fluid landscape itself. A diary entry from 1955 stated, "Now it become clear to me that not only the whole landscape in East Bengal is unstable and of a changing shape, form and structure but also that policies in this area will remain uncertain for many years to come."[40] Because of such fluidity and uncertainty,

Doxiadis explained, the Bengalis were less aware of their political existence and consciousness than other ethnic groups across the region [Figs. 2–3]: "People live isolated in such small groups of houses and there is no community feeling at all as in other parts of Pakistan, as for example in Punjab."[41]

In other places in his diary, Doxiadis observed how the frequency of natural disasters did not allow the Bengalis to imagine and aspire to any permanent monumental – that is to say, *architectural* or *urban* – presence, and this led to a lack of collective aspiration for the future. As such, the Bengalis' alleged lack of aspiration was attributed to political underdevelopment due to lack of education but also to an essential characteristic of an ethnic group that was capable only of "elementary" levels of human expression, having been overpowered and dominated by natural forces. Doxiadis was impressed by the "artistic" ability of the Bengalis as observed in different forms of folk art, clothing, boats and utensils.[42] Yet, while he saw great potential in those art forms, he explained that the hostile landscape, in tandem with prolonged foreign rule, had halted their evolution to a superior aesthetic level:

> Thinking of all the expressions of folk-art I am more and more convinced that this is an area with a big artistic potential which has not been developed up to now in higher forms of art. Is this not due perhaps to the fact that life as a whole has not been developed into higher forms in this area and that over major periods this area has been ruled by foreigners?
>
> Is not this situation mainly due to the fact that Bengal is still controlled by elemental forces of nature and dominated by them? Is it not important that the big rivers do flood the country continuously and change their course from time to time destroying everything and forcing the people to begin their life again? Is not this the reason [for] a philosophic resignation, of a fear for the unknown and a fatalism which is apparent in Bengal?
>
> I think that Bengal is entering the era during which it will have the opportunity to develop its own expressions of life not only at the lowest level but up to the highest. The elementary forces are there, the problem is how to develop them in form of their order.[43]

On the basis of this largely spatio-geographical assessment of the problem, DA's task was to develop different prototypes for primary- and secondary-

In a few more minutes the land seems to be not so low and the area of it which is regularly flooded seems to be smaller in extent. The areas which lie regularly above water are covering greater spaces; the highest part of them have trees but there are parts which are divided into regular gardens with some trees and hedges which prove that these areas are not regularly submerged.

Then the number of trees increases, they are even planted along all hedges and boundaries of properties and the area submerged becomes even smaller in extent, sometimes reminding of broad river beds in between fertile land tracks.

Same is the landscape further down, the only difference is that the parts of the land covered with trees are even greater, some tracks of land are even covered with bushes and here and there there are big rectangular water tanks.

Fig. 1 A page from Doxiadis's diary shows aerial photographs of villages in East Pakistan taken by Doxiadis.

level schools and to lay out policy for the overall physical development and provision of primary and secondary education in East Pakistan. The firm's involvement in East Pakistan thus moved into documenting the physical condition of its existing stock of school buildings. In order to create a database for the physical condition of the country's educational facilities, DA initiated a colossal survey in which a special DA team, organized by the firm's headquarters in Dhaka, visited every town and district in the province and created a sample survey of some 200 schools [Fig. 4]. "Investigation," as DA termed their survey activity, was broken into seven different categories: climate, life and culture, the educational system, the existing stock of school buildings, methods of construction, availability, and material and cost.[44]

A typical survey sheet was divided into two sections. The first section offered a sketch of the educational building and site plan, the main dimensions of the building and photographs from inside and out. The second section contained a chart that recorded all quantitative data [Fig. 5].[45] A typical diagrammatic section of the existing facility was also drawn and analyzed to illustrate the height and elevation of the building and the means of natural ventilation. The information was plotted into a numeric table to present broad comparative data on every school that DA surveyed. The objective of this survey was to identify the common fundamental geometric and climatic attributes of "traditional" school building.[46] Although by "traditional" DA meant the existing school buildings, it is noteworthy here that all of the buildings surveyed by the firm had been built during the British colonial period. In other words, Doxiadis directed an extensive survey of the school-building typology that the colonial government had haphazardly established to provide their education system as a modern alternative to the existing indigenous educational system (madrassa) in Urdu and Farsi that gave emphasis to religious education.[47]

Ayub Khan argued that, although the madrassa had been developed by the Mughals as a holistic educational system in which topics of science, philosophy and logic had become fundamental components over time, the system had lost its relevance. Political scientist Ali Riaz has observed that, during the colonial period, madrassa educators were among the most uncompromising critics of the colonial system and, in protest, had completely detached themselves from the mainstream of colonial modernization, which was the beginning of the chasm between so-called modern and traditional educational systems.[48] During colonial times, the ulama (Islamic

Figs. 2–3 Comparison of the "human types from the East and the North West" of Pakistan.

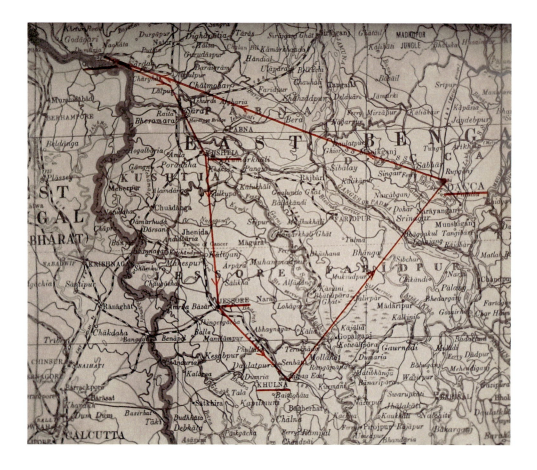

educators and pedagogues) on the Indian subcontinent had conceived of the madrassa as a counter-pedagogy focusing exclusively on the Qur'an and hadiths (sayings of the Prophet), which meant that it was irreconcilable with the secular Western model of education.[49] One of the main objectives of this new system was to free Muslim education from the customs and traditions of both Hindu culture and colonial values.[50] Within the colonial system of knowledge production and pedagogy, the madrassa had been increasingly marginalized.[51]

Based on this comparative data, DA provided the basis for what they argued to be effective and economic production processes for standardized school-building prototypes. In the report, DA suggested that, to modernize the inadequate educational infrastructure that the colonial government had left behind, a new standard was needed that was grounded in the existing

Fig. 4 Map showing C. A. Doxiadis's travel route in East Bengal.

construction culture in East Pakistan. All government buildings and public projects in the province were designed and constructed by the Public Works Department (PWD) of East Pakistan, which had been established during the colonial period. In the decades immediately after independence, the PWD maintained and continued colonial construction practices that, according to Doxiadis, were insensitive to the local climate and construction culture.[52] Doxiadis eventually interpreted East Pakistan's educational difficulties exclusively as a technical problem of the region's construction industry.[53] The preliminary report states:

> In order to formulate such a system it is necessary to have a common factor of design and planning, which will not only remain unaffected by all aforementioned variations, but on the contrary, it will help the architect to find the best design for each one of the problems which he is called upon to resolve.[54]

Doxiadis suggested that, for traditional knowledge to be more effective, it should be organized "rationally" so that it could be reproduced, implemented and improvised evenly across the region.

To achieve the desired rational organization of knowledge, Doxiadis proposed that architecture be understood through two basic "Moduli": the "Man-use Modulus" [Fig. 6] and the "Structural-use Modulus" [Fig. 7]. The first modulus entails the standard spatial parameters based on the human body, as "space is the container of man's body and activities."[55] Doxiadis repeatedly emphasized the need to understand architecture in regard to the specifics of the human body: "Since man's body has a certain size, with limited deviations, the dimensions of the container and consequently of the building, must bear a relationship to human dimensions."[56] In contrast, the Structural-use Modulus is based on the material units and structural principles of the building itself: "the construction of the building calls for the use of building materials assembled together in precisely predetermined ways, by certain structural methods so that characteristic elements of each building will be produced."[57] The prescribed resultant modulus, which he termed the "Metron," was in effect the optimization of these two moduli [Fig. 8]. Metron served as the dimensional coordination or "reference system" that helped to create a three-dimensional grid that could be used to develop different variations upon the basic prototypes.[58] To this end, Doxiadis

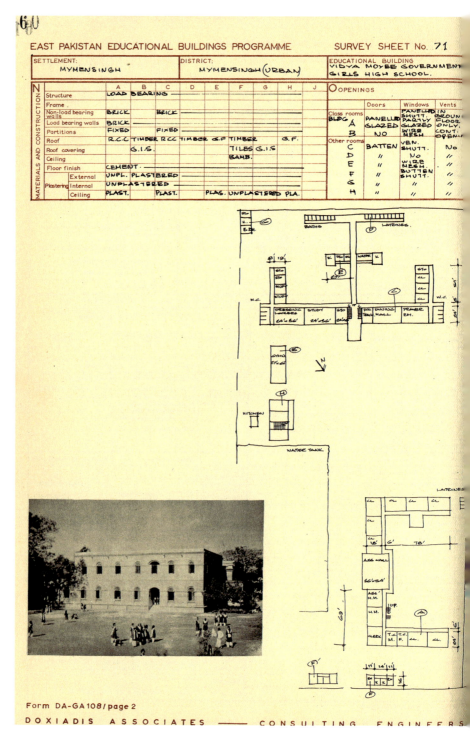

Fig. 5 An example of a field-survey log that records various data on primary-school buildings in East Pakistan.

EAST PAKISTAN EDUCATIONAL BUILDINGS PROGRAMME — SURVEY SHEET No. 75 A

SETTLEMENT	MYMENSINGH
DISTRICT	MYMENSINGH (URBAN)
EDUCATIONAL BUILDING	NASIRABAD COLLEGE

EDUCATIONAL BUILDING

- Educational level: PRIMARY, JUNIOR SECONDARY, SECONDARY, HIGH SECONDARY, GRADUATE SECTION (IN NIGHT COURSES)
- Classes: I II III IV V VI VII VIII IX X XI XII
- Sections: 1 1 1 1 2 1 1 2 1 1
- Elective subjects: HUMANITIES, LANGUAGES, ISLAMIC STUDIES, SCIENCE (GENERAL)

SHIFTS

	One shift	Two shifts 1st	Two shifts 2nd	Co-Ed
Boys	I–X : 360	XI–XII : 250	G.S : 80	YES
Girls	40			
Total	400	250	80	

STAFF / TEACHING

- Teaching: 20 MALE (I–X), 10 (XI to DEGREE)
- Other: ADMINISTRATIVE 3, PEONS 3, DARWAN 1
- To what grade: PRIM. SECTION

SPONSORING / AUTHORITY
- PRIVATE, REGISTERED
- No. of settlements / Total population / Distance from nearest school of the same type

AREA SERVED / PLOT AREA / PLAYGROUNDS
- PLOT AREA: 22338 sq. ft.
- PLAYGROUNDS: 13,140 sq. ft.
- BOUNDARY WALL — Height: 5'-0", Material: BRICK, Plastering: YES
- Type: YARD, No: ONE

UNITS / BUILDING

No. of independent bldgs or units	6
A	1
B	2
C	1
D	1
E	1
F	1
Number of floors	
Original use (if other than school)	
Date of construction	1924 1950 1958
Method of construction	SELF HELP
Total cost	
Financed by	THE GOVERNMENT 20%, PRIVATE SOURCES 80% (FOR THE NEW CONSTRUCTION)
State of maintenance	BAD
Maintained by	COMMITTEE
Effects of 1960 cyclones	NONE

SANITATION

	No.	Type
W.Cs	2	
Urinals	2	
Showers		
Wash basins		
Source of supply	TUBE WELL	
Method of storage	IN DRUMS	
No. of taps		
Remarks		

SCHOOL ACCOMMODATION

Room	Length	Width	Height	Area sq.ft
PRINCIPAL'S ROOM	18'	18'	12'	
VICE PRINCIPAL'S RM	18'	10'	12'	
OFFICE	18'	10'	12'	
2 CLASSROOMS FOR SCHOOL				
CLASSROOMS FOR COLLEGE				
TEACHER'S COMMON ROOM	24'	18'	12'	
LIBRARY (3200 BOOKS)				
TEACHERS COMMON-CUM-LIBRARY	24'	18'	12'	
STUDENTS' COMMON SITTING RM. (MALE)	33'	18'	10'	
DINING HALL / KITCHEN	FOR HOSTEL BOARDERS ONLY (SEE HOSTEL)			
PRAYER ROOM	IN A MOSQUE. IT IS A PUBLIC ONE, BUT WITHIN THE COMPOUND OF THE SCHOOL			

Net covered area: [blank]

RESIDENTIAL ACCOMMODATION

	Principal's residence	Darwan's or caretaker quarters
Inside school grounds		
Outside school grounds	YES — Distance from school ¼ MILE	YES — Distance from school
Ownership	OWN	
Type of construction	PUCCA	
Number size and type of rooms and other relative information	4 ROOMS	

	Staff quarters	Quarters for menial staff
Total No of dwelling units		
Inside school grounds		
Outside school grounds	ALL OUTSIDE — Distance from school	ALL OUTSIDE — Distance from school
Ownership		
Type of construction		
Number size and type of rooms and other relative information		

Hostel: YES, OWNERSHIP: COLLEGE

Number of boarders	15
Number of bedrooms	4
Ownership	
Number of boarders/brm	4
Type of construction	
Bedrooms	16' × 22' — SUPERINTENDENT'S ROOM 16' × 22'
Toilets	IN SCHOOL'S W.C'S
Dining hall	20' × 9'
Kitchen	7' × 9"

FB DIAGRAMS SECTION.

DOXIADIS ASSOCIATES — CONSULTING ENGINEERS

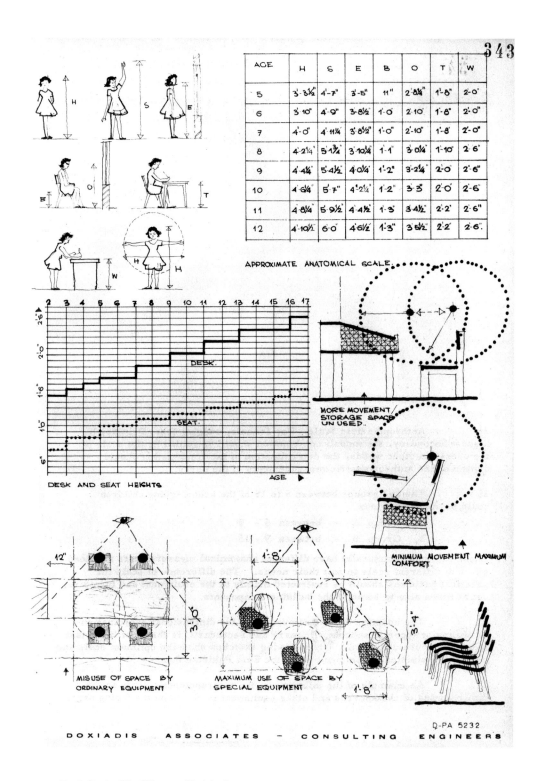

Fig. 6 Study of the "Man-use Modulus."

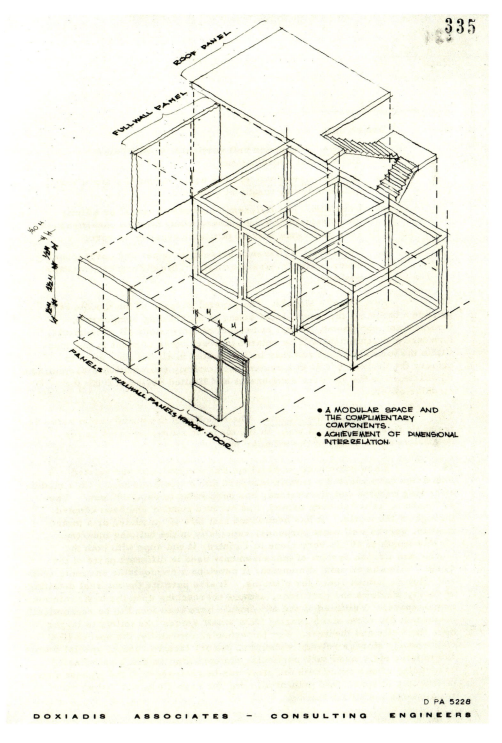

Fig. 7 The "Structural-use Modulus," showing the interrelation of various building components and modular spaces to produce a prototypical unit for school building.

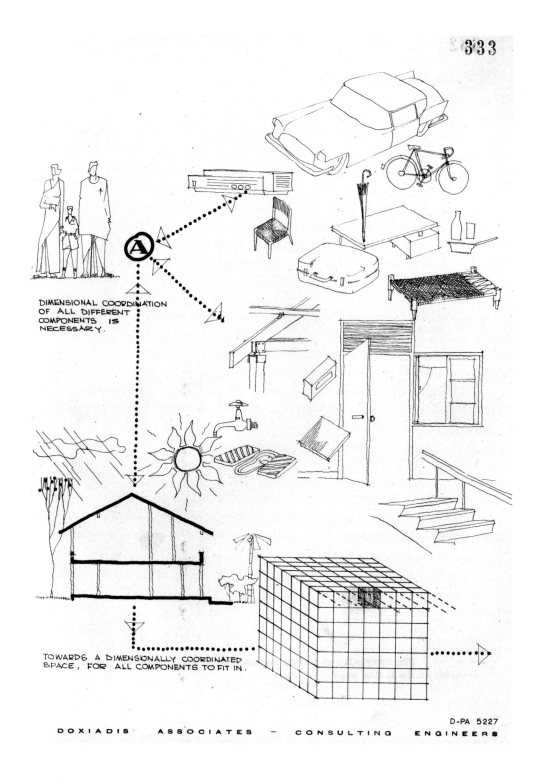

Fig. 8 Study of the "Man-use Modulus."

Associates offered a two-phase process, first by developing a modular prototype that would form a self-regulating system in which the prototype would adapt to different contexts by carrying out the required dimensional adjustment. The system thus conceived was omnipotent, omnidirectional and ubiquitous – and one that could address any level of contingency [Figs. 9–10].

DA meticulously recorded the full spectrum of the construction practices and standards, and the various supply chains of construction materials – both those that were industrially produced, such as cement and streel, and traditional materials, such as bamboo – to determine and derive the Structural-use Modulus. To define the Man-use Modulus, DA researchers presented an "anatomical scale" (mainly from Otto Neurath's ergonomic study of the human body) for architectural space based on the bodily measurement of an average child and adult. Thus, on the basis of the physical dimensions of East Pakistan children and adults, Doxiadis offered a two-phase process: first developing a modular prototype that would form a self-regulating system in which the prototype would mutate in different contexts by adjusting its referential dimensions.

Doxiadis published his study as the report "'New School for East Pakistan': East Pakistan School Building Programme,"[59] which presented the fundamentals of the method through which he derived the moduli, different possible ways of implementing the moduli as prototype buildings and the ways in which the protypes could eventually be used as school buildings.[60] Doxiadis explained that the complete process – from collecting data in the field to producing repeatable prototypes – followed a strict scientific method. The result of this scientific exercise, he proposed, would be the establishment of an economic, human and structural rationale for the standardized prototypes of different categories of school buildings. DA estimated that, despite the limited economic and human resources available, the East Pakistan government could aspire to build 7,000 primary and 500 secondary schools, 350 high schools, and a considerable number of colleges and other academic institutions in the first five-year period of the program.

The structural- and spatial-prototype diagrams presented in DA's modular plan, section and axonometric drawings not only indicated the physical attributes of form and space but also related to the social aspects of education, signaling thereby the democratization of and free access to education. The repeatable prototypes and the diagrammatic presentation of a basic unit that could be reproduced to generate a collection of diverse bodies can be connected to Doxiadis's appropriation of Otto Neurath's method of Isotype drawing.[61] Doxiadis used Isotype drawing and prototypical diagrams as an important technique to make the complex process of architectural ideas legible to the general public, and to create a physical condition that could trigger diverse yet equitable social conditions. Doxiadis's early use of Isotype diagrams featured in the display panels at the exhibition of Greek reconstruction, and since then he had used different forms of Isotype drawing throughout his career.[62] The transformation of verbal and numerical information into visual statements allows for multiple readings and therefore is critical for Isotypes as effective statements of fact from which new theses or plans about the future can be constructed.

Many of DA's housing projects could be considered as a collective Isotype language, not because Doxiadis created an image of identical, repetitive individual houses nor that he simplified the complex cultural meaning of home but because he transformed the "house" as a communicative and didactic mechanism to inform the community as to how to live in an ideal Ekistical environment even in the face of dire economic constraints. Similarly, in the education project for East Pakistan Doxiadis did not suggest that in every instance the ideal prototype would be built in its original form but, on the contrary, he imagined that the standard prototype would introduce new possibilities for free improvisation in response to specific local needs. The final physical manifestation of the school building, therefore, was conceived as a self-contained approximation of an ideal.

The Universalizing Model of Education in East Pakistan

In his investigation into traditional knowledge about and practices of school building, Doxiadis mainly depended on existing buildings for his prime evidence. The scope of his survey and research was based on the conviction that formal and typological studies would reveal the collective desire of society. The formalist premise of Doxiadis's approach to education was grounded in Ekistics theory, in which he theorized the evolution of the built environment as a result of collective social action. But Ekistics in practice is different from Ekistics in theory.[63] While in Ekistics theory the physical evolution of human settlements is akin to natural evolution and is driven by complex cultural and natural forces that can be studied in quantitative terms, the theory presumes that the human and political agencies of change cannot be located or identified precisely. They are objective, universal forces.[64]

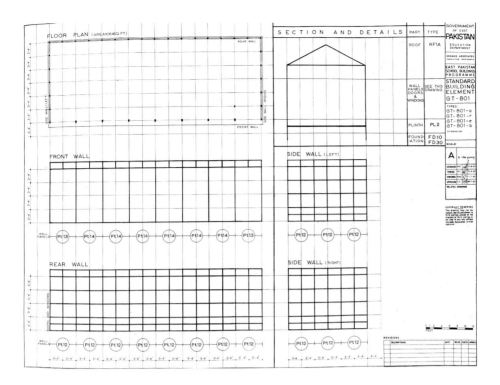

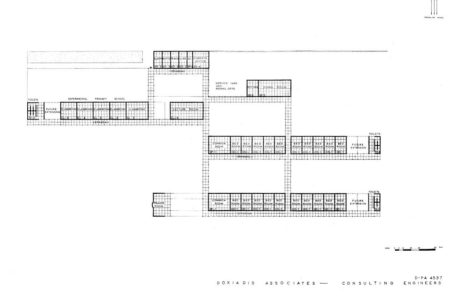

Fig. 9 Standard building element GT – 801, which shows how a set of standard elements can create repeatable modular space.

Fig. 10 Indicative layout of a primary training institute for a higher, secondary-level school building.

In his analysis of Pakistan, Doxiadis located much of this in the unique spatio-geographical circumstances of the region. In reality, however, the agents of change – or the *stakeholders* perhaps – and the nature and course of evolution in the region are very much identifiable and comprehensible, as are the structural conditions and discriminatory policies. For instance, the role of Ayub Khan's authoritarian state and his theory of Basic Democracy, along with the political power dynamic between East and West Pakistan, were among the major factors that caused the decline of public education in East Pakistan. Yet, Doxiadis's methodology of investigation was not equipped to identify let alone address those issues – nor indeed would it have been expedient from a professional standpoint. As a result, the Pakistan central government's approach to solving the education problem in East Pakistan was also formalist, leaving aside the uneven structural relationship between the new nation's two wings, and the other discriminatory policies that led to the downfall of the educational infrastructure in East Pakistan. This approach prevented Doxiadis from factoring in the core problem of education in East Pakistan, which was not formal but political. But as for any architect–planner operating in a political sphere, it often does not do to identify the problem in the commissioners themselves.

As scholars have indicated, the major problem with East Pakistan's educational system lay in the growing disparities and uneven resource allocation between East and West Pakistan schools. Since independence, East Pakistan had experienced a rapid decline in the extent and quality of its educational infrastructure. Within a decade after Partition, West Pakistan received 35,287 additional primary schools, but East Pakistan – despite its larger number of school-going children – had experienced a decline of 902 schools by 1971.[65] The exact reason for this disparity is not well researched. And on the basis of all the other contemporary economic and political inequities between West and East Pakistan, it may be assumed that it was the result of systematic structural discrimination against East Pakistan. Policy-makers were well aware of this decline and of the structural injustice from the reports of the two national commissions on education: the 1959 Sharif Commission and the 1968 Nur Khan Commission. Instead of suggesting any practical program to overcome this disparity, the 1959 National Report of the Commission on National Education defined the objective of education as follows:

> Our education system must play a fundamental part in the preservation of the ideals which lead to the creation of Pakistan and strengthen the concept of it as a unified nation. [...] We lay stress on the necessity to develop an educational programme [...] which will cultivate this sense of unity.[66]

In summary, while in theory and according to his ideology Doxiadis did not wish to consider the state and politics as an integral part of the evolution of the built environment, it is ironic that the assumption derived from Ekistics and its methods was in this case one that meshed so completely with the main thrust of Pakistani state governance.

Another major challenge that demanded serious intervention and planning was how to address the irreconcilable difference between the madrassa education or school system, based on religious teaching, and the "modern" system as established by the colonial government. In his initial survey, Doxiadis was aware of the parallel existence of two systems of education in East Pakistan, but in the calculation and projection of the need for primary schools the issue of madrassas was omitted.[67] The approach of the Pakistan education ministries was exclusive as it omitted the issue of madrassas altogether in any discussion of education reformation and channeled all existing resources into developing only one modern educational system.[68] Restructuring the modern school system was also conceived as part of the broader "rural development program" in Pakistan for which Doxiadis was designing two educational buildings: one in Comilla in East Pakistan and the second one in Rawalpindi in West Pakistan.[69] In general, the educational backwardness of East Pakistan was conceived as a result of the extremely rural condition of the province. In the other words, illiteracy and rurality were imagined as complementary factors, and developing rural environments was thought to be the primary means of educating the East Pakistani population. Comilla Academy was established with financial and technical help from the US government and the Ford Foundation, but the local administrators of the academy took special pride in being independent of US influence and in having evolved in a different way from the typical American community-development approach.[70] And this difference, according to the administrators of the academy, was the result of their focus on research and evidence-based operation with a special focus on reforming the psychology of the East Pakistani people through education.[71] Whether this claim is correct is not the concern here; what is important is how educational reformation was seen as one convoluted problem intertwined with issues related to rural development and how architecture was used to address that problem. Like any other rural-development initiative of its time, Comilla Academy's main goal was to train and develop the capacity of local agents, who would be the technical persons able to advise on agricultural matters but who would, at the same time, act as local educators. The Comilla Academy model emphasized that only by training the community leaders as development agents would true change come about. The country ought to make its future citizens willing and capable of accommodating the state's development missions. Put simply: rural-development initiatives would be useless if the country failed to train its village children in modern education.

The idea of rural development thus coincides with a national pedagogical mission – to teach the rural and seemingly apolitical "masses" to became active yet docile and agreeable citizens. Comilla Academy contrasted with the contemporary model of rural-development initiatives epitomized in the Etawah pilot project in India. Etawah was led by American architect Albert Meyer and supported by technical assistance from USAID and the Ford Foundation. The project's mantra was to awaken the inner entrepreneurial spirit of village populations by encouraging them to engage in site-specific, hands-on, self-help projects.[72] In contrast, Comilla Academy's model was to promote universally applicable development knowledge to trigger national-level development in East Pakistan. The inevitable connection between education and rural development was aptly reflected in a speech delivered by Akhter Hameed Khan, Director of the Comilla Rural Development Academy in East Pakistan, at Michigan State University in 1964:

> About the talk today, I am afraid that what I am going to discuss might appear rather irrelevant to you. [...] I will talk about the problems of education in East Pakistan. Now, I could begin with the ordinary problems such as the lack of resources, [...] But still, these are not the basic problems.[73]

Khan went on to elaborate on what he considered to be the fundamental limitations of the East Pakistan educational system – the chasm between two irreconcilable educational systems.

Doxiadis was aware of the fact that the school-building program was a part of the secularization of public education and the rural-development program. Although he argued that it was the "special and fundamental responsibility of women to develop the character of their children,"[74] the local people in DA's research were considered only as the passive recipients of knowledge. The reports that DA produced did not include any interviews with or record the opinions of the local users – students, parents, administrators or teachers – of the schools.[75] Only the students were consulted, but this was merely for their bodily dimensions to be collected as numeric data in the survey sheets. Education, to the government of East Pakistan, was considered as a question of development and a problem of form: a technicality that could be addressed through the production of building stock and not a problem of policy and politics. Doxiadis, through his scientific study and architectural suggestions, worked as an active partner to reify those claims: in short, Ekistics lent a rhetoric of objectivity to the policies of Ayub Khan.

For instance, Doxiadis suggested an economic model of education, with a graph that showed that the quality of education was reciprocally related to the money invested in it. As a whole, the endeavor of school building took on the form of assembly-line production in which the state resembled the factory and the educators and pupils were the consumers of education. Mary McLeod has explained that architects from the 1920s and 1930s justified their "apolitical" approaches of conflating industrial Taylorism with stewarding social development.[76] In a similar vein, we can consider Doxiadis's approach as a reminiscence of this modern "Taylorist" mindset. Doxiadis also justified his role as an architect in this assembly-line production model as he explained the production process of architectural drawing in terms of numbers and time. He explained that a typical school of modest size would require on average 83 drawings (12 architectural, 11 structural and 60 detail drawings), which meant that the 8,400 schools in his plan would require 697,200 drawings – an impossible task by any standard if one were to consider custom-designing each school.[77] So Doxiadis concluded that standardization was not only the pragmatic solution to this problem but the *only* solution. However, the assembly-line model was not without its didactic mission as the school-building project was often equated with nation building. Doxiadis summarized this as follows:

> In order to meet the basic needs and the high aspirations of the country, it is the aim of the Government of East Pakistan to spare no effort in raising the educational standards of its people by carrying out a number of reforms which will assist all individuals to lead a more productive public life as well as a fuller personal one according to the talents and interests of each one of them.[78]

Doxiadis's approach to developing the modular prototype of the school building was ambivalent, as it aspired to be both site-specific and site-less at the same time. In this project, Doxiadis explored aspects that were both physically and notionally rooted in the landscape and agrarian history, yet free floating and industrially reproducible – prototypes that would provide a regional–spatial armature for cultivating a universal modernism. DA's suggestions for streamlining the production of school buildings in East Pakistan were never realized; the findings and recommendations outlined in their report were also never utilized when, during the mid-1960s, a substantial number of urban and rural schools were built across the nation. With hindsight, we might surmise that the commissioning of the report was part of the central government's strategy to tackle East Pakistan's growing grievances against the discriminatory educational policy being imposed upon them.

1. Faisal Devji, *Muslim Zion: Pakistan as a Political Idea* (Cambridge, MA: Harvard University Press, 2013).
2. Salim M. Khalid and M. Fayaaz Khan, "Pakistan: The State of Education," *Muslim World* 96, no. 2 (2006), 305–22.
3. Naveeda Khan, *Muslim Becoming: Aspiration and Skepticism in Pakistan* (Durham, NC: Duke University Press, 2012).
4. Alan Peshkin, "Education, the Muslim Elite, and the Creation of Pakistan," *Comparative Education Review* 6, no. 2 (October 1962), 152–59.
5. M. Daechsel, "Misplaced Ekistics: Islamabad and the Politics of Urban Development in Pakistan," *South Asian History and Culture* 4, no. 1 (2013), 87–106.
6. Farhat Mahmud, *A History of US–Pakistan Relations* (Lahore: Vanguard Books, 1991).
7. A. Tzonis and A. P. Rodi, *Greece: Modern Architectures in History* (London: Reaktion Books, 2013).
8. Ministry of the Interior (Education Division), *Proceedings of the Pakistan Educational Conference* (Karachi: Government of Pakistan, 1947), 8.
9. N. U. Haque, M. H. Khan and A. R. Kemal, "The Economics Profession in Pakistan: A Historical Analysis [with Comments]," *Pakistan Development Review* 37, no. 4 (1998), 431–52.
10. G. Papanek, *Pakistan's Development, Social Goals and Private Incentives* (Cambridge, MA: Harvard University Press, 1967).
11. Crane worked as a consultant in the United States and twenty-five other countries. He served as a consultant to many government agencies, including the Tennessee Valley Authority, the National Resources Planning Board, the Federal Housing Administration, the United States Housing Authority, Defense Housing, the Housing and Home Finance Agency and the Division of Urban Development of the National Housing Agency.
12. Ford Foundation Grant Files, Reel #862, 863, 864 Grant #54-1, Archives of Rockefeller Foundation, New York.
13. Ibid.
14. B. L. Dean, "Citizenship Education in Pakistani Schools: Problems and Possibilities," *International Journal of Citizenship and Teacher Education* 1, no. 2 (2005), 35–55.
15. (Education Division), M.o.I.E., *Report of the Commission on National Education* (Islamabad: Government of Pakistan, 1959).

16 Ayub Khan, *Friends Not Masters: A Political Autobiography* (Oxford: Oxford University Press, 1967), 11.
17 Haque et al., "The Economics Profession in Pakistan," 431–52.
18 Ijlal Muzaffar, "Boundary Games: Ecochard, Doxiadis, and the Refugee Housing Projects under Military Rule in Pakistan, 1953–1959," in Aggregate Architectural History Collaborative (ed.), *Governing by Design: Architecture, Economy, and Politics in the Twentieth Century* (Pittsburgh, PA: University of Pittsburgh Press, 2012), 142–78.
19 "The Basic Democracies Order, 1959," *The Gazette of Pakistan Extra Ordinary*, October 27, 1959.
20 Ayub Khan, "A Short Appreciation of Present and Future Problems of Pakistan (4 October 1954)," in Nadia Ghani (transcribed and edited), *Field Marshall Mohammad Ayub Khan: A Selection of Talks and Interviews 1964–1967* (Oxford: Oxford University Press, 2008), 291; for a critical discussion about Basic Democracy, see Tahir H. Naqvi, "Nation, Space, and Exception: Pakistan's Basic Democracies Experiment," *Comparative Studies of South Asia, Africa and the Middle East* 33, no. 3 (2013): 279–94.
21 William Cummings, "Pakistan's Plan for 'Basic Democracies'," *World Affairs* 122, no. 4 (1959), 111.
22 Khalid B. Sayeed, "Pakistan's Basic Democracy," *Middle East Journal* 15, no. 3 (1961), 249–63. A total of 6,500 active politicians (3,500 in West and 3,000 in East Pakistan) were disqualified from taking part in elections from the introduction of the Basic Democracy Order in 1959 until December 31, 1966, following the accusation that these politicians were "corrupt."
23 Daniel Immerwahr, *Thinking Small: The United States and the Lure of Community Development* (Cambridge, MA: Harvard University Press, 2018).
24 Victoria d'Auria, "Retracing the Emergence of a Human Settlement Approach: Designing in, from and with Contexts of Development," in Farhan Karim (ed.), *The Routledge Companion to Architecture and Social Engagement* (New York: Routledge, 2018), 49–63; Kim De Raedt, "Tracing the History of Socially Engaged Architecture: School Building as Development Aid in Postcolonial Sub-Saharan Africa," in ibid., 71–86; Nancy Kwak, *A World of Homeowners: American Power and the Politics of Housing Aids* (Chicago: University of Chicago Press, 2015).
25 By politics I mean the power struggle between different groups and classes. See Vincent Lyon-Callo and Susan Brin Hyatt, "The Neoliberal State and the Depoliticization of Poverty: Activist Anthropology and 'Ethnography from Below'," *Urban Anthropology and Studies of Cultural Systems and World Economic Development* 32, no. 2, Anthropology and Political Engagement (Summer 2003), 175–204.
26 Hannah Arendt, "The Crisis in Education" (1961), in Arendt, *Between Past and Future: Six Exercises in Political Thought* (London: Penguin Books, 1993), 173–95.
27 Andrew Hartman, *Education and the Cold War: The Battle for the American School* (London: Palgrave Macmillan, 2012); Matthew Levin, *Cold War University: Madison and the New Left in the Sixties* (Madison: University of Wisconsin Press, 2013); Noam Chomsky, Laura Nader, Richard C. Lewontin and Richard Ohman, *The Cold War & the University: Toward an Intellectual History of the Postwar Years* (New York: The New Press, 1998).
28 Matthew K. Shannon, *Losing Hearts and Minds: American–Iranian Relations and International Education during the Cold War* (Ithaca, NY: Cornell University Press, 2017).
29 Ibid.
30 Burak Erdim, *Landed Internationals: Planning Cultures, the Academy, and the Making of the Modern Middle East* (Austin: University of Texas Press, 2020).
31 Tim Livsey, *Nigeria's University Age: Reframing Decolonisation and Development* (London: Palgrave Macmillan, 2017).
32 Inderjeet Parmer, *Foundations of the American Century: The Ford, Carnegie, and Rockefeller Foundations in the Rise of American Power* (New York: University of Columbia Press, 2012).
33 Ibid.
34 Poromesh Acharya, "Bengali 'Bhadralok' and Educational Development in 19th Century Bengal," *Economic and Political Weekly* 30, no. 13 (April 1995), 670–73; "Education," Banglapedia: National Encyclopedia of Bangladesh, http://en.banglapedia.org/index.php?title=Education (accessed May 6, 2024); Nilanjana Paul, "Muslim Education and Communal Conflict in Colonial Bengal: British Policies and Muslim Responses from 1854 to 1947," Ph.D. dissertation, Eberly College of Arts and Sciences at West Virginia University.
35 Peter D. Bell, "The Ford Foundation as a Transnational Actor," *International Organization* 25, no. 3, Transnational Relations and World Politics (Summer 1971), 465–78; J. Donald Kingsley, "The Ford Foundation and Education in Africa," *African Studies Bulletin* 9, no. 3 (December 1966), 1–7.
36 Peshkin, "Education, the Muslim Elite," 152–59; A. Peshkin, "The Shaping of Secondary Education in Pakistan," *History of Education Quarterly* 3, no. 1 (1963), 4–18; David J. Roof, "Problems of Common Interest: The Shaping of Education in Pakistan, 1970–2014," *Pakistan Journal of Commerce and Social Sciences* 9, no. 1 (2015), 35–51; A. H. Khan, "Education in Pakistan: Fifty Years of Neglect," *Pakistan Development Review* 36, no. 4 (1998), 647–67.
37 Doxiadis Archives, "Pakistan," vol. 4, Diary DOX-PP 40, January–February 1955, 134.
38 Ibid.
39 Markus Daechsel, *Islamabad and the Politics of International Development* (Cambridge: Cambridge University Press, 2015), 90–105.

40 Doxiadis Archives, "Pakistan," vol. 4, Diary DOX-PP 40, January–February 1955, 48.
41 Ibid., 134.
42 Ibid., 144.
43 Ibid., 146 (emphasis in original).
44 Doxiadis Diaries, vol. 128, "Pakistan Reports, East Pakistan School Building Programme," 1962, unpaginated.
45 Ibid.
46 Ibid.
47 Ibid.
48 Ali Riaz, "Madrassah Education in Pre-colonial and Colonial South Asia," *Journal of Asian and African Studies* 46, no. 1 (2010), 69–86; see also Ali Riaz, *Faithful Education: Madrassahs in South Asia* (New Brunswick, NJ: Rutgers University Press, 2008).
49 Barbara Daly Metcalf, *Islamic Revival in British India: Deoband, 1860–1900* (Karachi: Karachi Royal Book Company, 2004).
50 Barbara Daly Metcalf, *Bihisti Zewar: Perfecting Woman (Maulana Ashraf Ali Thanwi's Bihisti Zewar, A Partial Translation with Commentary)* (Lahore: Idara-e-Islamiat, 1997); Faisal Devji, "Apologetic Modernity," *Modern Intellectual History* 4, no. 1 (2007), 61–76.
51 For a review of colonial pedagogy, see Indra Sengupta and Daud Ali (eds), *Knowledge Production, Pedagogy, and Institutions in Colonial India* (London: Palgrave Macmillan, 2011).
52 For a critical history of the PWD shaping the built environment of colonial and post-colonial South Asia, see Peter Scriver and Amit Srivastava, *India: Modern Architectures in History* (New York: Reaktion Books, 2015).
53 Doxiadis Associates, "'New School for East Pakistan': East Pakistan School Building Programme," *DA Monthly Bulletin* 52 (February 1963), unpaginated.
54 Doxiadis Associates, preliminary reports "East Pakistan School Building Program," DOX-PA 162–67, 174, January–June 1962, vol. 127, no. 23658 (emphasis in original).
55 Preliminary reports, Dimensional coordinates, 2.
56 Ibid.
57 Ibid.
58 Ibid., 1.
59 Doxiadis Associates, "'New School for East Pakistan'."
60 The newly formed Education Commission of Pakistan (1959) considered the general improvement of secondary education to be an inevitable part of tertiary-education reform. A national report on the development of engineering education mentioned that secondary-school teachers "consider that no attempt to improve the quality of students will be completely successful unless the level of teaching in secondary schools is substantially raised. This observation […] requires careful consideration as in the post-war field, engineering without a good general education [is] apt to prove a failure." See Pakistan Commission on National Education, *Report, January–August, 1959, Department of Education, Government of East Pakistan* (Karachi: Manager of Publication Pakistan, 1960), 5.
61 Neurath's conception of an "Isotype" (International System of Typographic Picture Education) language was founded on the idea that a sign is not arbitrary but is instead rooted in the world, as the Isotype figure is pictorial but not realistic. For Neurath, of the principal didactic purposes of Isotype was "the teaching of how to argue" (Kostas Tsiambaos, "Isotype Diagrams from Neurath to Doxiadis," *Architectural Research Quarterly* 16, no. 1 (2012), 49–57; Sophie Hochhaeusl, "Otto Neurath – The Other Modern: Proposing a Socio-political Map for Urbanism," M.A. dissertation, Cornell University, 2010). Although contemporary CIAM (Congrès Internationaux d'Architecture Moderne) architects were drawn to the visual appeal of Neurath's Isotype, architects in general were not interested in his social method – the transformation and generalization of social information – because they saw Neurath's language as incompatible with architectural communication, which is very specific and cannot be generalized.
62 During the German occupation of Greece in 1942, Doxiadis joined the Ministry of Public Works as a civil servant. Doxiadis and his team began gathering data on war damage that included bombing by the Allied forces, sabotage by guerillas and destruction by the occupying forces. The data were passed on to the National Resistance Group known as Hephaestus, and from there via Turkey to the Allies in the Middle East. On October 12, 1944, the Germans withdrew from Athens and in 1946 Doxiadis's data were published under the title *The Sacrifice of Greece in the Second World War* in association with a traveling exhibition to London and Paris. The exhibition attracted much attention from the US press. The *New York Times* published a story and CBS Radio interviewed Doxiadis. In his public appearance in the US, Doxiadis argued that without a global master plan for a post-war global reconstruction there was little hope for the future of humankind. He was arguing for an international and coherent global development strategy (Alexandros-Andreas Kyrtsis (ed.), *Constantinos A. Doxiadis, Texts, Design Drawings, Settlements* (Athens: Ikaros, 2006), 337–57).
63 Daechsel, "Misplaced Ekistics," 87–106.
64 Constantinos Doxiadis, *Ekistics: An Introduction to the Science of Human Settlements* (London: Hutchinson, 1968), 44–56.
65 Mohammad Niaz Asadullah, "Educational Disparity in East and West Pakistan, 1947–71: Was East Pakistan Discriminated Against?" *Bangladesh Development Studies* 33, no. 3 (September 2010), 1–46.
66 Department of Education, Government of East Pakistan, *Commission on National Education*, 10.
67 J. W. Thomas, *Rural Public Works and East Pakistan's Development*, Harvard University Development

Advisory Service Economic Development Report (Cambridge, MA: Development Advisory Service, Center for International Affairs, Harvard University, 1968).

68 Doxiadis Archives, "Pakistan Reports, East Pakistan School Building Program," DOX-PA 162–67, 174, January–June 1962, vol. 127, no. 23658.

69 Farhan Karim, "Interpreting Rural: Doxiadis vis-à-vis East Pakistan," *South Asia Chronicle* 9 (2019), 243–80.

70 Harvey M. Choldin, "An Organizational Analysis of Rural Development Projects at Comilla, East Pakistan," *Economic Development and Cultural Change* 20, no. 4 (1972), 671–90; Harvey M. Choldin, "The Development Project as Natural Experiment: The Comilla, Pakistan, Projects," *Economic Development and Cultural Change* 17, no. 4 (1969), 483–500.

71 Arthur Franklin Raper, *Rural Development in Action: The Comprehensive Experiment at Comilla, East Pakistan* (Ithaca, NY: Cornell University Press, 1970); Howard Schuman, *Economic Development and Individual Change: A Social-Psychological Study of the Comilla Experiment in Pakistan* (Cambridge, MA: Center for International Affairs, Harvard University, 1967); Alex Inkeles, "Harvard Project on the Sociocultural Aspects of Development," *Sociological Inquiry* 39 (1969), 100–2.

72 Farhan Karim, *Of Greater Dignity than Riches: Austerity and Housing Design in India* (Pittsburgh, PA: University of Pittsburgh Press, 2019).

73 Akhter Hameed Khan, *Rural Development in East Pakistan: Speeches by Akhter Hameed Khan* (East Lansing, MI: Asian Studies Center, Michigan State University, 1964), 1.

74 Doxiadis Archives, "Pakistan Reports 1961," vol. 99; "Pakistan Reports 1962," DOX-PA 183–84, vol. 128, 165.

75 Doxiadis Archives, "Pakistan Reports 1961," vol. 99; "Pakistan Reports 1962," DOX-PA 183–84, vol. 128.

76 Mary McLeod, "'Architecture or Revolution': Taylorism, Technocracy, and Social Change," *Art Journal* 43, no. 2 (1983), 132–47.

77 Doxiadis Archives, "Pakistan Reports 1961," vol. 99; "Pakistan Reports 1962," DOX-PA 183–84, vol. 128.

78 Ibid., 1.

Shaping Ekistics
From Baghdad to Detroit
Lefteris Theodosis

Introduction

Flying from Karachi to Baghdad we stop in the evening at 8 o'clock at the airport of Dhahran of Saudi Arabia for which a special visa is required. We enter into an air-conditioned room and then to an air-conditioned bar and soda-fountain which is run by Americans selling American products, breakfast ice-cream and so on. Everything is clean as in the U.S.A. [...] It is characteristic that the poor fellah of the arabic desert who has been struggling a few years ago for survival is now able to eat, and pay for it with his own profits, at an American restaurant. [...] I wonder where do these arabs belong? What is their world?[1]

It is August 29, 1955. Constantinos A. Doxiadis is on his way to Baghdad to discuss with the Prime Minister, Nuri al-Said, the National Housing Program of Iraq (NHPI). The project is part of a great modernization effort driven by oil revenues, promoted by the monarch who would be the last of the Hashemite line, King Faisal II, and orchestrated by the newly established Development Board.[2] Among the national development schemes launched are large infrastructure interventions (roads, sewage, transportation, irrigation and flood control) but also grandiose architectural projects destined for the embellishment of Baghdad.[3] Projects authored by renowned architects such as Frank Lloyd Wright, Walter Gropius, Le Corbusier, Josep Lluís Sert, Alvar Aalto, Gio Ponti and Willem Dudok, to name just a few, aim to put Baghdad on the map of modern capitals.[4] Compared with those "star-architects," Constantinos Doxiadis is relatively unknown; nonetheless, his connection to Jacob L. Crane – a housing expert and head of the international office of the US Housing and Home Finance Agency – and his exceptional record of administrating the Greek post-war reconstruction and recovery program open the doors to the commission for him.[5] The NHPI becomes the first large-scale project of Doxiadis Associates (DA), which was established only two years earlier in 1953. It is the project that will solidify Doxiadis's reputation as a planning expert and boost DA from a small group of architects and engineers to become an international organization of planning and consultancy services.[6] The working methods, housing types and urban-planning models used thereafter in emblematic DA projects all over the world will unfold for the first time within the NHPI. The Iraqi commission is also Doxiadis's first opportunity to plan an Arab metropolis.

In March 1964, Doxiadis travels to Detroit to initiate a partnership with the Detroit Edison Company and Wayne State University on a planning research program for Michigan. He is endorsed by the chairman of the Edison Company Board, Walker L. Cisler, a Marshall Plan acquaintance and an expert in power networks who contributed significantly to the rebuilding of electrical power plants in war-torn Europe.[7] At the initial stage, DA is tasked with inquiring into the regional expansion of the company's energy-infrastructure system; however, Doxiadis seizes the opportunity to broaden the scope of the study and to propose strategies for urban and regional development.[8] The $3 million Urban Detroit Area (UDA) project becomes Doxiadis's greatest challenge in North America: it lasts for more than five years, is financed by one of the biggest companies in Michigan and draws on the new-towns incentives promoted by President Lyndon Johnson's New Communities Act of 1968.[9] And yet, the UDA will prove to be one of the failed attempts to revitalize Detroit after the destructive and bloody 1967 riots.

The NHPI and the UDA are turning points in Doxiadis's professional career: the first is where the extraordinary trajectory of DA starts, while the latter marks the beginning of the company's withdrawal from the international arena. In the period between the two programs, the Athens Center of Ekistics (ACE) is established to promote and debate Doxiadis's ideas at the international level through research and educational programs, the journal *Ekistics* and the celebrated Delos Symposia.[10] Ekistics evolves into an international movement with the participation of distinguished intellectuals and prominent experts who influence Doxiadis's thinking. Slowly but surely, it embraces emerging epistemological paradigms, such as the systems approach to planning and environmentalism, while Doxiadis makes use of techno-scientific metaphors in his writings to describe the city as an evolving biological organism.[11]

Juxtaposing Doxiadis's housing program in the developing but politically unstable Iraq with the comprehensive strategy unfolded to guide Detroit's growth, this study discusses the application of Ekistic concepts and models in different latitudes and contexts. Both projects interlace with Doxiadis's efforts to preserve local identities in the increasingly globalized world he described as the Ecumenopolis. It is against that background that the chapter reflects on the transformation of Doxiadis's planning philosophy from a pragmatic and hands-on approach to a more systemic and technocratic understanding of urbanization problems.

Planning the Steppe of Iraq

The NHPI was a fairly complex program that integrated policies and projects of differing natures, scopes and scales. It was developed to meet critical housing needs across the country, exacerbated by rural-to-urban migration amid nation building and Cold War politics in the Middle East. As might be understood from Doxiadis's discussions with Iraqi officials, as depicted in his travel diaries, the program was adjusted to cope with the requests of those officials who often raised competing demands according to their personal agendas.[12] The proposed projects were the eventual outcome of Doxiadis's constant negotiation both in administrative circles and in situ at the construction site. Rather than a "closed" program, the NHPI is best understood as a work in progress that navigated through the structural changes wrought by the modernization campaign of the Hashemite monarchy. While a detailed analysis of the DA projects in Iraq is beyond the scope of this study, it is important to examine how Doxiadis responded to the manifold challenges according to his expertise and experience while experimenting with construction materials, building systems and organizational and management methods.

When DA started to work in Iraq, several housing projects were already under construction across the country. These were promoted by the Iraqi Ministries of Social Affairs and Public Works, quasi-public transportation companies or private ones such as the Iraq Petroleum Company (IPC), albeit not always successfully. The first DA assignments – classified as technical assistance projects (TAPs) – involved consultancy services and technical assistance to third parties or direct work on the completion of other contractors' housing schemes. Doxiadis seized the opportunity to point out the faults of the pilot projects of the British company Wimpey, and to propose alternative solutions suitable for tropical climates.[13] Over lengthy discussions and site visits, he gained the trust of the Iraqi officials and soon DA was undertaking numerous housing projects from scratch, including modern houses for government officials, mass housing for low-income communities, settlements for industrial workers and rural villages for relocating populations displaced by agricultural, flood control and irrigation policies. Depending on the case, DA also provided the basic infrastructure or community facilities plans. For the most part, these schemes were catalogued as general housing projects (GHP), a category that came to include related DA activities such as the foundation of the Ekistic Center in western Baghdad for conducting research on building materials. All projects, however, came under the umbrella of the National Housing Program of Iraq, which proved to be an early stage in the exceptional trajectory of DA's international practice.

As reflected in the structure of the program, time was the most decisive factor in responding to the critical housing challenges. Since the late 1940s, massive protests and widespread strikes had put the country's pro-Western government on the ropes.[14] The demonstrations were driven by demands for social and economic justice, and fueled by the anti-colonial sentiments spreading throughout the region. Under the looming threat of another public uprising, the Iraqi establishment was compelled to provide housing for rural-to-urban migrants and the multi-ethnic, often nomadic, populations that settled in the so-called *sarifas*. These were precarious reed and mud-hut settlements that mushroomed both on the outskirts and in the open spaces of the old city of Baghdad despite being vulnerable to floods and government interventions alike [Fig. 1].[15]

As Doxiadis explained to Crane, public pressure for housing was growing stronger and thus "it would be impossible to tell to the public of Iraq that they have hired housing experts who will come back in 12 months' time with some big volumes on housing but without having built anything yet."[16] Hence, he proposed a twofold strategy to address both the immediate housing crisis and long-term planning objectives. On the one hand, the Special Program of Action (SPA) contained fast-track projects meant to meet the needs of – but also to mitigate the political risks of – an impoverished

Fig. 1 Reed- and mud-hut settlements in the *sarifa* area of Baghdad, c. 1956.

population. Slum-clearance projects and the resettlement of rural migrants in low-cost housing communities built from scratch were considered an effective measure. In some cases, *sarifa*-dwelling families were resettled in aided self-help housing schemes, where they were given a constructed nucleus with basic sanitation facilities and the possibility of extending the housing unit over time in accordance with their financial capacity. Moreover, the SPA also included the Experimental Housing Program (EHP), which was principally implemented in western Baghdad.[17] This involved the construction of housing units for occupants of different income levels, and explored three main avenues: the first focused on the building process per se and the second examined the application of different building materials and construction systems, while the third concerned the organization of competitions for contractors willing to undertake construction based on DA housing types and plans. Among the participating companies was the American International Basic Economy Corporation (IBEC), which applied its own cast-in-place concrete system in mass-produced prefabricated housing

Shaping Ekistics

schemes.[18] Essentially, the EHP proposed a trial-and-error approach in which the objective was to calculate and narrow down costs and time expenditure in mass housing.

The second leg of Doxiadis's strategy was the five-year Basic Foundation Program (BFP) which, as a rule, included master plans for other cities (Basra, Mosul, Amara, Kerbala, Kirkuk, Nejef, Kufa, Suleimaniya, Erbil, Diwaniya, Kut and Nasiriya), rural development projects and community facilities schemes, as well as administration projects. These projects unfolded in parallel with the DA work in Baghdad; however, they were meant to both decentralize and diversify the NHPI by focusing on rural areas where housing had to be developed in tandem with agricultural policies, flood control, irrigation and drainage measures. For example, the Greater Musayyib (or Mussayib) project (1957–1958) examined an area of 75,000 hectares south of Baghdad where DA were asked to build settlements for the relocation of rural families. The plan featured hexagonal patterns centered around the city of Hilla, undeniably indebted to Walter Christaller's central place theory principles and in support of Doxiadis's explorations of "scientific" planning methodologies.[19] Indeed, this is one of the first DA projects where Doxiadis's fascination with statistics and mathematics, and the need to quantify even natural phenomena (in this case, the prevailing winds in the region) is manifested [Fig. 2].[20]

Basically, the BFP program set the mid-term goals of the NHPI and was the backbone of the DA planning campaign in Iraq. Its main objective was to create "a suitable framework for the further development of all the complex activities constituting the national housing effort" and lay the foundations for a twenty-five-year National Housing Charter.[21] The twofold strategy (SPA-BFP) was welcomed by the minister of development, who responded to Doxiadis that only such a double program could save the country.[22] The immediate response and hands-on approach of the SPA projects would give the Iraqi government a chance to justify its modernization efforts in the eyes of the *sarifa* dwellers, while a comprehensive housing program would lay the foundations for further socioeconomic development. Considering the above, part of Doxiadis's discussions with Iraqi ministers focused on the ownership of the prospective housing units and on the need to develop a qualified and competent labor force. In point of fact, the scarcity of skilled workers was one of the major constraints on housing construction on a massive scale, the other one being the shortage of building materials. As an

AVERAGE NUMBER OF DAYS PER MONTH WITH WINDS BLOWING FROM SPECIFIED DIRECTIONS AT 0500, 1100 AND 1600 GMT.

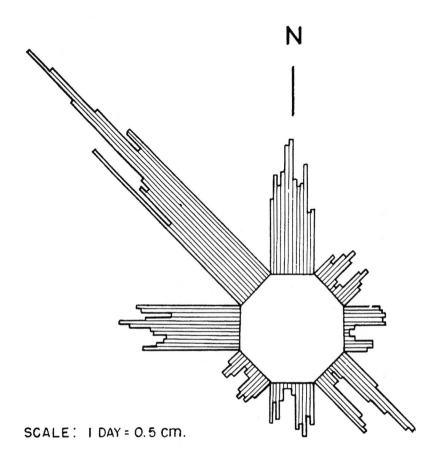

SCALE: 1 DAY = 0.5 cm.

NOTES:
1. Data of the years 1908 - 1913 from Babylon meteorological Station.
2. Projecting from each side of the octagon are twelve columns representing the twelve months of the year working round clockwise from January to December.

Fig. 2 Graphic representation of the prevailing winds in the Greater Musayyib region based on statistical data.

Shaping Ekistics

answer, Doxiadis suggested systematizing traditional building practices for producing basic building materials (e.g. clay bricks) and importing prefabricated components (e.g. door and window frames), whereas to speed up construction Crane proposed the use of mechanical methods and standardized systems.[23] Moreover, to meet the critical demand for construction workers Doxiadis proposed the establishment of vocational schools for building tradespeople such as masons, plumbers and electricians [Fig. 3].[24]

Training a new generation of workers was an ambitious goal that perfectly matched the long-term modernization promises of national emancipation and independence described by Doxiadis as "a genuine national life which will be created and developed by the Iraqis themselves."[25] To his credit, the first school was already operating in western Baghdad by 1957 and had overall a positive impact considering both the number of students it educated and the connections it established between construction labor, material progress and a new pedagogical tradition.[26] While similar concepts had already been promoted by the IPC and the British government in Kirkuk, these reflected a colonial and restrictive attitude towards Iraqi oil workers.[27]

In January 1960, DA published the Master Plan of Baghdad, integrating constructed and ongoing projects in a comprehensive scheme that, for the first time, featured key Ekistic concepts – namely, the Dynapolis urban-development pattern and the Human Sector (HS) neighborhood-unit pattern.[28] Doxiadis had already started working on the master plan in 1958, possibly as spin-off of the NHPI and with a view to superseding the standing plan of the British firm Minoprio, Spencely and MacFarlane, which was heavily criticized by Iraqi officials for lacking a solid empirical base.[29] Doxiadis himself considered the Minoprio plan to be of "low quality" and did "not expect new ideas [from] this team" – hence, the drafting of a new master plan seemed a good opportunity to present Ekistics as an innovative approach to the urbanization challenges of Baghdad.[30] Be that as it may, on July 14, 1958, the Nasser-inspired Free Officers movement headed by General Abd al-Karim Qasim overthrew the Hashemite monarchy in a violent coup that brought the Pan-Arab revolutionist movement into Iraq under the flag of a newborn republic. In the aftermath, a great portion of the development board's programs was put on hold or canceled, while most of the foreign companies and consultants were forced to abandon the country.[31] The Greek firm was among the ones that were granted permission to stay, though only for a short time: by the second half of 1959, DA had

Fig. 3 Cover of the booklet *Vocational Schools for Building Trades*, March 1957.

handed over to the Iraqi authorities the responsibility for implementing the housing schemes and slum-clearance projects that were in progress.[32] Among these were the opening of the Army Canal, a fairly large infrastructure project that initiated the urbanization of eastern Baghdad, where the notorious Sadr City (originally known as Al-Thawra) lies. While the former project is scarcely attributed to DA, the latter has become synonymous with "weaponized" architecture and the failure of planning and modernizing Iraqi cities according to a Western model.[33]

Planning the Motor City

Constantinos Doxiadis's reputation as a housing expert grew rapidly after the NHPI projects, and soon DA was contracted in Syria, Lebanon, Libya and, most notably, Pakistan, where the firm planned among other projects the new capital city, Islamabad. By the mid-1960s, DA had already established branch offices in Washington, DC (1959), Rawalpindi (1959), Accra and Philadelphia (1960), Addis Ababa (1961), Takoradi in Ghana (1963), Rio de Janeiro and Detroit (1964), paving the way for an extraordinary track record of spatial-development programs commissioned by both public bodies and private organizations. Interestingly enough, as in the case of Iraq, the DA projects in the Middle East, South Asia and West Africa took place against the background of rivalry between global socialism and Western-driven modernization.[34] Doxiadis, who had been an outspoken advocate of European cooperation under US auspices since the post-war reconstruction period, saw his career taking off with the help of a remarkable network of US experts – and in some cases aided by Ford Foundation dollars.[35] Nonetheless, he had a proper planning philosophy and a globalization vision that he tirelessly promoted vis-à-vis the urban crisis. His ardent desire was to spread the Ekistic word beyond the developing world to the center of decision-making – that is, the United States.[36] Premised on the belief that urbanization challenges were similar across the globe, he felt that the planning experience gained in the East might "be useful to many Western problems" and he expressed his confidence that "certain principles and techniques" of his organization could contribute to the regeneration of the American city.[37]

The first steps were taken with the master plan for Washington, DC (1958–1959), the planning and design of 323 housing units in Cincinnati, Ohio (1960–1962) and the Eastwick Philadelphia scheme (1960–1962) marketed by the Director of the Philadelphia City Planning Commission, Ed

Bacon, as the largest redevelopment project of the century.³⁸ The last-named project sought the development of a racially mixed community based on a joint proposal of the Reynolds Metals Company, the Samuel and Henry Berger construction firm and DA, which drew up a master plan featuring clusters of single-family units, garden apartments, a network of streets, cul-de-sacs and parking areas, a shopping center and a pedestrian esplanade. In 1960, the National Association of Housing and Redevelopment Officials (NAHRO) asked Doxiadis to present his views on urban renewal and "to develop a set of principles and criteria by which renewal agencies [could] appraise their progress and formulate programs for the future."³⁹ To the disappointment of these officials, the outcome of this Ford Foundation-funded study was detached from the socioeconomic conditions of America's slums and ghettos, and advanced – rather unfortunately at a time when participatory community planning was gaining ground – the centralized and comprehensive approach of Ekistics as a remedy for the ills of a so-called typical urban renewal area, or TURA.⁴⁰

At the same time, the UDA opened a window of opportunity for Doxiadis to carry out his large-scale vision for planning the contemporary city as an integral part of a system of urbanized areas. Actually, the general guidelines behind this vision originated from the Great Lakes Megalopolis (GLM) research project, which examined the formation of urban clusters in an area stretching from Milwaukee–Chicago to Detroit–Cleveland–Pittsburgh–Buffalo and towards the Canadian Toronto–Montreal–Quebec City cluster. This concept was in accordance with the seminal "Megalopolis" of the French geographer Jean Gottmann (1961); however, Doxiadis went even further and considered the emergence of such systems as steps in a process of urbanization towards the inevitable worldwide web of settlements, otherwise called Ecumenopolis.⁴¹ That said, the UDA provides a good example of how Doxiadis understood not only the planning of a city in the context of his planetary urbanization theory but also how Ekistics was applied as both a systemic methodology of analysis and a set of tools for planning development. More specifically, in relation to the latter, the UDA stands out as the testing ground for the Ekistic mission of planning a multidimensional city that would preserve the human scale in harmony with technological advances. Throughout his career, Doxiadis pointed out with fervor the alterations the "machine" brought to everyday life. To that end, he often used "the story of a square," which describes the transformation of a public plaza where he used to play as a boy after the cutting down of trees and the paving of streets.[42] As car accidents rose and environmental pollution worsened, the Greek planner called for neighborhoods to be shielded from the automobile's malicious effects and for the human scale to be preserved in the world's ever-growing cities.

As would be expected, the Motor City was the perfect setting for Doxiadis's confrontation with the automobile. Both the unparalleled economic growth and the disintegration of Detroit were intrinsically connected to the development and decentralization of the production line of the "Big Three" – namely, the corporate giants Ford, General Motors and Chrysler.[43] In fact, the very idea of planning the American city was subject to the automobile's "voracious appetite for land," as typified by the 1956 Interstate Highway Act, which fostered suburbia while impacting downtown areas.[44] In Detroit especially, the construction of the Chrysler freeway (Interstate 75) brought forced evictions and demolitions to the heart of the African American neighborhoods Black Bottom and Paradise Valley. The subsequent urban-renewal programs – otherwise nicknamed "Black Removal" – largely failed to accomplish their stated objectives and further aggravated the crisis. Eventually, anger at deep-rooted and long-standing injustice, inequalities and racially based economics exploded after police raided a speakeasy bar on the Near West Side in July 1967, bringing about one of the bloodiest riots in US history.

In Doxiadis's eyes, the decline of Detroit was intrinsically connected to the predominance of the automobile over public space, and yet he had a peculiar way of interpreting the problem. In a series of chronological maps, he depicted the deterioration of the city's central business district (CBD) as the outcome of the increasing volume of urban space "devoured" by freeways and parking lots [Fig. 4].[45]

The "footprint" of the automobile had increased to such an extent, Doxiadis explained, that it dispersed the urban fabric, dismantled community life and eventually drove away upper-class residents.[46] Consequently, he argued, their empty houses were converted to apartments and rented to middle- or low-class workers, leading to socioeconomic decline and ghettoization. Instead of looking into the socioeconomic challenges of the urban crisis reflected both in housing policies and everyday practices (e.g. the Federal Housing Association protocols or bank "redlining," which excluded racial minorities and Black people from receiving mortgages and

YEAR 1916   Fig. 203   YEAR 1950   Fig. 204

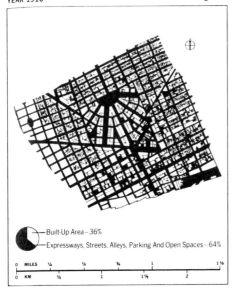
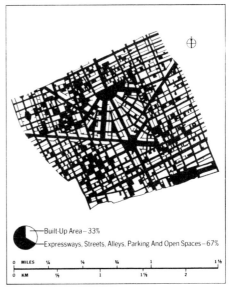

YEAR 1960   Fig. 205   YEAR 1969   Fig. 206

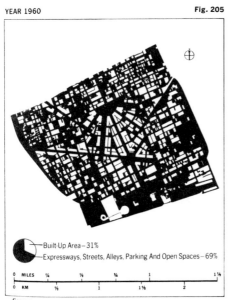
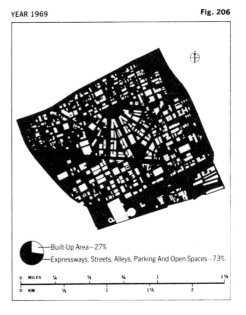

Source:
Baist's, *Real Estate Atlas, Surveys of Detroit and Suburbs, 1916*. City of Detroit, Department of Streets and Traffic, *Off Street Parking Facilities, 1950, 1960 and 1968*.

Fig. 4 Evolution of physical decline in Detroit's central business district (CBD) 1916–1969.

home improvement funding), Doxiadis interpreted this "white flight" as the outcome of the predominance of the car and a defective transportation system.[47] Moreover, to illustrate the capital outflow and the deepening of these central areas' decline, Doxiadis used an analysis diagram that depicted the per capita income of the inhabitants in relation to their area's distance from the CBD. In what would today be considered politically incorrect language, he dubbed central Detroit a "bottomless pit," while, after calculating the speed of the increasing poverty by comparing the curves of 1949 and 1959, he announced to Cisler that "the bottomless pit widens at the speed of 1.5 inch every hour" [Fig. 5].[48]

Both the aforementioned diagrams are characteristic of Doxiadis's quantitative and rational approach, which somehow brushed off social and racial concerns. Prompted by his faith in planning, the UDA analysis focused on the spatial aspects of Detroit's decline while vastly oversimplifying its complexity. In his eyes, even the 1967 riots were a symptom of a crisis originating in "territorial forces," while segregation was not just racial or economic but principally originated from the differences between urban and rural areas.[49] If Detroit's urban ills were to be understood as the outcome solely of spatial disorders, then a scientifically developed urban and regional system might, after all, bring order to chaos.[50]

Indeed, Doxiadis's proposal was the outcome of a systemic methodology, forecasting large-scale models and projections of trends – altogether, a laborious process carried out with the support of the Doxiadis Associates Computer Center, or DACC.[51] It was selected out of 49 million alternatives generated by the combination of planning parameters (e.g. population distribution, densities, transportation networks and speeds of transportation and maximum travel time), with basic assumptions for locating new urban centers, industrial poles or transportation nodes (ports, airports, etc.). For the selection of the optimal solution, then, Doxiadis applied the so-called Isolation of Dimensions and Elimination of Alternatives (IDEA) method. This was a methodological funnel for comparing, evaluating and eliminating alternatives in eight steps, "progressing from a theoretical number of tens of millions of alternatives to some tens, a few and finally one" [Fig. 6].[52]

The proposed solution, called the "Concept-Plan," was a comprehensive development strategy that promoted actions "at all scales, on all types of structures and functions" in three phases.[53] Forty programs were meant to be pursued by a coalition of public agencies and institutions thereafter,

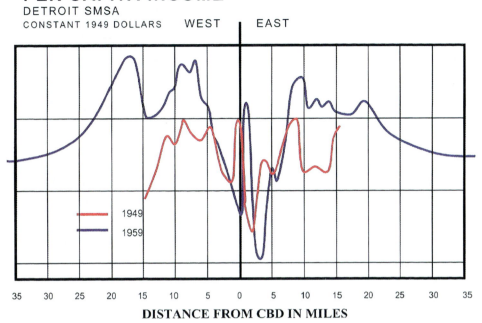

mobilizing private developers and stakeholders willing to support the regeneration of Detroit. According to Doxiadis, this was an "interrelated system" of actions that had to be carried out as a whole and as planned. The UDA prioritized five key programs that were expected to contribute to the solution of the largest number of identified problems and thereafter to pave the way for the implementation of the Concept-Plan. Apart from the first one, which concerned the revitalization of Detroit's center, the other four programs were large-scale interventions and infrastructure projects of regional scope. For example, in order to balance the "urban forces sprawling uncontrollably throughout the area" the UDA proposed the creation of a twin city for Detroit in St. Clair County (some 100 kilometers from the CBD) and of ten new towns located strategically in the broader region.[54] To facilitate commuting and commerce, it put forward a transportation system that included the development of a major east–west international corridor to directly connect Detroit's new twin city with Canada.

Fig. 5 Analysis chart showing per capita income in relation to distance from Detroit's CBD, a situation dubbed the "bottomless pit."

Shaping Ekistics

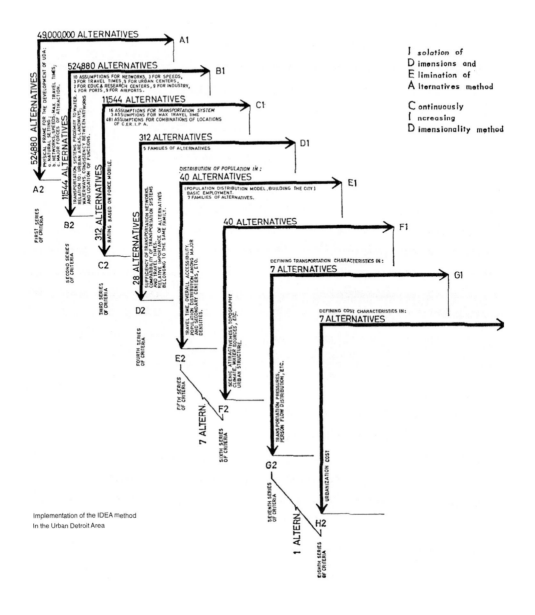

Fig. 6 The IDEA and CID methodology funnel used to select the optimal solution from a pool of 49 million alternatives.

The rationale behind such massive investments was unprecedented regional growth, which Doxiadis intended would transform the Motor City into the economic and administrative epicenter of a prosperous Great Lakes Megalopolis. Nonetheless, the overdependence of the Motor City on the automobile industry was a two-edged sword. The accelerated globalization of the economy in the 1960s, the outsourcing of services and the introduction of automation choked off the regional economy and brought mass unemployment and poverty.[55] When the effects of global economic transformations converged with the accumulated ills of white flight, racial conflict and housing segregation, Detroit fell into a downward spiral. Between the 1967 riots and the beginning of the twenty-first century, the city witnessed a major loss of population and its annual growth rate decreased from 2.15 percent almost to 0.5 percent and eventually filed for bankruptcy in July 2013. Detroit has exemplified the urban decay and economic decline of the US Rust Belt.

Beyond this, the only DA project that was implemented in Detroit was the Edison Center Development (1970–1973). Stripped of Doxiadis's scientific assumptions, this was a mixed-use plan that integrated the company's headquarters, housing, retail and parking facilities in developing a 21-hectare area in the vicinity of the CBD. Not unlike other urban-renewal interventions elsewhere, this project was mainly driven by the real-estate market while its design principles had little to do with Ekistic theory or models. For example, a total of 600 residential units appeared here in the form of high-rise buildings despite Doxiadis having condemned skyscrapers and high-rise condominiums several times.[56] At the core of the complex stood the Edison Plaza, which was practically a mall rebranded here as an air-conditioned *public* space [Fig. 7].

In Doxiadis's words, the plaza in principle was a miniature of a city's "properly operating downtown," a space where human contact and communication could flourish "without being exposed to the usual dangers of declining downtown areas."[57]

Applying Ekistics in Baghdad and Detroit: Successes and Failures

The comprehensive plan for Detroit was in every respect different from the NHPI, and yet the planning concepts and development-design patterns used in the UDA were featured for the first time in the Master Plan of Baghdad. In particular, the Dynapolis model and the Human Sector typify

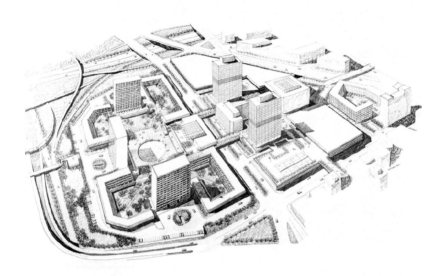

Doxiadis's efforts to harmonize community planning with urban development, and advance Ekistics as an integrated planning system that involved an array of scales, from the "bubble" that surrounds the individual up to the Ecumenopolis.[58]

Standing for the dynamic growth of the contemporary city in contrast to its "static" past, the Dynapolis model proposed development along a predetermined axis – most often a major transportation corridor – and a grid that expanded incrementally as a parabola to integrate new urban areas [Fig. 8].

According to Doxiadis, unlike concentric expansion models, Dynapolis made infinite *natural* growth possible "without allowing the new additions to break up the already existing pattern" – hence, safeguarding the historic city.[59] To all intents and purposes, Dynapolis was the principal urban-development model within Ekistics applied by DA for both the expansion of existing cities (e.g. Khartoum in Sudan) and the creation of

Fig. 7 "The Edison Center Development –
Bird's-Eye View of Complete Development,"
with Edison Plaza at its core.

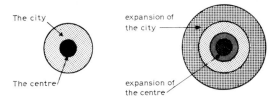

Fig. 35. From static to dynamic cities: the expansion in one direction allows the centre to expand without difficulty

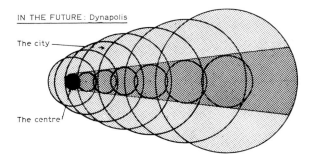

new towns – the most exemplary being the new capital of Pakistan: Islamabad.[60] In publicizing Dynapolis, Doxiadis not only avoided making reference to illustrious paradigms (e.g. Ivan Leonidov's competition proposal for Magnitogorsk or the MARS group's plan for London) but considered any comparison with linear cities confusing. For example, when Milton Keynes planner and core-group Delian Lord Richard Llewelyn-Davies cited Arturo Soria y Mata and Doxiadis as "the first attempts to add facility for growth to the traditional concepts of town design [that] led to the proposals for linear towns," the Greek planner denied any parallelism and argued that Dynapolis was quite different from the "corridor-like expansion of cities," which concerned only specific urban parts.[61] Instead, Dynapolis was a comprehensive concept meant to anticipate urban growth along specific axes in accordance with the Ecumenopolis theory.

The Ekistic paradigm for planning urban areas flanked by the main roads of the Dynapolis grid was the Human Sector. Unequivocally reminis-

Fig. 8 Doxiadis's Dynapolis urban-development rationale: "From static to dynamic cities."

cent of Clarence Perry's "neighborhood unit," the HS proposed a mixed-use urban area of reduced vehicle traffic that included community facilities and a pedestrian network so that a child could walk safely to school [Fig. 9].

Faithful to modern precepts, Doxiadis considered the separation of traffic flows to be a sine qua non for the preservation of the human scale in the city of the future. In fact, within Ekistics the HS was the largest unit where architecture remained "in direct relation to man without the interference of the machine,"[62] and was essentially conceived to both "replace the old-fashioned city block" and respond to the challenges of the automobile.[63] To "scientifically" define the spatial and programmatic features of the Human Sector, in 1961 the ACE launched the Human Community (HUCO) research program, a pioneering interdisciplinary study that analyzed selected Athenian neighborhoods on the basis of empirical knowledge, social surveys, statistical analysis and mathematics with systems analysis as a general methodological framework.[64] Despite HUCO not yielding the specific results that Doxiadis longed to apply in the design of DA's neighborhoods, it typified his persistent efforts to develop a planning approach at the intersection of theory, research and expertise.

In practice, however, the application of the HS and Dynapolis was shaped by the particularities of each project and depended on conditions on the ground. For example, in the case of Baghdad, the Dynapolis's axis was defined by the Tigris River, undeniably the most prominent natural element in the region, which was intrinsically linked to the historical evolution of the city and which played a major bioclimatic role in its everyday life. Parallel and at right angles to that axis were the road connections to other major Iraqi cities, which also delimited the future residential sectors. In order to create a pleasant micro-climate for the communities that were not adjacent to the river, the plan also proposed the construction of a system of canals and parks [Fig. 10].[65]

This concept sought to embed the gridiron plan in the landscape and was inspired by the flood-control and irrigation system, a practice as old in the Mesopotamia region as its cities – arguably the first proper cities in human civilization. Doxiadis gave a theoretical spin to the DA master plan, arguing that Baghdad's future should come out of its own past. Eventually, this imaginative proposal was only partly implemented with the opening of the Army Canal or Qanat al-Jaish, which today runs parallel to Imam Ali Street in the northeast and Omar Bin Al Khatab Street in the southeast.

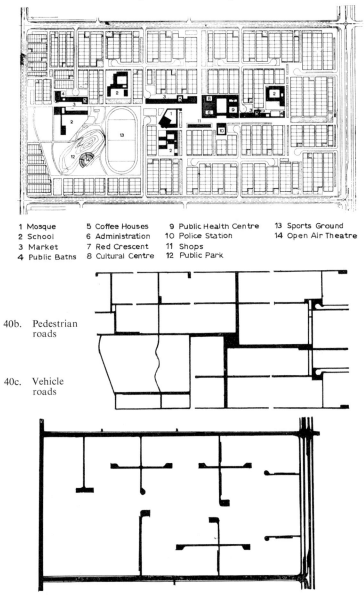

Fig. 9 "A representative human sector built in Western Baghdad."

At the same time, and despite Doxiadis's claims of regional and topographic sensitivity, the monolithic design and overwhelming scale of the Dynapolis made its pattern seem alien to the existing city. Perhaps this could be the reason for the critical interpretation of the DA master plan as a call for the demolition of the city's old quarters.[66] Nonetheless, compared with the Minoprio master plan, which proposed razing large parts of the Rusafa area for the building of emblematic architectural projects, the DA plan paid more attention to the existing city precisely because its grid embraced – instead of cutting through – Baghdad's center.[67]

By the same token, the HS sought to provide a model for integrating into the prospective communities some of the uses and spatial qualities that characterized the traditional Arab city. Apart from a school, administration buildings, shops and a cultural center, the HS included tea houses; public baths; a bazaar, or souk; and a mosque, which became an issue of dispute between DA and the development board. Apparently, the Iraqi officials argued that DA could not use the financial resources of the board for the study and design of mosques, to which Doxiadis answered that should local authorities wish to include a mosque in their community DA would provide the necessary plans for free.[68] Eventually, as reported in a DA internal document on the evolution of the constructed neighborhoods in Baghdad, two mosques instead of one were raised – one for Shias and the other one for Sunnis.[69]

Another focal point of the discussions between Doxiadis and Iraqi officials concerned the design of public space and, in particular, the width of the local roads. As Doxiadis explained, a common error in planning new towns or communities was the construction of wide roads, which required "higher cost of land, higher cost of development, [and] higher cost of maintenance."[70] At the same time, he observed, in Middle Eastern cities the narrow roads or alleys that served as entranceways to private households constituted an intermediate space between the private and public spheres, which better suited the warm climate. Doxiadis proposed using this concept for organizing the rowhouses in the DA community schemes, adding that "only narrow streets can have some shadow which will allow the people to circulate in them with certain comfort,"[71] an argument that was central in advocating a community-oriented architecture adjusted to local conditions.[72]

For the same reason, each row of houses was complemented by a miniature communal space with a small amount of vegetation, benches and a

THE RIVER

The Tigris River, the only outstanding natural element in the surrounding desert, imposes an axis along which the city of Baghdad should develop. Microclimatic effects, the pleasant view, vegetation and facilities for transport, justify the growth of the city along the river.

POSSIBILITY FOR EXPANSION

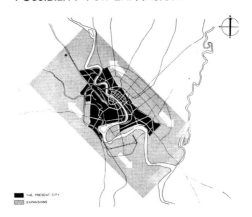

Existing conditions, and the limitations which the present road pattern imposes, must not adversely influence the natural development of Greater Baghdad or the wider Baghdad area. The general plan must follow the axis which runs parallel to the main direction of the river.

THE ROAD SYSTEM

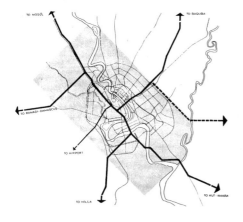

The plan must also provide for the easy connection of the city with the country through a system of roads adapted to the rectangular road pattern.

THE CANAL SYSTEM

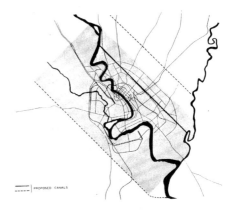

As only a part of the city will be in direct proximity to the river, canals have to be provided for the present and future development in order to create better climatic conditions for the more remote parts. That is why a complete net of canals was proposed, one of which is now under construction.

Fig. 10 The main premises for Baghdad's growth along the Tigris River Axis: "The River; Possibility for Expansion; The Road System; The Canal System."

fountain – the so-called gossip square [Fig. 11]. Apparently, this peculiar name was inspired by the neighborhood spots where casual meetings and informal gatherings were taking place; nonetheless, in the first place the concept emerged from the necessity of providing water facilities to the families of every housing module. During preliminary discussions with Iraqi officials, Doxiadis proposed installing "one tap of water for every group of families" at the end of every housing row instead of "connecting every household," which he considered uneconomical or even wasteful. Besides, having a point of water supply in every neighborhood would permit "the women folk to meet and gossip and [thus] be seen by the prospective husbands."[73] Despite the fact that Doxiadis's rationale reflected gender and cultural stereotypes, the name was successful in depicting the scale, character and use of a public space that were quite different from those of Western piazzas. The gossip square, in fact, received a great deal of press attention and was both acclaimed for its vernacular character and criticized as a stereotype of Middle Eastern culture. Nevertheless, in Doxiadis's mind "gossiping" was a universal characteristic and not peculiar to the Iraqi people. He used the term broadly to denote the human need for communication and social contacts – thus advocating for planning car-free neighborhoods, as in the case of the Eastwick project.[74] Finally, when he became aware of the gossiping about the gossip square, he instructed his associates to change the term to "community squares of first degree."[75]

While the Master Plan of Baghdad arguably exemplified Doxiadis's efforts for urban growth in tandem with the preservation of the historic city and the local culture, the principal objective of the Urban Detroit Area project was the development of a balanced regional system and the management of sprawl. In this latter case, the HS and Dynapolis were the main references for planning the new towns that were located on the regional transportation axes resulting from the Great Lakes Megalopolis study. These featured the typical community organization of Ekistics – that is, from small residential communities (Class IV) to urban communities (Class VI), while the central areas were foreseen as superblocks of metropolitan and regional importance (Classes VII and VIII). As could not be otherwise, emphasis was placed on the separation of traffic flows and the development of a people-friendly city with recreational and pedestrian networks. For the renovation of Detroit's central areas, for example, the plan proposed the transformation of selected local streets into green boulevards portraying low-density

residential areas where "gossiping" would take place in landscaped promenades instead of small squares [Figs. 12-13]. And again, as expected, no references were made to the race, ethnicity or social status of the residents. Instead, as published in a special supplement to the *Detroit News*, the plan unveiled a futuristic scenario of computerized, dual-mode vehicles and high-speed trains going underground through Detroit's CBD and Twin Urban Center.[76]

Lecturing at the Economic Club of Detroit in February 1967, Doxiadis used the metaphor of the human body, referring to how the speed of blood increases in the arteries and veins, and arguing therefore that "in order to achieve the highest possible speeds with the maximum economy of the most direct connections" traffic should move underground.[77] He pictured future cities as a system consisting of cells – essentially, human communities interconnected by transit lines. Transportation networks were the key to planned growth. A chaotic network, in contrast, would lead to the disintegration of the city, a concept Doxiadis chose to illustrate by juxtaposing the photographs of a spider's web before and after the arachnid was fed with sugar water containing dextro-amphetamine.[78] Indeed, the UDA is one of the foremost examples of a Doxiadis project in which biological metaphors and techno-scientific solutions mesh fully together.

Fig. 11 Gossip square with a fountain in the Western Baghdad Development, April 1958.

Figs. 12–13 Low-density residential communities with pedestrian streets and green boulevards.

Most importantly, it is perhaps the project that best exemplifies the comprehensive approach of Ekistics in developing interlocked projects in a layered structure. Unlike other DA plans marked by the directional growth of the Dynapolis pattern (e.g. the master plan of Washington, DC), the most distinguished feature of the UDA was the grid. This extended to the broader region of study, integrating new and existing towns including Detroit. The design logic of the grid was to a certain extent fractal: zooming in and out on the plan, one would see similar patterns of different scale nesting within each other [Fig. 14].[79] The neighborhood, the city, the metropolis and the Megalopolis itself were organized according to the endogenous principles of an expanding system where every pixel was assigned properties that stemmed from the DA comprehensive and visionary program [Fig. 15].

The landscape was also part of the UDA mosaic. In particular, the fifth key program of the Concept-Plan postulated the reserving of natural areas for recreational purposes and the preservation of the natural environment against land spoliation or resource depletion. Such concepts were consistent with the emergence of environmental awareness and the criticism of unrestrained growth that began taking shape in the early 1960s. Doxiadis embraced such theoretical currents in order to develop the concept of the Ecumenokepos – or the "global garden" – which complemented the worldwide Ecumenopolis in equipoise and harmony. Within Ekistics, urban and infrastructural development went hand in hand with environmentalism – at least, in principle.

And yet, the assumption of growth on which Doxiadis's vision was premised was a paradox at a time when a number of important US cities were rapidly losing population. Already in the early 1960s, shopping-mall pioneer architect Victor Gruen had argued for tightening up "inner sprawl" instead of elongating the city with Dynapolis "Miracle Miles."[80] Indeed, Detroit's urban center was not merely drifting across predetermined axes but was being hollowed out, leaving behind disconnected pockets of land: inner city decline, white flight, the retreat to Cold War suburbia or the shrinking economy of the Rust Belt were all interlaced processes that contributed to the disintegration of both its central neighborhoods and its metropolitan area. Doxiadis's phased program sought to combat this carcinogenic process and reconfigure the entire region based on comprehensive planning; scientific methods; and, above all, relentless optimism.

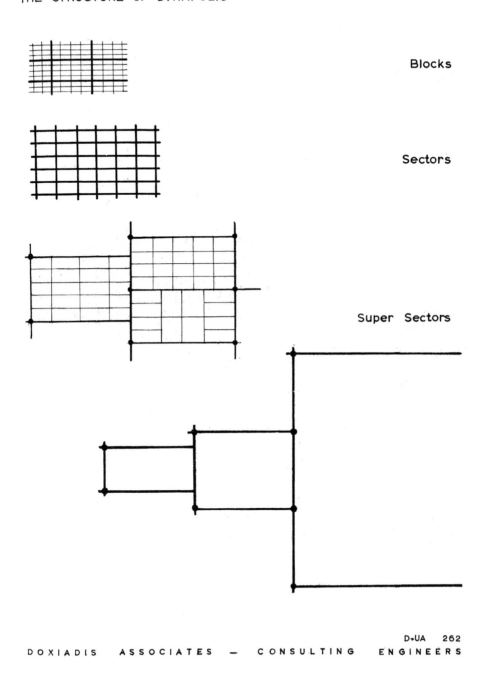

Fig. 14 From the Human Sector to the
Super Sector – "The Structure of Dynapolis."

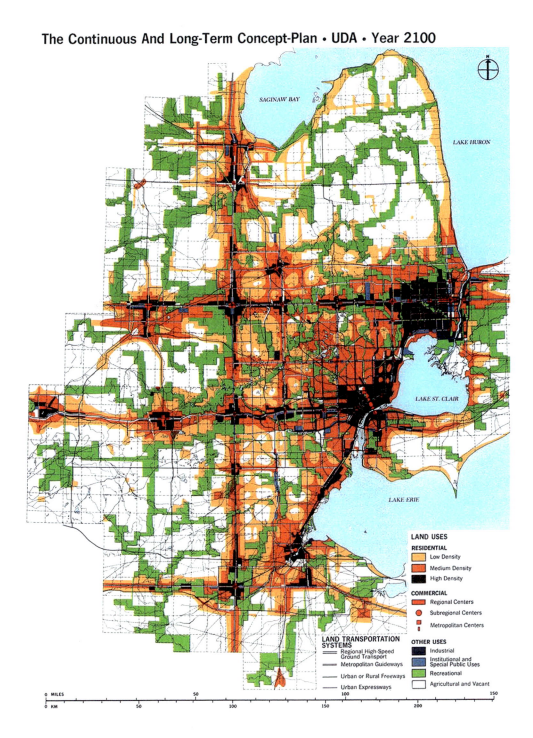

Fig. 15 "The Continuous and Long-Term Concept-Plan – UDA – Year 2100," featuring Detroit's twin city in Port Huron and a number of new cities interconnected by a high-speed transportation network.

From the Steppe of Iraq to the Highways of Detroit

In December 1960, Doxiadis was in Cairo along with other distinguished architect–planners to participate in the international seminar "The New Metropolis in the Arab World."[81] The event was organized by the Egyptian Society of Engineers and was sponsored by the Congress for Cultural Freedom, which was the most active American institution promoting an anti-communist cultural agenda – essentially, it was one of the "CIA's more daring and effective Cold War covert operations."[82] Despite the fact that Doxiadis was essentially pro-American, his discourse was politically neutral – by choice and by stratagem. During this "Arab Metropolis" conference, he discussed cities and societies as amalgams of local and universal elements, therefore arguing for the need to balance modernity and tradition in planning the city of tomorrow.[83] Coexistence was possible, he argued, when the architect or planner considered the necessary phenomena and processes at different scales. The harbor, the airport, the railway station and the automobile were the carriers of modernization and represented the international forces that shaped the larger scales of the metropolis. At the same time, the neighborhood, the narrow streets, the arcades and the souk were elements rooted in Arab tradition that characterized the smaller urban scale. Considering that, the binary Dynapolis–Human Sector was meant to guide dynamic growth and domesticate "international forces" in tandem with preserving the historic city, the human scale and the vernacular. To illustrate the above, Doxiadis juxtaposed the DA plans for Baghdad and Eastwick, Philadelphia, arguing that "these communities, although similar in their conception, differ in their expressions."[84] Therefore, despite the universalizing design method, it was legitimate – he claimed – for "the first community to be called an Iraqi community and the second one an American community."[85] These words perfectly capture Doxiadis's rationale, which understood Ekistics as a universal development approach that nevertheless safeguarded the local. And surely it is also the case that this approach allowed Doxiadis to dodge the complex socioeconomic, political and even racial factors that determined conditions on the ground in the places where he sought to operate.

DA embarked on their extraordinary trajectory in the steppes of Iraq, where Doxiadis received his first opportunity to plan an Arab metropolis. Some years later, he presented a comprehensive vision for an emblematic American city in decline. In Doxiadis's eyes, planning Baghdad or Detroit was part of a broader challenge – that is, planning the worldwide city of the future. In fact, he considered both Baghdad and Detroit as pieces in the Ecumenopolis puzzle that had to be integrated into broader urban and regional systems. Naivety aside, Doxiadis believed in an egalitarian world shared by the "poor fellah of the arabic desert" wandering around the airport and the American urbanite driving along endless highways.[86] Ekistics would ensure that a universal urban future could be planned, preserving traditional patterns and local cultures. Ironically enough, a DA internal document drafted in the early 1970s on the evolution of the implemented projects in Baghdad reported on the difficulty that large US-made cars had in turning in the small alleys of the planned neighborhoods.[87] By that time, Detroit was already caught in the vicious downward spiral that continues up to the present. The failure of the two programs and, above all, the unfortunate subsequent development of the two cities concerned tell us a great deal about the fragility of architecture and urban planning that have been conceived through universalizing models detached from local realities.

1. See Constantinos A. Doxiadis, diary entry, 1955, DA Projects: Iraq V.1 – Diaries DOX.Q, File 23873, Constantinos A. Doxiadis Archives, Benaki Museum, Athens (hereafter Doxiadis Archives).
2. Fahim I. Qubain, *The Reconstruction of Iraq, 1950–1957* (New York: F. A. Praeger, 1958). On the constitution and role of the Development Board, see also Mina Marefat, "1950s Baghdad – Modern and International," *Taarii Newsletter* 2, no. 2 (Fall 2007), 1–7.
3. Hoshiar Nooraddin, "Globalization and the Search for Modern Local Architecture: Learning from Baghdad," in Yasser Elsheshtawy (ed.), *Planning Middle Eastern Cities: An Urban Kaleidoscope in a Globalizing World* (London: Routledge, 2004), 59–84.
4. Pedro Azara (ed.), *City of Mirages: Baghdad, from Wright to Venturi* (Barcelona: Departament de Composició Arquitectònica, ETSAB-UPC, 2008). This most interesting chapter in the history of modern architecture in Iraq was presented in the itinerary exhibition *City of Mirages*, which opened in Barcelona in 2008.
5. Jacob Crane, George Reed and George Speer collaborated with Doxiadis on the implementation of the aided self-help housing program in Greece during the country's reconstruction and recovery period. See Konstantina Kalfa, *Self-Sheltering, Now! The Invisible Side of American Aid to Greece* [in Greek] (Athens: Futura, 2019); Richard Harris, "The Silence of the Experts: 'Aided Self-Help Housing,' 1939–1954," *Habitat International* 22, no. 2 (June 1998), 165–89, https://doi.org/10.1016/S0197-3975(97)00038-6 (accessed April 1, 2024). It was Jacob Crane who pulled strings to get Doxiadis on board with the Development Board's projects. Crane joined Doxiadis Associates as a senior consultant in 1955. See Lefteris Theodosis, "'Containing' Baghdad: Constantinos Doxiadis' Program for a Developing Nation," in Azara (ed.), *City of Mirages*, 167–72.
6. Athanasios Xatzopoulos, "The National Housing Program of Iraq," in G. Kazazi and N. Gounari (eds), *Ο Κωνσταντίνος Δοξιάδης και το έργο του, δεύτερος τόμος* [*Constantinos Doxiadis and His Work*] (Athens: Technical Chamber of Greece, 2009), vol. 2, 5–15. Xatzopoulos (Chatzopoulos) was one of the DA collaborators who were sent to Iraq for the purposes of the NHPI. The DA branch office in Baghdad was established in September 1955 with a workforce of four architect–engineers, eventually reaching up to 90 employees. During the same period, the DA headquarters in Athens established separate departments in architectural design, regional and urban planning, transportation and hydraulics.
7. Walker Cisler and Constantinos Doxiadis had a deep respect for each other and valued highly their professional and personal relationship, fostered over the years. According to Philip Deane, Cisler was a fervent supporter of Doxiadis's ideas. See Philip Deane, *Constantinos Doxiadis: Master Builder for Free Men* (New York: Oceana Publications, 1965), 130.
8. Lefteris Theodosis, "Previendo el Pasado – El Plan 'Doxiadis' para Detroit y el futuro de la Megalópolis de los Grandes Lagos," in Román Caracciolo,

Pablo Elinbaum, Biel Horrach and Mariana Debat (eds), *La metropolis Iberoamericana en sus propios terminos* (Barcelona: RIURB Editores, 2013), 157–79. Actually, the first DA project commissioned by the Detroit Edison in 1965 was a new town-planning scheme titled "All-Electric Community." During that period, several American corporations such as General Motors, Goodyear, the Reynolds Metals Development Corporation and United States Steel invested in the growing sectors of real estate and urban development. See Thomas E. Bray, "Building Cities: More Companies Enter Business of Developing Complete New Towns," *Wall Street Journal*, January 7, 1965.

9   Roger Biles, "New Towns for the Great Society: A Case Study in Politics and Planning," *Planning Perspectives* 13, no. 2 (January 1998), 113–32, https://doi.org/10.1080/026654398364491 (accessed April 1, 2024).

10 Panayis Psomopoulos, "Athens Technological Organization: Programs for Greece and the World," in Kazazi and Gounari (eds), *Ο Κωνσταντίνος Δοξιάδης και το έργο του, δεύτερος τόμος* [*Constantinos Doxiadis and His Work*], vol. 1, 95–138.

11 See Lefteris Theodosis, "Systemic Methods and Large-Scale Models in Ekistics," *Nexus Network Journal* 23, no. 1 (March 2021), 171–86, https://doi.org/10.1007/s00004-020-00531-y (accessed April 1, 2024); Panayiota Pyla, "Planetary Home and Garden: Ekistics and Environmental-Developmental Politics," *Grey Room*, no. 36 (July 2009), 6–35; Mark Wigley, "Network Fever," *Grey Room*, no. 4 (June 2001), 82–122, https://doi.org/10.1162/152638101750420825 (accessed April 1, 2024).

12 The publication of his travel diaries has been a most valuable contribution to the understanding of Doxiadis's work. See Dimitris Philippides (ed.), *Travel Diaries 1954–1956* [in Greek] (Athens: Melissa Books, 2019).

13 See Constantinos A. Doxiadis, diary entry, IRAQ V.3 – DIARIES DOX.Q, January 1956, File 23875, Doxiadis Archives.

14 Samira Haj, *The Making of Iraq, 1900–1963: Capital, Power, and Ideology* (Albany: State University of New York Press, 1997). The uprising of 1948, popularly known as *al-Wathba* ("the leap"), was initially a protest against the Portsmouth Treaty and British military dominance; however, it turned into a massive cry for "bread and clothes" and democracy. After three months of turmoil, the protests spread all over the country, culminating in "the great march" (*al-Masira*), in which thousands of the IPC's K3 oil-station workers decided to march 250 km to Baghdad. Some years later, in 1952, a new wave of strikes and student protests, known as *al-Intifada* ("the tremor"), added to the unrest, which was halted by the declaration of martial law. The Iraqi Communist Party's support of the revolts was met with violent measures from the government.

15 Huma Gupta, "Staging Baghdad as a Problem of Development," *International Journal of Islamic Architecture* 8, no. 2 (July 1, 2019), 337–61, https://doi.org/10.1386/ijia.8.2.337_1 (accessed April 1, 2024).

16 Constantinos Doxiadis to Jacob Crane, July 30, 1955, Correspondence between C. A. Doxiadis and J. L. Crane (1954–1957), File 19255, Doxiadis Archives.

17 Doxiadis Associates, *Experimental Housing Projects* (Baghdad: Development Board, Ministry of Development of the Government of Iraq, 1957).

18 Dalal Musaed Alsayer, "'Bringing the Machine to the House': The IBEC System and Experimental Housing in Baghdad, Iraq, 1953–58," Rockefeller Archive Center Research Reports, https://rockarch.issuelab.org/resource/bringing-the-machine-to-the-house-the-ibec-system-and-experimental-housing-in-baghdad-iraq-1953-58.html (accessed August 27, 2019).

19 Constantinos A. Doxiadis, lecture, 1958, "No More Regional Planning: A Move towards Regional Development Programs," File 2509, Doxiadis Archives.

20 Ibid. For example, one of the most characteristic graphs depicted the "average number of days per month with winds blowing from specified directions at 0500, 1100 and 1600 GMT" using data from the period 1908–1913.

21 See Doxiadis Associates, *Iraq Housing Program* (Athens: Doxiadis Associates, 1959), and Constantinos A. Doxiadis, report (R-QA 255), October 9, 1956, "On the National Housing Charter," File 28546, Doxiadis Archives.

22 Doxiadis discussed this strategy with the Minister of Development during his second visit to Iraq, on July 21, 1955. See Constantinos A. Doxiadis, diary entry, 1955, DA Projects: Iraq V.1 – Diaries DOX.Q, File 23873, Doxiadis Archives.

23 See Constantinos A. Doxiadis, report (Q.A.22), 1956, "Approval of Our Recommendations on the SPA and the BFP," File 23877, Doxiadis Archives. For Crane's complementary proposals, see Jacob Crane, report (Q.A.42), December 10, 1955, "Opinion of Mr. Jacob L. Crane on Our Iraqi Projects," File 23877, Doxiadis Archives.

24 In Mosul, where stone was in abundance, artisans from the northern areas of Greece were brought in to teach stone craft. In parallel, young Iraqi planners, architects and engineers were trained by DA both at their Athenian headquarters and at the Baghdad office. The ultimate objective was to staff the public housing authorities and continue the initiated programs once the foreign firms and missions had left the country. See Xatzopoulos, "The National Housing Program of Iraq."

25 Doxiadis Associates, *Experimental Housing Projects* (Baghdad: Development Board, Ministry of Development of the Government of Iraq, 1957).

26 Andrew Alger, "Homes for the Poor? Public Housing and the Social Construction of Space in Baghdad,

27 Arbella Bet-Shlimon, *City of Black Gold: Oil, Ethnicity, and the Making of Modern Kirkuk* (Stanford: Stanford University Press, 2019).
28 Doxiadis Associates, "The Master Plan of Baghdad," *DA Monthly Bulletin* 9 (1960).
29 Łukasz Stanek, *Architecture in Global Socialism: Eastern Europe, West Africa, and the Middle East in the Cold War* (Princeton, NJ: Princeton University Press, 2020), 178. The Minoprio, Spencely and MacFarlane plan was drafted in 1954. The change of regime was decisive for the British architects, and eventually their contract for the civic center project was canceled with the excuse that funds were not available anymore. In September 1960, the scheme was entrusted to Josep Lluís Sert. See Pedro Azara, "The Baghdad Civic Center Project (1960–1964)," *Taarii Newsletter* 6, no. 1 (Spring 2011), 4–8.
30 Doxiadis, report (Q.A.22), 1956.
31 Azara, "The Baghdad Civic Center Project," 4–8.
32 As stated in several reports from the MR-QA series written in 1959, "[f]ollowing the compulsory suspension of Doxiadis Associates activities in Iraq this housing scheme was handed over to the representative of the competent Iraqi authority." See, for example, Doxiadis Associates, report (MR-QA 46), 1959, File 24019, Doxiadis Archives.
33 Michelle Provoost, "New Towns on the Cold War Frontier," *Archplus* 183 (May 2007), 63–67.
34 See Stanek, *Architecture in Global Socialism*.
35 See Constantinos A. Doxiadis, "European Cooperation: The Perspective of Possibilities" [in Greek], *To Vima*, September 24, 1947. The cornerstone of such European cooperation was laid by the illustrious Marshall Plan.
36 For an insightful analysis of Doxiadis's professional action and projects in the United States, see Dimitris Philippides, *Constantinos A. Doxiadis: Report to Hippodamus* [in Greek] (Athens: Melissa Books, 2015), 274–78.
37 Constantinos A. Doxiadis to Walker L. Cisler, May 9, 1959, File 23387, Doxiadis Archives. Doxiadis announced to Cisler the opening of the Washington, DC office, saying that "[o]ur presence in the Western hemisphere will give our office a broader standing since our experience in the Eastern hemisphere can be supplemented by the experience to be gained in Western industrialized countries. On the other hand, this very experience of the East and the concepts developed there may be useful to many Western problems."
38 See Gregory L. Heller, *Ed Bacon: Planning, Politics, and the Building of Modern Philadelphia* (Philadelphia: University of Pennsylvania Press, 2013), 68–69.
39 Constantinos A. Doxiadis, *Urban Renewal and the Future of the American City* (Chicago: Public Administration Service, 1966).
40 Winnick Louis, "Philanthropy's Adaptation to the Urban Crisis 1987–1989," report, May 1989, Ford Foundation Urban History, Ford Foundation Archives.
41 On the relationship and intellectual exchange between Doxiadis and Gottmann, see Luca Muscarà, "The Doxiadis–Gottmann Exchange," in Kazazi and Gounari (eds), *Ο Κωνσταντίνος Δοξιάδης και το έργο του, δεύτερος τόμος* [*Constantinos Doxiadis and His Work*], vol. 2, 200–8. Ecumenopolis was both a vision and a warning that described world population trends as depicted in graphs and maps. See Constantinos A. Doxiadis and John G. Papaioannou, *Ecumenopolis: The Inevitable City of the Future* (New York: Norton, 1974). For a current reconsideration of Ecumenopolis in relation to the planetary urbanization discourse, see, for example, Nikos Katsikis, "Two Approaches to 'World Management': C. A. Doxiadis and R. B. Fuller," in Neil Brenner (ed.), *Implosions – Explosions: Towards a Study of Planetary Urbanization* (Berlin: Jovis, 2017), 480–504.
42 Constantinos A. Doxiadis, "The Death of Our Cities," *Ekistics* 10, no. 61 (November 1960), 298–307. The article is abstracted from a speech delivered during the fifth Working Conference on Urban Renewal, NAHRO, March 21, 1960. Doxiadis also addressed the twenty-eighth NAHRO conference that took place in Washington, DC in 1961, where he presented the theory of Ecumenopolis.
43 Patrik Schumacher and Christian Rogner, "After Ford," in Georgia Daskalakis, Charles Waldheim and Jason Young (eds), *Stalking Detroit* (Barcelona: Actar, 2001), 48–56.
44 See Martin V. Melosi, "The Automobile Shapes the City," Automobile in American Life and Society, 2005, http://www.autolife.umd.umich.edu/Environment/E_Casestudy/E_casestudy.htm (accessed April 25, 2022).
45 Doxiadis used the same maps in his lecture at the University of Michigan in Ann Arbor, which was attended by Governor George Romney. He concluded by saying, "Here Gentlemen, you see already the cancer of traffic pressures eating away the healthy urban tissue." See John Palaiokrassas, "C. A. Doxiadis' Way of Working in USA," in Kazazi and Gounari (eds), *Ο Κωνσταντίνος Δοξιάδης και το έργο του, δεύτερος τόμος* [*Constantinos Doxiadis and His Work*], vol. 1, 66.
46 According to Martin V. Melosi, in 1953 Detroit, "streets and parking made up 49.5 percent of the central city." See Melosi, "The Automobile Shapes the City."
47 Doxiadis's rationale was severely criticized by K. Kollarou, who argued that the worsening of the transportation system was a result instead of a cause of the overall decline. See K. Kollarou, report (CR-USA-A 16), 1967, "Comments on the Draft Report Entitled 'Considerations for a Program Tending to Face the Problems of the City of Detroit' Dictated by D," File 25364, Doxiadis Archives.

48 See Palaiokrassas, "C. A. Doxiadis' Way of Working in USA," 66. As Doxiadis explained to his collaborators, "we shall mean by Pit the total area which lies between the center of a city, if it declines and once it starts declining, and the highest region around. This pit is represented mostly by incomes of people although this may coincide with other phenomena." See Constantinos A. Doxiadis, report (R-USA-DT 80), 1967, "Considerations on the Central Region," File 23476, Doxiadis Archives.

49 See Sharon Woodson, "Doxiadis Terms Detroit Riots Only a Symptom of Crisis," *Ann Arbor News*, December 17, 1969. In Doxiadis's own words, "more and more I am convinced that we have two types of forces related to human settlements, not national nor racial not economic but territorial and non-territorial, this is my case." See Constantinos A. Doxiadis, report (R-USA-A 197), 1970, "Considerations on GLM Strategy," File 23523, Doxiadis Archives.

50 Commenting on safety in city centers, Doxiadis ascribed the problems of order and control to the physical characteristics of the built environment: "first, we lose security because, instead of having streets, we have a wild pattern of open lots. There is no structure; therefore, there is no order [...]." See Constantinos A. Doxiadis, report (R-DUS-WS 2), 1970, "Considerations and Information on Security and Safety in Central Cities," File 23523, Doxiadis Archives.

51 On the history of the DACC, see Andreas Drimiotis, "The Contribution of C. A. Doxiadis in the Development of the Information Technology in Greece," in Kazazi et al. (eds), *Ο Κωνσταντίνος Δοξιάδης και το έργο του, δεύτερος τόμος* [*Constantinos Doxiadis and His Work*], vol. 1, 50–59.

52 Constantinos A. Doxiadis, "Method for Synthesis: The I.D.E.A. and C.I.D. Methods," *Ekistics* 72, no. 430–35 (December 2005), 131–40, quotation 132.

53 Constantinos A. Doxiadis, "Toward the Implementation of the Concept-Plan," *Ekistics* 72, no. 430–35 (December 2005), 141–64.

54 Ibid., 141.

55 See Thomas J. Sugrue, *The Origins of the Urban Crisis: Race and Inequality in Postwar Detroit* (Princeton, NJ: Princeton University Press, 1996).

56 Constantinos A. Doxiadis, "Confessions of a Criminal," *Ekistics* 32, no. 191 (October 1971), 249–54.

57 Constantinos A. Doxiadis, "Downtown Detroit Recreates History," *CBDA Newsletter*, July 1971.

58 On Doxiadis's work at different scales, see Suzanne Keller, "Planning at Two Scales: The Work of C. A. Doxiadis," *Ekistics*, no. 282 (June 1980), 172–74. On Doxiadis's commitment to the smaller scales of architecture, see Simon Richards, "'Halfway between the Electron and the Universe': Doxiadis and the Delos Symposia," in Gerald Adler, Timothy Brittain-Catlin and Gordana Fontana-Giusti (eds), *Scale: Imagination, Perception and Practice in Architecture* (London: Routledge, 2012), 170–81.

59 See Jaqueline Tyrwhitt (ed.) "C. A. Doxiadis 1913–75: Pursuit of an Attainable Ideal," *Ekistics* 41, no. 247 (June 1976), 309–88. Also Constantinos A. Doxiadis, "Ecumenopolis: The Coming World-City," *Ekistics* 72, no. 430–35 (December 2005), 189–206.

60 Constantinos A. Doxiadis, *Architecture in Transition* (New York: Oxford University Press, 1963), 103.

61 Richard Llewelyn-Davies, "Town Design," *Town Planning Review* 37, no. 3 (October 1966), 157–72. Llewelyn-Davies was a Professor of Architecture and Urban Planning broadly known for his participation in the design of the new town Milton Keynes, once dubbed "little Los Angeles in Buckinghamshire." He was acquainted with Doxiadis and participated in several Delos Symposia. Doxiadis replied that "Soria was not thinking of cities but of parts of cities only, as well as of very long connections between distant cities. These parts of cities have no central functions and therefore do not form cities." See Constantinos A. Doxiadis, "On Linear Cities," *Town Planning Review* 38, no. 1 (April 1967), 35–42. The public discussion between the two architects ended with another article by Llewelyn-Davies wherein he "apologized" to Doxiadis, corroborating his arguments with paradigms of linear proposals – albeit based on transportation lines. In his closing statement, he advocated poly-nuclear patterns for the growth and management of the metropolis. See Richard Llewelyn-Davies, "Some Further Thoughts on Linear Cities," *Town Planning Review* 38, no. 3 (October 1966), 202–3.

62 Doxiadis, *Architecture in Transition*, 106.

63 Constantinos A. Doxiadis, lecture, 1960, "The Arab Metropolis," File 2556, 25, Doxiadis Archives. To exemplify the destructive forces of the automobile, Doxiadis often used in his lectures and writings "the story of a square." This parable describes the transformation of the neighborhood square where he used to play as a boy after trees had been cut down to pave the way for the automobile. Following the arrival of the "machine," the square, the neighborhood and, eventually, the whole city were never the same. One of the Ekistic objectives, then, was to plan a "human city" compatible with the automobile. See Doxiadis, "The Death of Our Cities," 298–307.

64 See Theodosis, "Systemic Methods and Large-Scale Models," 171–86.

65 Doxiadis Associates, *The Master Plan of Baghdad*.

66 Akram J. M. Al-Akkam, "Urban Heritage in Baghdad: Toward a Comprehensive Sustainable Framework," *Journal of Sustainable Development* 6, no. 2 (January 17, 2013), 39–55, https://doi.org/10.5539/jsd.v6n2p39 (accessed April 2, 2024). According to Al-Akkam, the master plans of both Minoprio, Spencely and MacFarlane and Doxiadis Associates "not only ignored the concerns of conservation but positively

advocated the total demolition of Baghdad's historic areas" (Al-Akkam, "Urban Heritage in Baghdad," 46).

67 See Panayiota Pyla, "Back to the Future: Doxiadis's Plans for Baghdad," *Journal of Planning History* 7, no. 1 (February 1, 2008), 3–19, 10, https://doi.org/10.1177/1538513207304697 (accessed April 2, 2024). Also see Stanek, *Architecture in Global Socialism*, 178.

68 See Constantinos A. Doxiadis, report (R-QA 773), October 14, 1957, File 28546, Doxiadis Archives.

69 See, G. Papageorgiou, report draft, October 1971, "Baghdad – October 1971," File 28978, Doxiadis Archives.

70 See Constantinos A. Doxiadis, report (R-QA 1), "SPA," 1955, File 23877, 8, Doxiadis Archives.

71 Ibid., 9.

72 Doxiadis, *Architecture in Transition*, 13.

73 Doxiadis, report (R-QA 1), 9.

74 Constantinos A. Doxiadis, "Man, City, and Automobile," *Ekistics*, no. 146 (January 1968), 13–16.

75 See Constantinos A. Doxiadis, memo, May 4, 1957, File 8032, Doxiadis Archives. Nonetheless, Doxiadis did not use the term "gossip" as a cultural stereotype. It actually appeared in several of his writings, one of which referred to the Eastwick community project in Philadelphia. See Doxiadis, "Man, City, and Automobile." In Doxiadis's eyes, then, "gossiping" was a universal characteristic.

76 The technological futurism of the UDA is depicted in the special supplement to the *Detroit News*, "Into the 21st Century: The Story of the Developing Urban Detroit Area," October 1969.

77 Doxiadis, "Man, City, and Automobile."

78 Constantinos A. Doxiadis, "The Two-Headed Eagle: From the Past to the Future of Human Settlements," *Ekistics* 33, no. 198 (May 1972), 406–20.

79 Doxiadis, *Urban Renewal and the Future of the American City*, 101–8.

80 See Gruen quoted in Ezra Ehrenkrantz and Ogden Tanner, "The Remarkable Dr. Doxiadis," *Architectural Forum* 114, no. 5 (May 1961), 112–16, 154. "More 'Miracle Miles,'" groaned Gruen: "Our downtown cores are already much too large and loose, including many uses which don't belong. The job is to tighten up this inner sprawl, not eat up more and more land by elongating the city core, and having the older end die off."

81 Apart from Doxiadis, the seminar featured the participation of eminent architects such as Michel Écochard, Cornelis van Eesteren, Maxwell Fry, Ernesto Rogers and Hassan Fathy, who at that time was collaborating with DA.

82 Michael Warner, "Origins of the Congress for Cultural Freedom, 1949–50," *Studies in Intelligence* 38, no. 5 (1995), 89–98. This article is an excerpt from a larger, classified draft study of CIA involvement with anti-communist groups in the Cold War.

83 Doxiadis, "The Arab Metropolis."

84 Ibid., 26.

85 Ibid.

86 See the epigraph to this chapter from Constantinos A. Doxiadis, diary entry, 1955 (n. 1).

87 See, Papageorgiou, "Baghdad – October 1971."

The Visionary in the Marsh
Doxiadis and the Dream of Eastwick
Harrison Blackman

The Planning Oracle in the Senate

On December 5, 1966, within the ornate chambers of the United States Capitol, Senator Abraham Ribicoff called the Senate Subcommittee on Executive Reorganization to order. Nine senators sat at their elevated desks, examining the celebrated figure sitting before them. Besides Ribicoff, one other lawmaker was intent on making the most of this hearing. This particular senator wanted to know what their guest – this world-famous architect and city planner – could do to address the urban crisis then afflicting cities in the United States.[1]

Ribicoff leaned into the microphone: "Mr. Doxiadis, you may proceed as you will. Go at your own pace […] after you are through, we might have a few questions."[2]

"I consider it a great honor, and a great challenge," Constantinos A. Doxiadis replied.[3] The Athenian architect was fifty-three years old, and his impeccably coiffed hair and mustache had begun to gray.[4] In many ways, Doxiadis had reached the pinnacle of his career. By this point, a constellation of institutions based out of his headquarters on the slopes of Athens's Mount Lycabettus brought business, education and cultural outreach to the city and to those who came to study Doxiadis's planning theories in Greece. These organizations included Doxiadis Associates, his architecture and planning firm employing 700 draftspeople, planners and engineers; the Athens Technological Institute, his undergraduate and graduate school in planning; and the Athens Center for Ekistics, his think tank, as well as *Ekistics* magazine, his scholarly journal spotlighting exciting developments in the field of human settlements.[5] Additionally, by this time the Delos

Symposia, Doxiadis's human-settlement-themed conference cruise on the Aegean, had run for its third year, in the process becoming a noted event for intellectuals the world over.[6] Six months earlier, Doxiadis had been given the Aspen Award in Colorado for his lifetime of work on human settlements in at least forty countries; by the *New Yorker*'s estimate, his work had already impacted the lives of 10 million people.[7]

"I was impressed by your letter to me," Doxiadis told Ribicoff. "One thing you said was: 'We don't know enough about the problems; we know even less about the solutions.' Allow me to support that statement […] I can only add that, because we now have the courage to make such admissions […] we are beginning to learn." Immediately, Doxiadis entered into a detailed, eloquent twelve-point description of his life's work – his design philosophy of Ekistics, the science of human settlements and his findings derived from a lifetime of studying and planning communities around the globe. In the course of this "lecture," he shared his firm's maps; his drawings of the five elements; his iconic, often comical, sketching style.[8] It was a lecture he had given many times, and it was hardly the first time he had given it in Washington, DC.

Georgetown was the home of Doxiadis's American headquarters, along the historic Chesapeake and Ohio Canal.[9] Noting the high-speed water taxis in operation at the time in Venice, Doxiadis was of the opinion the same might be useful for Washington, since the Potomac River linked Maryland, Virginia and the District of Columbia, and therefore might be the perfect vehicle to shuttle commuters back and forth between their various shoreline communities. "The river is a cheap, ready-made means of transportation that will cost nothing to maintain," Doxiadis had told a Washington newspaper in 1958 – a sunny suggestion few took to heart.[10]

But, as Doxiadis went through his projector slides – his drawings of cities expanding, ballooning and intersecting in wavy, curvilinear forms – the interested senator, who had been listening so intently, could not contain himself any longer.

"Could I see the last painting again?" Senator Robert F. Kennedy of New York asked, in his iconic New England accent. "Did you do that yourself?"[11]

"Yes," Doxiadis said – they were indeed drawings by his own hand, and he said as much to the brother of the beloved American president who had been slain three years earlier in Dallas, to the man who would intend to run for president in two years, the man who would then be assassinated in the kitchen of the Ambassador Hotel in Los Angeles. Here and now, Robert Kennedy allowed Doxiadis to continue for a few more minutes, before he interjected again: "Could I just interrupt? I know it is wrong of me, but I don't understand some of this."[12]

In that moment, out of this interruption, something remarkable happened. Over the course of the next hour – more than thirty pages of transcript – Doxiadis and Kennedy traded their opinions on the state of cities in their time: the problems of urban decay, the failure of public housing and how to provide a future for many minorities left behind in cities while more affluent white populations fled to the suburbs.[13]

Repeatedly, Kennedy asked Doxiadis: *What would he do? How would he do it?* Finally, when Doxiadis concluded with his points – and his responses to Kennedy – Senator Ribicoff asked some questions himself: "Are you doing work for any cities in the United States today?"[14]

"Yes, sir," Doxiadis said. "One of the urban areas we are working with is in the city of Philadelphia, where we have an urban renewal project to create a city within a city for almost ten thousand families. It is called the Eastwick area, and there we try to carry out the principles of communities in a human scale" [Fig. 1].[15]

Several minutes later, as the committee was just about to adjourn, Kennedy spoke up once more: "Mr. Doxiadis, I am going this afternoon to Philadelphia to see your project […] I have heard of it and some of the other work that is being done in Philadelphia, and I wanted to look at it and see whether we can do something like that in the city of New York. I am looking forward to it."[16]

The Mystery of Eastwick

Fifty-two years after Robert Kennedy said he would visit the Eastwick neighborhood of Philadelphia, I did. It was a bitterly cold weekend day in March 2018 when I took the pitted I-95 south from Princeton to the City of Brotherly Love. I drove through downtown, past City Hall and the Comcast Tower; I drove up and through the double-decker, traversed Girard Point Bridge, crossing the Schuylkill River. I took the exit for Penrose Avenue and entered the district of Eastwick, though there are few signs announcing the fact. From a metropolitan standpoint, the area's most important amenity is Philadelphia International Airport. Outside of the airport, one can find industrial sites, landfills, strip malls, a public library branch and a SEPTA

Fig. 1 Promotional material about the Eastwick project from Doxiadis Associates' *DA Monthly Bulletin*, 1963.

Harrison Blackman

suburban-rail station that can take you out of this somewhat forlorn place and back downtown.[17] The original phases of rowhouses planned and designed by Doxiadis Associates are still there, and the houses subsequently built and designed by later development corporations – though you would never know that if you weren't familiar with the history of Eastwick. This is astonishing because in the 1960s this neighborhood was the site of what was the largest urban-renewal project in US history, costing a whopping $78 million – the equivalent of more than half a billion dollars today.[18] Eastwick was so nationally prominent that it was even floated as the location for a failed bid to host the 1972 Olympic Games.[19] And yet, this is not a historic planned community such as Frank Lloyd Wright's Usonia, New York; or the original Levittown in Long Island; or James Rouse's celebrated Columbia, Maryland. There are no *signs*.

On this cold March day, the only way I could deduce I was in the right place – that I had entered the network of a Doxiadis plan – was through the street layout, which is highly engineered. The streamlined collector roads made it extremely difficult to enter the residential neighborhoods. Again and again, I was steered onto other major streets, pushed in the direction of the highway, down one-way streets and circles that led to empty blocks covered in weeds and trash – abandoned and deteriorating housing; the borders of the marsh, where all this had been built. Finally, after more than an hour of navigating this labyrinth, I came to a neighborhood that had, in many ways, held up relatively well. One house even had solar panels. Here, I finally stopped [Fig. 2].

About 12,000 people live in Eastwick.[20] The median household income is $39,000 a year – for a Northeastern city, this is a lower-income area.[21] The neighborhood is 76 percent African American.[22] Like some other parts of Philadelphia, it is a place frequently tested by violence – with eighteen reported homicides from 2010 to 2017.[23]

The gulf between Doxiadis's high-minded rhetoric of Eastwick and the disappointing reality is stark and demands explanation. For a moment, consider Doxiadis's background. The Athenian was no stranger to working in less-than-ideal conditions – in Greece, he had led a resistance group against the Axis occupation; in Iraq, his team of architects survived a coup d'état; in Pakistan, he had realized an entire capital city from the ground up.[24] Doxiadis's efforts in Eastwick were no less ambitious – and in some ways, perhaps they were even greater. Despite the praise of its initial residents, the redeveloped Eastwick never took off, and today, to the untrained eye, it appears an unremarkable low-income suburb on the fringes of the Philadelphia airport. What happened to Eastwick? The answer lies not in the idealistic vision of its international master planner but in what his dream ran up against. At the heart of Eastwick's disappointment was a deep-seated American phenomenon: the racial prejudice of its prospective inhabitants.

The Meadows and the Marsh

Southwest Philadelphia was a melting pot for different cultures in America long before there was a United States. The former township name of Kingsessing derives from the Lenape (Delaware Indian) word for "bog meadow."[25] The first settlers in the area were Scandinavians who arrived in 1643, thirty-nine years ahead of William Penn, who founded the city on the opposite bank of the Schuylkill in 1682.[26] Penn named the city Philadelphia after the Greek for "brotherly love." It was the Dutch who named the Schuylkill, which meant "hidden river."[27]

In 1810, a man named Andrew M. Eastwick was born in Philadelphia, who eventually became an accomplished locomotive manufacturer. In 1840, two Russian envoys met Eastwick – and signed him to a $3 million contract to supply locomotives for Russia's early railroad network. In 1851, flush with this new fortune, Mr. Eastwick built a mansion in southwest Philadelphia. He died in 1879; less than a decade later, the Eastwick mansion, a lavish Victorian palace, burned down and was subsequently demolished.[28]

But Eastwick lived on in the 1,200-hectare (3,000-acre) community later named after him.[29] That community was primarily rural, and it went by other names before it was known as Eastwick. Most of its residents – a racially integrated population of people with low incomes – knew it as the Native Americans once did, as "The Meadows."[30] But such a name would belie the appalling state of decay the neighborhood had reached in the early 1950s (as well as its unsuitable environmental conditions). As urban historian Guian McKee noted in his groundbreaking study of Eastwick, the houses were crumbling. There were illegal dumps, abandoned cars and trash fires. There was no sewer system. In some areas, the land was 3.6 meters (12 feet) below the level of the river, which made it vulnerable to flooding and, when it rained, the sewage and water would stew together, attracting rats. And, worst of all – at least to city officials – 84 percent of Eastwick residents didn't pay their taxes.[31]

This was the site that greeted Doxiadis in 1958.³² In an interview televised in 1964, Doxiadis described his experience on visiting the location for the first time:

> Now you can understand the disappointment of someone visiting an area that is, half of which are covered by swamps of the worst kind, and the other half by slums some of which were already demolished, but most of which already were still around, many of them still inhabited [...] it was not inspiring for anyone who wanted to create something on it.³³

But Doxiadis, being Doxiadis, apparently found his inspiration quickly. While walking around, he reported meeting an "old friend," who asked him what he was doing there.

Doxiadis said he was studying the possibility of building a new Eastwick. "You are crazy," the friend said. "I did not know what to do," Doxiadis thought after the encounter. After touring the site, he met the city officials and planners. He was impressed with what they had to say, particularly with City Planning Commissioner Edmund Bacon's preference for separating traffic from pedestrians – a view that coincided with his own.³⁴ He

Fig. 2 Eastwick homes, as seen in 2018.

apparently deemed Philadelphia the first American city he had seen to possess quality planning. "And then I said to myself [...] why should [there] not be also any good plan for Eastwick?" Doxiadis asked rhetorically. "And so I concluded we were crazy enough to undertake it, if we started the job."[35]

"No Visible Scars"

To further understand Doxiadis's role in Philadelphia, we have to travel to Athens. The Benaki Museum's sleek Piraeus Street annex is home to the Doxiadis Archive of the Constantinos and Emma Doxiadis Foundation, a vast collection of papers and ephemera from the Doxiadis Associates office. In June 2018, I watched some of the digitized videos on file. It was stunning how a two-part documentary – *Eastwick: Design for the City Within* and *Eastwick: The Painful Transition* – broadcast on a Washington, DC NBC TV affiliate in 1964, could reveal so much in just forty-seven minutes of tape. The documentary's second segment opened with the following voiceover overture:

> Children play and people live on what was once an area of marshland [...] to all outward appearances, Eastwick is just another "new community." The problems it faced left no visible scars, except that there aren't as many houses as people expected. The one developed lived-in section is positioned in a sea of open fields.[36]

Eastwick, the documentary stated, was supposed to feature 10,000 new homes. But four years into its development only 272 houses had been built. The first development corporation had "put itself out of the home-building business." A new company, the Korman Corporation, had taken over the project.[37] The question was, why? One only had to watch the rest of the film for the answer to leak out slowly, then announce itself in horrifyingly vivid terms.

One reason for Eastwick's lack of momentum, the documentary related, was the perceived quality of the Doxiadis-designed houses. Doxiadis had chosen rowhouses because they had been the traditional housing style of Philadelphia since colonial times and because they were among the most economical of housing types. But one Philadelphia politician reportedly called the houses "claptrap junk."[38] Some local planners shared this nega-

tive view – among them David Crane, who once wrote to the Rockefeller Foundation that he "got a little bit worried [...] when [Doxiadis suggested] the same form of approach used in Bagdad [*sic*] would be just as appropriate for Eastwick in Philadelphia" [Fig. 3].[39]

But in this curious public-access documentary, almost the sole occasion on which we can see and hear the voices of Eastwick's new residents, most of the interviewed subjects considered the houses to have been well designed.

For one, there was the opinion of a white couple, Bernard and Emily Knoll. Bernard told the interviewer, "We came to the conclusion that you couldn't get a finer house for the money that was spent than you can here in Eastwick." Emily looked like she had something to say, but she held it back for the moment.[40]

The comments of Don Davis, another white homeowner in Eastwick also speaking for his wife, tended to agree with that of Mr. and Mrs. Knoll:

> We [...] took a look at the samples, and soon, we fell in love with them, and we went back several times, and we finally decided to buy a house that was a little more expensive than the one we originally decided on.[41]

Fig. 3 Photograph of the model rowhouses of the Doxiadis Associates design in Eastwick.

Then there was the opinion of John James, an African American resident, whom the interviewer interrogated in an accusatorial tone – which, however, didn't seem to ruffle the speaker:

> Why, we like it very much [...] It's very quiet, no thru-traffic, it's a play area for the children [...] As far as the other side, why, we're a bit disappointed inasmuch as we haven't gotten the shopping centers yet, or the esplanade and backwoods, but I suppose in time we will have them, and when we do, it will be a very beautiful area.[42]

The documentary noted that the community was supposed to have 2,000 homes in the first five years. As I have stated previously, only 272 had been built – but only eighty-one of that number had been occupied, by lease-purchase agreements.[43] Apparently, by this point, they hadn't even "sold" any homes. As to the reason why, it was about to become abundantly clear.

During the interview, Bernard Knoll also stated, "the only thing slowing our growth here is that many people are frightened of living in an integrated neighborhood." At this moment, his wife Emily spoke up for the first time, describing a scene indicative of race relations in the 1960s:

> We know many people personally who have come out here and even put deposits on a home, and then they would [...] perhaps drive around on a Sunday afternoon and see white children playing with colored children, and it really bothered them so much that they just took their deposits back, they were just so worried about the integration problem.[44]

The modern horror of this anecdote aside, many of the residents felt proud of their role in Eastwick – that, by living in an integrated community, they considered themselves pioneers, leading the way into the future. White resident Anthony Pocinella told the TV crew, "the people here [felt] that because it started off as integrated, from the very beginning, they [were] more or less now adapted to the idea that this [was] something that [had] to be, something that [would] eventually *be* throughout the entire country."[45] This was the opinion, of course, of someone who had self-selected to live in an integrated community.

In the film, William Rafsky, the Director of the Philadelphia Redevelopment Authority and a local power broker in his own right, said that a city study had revealed "that many of the potential homebuyers, who could have their pick from any house in the area, were avoiding Eastwick even though they admitted it was a good housing buy, because they were not quite ready to live in an integrated neighborhood."[46]

One result of the looming shadow racism cast over the development was that, after four years and the bankruptcy of the original developer, all efforts to promote the Eastwick name ended. The new developer, the Korman Corporation, had dubbed its latest houses the community of "Blue Bell," a transparent effort at rebranding. Perhaps by 1975, the documentary suggested, Eastwick would overcome its difficulties and be transformed into the "city-within-a-city" of Doxiadis's vision, echoing Bacon's optimistic 1959 prophecy in *Philadelphia Magazine*, when he foresaw "by the year 2009, no part of Philadelphia [being] ugly or depressed."[47]

The Planning of Eastwick, before Doxiadis

The documentary, as revealing as it was, left out a few key details. In 1949, long before Doxiadis had arrived on the scene (in fact, while he was supervising the post-war reconstruction of Greece under the Marshall Plan), Eastwick had been targeted for urban renewal – but with aims that seem decidedly nefarious today.[48] At that point, Philadelphia city leaders reportedly wanted to build public housing in Eastwick to absorb and house African Americans displaced by the city's other urban-renewal projects. Essentially, Eastwick was supposed to be the city's brand-new ghetto.[49]

Edmund Bacon opposed this plan. The planner and architect was a complicated, polarizing figure in Philadelphia. In the 1964 issue of *Time* magazine in which he was featured on the front cover, he was described as a "Philadelphian with sharp blue eyes and an intensely intellectual air that hardly seems the right equipment for moving and shaking a major city," his saving grace being "his total dedication to his special art and to his native town – plus an impressive gift of gab."[50] For two decades, from 1949 to 1970, Bacon was in charge of the Philadelphia City Planning Commission. While that longevity might have made him seem like Philadelphia's counterpart to New York's Robert Moses, Bacon's biographer Gregory Heller described the Philadelphia planning board as having very little power.[51] It mostly made recommendations, framed initiatives and helped interface the city government with private firms. While some of his initiatives were, on their own terms, "successful" – such as his revitalization of the historic and charming

Society Hill neighborhood – Bacon had a mixed track record, but one with tremendous impact.[52]

The planning of Eastwick was part of a larger pattern of Philadelphia post-war redevelopment schemes and marketing efforts – one that preached inclusivity and progressive futurism while sidestepping the politics of race, class and gender that vitally required consideration in such visions. As planning historian Amy E. Menzer outlined in her article regarding the Philadelphia City Planning Commission's 1947 *Better Philadelphia Exhibition*, Bacon's commission marketed planning to the Philadelphia public as a way to meet the challenges of urban growth while at the same time achieving a sense of unity across the socioeconomic spectrum to march toward an idyllic future.[53] In that exhibition, held on the fifth floor of the downtown Gimbels department store, Menzer wrote, "the immediate conflicts between the city's economic and ecological future and that of the suburbs were reconciled through the invocation of a greater, regional scale of unity, and competition was displaced from being within the Philadelphia metropolitan region to occurring between it and other regions."[54] However, to generate such a sense of unity in the exhibition's messaging, Menzer argued, "the exhibition simultaneously evaded complicated questions of social difference – racial segregation, class hierarchy, and gender inequity – even as it introduced a participatory planning process that would require engagement with these fissures in the 'vital center' of Philadelphia and American life."[55]

As Menzer discussed, Bacon had previously advocated for the adoption of a housing rehabilitation policy (the idea of repairing the existing urban fabric as opposed to demolishing blocks and displacing communities so as to clear the ground for massive public-housing projects) as a potential solution for guaranteeing Philadelphia's urban renewal. Menzer wrote, "rehabilitation did not significantly challenge pre-existing patterns of racial and class segregation by minimizing the conflict that might arise from the perceived encroachment of poor blacks, who were in disproportionate need, on white ethnic and black middle-class enclaves."[56]

In Bacon's mind, the advantages and disadvantages of housing rehabilitation could contain the problems of racial discord by not creating a situation where a new public-housing project targeting the poorer, Black community spurred on white flight to the suburbs. Whether that theory was correct or not, Bacon could not rely on that strategy for Eastwick – though his presumption was in some ways prescient in explaining the consequences that project faced.

Menzer further argued that, "by dovetailing simultaneously with various political outcomes, rehabilitation may have been more politically palatable, but the pressures of postwar housing shortages and deterioration left most policy makers unconvinced that it was enough."[57] Though the urban-renewal project at Eastwick would seek to upgrade a neighborhood, it would be more than merely rehabilitation, being a full-scale intervention.

Bacon eventually came to have grander plans for Eastwick than his writings on rehabilitation suggested. He was not satisfied with the idea of using Eastwick as a dumping ground for minorities pushed out of other Philadelphia districts.[58] He had also long admired the design of Radburn, New Jersey, an influential "new town" built in 1929 to separate motor vehicles from pedestrians.[59] His eventual advocacy for Doxiadis as master planner arose in part because the architect's philosophy of Ekistics, the science of human settlements, had similar principles to those embedded in the design for Radburn.[60] With Eastwick, Bacon could use the town as a demonstration project for the ideal future of the American suburbs – pedestrian-friendly, community-oriented and, critically, racially integrated.

In 1953, city planner Henry Churchill developed the first plan for a new Eastwick, introducing the idea of a "balanced community" as a showpiece for the city. Churchill's plan suggested a neighborhood to be designed for 45,000 residents with a variety of housing types and community amenities in the form of parks, schools and commercial services. Like the Doxiadis plan that followed, collector roads would also keep cars out of neighborhoods.[61]

Following the landmark 1954 Supreme Court case *Brown v. Board of Education*, racial integration became a primary goal for Philadelphia – which must be emphasized as a quite remarkable goal for this time period. Some of the reasons for this were, admittedly, pragmatic. McKee attributed this to the fact that to build a community of this scale, with enough housing units to accommodate 45,000 people, necessitated attracting buyers from both African American and white communities. With only African American buyers, the community would not be able to take off – at least, that's how the theory went.[62]

To build a new Eastwick at this scale, the city needed to relocate and displace a portion of Eastwick's extant residents – 8,636 of them. For many of Eastwick's residents, this was unacceptable. They didn't want a brand-new, demonstration project of an ideal city. They just wanted the city to build the services that were necessary for a modern lifestyle: sewers, sidewalks, flood control. As McKee recounted, a series of protests, unruly town halls and even bomb threats slowed down the project, which, in many ways, had failed to consult with a community that was already integrated. One main tenet of the protest movement was that the redevelopment of Eastwick would lead to the *de facto* segregation of Eastwick – fears that seemed pretty rational in retrospect.[63]

By 1957, the Eastwick plans seemed to hit a wall they could not bulldoze through. But one force kept them alive – the promise of federal funding. If Eastwick were to be canceled, McKee reported, the city would lose $54 million in federal urban-renewal grants. *That* was unacceptable. And so, to the enduring anger of the existing Eastwick community, which called the Meadows their home, warts and all, Eastwick went forward to redevelopment. Crucially, the federal funding required that the housing be integrated.[64]

By 1959, after much of the extant housing had been demolished, Doxiadis arrived on the scene – initially disappointed with the aesthetics and potentials of the industrial and marshy site. However, he retained his characteristic resolve, and in Eastwick it was no different.[65] A year later, Doxiadis Associates won the bid to develop a new plan for Eastwick.[66] In 1961, the development broke ground.[67]

The City-within-a-City: The Doxiadis Plan

The 1960 Doxiadis Associates plan recognized the need to craft a self-sustaining group of neighborhoods that could in turn become a fully functioning district of Greater Philadelphia, thereby attaining the lofty goal of a city-within-a-city [Fig. 4].

To do this, DA planned for a network of collector roads and suburban streets to join the existing highways and railways in the area. From a small cul-de-sac, the typical motorist could depart their house, drive onto a collector road and then onto the highway. This may seem to be typical of many American suburban developments, but these cul-de-sacs were especially narrow and small, along straight lines, and siloed off through traffic patterns. Thus, this layout prioritized pedestrian safety and supported a more intriguing phenomenological experience of passing through a neighborhood via its unconventional network of sidewalks [Fig. 5].[68]

In keeping with Doxiadis's interest in maintaining the human scale, the plan was designed to allow for pedestrians to walk through all of Eastwick and for each of the sectors to be easily reached both on foot and by car. The twin needs of the modern citizen were thus addressed in an "intermeshed" fashion [Fig. 6].[69]

Within the residential neighborhoods, conceived as "minor" communities of forty or fifty houses, Doxiadis Associates stipulated the creation of gardens where children might play and adults could connect; this concept, in particular, mirrored DA's development of so-called gossip squares in Iraq, perhaps motivating Crane's previously mentioned comment about Eastwick and Baghdad.[70] As the DA plan published in *Ekistics* states:

> Everybody, entering by car such a community, will enter from a road where he will get the impression of an urban landscape in which he belongs. The lawn will not be long enough to be tiresome, but it will give a feeling of proper urban space, at the end of this road. As soon as he enters, however, the parking lot, placed vertically to the access road, he will get the feeling of being in a courtyard, the basic element of which is in the car. Finally, the third aesthetic element to the access road and the parking lot is the garden space between the houses, which inspires a rather rural feeling.[71]

Shops were to be placed on the corners of these clustered neighborhoods, ensuring the mixed-use nature of the project. The plan further stated, "This means that even such a small community of forty or fifty families, the elemental 'cluster' of houses, is really a living entity with its own character and spirit, composed of a good number of elements which contribute to community life and atmosphere" [Fig. 7].[72]

When Doxiadis spoke with Kennedy in the Senate, he recalled meeting a resident of the new Eastwick, "a lady of Italian descent with a very bad accent, worse than [his own] if [Kennedy could] imagine," and she told Doxiadis that "her children [could] play free outside of her home, out in the streets, and that she [did] not worry any more about them." Doxiadis concluded, "Even if only this can be achieved – that is, freedom to play in the streets – I think we are justified in our efforts."[73]

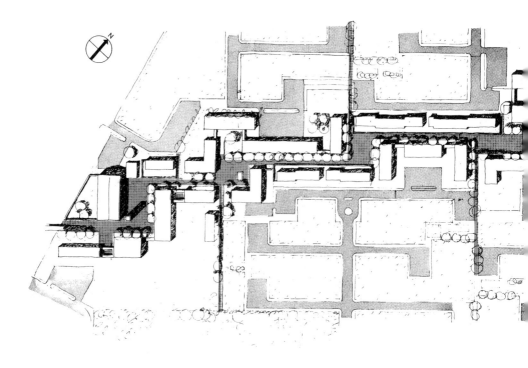

Fig. 4 The Doxiadis Associates map of a "typical residential sector" in Stage 1 of the implementation of the Eastwick plan.

Fig. 5 The "esplanade" of the Eastwick plan was conceived as a pedestrian corridor to form the backbone of the community.

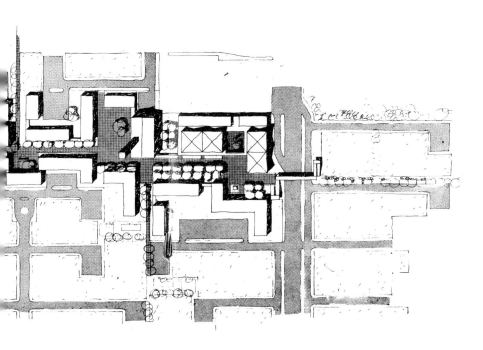

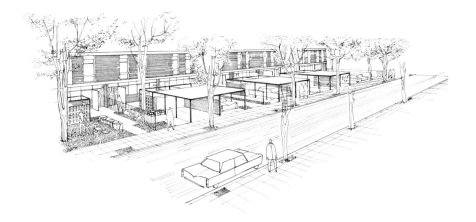

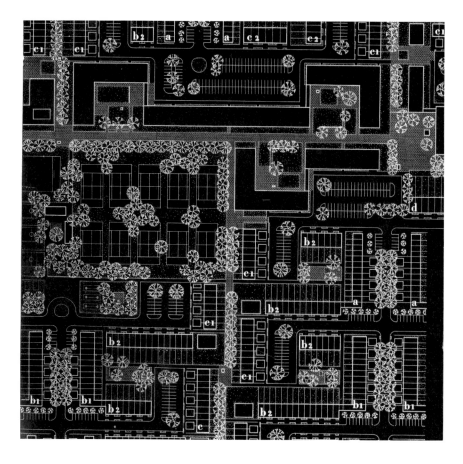

Fig. 6 A rendering of a Doxiadis Associates-planned Eastwick street lined with rowhouses that would, like most American suburbs, incorporate the car but in restrained fashion.

Fig. 7 The Doxiadis Associates plan for Eastwick sought to create "clusters" that would help facilitate community space.

Eastwick under Construction

While Doxiadis Associates were responsible for the plans and architectural designs of Eastwick's first homes – and figured highly in the marketing for the project – DA were not responsible for the construction or the manner in which they were sold.[74] The plans and designs of Doxiadis Associates were implemented by the New Eastwick Corporation, a collaboration between the small, local building firm of Samuel and Henry Berger and the Reynolds Aluminum Service Corporation. The latter was a manufacturer known for aluminum foil, which invested in Eastwick ostensibly because the company believed, in the *Jetsons*-mindset of the future, that aluminum was going to be used throughout the home-of-tomorrow.[75]

The first phase of the project was completed in 1962, with the construction of 272 homes, and sales stalled.[76] Soon, city officials and the New Eastwick Corporation feared that if the proportion of the African American population of Eastwick became too great, no white buyers would ever move there. As McKee noted, "during the early stages of marketing, as many as two-thirds of white customers lost interest on learning that Eastwick would be integrated at all." And so, the New Eastwick Corporation, with the acquiescence of the city, quietly – and quite illegally – implemented a racial quota for Eastwick. Only 20 percent of the houses could be sold to African Americans. To integrate Eastwick, the NEC decided that it needed to discriminate.[77] To achieve this morally dubious policy – one that, in the end, would still be ineffective at attracting enough sales to build the community at its planned scale – sales agents employed underhand tactics. The housing prices were raised from $10,000 to $12,000 to place the dwellings financially out of reach for many Black families in the area.[78] Salesmen strained every sinew to calm and assuage the reservations of the prototypical white homebuyer. In the words of McKee, "such tactics placed the burden of overcoming racism almost exclusively on African American homebuyers."[79]

In 1962, the National Association for the Advancement of Colored People (NAACP) filed a complaint on behalf of African American families who had been denied the opportunity to find a home in Eastwick. The restrictive practices were ostensibly ended but, in reality, they continued for a number of years through more insidious means – including a practice whereby potential Black buyers were advised that no homes would be available until the following year, whereas potential white buyers were told that units were immediately available.[80]

The Turning of the Page

The New Eastwick Corporation, now known as the Korman Corporation, has held onto most of the development rights of Eastwick's acreage over the past half-century.[81] However, the active involvement of Doxiadis Associates did not extend much past the release of its initial plans and designs in 1962.[82] Bacon retired in 1970, and Doxiadis passed away in 1975 of ALS (amyotrophic lateral sclerosis, also known as motor neurone disease) at the age of sixty-two.[83] A generation had passed, and Eastwick moved forward – albeit more slowly than had ever been anticipated.

By 1982, Eastwick had "4,022 housing units, three shopping centers, two schools, a library, and a pedestrian greenway."[84] Eastwick's population had reached 18,000 – just under the 19,000 it had possessed *before* the redevelopment.[85] It was hardly the 60,000-strong, city-within-a-city of the Doxiadis vision, but it was one of the few Philadelphia neighborhoods that had grown at all in the run-up to 1990 as the entire city contracted from a peak of 2 million in the 1950s to today's hollowed-out population of 1.5 million.[86] In 1982, the Philadelphia Urban Planning Commission declared Eastwick a "success" in that it was an urban community; it was racially integrated; and, "in future years, Eastwick is certain to be recognized as one of Philadelphia's most valued residential communities."[87]

But demographics changed, and quickly. In 2011, Pew Research reported that from 1990 to 2010, the population of Eastwick had transformed from 42.3 percent African American to 76.1 percent African American. More than 5,000 white residents had left the neighborhood over that period, Eastwick's population having been reduced to just 12,000 people in total in 2010.[88] Meanwhile, in 2001, the US Environmental Protection Agency declared Eastwick's Clearview Landfill one of the nation's most contaminated Superfund sites.[89] The twenty-first-century fate of Eastwick would seem to end talk of a city-within-a-city, but, as many have already discovered, the twenty-first century is full of surprises.

A New Beginning?

As recently as 2015, the winds of southwest Philadelphia seemed to have been blowing in a new direction. That was when the Korman Corporation reached a deal with the city to return 54 hectares (134 acres) of its Eastwick land to the public, officially ending the largest urban-renewal project in US history.

In 2016, the Philadelphia planning firm Interface Studio was contracted to develop a new "vision plan" for the returned acres – this time, with input from community residents. Action had long been needed, and finally some action had arrived – this time, with the input of stakeholders. The plan was completed in 2019 to the tune of $254,985.[90] Its principal concept was that Eastwick would one day comprise a "*village-in-the-city*," an irony that seemed to have been lost on its proponents.[91]

Lessons from the Marsh

Unfairly, modern articles about the Eastwick plan deem it an unambiguous disaster, though none of them care to mention Doxiadis specifically or acknowledge that the design elements of his plan were forward-thinking at the time – probably because the conventional journalist is not likely to discover, from the sources that are immediately available, that Doxiadis's involvement and sophisticated plans were such a large part of the selling point for this community.[92]

Bacon, Doxiadis and even Kennedy had high hopes for Eastwick. From their work and rhetoric, it seems that they sincerely believed they could turn around a neighborhood and salvage a controversial urban-renewal project. Ultimately, their design preferences were well-intentioned. Doxiadis's design for the road network and the first set of houses proved to be functional and well received by their initial inhabitants. With its focus on pedestrian streets and hope for mixed-use neighborhoods, this application of Ekistics might be seen as a precursor to the New Urbanism movement in the United States. As Bacon claimed in 1985, "Eastwick is an important statement in the development of urban thinking. Its significance has not been widely recognized. It does represent a very courageous concept which has been carried to completion on a large scale."[93]

As for the dream of integration, it was also noble. How that particular aspect was attempted by the authorities on the ground is an uncomfortable matter that modern historians and planners must reckon with. But despite the controversial means by which the city and the New Eastwick Corporation achieved the integration, some other aspects of this project remain noteworthy.

For a brand-new development to be built and not automatically price out all lower-income groups, that is quite remarkable. The Eastwick project sought to build quality housing for low-income households, and in this sense it delivered. Nowadays, we see new apartments rise all the time, but these forms of housing are almost always luxury apartments built for gentrifying young urban professionals and their deep pockets. With Eastwick, Philadelphia authorities removed many of the appalling living conditions of the site and replaced them with a plan and building format with the *potential* to become the thriving city-within-a-city of Doxiadis's dreams: a city of the future where white and Black residents might have lived together – this time, with the proper amenities of a developed nation.

Eastwick never reached its full potential because, despite efforts to persuade prospective white families to live alongside Black families, the racial prejudice of the former proved a potent, unshakeable force that justified the discriminatory policies of the New Eastwick Corporation and eventually bankrupted it. The fact that Philadelphia has dramatically shrunk in population over the past fifty years has not helped Eastwick become the burgeoning neighborhood it was conceived to be. As a result, one of Doxiadis's most heralded projects in the US fell out of the public discourse, and perhaps Eastwick's disappointing outcome is one of the factors that led to Doxiadis's relative obscurity in the US today. While the visionary striding forth along the marsh in 1959 could see a brighter future despite even his own reservations, the tumultuous social climate of the 1960s conspired against his efforts. Today, the marsh still needs attention; the dream is still unrealized. But in the capital city where he testified half a century ago, some of his more futuristic predictions have become reality.

The Oracle of Washington, DC

In July 2018, my brother and I visited Georgetown. Doxiadis Associates' former offices along the canal still exist – today, they house another architecture firm. More names have changed, though. The gentrification of Georgetown, for good or ill, has become all-encompassing. On the same block as Doxiadis's former offices is a brick-and-mortar Amazon bookstore, then one of the few of its kind in existence, and the popular Baked & Wired cupcake shop.[94]

My brother and I proceeded to the Georgetown waterfront, where we boarded a water taxi. Though the Potomac Riverboat Company has operated these vessels in the district for thirty years, it was only in 2018, five decades after Doxiadis proposed high-speed water taxis as an alternative to car commuting, that the company established a water-taxi network between the Georgetown, Alexandria, National Harbor and Wharf neighborhoods.[95] During a Metro subway shutdown in summer 2019, the taxis became a viable alternative for commuters between Alexandria and the District.[96]

In certain stretches, these taxis jet across the river at speeds that rival the highway traffic. My brother and I marveled as we raced past the Watergate Hotel and the Lincoln Memorial. I thought of Doxiadis's words about being patient with difficult plans, as in Eastwick:

> We are at the beginning of a long process. People are asking me why it takes so long. I answer – because urban renewal is a new affair. Humanity did not know before, how to carry urban renewal projects […][97]

In that same interview, he also said, "The cities that don't have the courage to try such schemes. are cities which are not going to survive."[98]

1. US Government Printing Office, "Federal Role in Urban Affairs: Hearings before the Subcommittee on Executive Reorganization of the Committee on Government Operations, United States Senate. Eighty-Ninth Congress, Second Session, December 2 and 5, 1966, Part 8," 1966, Box 10, Folder 13: Federal Role in Urban Affairs. U.S. Senate Hearings, 1966, Walter P. Reuther Library, Archives of Labor and Urban Affairs, Wayne State University, Detroit, MI, 1713; "Senate Resuming Urban Hearings: Ribicoff Opens Sessions on 'Crisis in Cities' Tuesday," *New York Times*, November 27, 1966.
2. US Government Printing Office, "Federal Role in Urban Affairs," 1713.
3. Ibid.
4. Christopher Rand, "Profiles: The Ekistic World," *New Yorker* (May 1963), 49.
5. Constantinos and Emma Doxiadis Foundation. "Biographical Note," 2019; A. L. Huxtable, "Urban Planning Boasts a World Supersalesman," *New York Times*, July 8, 1969; Louis Winnick, "Philanthropy's Adaptation to the Urban Crisis, 11 Volumes (Ford History)," 1987, Ford Foundation Archives, Catalogued Reports, Box 575, Report 012158, Rockefeller Archive Center, Sleepy Hollow, NY, Ch. VII, Pt. III, 1–69.
6. "World Experts Hunt Way to End Threat of Chaos in Urban Living: Fuller and Abrams on Panel on Vessel in the Aegean – 12 Nations Represented," *New York Times*, July 7, 1963; Alexandros-Andreas Kyrtsis (ed.), *Constantinos A. Doxiadis: Texts, Design Drawings, Settlements* (Athens: Ikaros, 2006), 455–56.
7. "3D Aspen Award Goes to Doxiadis," *New York Times*, July 30, 1966; Doxiadis Foundation. "Biographical Note," 2019; Rand, "Profiles: The Ekistic World."
8. US Government Printing Office, "Federal Role in Urban Affairs," 1713–63.
9. Constantinos A. Doxiadis, "From Athens to Washington: A Common Plight," *Washington Post*, February 28, 1965, Articles – Papers, 2721, Doxiadis Archive, Athens.
10. Alfred P. Alibrando, "Huge Mall Center Urged by Adviser: Greek Planner Sees Need to Preserve Land," *Evening Star*, November 26, 1958, in "Dr. CA. Doxiadis in the U.S.A.: as Reported by the Press," Doxiadis Archive, Articles – Papers, 6922, Athens.
11. US Government Printing Office, "Federal Role in Urban Affairs," 1730.
12. Ibid., 1746.
13. Ibid., 1730–63.
14. Ibid., 1786.
15. Ibid., 1786–87.
16. Ibid., 1797.
17. Wikipedia, "Eastwick, Philadelphia," 2020, https://en.wikipedia.org/wiki/Eastwick,_Philadelphia (accessed March 18, 2024).
18. Guian McKee, "Liberal Ends through Illiberal Means: Race, Urban Renewal, and Community in the Eastwick Section of Philadelphia, 1949–1990," *Journal of Urban History* 27, no. 5 (July 2001), 547.
19. Scott Gabriel Knowles, "Staying Too Long at the Fair: Philadelphia Planning and the Debacle of 1976," in Scott Gabriel Knowles (ed.), *Imagining Philadelphia: Edmund Bacon and the Future of the City* (Philadelphia: University of Pennsylvania Press, 2009), 94.
20. Pew Charitable Trust, "A City Transformed: The Racial and Ethnic Changes in Philadelphia Over the Last 20 Years," Philadelphia Research Initiative, June 1,

2011, https://www.pewtrusts.org/en/research-and-analysis/reports/2011/06/01/a-city-transformed-the-racial-and-ethnic-changes-in-philadelphia-over-the-last-20-years (accessed August 30, 2024).
21 AreaVibes, "Eastwick, Philadelphia, PA Employment," 2020, https://www.areavibes.com/philadelphia-pa/eastwick/employment/ (accessed March 18, 2024).
22 Pew Charitable Trust, "A City Transformed."
23 "Philadelphia Homicides 1988–2017'," *Philadelphia Inquirer*, 2020, https://data.philly.com/philly/crime/homicides/ (accessed April 17, 2024).
24 Kyrtsis (ed.), *Constantinos A. Doxiadis*, 311–463.
25 Anne E. Krulikowski, "Southwest Philadelphia," *The Encyclopedia of Greater Philadelphia,* 2014, https://philadelphiaencyclopedia.org/essays/southwest-philadelphia-essay/ (accessed April 17, 2024).
26 Ibid.; Frederick B. Tolles, "William Penn: English Quaker and Colonist," *Encyclopedia Britannica*, 2019, https://www.britannica.com/biography/William-Penn-English-Quaker-leader-and-colonist (accessed April 17, 2024).
27 Howard Gillette Jr., "Schuylkill River," *Encyclopedia of Greater Philadelphia,* 2024, https://philadelphiaencyclopedia.org/essays/schuylkill-river/ (accessed April 17, 2024).
28 "Andrew McCalla Eastwick," *The Encyclopedia of Pennsylvania Biography*, vol. 14 (New York: Lewis Publishing, 1923), 10–12; Joel T. Fry, "John Bartram House and Garden (Bartram's Garden)," Historic American Landscapes Survey, US National Park Service, HALS No. PA-1, 2002, 80.
29 McKee, "Liberal Ends through Illiberal Means," 547.
30 Krulikowski, "Southwest Philadelphia."
31 McKee, "Liberal Ends through Illiberal Means," 547; Albert M. Cole, "Eastwick Revisited," *Ekistics* 52, no. 312 (May/June 1985), 241–42.
32 *Eastwick: Design for the City Within* and *Eastwick: The Painful Transition*, WRCV-TV; produced by Bill Leonard, 1964, File 29083, Doxiadis Archives.
33 Ibid.
34 Gregory L. Heller, *Ed Bacon: Planning, Politics, and the Building of Modern Philadelphia* (Philadelphia: University of Pennsylvania Press, 2013), 69.
35 *Eastwick: Design for the City Within – The Painful Transition*.
36 Ibid.
37 Ibid.
38 Ibid.
39 David A. Crane, Letter from D. A. Crane to C. Gilpatric, February 23, 1961, Rockefeller Foundation Records, projects, RG 1.2, Series: 749 Greece, Subseries 749.R, Greece – Humanities and Arts, Box 1, Folder 9, FA387, Rockefeller Archive Center, Sleepy Hollow, NY.
40 *Eastwick: Design for the City Within – The Painful Transition*.
41 Ibid.
42 Ibid.
43 Ibid.
44 Ibid.
45 Ibid.
46 Ibid.; Heller, *Ed Bacon*, 10.
47 *Eastwick: Design for the City Within – The Painful Transition*; Edmund Bacon, "Philadelphia in the Year 2009," in Scott Gabriel Knowles (ed.), *Imagining Philadelphia: Edmund Bacon and the Future of the City* (Philadelphia: University of Pennsylvania Press, 2009), 8–18.
48 Kyrtsis (ed.), *Constantinos A. Doxiadis*, 349–52.
49 McKee, "Liberal Ends through Illiberal Means," 552; Heller, *Ed Bacon*, 70.
50 "Modern Living: The City: Under the Knife, or All for Their Own Good," *Time* 84, no. 64 (November 6, 1964), 69.
51 Heller, *Ed Bacon*, 10.
52 Ibid., 1–15.
53 Amy E. Menzer, "Exhibiting Philadelphia's Vital Center: Negotiating Environmental and Civic Reform in a Popular Postwar Planning Vision," in Alan C. Braddock and Laura Turner Igoe (eds), *A Greene Country Towne: Philadelphia's Ecology in the Cultural Imagination* (University Park: Pennsylvania State University Press, 2016), Kindle edition, loc. 4234–441; Stephen Napa, "Better Philadelphia Exhibition (1947)," in *The Encyclopedia of Greater Philadelphia,* 2016, https://philadelphiaencyclopedia.org/archive/better-philadelphia-exhibition-1947/ (accessed March 18, 2024).
54 Menzer, "Exhibiting Philadelphia's Vital Center," loc. 4441.
55 Ibid., loc. 4480.
56 Ibid., loc. 4480–98.
57 Ibid., loc. 4498.
58 Heller, *Ed Bacon*, 69–72.
59 Ibid., 5.
60 Ibid., 69.
61 McKee, "Liberal Ends through Illiberal Means," 552–53.
62 Ibid., 553–54.
63 Ibid., 554–58.
64 Ibid., 558–59.
65 *Eastwick: Design for the City Within – The Painful Transition*.
66 Redevelopment Authority of the City of Philadelphia, "Urban Redevelopment: Eastwick Philadelphia, USA," *Ekistics* 16, no. 94 (September 1963), 166.
67 Heller, *Ed Bacon*, 69.
68 Doxiadis Associates, "Eastwick Redevelopment Project," *Ekistics* 10, no. 59 (September 1960), 202.
69 Ibid., 204.
70 Ibid.; Panayiota Pyla, "Gossip on the Doxiadis 'Gossip Square': Unpacking the Histories of an Unglamorous Public Space," *Architectural Histories* 1, no. 1 (2013), art. 28, 1–6.
71 Doxiadis Associates, "Eastwick Redevelopment Project," *Ekistics* 10, no. 59 (September 1960), 214.

72 Ibid.
73 US Government Printing Office, "Federal Role in Urban Affairs," 1797.
74 Doxiadis Associates, "Eastwick Redevelopment Project," 195; Redevelopment Authority of the City of Philadelphia, "Urban Redevelopment: Eastwick Philadelphia, USA," 166.
75 Heller, *Ed Bacon*, 69.
76 *Eastwick: Design for the City Within – The Painful Transition*.
77 McKee, "Liberal Ends through Illiberal Means," 561–65; Heller, *Ed Bacon*, 73.
78 McKee, "Liberal Ends through Illiberal Means," 562; Heller, *Ed Bacon*, 73.
79 McKee, "Liberal Ends through Illiberal Means," 562.
80 Ibid.
81 Catalina Jaramillo, "How Philadelphia Built a Neighborhood on Toxic Soil," WHYY, October 14, 2019.
82 Kyrtsis (ed.), *Constantinos A. Doxiadis*, 406.
83 Heller, *Ed Bacon*, 198; Doxiadis Foundation, "Biographical Note," 2019.
84 McKee, "Liberal Ends through Illiberal Means," 563.
85 Ibid.; Heller, *Ed Bacon*, 68.
86 McKee, "Liberal Ends through Illiberal Means," 567; Redevelopment Authority of the City of Philadelphia, "Urban Redevelopment: Eastwick Philadelphia, USA," 195.
87 Cole, "Eastwick Revisited," 246.
88 Pew Charitable Trust, "A City Transformed."
89 Jaramillo, "How Philadelphia Built a Neighborhood on Toxic Soil."
90 Jared Brey, "Philadelphia Wants to Remedy an Urban Renewal Failure," *Next City*, June 5, 2017; Catalina Jaramillo, "New Path for Eastwick Opens Up One Year after Termination of Urban-renewal Agreement," WHYY, December 28, 2016.
91 Catalina Jaramillo, "Philadelphia Seeks to Heal Old Eastwick Wound with a 'Village in the City'," WHYY, March 27, 2019.
92 Ibid.; Brey, "Philadelphia Wants to Remedy an Urban Renewal Failure"; Jaramillo, "How Philadelphia Built a Neighborhood on Toxic Soil"; Jaramillo, "New Path for Eastwick Opens Up One Year after Termination of Urban-renewal Agreement."
93 Cole, "Eastwick Revisited," 240.
94 Ally Schweitzer, "At D.C.'s New Amazon Store, Come for the Books, Leave with a Blender," WAMU, March 13, 2018, https://wamu.org/story/18/03/14/d-c-s-new-amazon-store-come-books-leave-blender/ (accessed April 17, 2024).
95 Rebecca Cooper, "The Wharf to Bring New Daily D.C. Water Taxi," *Washington Business Journal*, November 16, 2016; "Potomac Water Taxi," City Experiences, 2024, https://www.cityexperiences.com/washington-dc/city-cruises/water-taxi/ (accessed April 17, 2024).
96 Kery Murakami, "During the Metro Shutdown, Riders Could Turn to Water Taxis for Transportation," *Washington Post*, May 14, 2019; Kery Murakami, "On the Water Taxi, a Different Kind of Metro Shutdown," *Washington Post*, June 9, 2019.
97 *Eastwick: Design for the City Within – The Painful Transition*.
98 Ibid.

Futures and Legacies

Section III

313 **Metacriticisms of Ekistics' Environmental Design**
Panayiota Pyla

337 **Urban Ecosystems and Global Ecological Balance**
Rethinking Doxiadis's Legacy as Nature–Settlement Dialectics
Ahmed Z. Khan

383 **Bio-systemic Thinking for Holistic Design**
On the Legacy of the Delos Symposia in Contemporary Environmental Thinking and Environmentally Conscious Design
Yannis Zavoleas

407 **Japanese Delos in 27 Points**
Tilemachos Andrianopoulos

439 **Doxiadis Associates' Master Plan for Skopje and the Global Ecological Balance**
The Element of Nature
Thomas Doxiadis

Metacriticisms of Ekistics' Environmental Design

Panayiota Pyla

Introduction

As scholarship on Constantinos A. Doxiadis and the Delos Symposia grows, and as more historical complexities are uncovered regarding the intellectual provenance of their ideas or their alignments with various political or socio-economic postures, Ekistics and the enterprise of the Delos network have been criticized using a variety of theoretical tools. Historiographic critiques of modernism that expose the pitfalls of rationalism and functionalism; Foucauldian critiques of power and governmentality that expose the paternalism of development expertise; Marxist critiques of development that challenge its economistic biases; environmental critiques of anthropocentrism's dominance over nature; and critiques of planning politics that have uncovered race or class inequalities in specific locales – these are just a few of the theoretical perspectives that have uncovered problematic aspects in the rationalist, bureaucratic or developmentalist visions of mid-twentieth-century architectural and planning visionaries and have challenged Doxiadis's enterprise of Ekistics, the practice of Doxiadis Associates and the ideas professed by Delos members.[1] Such recent, and sometimes powerful, critiques have permeated current scholarly knowledge at large – so much so that it is no longer possible to claim that urban transformations involve solely technocratic or apolitical processes. There *is* a more or less established understanding that science and centralized management are *not* neutral and that development bureaucracy is *not* entirely benign. Just as the entire architectural and planning production of that era came under scrutiny, so Doxiadis and his enterprise too are interrogated under such critical lenses.

Given the new level of criticality that has entered current discourse, today's architectural culture seems to have changed quite drastically since the heroic era of 1950s–1960s modernism. Nonetheless, practices that attempt to tackle contemporary emergencies insistently rehash issues of the role of science, development, the environment and interdisciplinarity in ways that indeed resonate with key themes contemplated by Doxiadis, Ekistics and the Delians. Even if those mid-twentieth-century methods and their materialized interventions have been challenged, the questions they posed still linger. We are still debating how buildings should negotiate between their economic and ecological priorities; there are still disputes on the ways in which technical know-how can permeate policy-making; and the old concept of international development still haunts world politics, even if there is a new version of geo-economics, fashioned in terms of market economics and global corporations.[2] The terms in which we now ponder the social and environmental role of architecture and planning or the relationships of science and technology to policy and society may be different from those in which Doxiadis and the Delians formulated these questions. However, the issues raised in Doxiadis's writings and the debates of the Delos Symposia insistently creep up on today's architectural disciplinary domain in some shape or form.

Let us contemplate the issue of the environment, on which this chapter focuses: even if the radical effects of climate change, the melting of ice and greenhouse-gas emissions make today's global environmental problems seem unprecedented, the strategies aimed at addressing these problems are very much rooted in 1950–1960s thought and often remind us of Ekistics specifically. Current strategies to make buildings responsive to combined economic, social and ecological priorities resonate with Doxiadis's dubious techno-scientific search for synthesizing the disciplines that shape the built environment. Similarly, trends in sustainable architecture, such as "natural design" or "eco-masterplanning," that are in step with market demands also resonate with Doxiadis's attempts to marry his increasing environmental concerns with a commitment to that era's drive for economic growth.[3] Furthermore, current design strategies that aim for moderation of resource use, energy-efficient buildings, self-sufficient solar homes, nontoxic materials, etc. do resonate with the ethic, if not the form and aesthetics, of Doxiadis's reconciliatory concept of an "ecological balance."[4] All in all, there are numerous conceptual continuities between mid-twentieth-century design strategies and current practices that profess architecture's relationship to science, economy and environment. As environmental imperatives increase even more and their impact on design strategies is all the more augmented, it becomes obvious that not only Ekistics' insights but also the critique that has surrounded its more problematic aspects could offer a useful lens through which to understand contemporary design practice and architectural theory.

This chapter examines the current relevance of the critique of Ekistics, at least to the extent that it pertains to concepts of environment and sustainability. To that end, it focuses on three themes that were advanced by Ekistics that also resonate quite well with current versions of environmental strategies in architecture, namely, 1) an emphasis on scientific comprehensiveness and interdisciplinarity as important to understanding the environment; 2) the alignment of design and ecology with development and market economics; and 3) conceptions of moderation as a way to manage resource use and exploitation. These will be interrogated in terms of the critiques that have been, or could be, leveled against these conceptual themes to ultimately contemplate the current resonance of this critique. Clearly, this is by no means an exercise in refashioning Ekistics. Rather, the purpose is to critically reflect on the *critique* of Ekistics. As though proposing a metacriticism, the chapter interrogates how critical perspectives on these three themes of Ekistics can also inform current predicaments of design and the environment.

Scientific Comprehensiveness and the Dubious Role of Interdisciplinarity – Or, Are the Social, Economic and Ecological Mandates Treated Equally in Sustainable Design?

Ekistics was well positioned to enter the ecological debates of the late 1960s because, since its earlier, developmentalist phase, it had already been extensively experimenting with key ecologically minded concepts – among them, an expanded notion of the environment of buildings. This was captured by the five Ekistic elements of nature, networks, society, shells and humans; the multiple scales of settlements that extended from small communities to large urban agglomerations and the global city of Ecumenopolis; and a notion of interdisciplinarity that took various forms. Let us focus on the last-named concept, with which Doxiadis experimented in at least two very different ways. The first concept of interdisciplinarity was reflected in the

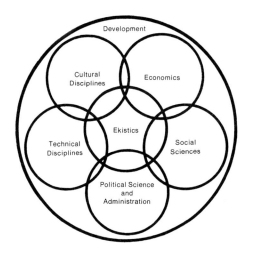

idea of "synthesis of disciplines," which was advanced from the very inception of Ekistics in the 1940s and aimed to forge alignments between architecture and planning and other forms of knowledge. The second was the Delos Symposia, which began in 1963, bringing together different experts from diverse backgrounds to discuss housing, urban planning and the larger physical environment. If the first was trying to "synthesize disciplines" in order to enlarge disciplinary knowledge on the built environment, the second tactic was trying to "synthesize processes" – to expand the powers and reach of the architect–planners themselves into other epistemological and policy realms. Both could fall under the umbrella of interdisciplinarity, which has been a key term in the ecological debate ever since its advent in the early 1960s.[5]

Ekistics' goal to synthesize various disciplines was captured in a diagram that became like a trademark for Doxiadis Associates. Titled "Ekistics and the sciences directly contributing to it," the diagram represented Ekistics as a science in its own right, with "economics," "social sciences," "political science and administration," "technical disciplines" and "cultural disciplines" all feeding in [Fig. 1]. The idea of incorporating the input of the social sciences to increase architecture's social instrumentality was, of course, not uncommon in post-war architectural discourse. Social scientists themselves initiated such collaborations in an effort to grasp the impact of the physical environment on human behavior and social patterns. Ekistics aspired to bring these collaborations to the domain of physical planning, and this too was already very much in tune with larger post-war architectural critiques of pre-war CIAM's (Congrès Internationaux d'Architecture Moderne's) mechanistic conception of function. Doxiadis's efforts to transcend functionalism did not follow those post-war trends that turned to symbolic representations or aestheticism (e.g. Jørn Utzon's experiments) and did not reject the professional disciplines of architecture and planning

Fig. 1 Constantinos A. Doxiadis's diagram illustrating Ekistics' multidisciplinary ethos.

in favor of the vernacular (e.g. Bernard Rudofsky's search for an architecture without architects). Instead, Doxiadis joined the ranks of those post-war architects who tried to humanize modernism by establishing new alignments with the conceptual framework of science. His own "Ekistics," as the "science of human settlements," aimed to amend the rationalization of architectural production and to address the "the totality of human needs" that would reconcile functionalism with humanistic concerns.[6] Another factor that differentiated Doxiadis's Ekistics from other architectural investigations of extra-technological and non-functionalist concerns was its methods of aligning architecture and planning with the modes of post-war development – but this will be discussed later, under the second theme.

The diagram of the "synthesis of disciplines" that captured Ekistics' interdisciplinary ethos presented five types of discipline with slight overlaps between them and with Ekistics as a central circle that drew on all of them to form what has now come to be called a "metadiscipline": a methodological means of pursuing "novel collaborations" to arrive at an interdisciplinary synthesis by making exactly what Harvey J. Graff describes in "The 'Problem' of Interdisciplinarity in Theory, Practice, and History" – namely, a "heavy use of the knowledge provided by the relevant disciplines but combined and transformed to form new knowledge not directly deducible from the disciplines themselves."[7] Putting aside the fact that the diagram separated economics from other social sciences and gave it a circle in and of itself, it is striking how deductive knowledge ("technical disciplines") was to be combined with the evaluative knowledge of "cultural disciplines" in an entirely static and symmetrical relationship through a conflict-free process whereby Ekistics (the central circle) would integrate elements from a variety of disciplines that included anthropology and building physics, economics and health, to approach the design of settlements in a new way. This romanticized combination remained unaware of the complicated incommensurability between different types of knowledge and ignored the danger that transcending dichotomies between disciplines can lead to reductionism.[8] This is not to mention that this schema also ignored the fact that each circle overlapping the Ekistics "synthesis of disciplines" embodies its own conflicts, limits and contradictions, constituting "interdisciplinarity within a discipline."[9] How exactly would Ekistics resolve the tensions or antagonisms of the different scientific knowledges gathered under its umbrella (or into its circle, so to speak)? The term "synthesis," so favored by Doxiadis, recognized no epistemological gap between the social aspects of space and the different aspects of knowledge that were supposedly in tune with each other to produce more knowledge.

The incommensurability described above would also surface in Doxiadis's other interdisciplinary experiment – namely, the Delos Symposia. These Symposia were annual week-long events between 1963 and 1975 that were initially modeled after the earlier congresses of the modern movement, CIAM but, contrary to their predecessor, projected a more diverse outlook as the invited participants had more varied backgrounds in terms of geographies and disciplines [Fig. 2]. The Delos Symposia tried to augment the voice of planners and architects (and the importance of housing and planning) by organizing a new professional society that would include not only architects and planners but also scientists and administrators. These meetings attempted to boost the bureaucratic and technocratic aura of Ekistics and the entire Doxiadis Associates enterprise, and to forge a dialogue with the specific disciplines that Ekistics wanted to embrace yet also build bridges to the realm of policy-making and action.

Doxiadis, having established himself as a player in the scene of international development consulting – after being a coordinator of Marshall Plan aid to Greece, he participated in United Nations (UN) and World Bank Technical Assistance missions, and he became consultant to several newly established nation-states in the post-colonial world – recognized that the expansion of disciplinary knowledge was not enough and that architectural and planning visions had to also reach out to technocrats, state powers and international development institutions. This view, which he expressed in his first book, *Architecture in Transition*, echoed the Taylorist ethos of the "Athens Charter," the 1933 manifesto of modernist urbanism that advocated rational and efficient urbanism be carried out by a central state power under the guidance of expert planners.[10] Doxiadis embraced the social optimism of this technocratic model, which appeared even more appealing after World War II, when the daunting tasks of reconstruction, rehousing and urbanization in many parts of the globe augmented the need to objectify, chart and analyze needs, resources and social relationships.[11]

By building personal and professional networks and by forming loose alliances with various disciplines and with policy-makers (some of whom were highly placed in international institutions or national governments around the world), the Delos Symposia constituted an alternative space for

architectural, planning, administrative and political debates on urbanism.[12] This space was created literally on ships cruising the Aegean, and it was also created metaphorically by diverse personas and competing agendas that converged on annual themes such as urban density, networks, education, development and environmental quality.

The first Delos Symposia included renowned scientists such as the anthropologist Margaret Mead and the economist Barbara Ward – global activists in their own right and reportedly "the stars of the cruise"; communications expert Marshall McLuhan, soon to become Director of the Center for the Study of the Extensions of Man at the University of Toronto; the geneticist and professor at Edinburgh University Conrad Waddington; and the sociologist Eiichi Isomura, professor at Tokyo Metropolitan University and also Director of the Japanese Bureaus on Planning and on Social Development. Simultaneously, the involvement of United Nations officials and various top government officials from around the world underlined the desire for this new professional society to be directly inserted into policy-decision processes. Meanwhile, the realm of architecture and planning was represented at the first Delos meeting by such figures as Sigfried Giedion

Fig. 2 Photo from the third Delos Symposion, 1965, showing one of the sessions on board. Seated in the first two rows, from left to right, are W. Nielsen, B. Ward, J. M. Richards, E. Mason, G. Danos, C. H. Waddington, Ms. Wolfe, S. Giedion, L. B. Granger and M. Mead.

and Jaqueline Tyrwhitt, who underlined the link between CIAM and Ekistics, as well as such personalities as Richard Buckminster Fuller, who boosted the meeting's media appeal.[13]

The debates that took place in this interdisciplinary encounter had many frustrating incongruities. Not everyone agreed with Doxiadis's projections of the future. Some thought they overlooked the unpredictability of human behavior or chance, while others thought that the emphasis on physical space and human scale was outdated and static.[14] These incongruities were mediated by the particularly pleasant venues of the meetings (cruise ships, visits to islands and archaeological sites), and the relaxed atmosphere of food and drink helped finesse differences and allowed the strong-minded intellectuals, highbrow bureaucrats and overconfident academics to all converse with each other. This is what Hashim Sarkis, discussing the first Delos Symposion, described insightfully as "dancing" around disciplines.[15] The fact that Delian conversations had the laid-back, improvisational and playful character of dancing (as opposed to the diligent and uptight rigors of negotiation, let us say) is quite significant in explaining how the scientific perspectives that each Delian brought from their respective fields could become neatly entangled with intuitive assertions or impossible generalizations about the "expansion of cities," "the totality of human needs" and the like [Fig. 3].

Having the character of a leisurely retreat, the cruise was a venue for negotiation that tolerated, much more than resolved, disciplinary contrasts and ideological antagonisms. This more playful than usual contemplation of scientific (but often also other) themes can explain, for example, how Tyrwhitt's diligent insistence on the human scale could coexist with McLuhan's and Buckminster Fuller's abstract aestheticization of global networks and mobility. And it would explain why a microbiologist such as René Dubos participated in Delos just once, because apparently not much common ground was found, only to find himself in the midst of discussions on building and city design. The fact that the delegates were not able to agree on a plan of action in the form of a charter and could only settle for a more general "declaration" about urban problems is telling about the incommensurability of their perspectives and the tensions between their disciplines. Thus, ultimately, what the Delos Symposia's interdisciplinary experiment showed most vividly was that, even if there is a common concern about the shape of cities, the lack of housing or environmental degradation, common goals are neither obvious nor so easily agreed upon because their priorities

can be contested, their presuppositions can be conflicting and their beneficiaries can be divided – not to mention that particular desires can be filtered through political agendas or media tactics.

What does the above history tell us for the present? Today, we again see design trends that unequivocally advocate interdisciplinary collaborations and echo Doxiadis's belief that (techno-)scientific rationality can address environmental exigencies. Today's discussions on sustainability readily accept it as a quintessentially interdisciplinary issue. And, even if most current interdisciplinary encounters lack the Delos meetings' interpersonal relationships and charming setting, the concept of interdisciplinarity itself

Fig. 3 Photo from the first Delos Symposion, 1963, showing the visit to Hydra.

still manages to evoke what Graff called "a feeling of communicative warmth and power"[16] that allows interdisciplinarity to appear often as some kind of "epistemological panacea" that can cure all ills.[17] Meanwhile, however, we are also coming to realize that interdisciplinarity, as a complex and rather contradictory process, is often also characterized by "exaggerated promises and unrealistic expectations."[18] Tangible examples of such problems of interdisciplinarity can be encountered in current practices of sustainability. Let us reflect on an account offered by environmental historian Donald Worster writing about the emergence of "sustainable development," first in the World Conservation Strategy of the International Union for the Conservation of Nature in 1980 and then in the meetings that followed, culminating with the World Commission on Environment and Development in 1987:

> Lots of lobbyists coming together, lots of blurring going on – inevitably, lots of shallow thinking resulted […] Like most popular slogans, sustainable development begins to wear thin after a while. Although it seems to have gained a wide acceptance, it has done so by sacrificing real substance.[19]

Worster also makes another point that highlights the blind spots in the purportedly global reach of sustainability strategies:

> The North and the South, we were told, could now make common cause without much difficulty. The capitalist and the socialist, the scientist and the economist, the impoverished masses and the urban elites could now all happily march together on a straight and easy path, if they did not ask too many potentially divisive questions about where they were going.[20]

The problem that Worster highlights is that all the "blurring" of disciplinary or geographical boundaries creates uneven dynamics both in regard to disciplinary domains and to international encounters. When economists and ecologists sit around a table to discuss environmentalism, or, more generally, when "hard" and "soft" sciences engage in collaborations regarding sustainability, not all perspectives are discussed on equal terms because the utilitarian and the economic – which can be discussed in more concrete terms – take precedence over the ethical and the cultural.[21] This was a problem that characterized Doxiadis Associates' practice and Ekistics' claims –

and, as Worster shows, it continues to characterize environmental strategies. Ultimately, Worster warns,

> Worse yet, the slogan [of sustainability] may turn out to be irredeemable for environmentalist use because it may inescapably compel us to adopt a narrow economic language, standard of judgement, and world view in approaching and utilizing the earth [...][22]

What Worster says about sustainable development in general applies to architecture and its attempts at sustainable design approaches in particular. Technical questions on energy consumption, materials and building footprints are considered very important in lessening the impact of buildings on the environment, and they typically take the upper hand even when environmental and social justice questions are purportedly considered.

One can spot many other inconsistencies and inequalities lurking behind the rhetoric of interdisciplinary approaches that claim to be comprehensive in considering all social and environmental concerns. Trends like adaptive reuse are often celebrated as sustainable, mainly because they combine economy of resources with corporate profit, while this celebration hardly takes into account the consequences of gentrification.[23] Even the LEED certification system (the US-based Leadership in Energy and Environmental Design program) runs into similar problems, and, although it claims to take into account social and ecological mandates, it does not account for them with the same rigor as it accords other aspects of building design.[24] Furthermore, why does design research and innovation that accumulates important data on environmentally sensitive construction materials and methods not also consider with analogous rigor the ethical questions around the corporate ownership and limited dissemination of this knowledge? I am referring here to patents for environmentally sensitive materials, drawing on Aetzel Griffioen's critique of William McDonough and Michael Braungart's *Cradle to Cradle*, which, for all its embrace of sustainability, restricts the use of raw materials and knowledge. As an alternative, Griffioen presents Dennis Kaspori's plea for open-source architecture and André Gorz's favoring of methods of "personal fabrication," or "fabbing," that one can use to develop one's own high-tech machines using free shared knowledge and cheap resources – a method that shifts the typical profit-driven market model to a community-based approach.[25]

The type of blurring and inaccuracies that Worster diagnosed in interdisciplinary collaborations for sustainable development is a warning for the more immediate present. Current combinations of techno-scientific approaches to environmental design with "softer" disciplines that encompass issues of society, behavior, ethics or aesthetics do not automatically produce a well-rounded approach to sustainability and do not readily guarantee a more balanced or fair approach to design any more than Doxiadis's "synthesis of disciplines" did. Interdisciplinarity is not, in and of itself, a solution to a problem, and it does not automatically guarantee success. There is a wide spectrum of interdisciplinary relationships, various methods and practices to achieve interdisciplinarity and a variety of meanings imposing limits and framing novelties of the notion of interdisciplinarity. If some kind of synergy (of knowledge, perspectives or goals) can emerge from an interdisciplinary encounter in ways that can indeed overcome fragmentation or reductionism, this can only be a beginning for contemplating a solution to a problem.

Development, Market and Their Conflicts – Or, Is the Alignment of Ecology with Capital Good for the Environment?

Arguably, one of the major contributions of Doxiadis was that his writings and practice inserted architecture and planning into global debates on post-war reconstruction and international development. Not only did he call on architects to reconceptualize the architectural profession and to reinvent themselves as global planners and development experts, but he also achieved the opposite – namely, framing 1950s and 1960s developmentalism in spatial terms.[26] In advising UN bodies and funding institutions, or in speaking at the US Senate or in radio broadcasts, Doxiadis highlighted spatial concepts on housing, highways, urban centers and the like to introduce such considerations into the mechanisms of international decision-making power. He even spoke of a gap in UN bureaucracy: that it lacked a body analogous to its World Health Organization (WHO) or Food and Agriculture Organization (FAO) that could be dedicated to housing. Conversely, it is quite telling that in the diagram of interdisciplinary collaborations discussed in the previous section there was a larger circle circumscribing all the other processes, and this was "Development" – as though nothing, in the Ekistics worldview, was to fall outside the developmentalist logic.

As Doxiadis moved comfortably in many development spheres, what seems to have distinguished him from many other fellow "experts" was indeed an emphasis on the spatial and physical dimension of socioeconomic development – namely, urbanization and the overall transformation of the physical environment. If he aspired to the modernization of the planet, this modernization was imagined in terms of the physical environment and not, for example, of industrialization or communication networks.[27]

In Doxiadis's rhetoric, the restructuring of human settlements was a matter of the realistic acceptance of the dominant post-war trends. Influenced by such trends in regional planning, which tied urban industrialization to economic growth, Doxiadis accepted the expansion of cities as irreversible while also arguing for the modernization potentials of rural development.[28] The challenge, then, for the architect–planner was not to halt metropolitan or rural development but to manage growth so as to temper the effects of urbanization and the impact of modernization.[29] Of course, Doxiadis's ostensibly "realistic" compliance with dominant socioeconomic trends implied specific political preferences. Even if Doxiadis would frame his enterprise as apolitical and technocratic, his projects aimed to facilitate the integration of the so-called underdeveloped countries into the post-war economic and political structure favored by the US government, the United Nations and other development institutions. Similarly, his rhetoric on the role of the architect and the overall logic of "growth" in Ekistic analyses clearly embraced the logic of capitalist expansion. All these were, of course, intertwined with the geopolitical antagonisms of the Cold War.

Recent scholarship has critiqued, sometimes strongly, Doxiadis's alignment with international institutions and governmental organizations, showing that centralized management is not necessarily benign and that the drive to integrate the non-industrialized world into the post-war economic and political structure of the Global North serves biopolitical purposes.[30] There have been critiques of governmentality and technocratic expertise that can be further applied to the practice of Doxiadis.[31] We have come to challenge the assumption that modernization and development will overcome the unequal social contours of either local societies or geopolitical dynamics.[32] And we now realize that development has involved conflict of many types because, despite its scientific claims to neutrality, it was entwined with (or became appropriated by) geopolitical agendas or other types of politics.

The same critique could be leveled against the environmental strategies of Ekistics because these too were entwined with the development discourse. The concern for the environment that Ekistics increasingly expressed in the

1960s was a concern that eventually permeated the entire apparatus of development, and this is what ultimately led to the 1980s idea of sustainable development, advanced by the UN and other international institutions – a concept that tried to marry development with the environment.[33] This, as critics of sustainable development point out, was a concept that aspired not to halt development but to ensure the continuation of its logic. Ultimately, sustainable development inserted the environment into the realm of developmentalism, which promoted the global management of resources, leaving intact the logic of development economics, which measured the advancement and worth of nations in terms of products and services produced.[34]

Today, the heroic era of development economics and international bureaucracies may have taken a back seat to market economics, but most design strategies take for granted the alignment of ecology with new forms of capital. Some environmental strategies embrace the "corporate biosphere" or see a "win-win situation" where "you make money and save the planet too," echoing the 1960s–1970s marriage of development and environment, which later scholarship has criticized for its biased favoring of economistic criteria.[35] Consider for example, the invention of ecologically friendly materials, which combines ecological/ethical imperatives with the patenting of technological knowledge to secure company profits. Such postures may not aspire to international development and may not share modernization theory's paternalism of the 1960s, yet they nonetheless turn the protection of nature into a managerial task of economic profit-making, thus sustaining the dominant productivist accumulation ethic – even an ethic of excessive consumption. In other words, these optimistic and consumer-happy solutions are mostly maintaining a status quo, and their diligent dodging of challenging established practices is very similar to the tactics of the vigorously criticized "marriage of development and environment" of the 1970s.[36]

Environmental Balances of Sorts – Or, Whose Balance and for How Long?

As already mentioned, Doxiadis aspired to temper the developmentalist ethos of Ekistics with an increasing emphasis on the environment and ecology. Still very much inscribed within his modernist, rationalist and developmentalist preoccupations, his efforts to humanize development set a "harmonious physical environment" as their target. To interrogate what this meant, let us focus on his vision of an ideal Metropolis, which he envi-

sioned for 2100 CE and which was presented by Doxiadis Associates in a rendering [Fig. 4]. This ideal Metropolis was to temper the effects of industrialization and modernization and to provide a harmonious urban environment. Much as with his plans for many other cities, this "harmony" was tied to a call for attentiveness to the human scale, which, for Doxiadis, meant an emphasis on low densities; the avoidance of tall buildings or any kind of self-conscious forms; and, overall, an aesthetic of order that emphasized the readability of the plan. All in all, his harmonious urban environment was manifested as an anti-urban, low-density, sprawling metropolis.

Doxiadis's partiality to a visual order was pushed to its limits in the projection of a future "Mediterranean Metropolis" in which modern means of transport were placed underground. Highways would be replaced by what Doxiadis called "deepways," and factories were also to exist underground – either beneath public installations or below green open spaces. It is as though harmony would be achieved by placing all intrusions of mechanization out of sight. Of course, we can wonder about the immense cost of the great amounts of energy required to keep these intrusions of mechanization out of sight and to transfer roads and cumbersome mechanical

Fig. 4 Constantinos A. Doxiadis in front of a painting of "Entopia" as Mediterranean Metropolis.

systems underground.³⁷ Furthermore, the placing of factories underground was premised on a view of them as purely utilitarian elements and not as places inhabited by countless workers in need of decent living and working conditions. This extremely inflexible functional division echoed the rigid zoning logic of the "Athens Charter," which did not acknowledge the multiplicity of uses in spaces of work or circulation.³⁸

The above critique by may be refuted by proposing that the Mediterranean Metropolis was not meant to be taken literally and that it served the purposes of a radical manifesto, criticizing the present and provoking people into action. Even we were to accept this urban vision as a conceptual tool, the proposal's insistence on an aesthetic of order and the ways this aesthetic would be transferred to the logic of social ordering remain in question. The rendering shows a sprawling metropolis organized as a blend of communities obeying common zoning laws. Some communities, such as the ones on the hill to the left in Figure 4, were composed of old structures that would be preserved out of respect for traditional patterns of living; others comprised new buildings, apparently for purposes of economy and efficiency. Most communities were open to all religious groups, whereas some were religiously homogeneous – ostensibly to accommodate distinct religious needs. This unsophisticated inclusionary strategy extended to the incorporation of a nudist community that, like the traditionalist and the religious, was assumed to be readily assimilated into the larger social and physical space. All in all, the Mediterranean Metropolis's social ordering advanced an uncomplicated version of pluralism, which assumed that social tensions would be resolved and that even though each community would have "its own special character," all would be "integrated into a harmonious whole."³⁹ Ultimately, the Mediterranean Metropolis was the epitome of Doxiadis's optimistic vision of a peaceful egalitarian future where ethnic, racial and gender struggles would be perceived through the prism of a cosmopolitan idealism that rendered politics obsolete.

The rhetoric of serenity and harmony that accompanied Doxiadis's description of the Mediterranean Metropolis was emblematic of his larger environmental vision. As explained above, when environmental concerns had become widespread by the late 1960s, Doxiadis also increasingly reconceptualized his long-standing efforts to contain and manage urbanization and industrialization in terms of environmental exigencies. In light of the global environmental problems that became increasingly evident in the late

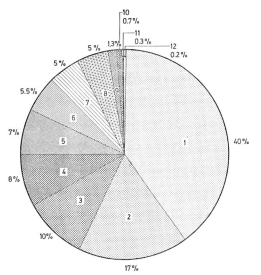

1960s, Doxiadis framed the large urban agglomerations he had envisioned (Dynapolis and Megalopolis all the way up to Ecumenopolis) as a means to restore the "balance of the human environment." In his last book, *Ecology and Ekistics*, he even advanced an argument about balancing nature and society, and this was quite telling about the way he perceived the environmental problems of the time and their solution.

The management of land and resources in Ecumenopolis was purposefully organized to inclusively accommodate human needs. Using a pie chart, Doxiadis divided Earth's land with decimal-point precision, considering the need for industrial progress, scientific advancement, access to nature and alternative lifestyles in an effort to achieve what he called an "ecological balance" between nature, society and humans [Fig. 5]. This planetary pie chart had no reference to specific places or situations, avoiding entirely the otherwise inescapable political questions. Instead, issues related to national resources, technological and military power, and international trade were all to be controlled and managed, it seems, by some supra-political expert management body with the overarching and noble aim of "balance" and the assumption that no disenfranchised individuals and groups would emerge out of all this. Once political antagonisms were bracketed, then the managerial expert's (or the Ekistician's) ecological task was the selective recovery of lost physical qualities, their enlightened reorganization and large-scale dissemination.[40]

The Mediterranean Metropolis did not materialize in any built project, and Doxiadis's ambition for a global distribution of resources appears to us now as symptomatic of late modernism's fixation on comprehensiveness, functionalism and an aesthetic of order. Still, this outdated urban vision has aspects that resonate today. First, its assumption of a post-political future where all antagonisms would be managed away by a developmentalist ethos

Fig. 5 A pie chart dividing Earth's land according to need and "ecological balance."

resonates with today's "sustainability culture," whose engagement with problems of environmental exploitation and social injustice is bound up with the logic of late capitalism.[41] In much the same way that Doxiadis's vision of a post-political future ignored global geopolitical antagonisms, so too does the productive force of sustainability culture, as Adrian Parr has shown, overlook the needs of the world's most impotent inhabitants: the poor.[42] For example, McDonough's dictum of waste = food is a contemporary version of an apparently apolitical and universal claim that also brushes over real and present inequalities that produce "human waste," which, as Griffioen explains, relate to issues of unemployment, poverty and powerlessness in areas that cannot keep up with the corporate production of green materials.[43]

Along with its apolitical claims, a second aspect of the Mediterranean Metropolis that is useful for reflecting on the present is the low-tech familiarity of the resulting settlements in that future landscape. This may have been consistent with Doxiadis's claims to prudence and pragmatism, but a critical look at his Mediterranean Metropolis reveals that, despite the apparent low-tech familiarity of the rendering, the realization of such an urban vision would actually require radical technological interventions, including the reshuffling of population and transportation networks and the creation of enormous underground structures.

The low-tech and somewhat anti-urban vision advanced by Doxiadis is not irrelevant to current debates. In many ways, it alludes to current strategies that express their environmental sensitivity with self-build, off-the-grid, self-sufficient communities made of low-tech materials, and it also resonates with experiments with current reinventions of traditional construction materials such as earth or bamboo [Fig. 6].[44] Many of today's "vernacular" forms or anti-urban, low-density formations face a similar irony as Doxiadis's: they too demand high embodied energy and depend on transportation infrastructures and networks, raising similar concerns.

Another analogy between the Mediterranean Metropolis and our present is the notion of moderation and balance, which continues to bounce around in debates on design/construction and the environment. It may not be possible in the current climate to produce the kind of visionary designers from the previous century, who worked across space and time rationalizing the processes of the built environment and the distribution of planetary resources. Such magic formulas are no longer assumed to exist, because, if for no other reason, nature's own constant flux defies definitive prescriptions for the appropriate type or limits of human intervention. Still, there are many design strategies seeking to approach an "appropriate" human intervention and to assume responsibility for protecting our collective biological whole by moderating the impact on it. Indeed, this is a direction supported by ecologists, who more or less consent that "slow rates of change in ecosystems are 'more natural,' and therefore more desirable, than fast rates."[45] Following that logic, many design strategies, too, focus their objectives on tempering the impact of human production and embrace this philosophy of moderation as the direction toward which much current practice in green or ecological design has been moving.[46]

No matter how reassuring such reconciliatory tactics may appear, they end up triggering more questions and doubts about the way criteria and priorities are defined. Even if we were to make the big assumption that global society could coordinate its efforts in an equitable manner, should it protect nature by managing its resources for human use? Or should it be less hubristic and nurse it as a fragile entity or as natural beauty? Or is it impossible to save nature unless humanity were to radically challenge the impulse to perpetuate growth? How different are approaches that assign to humans, with their current knowledge, the task of correcting the previous harm humanity has inflicted on nature from hubristic views of humans as masters of nature, but in reverse?[47] Conversely, for approaches that pose much more uncomfortable questions about our mode of living and seek a radical restructuring of our societies and their economics – following the lead of a line of thinkers from E. F. Schumacher to V. Shiva – one question that keeps reappearing is how their radicalism can guard against corruption by dominant forms of power.[48] And, as for those strategies that diametrically oppose anthropocentrism in favor of eco-centric approaches, to what extent should they also include, as part of their assessment of ecological processes, the transformative actions of human beings during the past few centuries?[49]

These questions highlight the biggest pitfall in Doxiadis's notion of balance and also offer a critical lens through which to scrutinize current claims of moderation. Environmental historians have shown us how the very notion of balance is culturally and historically constructed, and that nature has no "norm" around which specific sustainability targets can be set.[50] Ecologists themselves speak of nature as inherently disorderly, and can no longer claim to set the standards for a "healthy nature" with certainty

Fig. 6 The Telaithrion Project, a contemporary version of low-tech and low-density urbanism.

(there can be no set "steady-state population" for fish, nor an "optimum yield" for a forest, for example).[51] Consequently, if the science of ecology cannot determine the targets for the sustainable use of seas and forests, how can we set paths for sustainability in other realms of practice?

A final reflection: Doxiadis was operating at a time before ecology had become what Wolfgang Sachs called "a knowledge of domination." Sachs was a pioneer in the bureaucratization of the environment, and we may critique this in terms of issues of power expertise, but it was important that he inserted architecture and the physical into this debate on ecology – especially given that he did not perceive ecology to be a commodity. Ideas about protecting the environment, for example, or about climate change as it is now called, are tossed around as an ethical framework, a managerial method, a governance mode or even a business model without contemplating a most important predicament: now that the environment and ecology are burdened with the status of no longer being at the margins but at the hegemonic center of design concerns, the realm of design has the responsibility to carefully consider how this magic word of consensus came about and how its goals, whatever they are, allow room for complexity and nuance. The historical perspective presented here, which overlays the critique of Ekistics with a critique of current environmental strategies, is aiming at precisely this kind of nuance.

1   Ahmed Zaib Khan, "Representing the State: Symbolism and Ideology in Doxiadis's Plan of Islamabad," in Mark Swenarton, Igea Troiani and Helena Webster (eds), *The Politics of Making* (London and New York: Routledge, 2007), 61–75; Ali Madanipour, "The Limits of Scientific Planning: Doxiadis and the Tehran Action Plan," *Planning Perspectives* 25, no. 4 (2010), 485–504; Arbella Bet-Shlimon, "The Politics and Ideology of Urban Development in Iraq's Oil City: Kirkuk 1946–1958," *Comparative Studies of South Asia, Africa, and the Middle East* 33, no. 1 (2013), 26–40; Dimitris Philippides, *Κωνσταντίνος Α. Δοξιάδης (1913–1975): Αναφορά στον Ιππόδαμο* [*Konstantinos A. Doxiadis (1913–1975): Reference to Hippodamus*] (Athens: Melissa Books, 2015); Farhan Karim, "Between Self and Citizenship: Doxiadis Associates in Postcolonial Pakistan, 1958–1968," *International Journal of Islamic Architecture* 5, no. 1 (2016), 135–61; Hashim Sarkis, *Circa 1958: Lebanon in the Pictures and Plans of Constantinos Doxiadis* (Beirut: Dar An-Nahar, 2003); Ijlal Muzaffar, "Boundary Games: Ecochard, Doxiadis, and the Refugee Housing Projects under Military Rule in Pakistan, 1953–1959," in Aggregate Architectural History Collaborative (ed.), *Governing by Design: Architecture, Economy, and Politics in the Twentieth Century* (Pittsburgh, PA: University of Pittsburgh Press, 2012), 147–76; Mark Wigley, "Network Fever," *Grey Room*, no. 4 (Summer 2001), 82–122; Markus Daeshsel, *Islamabad and the Politics of International Development in Pakistan* (Cambridge: Cambridge University Press, 2015); Panayiota Pyla, "Back to the Future: Doxiadis's Plans for Baghdad," *Journal of Planning History* 7, no. 1 (2008), 3–19; Panayiota Pyla and Giannis Papadopoulos, "Doxiadis's One Big Pan-Africa," in Benno Albrecht (ed.), *Africa: Big Change, Big Chance* (Bologna: Editrice Compositori, 2014), 67–70; Petros Phokaides, "De-tropicalising Africa: Architecture, Planning, and Climate in the 1950s and the 1960s," *Docomomo Journal* 48, no. 1 (2013), 76–82; Saboohi Sarshar, "Power and Identity: The Case of Islamabad," *Journal of Urban History* 45, no. 2 (2019 [2017]), 247–64; Simon Richards, "'Halfway between the Electron and the Universe': Doxiadis and the Delos Symposia," in Gerry Adler, Timothy Brittain-Catlin and Gordana Fontana-Giusti (eds), *Scale, Imagination, Perception,*

and Practice in Architecture (London: Routledge, 2012), 170–81; Tom Avermaete and Casciato Maristella, *Casablanca Chandigarh: A Report on Modernisation* (Zurich: Park Books and Canadian Centre for Architecture, 2014), 339–43; Viviana d'Auria, "From Tropical Transitions to Ekistics Experimentation: Doxiadis Associates in Tema, Ghana," *Positions*, no. 1 (2010), 40–63.

2 Wolfgang Sachs (ed.), *The Development Dictionary: A Guide to Knowledge as Power* (London and New York: Zed Books, 2019 [1992]), ix–xvii.

3 For "natural design," see William McDonough and Michael Braungart, *Cradle to Cradle: Remaking the Way We Make Things* (New York: North Point Press, 2002). Regarding "eco-masterplanning," see Ken Yeang, "Ecomasterplanning," *Architectural Design* 78, no. 5 (2008–2009), 128–31.

4 Constantinos A. Doxiadis, "The Future of the City," draft prepared by Doxiadis for *Newsweek International* (March 1968), 1–4, quotation 4.

5 Robert Frodeman (ed.), *The Oxford Handbook of Interdisciplinarity* (Oxford: Oxford University Press, 2017). For the purposes of this analysis, we will not dwell on the distinction made between interdisciplinarity and transdisciplinary aspects of sustainability that could relate to the synthesis of processes.

6 Constantinos A. Doxiadis, *Architecture in Transition* (London: Hutchinson & Co., 1963), 24. Attempts to rationalize and systematize architectural production stretch from Gottfried Semper's notions of functionalism and Eugène Viollet-le-Duc's rational philosophy of architectural structure in the nineteenth century to CIAM's doctrines for functional determination and technical advancement in the early twentieth century.

7 Harvey J. Graff, "The 'Problem' of Interdisciplinarity in Theory, Practice, and History," *Social Science History* 40, no. 4 (Winter 2016), 775–803, quotation 776; Donald G. Richards, "The Meaning and Relevance of 'Synthesis' in Interdisciplinary Studies," *Journal of General Education* 45, no. 2 (1996), 119.

8 Panayiota I. Pyla, "Baghdad's Urban Restructuring, 1958: Aesthetics and Politics of Nation Building," in Sandy Isenstadt and Kishwar Rizvi (eds), *Modernism and the Middle East: Architecture and Politics in the Twentieth Century* (Seattle: University of Washington Press, 2008), 97–115; Muzaffar, "Boundary Games," 147–76.

9 Graff, "The 'Problem' of Interdisciplinarity," 800.

10 The authors of the "Athens Charter" had drawn on Frederick Taylor's *Principles of Scientific Management* (1911), which traces its roots back to Saint-Simon's proposals for the rational engineering of social life. As such, the "Athens Charter" captured the technocratic preoccupations of CIAM members in the 1930s. See Mary McLeod, "Architecture or Revolution: Taylorism, Technocracy and Social Change," *Art Journal* (Summer 1983), 132–47.

11 For a brief history of the Delos Symposia, see Panayiota Pyla, "Delos Symposion: Leaving Earth to Save It," in Giovanna Borasi (ed.), *The Other Architect* (Leipzig: Spector Books; Montreal: Center for Canadian Architecture, 2015), 406–7; Ellen Shoshkes, *Jaqueline Tyrwhitt: A Transnational Life in Urban Planning and Design* (Farnham, Surrey: Ashgate Publishing, 2013); Richards, "'Halfway between the Electron and the Universe': Doxiadis and the Delos Symposia," 170–81; and Wigley, "Network Fever," 82–122.

12 Pyla, "Delos Symposion," 406–7.

13 Panayiota Pyla, "Planetary Home and Garden: Ekistics and Environmental–Developmental Politics," *Grey Room*, no. 36 (Summer 2009), 6–35.

14 Pyla, "Planetary Home and Garden," 13.

15 Hashim Sarkis, "Dances with Margaret Mead: Planning Beirut since 1958," in Peter Rowe and Hashim Sarkis (eds), *Projecting Beirut: Episodes in the Construction and Reconstruction of a Modern City* (New York: Prestel, 1998), 187–201.

16 Graff, "The 'Problem' of Interdisciplinarity," 785.

17 Georges Gusdorf, "Past, Present, and Future in Interdisciplinary Research," *International Social Science Journal* 29 (1977), 580.

18 Graff, "The 'Problem' of Interdisciplinarity," 778.

19 Donald Worster, "The Shaky Ground of Sustainability," in Wolfgang Sachs (ed.), *Global Ecology: A New Arena of Political Conflict* (London and New York: Zed Books, 1993), 133.

20 Ibid.; Gustavo Esteva, "Development," in Wolfgang Sachs (ed.), *The Development Dictionary. A Guide to Knowledge as Power* (London: Zed Books, 1992), 6–25; Panayiota Pyla, "Counter-Histories of Sustainability," *Volume #18: After Zero* (December 2008), 14–17.

21 Worster, "The Shaky Ground of Sustainability," 133.

22 Ibid.

23 Daniel M. Abramson, "Reversing Obsolescence," in *Obsolescence: An Architectural History* (Chicago and London: University of Chicago Press, 2016), 107–34, quotation 116.

24 Michael Zaretsky, "LEED after Ten Years," in Adrian Parr and Michael Zaretsky (eds), *New Directions in Sustainable Design* (London: Routledge, 2010), 197; Barbara Wilson, "The Architectural Bat-Signal: Exploring the Relationship between Justice and Design," in Bryan Bell and Katie Wakeford (eds), *Expanding Architecture: Design as Activism* (New York: Metropolis Books, 2008), 29.

25 Aetzel Griffioen, "Untying Cradle to Cradle: Towards an Open Source Sharing Model for Unrestricted Use," *Volume #18: After Zero* (December 2008), 122–25.

26 Doxiadis emphasized this in his first book: see Doxiadis, *Architecture in Transition*.

27 Muzaffar, "Boundary Games," 147–76; Panayiota Pyla, "Architects as Development Experts," in Panayiota Pyla (ed.), *Landscapes of Development: The Impact of Modernization Discourses on the Physical*

Environment of the Eastern Mediterranean (Cambridge, MA: Harvard University Press, 2013).
28 For more on the rural projects of Doxiadis Associates and their key role in Doxiadis's urbanism and modernization concepts, see Petros Phokaides, "Rural Networks and Planned Communities: Doxiadis Associates' Plans for Rural Settlements in Post-Independence Zambia," *Journal of Architecture* (April 2018), 472–97.
29 Constantinos A. Doxiadis and Truman Douglass, *The New World of Urban Man* (Philadelphia, PA and Boston, MA: United Church Press, 1965).
30 See n. 1 above.
31 Sheila Jasanoff, *Can Science Make Sense of Life?* (Cambridge: Polity Press, 2019); Sheila Jasanoff and Sang-Hyun Kim (eds), *Dreamscapes of Modernity: Sociotechnical imaginaries and the Fabrication of Power* (Chicago: University of Chicago Press, 2015); Timothy Mitchell, *Rule of Experts: Egypt, Techno-Politics, Modernity* (Berkeley: University of California Press, 2002).
32 Panayiota Pyla, "Constantinos A. Doxiadis and His Entopia: Promises of a Moderate Utopia and a Humanized Modernism," *FAM Magazine* (2019), 104.
33 For a critique of the marriage of development and the environment, see Sachs, *The Development Dictionary*, 26–37.
34 Sachs, *The Development Dictionary*, passim.
35 David Serlin, "Rethinking the Corporate Biosphere: The Social Ecology of Sustainable Architecture," in David Gissen (ed.), *Big & Green: Toward Sustainable Architecture in the 21st Century* (New York: Princeton Architectural Press, 2003), 144–54; William McDonough and Michael Braungart, *The Upcycle: Beyond Sustainability – Designing for Abundance* (New York: North Point Press, 2013).
36 Teddy Cruz, "Letter to the Profession of Architecture," in Adrian Parr and Michael Zaretsky (eds), *New Directions in Sustainable Design* (London: Routledge, 2010), 3.
37 Constantinos A. Doxiadis, "Energy and Human Settlements," lecture, Edison Electric Institute, New York, January 31, 1968.
38 Pyla, "Planetary Home and Garden," 6–35.
39 Constantinos A. Doxiadis, *Between Dystopia and Utopia* (Hartford, CT: Trinity College Press, 1966); Constantinos A. Doxiadis, "Entopia" (short description accompanying a rendering of Entopia printed on Doxiadis Associates' greeting cards, 1974).
40 Reinhold Martin, "Crystal Balls," *Any*, no. 17 (1997), 35–39.
41 Adrian Parr, *Hijacking Sustainability* (Cambridge, MA: MIT Press, 2009), 3–4.
42 Ibid., 5.
43 Griffioen, "Untying Cradle to Cradle," 124.
44 See, for example, Free and Real: The Telaithrion Project, in Agios Village, Evia Island, Greece; IBUKU, a green village made of bamboo; or the work of Michael Green, an advocate for constructing high-rise buildings with timber: "FreeandReal," Facebook page of Free and Real Environmental Conservation Organization, updated January 17, 2021, https://www.facebook.com/FreeandReal (accessed April 4, 2024); Michael Green, "Why We Should Build Wooden Skyscrapers," https://www.ted.com/talks/michael_green_why_we_should_build_wooden_skyscrapers (accessed January 17, 2021).
45 Worster, "The Shaky Ground of Sustainability," 141.
46 See Panayiota Pyla, "Sustainability's Prehistories: Beyond Smooth Talk: Oxymorons, Ambivalences, and Other Current Realities of Sustainability," *Design and Culture* 4, no. 3 (2012), 275.
47 David Harvey, "The Body as an Accumulation Strategy," *Environment and Planning: Society and Space* 16, no. 3 (August 1998), 328.
48 E. F. Schumacher, *Small Is Beautiful: A Study of Economics As If People Mattered* (London: Blond & Briggs, 1973); Vandana Shiva, *Staying Alive: Women, Ecology, and Development* (Berkeley, CA: North Atlantic Books, 2016).
49 Pyla, "Sustainability's Prehistories," 275.
50 Worster, "The Shaky Ground of Sustainability," 133–45.
51 Ibid., 133–34.

Urban Ecosystems and Global Ecological Balance
Rethinking Doxiadis's Legacy as Nature–Settlement Dialectics
Ahmed Z. Khan

Introduction

In the context of global climate change and environmental crisis, urban-sustainability concerns have triggered a tremendous interest in reconceptualizing nature–city relations and calls for renaturing cities. New disciplinary realignments, concepts and discourses have emerged, such as landscape urbanism; ecological urbanism; resilience; transitions; sustainable urban design; urban ecosystem services (UES); and, more recently, nature-based solutions (NBS). In this process, while several historical figures of twentieth-century modernism have also been revisited and their environmental ideas and concepts rediscovered, there seems to be an attempt to develop a broader framework of environmentalism and green consciousness in architecture culture. However, despite his significant contributions to both the theory and the practice of environmentalism, the figure of the Greek architect–urbanist C. A. Doxiadis remains a blind spot. The ambition of this chapter is to rethink Doxiadis's environmental legacy with a twofold objective: to trace his key environmental ideas, design concepts and strategies in the context of the 1950s–1970s, and to articulate their contemporary relevance for urban-sustainability theory and practice.

Interest in reconceptualizing nature–city relationships has grown across disciplinary domains. On the one hand, works in geography and the social and natural/environmental sciences have unfolded conceptual and theoretical constructs such as socio-ecological systems (SES), UES and NBS, which are championed as fields of scientific research, policy and practice aimed at shifting urban systems towards sustainability. For instance, the development and mainstreaming of the concept of SES is considered, among other things, as an interdisciplinary framework bridging the nature–culture (natural and social sciences) divide.[1] Tremendous interest has emerged around UES as a concept and approach that is commonly classified into four main categories: provisioning services, regulating services, habitat or supporting services and cultural services.[2] More recently, the emergence of NBS as an umbrella concept for ecosystem-related approaches for renaturing cities is gaining uptake across scientific disciplines and policy and practice fields aimed at urban sustainability.[3]

At the same time, major strands of nature–city reconceptualization among design disciplines have yielded several paradigmatic shifts in sustainable design concepts and approaches, as well as steering new disciplinary realignments. For instance, Janine Benyus and Julian Vincent's pioneering work on "biomimicry and biomimetic design" and William McDonough and Michael Braungart's idea of "cradle-to-cradle"-based design approaches are considered as paradigmatic shifts in design culture aimed at sustainability.[4] Among the new disciplinary realignments, "landscape urbanism" has emerged as a meta-discipline – both a field of theory and practice.[5] Among its proponents, the intellectual foundations of landscape urbanism are often traced back to the "Parc de la Villete" (1982) design competition entries of Bernard Tschumi and Rem Koolhaas, and in some accounts – albeit less enthusiastically – to the trajectory of modern urbanism during the 1950s–1960s, with references to such figures as Ludwig Hilberseimer and Ian McHarg.[6] In addition to the absence of a coherent framework, scholarship on the trajectory of nature–city conceptualization in modern architecture and urbanism, especially during the 1950s–1970s, is scant and fragmented despite the emergence of themes such as landscape, nature, climate and the vernacular during this period – themes that are of continued relevance for sustainable design.

Seen in a broader historical perspective, it can be argued that nature–city relationships have been a profound concern characterizing the development of modern urbanism. The quest for "nature in the city – the parks movement" (F. L. Olmstead), a synthesis of "town and country – the garden city" (E. Howard), "city in nature – Broadacre City" (F. L. Wright), "isolated towers in sun, space and green – the Modernist city" (Le Corbusier) and so on have been influential paradigms setting the contours of nature–city relationships in modern urbanism. These varied nature–city conceptions were employed in a variety of configurations by post-World War II urbanists dealing with the explosive urbanization of the era and in the new towns movement from the 1950s to the 1970s. Seminal works on landscape, such as those by Ian McHarg and others, emerged during this period. The role of landscape as a means to "mitigate the perceived impersonality of international modernism" and to experiment in developing a modernist aesthetic in landscape by such figures as Garrett Eckbo, Roberto Burle Marx and Christopher Tunnard were instrumental in defining its autonomy and as an alternative frame of reference for urbanism.[7] More generally, scholarship on the trajectory of nature–city conceptualization in modern architecture and urbanism during the 1950s–1960s reveals three emblematic shifts that are relatively well-established works of continued relevance for sustainable design: "Design with Climate" (Victor Olgyay 1963), the (re)discovery of the vernacular (Bernard Rudofsky 1964) and "Design with Nature" (Ian McHarg 1969).[8]

Design with Climate (1963) mainstreamed the idea of thermal comfort and solar-responsive design, which in many ways also owes its origins to the climatic concerns of modernism, especially Bauhaus teachings, and the whole tropical-architecture movement of the 1950s–1960s. The exhibition and publication of *Architecture without Architects* (1964), albeit controversially received during the 1960s, have nevertheless mainstreamed the idea of vernacular architecture as a body of design knowledge for passive and resource-efficient architecture.[9] The emergence of Ian McHarg's *Design with Nature* (1969) owes much to, among other things, the socio-environmental concerns and the emerging currents of landscape thinking in the post-war years (Garrett Eckbo and Christopher Tunnard, etc.).[10] This inspired experimentation in nature–city integration, with concepts such as "green-ways" that underpinned the new-towns movement and also found its way into Le Corbusier's plan for Chandigarh. In this context, *Design with Nature* is credited with the idea of mainstreaming "ecology as a basis for design and planning": the "relationship between the built environment and nature can be used to their [*sic*] full potential without being detrimental or destructive to each other," or, put simply, "human cooperation and biological partnership" in design and ecological planning.[11]

Ranging across these shifts – design with climate, nature, vernacular and more, such as the split within design disciplines (architecture, landscape, urban design, urban planning) – that characterize the trajectory of green/environmental consciousness in architecture culture during the 1960s, Doxiadis's oeuvre offers a fascinating view and, in some ways, an attempt to integrate, synthesize and transcend these various shifts.

Doxiadis offered a unique blend of theory and practice, which he proclaimed as a new synthetic discipline – naming it "Ekistics": the science of human settlements – concerning spatial issues across scales (from local, building and city to metropolitan and global scales) and design disciplines (interior design, architecture, urban design, landscape and regional planning).[12] On the back of a proliferating practice (Doxiadis Associates), which had projects on five continents in over forty-five countries, Doxiadis established the "Delos Symposion" as an agora for debating global urban futures during the 1960s–1970s. Many luminaries of that time from a variety of disciplinary backgrounds were onboard these intellectual "charettes," giving Delos a semblance of a sort of CIAM 2.0 (a new version of the Congrès Internationaux d'Architecture Moderne).[13] The Delos Symposia (1963–1974) included participants such as CIAM veterans Sigfried Giedion and Jaqueline Tyrwhitt; other architects/planners such as Richard Buckminster Fuller, Sir Robert Matthew, Charles Abrams, Jacob Crane, Edmund Bacon, Kenzo Tange and Hassan Fathy; development experts such as Edward Mason; the anthropologist Margaret Mead; economists such as Barbara Ward, David Owen and Stewart Bates; communication guru Marshall McLuhan; geneticist Conrad Waddington; and sociologist Eiichi Isomura. Many of the participants, including Giedion, emphasized the parallels between the 1930 CIAM and the Delos Symposia. Building upon the CIAM prototype, however, Delos's forte evolved as more multidisciplinary, international and cross-cultural, placing a sharper focus on the environmental crisis while imagining global urban futures.[14]

In the albeit limited recent scholarship on the figure of Doxiadis, he is being rediscovered as a global visionary, a coalition builder and a pioneer in environmental thought, and his oeuvre is being considered a precursor to sustainable development.[15] Despite his contributions, however, he remains a blind spot in the history and theory of modern architecture and urbanism.[16] In particular, his contributions to the environmental trajectory leading to sustainable development are intriguing and have received growing interest.[17] The main argument that I will develop in this chapter is that the way Doxiadis deals with the element of "nature" – conceptualized in relation to landscape, townscape, microclimate and urban environmental quality, anticipating several notions of contemporary relevance such as adaptation, recycling and alternative futures – reveals a sophisticated reconceptualization of nature–city relations that is of particular relevance for today's concerns for renaturing cities and sustainable urban design. Therefore, the main objective of this chapter is to trace and rethink Doxiadis's environmental legacy for its value and contemporary relevance for advancing urban sustainability theory and practice. This rethinking is articulated through addressing a series of questions: What is Doxiadis's notion of nature and landscape? How does Doxiadis spatially articulate the integration of nature and the city in practice? How does Doxiadis theorize the influence of nature on the settlement and vice versa? What is the role of diagrammatic reasoning, interdisciplinarity and multi-scalarity in the development of the concept of global ecological balance (GEB)? What is the relevance of nature–settlement dialectics and GEB for the contemporary theory and practice of sustainable architecture and urbanism?

From a methodological perspective, the chapter first traces Doxiadis's notion of landscape and ideas about nature and the city as they developed in his practice – using Islamabad (1959–1963) and the Great Lakes Megalopolis (1966–1970) as two emblematic projects – through the analysis of historical documents and publications. Second, the evolution of his ideas in theory is explored through examining the taxonomic and epistemological development of Ekistics with a particular focus on diagrammatic reasoning. Third, the development of his concept of the GEB as iteration of his theory and practice is analyzed for its underlying ideas of urbanism and their relevance today. The chapter interprets Doxiadis's legacy as nature–settlement dialectics and portrays its contemporary relevance to urban ecosystems and GEB – an overarching conceptualization that underpins many of the proliferating discourses in urbanism aimed at sustainability.

The main argument of nature–settlement dialectics is advanced through discerning and analyzing a double thought structure in the practice and theory of Doxiadis dealing with nature: 1) nature as part (element) of a whole (settlement); 2) nature, occasionally drawn out as a system in itself, to be formulated at various scale levels. Of particular interest is the attempt at transcending previous notions of nature in the city (garden, parks, green belts, etc.) through the infiltration of nature into the settlement as a framework with specific design concepts and strategies at different scale levels. At the same time, the settlement design also transcends the previous (mainstream modernist) notions of functional zoning (work, dwelling, mobility and recreation), which are interpreted as urban ecosystems organized at different scale levels. It is the multi-scalarity in the nature–city integration that activates the dialectics – and thus multiple relationships responding to many of the contemporary challenges, such as urban sprawl and environmental degradation – albeit the critical human (as agency) factor remains largely an abstract notion. The agenda pursued through such a framework is clearly a top-down, technocratic/managerial approach towards the simultaneous development of landscape and townscape and the amelioration of climatic conditions to ensure environmental quality (seen by Doxiadis as a measure of the success of his ideal city of the future).

Urban Environmental Quality: Doxiadis's Notion of Landscape, Townscape and Climate

Nature expresses itself through landscape and then climate.[18] With this view, Doxiadis approaches urban environmental quality (UEQ) as a matter of the continual improvement of "Landscape, Townscape and Climate" to ensure "relative harmony" between natural and built environments. This peculiar notion of UEQ was developed during the planning of Islamabad (the new capital city of Pakistan) in 1959–1963, where he conducted a detailed survey and analysis of the existing landscape and climate conditions.[19] UEQ was considered of "fundamental importance" as it would determine the "success of the city," and it required "relative harmony" between "Landscape, Townscape and Climate" and their simultaneous and continuous improvement for the wellbeing of inhabitants.[20] With landscape and climate being central to Doxiadis's idea of nature, the question is what exactly these two notions meant to him and why he accorded so much attention to them in the context of a post-war urbanism typically dominated by concerns for social issues, technological progress and development.

In developing the notion of landscape during the planning of Islamabad, Doxiadis advances several arguments. While meticulously documenting the local vernacular tradition, he develops the argument for landscape as a means to bridge tradition and modernism and to further (national) identity – a current just emerging in the discipline of landscape architecture at the time [Fig. 1].[21] His analysis of the existing landscape was driven by the notions of unlocking its "potential" through an "imaginary restitution," "renewal and restoration" of the landscape. These notions followed a survey of the morphology of the ground, soil and vegetation to derive the ecological structure and landscape pattern of the area, identifying challenges (the denuding of steep slopes, soil erosion, etc.) as well as opportunities (the Margalla Hills as a majestic natural backdrop, natural drainage patterns and

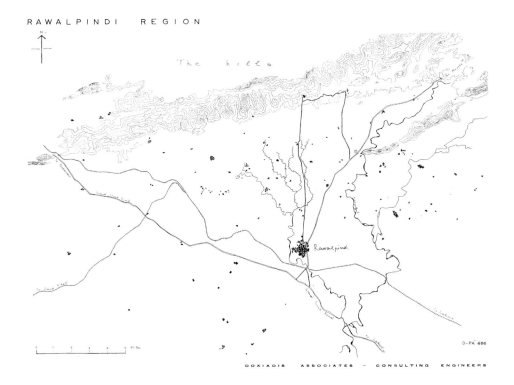

ravines as the most characteristic feature, etc.) for the development of this landscape. What emerges from his analysis is a keen sense of awareness about the benefits of nature as landscape (in relation to the city), which regulates thermal comfort/microclimate, provides natural drainage, serves the inhabitants' health and recreation needs, enhances social and cultural life, and provides aesthetic satisfaction and economic development.[22] In short, this is the idea that the "integration of nature and city enhances citizen's [sic] sense of well-being," which had been underpinning Doxiadis's design thinking since the doctoral dissertation that he defended at the Technical University (TU) Berlin in 1936, which was later translated by Jaqueline Tyrwhitt and published by the MIT Press.[23]

When it comes to climate, the argument Doxiadis develops is that of a dialectics between climate and the city. With the aim of "creating a milieu" for balanced life, work and mobility, Doxiadis considers climate and "its possible effects on the elements of the city and, inversely, the effect of the

Fig. 1 The vernacular settlement pattern of villages and the surrounding landscape of the new capital site, just north of Rawalpindi.

city's elements on climate," and argues that they are "inseparable to an extent that we have to deal with them as a whole."[24] Based on an exhaustive study of meteorological data (over the period 1881–1960), the climatic elements influencing the settlement/city in Doxiadis's analysis include: different "Seasons" and their variations (from very hot to very cold, dry to humid and a wider diurnal range); "Air" (temperature, humidity and their extreme fluctuation); and "Atmospheric Pressure and Winds" (cloud cover, rainfall, thunderstorms and hail, wind and dust storms, etc.).[25] His analysis of the influence of these elements on the settlement – deconstructed into five elements: Man, Plan, Buildings, Community Facilities and Landscape – leads to the development of a wide range of strategies of what we would call today bioclimatic design – ranging from thermal comfort, orientation and materials choice to types of open spaces, vegetation, landscape and ravines for natural drainage, the arresting of soil erosion and ventilation at different scales of the metropolitan area in order to ameliorate (micro)climatic conditions.[26]

In terms of the influence of city elements on the climate, Doxiadis argues that the mass of buildings and the components of the city, including both built-up (buildings, infrastructures, etc.) and open (public spaces, landscaped areas) spaces, modifies the existing microclimate. Anticipating the notion of the urban heat island (UHI) effect, he identifies that this influence "will be felt in small increases in temperature, moderation of wind velocity, and a fall in humidity."[27] Moreover, this influence is a dynamic one for Doxiadis – i.e. as the city development continues, it will continue to affect microclimatic conditions.[28] Synthesizing the dialectics of climate and city influences, Doxiadis includes three elements (along with existing and future changes in them) that influence the formation of the microclimate of the city: morphological and topographical features of the landscape (hills, water streams, the plain, vegetation and soil types); city elements (houses, roads, parks and open spaces, public buildings and public utility works, other land uses, etc.); and building-mass distribution pattern (dense, uniform, continuous, distributed, height, width, etc.).[29]

Simultaneously seeing nature as part of the settlement system and nature as a system itself is a distinctive double-thought structure that Doxiadis develops. On the one hand, the provision of nature at various scale levels – from house and street to metropolis – as part of the settlement system ensures and optimizes the beneficial aspects of nature for the settlement. On the other hand, seeing nature as a system implies stewardship of nature and a reduction or mitigation of the detrimental effects of urbanization on nature. Among the attempts at different classification systems in this double relationship, we see Doxiadis developing analysis by type and scale, geography and dimension, degrees of public and private, degrees of intervention, quality and quantity of landscape and so on. For instance, in the case of Islamabad, the classification of landscape by type and scale in relation to the city shows six categories on the Y-axis and, on the X-axis, an attempt to portray nature as a system in itself – that is, the Margalla and Murree Hills, the National Park and the south-east and south-west landscapes comprising ravines, plains, etc. [Fig. 2].[30] Conceptualizing such a nature–settlement dialectic is thus about the reformulation of a nature that Doxiadis sees as a "service to climate, health, various functions, social life, economy and aesthetics" – in short, UEQ. Understanding UEQ as a dialectic between nature – "climate" and "landscape" – and the development of the settlement – "townscape" – also implies a continual process of improvement of what Doxiadis sees as "the environment in which man lives, whether this environment is natural or artificial."[31] Such an integrative understanding of UEQ shows how Doxiadis's views anticipated, and somewhat transcended, the shifts – design with climate, nature and vernacular, etc. – that emerged in the environmental trajectory of architecture and urbanism during the 1960s.

Design and Planning with Nature–Settlement Dialectics

> Nature provides the foundation upon which the settlements are created, and the frame within which they function.[32]

With nature–settlement dialectics as a design-and-planning framework, a whole range of design concepts and strategies at multiple scale levels are discernible from Doxiadis's practice. Bearing in mind their relevance to contemporary sustainable urbanism, my analysis now focuses on two of the most emblematic DA projects demonstrating these concepts and strategies: Islamabad (1959–1963) and the Great Lakes Megalopolis (1966–1970).

Designed as a "city of the future" (COF) for 3 million inhabitants, Islamabad in Doxiadis's plan represents a unique urban form [Fig. 3]. Half-nature and half-settlement, the urban form embodies nature–settlement dialectics at multiple scale levels. Underpinning the design of such an urban

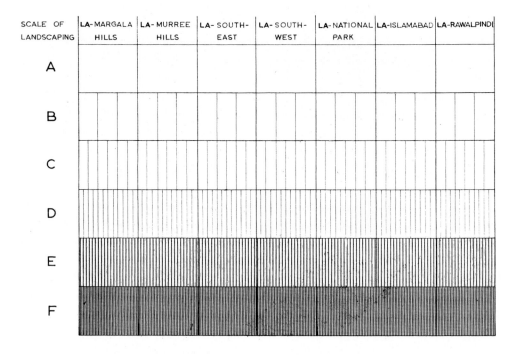

form is Doxiadis's stated ambition of the simultaneous development of "landscape" and "townscape," and amelioration of local "climate" conditions to ensure "environmental quality," seen as a measure for the success of this COF.[33] This is achieved through the integration of nature and the city by incorporating a nature–settlement dialectics that are spatially implemented through a range of design concepts and planning strategies at different scale levels – from the regional, metropolitan, city and neighborhood down to individual building scales.

The Regional Scale

The spatial articulation of the metropolitan area (1,165 km²) of Islamabad was framed within a regional dimension, with proposals and strategies for the planning and coordination of a greater region [Fig. 4]. The specified area of this greater region (3,626 km²), comprising a large part of Pothwar Plateau in northern Pakistan, was notified under the Capital Development Authority (CDA) Ordinance 1960.[34] Anticipating the potential influence of the devel-

Fig. 2 Landscape areas, scales of landscaping and the schematic representation of the degree of interventions in the planning of Islamabad.

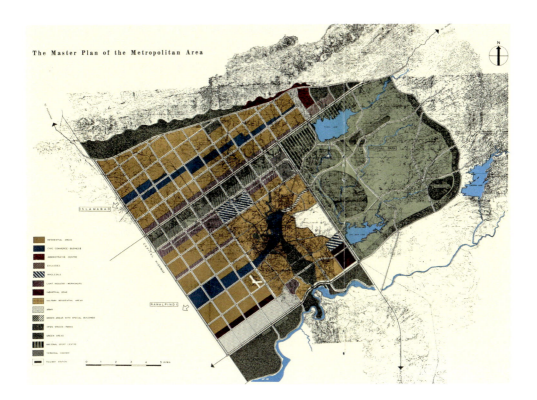

opment of the new city, Doxiadis emphasized coordination and planning at the greater regional level in order to bring together synergies for a coherent and integrated development. Underpinning this greater regional planning and coordination was the intention to effectively organize and manage the flows of energy, water, food, materials and a coherent socioeconomic development of the region – and thus to facilitate the unfolding of a vibrant development pole in the northern part of the country. It is to be noted that, in parallel to the planning of Islamabad, large-scale spatial restructuring and strategic development projects (dams and agriculture – for securing water, food and energy supplies – and industries, etc.) were integrated with the planning process of the capital in order to define the scale and ambition of the metropolitan area envisaged by Doxiadis as a COF.[35]

The Metropolitan Scale

The original "Master Plan of the Metropolitan Area," spread over 1,165 km², proposed the integration of the following four entities: 1) Islamabad,

Fig. 3 Islamabad: "The Master Plan of the Metropolitan Area."

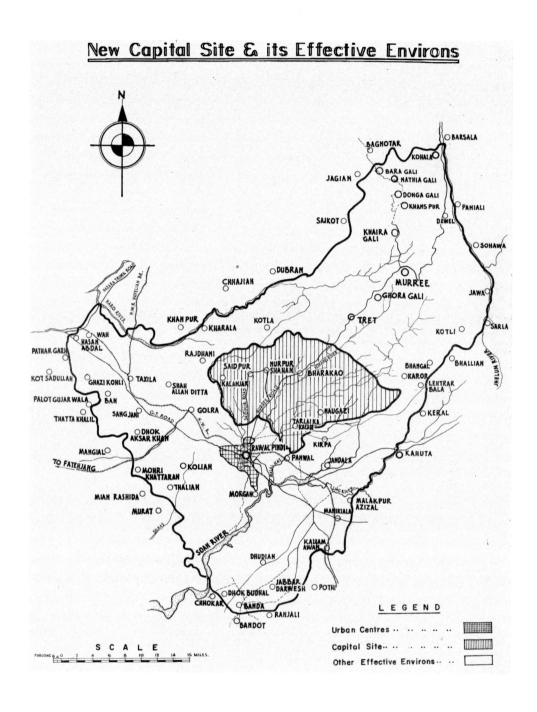

Fig. 4 The specified area (3,626 km²) of the region for the planning of the new capital city of Islamabad.

220 km²; 2) Rawalpindi, 259 km²; 3) National Park, 220 km²; and 4) Islamabad Rural Area, 466 km².[36] The metropolitan urban form thus proposed, through the spatial articulation of its main axes, organized and structured the settlement (Islamabad and the existing city of Rawalpindi, 479 km²) and nature (National Park including rural area, 686 km²) as the constituent components of the metropolitan area. Embodying the nature–settlement dialectics in the articulation of the main axes, on the one hand, the northeast–southwest principal axis is derived from an analysis of the deepest lines of the landscape patterns marked by the parallel rivers and valley structure [Figs. 5-6]. Such alignment along the deepest lines of the landscape structure secures the economy of future infrastructures along this axis. Setting aside any environmental concerns that such river-valley landscapes may evoke, however, shows Doxiadis's settlement bias in the dialectic. On the other hand, the northeast–southwest principal axis is derived from an analysis of the settlement structure – in particular, the role of the historic Grand Trunk Road (GT Road). The strategy behind such an articulation of the main axes, and leaving very wide strips of green along them and also along all the major streams of the specified area, is to simultaneously buffer noise and air pollution (main axes), to preserve and enhance nature (major streams) and to connect the metropolitan urban environment (city) with the larger surrounding landscape (nature). Several landscape strategies aimed at ameliorating the local climatic conditions of the metropolitan area (in Doxiadis's parlance, and what we would today call addressing the UHI effect, implementing NBS, etc.) can be discerned, such as a large plantation buffer up to 2 km wide along the southern bank of the Soan River for offloading and cooling the dust-laden winds from the south during summer; an alternating barrage formation of landscape plantation over the Margalla Hills to protect the metropolitan area from cold northeastern winds during winter; and green rights-of-way (ROW) along the formal grid and ravines (ecological grid) to provide ventilation to the metropolitan area [Fig. 7].[37] The dedication of almost half of the metropolitan area (National Park and Margalla Hills ecological corridor, wide ROWs, open spaces around and within the sectors) for nature, green space and (urban) agriculture is to ensure what we would call today a wide range of ecosystemic benefits encompassing regulating, support and cultural ecosystem services (such as environmental, air quality, hydrological, food production, biodiversity, cultural–recreational and so on).[38]

The City and Neighborhood Scales

When it comes to the city and neighborhood scales, the design of nature (the landscape and vegetation pattern, water, open space system, etc.) in and around the "sector" and the design of the built city elements (building-mass configurations, streets and roads, spatial layout, etc.), constitute – respectively – the nature and the settlement parts of the dialectic.[39] The sector is a spatial unit marked by 2 × 2 km "formal grid" lines, which constitutes a 4 km² module of the metropolitan area representing, according to Doxiadis, the average size and scale of a typical historic city.[40] Each sector is surrounded by ample green spaces (mimicking historic cities surrounded by landscape) to buffer noise and pollution from the "utilidors" (Doxiadis's concept for the main infrastructures and transportation arteries surrounding the sector). Within each sector, the preservation and enhancement of smaller streams running diagonally form the ecological, green-and-blue network called the "eco grid."[41] The eco grid typifies the organic natural and

Figs. 5–6 The principal axis (NE–SW) in the planning of Islamabad (opposite), derived from an analysis of the deepest lines of the landscape patterns marked by the parallel rivers and valley structure (above).

Ahmed Z. Khan

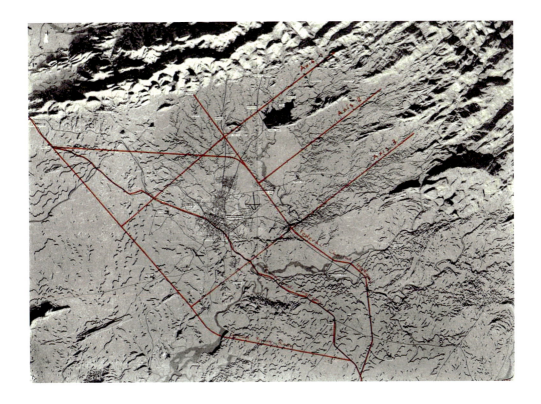

Fig. 7 Landscape strategies at the metropolitan scale of Islamabad.

systemic structure of the area – including both of what are called today "green" and "blue" networks (rivers and vegetated lands) – characterized by *nallas* (ravines) organically flowing within the sectors and across the metropolitan area, most of them draining the Margalla Hills into the Soan River in the south.

The overlapping of the formal grid (2 × 2 km) over the eco grid [Fig. 8], and the leaving of ample ROWs of green space for both of them are what give Islamabad its distinctive green character and high environmental quality. While this overlapping forms the spatial structure of the city where open space (or nature) dominates, careful design of the detailed landscape strategies in the central areas, streets and squares helps improve local climatic conditions (air flow, moderation of temperatures, orientation, etc.) and thermal comfort by creating ample shade and evapotranspiration-based cooling, and makes nature part of urbanity.

Such an overlapping also creates an articulation of the settlement part of the dialectic that results in a very distinctive urban design and typo-morphology of the city. On the one hand, the urban design shows a synthesis of nature–city elements [Fig. 9]. With the linear form of the (Margalla)

Fig. 8 City- and neighborhood-scale strategies. The overlapping of the formal (2 × 2 km) grid and the eco grid gives Islamabad its distinctive green character and high environmental quality.

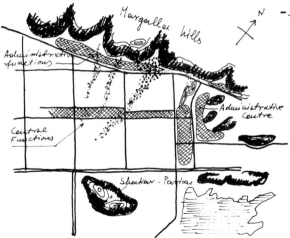

- Fundamental component elements of the area:

  Natural: — Margalla hills which create a wall to the north.
  — The group of hills in the area of the Administrative Centre, and Shakar-Parian hill, forming a horseshoe.
  — The vegetation which penetrates the plain along the Nullachs.

  Artificial: — The building mass in the areas of Administrative and central functions.

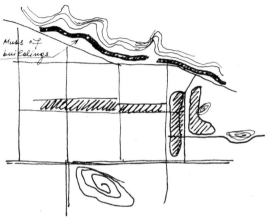

The synthesis follows the Landscape:

- Creation of a moving mass of buildings, as a wall along Margalla hills
- Creation of the
- The cohesion of the area is achieved through sequence.

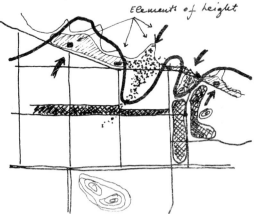

Landscape and city appear interlocked:

- Cohesion of the area is attained through elements of height.

D-PA 6136

Fig. 9 Natural landscape and the city interlocked.

hills and vegetation penetrating the city along ravines, the Central Business District (CBD – the commercial/central, mixed-use, cultural and administrative areas of the city) is articulated as a linear spine that, together with the elements of height and sequence, creates cohesion and interlocking of the city with nature. However, the residential areas are spatially articulated in the voids between these elements of nature and the linear CBD [Fig.8]. Such an integration of housing and the public realm with nature also creates variety of spaces, economy of infrastructures and a different kind of urbanity that, according to Doxiadis, enhances the citizen's sense of wellbeing.[42] On the other hand, such an urban design defies conventional/modernist notions of the functional zoning of the city (work, dwelling, mobility and recreation) by articulating the urban areas as distinctive urban ecosystems: central areas as linear spines capable of gradual extension, residential areas as neighborhoods of different sizes, the connecting and supporting recreational (eco grid) and mobility/infrastructure (formal grid) systems. Designing the cohesion, interlocking and interdependence of both the natural and the urban ecosystems at multiple scales shows a symbiotic relationship due to the embodiment of nature–settlement dialectic as a design framework in the case of Islamabad.

Doxiadis's plan for Islamabad thus demonstrates a transcendence of previous/conventional notions of nature in the city (garden, parks, green belts, etc.) through the infiltration of nature into the settlement as a framework with specific design logics at different scale levels. At the same time, the settlement design also transcends previous notions of functional zoning (work, dwelling, mobility and recreation), which are interpreted as urban ecosystems organized at different scale levels [Fig. 10]. These urban ecosystems include those of "centralities" (two CBDs, central–commercial citywide activities), "human communities" of residential areas/enclaves, "mobility infrastructure and industries" (light industry, craft, trading, wholesale markets, etc.), the linear "metropolitan ecologies of nature areas" (green-and-blue networks, Margalla Hills and Soan River ecological corridors and the inter-urban green) for recreation and preservation, and urban "agriculture" (National Park and rural area/agro-model villages). Designing with nature–settlement dialectics to ensure urban environmental quality thus implies the integration of urban, industrial, agricultural and natural realms/landscapes at multiple scale levels to deliver what we would call today UES: local food provision, local watershed maintenance, clean water supply, air quality,

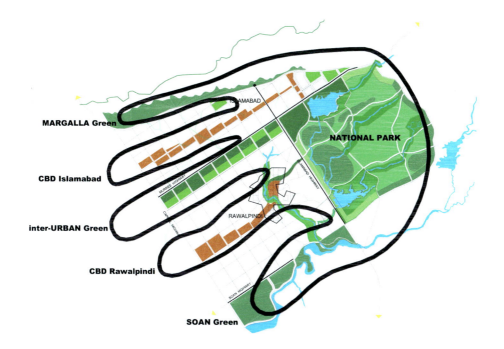

biodiversity and local climate amelioration. In the plan for Islamabad, it is the multi-scalarity in the nature–city integration that activates the dialectics and, thus, multiple relationships responding to many contemporary challenges such as sprawl and environmental degradation. The plan embodying nature–settlement dialectics as a design framework shows how urbanization can go hand-in-hand with environmental protection and enhancement, developing a symbiotic relationship between the two for what Doxiadis called "enhancing the citizen's [sic] sense of wellbeing."

Doxiadis continued to pursue such nature–settlement dialectics in several projects throughout the 1960s. Integrating an element of nature – such as the Tigris in the case of Baghdad or the Potomac River in his plan for Washington, DC – as part of the settlement dialectics remained central to Doxiadis's practice. Moving towards larger scales, his plan for the Great Lakes Megalopolis represents yet another very particular episode of nature–settlements dialectics. In this case, the Detroit Edison Company commissioned DA to conduct a study of the future urbanization of the Great Lakes region. The study, spanning four years (1966–1970), included "Analysis,"

Fig. 10 Urban ecosystems of the metropolitan area organized at different scale levels: the linear "metropolitan ecologies of nature areas" (green-and-blue networks), the "centralities" of two CBDs, the "human communities" of residential areas, "mobility infrastructures and industries" and urban "agriculture" and rural communities (National Park area).

"Future Alternatives" and a "Concept for Future Development" centered on the potential of energy and water flows (both in abundance due to the Great Lakes, one of the world's largest freshwater resources, and their potential for harnessing hydropower) as structural elements for the spatial organization of the future urbanization of this region.[43] In DA's concept plan for the year 2100, we see the settlement part organized into residential, commercial, institutional and industrial land uses at three levels of densification: low, medium and high densities of the settlement [Fig. 11]. The two principal grids structuring this settlement of varying densities are the formal (larger) grid, comprising the different levels of transport infrastructure lines, while the nature part/eco grid is the diagonal green network providing recreation and surrounding areas for agriculture across the Megalopolis. At the city scale, the urban-design scheme for the proposed new urban centers shows eco and formal grids structuring urban communities of varying densities and a peculiar multi-layer design for the CBD/central area. The design strategy of layering the CBD – multi-level separation of flows with transport and parking below ground, multiple levels of public space and green areas above for pedestrian movement, and surrounded by high-density and mixed-use buildings – can be seen as a precedent for the pedestrianization strategies of city centers that would unfold in the urban regeneration of historic cities in Europe from the 1980s and that continues today. This iteration of nature–settlement dialectics embodied in the plans for the Great Lakes Megalopolis shows a model of urbanization with resource (energy, water, etc.) efficiency and environmental awareness. Designing with nature–settlement dialectics, as both of these cases demonstrate, is thus about linking urbanism with resource flows (water, energy, mobility, etc.) and the value of landscape, resulting in a wide range of ecosystemic benefits for urban systems.

Theorizing Nature–Settlement Dialectics

In Doxiadis's oeuvre, we find a fascinating interaction between practice and consistent attempts at theorization. Straddling across disciplines (from social sciences and humanities to engineering and health sciences), or what Hashim Sarkis calls "dancing with disciplines," on the one hand, this theorization attempts to build up the epistemology of a unified/synthesis discipline – of architecture, urban design, planning – concerning the spatial aspects of settlement organization at large that he names Ekistics as a "science of human settlements."[44] Ekistics epistemology has been considered

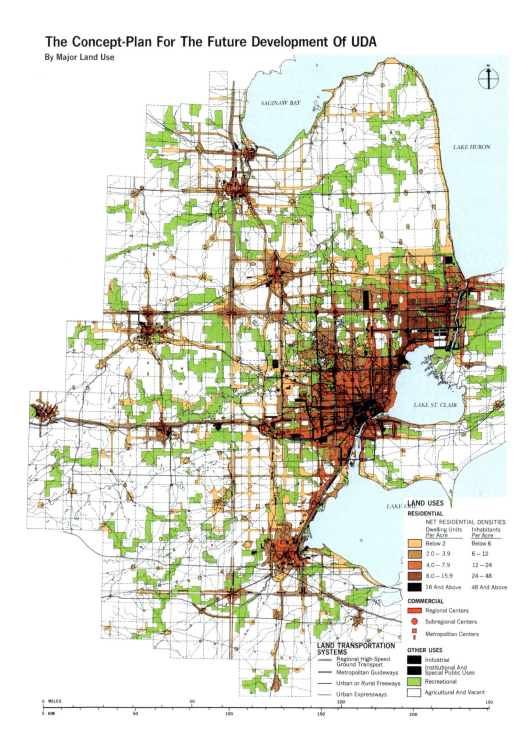

Fig. 11 Concept plan for the Detroit region for 2100 as part of the larger Great Lakes Megalopolis.

Settlement Elements (Evolution)

Settlement as Organism

1961	1963	1965	1968		1975	
					Elements	Forces
Man	Man	Nature	Nature	1 Geological Resources 2 Topographical Resources 3 Soil Resources 4 Plant Life 5 Water Sources 6 Animal Life 7 Climate	Nature	1 Gravity 2 Geographical – Land, Water 3 Geographical – Air, Climate
Plan	Society	Man	Man	1 Biological Needs (Space, Air, Temp.) 2 Sensation and Perceptions 3 Emotional Needs 4 Moral Values	Man	4 Biological 5 Physiological
Buildings	Shells	Society	Society	1 Population Composition and Density 2 Social Stratification 3 Cultural Patterns 4 Economic Development 5 Education 6 Health and Welfare 7 Law and Admin	Society	6 Inner Structure 7 External Structure 8 Social Structure
Community Facilities	Functions	Shells Houses + Buildings	Shells	1 Housing 2 Community Services 3 Shopping and Markets 4 Recreational Facilities (Theater, Museum, etc.) 5 CBD 6 Industry 7 Transport Centers	Shells	9 Growth 10 Organisation
Landscape	Nature	Networks Roads, Power, etc.	Networks	1 Water Supply System 2 Power Supply System 3 Transport Supply System (Water, Air, Road, Rail) 4 Communication Supply System (Tel, Radio, TV, etc.) 5 Sewerage and Drainage 6 Physical Layout (Ekistics Plan)	Networks	11 Movement

Le-Play: Plage, Work, Family (*Lieu, Travail, Famille*) (1964)

Geddes: Plage, Work, Folk

CIAM: Dwelling, Work, Circulation, Recreation (1933–1942)

Fig. 12 Taxonomic and epistemological development of Ekistics: the evolution of settlements and elements (Man, Nature, Society, Shells and Networks).

a major attempt at incorporating systems theory and interdisciplinarity in architecture and aligning it with the post-World War II international development context.[45] On the other hand, Doxiadis's peculiar form of theorization establishes a dialectics between practice and theory through deploying three main discernible strategies that underpin the epistemology of Ekistics: 1) the creation of (new) taxonomies and classification systems – e.g. settlement "elements" and spatial "scales"; 2) conceptualization through "diagrammatic reasoning"; and 3) historicization and discourse evolution. In the following analysis, an attempt is made to show how nature–settlement dialectics plays out, and evolves, across these strategies of theorization.

Doxiadis's intellectual trajectory, and that of Ekistics' taxonomic and epistemological development, is underpinned by a remarkable obsession with the creation of (new) taxonomies and classification systems. Tracing the classification of settlement elements over the period 1961–1975, we see, on the one hand, an attempt at rethinking and synthesizing other known classifications such as Frédéric Le Play's Place, Work and Family (*lieu, travail, famille*); Patrick Geddes's Place, Work and Folk; and CIAM's Dwelling, Work, Circulation and Recreation [Fig. 12].[46] On the other hand, we see the evolution within the settlement elements and what they denote, with a consistent tendency to theorize settlements as organisms. For instance, in 1961, Doxiadis identifies five elements as an attempt to theorize climate influence on settlement and vice versa: Man, Plan, Buildings, Community Facilities and Landscape.[47] Over the course of the next four years, we see Doxiadis arriving at the more familiar Ekistics elements: Nature, Man, Society, Shells and Networks. Between 1968 and 1975, we observe that "Anthropos" replaces "Man" and a broader, more ecological, content of each of the elements is delineated. In addition to qualifying settlement as organism, through such classification Doxiadis attempts to establish the co-relation between these elements as the very foundation of Ekistics epistemology – and, by extension, that of urbanism.

In addition to settlement elements, spatial scales are central to Doxiadis's theorization – in particular, multi-scalarity as a major contribution.[48] Among one of the earliest attempts (in 1962), we see the insertion of multiple scales into the organization of CIAM's four functions (Residence, Work, Recreation and Circulation) [Fig. 13].[49] These multiple scales ranged from "Family" and "Community Classes" I to VIII, denoting small neighborhoods, to "City" and "Metropolis" levels. By 1963, we see the delineation of

Fig. 13 Theorizing the settlement aspect: evolution of the concept of multiple scale levels in relation to the organization of urban functions and urban design.

eight scale levels ranging from "Room" and "Building" to "Ecumenopolis." By 1964, we see the addition of "House," "Plot," "Block," "Small Town," "Large City," "Metropolis" and "Large Region." By 1965, the term "Terrestrial Space Units" has been coined for spatial scales and included "Man" and "Earth." Between 1968 and 1976, several neologisms come in with the ELS (Ekistics Logarithmic Scale), etc., which now contains the familiar fifteen spatial scales and each with a population size marking 30 to 50 billion people for the future inhabited Earth – the so-called Ecumenopolis. However, while the earlier organization of urbanism functions at multiple scales, unfolding the concept of multi-scalarity as a major contribution to urban design, the later iterations of scales were too quick and thinned out of content as they reached the global scale.

While the settlement elements and spatial scales establish a holistic framework for Ekistics, Doxiadis attempts to address the inevitable complexity of such a framework through emphasizing "spatial synthesis" as the main focus, with disciplinary realignments and interdisciplinarity. On the one hand, Doxiadis's aim is to distinguish Ekistics from geography and the newly emerging "regional science." He articulates Ekistics as a unified "spatial/synthesis" discipline transcending the silos of spatial disciplines such as architecture, urban design and physical planning.[50] In his theorization of spatial disciplines, he considers two main groups – one focusing on analysis (exemplified by Patrick Geddes, Camillo Sitte, Walter Christaller, etc.) and the other focusing on the creation of new forms (CIAM) – that the synthesis focus of Ekistics will transcend.[51] On the other hand, he positions Ekistics and its elements to derive and synthesize knowledge from a range of disciplines: economics, the social sciences, cultural disciplines, technical/engineering subjects and the political sciences [Fig. 14].[52] Seeing each of the elements from different disciplinary perspectives requires the kind of synthesis that Doxiadis claims for Ekistics as its raison d'être as a discipline at the very heart of spatial development. Spatial development, practice and policy-making were thus to be Ekistics' forte; the other disciplines remained at the margins of Doxiadis's vision of development. An Ekistician, in Edward Bacon's words, was to be "a specialist in generalities"[53] – someone able to situate architecture in the context of international development, infrastructure, master planning and national housing programs. Clearly, this needed a wide range of disciplinary expertise and coordination, moving towards an integrated and interdisciplinary approach. However, placing

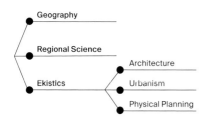
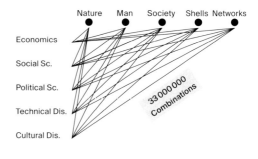
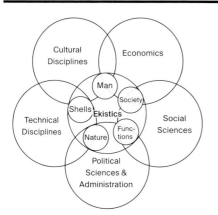
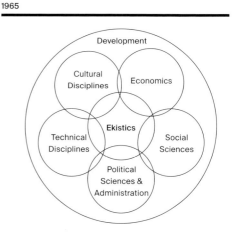

disciplines side by side is one thing, and evolving 'interdisciplinarity' is another: Doxiadis's vision of interdisciplinarity was his alone and rarely shared by other disciplines or within architecture during the 1960s.

Parallel to taxonomic classification and interdisciplinarity, a peculiar pathway underpinning Doxiadis's intellectual trajectory in theorizing Ekistics is a form of conceptualization through diagrammatic reasoning.[54] In the case of nature–settlement dialectics, Doxiadis's conceptualization diagrams of 1968 operated on the principle that the "infiltration of Nature into the human settlement is much better than a large park" [Fig. 15]. However, while this strategy is implemented in the plan for Islamabad (1959–1963), Doxiadis presents it more as a general theoretical principle based on diagnosis through diagrammatic reasoning, as illustrated in Figure 16, where "the city which grows concentrically [is said to increase] the distance between

Fig. 14 Disciplinary alignments and interdisciplinarity: author's mapping of Doxiadis's attempt at evolving Ekistics into an interdisciplinary synthesis discipline.

Man and Nature," while "the city which grows naturally decreases the distance."⁵⁵ Infiltration, therefore, is seen as the best way to bring nature and humanity together in settlement design. Doxiadis's illustration of the relationship between nature, machine and humankind is yet another example of the conceptualization of nature–settlement dialectics through diagrammatic reasoning as a synthesis [Fig. 16]. Evoking Hilberseimer's flow and form and Louis Kahn's conceptualization of Philadelphia's mobility pattern as river flows, Doxiadis's synthesis articulates nature as a framework for settlement design organizing vehicular and pedestrian movement as well as public space and communities. Doxiadis deploys such diagrammatic reasoning to illustrate the historical evolution of nature–settlement dialectics only to show/qualify a view of history (diagnosis) that fits his prognosis – that is, how nature's and settlements' relationship ought to be in the future. Conceptualization through diagrammatic reasoning is both a diagnostic and an analytical tool, as well as a tool for synthesis, communicating complex ideas and interactions. As a step between practice and theory, Doxiadis uses diagrammatic reasoning as a way of generating reflections on practice and deploys strategic simplification as an operating tool to conceptualize, illustrate and express complex ideas and relationships as his distinctive form of theorization. During the last decade of his life, as the practice receded, Doxiadis sought comfort in constructing an ivory tower of theory. After *Ekistics: An Introduction to the Science of Human Settlements* (1968), his work aimed more at adumbrating Ekistical theorems in relation to ecology, becoming more prophetic in tone with increasingly normative ideas, assertions, statements and manifestos while giving an impression of being simultaneously scientific–analytical and historic–evolutionary and having projective–futuristic goals.

Urban Ecosystems and Global Ecological Balance

The concept of global ecological balance – and its spatialization through Ecumenopolis (the global city) and Ecumenokepos (the global garden) – is a major contribution of Doxiadis's, articulated during the last years of his life. While presenting an extended articulation of this concept in a paper in 1974 entitled "Global Ecological Balance," he called for a United Nations declaration on GEB and for the establishment of a new UN agency for its implementation.⁵⁶ The full extent of the concept was published posthumously in his book *Ecology and Ekistics* in 1977.⁵⁷

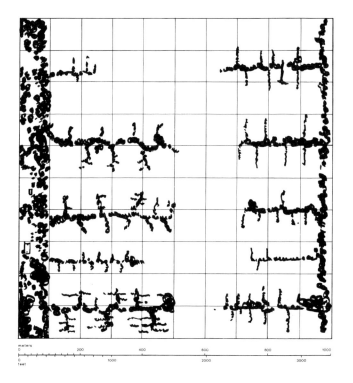

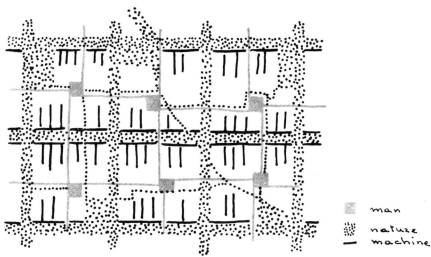

Fig. 15 Diagrammatic reasoning as a mode of visual thinking and persuasion, bridging theory and practice, with strategic simplification as an operating tool. The illustration shows Doxiadis's prognosis that the "infiltration of Nature into the human settlement is much better than a large park."

Fig. 16 Doxiadis's conceptualization of nature–settlement dialectics through diagrammatic reasoning as a synthesis that articulates nature as a framework for settlement design organizing vehicular and pedestrian movement as well as public space and communities.

With Ecumenopolis, Doxiadis attempts to encapsulate urbanization at large as global urban ecosystems; all types of human settlements are treated as organisms, as are their relationships to each other and to urbanization as a whole over time – that is, their past, present and probable future states. Ecumenokepos, in contrast, implies all types of nature areas – from home gardens, street greens and citywide green infrastructures to agricultural areas, forests, coasts, mountain ranges, deserts and so on. Doxiadis imagined not only that the explosive growth of global urbanization would be a great threat to global nature but also that the endangering of the latter would lead to the collapse of urban ecosystems. To address this problematic, he began to articulate the pragmatic concept of GEB.

Several intellectual pathways underpin Doxiadis's conceptualization of GEB: 1) the iteration of his theory and practice within the framework of the COF research project; 2) the rethinking of human settlements as biological organisms with metabolic needs and processes (energy, mobility, air, water, food, raw materials, etc.) that are capable of growth, expansion and decay as urban ecosystems; and 3) the aligning of Ekistics, as a science of urban ecosystems, more closely with ecology and emerging environmental concerns.[58] For instance, Doxiadis's description of a metabolic understanding of the settlement system remains an overarching and comprehensive one that includes spatial and social aspects:

> Settlements are biological organisms which take in energy and raw materials and, overcoming internal resistances, transform them into useful products, generating unwanted by-products and waste in the process [...] Goods, energy, people, information and services now pass through the system in unprecedented quantities, varieties and speeds [...] waste disposal systems have been overloaded, transport and communication systems have grown too complex for efficient action, and the matrix of social relationships with human communities has suffered and dissolved under repeated stress.[59]

Thanks to Doxiadis's interactions with the Delians on environmental themes, such as "interdependence" and "adaptation" (René Dubos) and the "inner limits" and "outer limits" of Barbara Ward's *Spaceship Earth* (1966), Doxiadis's post-1968 environmental thinking in search of synthesis is pragmatic: it coalesces around the idea of "balance." If nature was seen by

Doxiadis as that which "provides the foundation upon which Human Settlements are created and the frame within which they function," he also began to acknowledge that "the development of Ecology and increased awareness of the relationships between living organisms and their surroundings has led to the development of Ekistics, first as a discipline, and later as a science of Human Settlements, through which settlements may be planned in *balance* [emphasis added] with Nature."[60]

Balance(s) and Adaptation(s)

In Doxiadis's idea of "balance(s)" between nature (Ecumenokepos) and settlement or city (Ecumenopolis) underpinning the concept of GEB, we can discern at least four main themes: 1) technology versus space; 2) dynamic balance; 3) urban environmental quality; and 4) alternative futures. The need for a balance between "technological optimism and spatial finitude" owes much to Doxiadis's belief that the recycling of resources and production, and the carrying capacity of ecological systems can be increased, whereas terrestrial space can neither be recycled nor expanded.[61] Doxiadis suggests "dynamic balance" to be neither specific nor definitive: both nature and settlements are neither a normal condition nor a stable one; they are both in evolution, and therefore achieving a dynamic balance in nature–settlement dialectics is about "adaptation" at multiple scale levels. He argues that "Man is adjusted to Nature, but Nature must also be adjusted to Man [...] when it is, the ensuing balance will mean a healthy settlement."[62] While evoking Ian McHarg's ideas – "Man and his environment" and "Design with Nature," which he also cites – Doxiadis brings the issue of scale and dialectics to his idea of dynamic balance: "Man adjusts himself to natural conditions by creating a different environment for himself on a micro or macro scale and [...] this scale increases as time passes [...] Both Man, with his actions, and Nature, will be evolving; they will influence each other; we must think of both in proper balance, a balance which will be dynamic."[63] Doxiadis's pragmatic view of nature and Anthropos is thus that of systems that evolve a dynamic balance through adaptation. Doxiadis characterizes this with three phases: "first, attack by nature, second counter attack by Man which ranges from burning forests to global pollution [...] Third, peace between the two; either by adaptation of Man to Nature or of Nature to Man or by a compromise."[64]

Linking dynamic balance with urban environmental quality and its evaluation, Doxiadis initially developed the notion of a simultaneous development of landscape, townscape and climate. Towards the end of his career, his synthesis *Building Entopia* brings to the fore the idea of "balance and harmony" between the five Ekistics elements (Nature, Anthropos, Society, Shells and Networks) and five principles to achieve quality (1. maximization of potential contacts; 2. minimization of effort in terms of energy, time and cost; 3. optimization of Anthropos's protective space; 4. optimization of the quality of Anthropos's relationship with "his" system of life; and 5. balance through optimization and synthesis of the four principles) as central to ensuring UEQ with much broader criteria. These criteria now included the "satisfaction" (of the average Anthropos) with safety and happiness, (social) "equality" (among Anthropos), equal rights and "humane development."[65]

Doxiadis develops the notion of balance between (alternative) futures – the fourth theme underlying GEB – through a "desirability" and "feasibility" approach. In his book *Between Dystopia and Utopia* (1966), Doxiadis positions "dystopia or the bad city" as undesirable and "Utopia or the non-feasible city" as counter-extremes to his future vision of "Entopia or the desirable and feasible city." While elaborating on this notion more comprehensively in his later book *Building Entopia* (1975), Doxiadis articulates five futures – the constant, the declining, the continuing, the creative and the unexpected futures – and connects them with criteria of probability, desirability and feasibility to achieve balance.[66]

Seen through the thematic categories of technology, space, change dynamics and evolution, quality and futures, nature–settlement dialectics thus become multiple perspectives underlying Doxiadis's conception of GEB. Such perspectives generate contemporary relevance – for example, spatial finitude and the recycling of resources, urban environmental quality and alternative futures are major themes in contemporary sustainable urbanism. Adaptation, and that also at multiple scale levels, has emerged as a major theme in the contemporary discourse on climate change and sustainability.

Spatializing GEB

A particularly distinctive attribute of GEB is that it is a spatially articulated and developed concept. In this spatialized approach, Doxiadis's – and his multidisciplinary COF team's – mapping and juxtaposition of two overarching ideas play a central role: these are "Ecumenopolis," the global city of Anthropos or the city of the inhabited globe, and "Ecumenokepos," the global garden [Fig. 17]. Underlying both these ideas is a peculiar form of theorization or, more accurately, a series of (normative) assumptions. Ecumenopolis is, first and foremost, Doxiadis's vision of unchecked patterns of urbanization over centuries (until the year 2125, in fact): a system of human settlements encircling the whole globe, made up of several types of cities, towns and villages that will be interconnected into broader urbanized areas. Ecumenopolis, argues Doxiadis, "will consist of parts with very different densities ranging from very high to very low, and of continuous built-up areas as well as separate areas interconnected by several types of transportation and communication lines."[67] While reaching its maximum extent by 2125, Ecumenopolis may, if Ekistics' ecological and environmental tenets and prescriptions are adhered to – in short, a "successful marriage between Ecumenopolis and Ecumenokepos" – become Entopia, Doxiadis's ideal city, which will be of the highest standard that Anthropos (humanity) can dream of.[68] Ecumenopolis is thus a doomsday scenario or dys-topia as well as an ideal/Entopian vision of Anthropos living in harmony with nature.

Amidst the explosive urbanization of the 1960s, Doxiadis articulates the temporal scale of Ecumenopolis, spanning over three centuries: from 1825, the beginning of the Industrial Revolution, to 2125, by which time the forces unleashed by the industrial era would have stabilized. Ecumenopolis for Doxiadis is inevitable: "Because humanity has entered [since 1825] a new era of science and industry, Ecumenopolis is as inevitable as the village after the agricultural revolution."[69] He characterizes this as the "era of explosion," underpinned by several forces: of demography/population; the economy, trade and income; energy; technology; mobility and the means of communication. The transformative changes unleashed and driven by these forces include the shift from the uni-speed to the multi-speed city and from isolated built-up areas to broader urbanized systems, and the explosion of knowledge, choices and communication technologies.[70] In several publications (all part of COF), Doxiadis presents in-depth documentation and meticulous analysis of these forces that had increased the "complexity of life" – such as the facts that, between 1860 and 1960, the population of the average Western city increased by 47 times, its area expanded by 62 times, its economy grew 400-fold and the energy it used ballooned by 550 times.[71] Extrapolating these trends, Doxiadis graphically demonstrates that the global population will level off by 2150, that average per capita income will increase

Ecumenopolis

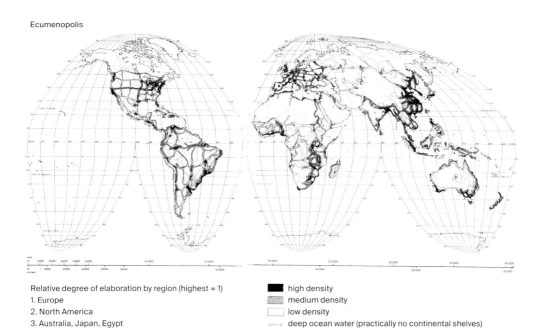

Relative degree of elaboration by region (highest = 1)
1. Europe
2. North America
3. Australia, Japan, Egypt
4. Africa south of Equator, SE Asia
5. Other

■ high density
▨ medium density
□ low density
⋯ deep ocean water (practically no continental shelves)
⋯ deep ocean water (greater depths)

Ecumenopolis and Ecumenokepos

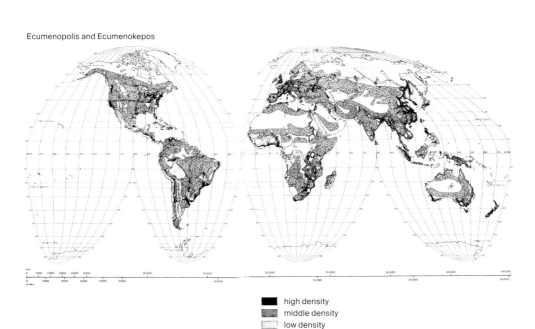

■ high density
▨ middle density
□ low density
▥ Ecumenokepos

Fig. 17 Spatializing global ecological balance (GEB). Ecumenopolis, the global city of Anthropos or the city of the inhabited globe (top), in balance and harmony with Ecumenokepos, the global garden/nature areas (bottom).

Urban Ecosystems and Global Ecological Balance

enormously until the twenty-second century and that global per capita energy consumption will continue to increase, especially in the twenty-first century.[72] Even if the population did not grow, Doxiadis held the belief that increasing energy availability and income would give humanity the ability to move further out of the city, with the resulting system of settlements becoming more and more complex.

Disputing the popularly held notion of implosion, or a shrinking world, or the idea – spearheaded by media visionaries such as Marshall McLuhan – of a "global village" that would be brought about by innovations in communication technologies, Doxiadis argued that the "road to Ecumenopolis leads from civilization to ecumenization," whereby humanity would continue to expand in space and spatial relations while reducing the notion of time – that is, it would become more interconnected – and that, demographically, if civilizations were underpinned by a jump of a hundred times that took thousands of years, ecumenization would be unfolded by a jump of a million times over only 300 years.[73]

In the spatial articulation of Ecumenopolis, Doxiadis forecasts the global population to level off at around 15–20 billion people by the mid-twenty-second century.[74] The development of the economy and of energy are not going to level off in the same way – nor should they, according to Doxiadis.[75] If we don't understand that progress depends on them, he argued, let us at least not forget the low-income groups that badly need higher incomes and much more energy.[76] In terms of spatial distribution, Doxiadis uses two main ideas in shaping the form of Ecumenopolis: varying "densities" and "forces conditioning the shape of urban systems." He articulates the probable distribution of the global population in terms of densities with a rather simple distinction: low densities (what we call today diffused urbanization/*città diffusa*, villages, rural and small settlements), medium densities (clusters of towns, cities and metropolises) and high densities (cores of highly urbanized regions).[77] Doxiadis distinguishes three forces that will shape the structure and form of Ecumenopolis: concentric "economic" forces, forces attracting many elements towards main lines of "transportation" infrastructures and "aesthetic" forces attracting urbanization towards coastal and aesthetically pleasing areas.[78] Ridiculing the modernist notion of design, Doxiadis argued that the shape, form and structure of the settlements of the future at the large scale are "going to have nothing whatever to do with anyone's personal and aesthetic theories of design; it is going to depend on the laws imposed by nature, on Anthropos real needs, and on his ability to organize the use of technology to serve those needs."[79] While cognizant of the complexity of spatial design, planning and policy at larger scale, what Doxiadis offers as a strategic ambition to realize Entopia through the concept of GEB is "enabl[ing] the forces to expand in the least harmful way until they slow down. In the meantime, protect all the values of the past from the explosion: people, nature and culture."[80] In the cause of realizing Entopia through achieving GEB, Doxiadis dedicated the last years of his life to articulating a detailed road map in his final book, *Ecology and Ekistics*, which expands "land-use" planning to grand new horizons encompassing terrestrial and ecological types of global space design and planning.

Ecological Design and Planning for GEB

Doxiadis develops a peculiar form of design and planning for realizing GEB that we would today call ecological urbanism: by (re)articulating his Ekistics elements and terminologies in relation to global and ecological scales. Global space is articulated through spatial areas, ecological zones and terrestrial space including Land, Water, Coastal and Air [Fig. 18]. Four types of "spatial areas" comprising twelve "ecological zones" include "Naturareas" (five types of "nature" zone), "Cultivareas" (two types of agriculture zone), "Anthro-poareas" (four types of urban area/human settlement) and "Industrareas" (heavy industry, waste and recycling areas). A similar type of zoning is defined, albeit at a lower resolution than land zones, for the water (on land and ocean), coastal and air zones.[81] The vision of Ecumenopolis-turned-Entopia that emerges from this ecological zoning is one in which humanity (about 20 billion people) has transcended urban sprawl and is now settled in an urban system that covers 7.3 percent of the global land area, distinguished into low, medium and high densities (1.3, 0.7 and 0.3 percent, respectively) and natural area for recreation (5 percent of natural areas for sports, resorts of different types). Industrial activity – including waste treatment, recycling and reuse – is restricted to 0.2 percent of the global land surface, overcoming pollution and resource depletion in a system akin to what we would today call the circular economy. This also involved dedicating 5.5 percent of global area to natural agriculture and fishing, and 0.5 percent to industrial cultivation and mariculture in order to establish food security. The GEB for this human settlement and range of activities is established by designating 82 percent of global land and water/oceans as protected nature areas, including regulations for air quality. With such a spatial articulation of the Earth system, Doxiadis imagined the "balance of the global ecosystem on the one hand and human settlements and other interventions by mankind on the other hand, resulting in a situation suitable for the continuation of human life and of nature."[82]

He saw GEB as an ultimate goal that was "dependent on achievement and [the] maintenance of a complex series of balances at lower scales."[83] This implies that he saw GEB as a framework for the organization of the natural, agricultural, industrial and urban realms at the larger scales, and also for the metropolitan-scale integration of urban, industrial, agricultural and natural realms/landscapes. Echoing contemporary calls for nature-based solutions and the greening of cities, he argued, "We have to save Nature. We must conserve, preserve, and also develop. We have to bring Nature into the city of Man and not keep it out to be visited only during long weekends."[84]

With an unwavering belief in the promise and potential of such a union of nature and the city through GEB for the broadest human interests, Doxiadis outlined the qualities of this "desirable and feasible" city of the future as the one that "makes people happy and safe and helps them to develop more and more."[85] Echoing this belief in GEB for achieving quality of life, Doxiadis imagined that

> [t]he surface of the city will allow the flora to spread again, beginning from the small gardens within the cells, to major zones of forests above the tunnels of the networks, to big farming areas and natural reserves where man will find the rough conditions which he also needs. In this city we can hope that man, relieved of all stresses that arise from his conflict with the machine, will allow his body to dance, his senses to express themselves through the arts, his mind to dedicate itself to philosophy or mathematics, and his soul to love and to dream.[86]

While the concept of GEB and the vision of Entopia are based on the lofty ideals of the continuation and improvement of quality of life (both human and nature), human development and wellbeing, they also represent an a-political and a-social theorization of the Earth system from a spatial/land-use and ecological planning perspective. They assume that somehow political and administrative boundaries, property rights, political ideologies and

Ecological Types of Space

Spatial Areas	Ecological Zones (Type of)		Terrestrial / Space (Use Zones)			Coastal	Air
			Land 100%	Water			
				Land (incl. u'ground)	Ocean		
Naturareas (N)	As nearly virgin as possible	①	Real wildlife (RW) 40%	RW	RW	(N)	
	Visited by some humans but without permanent human installations	②	Wildlife visited (WV) 17%	WV	WV		Eco-climatology Base Zones Beneath
	Humans enter and stay but without machines	③	Wildlife embraced (WE) 10%	WE	WE		
	Similar to ③, but human settlements built of natural materials	④	Wildlife invaded (WI) 8%	WI	WI		
	Nature prevails but humans enter with machines and can use the zone (forests) by stages and sections	⑤	Wildlife conquered (WC) 7%	WC	WC		
Cultivareas (C)	Natural cultivation in traditional ways, without coverage of plants and animals by artificial roofs, without controlled climate	⑥	Natural cultivation (NC) 5.5%	NC	Natural fishing		
	Cultivation with new methods allowing for much greater exploitation and higher production	⑦	Industrial cultivation (IC) 5%	IC	Industrial mariculture		
Anthropareas (A)	Natural areas used as resorts for sports, etc.	⑧	Physical human life (PH) 5%	PH		(A)	
	Inhabited at the lowest reasonable density	⑨	Low density city (LD) 1.3%	LD	LD		
	Inhabited at middle densities	⑩	Middle density city (MD) 0.7%	MD	MD		
	Inhabited at the highest reasonable density	⑪	High-density city (HD) 0.3%	HD	HD		
Industrareas (I)	Every possible use for achieving the goal of the best industrialization	⑫	Heavy industry and waste zone (HW) 0.2%	HW	Waste disposal zone	(I)	

Fig. 18 Ecological types of space and land-use planning for achieving global ecological balance.

Urban Ecosystems and Global Ecological Balance

conflicts – and even the very idea of the nation-state – would disappear in favor of an eco-centric global government that would guarantee the implementation and maintenance of the ecological zones as global "commons." Moreover, social inequalities and inequalities between nations (developed and developing countries) would somehow cease to exist. In short, Entopia illustrates a vision of a planetary form of urbanism wherein humanity has transcended the forces of history, politics, religion and capitalism, and attained an ecumenic, happy, safe and stabilized form of life by living in balance and harmony with nature.

Conclusion: Nature–Settlement Dialectics and (Urban) Sustainability

Rethinking nature–settlement dialectics in terms of urban ecosystems and global ecological balance offers a holistic and interdisciplinary framing of the contemporary discourse on urban sustainability, which is fragmented across different disciplinary silos. While connecting partial categories of understanding of urban-sustainability issues to work towards synthesis and shared understanding, this dialectical framing could facilitate a qualitative transformation in the direction of the discourse. To make this discussion more precise, the four main categories of nature–settlement dialectics viewed as such a framework can be articulated as a matrix: A) nature as part of the settlement; B) nature as a system in itself; C) climate influences on the settlement and D) settlement influences on the climate [Fig. 19].

Over the last few decades, we have seen tremendous developments in each of these categories of understanding sustainability issues. For instance, the theory and practice of urban green infrastructure; the green–blue network in cities; landscape urbanism; greening cities; and, more recently, urban ecosystem services and nature-based solutions have mainstreamed the idea of nature–city integration for addressing a wide range of urban-sustainability issues – that is, nature as part of the settlement system (A above). At the same time, research in the fields of ecosystem services, nature conservation and protection, biodiversity and resources management has highlighted the incredible importance of nature and biodiversity for the very survival of human life on Planet Earth. Cognizant of the need for viewing nature as a system in itself (B), the contemporary (urban) sustainability discourse often finds affinity with conceptualizations such as "natural capital" and "biological cycle," and as a renewable "resource base." Such conceptualizations highlight the regenerative role of nature for the very survival

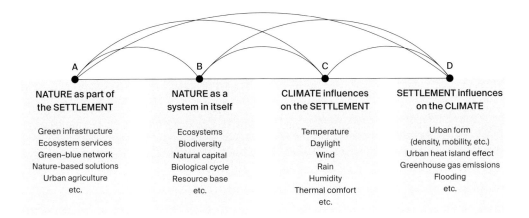

Fig. 19 Nature–settlement dialectics framework for urban sustainability.

of any settlement system that increasingly relies on renewable flows of energy, food, water and materials for its sustainable metabolic functioning. Little wonder, then, that Doxiadis so prophetically acclaimed "Nature" as the "foundation upon which settlements are created and the framework within which they function."

Triggered by the contemporary challenges of global warming and climate change, a wide range of disciplines are engaged in developing our understanding of the two other categories of nature–settlement dialectics – that is, climate influences on settlement (C) and settlements' influences on climate (D). Whether building upon research in the fields of climatology, meteorology and other sciences or rediscovering the climatic concerns within modernism (from the Bauhaus to the tropical-architecture movement and the rediscovery of the vernacular) and the pioneering work of Victor Olgyay ("Design with Climate"), we have seen tremendous advances over the last few decades in understanding climatic influences on settlements. These advances include sophisticated modeling and simulation platforms that facilitate our understanding of how climatic factors (temperature, wind, precipitation, daylight, etc.) influence settlements in terms of visual and thermal comfort and air quality at the interior to building scales and in their urban spatial arrangements. Equipped with these technologies, and a new generation of bioclimatic and passive design strategies, a new era of regenerative and sustainable architecture is emerging with the ambition of ensuring visual and thermal comfort using renewable and natural energies (solar gain, natural ventilation, thermal mass, etc.) as a response to sustainability challenges. At the same time, and with the constitution of the IPCC (Intergovernmental Panel on Climate Change) in 1988, among other developments, a large body of scientific knowledge and societal awareness is emerging on the influences that urbanization at large or settlements have on climate (D). As demonstrated by MEFA (material and energy flow analysis) and urban metabolism studies over the last two decades, human activities in urban settlements (transport, construction, work, dwelling, recreation, etc.) induce large inflows of resources (water, energy, materials, food, etc.) that provide necessary services or add to the built stocks and generate waste flows (liquid, solid and gaseous, i.e. greenhouse-gas [GHG] emissions) in a linear way.[87] These unrelenting waste and emissions flows pollute oceans and increase GHG concentration in the atmosphere, leading to pollution, global warming and climate change. Several studies attribute the ways in which urban form is configured and population growth, density and mobility are organized, along with the overall levels of permeability of urban surfaces and so on, to vectors that produce what is called the urban heat island effect and contribute to influences on climate change.

Rethinking urban-sustainability issues through the framework of nature–settlement dialectics as urban ecosystems and GEB thus offers a more holistic and interdisciplinary framework. On the one hand, seeing human activities and settlements as urban ecosystems implies a human habitat or built environment constituted by human activities (a broader view of "work" – industry, agriculture, services, etc. – "dwelling," "mobility," "recreation," etc.) that are organized at different scales of settlements (from small hamlet to large metropolis), their relationships with each other and with the urbanization at large, that is, the global urban system. Bringing nature–settlement dialectics to understanding the multi-scalar and multi-dimensional aspects of such relationships calls for a reinterpretation of Doxiadis's Anthropocosmos model as an example to illustrate the complexity of the more integrated and interdisciplinary knowledge base needed for transitioning towards sustainable built environments [Fig. 20].[88] On the other hand, the nature–settlement dialectic framework brings with it a systemic view of the implications of urban ecosystems for GEB; nature can be integrated as part of the settlement (to address many urban-sustainability challenges) but it also needs to be viewed as a system in itself, and our focus should not only be framed by ameliorating or moderating climate influences on settlements (through design, technology, etc.) but also by the ways

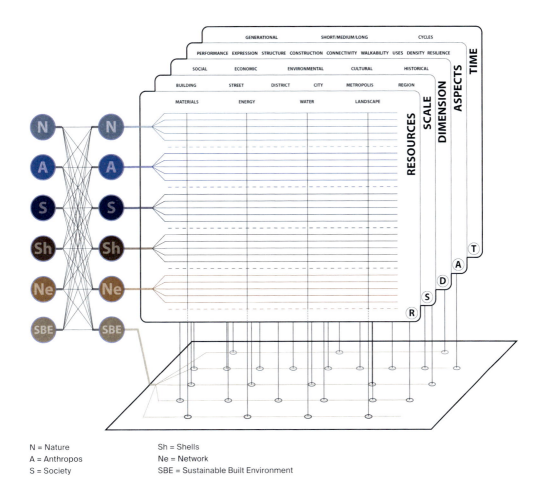

N = Nature
A = Anthropos
S = Society
Sh = Shells
Ne = Network
SBE = Sustainable Built Environment

in which settlement pattern influences climate – in other words, seeing climate, like nature, as a system in itself as well. Achieving GEB is thus not only about sustainability or energy efficiency at the building or urban scales but also about the protection of nature and climate from local to global scales.

While Doxiadis's conceptualization of GEB was visionary in many ways, the top-down technocratic/managerial approach towards its spatialization also reveals several contradictions inherent in the modernist thinking to which he adhered. Conceptualizing GEB offers a systemic view of the complexity of human settlements as adaptive systems at multiple scales. Establishing GEB as an "ultimate goal" anticipated the sustainability paradigm by almost two decades and – being explicit about notions of contemporary

Fig. 20 A reconfiguration of Doxiadis's Anthropocosmos model, illustrating the complexity of integrated and interdisciplinary knowledge for sustainable built environments.

relevance such as "climate change," "recycling," "adaptation," "transition" and "quality of life" – supports the visionary credentials of Doxiadis. At the same time, his spatialization of GEB reveals an apolitical and asocial theorization of the complexity of the Earth system that privileges spatial finitude (as demonstrated by his Earth habitability indexes) and zoning-based land-use planning perspectives. Achieving GEB through a static and apolitical division of the dynamic Earth system into four zones – Land, Water, Coastal and Air – and four basic spatial areas – Naturareas, Cultivareas, Anthropoareas and Industrareas – that are mutually exclusive reveals an intuitive and simplistic reasoning that contradicts the complexity of system dynamics and seems far from being an ecological approach. Biodiversity is also something that does not appear on his radar, while social differences and uneven development would somehow be managed away by a technocratic and environmentally benevolent global governance system.

Despite these inherent contradictions, Doxiadis's optimistic vision of a sustainable future Earth – inhabited by 20 billion people living in harmony with nature – through GEB remains appealing and relevant for addressing sustainability and climate challenges in a holistic and systemic way. On the one hand, the kind of top-down-conceived, large-scale, planetary visions for transition towards sustainability that Doxiadis pioneered recur in contemporary architectural thinking. The various manifestos of ecological and planetary urbanisms, with the latest one being the "Masterplanet" for 10 billion people by Bjarke Ingels that is currently in progress, highlights this distinctive genre of utopian yet pragmatic architectural thinking.[89] Moreover, zoning remains a powerful tool in broader land-use and regional planning domains. In particular, nature as "protected area" zones has historically been received favorably, as can be witnessed by the proliferation of environmental-protection agencies, national parks and protected areas around the world. Setting clear and simple targets facilitates the political mobilization necessary for environmental protection. The most recent and ambitious among such initiatives is the European Union's plans to have "at least 30% of EU land and seas […] protected by 2030 to halt the decline of biodiversity and restore carbon sinks to address climate change."[90] On the other hand, a wide range of bottom-up, socially innovative and participatory initiatives – from climate-justice activism to the transitions movement, and various innovations in circular- and shared-economy initiatives, resilience and urban-ecosystem services, nature-based solutions and urban agriculture, etc. – highlights the importance of behavioral change and inclusive and participatory processes as bedrocks of any move towards arresting ecological collapse. Between these two transition pathways – top-down and bottom-up – is perhaps where the relevance and potential lie for nature–settlement dialectics to develop the theory and practice of sustainable architecture and urbanism, and to facilitate the unfolding of sustainable futures.

1. Fikret Berkes and Carl Folke, *Linking Social and Ecological Systems* (Cambridge: Cambridge University Press, 1998).
2. Millennium Ecosystem Assessment, *Ecosystems and Human Well-Being: Synthesis* (Washington, DC: World Resources Institute, 2005).
3. N. Kabisch et al., "Nature-Based Solutions to Climate Change Mitigation and Adaptation in Urban Areas: Perspectives on Indicators, Knowledge Gaps, Barriers, and Opportunities for Action," *Ecology and Society* 21, no. 2 (2016), 39.
4. Janine Benyus, *Biomimicry: Innovation Inspired by Nature* (New York: William Morrow, 1997); Julian Vincent et al., "Biomimetics: Its Practice and Theory," *Journal of the Royal Society Interface* 3 (2006), 471–82; William McDonough and Michael Braungart, *Cradle to Cradle: Remaking the Way We Make Things* (New York: North Point Press, 2002).
5. Charles Waldheim, *The Landscape Urbanism Reader* (New York: Princeton Architectural Press, 2006).
6. See ibid.
7. Marc Treib (ed.), *The Architecture of Landscape, 1940–1960* (Philadelphia: University of Pennsylvania Press, 2002).
8. Victor Olgyay, *Design with Climate: Bioclimatic Approach to Architectural Regionalism* (Princeton, NJ: Princeton University Press, 1963); Bernard Rudofsky, *Architecture without Architects: A Short Introduction to Non-Pedigreed Architecture* (New York: Museum of Modern Art, 1964); and Ian McHarg, *Design with Nature* (Garden City, NY: Natural History Press/Doubleday, 1969).
9. For example, see Willi Weber and Simos Yannas, *Lessons from Vernacular Architecture* (Abingdon and New York: Routledge/Earthscan, 2014).
10. See Treib, *The Architecture of Landscape*.
11. F. Steiner and B. Fleming, "Design with Nature at 50: Its Enduring Significance to Socio-ecological Practice and Research in the Twenty-First Century," *Socio-ecological Practice Research* 1 (2019), 173–77.
12. For a comprehensive review of Doxiadis's oeuvre, see Alexandros-Andreas Kyrtsis (comp.), *Constantinos A. Doxiadis: Texts, Design Drawings, Settlements* (Athens: Ikaros Publishing, 2006).
13. The *Ekistics* issue on the Delos Symposion included in its appendix the CIAM Athens Charter, with the subtitle "Outcome of a Similar Effort," *Ekistics* 16, no. 95 (October 1963), 263–66.
14. For these distinctive aspects of the Delos Symposia, see Panayiota Pyla, "Planetary Home and Garden: Ekistics and Environmental–Developmental Politics," *Grey Room*, no. 36 (Summer 2009), 11–17; and Ahmed Z. Khan, "Rethinking Doxiadis' Ekistical Urbanism: Sustainability and Globalization as a Dialectical Framework for Design," *Positions: Modern Architecture and Urbanism – Histories and Theories* (2010), 6–39.
15. Ray Bromley, "Towards Global Human Settlements: Constantinos Doxiadis as Entrepreneur, Coalition-Builder and Visionary," in Joseph Nasr and Mercedes Volait (eds), *Urbanism: Imported or Exported?* (New York: John Wiley and Sons, 2003), 316–40; Panayiota Pyla, "Ekistics, Architecture, and Environmental Politics, 1945–1976: A Prehistory of Sustainable Development," Ph.D. dissertation, Massachusetts Institute of Technology, 2002; Pyla, "Planetary Home and Garden," 9; Ahmed Z. Khan, "Constantinos A. Doxiadis' Plan for Islamabad: The Making of a 'City of the Future' 1959–1963," Ph.D. dissertation, KU Leuven, April 2008; and Khan, "Rethinking Doxiadis' Ekistical Urbanism."
16. For example, Wouter Vanstiphout, "How to Survive the Twentieth Century," in Kees Christiaanse (ed.), *Situations: KCAP Architects and Planners* (Rotterdam: Nai Publishers, 2005); Mark Wigley, "Network Fever," *Grey Room*, no. 4 (2001), 82–122; and also Khan, "Rethinking Doxiadis' Ekistical Urbanism," 10–12.
17. Pyla, "Ekistics, Architecture, and Environmental Politics"; Pyla, "Planetary Home and Garden"; Panayiota Pyla, "Counter-Histories of Sustainability," *Volume #18: After Zero* (December 2008): 14–16; Kyrtsis, *Texts, Design Drawings, Settlements*; Khan, "Constantinos A. Doxiadis' Plan for Islamabad," 381–87; and Khan, "Rethinking Doxiadis' Ekistical Urbanism."
18. C. A. Doxiadis, *Ekistics: An Introduction to the Science of Human Settlements* (New York: Oxford University Press, 1968), 299.
19. Compiled and issued in the form of four reports: Doxiadis Associates (hereafter DA), "Landscape Design – Existing Conditions," DOX-PA 159, 1962; DA, "The Climate and Its influence on the Capital," DOX-PA 161, 1962a; DA, "Landscape," DOX-PA 168,

1962b; and DA, "Landscape and Climate," DOX-PA 169, 1962c. These reports were part of the Islamabad Master Plan and Program, prepared and issued by the DA office in Athens, which includes 138 such reports in total. They are available at both Doxiadis Archives (Athens) and Capital Development Authority Archives (Library Iqbal Hall, Islamabad). For a complete list of all these reports by DA, and also those prepared by the FCC (Federal Capital Commission), see Khan, "Constantinos A. Doxiadis' Plan for Islamabad," 478–84.

20 For detailed elaboration, see Khan, "Constantinos A. Doxiadis' Plan for Islamabad," 343–44.

21 For Doxiadis's notion of the vernacular, see ibid., 346; and Ahmed Z. Khan, "Representing the State: Symbolism and Ideology in Doxiadis' Plan for Islamabad," in Mark Swenarton, Igea Troiani and Helena Webster (eds), *The Politics of Making* (London and New York: Routledge, 2007), 61–75. For the thinking in the landscape discipline, see Treib, *The Architecture of Landscape*.

22 For the detailed elaboration of these benefits by Doxiadis, see DA, "The Climate," 1962a, 108; and DA, "Landscape," 1962b, 15, 69.

23 C. A. Doxiadis, *Architectural Space in Ancient Greece*, edited and translated by Jaqueline Tyrwhitt (Cambridge, MA: MIT Press, 1972); and Khan, "Constantinos A. Doxiadis' Plan for Islamabad."

24 DA, "The Climate," 1962a, 1.

25 Ibid., 2–99.

26 Ibid., 103.

27 Ibid., 1, 110.

28 Ibid., 1; and Khan, "Constantinos A. Doxiadis' Plan for Islamabad," 110–11.

29 DA, "The Climate," 1962a

30 Khan, "Constantinos A. Doxiadis' Plan for Islamabad," 350–58.

31 DA, "The Climate," 1962a.

32 Doxiadis, *Ekistics: An Introduction*, 517.

33 DA, "Landscape Design," 1962; DA, "The Climate," 1962a; DA, "Landscape," 1962b; and Khan, "Constantinos A. Doxiadis' Plan for Islamabad," 339–90.

34 Khan, "Constantinos A. Doxiadis' Plan for Islamabad."

35 These included the Tarbela and Mangla dams, and a series of small dams on the Pothwar Plateau to ensure energy, water and food production in the broader region; and HMC (Heavy Mechanical Complex), POF (Pakistan Ordnance Factories, based in Wah Cantonment, Pakistan) and several other industries as an industrial base for the region, etc. For details, see Khan, "Constantinos A. Doxiadis' Plan for Islamabad."

36 Ibid.

37 Ibid., 377–79.

38 For instance, the National Park area includes land-use allocation for an urban agro-farming area; model agro-villages; and the preservation of existing rural–agro areas, national institutions (health, education, research, etc.) and exhibition grounds, nurseries and edge parks along the main rivers. See Khan, "Constantinos A. Doxiadis' Plan for Islamabad," 339–90.

39 Ibid., 350, 358–60; DA, "Landscape Design," 1962, 1, 25–29.

40 In the parallel theoretical COF research project, conceived with the aid of the Ford Foundation to facilitate the planning of Islamabad, several hundred historic cities (from before the industrial age) were documented. Their average size (2,000 m across) was argued by Doxiadis to form the constituent component or basic cell of the modern metropolis. See Khan, "Constantinos A. Doxiadis' Plan for Islamabad"; Khan, "Rethinking Doxiadis' Ekistical Urbanism."

41 For the conceptualization of the term "eco grid," see Khan, "Constantinos A. Doxiadis' Plan for Islamabad," 340–90; and Khan, "Rethinking Doxiadis' Ekistical Urbanism," 32–33.

42 Khan, "Constantinos A. Doxiadis' Plan for Islamabad," 380–81.

43 The three volumes of the DA study published by the Detroit Edison Co. (Detroit, MI) are: DA, *Emergence and Growth of an Urban Region, the Developing Urban Detroit Area*, vol. 1, *Analysis* (1966); vol. 2, *Future Alternatives* (1967); and vol. 3, *A Concept for Future Development* (1970).

44 Hashim Sarkis, *Circa 1958: Lebanon in the Pictures and Plans of Constantinos Doxiadis* (Beirut: Dar An-Nahar, 2003).

45 Khan, "Constantinos A. Doxiadis' Plan for Islamabad"; Lefteris Theodosis, "Systemic Methods and Large Scale Models in Ekistics," *Nexus Network Journal* 23 (2020), 171–86.

46 For the settlement elements by Le Play, Geddes and CIAM, see Doxiadis, *Ekistics: An Introduction*, 22–23. References (including for Figure 12 here) for 1961, see DA, "The Climate," 1962a; for 1963 and 1965, see Kyrtsis, *Texts, Design Drawings, Settlements*, 250, 49 and 181; for 1968, see Doxiadis, *Ekistics: An Introduction*, 35; for 1975, see C. A. Doxiadis, *Building Entopia* (Athens: Athens Publishing Centre, 1975).

47 DA, "The Climate," 1962a.

48 Khan, "Constantinos A. Doxiadis' Plan for Islamabad," 443–44; Khan, "Rethinking Doxiadis' Ekistical Urbanism."

49 References (including for Figure 13 here) for 1962, see DA, "Landscape," 1962b, 53; for 1963, see C. A. Doxiadis, *Architecture in Transition* (London: Hutchinson, 1963), also cited in Kyrtsis, *Texts, Design Drawings, Settlements*, 236; for 1964, see Kyrtsis, *Texts, Design Drawings, Settlements*, 203, and C. A. Doxiadis, "Ekistics and Regional Science," *Ekistics* 14, no. 84 (November 1962), 193–200; for 1965, see Kyrtsis, *Texts, Design Drawings, Settlements*, 49; for 1968, see Doxiadis, *Ekistics: An Introduction*; and for 1975, see Doxiadis, *Building Entopia*.

50 For synthesis as the main focus of Ekistics, see Doxiadis, "Ekistics and Regional Science."
51 Doxiadis, *Ekistics: An Introduction*, 48.
52 References (including for Figure 14 here) for 1962, see Doxiadis, "Ekistics and Regional Science"; for 1963, see Doxiadis, *Architecture in Transition*; for 1965, see Kyrtsis, *Texts, Design Drawings, Settlements*, 23, 49, 75.
53 Doxiadis, *Ekistics: An Introduction*, 76.
54 Kyrtsis, *Texts, Design Drawings, Settlements*.
55 C. A. Doxiadis, *Anthropopolis: City for Human Development* (New York: Norton, 1974), 115.
56 C. A. Doxiadis, "Global Ecological Balance (The Human Settlement that We Need)," paper for the Tyler Ecology Award (September 1974). In this paper, Doxiadis claims that he had presented the concept partially in several publications over the preceding two years, including C. A. Doxiadis, "Water and Human Environment," *Water for Peace*, vol. 1, International Conference on Water for Peace, Washington, DC, May 23–31, 1967 (Washington, DC: US Government Printing Office, 1967), 33–60.
57 C. A. Doxiadis, *Ecology and Ekistics*, edited by Gerald Dix (London: Paul Elek; Boulder, CO: Westview Press, 1977).
58 C. A. Doxiadis and John G. Papaioannou, *Ecumenopolis: The Inevitable City of the Future* (New York: Norton, 1974).
59 Ibid., 153.
60 See Doxiadis, *Ekistics: An Introduction*, 517, and Doxiadis, *Ecology and Ekistics*, 13 [emphasis added]. The idea of using Ekistics to achieve ecological balance is present in Doxiadis's discourse since at least 1966, for example: "Instead of […] urban planning and considering human needs only, we must try Ekistics planning which includes Nature and can lead us to the balance that we need between Nature and Anthropos," in C. A. Doxiadis, *Between Dystopia and Utopia* (London: Faber and Faber, 1966), 74.
61 Doxiadis and Papaioannou, *Ecumenopolis*, 8–9.
62 Doxiadis, *Ekistics: An Introduction*, 286.
63 Ibid., 411.
64 C. A. Doxiadis, *The Two-Headed Eagle: From the Past to the Future of Human Settlements* (Athens: Lycabettus Press, 1972), 68.
65 Doxiadis, *Building Entopia*, 6, 20–27, 24.
66 Ibid., 28–37, 53–54.
67 Ibid., 2.
68 Ibid., 3.
69 Ibid., 19.
70 Ibid., 8–10.
71 C. A. Doxiadis, *The Human Settlements That We Need* (New Delhi: TATA/McGraw-Hill, 1976), 66; and also Doxiadis, *Building Entopia*, 6–10.
72 Doxiadis, *Building Entopia*, 8–10.
73 Ibid., 231–32; Doxiadis, *Ekistics: An Introduction*, 449.
74 Doxiadis, *The Two-Headed Eagle*, 45; in later books, this becomes 20 billion: Doxiadis, *Building Entopia*, 8–9; Doxiadis and Papaioannou, *Ecumenopolis*.
75 Doxiadis, *Building Entopia*, 8–9.
76 Doxiadis, *The Two-Headed Eagle*, 45.
77 Doxiadis, *Building Entopia*, 232–36.
78 Ibid., 231–32; Doxiadis, *Ekistics: An Introduction*, 450.
79 Doxiadis and Papaioannou, *Ecumenopolis*, 308.
80 Doxiadis, *The Two-Headed Eagle*, 47.
81 For a detailed elaboration, see Doxiadis, *Ecology and Ekistics*, 14–47. For the rearticulation of Human Settlements, from the earlier five elements to these four spatial areas, see ibid., 66.
82 Doxiadis, *Ekistics and Ecology*, xxiii.
83 Ibid., 43.
84 Ibid.
85 Doxiadis, *Building Entopia*, 307.
86 Ibid.
87 C. Kennedy, S. Pincetl and P. Bunje, "The Study of Urban Metabolism and Its Applications to Urban Planning and Design," *Environmental Pollution* 159 (2011), 1965–73; A. Athanassiadis, P. Bouillard, R. Crawford and Ahmed Z. Khan, "Towards a Dynamic Approach to Urban Metabolism," *Journal of Industrial Ecology* 21 (2017), 307–19.
88 Doxiadis did evolve his Anthropocosmos model, the last iteration being an attempt to rearticulate it to fit the Ekistics–ecology nexus: see Doxiadis, *Ekistics and Ecology*, 49–72.
89 Ciara Nugent, "The Great Reset: The Climate Is Breaking Down: Architect Bjarke Ingels Has a Masterplan for That," *TIME*, October 21, 2020, https://time.com/collection/great-reset/5900743/bjarke-ingels-climate-change-architecture/ (accessed December 16, 2020).
90 European Commission, "EU Biodiversity Strategy for 2030: Bringing Nature Back into Our Lives," European Commission, Brussels, May 20, 2020, https://eur-lex.europa.eu/legal-content/EN/TXT/?uri=CELEX%3A52020DC0380 (accessed December 16, 2020).

Bio-systemic Thinking for Holistic Design
On the Legacy of the Delos Symposia in Contemporary Environmental Thinking and Environmentally Conscious Design

Yannis Zavoleas

Introduction

The Delos Symposia activities during the 1960s and early 1970s may be explained as a coordinated effort to reinforce cross-scientific knowledge in architecture and planning. By establishing the Delos group, Constantinos Doxiadis and Jaqueline Tyrwhitt gave shape to the idea that original solutions may emerge when mindsets of diverse training and background share their expertise and communicate their knowledge to larger audiences. To enable such an exchanging of views, science was viewed as a multifaceted platform and a reliable asset everyone could follow, relate with and build upon. An appreciation of science is evident in Doxiadis's exploration of a biological origin – or at least a parallel – for urban phenomena. Doxiadis employed systemic models as references to nature's sustainable practices directed to spatial management at all scales. Nature directs its resources through dynamic operations that reflect its adaptive, efficient and performative character. As such, Doxiadis observed, nature's overall complexity and richness are not accidental but may be attributed to the greater laws of physics, which designers must study and consider in their work. However diverse with regards to scale, context and subject matter, then, natural and human-made environments were governed by extensive data inputs and cause-and-effect relations. This belief laid the foundations for an all-systemic approach to design – from architecture through cities, regions and indeed the planet – which Doxiadis infused into the core ideology of the Delos Symposia. Responses to global sustainability ought to be drawn by a holistic scope aiming to bring Nature, Man (Human), Shells, Society and Networks – suggested as the five elements of human settlements – into some sort of

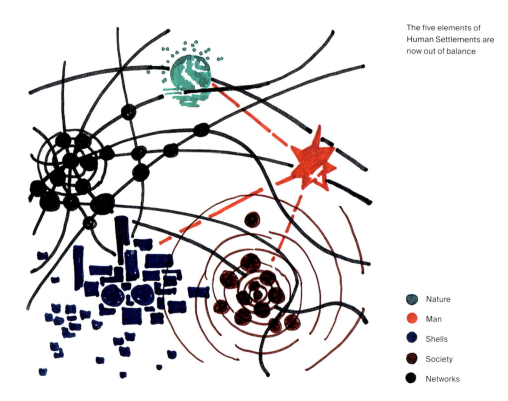

The five elements of Human Settlements are now out of balance

- Nature
- Man
- Shells
- Society
- Networks

balance [Figs. 1–2]. Eagerly embracing systemic thinking and making it central to Delos Symposia discourse, Doxiadis figured the nature–city dialectic as an idiosyncratic "algorithmic" system.

Building on Delos Symposia links with cross-scientific discourses, this chapter begins with a discussion of dynamic systems and their applicability to various scenarios, mainly in urban planning for more sustainable built-environment solutions. This ambition was generally aligned with modernism's appreciation of science as expressed through CIAM (Congrès Internationaux d'Architecture Moderne), although there it was often driven by a concern for machine-influenced style and aesthetics. To Doxiadis and his peers, science was clearly much more than an analogy for a new aesthetics. It was the vehicle to understand extended system structures through which the artificial environment could meet and mesh with the natural one, bringing together the totality of resources, parameters and constraints that are responsible for their joint future viability.

Figs. 1–2 Graphic depictions showing the five elements of Human Settlements out of balance. A future projection (opposite) suggests that the situation will only be exacerbated as cities become more populated and complex.

The five elements of Human Settlements will be completely out of balance in the future

The chapter then moves on to explore a connecting thread between physical space's dynamic qualities, identified during the Delos Symposia, and those currently studied in computational design culture. Computers execute calculations, yet computation suggests more than calculating numbers. The computer may be used not only as an explanatory aid in the usual sense but also as an evolutionary accelerator and a generative element, helping to envision "a new form of design artefact interacting and evolving in harmony with natural forces, including those of society."[1] The capacity to calculate at increasing speed translates to a complex understanding of phenomena by open system models that promote design's dynamic and holistic character rather than permanence, rigidity, fragmentation or finite procedures. In effect, computational processes can present compelling similarities with nature's adaptable and responsive character in producing new solutions while also dealing efficiently with resources. In 2003, Sanford Kwinter observed that "computers offer the possibility of apprehending developmental patterns of extraordinary and unprecedented depth and abstraction, offering tantalizing glimpses of the very freeform structure of time itself (chaos, complexity, self-organization)," adding, "This new tool [...] may well bear the potential to unlock the door on the universal laws that govern the appearance and destruction of form, and in so doing to free us from the multiple tyranny of determinism and from the poverty of a linear, numerical world."[2] Kwinter refers to the current production workflow that holds various specializations together through fully digitized platforms to better inform design decisions. These cross-disciplinary digital alliances are strikingly analogous to those systemic ones once suggested by Delos Symposia, and a new vision and role for architecture may lie in this direction.[3] Likewise, the environmental and population issues that architecture and planning currently need to grapple with were also noted at the Delos Symposia meetings over half a century ago [Fig. 3], at the same time as they broached their experimental computational solutions. This chapter investigates these historical aspects of the Delos Symposia to see what they might teach us about possible futures for the built environment and the challenges in architecture and urbanism that have yet to be met.

Extended Collaboration in Architecture and Urbanism
Dynamic Systems and Global Networks

The Delos Symposia introduced various ways to better describe physical space as a holistic phenomenon that dynamically relates a plurality of inputs. This view invokes Doxiadis's proposed analogies between biology and physical space, focusing on the systemic logic by which natural phenomena generally occur. Nature's systemic qualities may then be applied to understand the lifecycle patterns of the birth, growth, expansion and decay of human settlements. Nature consists of a poly-systemic entity, with multiple sub-systems co-evolving in partial autonomy and together, through which mutation, transformation and other time-, space-, matter- and energy-related activities unfold. Following the metaphor, form is viewed as a system made of sub-systems and as part of higher systems that can be read at different

Fig. 3 A newspaper cutting stored in an archive folder as a working file for the book *Architecture in Transition*, dated 1961.
It mentions the RIBA conference entitled "Designing for Survival" at Lancaster University, an occasion that – according to the opening words of Mr. Alex Gordon, President of the RIBA – "heralds the beginning of an important new course for the architectural [profession]." The architect is presented with a new code of ethics to "not perform any work which his conscience tells him is harmful to the best interests of the public."

According to this article, "the biggest danger was the unwillingness to adjust established social and political ideas quickly enough, and to know how to respond to commercial pressures strongly enough for the necessary changes to be made. If the profession refused, or moved too slowly, the changes would not be deliberate and controlled, but would be forced upon it in the form of catastrophe or cataclysm. Environmental deterioration could pass the point of no return before the danger was fully appreciated."

Architects face demands of environmental changes

BY H. A. N. BROCKMAN, ARCHITECTURE CORRESPONDENT

"I HAVE NO DOUBT this is one of the most important conferences we have ever held." These were the opening words of Mr. Alex Gordon, president of the Royal Institute of British Arhitects, in his address to mark yesterday's beginning of this year's RIBA conference at Lancaster University.

The conference title is "Designing for Survival" and in the president's view the occasion heralds the beginning of an important new course for the architectural progression. He quoted the chairman of the Royal Commission on Environmental Pollution, Sir Eric Ashby, who said last month: "We shall not survive another generation without fundamental changes in our social institutions, among them the values which guide business and industry in supplying the needs of man."

The current concern for the environment had undermined all the optimistically held assumptions that there would always be a reserve of power or a scientific development to clear up the mess or dispose of the rubbish. We had assumed, for instance, that there was still plenty of land to accommodate our new buildings and somebody to clear them away when their useful life was over. We now faced a future which would demand that we lived more carefully, did more with less and made no demands on nature which nature could not continue to answer: an indefinite period of reappraisal and change.

Code of ethics

In reviewing the RIBA code of conduct, the architect's responsibility to the community would have to be taken more seriously.

A draft Code of Ethics for architects of the Common Market already drawn up included clauses on moral as well as professional responsibility, requiring that "the architect should contribute by his work to the full development of mankind . . . and that he should not perform any work which his conscience tells him is harmful to the best interests of the public."

The conference, Mr. Gordon continued, should raise the level of understanding of the nature of the environmental crisis, should make architects look at the implications for them as the designers of buildings and human settlements at every scale, together with the social and political implications of these tasks.

The biggest danger was the unwillingness to adjust established social and political ideas quickly enough, and to know how to respond to commercial pressures strongly enough for the necessary changes to be made. If the profession refused, or moved too slowly, the changes would not be deliberate and controlled, but would be forced upon it in the form of catastrophe or cataclysm.

Environmental deterioration could pass the point of no return before the danger was fully appreciated. There was therefore a special rseponsibility on professional men and women to lead, to warn and to advise, and to be prepared to opt out when advance knowledge so demanded, even at the expense of personal sacrifices.

Role and values

An American scientist, Prof. Barry Commoner, said that modern technology was destroying the biological wealth of the world. He added that the environmental crisis was a "tragic paradox."

He rejected the argument that it was caused by overpopulation or by affluence.

Mr. Graham Ashworth, director of the Civic Trust for the North-West, raised questions about what it was we wanted to survive. Was there an optimum size for the community beyond which it became unmanageable? Could the architectural profession survive the necessary change from its traditional service to the private client and become part of a public service, without "losing its professional detachment." Under such circumstances, would architects, in fact, lose their creative role but at the same time continue to impose their own values?

To-morrow the Bishop of Kingston, the Rt. Revd. Hugh Montefiore, who will discuss the implications for architects and architecture of man's attitude to his environment, his fellow-men, to nature and to society. R. S. Scorer, Professor of Theoretical Mechanics at Imperial College, London, will speak on "the environment our children can expect."

levels.⁴ Studying nature's systemic character and adapting it to design is highly suggestive of deep analogies between nature and architecture.

The connection between nature and space as dynamic systems was solidified in the post-World War II era, mainly through research into cybernetics. Gordon Pask, for example, conceived a human-made spatial structure as a unit system that could interact with inhabitants and the environment in an open, renegotiable contract.⁵ Since a structure or unit was variously connected to its surroundings, it would have been unsafe to explain either of them separately or to draw conclusions as if they were independent. The resulting model assumes an extended understanding of "mutualism" with regards to context, behavioral patterns and developmental processes.⁶ A notion of holism is fundamental to spatial systems describing artificial and natural environments alike, operating alongside a quest for interconnectivity between the parts in constant reciprocity and exchange also with the whole. In studying human settlements, it is the evolutionary properties, relationships and rules that count the most, so that "growth is to be healthy rather than cancerous."⁷ Likewise, the Delos Symposia included meticulous explorations of spatial organizing, comparative data management and the detection of dynamic system patterns. The focus was rethought toward finding the principles that drive the evolution of cities as open systems. Like natural systems, cities follow the imperatives of change and renewability caused by dynamic factors.⁸ These are not static, nor is the world they describe undeniable, objective, fixed, finite or fully predictable. As a result, open systems were sought as alternatives to the up to then closed organizational structures of cities that were failing to adapt to change, as this would soon become the gravest challenge facing the human species.⁹

The main historical reference to this systemic approach was the research of Scottish biologist Patrick Geddes in the late nineteenth and early twentieth century.¹⁰ Driven by an interest in sociology and the designing of large urban regions, Geddes aimed to link settlements of various sizes together and then identify the mechanisms governing the evolution of spatial schemes during their lifespan.¹¹ His work evinces the interdependencies between energy flows and material resources and the environment, and also the distribution of wealth, labor and human needs within society. As in ecosystems, space and form evolve as the result of external (environmental) stimuli and internal (cultural) pressures, producing unique instances of an ever-expanding pluralism.¹² Applying Geddes's theory, Doxiadis employed natural systems to explain the city as a growing phenomenon expressed by the notion of Dynapolis.[13] Doxiadis also coined the term "Ecumenopolis," a version of the universal *polis* – that is, a future city with ubiquitous presence and active responses to fluctuating factors.[14] As these concepts suggest, buildings and urban settlements are never isolated or at rest, but they interact with one another to form extended network system structures.

Networks constituted a main theme in the Delos Symposia, both as structures explaining spatial aggregates and as infrastructures for the circulation of material, energy and electronic information. The network was a comprehensive idea explaining the urban phenomenon in its full physicality and expansion by means of the intakes and outtakes it hosts in analogy to biotic organisms.[15] The city ought to evolve much like a biological body, making an organism of a higher order. Its street patterns and electronic networks would form higher densities inward while also extending outward as tentacles, reaching toward and eventually meeting with those of other cities. This would create a web of arteries for interaction, communication and exchanging. These ideas find their culmination in a view of the world as a complex network of spatial nodes, whose size may be as small as the generic room-cell and which – through successive bouts of accumulation, articulation and growth – would form dwellings, dwelling groups, buildings and building blocks – then neighborhoods, districts, towns, cities, metropolitan areas, conurbations and groups of cities, urbanized regions and continents until they cover every part of Earth.[16] This whole articulation produces a "nested" hyper-organism made of units at every conceivable scale, interacting locally and across the globe within one gigantic system that represents constant material transformation and energy distribution.[17]

Cross-Scientific Agendas to Spatial Dynamics

But, as well as being a seductive reference and an ostensibly practicable approach for organizing space, the global system described above introduced a more exploratory framework by which to better gear up terrestrial discourse at the Delos Symposia with science-based research. Space's dynamic features set a challenge to be met with strategic planning solutions from the members of the group. Planning represented a new kind of continual learning and an enormous upgrading that stated the imperative need for open-endedness and flexibility by which to respond to unforeseen changes.[18] In support of this view, Delos Symposia members Marshall McLuhan and Richard Buckminster Fuller argued that technological advancement would cause conventional architecture and urbanism to lose their rigid character, and urban space to embrace the more ephemeral and instant qualities of the electronic flux.[19] Consequently, it would no longer be sufficient to represent space solely with the Euclidian shape that was supposed to be its "real material essence"; to this, one should add its "symbolic," "human," "subjective" or "iconic" value.[20] Such remarks conjure up the observation that physical space should be studied only along with the implications of time as its fourth dimension. Time describes space by its influences, which, according to an evolutionary logic, affect the decisions about a project, the finished form it may take and its life after completion – a condition that is profoundly represented at the Delos Symposia and in Doxiadis's philosophy too, being distilled in the analysis, the arguments and the appointed techniques through which the various data since the early phases of the Symposia were often given parametric significance [Fig. 4].

Moreover, Delians Sigfried Giedion and David Owen stressed a design scheme's profound linkage to political debates, requiring statistical inquiries and sociological studies.[21] Its plans must take into account a constellation of forces playing upon the decisional process and the capacity of the administrative machinery to carry out plans once they have been adopted.[22] A project undergoes continual transformation driven by criteria expressed during and after the end of this process, and causal and recursive features should be used to identify the generative forces that reshape the system. A proposed scheme ought to be flexible and adaptable in order to satisfy the requirements of internal and external forces and, at the same time, to manifest efficiency so that its routine operations may be completed successfully, safely and in a timely manner. Such a comprehensive understanding of a scheme causes us to revisit the practical and symbolic implication of typologies, shapes, patterns and structures – and often to update them with "softer" ones that are capable of responding to any of the socioeconomical, environmental and geopolitical inputs otherwise suppressed by grand centralized themes.[23] In that sense, the Delos Symposia redirected their aim toward more integrated methods and styles of work by which architecture is reunited with the other, broader activities – scientific, cultural, social and technical alike. Following such remarks, Doxiadis pointed out the need to establish a coordinated foundation for the study of physical spaces that would grant equal participation for each specialist.[24] A preference for extended

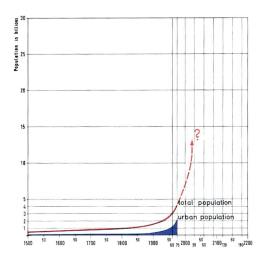
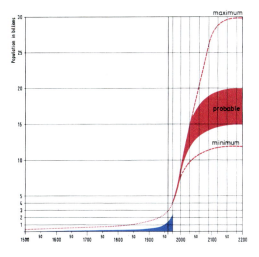
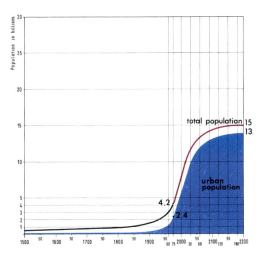

Fig. 4 Doxiadis's probability diagrams, showing the increasing rate of urban population growth and the consequences of its explosion since the early twentieth century in order to discuss its impact on the development of urban settlements in the future. In Doxiadis's work, analytical data were commonly expressed and then processed as parametric values right from the start, rather than as fixed values. With graphs, data were introduced to the project in a quest for time-related qualities by which to study space as a dynamic phenomenon.

organizational structures was common to all the Delos participants, guiding their actions and also being supported by the communication platforms that were rapidly expanding at a global scale.

Furthermore, under the collaborative efforts managed by the Athens Center of Ekistics and the *Ekistics* journal, new graduate programs of planning were sought under the theme of Ekistics to cope with the greater problems of urbanization and industrialization throughout the world – with majors in architecture, landscape architecture, engineering, sociology, anthropology, economics, law, public administration and public health.[25] Ekistics was a new cross-scientific academic field described as "the science of human settlements, which proposed to synthesize the economic, social, political, and administrative sciences, technology and aesthetics into one coherent whole."[26] An effort was made to integrate the systems of analysis used by different fields into a unified approach. Research was oriented toward methodologies and techniques for city planning applicable to local conditions, while professional consulting services were developed targeting various public and private agencies. Delian Richard Llewelyn-Davies further suggested that practitioners from several areas of expertise could act together in the broad arena to be found between the fields of pure theory and actual practice, approaching the problem of human settlements by programs of fundamental research that would examine the data of the present to make projections about the future.[27]

The range of topics covered in the journal *Ekistics* often extended to the study of spaces and the environment from a broader scope – which was then reflected back onto architecture to challenge its established themes, influences and practices. The broader concepts of ecology were central to this process, often tackling subjects from and interactions with external bodies of knowledge. A characteristic example is the experimental project called "Wildlife" presented in the journal; this involved a gaming simulation model of living biosystems developed in the 1960s with the aim of producing a gaming platform for the interactive study of natural phenomena.[28] Wildlife operated through guiding human behavior, and was initially intended to acquaint students of the natural sciences with concepts concerning community in the ecosystem that were otherwise difficult to transmit. In order to function properly, however, the model had to be stripped of all non-essential information to the point that the remaining level of complexity on the playing board "should generate a minimum of confusion, yet almost universal respect."[29] As this new realm of modeling was taken to the architects and landscape architects, its "mode of abstraction was not fully satisfying to the students recruited [from] these professions [...] [since] the potential for fantasy, a capacity that is treasured by those who seem born to design, had been ruled out by this purely objective, science-based approach."[30] Yet, projects such as Wildlife, developed under the aegis of Ekistics, pioneered an alternative mindset about the field of architecture, which manifested itself in the novelties being initiated concerning the methodology, the tools and the communication links it gave rise to with the scientific world.

By partaking in the academic faculty through Ekistics, and by actively engaging with science, the Delos Symposia group nourished a multifaceted strategy about the "unknown" as the expertise of various specializations was brought together and directed toward an extensive cross-fertilization of ideas. Their shared efforts described a sophisticated knowledge model intended to encompass the complexities and the multifaceted qualities of terrestrial space. But, drawing comparisons between versatile inputs and the views of experts was perhaps one of the most challenging issues facing the Delos Symposia peers, being the subject of coordinated negotiation and teamwork discussion as opposed to a sequential or deterministic processes – an issue that is reviewed in the following section.[31]

Delos Symposia and the Reforming of Architecture
New Protocols of Collaboration with Art, Science and Technology

Perhaps one of the main concerns around the Delos Symposia – especially over the introduction of scientific references to space-related debates – has to do with the belief that science's clear-cut answers do not always align with the ambiguous character of creative thinking. This discrepancy between science and creativity in general was known to the architects of the twentieth century. Hence, they often would not sit comfortably alongside scientists and other techno-specialists whose aspirations to, for example, introduce innovations into the field were thought to be too different – despite the observation that exchanges between various sources of knowledge are unavoidable and, indeed, mostly fruitful.[32] This section aims to draw attention to the protocols of collaboration between architecture and planning employed by the Delos Symposia, on the one hand, and the external influences and borrowings, specifically from science and technology, on the

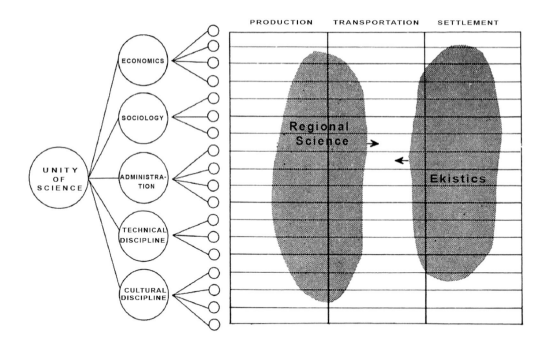

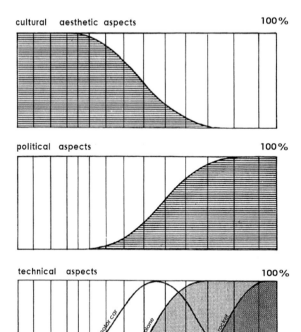

Fig. 5 Diagrams showing how different disciplinary activities such as culture, aesthetics, politics and technology may collaborate to produce a joint effect and a new dimension regarding space perceived through those disciplines (above), and the impact of different sciences such as economics, sociology, administration, technology and culture on regional science and Ekistics – also in relation to production, transportation and settlement (right).

Yannis Zavoleas

other. Ideally, a coordinated framing of such alliances would alleviate any of the drawbacks related to the deterministic translation of outside references into the broader field of architecture.

Crossing pathways between architecture, science and technology was a recurring theme in twentieth-century modernism. The Delos Symposia approach expanded CIAM's agenda, whereby a group of architects and urban planners collaborated with various intellectuals and technocrats specializing in nature-related and social matters.[33] Increasingly, architects were forging new ideas by introducing references, methods, techniques and tools from other scientific disciplines, while architectural thinking began to appropriate science-borne concepts – not least when it harbored technocratic ambitions. Doxiadis first ran up against this prospect as early as in 1933, when he attended the fourth CIAM meeting while a student at the National Technical University of Athens, the Athens Polytechnion. Tyrwhitt had also worked closely with prominent CIAM figures such as Giedion (later a Delian) and Josep Lluís Sert, and she was herself one of the main contributors to post-World War II CIAM. Drawn further into CIAM's trajectory, the Delos Symposia revived one of modern architecture's cornerstone aims: to engage with scientific and technological progress in order to validate its endeavors.

Aside from the significance of scientific knowledge and analysis as sources of evidence, it was observed that scientific language, with its homogeneity, could suggest a universal platform for critical thinking. For McLuhan and Giedion, science's vocabulary consisted of a common ground hosting theory and experimentation, upon which the various disciplines could meet and interact.[34] By virtue of the universal appeal of charts and tables, science's complex concepts, methods and techniques would be disseminated to wider audiences. Consequently, its respected modes of focus, analysis, explaining and reasoning set an overarching framework for all related activities to contribute to solving the problems of human settlements [Fig. 5]. Additionally, acclaimed scientists in the broader Delos Symposia circle fueled such a neo-humanistic approach engaging all specializations. Biologist Ludwig von Bertalanffy, whom Fuller pronounced to be one of his influences, envisioned a unifying of the perception and communication of knowledge by a general system theory that ran "vertically" through the universe of specialized fields – prompting critical analogies between them, and their integration into one common discourse.[35] In such a way, it was possible to draw comparisons across disciplines, along with an ability to discern the "isomorphy" of laws, understood as the operational analogies and the structural uniformities observed between different events or world realms.[36] The Delos Symposia served as a platform for these ideas, but also mirrored them in their very mode of operation: an amorphous forum for the free circulation of ideas, methods and principles, reflexively searching for a common discourse on global space.

The Delos Symposia's all-encompassing ideology infused its manner of working. Analysis would begin with precisely calibrated diagrams, statistics and numbers, and decision-making would often be driven by dynamic pattern recognition.[37] A solution was the output of a series of operations combining all scales, and expressing the ways in which the variables might interfere and negotiate with one another through mutual compromises and data tweaks. However, for an otherwise strictly rational approach solely driven by data, rules and equations, science was, rather, an intellectual framework by which to translate the collected information into a set of "functions" and hence to expand modernism's concept about functionalism to one that reflected a system's operative qualities. In its updated definition, the term "function" would also describe the sum of inputs and actions profoundly conditioned and linked together by the socioecological body – global and local, constructed and natural alike – including those related to production. The variables and influences of different specializations enriched the process with practicality and efficiency, manifested throughout the scheme and beyond to merge with its surroundings. In effect, it was possible to reunite spatial units from the microscopic to the mesoscopic, the macroscopic and the terrascopic scale, with sociopolitical dimensions and the greater ecology.

It may be noted that the expressive language by which ideas were developed in the Delos Symposia presents an intonation that is very different from typical architectural sketches and drawings. The mode by which concepts and strategies were illustrated was abstract – that is, completely detached from any aim to resemble or look like the realities being represented. For example, in one case, the graphics show data comparison and the superimposition of science-related graphics onto maps, such as organic aggregates describing patterns of evolution, growth, expansion, explosion, diffusion, mutation, transposition, self-division, articulations, dependencies and hierarchies common in human settlements [Fig. 6]; in another case, they present molecular and multicellular units layered upon geographical areas and

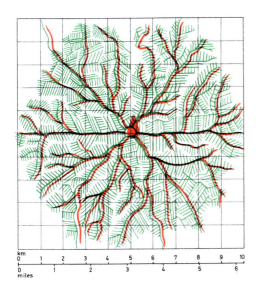

energy flowers

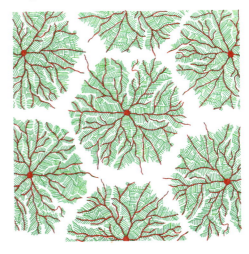

energy model of several villages which are not interconnected into a system

energy model of a system of settlements

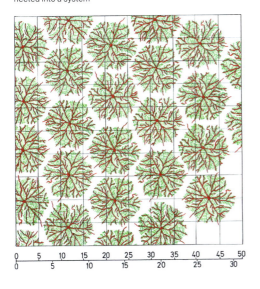

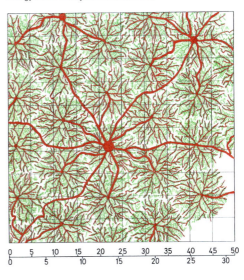

Human energy consumed for agricultural purposes in the fields

Daily energy consumption per capita 8000 Cal.

Human energy consumed for all other purposes in the village

Fig. 6 Diagrammatic depiction of an energy model, suggesting functional ways to connect individual villages, named "Energy Flowers," via a system of arteries for energy distribution, following a logic similar to that of tree branching – and also nervous and bloodstream circulatory systems. These energy models were presented in *Ekistics* in 1970 and consisted of abstract energy-flow schemes representing the movement and settlements of humans.

Bio-systemic Thinking for Holistic Design

dynamic expressions of atoms [Fig. 7]; in yet others, they consist of diagrammatic approximations explaining dynamic sociocultural phenomena related to diversity or the segregation and isolation of populations [Fig. 8]. These organograms and graphemes communicate rough information, being suggestive of how data are related but not of what may ultimately be developed as a scheme resulting straight *from* them. Such a distinctive style claims its intellectual placement somewhere between architecture and science, where the latter is employed as a manifold resource and mediated by the "raw" language it employs in order to deliver architectural content.

The Delos Symposia built upon a new collaborative setting wherein the body of knowledge produced could circulate freely between different experts as conceptual and technical assets toward creative goals and strategic solutions. Information could be drawn out of a wide spectrum of influences: some could be calculated accurately, while other ones could only be approximated. Science, with its direct yet non-descriptive modes, was used as a means to clarify intentions and decisions, thereby endowing the process with the openness and flexibility necessary to experiment critically. In consequence, the Delos Symposia promoted an alternative view about architecture as a discipline at large that rendered its methods and results more competent and broadly accessible. A hybrid working model would merge the various instances and means together, allowing ideas to diffuse, breed and evolve toward new theories, methods and solution schemes – forging the workplace and the nature of cross-disciplinary alliances for the future of architecture.

Anticipating the Future Scenario

Currently, the computer is involved, either directly or indirectly, in almost every activity in architecture, planning and beyond – and so, production has shifted to digitally shared information platforms as the emerging form of practice.[38] Meanwhile, the discipline of architecture is constantly being updated with new concepts, terminology and styles of work, further challenging enduring assumptions – for example, those referring to the architect's idioms or appreciated talent, which have influenced the profession and education for so long.[39] Consequently, the twentieth-century mentality of objectifying and representing reality with a system, a set of data and algorithmic procedures has prompted the computer's wholesale adoption into architecture at large as the main instrument that could effectively undertake such increasingly complex tasks.[40]

These changes have impacted upon the Delos Symposia's legacy with regards to active cross-scientific and cross-cultural participation; extensive data management; automation; and the introduction of computers into spatial analysis, design and strategic planning. At the Delos Symposia, it was evident that sustainable solutions to spatial problems could only be reached through coordinated contributions – an idea that was essentially an evolution of modernism's earlier views. For example, in CIAM's "La Sarraz Declaration" document of 1928, turning to scientific methods, tools and techniques was presented as a pathway toward reliable design solutions.[41] During the 1960s, Doxiadis further built on this approach and enriched it with holistic and systemic thinking. Meanwhile, he warned that by denying techno-scientific progress, architects would be marginalized and removed from the real needs of humanity and from the key roles of decision-making.[42] Consequently, he sought a constant updating of the field using whatever science and technology had to offer in order to catch up with changing phenomena – as, in doing so, architecture would "cease to be merely the practice of an art form and once again become a practice that serves all the people, in the best possible way."[43] The Delos Symposia members also expressed their conviction that any of the challenges faced by human settlements lay somewhere along the spectrum of science and technology. As stated in the "Declaration of Delos" document of 1963, "science and technology determine more and more of the processes of human living," and their advancement causes social behavior to be modified, too.[44] McLuhan was convinced of the potential for a combination of technology and electronic fusion to bring together all different functions and to creatively use the possibilities being offered – including those that, at the time, remained unforeseen. In simple words, to remain current and relevant to emerging themes, architecture had to reinforce its ties with other areas of knowledge. In the post-World War II world, this could be achieved by cross-scientific models combined with those pertaining to computing and networking. Tools and practices for data analysis, manipulation and further processing – even the language that was used in the Delos Symposia – were far from, and not to be confused with, architecture's repeated themes and technical stock typically related to drawings, sketches and representational models.

Meanwhile, the influences of scientific and technological progress had to be conditioned. Architects commonly notice a difference in how creativity is manifested in their discipline compared with others. The form of a

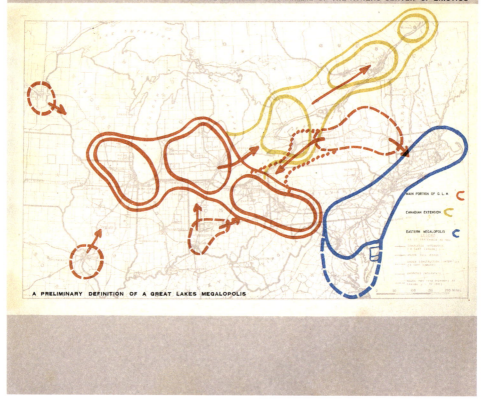

Fig. 7 Cover of *Ekistics* (July 1966) presenting the concept of Megalopolis, a polycentric network of cities in the Great Lakes area forming an urban aggregate that stretches out to connect Michigan, Ontario, Pennsylvania, Virginia, Philadelphia, New York and Boston. According to this scenario, the resulting entity evolves as a gigantic multi-cellular organism constantly expanding to engulf other adjacent areas found in its path.

people in the large city
segregation of different groups of people

people in the large city
segregation leads to isolation,
autocratic organization and conflict

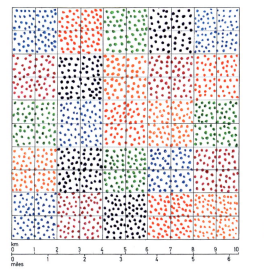

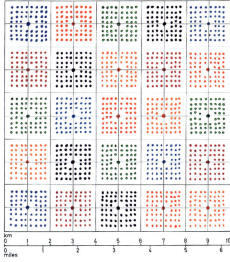

people in the large city
radiation of the blue people

people in the large city
synthesis of people

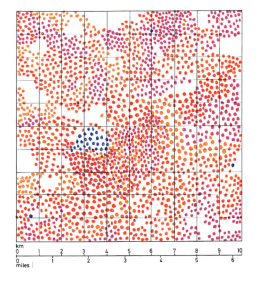

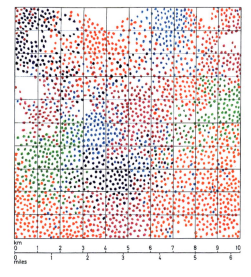

- blue people
- urban dwellers
- positive influence of the blue people
- negative influence of the blue people

Fig. 8 Diagrams roughly depicting the population fusion of different groups of people, further suggesting ways to promote either cultural diversity and richness, or segregation leading to "isolation, autocratic organization and conflict," as the original captions suggest.

Bio-systemic Thinking for Holistic Design

proposed scheme is not known from the start of the process but is, rather, discovered and reached gradually and quite similarly to natural models, through a series of iterations aiming to bring its different influences together in mutual recognition and compromise.[45] At the same time, technoscientific knowledge is typically specialized. Its appointed references are often too deterministic and do not always work well with, for example, contested information such as that arising from sociocultural constraints and long-term effects. Equally, its models of thought remain too fragmented or limiting to deal with the intricacies of a design project or to reconstruct the whole picture – processes that are, rather, best met through artistic means.

The Delos Symposia's response to the above was to mitigate enduring polarizations between architecture and other areas of knowledge by engaging with them while still on architecture's own terms.[46] A spatial proposal at any scale would be the outcome of a dynamic balance between technoscientific intentions on the one hand and artistic intuition on the other, at the intersection of architecture and planning with science, technology and art. This could be developed, for example, by the new graduates of the Ekistics program, who were trained specifically to manage such diverse languages, priorities and resources. Priorities were repositioned around social and eco-political forces, energies and relationships, and moved away from architecture's typical focus on typology, geometry and form. Through cross-disciplinary critical reflection, it was possible to discern the principles that linked disparate phenomena together and, moreover, to diffuse them into spatial concepts and strategies. Such an outward-looking stance about architecture's own transformation alongside science and technology raises a critical dimension that is relevant in current computational settings.

Conclusion: An Impending Paradigm Shift and What Delos Has to Offer

Digital workflow is supported by networking, information exchanging and collaboration and is further facilitated by automated routines and real-time access to datasets. Data-driven processes have been greatly enriched by extended computational models such as geographic information systems, building information modeling, big data and machine learning systems constantly feeding simulation and programming algorithms directed toward dynamic linking, iterative testing and decision-making. Such technologies support arguably the most innovative, collaborative research currently to be found in the academic curricula of renowned institutions, effectively forming a new framing by which to rethink architecture's intellectual and practical corpus.[47]

However, reservations are growing alongside this imminent shift, especially over the uncritical use of the computer for activities related to imaginative thinking.[48] Automation has added more reliability and speed but, for some, the processes being advertised seem often too precise, rigid and impersonal – thus not always granting sufficient freedom for intuitive action and the various forms of ambiguity and self-doubt inherent in creativity.[49] That is, architects still need some freedom to intervene if the result simply "does not look quite right." Macroscopic reflection on any of the intermediate steps (from the first ideas until the finalized scheme) is necessary in order to compare automatically produced results – or to fix similarly produced obvious errors. Considering that similar concerns have been present at least since the time of the Delos Symposia, their setting offers a pertinent case study by which to reconcile the tradition of architecture with rapidly evolving working trends.

Subjective inputs – once expressed through rough handcraft techniques – should, in a computational setting, still express an intuitive character. Aside from the technical advancements brought about by computing with regards to productivity, efficiency, detailing and information/knowledge distribution, there has been a parallel need for tools that approximate to dynamic phenomena such as socioecological inputs through fluctuating values and negotiated procedures. The dynamic features of advanced computing have prompted its users to envision the screen as the primary stage where data about activities and patterns of spatial occupation, site, materials, economy, energy flows, points of interest, orientation – even those about society and culture – may interact. Through simulation dynamics, topological defining, point cloud mapping and machine learning, diverse information can be given significance as part of the system model, then be translated spatially and further examined, resolved and finalized for construction and post-evaluation purposes. Ideas emerge through trial-end-error feedback procedures, during which early approximations evolve gradually to become refined proposals. In consequence, the project may not begin by drawing a scheme in a conventional sense but rather by introducing the conditions into the system, first as the influential factors by which the project will "occur" with a varying degree of fuzziness and intuition to complement accuracy and resolution in the ensuing phases. As such, the outcome is directly linked back to the context following an evolutionary mode that is analogous to bio-systemic processes, by mixing architectural styles, typologies and languages to produce unique results each time.

Given the profound analogies between the Delos Symposia ideology and advanced data-driven computing, it may be claimed that the Symposia heralded the current production workflow well before the latter was technologically possible. However, the present direction still needs to be supported by holistic, non-linear models of thought and action. Routine applications have often been responsible for reducing architectural activity to a set of repetitive tasks that grant insufficient room for critical intervention, which somewhat explains architects' reluctance to using computers – especially for creative tasks. The computer has been a fascinating tool, but it sets its own limits too, which architects must be able to recognize and then to manage. Invoking the Delos Symposia initiatives, there has been a renewed interest in readdressing architecture's synergies with science and technology, evidenced by the cross-disciplinary research agendas being pursued around the world. By taking advantage of key aspects of the digital culture – especially with regards to ubiquitous networking, information sharing and cross-disciplinary communication – it is possible to constantly realign architecture's aims with global challenges.

As it turns out, the Delos Symposia laid out a robust action model for architecture to catch up with the urgent priorities of the post-digital culture – one that required holistic processes, mutual participation and coordinated planning. Technological progress has facilitated critical changes with regards to the profession, the architect's role in the building industry and the style and kind of work that they undertake. Younger generations of architects are investing in these new trajectories by opening up the discourse, as they become increasingly acquainted with methods, strategies and toolsets from outside resources. Pulsating data – about signals, observations and recordings – are linked by DNA-like systemic code sets explaining a project task with scientific rigor – whose translation into form is, however, the result of artistic sensations and actions seeking their balance between deliberation, speculation, ingenuity and, to a certain extent, risk as true expressions of creativity. This approach bypasses disciplinary entrenchment, object-oriented strategies, symbolic representations and personal preferences, giving way to concepts and arguments supported by extended combinations of knowledge and expertise. This total hybridization of human and nature, analysis and synthesis, intention and intuition, science and art, and reason and dream expresses novelty in architecture, the prospect of which may not be built around techno-scientific phobia but around the hope that, with computation, humanity may just be able to imagine, design and actualize a well-informed paradigm about, for and with the world.[50]

1. John Frazer, *An Evolutionary Architecture* (London: Architectural Association, 1995), 10.
2. Sanford Kwinter, "The Computational Fallacy," *Thresholds – Denatured*, no. 26 (2003), 90–92.
3. Flora Samuel, *Why Architects Matter: Evidencing and Communicating the Value of Architects* (London and New York: Routledge, 2018), 13–28.
4. Michael Weinstock, "Morphogenesis and the Mathematics of Emergence," in Sean Ahlquist and Achim Menges (eds), *Computational Design Thinking* (Chichester: Wiley, 2011, originally published 1969), 166.
5. Gordon Pask, "The Architectural Relevance of Cybernetics," *Architectural Design*, no. 7/6 (1969), 494–96.
6. Ibid., 495–96.
7. Ibid., 495.
8. "The Delos Symposion," *Ekistics* 16, no. 95 (October 1963), https://www.jstor.org/stable/pdf/43622749.pdf?refreqid=excelsior%3Ac703117c2ee1d-5da5f95b0ed2be6b659 (accessed August 17, 2021).
9. Ibid.
10. Panayiota I. Pyla, "Ekistics, Architecture and Environmental Politics, 1945–1976: A Prehistory of Sustainable Development," Ph.D. dissertation, Massachusetts Institute of Technology, 2002, 46–47.
11. Patrick Geddes, "Paleotechnic and Neotechnic," in Patrick Geddes, *Cities in Evolution* (London: Williams & Norgate, 1949, originally published 1915), 60–83. Also, Yannis Zavoleas, *Η Μηχανή και το Δίκτυο ως Δομικά Πρότυπα στην Αρχιτεκτονική* [*Machine and Network as Structural Models in Architecture*] (Athens: Futura, 2013), 182.
12. Ariane Lourie Harrison, "Charting Posthuman Territory," in Ariane Lourie Harrison (ed.), *Architectural Theories of the Environment: Posthuman Territory* (New York: Routledge, 2013), 27. Also, Simon Guy, "Pragmatic Ecologies," in Harrison (ed.), *Architectural Theories of the Environment*, 141.
13. Constantinos A. Doxiadis, "Rural Housing in an Urbanizing World," *Ekistics* 24, no. 141 (August 1967), 131–34, https://www.jstor.org/stable/43614539 (accessed August 28, 2021).
14. Constantinos A. Doxiadis, *The Two-Headed Eagle: From the Past to the Future of Human Settlements* (Athens: Lycabettus Press, 1972).
15. Constantinos A. Doxiadis, *Ekistics: An Introduction to the Science of Human Settlements* (London and New York: Oxford University Press, 1968), 27–33. Also, Mark Wigley, "Network Fever," *Grey Room*, no. 4 (summer 2001), 83–122.
16. Constantinos A. Doxiadis, *Between Dystopia and Utopia* (London: Faber & Faber, 1966), 55. Also, Constantinos A. Doxiadis, "Ekistics Units," in "C.A. Doxiadis 1913–75: Pursuit of an Attainable Ideal," special issue, *Ekistics* 41, no. 247 (June 1976), 344.
17. Yannis Zavoleas and Panayotis Tournikiotis, "Archetypes in-Formation. Strategies of Transition in Architecture and Urban Design," in Marco Bovati, Michele Caja, Giancarlo Floridi and Martina Landsberger (eds), *Cities in Transformation, Research & Design: Ideas, Methods, Techniques, Tools, Case Studies*, vol. II (Milan and Brussels: Il Poligrafo and EAAE/ARCC, 2014), 1411–17.
18. "The Delos Symposion."
19. Wigley, "Network Fever," 83–122. Also, Marshall McLuhan, *Understanding Media: The Extensions of Man* (Cambridge, MA: MIT Press), 1994; Richard Buckminster Fuller, "Letter to Doxiadis," *Main Currents in Modern Thought*, vol. 25, no. 4 (March/April 1969), 87–97.
20. Bruno Latour and Albena Yaneva, "Give Me a Gun and I Will Make All Buildings Move: An ANT's View of Architecture," in Harrison (ed.), *Architectural Theories of the Environment*, 107–11.
21. "The Delos Symposion."
22. Ibid.
23. Pyla, "Ekistics, Architecture and Environmental Politics, 1945–1976," 84–87.
24. Ibid.
25. "New Schools of Planning and Ekistics," *Ekistics* 11, no. 68 (June 1961), 459–68, https://www.jstor.org/stable/43613518 (accessed August 28, 2021).
26. Constantinos A. Doxiadis, "Architecture," in David L. Sills and Robert King Merton (eds), *International Encyclopedia of the Social Sciences* (New York: Macmillan and Free Press, 1968), 8–10.
27. "The Delos Symposion."
28. Richard L. Meier, "Creating Wildlife: Synthesis of a Gaming Simulation," *Ekistics* 40, no. 239 (October 1975), 294, https://www.jstor.org/stable/43618587 (accessed August 28, 2021).
29. Ibid., 293.
30. Ibid., 297.
31. "The Delos Symposion."

32. Reyner Banham, *Theory and Design in the First Machine Age* (New York and Washington, DC: Praeger Publishers, 1960), 330.
33. Nader Vossoughian, "Mapping the Modern City: Otto Neurath, the International Congresses of Modern Architecture (CIAM), and the Politics of Information Design," *Design Issues* 22, no. 3 (Summer 2006), 48–65.
34. "The Delos Symposion."
35. Ludwig von Bertalanffy, "The Meaning of General System Theory," in Sean Ahlquist and Achim Menges (eds), *Computational Design Thinking* (Chichester: Wiley, 2011, originally published 1969), 51. Also, Ludwig von Bertalanffy, *General System Theory: Foundations, Development, Applications* (New York: George Braziller, 1968).
36. Bertalanffy, "The Meaning of General System Theory," 56.
37. Wigley, "Network Fever," 83–122.
38. The former is a concept that Vilém Flusser described eloquently in 1996, and one that others have followed in foreseeing dystopian futures, such as that of *The Matrix* film franchise directed by the Wachowskis, the first of which was released in 1999. Vilém Flusser, "Digital Apparition," in Timothy Druckrey (ed.), *Electronic Culture: Technology and Visual Representation* (London: Aperture, 1996) 242–45.
39. Garry Stevens, *The Favoured Circle: The Social Foundations of Architectural Distinction* (Cambridge, MA and London: MIT Press, 1998), 67.
40. Alberto Pérez-Gómez and Louise Pelletier, *Architectural Representation and the Perspective Hinge* (Cambridge, MA: MIT Press, 1997), 377.
41. See, for example, CIAM's positions expressed in the "La Sarraz Declaration," signed by twenty-four members of CIAM in La Sarraz, Switzerland in 1928.
42. Constantinos A. Doxiadis, "Architecture," in Sills and Merton (eds), *International Encyclopedia of the Social Sciences*, 7–10.
43. Ibid.
44. "The Delos Symposion."
45. Richard Garber, *BIM Design: Realising the Creative Potential of Building Information Modelling* (Chichester: Wiley, 2014), 23–25.
46. Constantinos A. Doxiadis, "A Technique to Control Technique," *Main Currents in Modern Thought* 22, no. 5 (May–June 1966), 3–15.
47. Theodore Spyropoulos, "Constructing Adaptive Ecologies: Towards a Behavioural Model for Architecture," *SAJ: Serbian Architectural Journal* 5, no. 2 (2013), 164–67.
48. Robert Temel, "The Means and the End," in Elke Krasny Basel (ed.), *The Force Is in the Mind: The Making of Architecture* (Boston and Berlin: Birkhauser, 2008), 140–43.
49. For example, prominent thinkers and designers have often criticized the computer for being too abstract, distant and far from reproducing real experience. See Yona Friedman, "I Am a Craftsman," in Basel (ed.), *The Force Is in the Mind*, 52–57. Also, Juhani Pallasmaa, *The Thinking Hand: Existential and Embodied Wisdom in Architecture* (Chichester: Wiley, 2009).
50. Doxiadis, "A Technique to Control Technique," 14–15.

Japanese Delos in 27 Points
Tilemachos Andrianopoulos

1963_1949_2000_1965_1973_1963_1964_1963_1965_
1966_1963_1973_1966_1973_1972_1960_1966_1965_
1970_1973_2000_1951_1964_1966_2000_1972_1952

1963: First Delos Symposion

Eiichi Isomura, sociologist, "the most frequent attendant not only among the Japanese but also among other members"[1] of the Delos meetings, fourth president of the World Society of Ekistics, states, "At a Japanese conference, just before leaving, I was unanimously asked to raise the problems resulting from the Hiroshima bomb and appeal for the peaceful uses of atomic energy. […] I deeply appreciate your kind consideration about Hiroshima. No more Hiroshimas."[2] Now a city of 1.2 million, Hiroshima has had its post-war identity reinvented using peace as its reconstruction vehicle. In 1945, the city was razed to the ground; the following year, a competition was organized for a memorial to be erected on the spot where, on August 6, 1945, the first atomic bomb had fallen.

Fig. 1 Cover of the *Ekistics* issue dedicated to the first Delos Symposion.

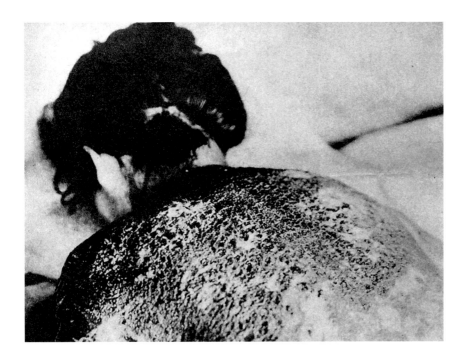

1949: Peace Memorial, Hiroshima

The plan that is accepted for execution is elaborated by Kenzo Tange; by 1956, construction is almost over.[3] Thirty-six years old by the time he entered the competition, it is Tange's first large-scale project in Japan. Articulated via a symmetrical axis that runs through it and the emblematic ruin of the Prefectural Industrial Hall, the memorial has as its dominant feature the museum: a rectilinear volume, elevated 6 meters above ground, perpendicular to the axis. Eiichi Isomura attends Delos 1 and, while accepting his personal invitation to Delos 2, he proposes to Constantinos Doxiadis that he also invite Tange.[4] Isomura had met Doxiadis in 1958 – for him, as he notes, "an energetic businessman rather than an academician."[5] In the same draft of a preface of his translation of *The Science of Ekistics*, he is both critical and complimentary: "From an academic point of view, the thoughts introduced in this book are rather crude. However, it is such seemingly simple thoughts that would save us from the academic labyrinth in which we have lost ourselves."[6]

Fig. 2 Hiroshima atomic-bombing victim.

2000: *De l'origine du XXIe siècle* [7]

On the Origin of the 21st Century. Short, labyrinthine film by Jean-Luc Godard. Quite anti-academic [Fig. 3]. An extract. (07.30-11.00 minutes into the film). Going back to the origins of the previous century, Godard uses mainly newsreel documentary material of war disasters starting from the 1990s siege of Sarajevo – always subtracting fifteen years, from 1990 to 1975 to 1960 to 1945 to 1930 to 1915, in order to conclude with 1900. We will also return to it.

Fig 3 Still from the film *De l'origine du XXIe siècle*, directed by J.-L. Godard, 2000.

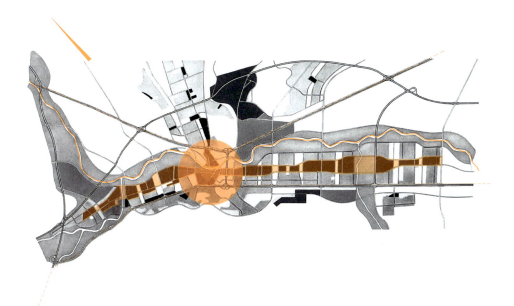

1965: Plan for Skopje

On July 26, 1963, thirteen days after the first Delos Symposium, in just seventeen seconds, 75 percent of the city of Skopje is completely destroyed. Two years after the earthquake, Tange is invited to Delos 3. He does not manage to attend, being concurrently engaged in submitting a winning scheme to the international competition for the reconstruction of Skopje – a tool for the physical rebuilding of the city and, at the same time, the conceptual redefinition of its identity. Before the competition, "a regional plan for the Skopje district, elaborated by the Greek firm of Doxiadis Associates and a Polish group, left the city center, of around 2 square kilometers open, in order, for this area […] to propose a detailed elaboration of the reconstruction scheme."[8] Tange's land-use plan [Fig. 4] most likely incorporates Doxiadis's regional plan. The intention to create a linear city along the Vardar River is clear; a green zone protecting the river runs parallel to the high-density residential area, also essentially linear. A quick look at a recent satellite image assures the viewer that neither of these zones was realized; instead, the city has acquired the usual centripetal form. The 1965 project was a joint United Nations–Yugoslavian initiative: "The key figure in the UN operations and in the Skopje project was Ernest Weissmann, a Yugoslavian […] appointed Director of Housing, Building and Planning to the UN Bureau of Social Affairs in 1948."[9]

Fig. 4 Kenzo Tange, "Land Use Plan for Skopje," highlighted in black, white and orange by the author of this chapter to show: circulation axes, river, linear city and center.

Japanese Delos in 27 Points

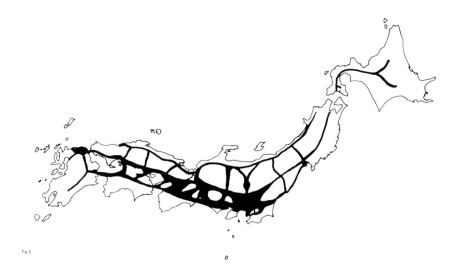

1973: Comparative Megalopolis Study

Proposing a triple-oriented research program for "the Tokaido Corridor in Japan [Fig. 5], the Eastern Sea-board Megalopolis in the U.S.A. and the North West European Mega Region,"[10] Ernest Weissmann visits Japan in 1972 in order to meet Kenzo Tange and Eiichi Isomura, attaching a handbook of the study for the last-named project in his letter to his three Japanese interlocutors.[11] A 1973 note to Doxiadis by Panagis Psomopoulos sums up this ambitious joint venture: "Isomura's center, financed by the Expo Foundation with a sum of approximately 30.000 USD has commissioned a 'Comparative Megalopolis Study' with three case studies: east coast USA megalopolis, West Europe Megalopolis and Tokaido area."[12] Psomopoulos adds, "It was Weissmann's idea […] It was discussed between Isomura, [Martin] Meyerson and [Jean] Gottmann in Delos and a group of young [participants] was formed under the supervision of Isomura. Kathy Nagassima [Catharine Nagashima – Jaqueline Tyrwhitt's niece] and Ikumi Hoshino participate, as well as two more urban planners, an economist and professor [Tatsuo] Ito."[13] He concludes, "The main issue that needs your attention is that we are not referenced at any point […] and that they do not intend to invite the Athens Center of Ekistics neither to participate in the research nor to the Tokyo conference. I asked Hoshino about that and he told me 'I think no – and this is what I understand from discussions. As you may understand, it is not me who decides'."[14]

Fig. 5 Kenzo Tange,
"Japan regarded as a Megalopolis."

1963: First Delos Symposion

Constantinos Doxiadis initiates the Delos Symposia as an ambitious networking tool, just four years after CIAM's (Congrès Internationaux d'Architecture Moderne's) dissolution in Otterlo [Fig. 6]. A draft unsigned text found in his archive testifies eloquently to this ambition.[15] Though calling for a collaborative meeting of the old and the new generation, the text seems clearly antagonistic to the "Charter of Athens," trying to underestimate its importance in relation to urban planning. Its naivety perhaps explains the fact that it was never published: "attention never focused on the large masses of people, perhaps because the phenomena of large population concentrations which accentuated the problems of good living have not been felt until recently. Lately, however, attention is shifting more and more away from 'The Building' and more towards 'the Settlement'."[16] For this reason, the first Symposion is, as noted, "a good opportunity to bring together the older generation of the Charter of Athens and the architecture that was represented in it to meet the younger and rising generation of planners who are working in terms of Settlements and to declare the Charter of Delos for the creation of better human settlements through a new scientific approach."[17] We understand from this that early modernism is degraded to a simplistic "architecture affair," and "working in terms of settlements" is clearly considered a brand new historical approach and an exclusive objective for the upcoming Delian Charter.

Fig. 6. Constantinos A. Doxiadis.

1964: Charter of City

Just after Delos 1, Eiichi Isomura conducts research at Tokyo University on "the problem of consciousness of Tokyo Metropolitan inhabitants."[18] Those who identify as Tokyoites are 55 percent of the whole sample, the rest are not conscious of belonging to a civic entity – or have no interest in answering. Isomura explains this fact: "In my country, it is said that the bigger the population size of cities become[s], the lower their autonomous consciousness goes down."[19] Based on this study, he proposes a "Charter of City," presented at Delos 2 and published in *Ekistics* [Fig. 7]. Though it is aimed at Japan it seems written as if it could claim global application, replacing the Athenian Charter. The main goals to be achieved are threefold: "1. To identify 'happiness' of civic life. 2. To clarify the importance of civic society. 3. To improve the environment of city life."[20] The first goal, civic "happiness," as vague as the term may be, seems crucial – and, as we will see, not only for Isomura.

Fig. 7 Eiichi Isomura.

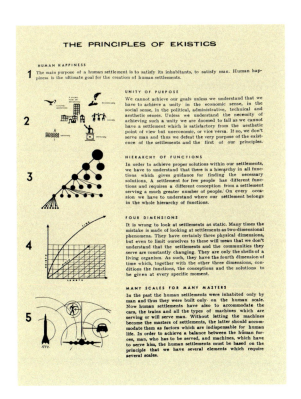

Fig. 8 "The Principles of Ekistics,"
back cover of the *Ekistics* issue dedicated
to the first Delos Symposion.

1963: First Delos Symposion

The *Ekistics* issue for the first Symposion includes "The Principles of Ekistics" [Fig. 8]. The first principle is human happiness: "The main purpose of a human settlement is to satisfy its inhabitants, to satisfy man. Human happiness is the ultimate goal for the creation of human settlements."[21] This first principle is not explained further. In the same issue, Sigfried Giedion, a distinguished member of the modernist old guard, begins his contributing text with a short report on CIAM IV and ends it by addressing the importance of its "satisfying" function par excellence – recreation: "we all knew that our period has up to now been incapable of creating a type of recreation to release us from the weariness caused by our type of civilization."[22] A few lines before, his argument is supported by antiquity: "Priene shows that a small community of 4–5.000 people [...] could afford to create on a highly difficult terrain two gymnasia [...], a large agora, a theatre, council chamber, etc. Today a city of two millions (like Boston) has no permanent theater [...]."[23]

1965: Plan for Skopje

Before the earthquake, Skopje was a city of just 172,000. Tange's project anticipates a doubling of this number. Its main features are the City Wall – a dense residential entity – and the City Gate: "City Gate Centre contains office high-risers, a library, banks, exhibition halls, three cinemas, a hotel, shops, restaurants – all connected up with the railway and bus terminal i.e. geared to it."[24] Three cinemas, but still no theater – even from a Japanese master planner. Recreation has its part in this symbolically charged civic entity but its main function is the management of the flow of traffic and information, and in a clearly monumental manner: "Under the concept of City Gate, Tange comprised all functions having to do with communications and business operations. All existing traffic systems are made to converge at this point: rail, motor, bus and pedestrian movements."[25]

Fig. 9 "Plan for Skopje," City Wall in orange lines, highlighted by the author of this chapter.

Fig. 10 Detail from "A Plan for Tokyo, 1960," showing the traffic system.

1966: Movement of Ideas and Information

In 1972, when Doxiadis has already formulated his theory on his anticipated Ecumenopolis network, a 1966 text by Kenzo Tange entitled "Movement of Ideas and Information" is retrospectively published in *Ekistics*. Tange advocates the importance of transportation not only per se but also as a channeling of information – proposing a ubiquitous network: "what are needed are not merely new thoroughfares and subway systems. It is a completely new way of structuring or system of urban relationship: a relationship between a region and another region, between a city and another city, a relationship between highways, streets, parking areas, plazas, buildings; between traffic systems and buildings; between stations and buildings; between one building and another building; and between each building and its component parts" [Fig. 10].[26] Tange adds, "We have begun to create a new nervous system in society using the advanced communication technology that will enable the social brain to function more effectively. […] Large metropolitan areas or metropolises in our day are becoming the brains for the body of modern society."[27] The organic manner in which this complex networking is envisioned by Tange is also advocated by Eiichi Isomura in a text prepared for Delos 4, also in 1966: "Without that mobility or fluidity of people, it is impossible to say that cities are human settlements. It might be better to express these movements as a 'metabolism' of urban society."[28] Metabolism's hypermodernity, as expressed mainly by Tange's projects, is at this time at its peak: complex highway interchanges, multiple elevated thoroughfares, extended parking facilities. CIAM IV's "transportation" as the fourth function seems now to be almost worshipped.

Fig. 11 A Mercedes-Benz 8/38 PS Roadster in front of Le Corbusier and P. Jeanneret's house on the Weissenhof Estate, Stuttgart, 1928.

1963: First Delos Symposion

Giedion admits in 1963 that thirty years earlier, in 1933, technology played a seductive game with modernism's old guard: "There are certain dangers of which we have to be aware. We were seduced through technical possibilities – for example the car – which then made [the] functioning of our cities impossible. We had become so hypnotized by inventions that they took possession of us" [Fig. 11].[29] Judging from Tange's belief in transportation, Giedion is right – this possibility is always open. His next remark may have irritated the Japanese designers, or even Doxiadis himself: "Another danger lies in our great confidence in statistics. This means an absolute faith that the present trends of development will continue in a straight line – statistically. This is highly unlikely."[30]

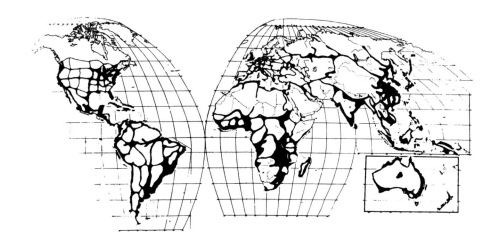

1973: Comparative Megalopolis Study

Weissmann's proposal for the comparative Megalopolis study is followed in Doxiadis's archive by Japanese geographer Tatsuo Ito's draft text of "The Formation of Japan Megalopolis," published later as "Tokaido-Megalopolis of Japan" cowritten with Catharine Nagashima. For Ito, "no consensus has been reached as to whether the urbanization of the Japanese archipelago has inevitably been leading to megalopolis formation, […] as to whether such a transformation in Japan is a desirable form of urban growth."[31] Ito's views on the Tokaido urban belt seem the opposite to the anticipation of Tange, who considered the formation of the Tokaido megalopolis "not only a natural development, but an excellent means of providing Japan with an organic composition of a very high degree."[32] For Ito, "Megalopolis," invented by Jean Gottmann as a proper name, denotes a concept that is generally misapplied – except by Doxiadis: "For a Greek like Doxiadis it seems quite natural to use the term megalopolis to indicate a population unit of higher order than metropolis. His scale of fifteen 'ekistic units' ranges from the individual man at the lower end, through the dwelling, the town (polis), the metropolis, the megalopolis, and finally to ecumenopolis or world city" [Fig. 12].[33] Nonetheless, Ito remains skeptical toward the concepts of Megalopolis or Ecumenopolis, and his remark on the latter is sharply accurate: "C. A. Doxiadis's 'ecumenopolis' is no concept at all, but a poetic vision."[34]

Fig. 12 Constantinos A. Doxiadis, "Ecumenopolis 2060."

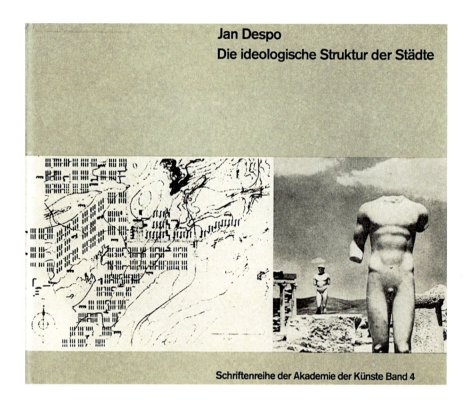

1966: *Die Ideologische Struktur der Städte*

Originally entitled "The ideological imprint of cities," Jan Despo's lecture at the Berlin Academy of the Arts is published during Delos 4 [Fig. 13]. Ioannis Despotopoulos, a second-generation militant Modernist and founding member of the Greek CIAM team, is an old antagonist of Doxiadis's – in 1941, they had both been candidates for a professorship at the National Technical University (Despo had clinched the post). He was consequently never invited to the Delos Symposia. At the end of his introductory text, entitled "The danger of the city of bliss," wherein he criticizes technologically driven modern prosperity, he attacks the possibility and therefore the very concept of Ecumenopolis: "a contiguous Ecumenopolis, a global 'pasture for cows of democratic prosperity,' has been organized and planned."[35]

Fig. 13 Jan Despo (Ioannis Despotopoulos), original cover of *Die ideologische Struktur der Städte*, lecture at the Berlin Academy of the Arts, 1966. The photomontage consists of a Soviet city plan (by an Ernst May "Brigade") and a picture taken in Delos.

1973: Comparative Megalopolis Study

Despo is not alone. In her "International Comparative Study of Megalopolis, Notes on Terminology," Catharine Nagashima shares Tatsuo Ito's distrust of the term and summarizes the reaction against it: "megalopolis smells of ecumenopolis, a concept some people feel they cannot possibly accept and therefore they prefer to reject both terms."[36] She adds, "The real problem is not what we call our phenomenon, but what it is, whether it really exists or whether it is ever likely to emerge."[37]

Fig. 14 Archigram, Instant City, 1969.

1972: Tenth Delos Symposion

Jean Gottmann, a loyal Delian, was the first to use the word "Megalopolis" in 1957 as a place name for the urbanization of the northeastern seaboard of the United States. Fifteen years later, the tone of his statement for the "Epilogue to the Declaration of Delos Ten" seems quite gloomy: "The evolution over the decade has been momentous, but the problems facing us are at least as bad as ten years ago. The basic difficulty was pointed out in Plato's laws. He stated that the New City should be established remote from the sea and foreign commerce, and influence an area sufficient to support a limited number of people of 'modest ambitions.' The way of life of the inhabitants of the island of Delos, as shown in the Homeric Hymn, indicates that the Delians were not men of modest ambitions, and history has followed this direction. Then the question arises of the stability and quality of the political process: Does megalopolitan growth provoke Leviathan?"[38]

Fig. 15 Detail from drawing of bird's-eye view of Delos's port and sanctuary by Francesco Comi, 1995.

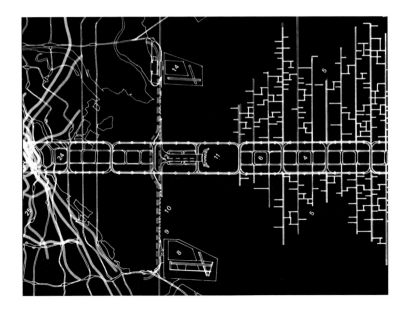

1960: A Plan for Tokyo – Ekistics

Kenzo Tange's magnus urban-planning opus, his meticulous study for the urbanization of Tokyo Bay, is presented in *Ekistics* in 1961, "abstracted for the 'Japan Architect'." Neither Tokyoites of the era nor Tange and his team were "men of modest ambitions." Furthermore, the city was never far from the sea nor from foreign commerce, as demanded by Plato. Jan Despo includes this work in the "Ideologische Struktur der Städte" as a "structural urban design, that is clear and convincing."[39] The project's structure is, as at Skopje, essentially linear: "We reject the concept of the metropolitan civic center in favor of a new concept which we call civic axis. This is tantamount to rejecting the closed organization of the centripetal pattern in favor of an open organization which makes possible a development along a linear pattern."[40] Tange insists on the novelty of the concept, though there had certainly been linear urban schemes in Russian modernism. His emphasis is again on transportation, explained through a catchy metaphor: "The cyclical transportation system supports linear development and the fact that it is composed of distinct units makes gradual development possible. This system is composed of unit cycles, somewhat like the vertebrae in the spine" [Fig. 16].[41]

Fig. 16 Inverted detail from "A Plan for Tokyo, 1960," showing the traffic system.

1966: Function, Structure and Symbol

The modernist Despo considers the Tokyo Bay design convincingly "structural,"[42] while the Metabolist Tange uses the symbolic power of an organic structure in order to describe it. In 1966, the latter writes a text entitled "Function, Structure and Symbol," in which he considers that the architectural and urbanist approach should involve both the process "of giving function and that of giving structure to spaces."[43] Surprisingly, the non-modernist notion of "Symbol" enters the field of "Structure." Tange states, "Giving a symbolic meaning to the structure itself is useful for elaborating design and making it understandable to people," adding, "We made an ample use of the attitude in the Plan for Skopje. For instance, in applying the name 'City Gate' to the center of Skopje, we not only gave ourselves the hint that we should use something gate-like in this area, but also planted in the minds of the people the understanding of the gate through which one enters the city of Skopje."[44] The second main design feature of the Skopje project is the City Wall, a high-density, residential, linear complex of blocks at the western and southeastern sides of the new center that defines its exterior built limits in synergy with the City Gate and Kale Fortress Hill [Fig. 17]. Tange emphasizes its symbolic structure as well: "The City Wall, too, gained fame, and even when opinions emerged that perhaps the Wall was an obstacle and that we should abandon it, the people of the city were opposed to this opinion. They said: 'The City Wall is familiar to us and in our imagination it has already become the symbol of the city center. We can no longer give it up.'"[45]

Fig. 17 Detail from "Plan for Skopje," showing an aerial view of the first phase of the City Wall.

Fig. 18 "Plan for Skopje," showing the third phase of the City Wall.

1965: Plan for Skopje

Tange and his team work on the project in three distinct phases. The "City Gate" of the third phase is less symmetrical and massive than earlier phases, with the residential blocks of the City Wall simplified in a more continuous form [Fig. 18]. The models and their dramatic photomontages of all phases express a powerfully Metabolist formalism. City Wall is not a wall, though: it is a vehicle for creating the identity of a twenty-first century European city where a wall is not needed. Even Tange's new linear city needed a center, and that was attempted by a symbolic element of the past – not functional anymore. Tange, who advocated that "from 1920 to 1960, there was a static and deterministic approach to the relationship between function and space," used the concept of "City Wall" as a tool that inscribes the center in an entity – in order to make it appear as an entity, so that it acquires an identity.[46] For Mirjana Lozanovska, "[t]he City Wall and the City Gate in Skopje are examples of how the functionalist basis of modernism was transcended."[47] The question is whether the transgression has been a successful one, both as scope and as execution. Concerning the latter, what is realized in Skopje is indeed disappointing compared with the architectural intensity of the original design. Arata Isozaki was part of both the competition and the design development team: "I actually don't know how it was realized in the end. I was having big fights every day in Skopje. I once even tore up the drawings and went home. I have bad memories."[48] Interviewed for *Project Japan* by Rem Koolhaas, he stresses the main reason for its failure: "more and more came in, more conservative people, over our heads. After a few months of working there, I was completely exhausted. I thought, 'My God, I can't do this anymore.' And Tange said, 'Ok, it's time to compromise and go home.' So we did. This was exactly when Tange started to work on Expo '70."[49]

Fig. 19 Expo '70, space-frame roof covering the Festival Piazza.

1970: Osaka Expo

The Osaka Expo is the culmination of Japan's post-war prosperity, visited by 60 million visitors and turning a $100 million profit.[50] "In October 1965, 'Progress and Harmony for Mankind' [is] chosen as the main theme."[51] The complex is articulated through the symbol zone (the "trunk") and the sub-plazas (the "branches"). "The Symbol Zone, an area one hundred and fifty meters wide by one thousand meters long running north and south, intersects the approaching highway to form the Main Gate" and is dominated by the Festival Piazza.[52] Covered by a megastructure, a vast space-frame roof, in the Festival Piazza, people, for Tange, "can have an environmental experience. To spend time in these exterior spaces and to experience the feeling of participation in some events or some happenings might be an unforgettable and psychologically satisfying moment" [Fig. 19].[53] Tange designs the frame and Arata Isozaki designs all the equipment underneath, including the suspended robot and the walking robot.[54] On this site for a national event, Isozaki conceives a scene for people whereby Tange imagines that, after the Expo, the site could eventually become a city of 500,000.[55] Contrary to that, a 1995 photograph depicts the site occupied by nature. Taro Okamoto's Tower of the Sun resides alone, without its accompanying roof.

Japanese Delos in 27 Points

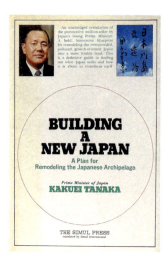

Fig. 20 Cover of Kakuei Tanaka's book *Building a New Japan*.

1973: Comparative Megalopolis Study

"How to represent the will of the nation was the fundamental framework of Tange's architectural conception up to Expo '70. His national-scaled 'megastructure' planning concept in the '60s also stemmed from this framework of thought."[56] Isomura, too, sees the possibility of a Tokaido Megalopolis as a crucial national motive: "Urbanization is about to bring forth a new kind of nationalism. [...] In the Japanese archipelago it is possible today to reach Tokyo in the matter of 2 to 3 hours even from the farthest point by means of the faster transportation."[57] He adds, "there is a growing sense of equating Japan with Tokyo – a sense that integrates the whole islands of Japan as a continual city expanse. We seem to be in this sort of mechanism which drives us to a nationalism of the new sense of the word."[58] The expression "Tokaido Megalopolis" indicates the area extending from Tokyo to Osaka. In 1966, Tange appears on national TV on New Year's Day presenting the Tokaido Megalopolis on the show *Designing the 21st Century*. Kakuei Tanaka, Japan's prime minister between 1972 and 1974, advocates the creation of 150 to 300 cities across the Japanese Archipelago. Constantinos Doxiadis responds in 1972 to a gift of his vision: "Dear Professor Isomura, I want to thank you warmly for your kindness to send me the Prime Minister's book 'Building a New Japan'. I am reading it now with great interest. Please transmit to Mr. Tanaka my very sincere thanks and give him my book 'Ecumenopolis: The inevitable city of the Future'."[59] Strongly identified with the construction industry and a central figure in several political scandals, Tanaka's political–economic direction is called *Doken Kokka*, or the "Construction State."[60]

2000: *De l'origine du XXIᵉ siècle*

From Sarajevo to Berlin, all the disasters depicted in Jean-Luc Godard's films are essentially state-driven [Fig. 21]. Repeating one of his borrowed excerpts, "Nothing conflicts more with the image of the beloved than that of the State. The State's rationale directly opposes the sovereign value of love. The State in no way possesses, or else it has lost, the power to embrace, before our eyes, the totality of the world, that totality of the universe offered externally via the loved one as object, and internally via the lover as subject."[61]

Fig. 21 United Nations patrol in front of the destroyed mosque of Ahinici, near Vitez, northwest of Sarajevo, on April 27, 1993.

1951: *L'amour d'un être mortel*

Godard provocatively opposes "State" as "City" and love, using excerpts from George Bataille's 1951 article "Love of a Mortal Being." In the following passage from his text, Bataille uses the two words, and consequently the notions of "State" and "City," interchangeably: "Neither the State nor the City are ever given to us in this way, in the silence of death where nothing seems to exist any more. The community can never provoke this impulse, really mad, that comes into play in the preference for a being" [Fig. 22].[62]

Fig. 22 Stills from the film *De l'origine du XXIe siècle*, directed by J.-L. Godard, 2000.

1964: Charter of City

In Eiichi Isomura's "Charter of City," each of his three goals is clarified by five points. Even after the clarification, the goal "happiness" remains relatively vague (since Isomura mainly focuses on matters of security, civic rights and civic duties); it returns, though, as a central notion at the very end of his charter: point 5 of the third goal for the "improvement of the environment of city life" is entitled "Development of recreation." Isomura concretizes it as follows: "In the arrangement of the city environment, recreation occupies a big part. Recreational facilities are designed in the socialized public spaces, and this point has an implication if we look at the problems from the viewpoint of housewives. Traditionally women have been bound to live just in the house but gradually they have come out to the recreational areas because of greatest freedom in city life. To include this implication on an actual city plan will be coincident with the purpose of 'charter of city' providing 'happiness' for each one of the inhabitants" [Fig. 23].[63] The fact that the city, for Isomura, ought to "provide" "happiness" indicates that it is conceived as an external entity – separable from its citizens – designated to "provide." The city is not its citizens anymore.

Fig. 23 Utagawa Toyoharu (1735–1814), *A Winter Party*, Edo period, Japan.

1966: *Die Ideologische Struktur der Städte*

Jan Despo is almost coeval to Isomura, who was born in 1903, having been born just three days after him. Giedion is older (b. 1888). We are now in the prosperous mid-1960s. The sense of community that Isomura and Giedion seek in happiness-as-recreation is commented on in Despo's text: "Material recreation for the many and futile intellect for the few. This inevitable evolution leads to the massive human-robot and the enjoyable city of bliss. It also leads to the 'pasture' of a non-ideological democracy of permanent prosperity. [...] The worst evolution would be that into this pasture, people turn serene and happy until they are immersed in the 'nothingness' of a choking bliss" [Fig. 24].[64]

Fig. 24 Osaka Expo '70, Festival Piazza.

2000: *De l'origine du XXIᵉ siècle*

Sarajevo's destruction proves that, even in Europe, the 1960s' "ideological democracy of permanent prosperity" foreseen by Despo cannot be that permanent [Fig. 25]. Unlike Skopje, twentieth-century Hiroshima is destroyed by humankind. Godard offers an enigmatic final scene as the origin of a catastrophic century – the last 1.30 seconds of *De l'origine du XXIᵉ siècle*.

Fig. 25 A young boy plays on a tank in the Sarajevo neighborhood of Grbavica, April 22, 1996.

1972: Tenth Delos Symposion

In the "Epilogue to the Declaration of Delos Ten," Eiichi Isomura states, "Ten years ago, I completed my few remarks in this theatre by saying: 'no more Hiroshimas!' Today, it is unnecessary to repeat this phrase."[65] Isomura's belief is somewhat justified, since the major problem that his era was starting to face – and which has climaxed in our era – is environmental. During World Wars I and II, the technological explosion of the nineteenth century turned into a bloodbath – cynically annihilating the hopes of directly correlating it to human happiness. In his text "Social Life and related environmental problem," though, Professor Isomura relies again on divine technology: "environmental disruption will have reached such a serious level that the continued existence of the human being will be questioned. The effort at that time to maintain the ecological system of the earth may require us to limit some of the human instincts themselves. And, on the other hand, technological progress may have invented a kind of operation to make the body feel happy by stimulating a certain part of the brain or taking drugs" [Fig. 26].[66]

Fig. 26 Portrait of Japanese youth in revolt, 1964.

1952: *Le plaisir*

Prosperous recreation is not strongly linked to happiness; the link may even turn destructive. The final words of Godard's film are not his own – as usual. They belong to Max Ophüls, and conclude his 1952 film entitled *Le plaisir* (Pleasure): "Isn't this perfect happiness?" – "Come on, you have to admit it's all pretty sad." – "But, my dear fellow, happiness isn't enjoyable."[67]

Fig. 27 Teenagers dance the twist around a radio/cassette recorder in a street in the Harajuku district of Shibuya, Tokyo, Japan, 1978.

1. Eiichi Isomura, "Message from Professor Eiichi Isomura," *Ekistics* 48, no. 289 (July/August 1981), 257.
2. Eiichi Isomura, "Eiichi Isomura, Japan," *Ekistics* 16, no. 95 (October 1963), 226.
3. Tange collaborated with Takashi Asda and Sachio Otani. See Udo Kultermann, "Plan for Skopje," in Udo Kultermann (ed.), *Kenzo Tange* (New York: Praeger Publishers, 1970), 17.
4. Eiichi Isomura, letter to C. Doxiadis, January 20, 1964. C. Doxiadis Archives, Benaki Museum, Athens.
5. Eiichi Isomura, "The science of Ekistics," typed text, May 1965. C. Doxiadis Archives, Benaki Museum.
6. Ibid.
7. Jean-Luc Godard and Anne-Marie Mieville, *De l'origine du XXIᵉ siècle*, 2000.
8. Kultermann, "Plan for Skopje," 262–63, quotation 262.
9. Mirjana Lozanovska, "Kenzo Tange's Forgotten Master Plan for the Reconstruction of Skopje," *JSAH* (Australia and New Zealand) 22, no. 2 (December 2012): 140–163, quotation 143.
10. Ernest Weissman, letter to Isomura, Tange and Honjo, January 12, 1972. Doxiadis Archives, Benaki Museum.
11. Ibid.
12. Panagis Psomopoulos, note to Constantinos Doxiadis, January 3, 1973, Doxiadis Archives, Benaki Museum.
13. Ibid.
14. Ibid.
15. "A proposal for a conference of planners on the island of Delos for the formulation and declaration of the Charter of Delos," unsigned, Doxiadis Archives, Benaki Museum.
16. Ibid.
17. Ibid.
18. Eiichi Isomura, "Charter of the City," *Ekistics* 18, no. 107 (October 1964), 248–50, quotation 248.
19. Ibid.
20. Ibid.
21. Anonymous, "The Principles of Ekistics," *Ekistics* 16, no. 95 (October 1963), back cover.
22. Sigfried Giedion, "Sigfried Giedion," *Ekistics* 16, no. 95 (October 1963), 255–57.
23. Ibid.
24. Kultermann, "Plan for Skopje," 262–63, quotation 264.
25. Ibid.
26. Kenzo Tange, "Movement of Ideas and Information," *Ekistics* 33, no. 197 (April 1972), 339–40, quotation 340.
27. Ibid.
28. Eiichi Isomura, "Sociological interpretation of Human Settlement," typed text. Doxiadis Archives, Benaki Museum.
29. Sigfried Giedion, "Sigfried Giedion," *Ekistics* 16, no. 95 (October 1963), 255–57, quotation 256.
30. Ibid.
31. Tatsuo Ito, "The Formation of Japan Megalopolis," draft. Doxiadis Archives, Benaki Museum.
32. Kenzo Tange, extract from paper, *Ekistics* 22, no. 131 (October 1966), 248–50.
33. Ito, "The Formation of Japan Megalopolis."
34. Ibid.
35. Ioannis Despotopoulos, *Η Ιδεολογική Δομή των Πόλεων* (*Die ideologische Struktur der Städte*) (Athens: NTUA Press, 1997 [1966]), 16.
36. Catharine Nagashima, "International Comparative Study of Megalopolis, Notes on Terminology," typed text. Doxiadis Archives, Benaki Museum.
37. Ibid.
38. Jean Gottman, "Epilogue to the Declaration of Delos Ten," *Ekistics* 34, no. 203 (October 1972), 289–93, quotation 290.
39. Despotopoulos, *Η Ιδεολογική Δομή των Πόλεων*, 161.
40. Kenzo Tange "A Plan for Tokyo, 1960," *Ekistics* 12, no. 69 (July 1961), 9–19, quotation 12.
41. Ibid.
42. Despotopoulos, *Η Ιδεολογική Δομή των Πόλεων*, pic. 130.
43. Kenzo Tange, "Function, Structure and Symbol," in Kultermann (ed.), *Kenzo Tange*, 244.
44. Ibid.
45. Ibid.
46. Ibid.
47. Lozanovska, "Kenzo Tange's Forgotten Master Plan," 149.
48. Arata Isozaki, interviewed in Rem Koolhaas and Hans Ulrich Obrist, *Project Japan: Metabolism Talks* (Cologne: Taschen, 2011), 45.
49. Ibid.
50. Ibid., 536.
51. Kultermann (ed.), *Kenzo Tange*, 282.
52. Kenzo Tange "The Basic Idea of the Exposition Masterplan," in Kultermann (ed.), *Kenzo Tange*, 284.
53. Koolhaas and Obrist, *Project Japan*, 523.
54. Arata Isozaki, interviewed in ibid., 45.
55. Koolhaas and Obrist, *Project Japan*, 45, 539.
56. Arata Isozaki, interviewed in ibid., 538.
57. Eiichi Isomura, "Changing Environments in Japan," typed text. Doxiadis Archives, Benaki Museum.
58. Ibid.
59. C. Doxiadis, letter to Eiichi Isomura, December 28, 1974. Doxiadis Archives, Benaki Museum.
60. https://en.wikipedia.org/wiki/Kakuei_Tanaka (accessed April 5, 2024).
61. Georges Bataille, "L'amour d'un être mortel," in *Oeuvres complètes*, vol. VIII (Paris: Gallimard, 1976 [1951]), 497, translated by the author.
62. Ibid.
63. Eiichi Isomura, "Charter of City," *Ekistics* 18, no. 107 (October 1964), 248–50, quotation 250.
64. Despotopoulos, *Η Ιδεολογική Δομή των Πόλεων*, 30.
65. Eiichi Isomura, "Epilogue to the Declaration of Delos Ten," *Ekistics* 34, no. 203 (October 1972), 289–93, quotation 291.

66 Eiichi Isomura, "Social life and related environmental problem," typed text. Doxiadis Archives, Benaki Museum.

67 "Est-ce que ce n'est pas le bonheur?" – "Tout de même, tu le vois, tout ça a l'air triste." – "Mais, mon cher, le bonheur n'est pas gai." Max Ophüls, *Le plaisir,* 1952.

Doxiadis Associates' Master Plan for Skopje and the Global Ecological Balance
The Element of Nature

Thomas Doxiadis

Research, Sketches: Chryssa Gkolemi, Alexandra Souvatzi

Introduction

The 1960s were a seminal period in ecological awakening, starting most notably with Rachel Carson's call to action in her 1962 *Silent Spring* and Barbara Ward's in her 1966 *Spaceship Earth,* and leading to ecology in spatial design in Ian McHarg's 1969 *Design with Nature.* In urbanism, Patrick Geddes's 1915 *Cities in Evolution: An Introduction to the Town Planning Movement and to the Study of Civics* had already established a view of cities as ecosystems, paralleling natural ones, and Frederick Kiesler's 1939 *Architectural Record* article "On Correalism and Biotechnique: A Definition and Test of a New Approach to Building Design" had created a framework for "the dynamics of continual interaction between man and his natural and technical environments."[1] Yet, in the 1960s, the field of urban ecology was still a decade or two in the future – as was urban design based on principles of ecology. Or was it? A group of practitioners were already convinced of the importance of ecology, writing but also practicing in the direction of ecological design; the work of Doxiadis Associates (DA), whose early adoption of ecological thought and practice is being re-examined, was a prime example.[2]

Half a century later, spatial design is strongly predicated on ecology, significant theoretical and practical know-how having been developed in the last few decades. Even today, the question of whether a proposal is earnestly in line with ecological principles or merely communicates adherence is valid. What of the 1960s? Do the designs of that era stand the test of compliance with the principles of ecology as understood at the time? Even more interestingly, if historically biased, do designs of that era pass muster with the ecological design principles of our own time?

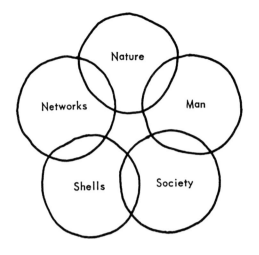

Six decades after its creation, the master plan for the metropolitan area of Skopje in then Yugoslavia (now North Macedonia), developed by DA after the devastating 1963 earthquake, is a good case in point. Constantinos Doxiadis and his associates were early adopters and developers of a holistic approach to the design of space whereby multiple factors interact and are designed for. Ekistics, the term coined by Doxiadis for this "science of human settlements,"[3] was developed over three decades and multiple books, articles, research projects and realized works, ranging from first principles to analysis and assessments and to specific design directions.

Doxiadis's integrative approach to human and natural systems is evident from the 1940s,[4] and could be traced to the Greek Immersionists of the early twentieth century such as Periklis Giannopoulos (Perikles Yannopoulos), Dimitris Pikionis and the Generation of the '30s; to Doxiadis's years in post-Bauhaus Germany; and to his own experiences in the humanitarian crises of the 1922 refugees, World War II and the Greek Civil War. The Ekistic system held "Nature" to be one of the five integral elements of the city of the future, always placed on top in the relevant diagram [Fig. 1]. With time, the focus of Doxiadis's thinking shifted ever more strongly to nature and ecology: "Once the concept of Ecumenopolis crystallized, the environmental considerations of ekistics went well beyond speculating on the dehumanizing effects of urbanization–modernization and began instead to outline specific strategies for the symbiosis of the global city with the natural world."[5] According to Panayiota Pyla, "Doxiadis and his enterprise began to reconceptualize issues of environmental interdependence on a truly global scale and to reinvent ekistics not only as a strategy for international development but also as a strategy for global environmental protection."[6] Many of his final articles and his last book – *Ecology and Ekistics*, published posthumously – put sustainability at the center.[7]

Fig. 1 The goal of Ekistics is to achieve a balance between the elements of human settlements.

Within this trajectory, the early 1960s are seminal to Doxiadis's thinking. In 1961, he produced the internal report "Ecumenopolis, 'The Settlement of the Future'," which argued for global urbanization achieved in "complete balance between its own forces and the forces of the countryside."[8] Pyla states that "Doxiadis voiced similar concerns in many international meetings in the early 1960s. In January 1963, when the United Nations (UN) Economic and Social Council (ECOSOC) convened its first Committee on Housing, Building, and Planning in New York to investigate the role of shelter in advancing growth rates in 'underdeveloped countries,' Doxiadis was one of the most vocal members."[9] The year 1963 was particularly important as it saw the first Delos Symposion, organized by Doxiadis:

> The event was a turning point in the history of ekistics not only because it increased its international visibility but also because it reshaped its agenda. Like Doxiadis's speeches at the UN a few months earlier, the multi-ethnic and interdisciplinary Aegean cruise pushed the debate on shelter well beyond the economics of efficiency, the aesthetics of order, the management of resources, or the engineering of social reform to inaugurate an even greater cause: saving the earth.[10]

Significantly, Barbara Ward was a key participant in the Symposion, whose *Spaceship Earth* was published three years later. It was at this point within DA's trajectory towards sustainability that the Skopje earthquake occurred – strangely, in July 1963, the same month as the first Delos Symposion.

The 1964 "Outline Plan for the City of Skopje" and the 1965–1966 "Skopje urban plan" thus provide a good opportunity to examine the relationship between ecological thought and practice at this crucial time in urban thinking.[11] Such an examination should include a search for information on sustainability discourses withing the masterplanning team, and between DA and third parties, including the clients. In this chapter, we examine another aspect: how the master plan really measures up in terms of ecology and natural sustainability. For this, we will examine the master plan for Skopje through the lens of early twenty-first-century landscape ecology, a field of knowledge that was significantly less developed at the time.

Approach

Our base data is the information contained in the DA master plan reports, the master plan drawing itself and the present structure of the Skopje region's ecological "mosaic." The last-named is based on topography and land cover garnered through Google Earth. From this, we can assess the overall ecological workings of the mosaic. On the Google Earth model, we then overlay the 1964 master plan [Figs. 2-3]. We then examine the master plan according to the following categories of landscape ecology and ecological site planning:

1. Topography
2. Hydrology
3. Soils
4. Biodiversity and Connectivity
    - Patches
    - Corridors
    - Mosaics
5. Green Infrastructure
6. Dynamic System

Through this lens, we will determine at a basic level the results of the DA masterplanning process.

1. Topography

The report highlights the primacy of north–south connections:

> The region forms an important part of the Balkan Peninsula. The peninsula is divided into two parts by massive mountains [sic] formations from the Adriatic Coast to the Black Sea. Thus, the only connections North and South of the mountains [sic] ranges are through narrow passages formed by the main rivers and the two narrow coastal strips. The two most important are those of the Vardar and Struma valleys.[12]

In fact, this is the central Balkan axis that appears on the DA projection for the future European continental Megalopolis [Figs. 4-5].

At the northern tip of this Vardar north–south axis, Skopje Valley is in fact perpendicular, on a west-northwest–east-southeast axis, joining the major north–south axis (now the E75 European highway joining Thessaloniki,

Figs. 2–3 The Skopje master plan overlaid on Google Earth.

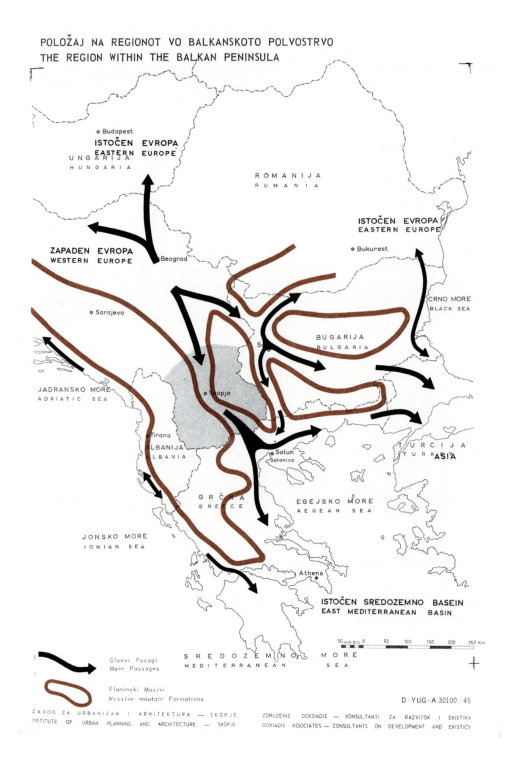

Fig. 4 The region within the Balkan Peninsula.

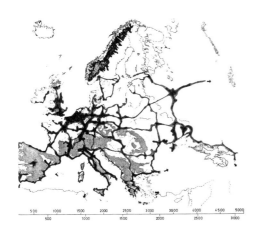

Skopje, Nis, Belgrade and Budapest) at the metropolitan area's eastern node (now the location of Skopje International Airport). DA identifies this crossing as the "Future Town," with old and future towns dynamically growing into each other [Fig. 6]. The master plan itself develops along these topographical corridors; indeed, topography is the main driver of the master plan. In typical DA fashion, a Cartesian grid is laid on the land – in this case, rotated to follow the direction of the valley.

To the south, the plan follows the (steeper) topography closely, while to the north a highway is planned in a more sweeping and generalized fit to the topography. The central element of the master plan is defined by the Vardar river itself, which forms the spine of a park system.

Overall, the master plan recognizes and respects existing topography, and can be considered successful in that sense by today's standards [Figs. 7-8].

2. Hydrology
The report highlights the fact that

> The region consists of a chain of mountains and a system of relatively narrow valleys formed by rivers which cross the area. The main axis of these valleys is the Vardar–Posinjia–Morava valley. All the other valleys are linked to it in a fishbone pattern.[13]

The Skopje Valley itself contains lowlands around the Vardar, which are identified as flood zones [Figs. 9-10].

> The river should be a very important element for the future city of Skopje.[14]

To the west and south, the master plan closely follows the hydrological network, creating a park system along the Vardar and its tributary streams.

Fig. 5 Ecumenopolis in Europe, 2060.

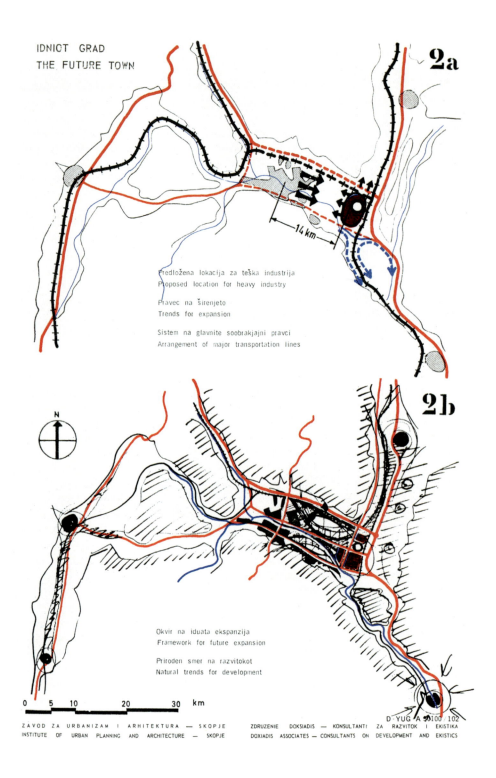

Fig. 6 The Future Town.

Figs. 7–8 Section of the Skopje master plan overlaid on Google Earth.

Doxiadis Associates' Master Plan for Skopje and the Global Ecological Balance

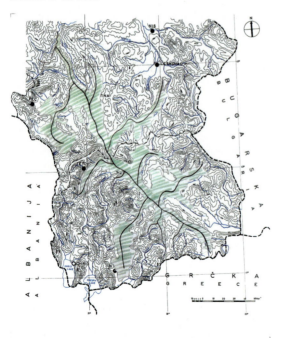

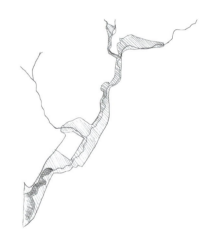

Fig. 9 (top left) Hydrology of the region.

Fig. 10 (bottom left) Sketch of a network of alluvial plains defined by the mountains.

Fig. 11 (above) Natural areas along the Vardar River corridor existing in the 1960s (top) and proposed under the DA master plan (bottom).

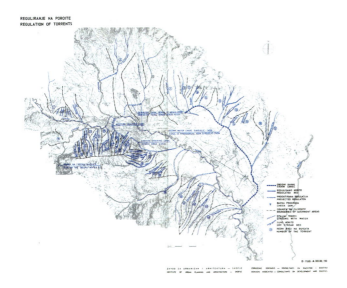

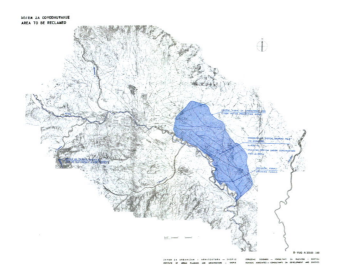

Fig. 12 (top) Regulation of torrents.

Figs. 13–14 (middle) "Area to be Reclaimed" compared to (bottom) the current area as seen on Google Earth.

Doxiadis Associates' Master Plan for Skopje and the Global Ecological Balance   449

By containing the river while respecting its dynamic, flooding is avoided, the land is reclaimed for other uses and a wide park system is created along the river on both sides, forming the heart of the city [Fig. 11].

To the north, however, rather than following the torrents, the master plan directs all the water to a storm canal, or culvert [Fig. 12]. This is successful in flood-control terms but not in terms of ecological connectivity. Furthermore, the large northeast segment of the flood zone is identified as "To be Reclaimed" [Figs. 13-14]. This area shows today as a much greener patch in the mosaic, probably due to the effect of this concentrated water on vegetation.

The city grid itself is primarily determined by hydrology. Its central spine follows the Vardar completely, in a confluence of existing forms and a new Hippodamian grid [Fig. 15]. Perpendicular to this, regular linear parks are placed that in turn direct the water from uplands to lowlands. To the east, the perpendicular system forms an idealized grid while, to the west, green "fingers" follow the existing streambeds and urban structure to break the Cartesian organization and provide for a much richer texture [Fig. 16].

Closer examination corroborates the finding that in the west – such as at Bardovtsi – the master plan follows the existing hydrology closely [Fig. 17], while in the east – such as here at Ilinden – a a Cartesian grid is imposed, hydrologically functional but ignoring the actual existing streams, which have been directed into the aforementioned culvert [Fig. 18]. The alignment of the city with the river follows the traditional pattern of cultivated fields, revealing an understanding of the local landscape dynamics and providing the best possible bioclimatic conditions as well as water-management opportunities. It is a Cartesian abstraction of the existing hydrological network, forming the new master plan with the hydrological system as its skeleton.

There is a genealogy to this approach – of green fingers following existing streams and rivers to break the Cartesian organization and provide for a much richer urban texture – from Chinese imperial cities to the DA plan for Islamabad [Figs. 19-20]. Significantly, both in Islamabad and here the stream-based green fingers form part of a continuous network, which complements the "Mecroads" – the network of roads for machines. This connected network of green spaces provides a clear case where one of the five key DA elements, "Nature," is designed through the lens of another one, "Networks."

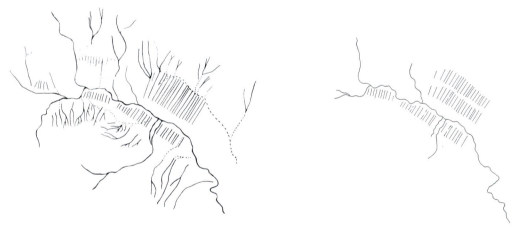

Overall, the master plan recognizes and respects existing hydrology and can be considered successful in that sense by today's standards, with the notable exception of the area to the northeast.

3. Soils

Soils do not seem to be dealt with in the report – indeed, the productive potential of the land does not appear to come into play at all.

Fig. 15 The Skopje master plan overlaid on Google Earth.

Fig. 16 Existing hydrology and the Skopje master plan stream corridors.

Fig. 17 Section of the Skopje master plan overlaid on Google Earth, showing Bardovtsi in the western part.

Fig. 18 Section of the Skopje master plan overlaid on Google Earth, showing Ilinden on the eastern part.

Thomas Doxiadis

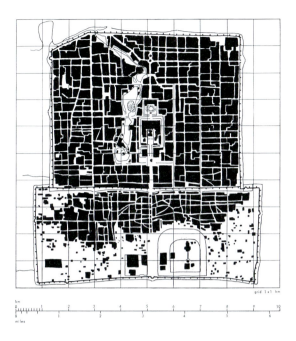

Fig. 19 "Monumental synthesis of the initial plan in a grand scale – Peking, China (A.D. 1409)."

Fig. 20 Aerial view of Islamabad.

Doxiadis Associates' Master Plan for Skopje and the Global Ecological Balance

4. Biodiversity and Connectivity

High levels of biodiversity and healthy ecosystems are the core values of contemporary ecology. Landscape ecology is the science of studying and improving relationships between ecological processes in the environment and, in particular, ecosystems.[15] Yet, while originating in the 1939 work of Carl Troll, the science did not come into its own until Robert MacArthur and E. O. Wilson's seminal *The Theory of Island Biogeography*, and the basic principles of landscape ecological design were not developed at the time of the DA Skopje master plan.[16] Here again, we will perform a post hoc assessment of the master plan based on our current understanding of these principles.[17]

Patches

Patches are relatively homogeneous areas that differ from their surroundings and form the basic spatial unit of landscape ecological analysis and design. Of particular importance to their ecological function are their number, scale, shape, size and content.

The DA master plan develops a wide variety of patches with respect to number, scale, shape and size, while content at this level is designated as green, corresponding to "Nature" in the Ekistic model, and to ecotopes, where primacy belongs to biological organisms other than humans [Fig. 21]. Significantly, Doxiadis's Ekistic thinking is scalar and patch-based when it comes to the human-primacy areas [Figs. 22–25].

Fig. 21 Section of the Skopje master plan nature areas.

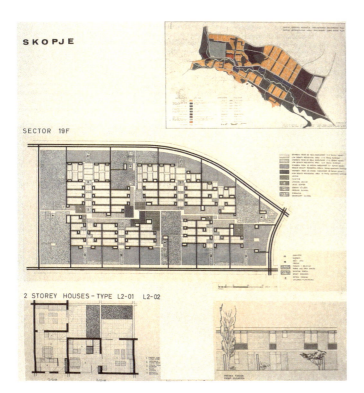

Corridors

Corridors are connectors, linear elements that serve the movement of organisms. Spatially, they may appear thin and insignificant; they are, however, the determinants for perhaps the most important parameter of an ecological system: its *connectivity*. Corridors are characterized by a number of variables, such as width and continuity, which in turn relate to the organism in question. The effectiveness of a corridor for each species boils down to how well it allows for the movement of that species along it. Stepping stones in a pond might be a suitable corridor for humans but are impassable for ants.

The DA master plan provides for good ecological connectivity by organizing green spaces along water corridors, themselves the most important connectors in a geography such as that of Skopje. A plan of the green connectors demonstrates this – especially when placed in the wider context of the rural, ecological patch. The Vardar River corridor is dominant, interrupted only by the existing fabric of the historic urban core.

Fig. 22 "Sector 19F: 2 Storey Houses –
Type L2-01 L2-02."

GROUPING OF RESIDENTIAL COMMUNITIES AND CORRESPONDING FUNCTIONS

FUNCTIONS	PURPOSE	N° OF INHABITANTS	COMMUNITY	CLASS
		100–200		I
1. CULTURAL & SOCIAL ESTABLISHMENTS 2. TRADE, CATERING AND SERVICES 3. OPEN SPACES, GREEN AND PLAYFIELDS	• PARLOUR • AUTOMATS, KIOSKS • PUBLIC TELEPHONE BOOTH • POST BOXES • SMALL PARK WITH CHILDREN'S PLAYGROUND	1000		II
1. PUBLIC EDUCATION 2. SOCIAL WELFARE ESTABLISHMENTS 3. TRADE, CATERING AND SERVICES 4. OPEN SPACES, GREEN AREAS & PLAYFIELDS	• PRIMARY SCHOOL • NURSERY (AGE 0-3) • KINDERGARTEN (AGE 3-7) • SHOP CENTRE • SNACK-BAR • SERVICES • OFFICES • PUBLIC W.C. • MEDIUM SIZE PARK • SMALL ATHLETIC FIELD (CONNECTED WITH THE PRIMARY SCHOOL)	4000		III
1. PUBLIC HEALTH 2. CULTURAL AND SOCIAL ESTABLISHMENTS 3. TRADE, CATERING AND SERVICES 4. OPEN SPACES, GREEN AREAS & PLAYFIELDS	• HEALTH STATION • PHARMACY • CULTURAL CLUB (MEETING HALL) • CINEMA • SHOP CENTRE • CAFE • RESTAURANT • PUBLIC BATHS, LAUNDRIES, • AUTO-SERVICE, E.T.C. • SERVICES • PARK	12000		IV
1. ADMINISTRATION 2. PUBLIC EDUCATION 3. CULTURAL & SOCIAL ESTABLISHMENTS 4. PUBLIC HEALTH 5. SOCIAL WELFARE ESTABLISHMENTS 6. TRADE, CATERING AND SERVICES 7. OPEN SPACES GREEN AREAS & PLAYGROUND	• COMMUNITY HEADQUARTERS • OFFICES • FIRE PROTECTION • POST OFFICE • PUBLIC MILITIA • INSURANCE INSTITUTE • BANK BRANCH • GYMNASIA (TWO) • CULTURAL CLUB • LIBRARY • PIONEER'S CLUB • HEALTH CENTRE • PHARMACY • HOUSE FOR PENSIONERS • SHOPPING CENTRE • LARGE PARK • ATHLETIC CENTRE (CONNECTED WITH THE GYMNASIA)	48000		V

ZAVOD ZA URBANIZAM I ARHITEKTURA — SKOPJE
INSTITUTE OF URBAN PLANNING AND ARCHITECTURE — SKOPJE

ZDRUZENIE DOKSIADIS — KONSULTANTI ZA RAZVITOK I EKISTIK
DOXIADIS ASSOCIATES — CONSULTANTS ON DEVELOPMENT AND EKISTIC

ORGANIZACIJA I STRUKTURA NA STANBENITE EDINICI
ORGANIZATION AND STRUCTURE OF RESIDENTIAL COMMUNITIES

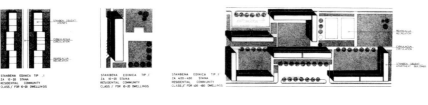

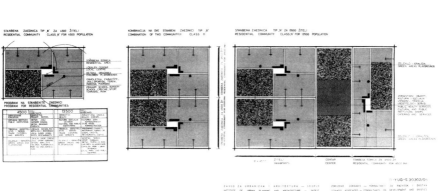

PEŠAČKI I AUTO DVIŽENJA - KLASIFIKACIJA NA PATIŠTA
PEDESTRIAN AND VEHICLE MOVEMENTS - ROAD CLASSIFICATION

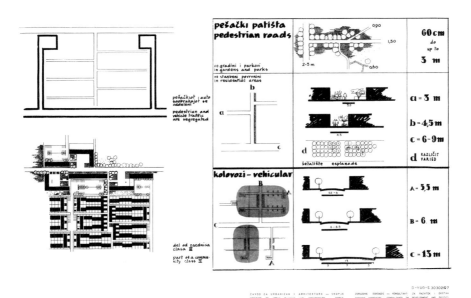

Fig. 23 (opposite) Grouping of residential communities and corresponding functions.

Fig. 24 (top) Organization and structure of residential communities.

Fig. 25 (bottom) Pedestrian and vehicle movements – road classification.

Doxiadis Associates' Master Plan for Skopje and the Global Ecological Balance

Contrary to common practice at the time, major highways are pulled inland rather than strewn along the river corridor, which is defined by a more local road network of lower-speed roads with wide green zones [Figs. 26-27].[18]

Yet it is not clear if ecological connectivity is carried through all the way, as the perpendicular green fingers are interrupted by the major highway system close to the river [Fig. 28]. Unless the thinking was to establish these at a finer scale or under the highways, this would break connectivity along the whole system.

Mosaics

Mosaics are the overall spatial arrangements of ecological elements in a given area. A number of characteristics determine whether a mosaic functions well in ecological terms – the most important being variety in patch size and distribution, and excellent overall connectivity.

In both these metrics, the DA master plan for Skopje performs well. Its nature areas have a scalar hierarchy, which in the east seems quite specific to location but in the west is more systematic and generic [Fig. 29]. The whole is arranged into a system with a high degree of connectivity. Knowing what we do of other DA master plans, such as that for Islamabad, it is safe to assume that in terms both of scale and of connectivity the natural mosaic would eventually extend into the neighborhoods and down to the scale of individual streets and buildings.

What is missing is the relationship to the wider spatial ecological context. Elements of natural space are inserted into the master plan but the master plan itself is not inserted into the wider ecological region, as will become standard good practice six decades later.

5. Green Infrastructure

While the previous criteria are centered on the needs of natural systems and ways to help them function better for their own sake, the lens of *green infrastructure* is anthropocentric, examining how natural elements can improve the lives of people.

> Referring to the major green areas indicated in the plan, the effort was to create a zone running along the river and the proposed central zone, which will provide adequate green and recreational spaces right in the heart of the city and in all its length.[19]

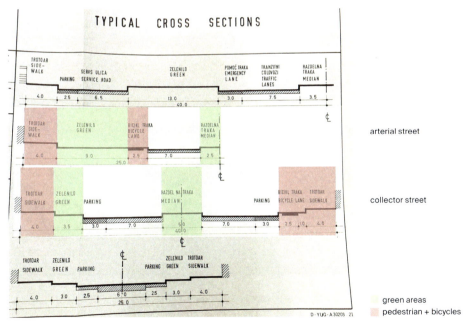

Fig. 26 Recommended 1981 road plan.

Fig. 27 Road classification: "Typical Cross-Sections."

Fig. 28 The Skopje master plan nature areas.

Fig. 29 The Skopje master plan overlaid on Google Earth.

Thomas Doxiadis

> Recent information on seismicity indicate[s] the areas which are allocated along the river for green and recreational purposes, as areas where no construction should take place, thus making necessary for another reason the proposed land use.[20]

Apart from the aforementioned central zone, the plan provides for the reservation of certain hilly areas for the same (recreational) purposes.

> The area to the North-West shown with a special indication has been allocated to a group of functions suitable for this location. Central and regional institutions, a part of the university and the secondary schools related to medical, agricultural, etc., education, the main sports center, the fair of Skopje, the main park and zoological garden, etc.[21]

Indeed, in this respect, the DA master plan fares well. Its green-infrastructure plan could easily pass for a master plan drawn up six decades later, forming the central green–blue corridor of the Vardar and connecting it at various scales out to the countryside and eventually up to the surrounding mountains [Fig. 30].

6. Dynamic System

A last lens through which to examine the environmental proposals of the master plan is that of its openness to change. Biological systems are now recognized as very dynamic, altering with time, and in this sense urban design too must accommodate unknown futures.

Dynamic change is central to DA thinking [Fig. 31]. In practice, in the master plan for Skopje this is accommodated at two scales. The first scale is that of the master plan as designed, where placeholders – such as the green fingers – accommodate things that are yet to be, and which will develop dynamically within these placeholders. The second scale lies in the recognition that the master plan is but a stage in a longer timescale – one in which the city will eventually expand to the east and be planned in the future. This was not to be, as Skopje has not yet followed the population growth projected by DA; however, this does not diminish the openness to change of the master plan itself.

A criticism on the level of spatial dynamics is that the DA master plan assigns specific bounded spaces to humans on the one hand and to natural

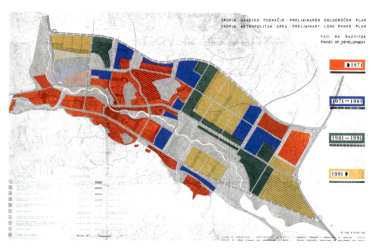

Fig. 30 Green infrastructure in the Skopje master plan.

Fig. 31 Skopje metropolitan area – preliminary long-range plan.

elements on the other – prioritizing clarity, functionality, diagrammatic legibility and probably realism in that natural areas tend to get overrun by other uses if they are not strictly delimited (or sometimes even when they are strictly delimited, as has recently been the case with Islamabad). The growing understanding six decades later that human, technological and biological systems need to be more closely connected was not obvious in the late 1960s.

Conclusion

The DA master plan for Skopje has been assessed through the principles of landscape ecology and ecological planning. A quick graphic representation of how the plan from six decades ago fares through our contemporary lens is presented below (colors indicate the level of success for each factor):

Topography
Hydrology
Soils
Biodiversity and Connectivity
    Patches
    Corridors
    Mosaics
Green infrastructure
Dynamic System

A contemporary ecological assessment of the DA master plan has indeed proven to be a possible and valid exercise. This chapter has made a first general attempt at such an assessment. Future works could provide very important further insights.

The master plan works well for most, but not all, of the categories investigated. Further research could provide a deeper understanding of the thinking and process within Doxiadis Associates and the master plan team that created an ecologically sound design.

A greater opportunity and task present themselves, however. As humanity is rapidly shifting gears to a greener and more climate-resilient future, the implementation of examples of urban design from the past can provide crucial case studies of successes and failures. The present rate of change, and perhaps the instability of our current spatial systems, is such that opportunities for reality checks of this kind should be grasped.

1. Lydia Kallipoliti, "History of Ecological Design," Oxford Research Encyclopedias online, 2018, https://oxfordre.com/environmentalscience/environmentalscience/view/10.1093/acrefore/9780199389414.001.0001/acrefore-9780199389414-e-144#acrefore-9780199389414-e-144-div1-3 (accessed December 1, 2022).
2. Panayiota Pyla, "Ekistics, Architecture and Environmental Politics, 1945–1976: A Prehistory of Sustainable Development," Ph.D. dissertation, Massachusetts Institute of Technology, 2002; Panayiota Pyla, "Planetary Home and Garden: Ekistics and Environmental–Developmental Politics," *Grey Room*, no. 36 (Summer 2009), 6–35.
3. Constantinos A. Doxiadis, *Ekistics: An Introduction to the Science of Human Settlements* (New York: Oxford University Press, 1968).
4. Pyla, "Planetary Home and Garden," 6–35.
5. Ibid., 9.
6. ibid., 10.
7. Constantinos A. Doxiadis, "Global Action for Man's Water Resources," paper submitted to the First World Congress on Water Resources, Chicago, IL, September 24–28, 1973; Constantinos A. Doxiadis, "Global Ecological Balance (The Human Settlement That We Need)," paper prepared for the Tyler Ecology Award, September 1974; Constantinos A. Doxiadis, "Marriage between Nature and City," *International Wildlife* 4, no. 1 (January–February 1974), 4–11; Constantinos A. Doxiadis, *Ecology and Ekistics* (London: Paul Elek, 1977).
8. Pyla, "Planetary Home and Garden," 10.
9. Ibid., 10.
10. Ibid., 12.
11. Doxiadis Associates, "Outline plan for the city of Skopje," vols. 1–2, August 14, 1964, DOX-YUG-A 1, Files 24766 and 24767, Doxiadis Archives; "Skopje urban plan," 1965–1966, September 30, 1965, DOX-YUG-A 58, File 24771, Doxiadis Archives.
12. Doxiadis Associates, "Outline Plan for the City of Skopje," 1964, vol. 1, 8 .
13. Ibid., 10.
14. Ibid., 188.
15. Wikipedia, "Landscape Ecology," http://en.wikipedia.org/wiki/Landscape_ecology (accessed May 29, 2022).
16. Robert MacArthur and E. O. Wilson, *The Theory of Island Biogeography* (Princeton, NJ: Princeton University Press, 1967).
17. W. Dramstad, J. D. Olson and R. Forman, *Landscape Ecology Principles in Landscape Architecture and Land-Use Planning* (Washington, DC: Island Press, 1996).
18. Doxiadis Associates, "Design of selected sections of the Skopie highway system," April 2–October 1, 1966, DOX-YUG-A 14, File 24773, Doxiadis Archives.
19. Doxiadis Associates, "Outline plan for the city of Skopje," 1964, vol. 1, 322.
20. Ibid.
21. Ibid.

Afterword
The Three Antiquities of C. A. Doxiadis and the Road to Eutopia
Panayotis Tournikiotis

The Delos Symposia have become a myth and the Delians of Doxiadis, the ideal inhabitants of mythical Delos, a distinct tribe – a sect of intellectuals, including architects and urban planners who envisioned a better world in the measure of universal human. Given the scope of the Symposia, it would be reasonable to look for archetypal references to Delos in Constantinos Doxiadis's doctoral thesis, in its original German published edition, *Raumordnung im griechischen Städtebau* of 1937, or its revised English translation by Jaqueline Tyrwhitt, *Architectural Space in Ancient Greece* of 1972.[1] The public space at the sanctuary of Apollo on Delos offered itself as the perfect place for an interpretative investigation into *Raumordnung* (spatial planning). In the introduction to the German edition, Doxiadis states that he traveled to Delos and other excavated sites of ancient Greece while still studying architecture in Athens, without reaching a conclusion because his observations were not logically coherent.[2] In the body of the book, he makes a brief reference to Delos, consisting of fourteen lines in total and a plan of the sanctuary from an encyclopedia, saying that he lacks sufficient data and an accurate plan with dating to make any observations with scientific accuracy – and that this is why he has decided not to include the island in his thesis.[3] However, in the well-known and well-read English version, there is no mention of Delos – not even the word itself.

Delos is thus not included in the interpretive framework of *Architectural Space*, nor is it part of the *Raumordnung*. One might expect, however, that it would be included in the Ancient Greek Cities Project, which was developed from 1963 to 1977, alongside the Delos Symposia, with the aim of expanding research on the organization of space in ancient Greek cities in collaboration with eminent archaeologists and historians. At that time, twenty-four monographs were published, with another twelve completed without being published, covering the entire Greek geographical and historical area.[4] But, even in this great research enterprise from the Athens Center of Ekistics, the small island is not included. Ancient Delos is latent and, despite the actual presence of the delegates in the physical environment of its archaeological site, it is *adelos* (invisible).[5] It seems to be closer to the space and time of Thomas More's Utopia island – metaphorically, of course, a political and social context for humanity and its future organization of life on a human scale. Could it be that Doxiadis's Delos is a retrospective construction of Utopia?

Doxiadis left for Berlin as soon as he finished his studies at the Architectural School of Athens and completed a doctoral thesis in a very short time, which received immediate recognition and little though severe criticism. He studied the organization of space in ancient Greece, mainly in sanctuaries and agorae, in search of an implicit and irreducible design order, which, when it later became evident through his own treatises, would allow us to see the ideal harmony of space in the ancient world as well as to design a correspondingly ideal modern world. To achieve this, he traveled less (when he did, it was to Asia Minor and Greece) and worked more, in the libraries of Berlin, on the published plans of archaeological research. To tease out the spatial relationships he had assumed in his research, he drew geometric ratios on the plans of archaeological sites – following the point of view of a mobile observer taking in the complexities of spatial perspective, like Michelangelo in Rome's Campidoglio; or moving through space in an architectural promenade, like Le Corbusier; or in a cinematic traveling, like Sergei Eisenstein. The geometric relationships that he inscribed on paper do not, however, reflect the relationship between the eye of the modern observer and the ruined ancient buildings in real space, but rather geometric ratios and mathematical proportions that derive from the Platonic harmony of the golden section and its Neoplatonic interpretations in the early twentieth century.

Doxiadis's thesis, although it was conducted in an archaeological context, was aimed not at the ancient but at the modern city and its future planning. *Raumordnung* begins with statements regarding town planning over the previous three decades, referring to new building materials and mechanical means of transport, which constituted a revolutionary change, and sets the goal "to find the right path for present and future town planning."[6] Doxiadis explains from the beginning his interest in the past:

> In order to understand the issues of present-day urbanism, one has to master its entire problem and delve particularly into its relation to life, in the broadest sense of the word, over time and place. It is necessary for this – avoiding a formalistic or superficial view – to have a thorough knowledge of past civilizations and their creations in order to grasp their meaning. With confidence in these ideas, I visited and studied [...] the excavated sites and cities of ancient Greece.[7]

At the same time, he clarifies that his aim was to formulate a theory: "The simple observations from where I had started developed into a broad theory that slowly spread to other areas, such as mathematics, philosophy, etc. This theory is the subject of my work."[8] Then, he concludes by making clear the programmatic aim of the design of space in a city – that is, the space between buildings – which was his life's main work: "In this study I deal with the most important part of man's general technical creation, with the shaping of space, not inside the building or in its details, but of space in a city, with the way space acts between buildings."[9]

The whole of *Raumordnung* refers, from here on to the very end, only to geometric ratios and other mathematical calculations about ancient cities, culminating in the revolving gaze, a panoramique that takes 30- or 36-degree steps (in a ten-part or a twelve-part system), with a preference for the latter because it follows the golden ratio. Thereby emerges an "aesthetic form [that] was created by man to give pleasure to man" because "the organization of every site was entirely rational and could be immediately comprehended from the entrance," with the conceptual objective made clear "by a clearly visible pathway."[10] However, the way in which Doxiadis "read" the ancient cities in *Raumordnung* will not concern him again. He almost immediately turns to the design of the modern city and modern inhabitation. But the antiquity of the thesis will never be forgotten, even if the geometric order of ancient space was not to be an obvious design tool in Doxiadis's office. However, it will provide an unexpected reference for the design of the site by his mentor, Dimitris Pikionis – both on the hills around the Acropolis and at Delphi. This was not only the support and promotion that Pikionis offered Doxiadis's thesis from 1937 onward.[11] The invisible harmony of space in Greek antiquity was recovered by Pikionis and was projected through his drawings into modern, visible reality – culminating in the configuration of the space on the hill of Philopappos. Pikionis, a father figure in

Doxiadis's studies and career, might have been the initiator – and he was certainly the intended audience – of this thesis.

Twenty-five years later, Doxiadis's office has already designed many housing complexes for human life as well as a capital city, Islamabad. In these large projects, which do not include the design of the contemporary agora and the contemporary sanctuary, the patterns of the thesis are not applied but the focus is on human communities and the design of residential complexes with reference to ancient Greek cities from a different perspective: scale, circulation, structure, human proportions. Doxiadis's ideal models are not only ancient Athens but also Olynthos and Hellenistic Priene. The relationship between the ancient and the modern city is developed in successive publications and, in my opinion, it is best summarized in Doxiadis's speech at the sixth Conference of the European Cultural Foundation, held in Athens in May 1964, together with an exhibition of drawings at the Athens Technological Institute, published as "The Ancient Greek City and the City of the Present" in both *Ekistics* and *Architektoniki*.[12] In this article, which has excellent illustrations comparing urban masses, agorae, squares and housing complexes at a common scale from around the world and across the ages, culminating in the relationship between Le Corbusier's Chandigarh and Doxiadis's Islamabad, the agora and sanctuary of Delos are illustrated but without special emphasis. The main issue is the definition of the human community, as explored in his research into ancient Athens and as rendered in perspective in ancient Priene and Islamabad, with the "common feature" of "human scale"[13] (see Fig. 7 on p. 56 in the Zarmakoupi chapter in this volume). The typological approach is timeless and translocal, following the thinking of Pikionis, and the representation is linear and abstract, both modern and classical (designed by Alexandros Tombazis).[14]

In Doxiadis's worldview, there are three antiquities. The first is the architectural antiquity of *Raumordnung*, with its modern, geometric and cinematic perspective of an idealized but now uninhabited world. Next is Thomas More's utopian antiquity, whose human community is inhabited by the "descendants" of the speakers of the Greek language who read ancient texts in the original language. And, finally, we have archaeological antiquity, in the form of the Ancient Greek Cities Project, which aspires to make the ancient city the property of the science of human-settlement design, with the interdisciplinarity that characterized the thought of Doxiadis and the documentation of the archaeologist.

I have already discussed the antiquity focus of *Raumordnung*. The notes, sketches and photographs preserved in Doxiadis's archive allow us to reconstruct the methodology, approach and weaving of his thesis. He selects published drawings from books; quotes from the ancient Greek geographer Pausanias; conveys in his own sketches the ordering of space in different places (including the "square before the great porticoes of Eleusis" and the square of the Capitol in Rome) with an implicit comparative intention; corresponds with professors and scholars for evidence and information (with Anastasios Orlandos about Sounion and Paul Lemerle for Delos); assembles successive photographic shots in the sequence of a revolving gaze, on the Acropolis or in Pergamon; and systematically works on the organization of the sites in plans and with diagrams, in search of dynamic and harmonious proportions, starting from, but not limited to, the golden ratio. A visit to Pergamon in 1936 brings him into contact with antiquity – with the altar of Zeus, for example – but his photographic representation does not document the altar and the ancient remains, which are lost in the vegetation, but explores the revolving gaze, constructing a panorama that finds no place, as a photograph, in his thesis [Fig. 1]. The corresponding photographic investigation of the Acropolis of Athens [Figs. 2-3] is followed by diagrams in plan [Figs. 4-5] with calculations that reveal a mathematical search for harmony in the order of space [Figs. 6-7]. I have found similar "operations" in the

Fig. 1 C. A. Doxiadis, collage of photographs from his visit to Pergamon in 1936.

sketchbooks of Le Corbusier, when he was designing the Villa Savoye. Obviously, Doxiadis has not seen these, but the way in which he looks at and analyzes space parallels that of Le Corbusier and reflects a conception of the order of space that combines the history of architecture (Auguste Choisy), the theories of harmonic ratios and the golden ratio (Matila Ghyka). Doxiadis is aware of these things.[15] His view is in no way archaeological but is totally modern and architectural – looking stealthily at history, searching for the logical structure without the visible form of the past in order to design the coming future. For him, analysis of space is design of space.

Much has been written about Thomas More's Utopia and its relationship to Plato's *Republic*, or the didactic projection onto this invisible island of a better democracy and an ideal human society, and I will not go into it again. More's subtitle is clear: "De optimo rei publicae statu deque nova insula Utopia" – that is, "Of a republic's best state and of the new island Utopia." Utopia, the invisible island, becomes visible and perceptible through More's writing: it becomes Delos. In a similar way to Delos and the Delos Symposia, in More's *Utopia* an urban, geographical and architectural organization and form is not represented and is not of interest because all interest belongs to the order of discourse. It is much more concerned

Figs. 2–3   C. A. Doxiadis, consecutive photographs taken on the Acropolis of Athens in 1936.

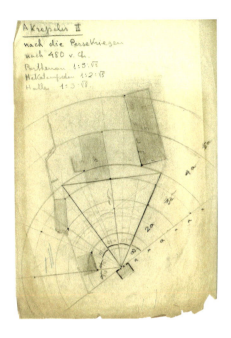 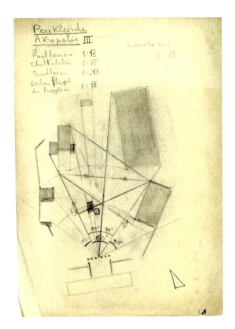

with the structure of the human community and ultimately its residential, rather than its morphological, expression. I have chosen two short passages from More's *Utopia*, concerning the housing structure:

> There be in the island fifty-four large and fair cities or shire-towns, agreeing all together in one tongue, in like manners, institutions, and laws. They be all set and situate alike, and in all points fashioned alike, as far forth as the place or plot suffereth.[16]

> The streets be appointed and set forth very commodious and handsome, both for carriage and also against the winds. The houses be of fair and gorgeous building, and on the street-side they stand joined together in a long row through the whole street without any partition or separation. The streets be twenty foot broad. On the back side of the houses, through the whole length of the street, lie large gardens, which be closed in round about with the back part of the streets. [...] Every man that will may go in, for there is nothing within the houses that is private or any man's own. And every ten years they change their houses by lot.[17]

Figs. 4–5 C. A. Doxiadis, diagrams of the panoramic view of the Acropolis of Athens in 1936.

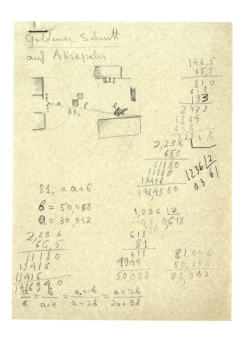
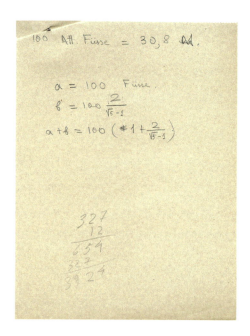

Leaving aside the archaic English of the translation from More's Latin text, the description could equally fit the human communities of Islamabad or the White Houses (Aspra Spitia).[18] One of the most interesting elements of More's *Utopia*, however, is that this human community, which was "lost" in the distant seas and had as its capital the "dreamy" Amaurote, derives its origin – like More – from the same Greek antiquity to which Doxiadis refers when he gathers men and women of spirit from all over the world to sign in the ancient theater of Delos a declaration for human settlements and for humanity itself.[19] I am sure that, if Thomas More had been alive, he would have been invited in 1963 to the Delos Symposion and would have signed the declaration. So, the Utopians are distant relatives of the Delians? More, speaking in the words of his interlocutor and narrator, Raphael Hythloday, states boldly about Utopia and the Utopians, "I believe verily: howsoever these decrees be, that there is in no place of the world neither a more excellent people, neither a more flourishing commonwealth" and "I think that this nation took their beginning of the Greeks, because their speech [...] keepeth divers signs and tokens of the Greek language in the names of their cities and of their magistrates."[20] Thanks to the books Hythloday provided

Figs. 6–7 C. A. Doxiadis, calculations that reveal the mathematical search for harmony in the order of space on the Acropolis of Athens.

them, in fact, they easily appropriated – even in the ancient original – "the most part of Plato's works, more of Aristotle's"; from the poets "Aristophanes, Homer, Euripides, and Sophocles in Aldus' small print"; and from the historians "Thucydides, Herodotus, and Herodian."[21]

Reading the "Declaration of Delos," we see that Doxiadis and the Delians are not content with the mere revival of ancient ideals in a distant and "invisible" utopia but wish to take the initiative to design this republic in the modern world – passing from dystopia to the implementation of utopia, which will be called Eutopia. In words similar to the introduction of the *Raumordnung*, the declaration aims for "the rational and dynamic planning of human settlements" that will "satisfy man not only as parent and worker, but as learner and artist and citizen" – an outcome that can only be reached by the establishment of "a new discipline of human settlements."[22]

Doxiadis will refer more extensively to this relationship between the "new discipline of human settlements" and Thomas More's creation in his book *Between Dystopia and Utopia*:

> The city we are building is worse than yesterday's city. In this sense it is definitely a bad place, a dystopia. [...] Then came a voice: "Why not build my Republic?" I recognized Plato. Sir Thomas More stole my answer: "It is too small. You had better turn to my Utopia." I then realized that my room was full of voices of the past and present representing dreams of the ideal city – philosophers, statesmen, architects, and many others [*sic*] everyone looking at it in his own way. J. V. Andreae proposed Christianopolis, Etienne Cabet his Icaria, Edward Bellamy his America, Le Corbusier his Ville Radieuse, Frank Lloyd Wright his Broadacre City, and Aldous Huxley his Island. I was following them through the ages as they built with words and drawings their dreamland for which there was no place – Utopia.[23]

Doxiadis then becomes more specific: "Man's dreams [...] do not only lead him to write about a utopia, but also to design it, and then it takes the name of Ideal City – the utopia of those who can think in terms of spatial forms." "Utopia may well be derived not only from the Greek ου-τοπία, utopia – no-place, but also from ευτοπία – the eutopia, [eftopia] [...] that is the good place. [...] Plato's Republic, for example, is high up towards the eftopian side." "Utopia began to lead man to think that paradise could not be in

BETWEEN DYSTOPIA AND UTOPIA
by Constantinos A. Doxiadis

heaven but had to be built."[24] However, is it possible to do all this? Even he himself is troubled, admitting that "[t]here is only one road left – with reason and dream – which should take us out of the bad place into a good place, which is not out of place, but in place – an entopia." "Entopia" is a term Doxiadis created to describe the "place which satisfies the dreamer and is accepted by the scientist, the place where the projections of the artist and the builder meet."[25]

The drawing on the cover of the book summarizes the relationship between dystopia and utopia, and shows the road to eutopia, which can only be in place in an Entopia [Fig. 8]. The circular structure of the utopian city (top left) contrasts with the dystopia of the growing city with its tall buildings and narrow streets, right, and finds a way out in the city of Entopia, with the rectangular network of mechanical accesses in which human communities are inscribed (bottom left). This form of entopia can be spread anywhere on Earth, all over Earth, to become the "skin of the earth" [Fig. 9]. According to Doxiadis, "[a]ny place on the Earth is of interest to man if he can settle on it so that it turns into his human settlement"[26] – as long as "he" applies "the five elements in Plato's republic" – that is, "nature, man, society, shells and networks." Doxiadis illustrates this critical relationship in an evaluation table, which compares the degree of reality, from topia/place to u-topia/no-place, and the degree of quality, from dys-topia/bad-place to ef-topia/good place. The possibility of healing dys-topia/bad-place if there is wisdom and knowledge brings back to the fore More's Hythloday and the "pursuit" of the good in Plato's *Theaetetus*.[27]

Fig. 8 Cover of C. A. Doxiadis's book *Between Dystopia and Utopia* (1966), juxtaposing dystopia, utopia and Entopia.

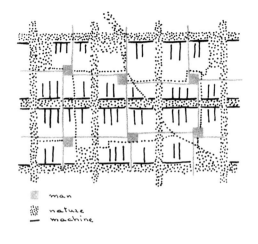

Only in a specific place and time – that is, in Entopia – can the world change, but even that is not enough because change ultimately depends on humanity itself. Doxiadis's anguish over this point is not hidden:

It is a dark night and I sit in my office and think about past, present and future [...] The city of Athens lies dark in the plain, but the first rays of the rising sun illuminate the Acropolis which sparkles in the half-light, and as I look at it I know that, yes, it is possible. It is up to man.[28] [Fig. 10]

This same thought, "[i]t is up to man," was already referred to in the quotation in the preface to both *Raumordnung* and *Architectural Space*, which Doxiadis took from Plato's *Theaetetus* (152A): "Man is the measure of all things, of the existence of the things that are and the nonexistence of the things that are not." "Man" is the only measure for both utopia and reality.

The Ancient Greek Cities Project was the continuation and completion of *Raumordnung*'s research at the meeting point of human-settlement science and archaeology.[29] The second volume of the series, *The Method for the Study of Ancient Greek Settlements*, authored by Doxiadis, begins with the statement "This study was undertaken to understand the general rules which influenced the settlements Man created in or under the influence of the ancient Greek world."[30] In terms of method, the research extends geographically from Spain to the Indus Valley – that is, it reaches Islamabad. It refers to "space influenced by Greek civilization" according to Isocrates's definition, which means that "Greeks are all those who share the Greek culture" – in other words, it includes Thomas More's Utopians.[31] It is limited in time to antiquity, ending in 330 CE, when Constantinople was founded – that is, it excludes the Byzantine era and modern times.[32] In addition, it refers specifically to the "ekistic phenomena of the areas," which are

Fig. 9 C. A. Doxiadis, Entopia as the "skin of the earth" in *Between Dystopia and Utopia*.

Afterword

"relative to the settlements themselves" and are examined "under the headings of Nature, Man, Society, Shells, and Networks" – that is, Doxiadis's five basic elements of Ekistics, echoing Plato's homologous elements of the *Republic*.[33] To shape the project, Doxiadis had advisers who were distinguished archaeologists, historians and philologists – such as John Travlos, Michael Sakellariou and Demetrios Maronitis – while most of the research was undertaken by archaeologists such as Demetrios Lazaridis and Nikolaos Faraklas. Doxiadis reserved for himself "the level of general conclusions" and "the total responsibility [...] to present a synthetic picture."[34] However, his life ended before the completion of this ambitious project, and thus the Ancient Greek Cities Project has neither conclusions nor a synthetic picture. However, by holding fast to his methodological contribution, Doxiadis subtly illuminates a part of the expected conclusions of this collective research on ancient Greek cities, which is summarized in a table of sizes and definitions starting from "the ekistic scale which divides all the space on earth – known as the anthropocosmos – into 15 units."[35]

Fig. 10 C. A. Doxiadis in contemplation, with the Parthenon in the background.

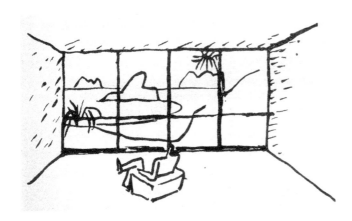

According to Doxiadis,

> in order to study more systematically the ancient Greek cities and in such a way come to a better understanding of them, and to be able to compare them with concepts that are today more clear to us, it became necessary to arrange the settlements into categories, enabling us to get a correct picture of Man's relationship to space, and each time we referred to a settlement of a certain order to employ the ekistic unit. For a start, we accepted that the village, the basic Greek settlement from ancient times to the present, correspond[ed] to ekistic unit 6, with an average population of 1,500 inhabitants, ranging from 500–3,000 inhabitants.[36]

Since the early 1960s, however, the settlement-scale approach to space and reference to antiquity have been the theoretical starting points for the design of cities by the Doxiadis office, with Islamabad being a typical example. The *archaeological antiquity* of the Ancient Greek Cities Project has as its starting point not the past but the expected future, and attempts a documented retrospective view of the settlement past of the Greeks in order to project it into the future of the whole world as an intrinsic memory of Eutopia. This view is not far from the inherent memory of the Greek language and the quick recovery of ancient Greek thought by More's Utopians, which Doxiadis attempts to revive by inviting their selected "descendants" from all over the world to the Delos Symposia to agree on the design of human

Fig. 11 Le Corbusier, drawing of a modern man's habitat in La Ville Radieuse.

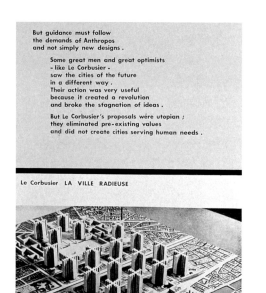

settlements for humanity itself. Is Greek antiquity the real utopia, and are the Delians distant relatives of the utopians?

In 1933 in Athens, during the fourth CIAM (Congrès Internationaux d'Architecture Moderne), Le Corbusier gave a lecture at the School of Architecture entitled "Air, Son, Lumière, expressing the basic ideas of *La Ville Radieuse*."[37] He subsequently illustrated them in 1942, in *La maison des hommes*, in a drawing showing a man seated behind the closed glass wall of his high-rise apartment enjoying the spectacle of beautiful nature in Rio de Janeiro – and perhaps in Algiers, Marseille, Oran, Nice, the Côte d'Azur or Barcelona – as both coastal and continental cities have admirable landscapes [Fig. 11].[38] This was Le Corbusier's answer to the fatal illness of the great cities, which could be cured, to his mind, with a set of utopian principles making the modern city radiant: the *ville radieuse*. Doxiadis had attended Le Corbusier's lecture in Athens while a student, and often refers to La Ville Radieuse. He also, in *Between Dystopia and Utopia*, compares its principles to the five elements in Plato's *Republic*, drawing another evaluation table. Doxiadis is critical of Le Corbusier, but at least gives him credit for utopia – including him, with reference to La Ville Radieuse, among those who "built with words and drawings their dreamland for which there was no place – Utopia."[39] His proposals were useful because they caused a revolution and broke the stagnation of ideas, but they were utopian because they emphasized design rather than the values and needs of humanity [Fig. 12].

Fig. 12 C. A. Doxiadis, "La Ville Radieuse by Le Corbusier," from the exhibition "Doxiadis: Building Tomorrow's Cities" at the Museum of Science and Industry, Chicago, May 24–July 21, 1974.

Fig. 13 (opposite, top) "Narrow street in the metropolis," drawing by A. Tombazis for C. A. Doxiadis's book *Ekistics: An Introduction to the Science of Human Settlements*.

In other words, Le Corbusier is placed alongside Thomas More, in Utopia, while Doxiadis maintains for his own theory the pursuit of the Eutopia that Entopia brings. He will bring Le Corbusier's man down to earth and remove the closed glass wall and the roof, in order to bring him closer to place – in direct relation to the natural and human environment, in a horizontal dimension of human community that extends infinitely into the Ecumenopolis. With the help of Alexandros Tombazis, he will adapt Le Corbusier's drawing and, instead of the narrow streets with the tall buildings of the dystopian metropolis, he will propose the streets of Islamabad, modelled on ancient Priene [Figs. 13–15]. It is on such a street that the Delians, in 1963, walk through the ancient neighborhood made visible by an archaeological excavation of a human community, to reach the theater (see Fig. 1 on p. 44 in the Zarmakoupi chapter in this volume). Delos is no longer an invisible place – no longer a non-place, a utopia. It is a prototype of Entopia. In the eyes of Doxiadis, utopia can and must become an achievable reality and the best possible reference to this

Fig. 14 (middle) "Man and his habitat," a revision of Le Corbusier's drawing as Entopia by A. Tombazis for C. A. Doxiadis's book *Ekistics: An Introduction to the Science of Human Settlements*.

Fig. 15 (bottom) "Islamabad," drawing of Entopia by A. Tombazis for C. A. Doxiadis's book *Ekistics: An Introduction to the Science of Human Settlements*.

ideal could not be Amaurote on the uncharted island of Utopia, nor a *ville radieuse*. It is an ancient Greek city with a settlement structure that is appropriate to the measure of humanity: Priene, Olynthus and, finally, Delos, which was invisible in his previous investigations but could be a real meeting place and not just an allegory. Following the 1933 journey of the moderns from Marseille to Athens, in 1963 Doxiadis organized the journey of the ancients from Utopia to Delos. And this, in my eyes, is a reversal, a transgression of the moderns that embraced the lesson of the ancients, in full analogy with that of the seventeenth century, when the rise of rationalism and science founded modernity on the awareness of antiquity.[40]

The three antiquities of Doxiadis coexist and overlap in his thought and work, from the years of his studies to the Delos Symposia. These architectural, utopian and archaeological perspectives are complementary approaches in a pursuit of the ideal world for humanity's creative survival. Having been formed in an environment of therapeutic positivism, refugee crisis and human resettlement, Doxiadis pursues a method that enables diagnosis, prognosis and treatment through the design of ideal and effective responses to real problems. His entire career is characterized by the coexistence and overlapping of idealism, pragmatism and positivism – approaches as different and seemingly contradictory as the three antiquities. But this is precisely his most interesting contribution. By bringing together what in this volume we have called "Foundations and Ideals" (Section I) and "Practices and Implementations" (Section II), Doxiadis gave a dynamic, interdisciplinary and executive direction to those who undertake to design a human space that is rooted in the experiences of the past, grounded upon the earth and looking towards "Futures and Legacies" (Section III).

1   K. A. Doxiadis, *Raumordnung im griechischen Städtebau* (Heidelberg and Berlin: Kurt Vowinckel Verlag, 1937); C. A. Doxiadis, *Architectural Space in Ancient Greece*, translated by Jaqueline Tyrwhitt (Cambridge, MA: MIT Press, 1972).
2   Doxiadis, *Raumordnung*, 3.
3   Ibid., 36. In Doxiadis's archive, however – in the folder of his dissertation notes – there is a handwritten detailed record of maps and drawings from the literature of Delos addressed to him by Paul Lemerle, then Secretary of the École française d'Athènes. Lemerle also pointed him to the exact bibliographical reference of a Delos plan from the Pauly–Wissowa encyclopedia, the one that Doxiadis actually used in his *Raumordnung* (Archive Files 18469).
4   Mantha Zarmakoupi, "Balancing Acts between Ancient and Modern Cities: The Ancient Greek Cities Project of C. A. Doxiadis," *Architectural Histories* 3, no. 1 (2015), 1–22.
5   Delos, Apollo's sacred birthplace, was an "Adelos island," an island that could not be seen, floating here and there in the Aegean Sea until Zeus asked Poseidon for a shelter for Leto to give birth to his twin children Apollo and Artemis, when the island settled and became visible as "Delos." See also the discussion in Mantha Zarmakoupi, "The Blue Marble of Greek Architectural History: Delos and the Delos Symposia," in M. Zarmakoupi (ed.), *Looking at the City: Architectural and Archaeological Perspectives* (Athens: Melissa Books, 2023), 206–33, 215; and Zarmakoupi in this volume.

6   Doxiadis, *Raumordnung*, 1–2.
7   Ibid., 2.
8   Ibid., 3.
9   Ibid., 7.
10 Doxiadis, *Architectural Space*, 23.
11 Δ. Πικιώνης, "Η Θεωρία του αρχιτέκτονος Κ. Α. Δοξιάδη για τη διαμόρφωση του χώρου εις την αρχαία αρχιτεκτονική [The Theory of the Architect C. A. Doxiadis on the Configuration of Space in Ancient Architecture]," *Το 3ο Μάτι* [*The Third Eye*], no. 7–12 (1937), unpaginated. I quote from the reprint, *Το 3ο Μάτι 1935–1937* (Athens: ELIA, 1982), 239–46.
12 Κ. Α. Δοξιάδης, "Η αρχαία ελληνική και η σημερινή πόλη [The Ancient Greek City and the City of the Present]," *Αρχιτεκτονική* [*Architecture*] 46 (July–August 1964), 46–59; C. A. Doxiadis, "The Ancient Greek City and the City of the Present," *Ekistics* 18, no. 108 (November 1964), 346–64.
13 Δοξιάδης, "Η αρχαία ελληνική και η σημερινή πόλη," 55–56.
14 The young architect Alexandros Tombazis had collaborated with Doxiadis in this design investigation, and, as he personally confirmed to me a few years ago, had produced the two perspectives of Priene and Islamabad.
15 Issue 7–12 of the magazine *Το 3ο Μάτι* [*The Third Eye*], published in 1937 and edited by N. Hadjikyriakos-Ghika and D. Pikionis, was devoted to the "Law of Number in Nature and Art" and included extensive references to Matila Ghyka, Jay Hambidge and others. Included in this issue was Pikionis's article on Doxiadis's thesis (see note 11) and, before that, an article by Constantinos Doxiadis himself entitled "Οι θεωρίες των αρμονικών χαράξεων εις την αρχιτεκτονικήν [The Theories of Harmonic Ratios in Architecture]," 213–25.
16 Thomas More, *The Utopia of Sir Thomas More*, edited with introduction, notes, and glossary by William Dallam Armes (New York: Macmillan, 1912 [1516]), 87–88.
17 More, *The Utopia of Sir Thomas More*, 94.
18 See discussion by Zarmakoupi in this volume.
19 Amaurote is derived from the ancient Greek *Amauros* (Αμαυρός): dim, hard to see. The word is first found in the *Odyssey* as a description of a vision or a ghost and meaning "dark, indistinct." In modern Greek, More's Amaurote has been translated as Oniropolis, "Dreamland" (Thomas More, translated by Giorgos Karagiannis as *Η Ουτοπία [Utopia]* (Athens: Kalvos, 1970), 63.
20 The name Hythloday, coined by More and given by him to his imaginary interlocutor, is borrowed from the ancient Greek word for nonsense, used by Plato in *Theaetetus* (176b) to contrast evil with good. Socrates says, in this dialogue, "it is necessary to have something contrary to good" in order to be able to overcome it, and that "this pursuit means becoming like God," which requires wisdom and knowledge. This probably accounts for the choice of the forename Raphael, meaning in Hebrew "God has healed," which More gave Hythloday – that is, God has healed nonsense with wisdom and knowledge. For the quotations, see More, *The Utopia of Sir Thomas More*, 149.
21 More, *The Utopia of Sir Thomas More*, 151, 152.
22 "The Declaration of Delos," July 12, 1963, unpaginated.
23 Constantinos A. Doxiadis, *Between Dystopia and Utopia* (Hartford, CT: Trinity College Press, 1966).
24 Ibid., 24, 25, 30.
25 Ibid., 49–50, 50–51.
26 Ibid., 38.
27 See note 19. See also discussion in Mantha Zarmakoupi, "Τόπος και εντοπία: τα Συμπόσια της Δήλου [Topos and Entopia: The Symposia of Delos]," in D. I. Kyrtatas, I. Konstantopoulos and C. Boulotis (eds), *Τόπος Τοπίο, Τιμητικός Τόμος για τον Δημήτρη Φιλιππίδη* [*Topos Topio, Honorary Volume for Dimitris Philippides*] (Athens: Melissa Books, 2018), 63–70.
28 Doxiadis, *Between Dystopia and Utopia*, 84.
29 See Zarmakoupi, "Balancing Acts between Ancient and Modern Cities," 1–22.
30 C. A. Doxiadis, *The Method for the Study of Ancient Greek Settlements* (Athens: Athens Center of Ekistics, 1972), viii. The first volume is authored by Arnold Toynbee and is entitled *An Ekistical Study of the Hellenic City State* (Athens: Athens Center of Ekistics, 1971).
31 Doxiadis, *Method for the Study of Ancient Greek Settlements*, 5.
32 Ibid., ix.
33 Ibid., 12; on these five basic elements, see C. A. Doxiadis, *Ekistics: An Introduction to the Science of Human Settlements* (New York: Oxford University Press, 1968).
34 Doxiadis, *Method for the Study of Ancient Greek Settlements*, xiii. See discussion in Zarmakoupi, "Balancing Acts between Ancient and Modern Cities."
35 Zarmakoupi, "Balancing Acts between Ancient and Modern Cities," 36.
36 Ibid., 36–37.
37 The lecture text was published as "Air, Son, Lumière" in *Annales Techniques*, no. 44–46 (1933), 1140–45, and as "Discours d'Athènes" in *L'Architecture d'Aujourd'hui*, no. 10 (1933), 80–89; see also Le Corbusier, *La ville radieuse* (Paris: Éditions de l'Architecture d'Aujourd'hui, 1935).
38 Le Corbusier, *La maison des hommes* (Paris: Plon, 1942), 69.
39 Doxiadis, *Between Dystopia and Utopia*, x.
40 See for instance Antoine Picon, *Architectes et ingénieurs au siècle des Lumières* (Marseille: Editions Parenthèses, 1988).

Acknowledgments

From its inception through to its completion, this project has enjoyed extraordinary support from the Constantinos and Emma Doxiadis Foundation. This support has been felt in various ways but particularly in the granting of privileged access and image copyright clearance through the Constantinos A. Doxiadis Archives at the Benaki Museum, as administered through their fabulously knowledgeable, helpful and forbearing archivist, Giota Pavlidou. A volume of this size and scope has very considerable production costs, and it would simply not have been possible to bring it to the public had it not been for the enlightened and extremely generous financial support of the Evangelos Pistiolis Foundation, Switzerland, and the Williams Publication Fund of the Department of the History of Art at the University of Pennsylvania.

This book project was developed in the context of a research networking grant from the Arts and Humanities Research Council that allowed us to gather international scholars and audiences across three workshops and begin to share our understanding of the Delos Symposia. We are grateful to the Arts and Humanities Research Council, as well as to the institutions – the Universities of Birmingham and Loughborough in the UK and the Benaki Museum in Athens – that hosted these workshops. The Bodossaki Foundation helped us reach new audiences by recording and disseminating the Athens papers through their "Bodossaki Lectures On Demand" portal, for which we are duly obliged. Likewise, to Lars Müller, Hester van den Bold, Esther Butterworth and the wider editorial and design team at Lars Müller Publishers, whose enthusiasm, efficiency and attention to detail have made the publishing process a pleasure. Thanks must also go to Markus Daechsel for his cogent and insightful reading of the manuscript, which helped us understand its contents more fully and reinforce its themes.

To all of the above – people, foundations, organizations – we offer our sincere thanks for your indispensable contributions in bringing this project to completion. At the same time, we must acknowledge that we have only begun to understand the importance of the Delos Network for the culture of its day and down through to ours, and so we look forward to the scholarship and insights to follow.

Appendix

About the Authors

Tilemachos Andrianopoulos is an architect, urban designer and Associate Professor in the School of Architecture at the National Technical University of Athens. He is the founder of Tense Architecture Network (2004). The practice's portfolio includes several competition-winning proposals – among them, the Regeneration of Athens City Center (2019) and the Regeneration of the Public Space of the Exarchia Metro Station (2023) – as well as private residences. Residence in Megara won a Häuser Award (2016), Residence in Heraklion was nominated for the Mies van der Rohe Award (2017) and Residence in Sikamino was shortlisted for the same award (2013).

Harrison Blackman is a writer, editor, journalist and screenwriter. He graduated from Princeton University and holds an MFA from the University of Nevada, Reno. A former Fulbright Scholar to Cyprus, he often writes about the modern urban history of the Mediterranean. His work has appeared internationally, in Greek translation and in outlets such as *The Brooklyn Rail*, *Literary Hub* and *The Los Angeles Review of Books*.

Filippo De Dominicis is an architect and Ph.D. in Architectural Design and Theory. At present, he serves as Associate Professor in Architecture at the University of L'Aquila. Previously, he conducted post-doctoral research at Sapienza University of Rome, University Iuav of Venice and MIT, where he was the Aga Khan Fellow in Islamic Architecture. His research focuses on large-scale planning and design strategies in relation to politics and the environment. He has published widely on this topic, including a monograph, the first in the Italian language, on Doxiadis's earliest formulations on world planning, *Il progetto del mondo: Doxiadis, città e futuro, 1955–1965* [*A Project for the World: Doxiadis' City of the Future*] (LetteraVentidue, 2020).

Thomas Doxiadis (Bachelor of Arts, 1992, and Master in Landscape Architecture, 1998, both from Harvard University) designs and studies the landscape, and through it the relationships between humans and the non-human. He does this as Director of the design practice doxiadis+, as an environmental volunteer currently heading the national Greek Adaptation of Landscapes to Climate Change program and as an occasional academic. Doxiadis has written about and participated in several conferences focusing on ecology, landscape and the city. Research-based projects include "Landscapes of Cohabitation" and "Entangled Kingdoms," the first ever fungal garden at the 2020–2021 Venice Architectural Biennale. He was a finalist in the 2018 International Landscape Rosa Barba Prize.

Farhan Karim is Associate Professor of Architectural History at Arizona State University. He is the author of *Of Greater Dignity than Riches: Austerity and Housing Design in India* (University of Pittsburgh Press, 2019) and has contributed as an editor to works including *The Routledge Companion to Architecture and Social Engagement* (Routledge, 2018); "Boundaries, Flows, and the Construction of Muslim Selves through Architecture" (special issue of *International Journal of Islamic Architecture*, 2018), *The Making of Modern Muslim Selves through Architecture*, co-edited with Patricia Blessing (Intellect, 2024); and *The History of Architectural Education in the Middle East and North Africa*, co-edited with Mohammad Gharipour (University of Edinburgh Press, 2024).

Ahmed Z. Khan is Professor of Sustainable Architecture and Urban Design, and Director of the Sustainable Urban Futures Institute (SUFI) at the Université Libre de Bruxelles. His research spans sustainability, climate change and spatial quality at different scales of the built environment. His scientific contributions and publications, stemming from numerous European and regional research projects, cover topics such as urban metabolism and the circular economy, ecosystem services and green infrastructure, urban energy dynamics, sustainable regeneration and bioclimatic design. Professor Khan is a fellow of several learned societies and regularly advises governments on sustainable architecture and urban development across Africa, Europe, the Middle East and South Asia.

Dimitris Philippides is an architect (graduate of the National Technical University in Athens, 1962, and Ph.D. in Architecture from the University of Michigan, 1973) and Professor Emeritus at the School of Architecture, NTU of Athens, where he taught urban design from 1975 to 2005. The range of his professional activity has extended from architectural design to urban planning. He was employed by Doxiadis Associates in Athens (1964–1967) and in Detroit, Michigan (1967–1970). He has also published extensively on Greek architecture and physical planning, traditional and modern, including a monograph on C. A. Doxiadis, *Constantinos Doxiadis (1913–1975): Report to Hippodamus* (Melissa Books, 2015).

Panayiota Pyla is an architectural historian and theorist and Professor of Architecture at the University of Cyprus (UCY), having previously served on the faculty of the University of Illinois at Urbana–Champaign. She holds a Ph.D. in the History and Theory of Architecture and Urbanism from the Massachusetts Institute of Technology. Among her works is the co-edited *Coastal Architectures and Politics of Tourism: Leisurescapes in the Global Sunbelt* (Routledge, 2022) and the edited *Landscapes of Development* (Harvard University Press, 2013) along with articles in *Architectural Histories, Journal of Architectural Education* and *e-flux*, among others. At UCY, she directs the Mesarch Lab (http://mesarch.ucy.ac.cy) and is currently Vice-Dean of the School of Engineering.

Simon Richards is an architectural historian with a particular interest in theory, aesthetics, tradition and heritage. He has published widely in these areas, including two monographs exploring the philosophies and psychologies of environmental determinism in architecture – *Le Corbusier and the Concept of Self* (Yale University Press, 2003) and *Architect Knows Best: Environmental Determinism in Architecture Culture from 1956 to the Present* (Ashgate, 2012) – as well as a co-edited volume exploring the concepts and histories of *Region* (Routledge, 2023). Currently, he is Programme Director of the undergraduate architecture program at Loughborough University, UK.

Ellen Shoshkes has practiced as an architect and planner in the fields of housing and urban design. Her scholarly work has focused on the creative dialogue between East and West in the evolution of modern regional urbanism. She has published extensively about the contributions of Jaqueline Tyrwhitt to that process, including *Jaqueline Tyrwhitt: A Transnational Life in Urban Planning and Design* (Ashgate, 2013) and numerous articles and chapters – most recently, studies of Tyrwhitt's collaboration with Marshall McLuhan and her engagement with the Regional Planning Association of America in the post-war discourse on urbanism. Ellen's current work digs deeper into Tyrwhitt's role in the Delos Symposia.

Ioanna Theocharopoulou is an architect and architectural historian. She trained at the Architectural Association in London and at Columbia University in New York. She holds a Ph.D. in Architectural History from Columbia University. She has participated in numerous academic conferences and publications and is the author of *Builders, Housewives and the Construction of Modern Athens* (Artifice Books, 2017; Onassis Foundation, 2022). Her book was used as the basis for an award-winning documentary film of the same title, directed by Tassos Langis and Yiannis Gaitanidis (Onassis Foundation, 2021). She is Lecturer at the Department of Art History and Archaeology, Columbia University.

Lefteris Theodosis is an architectural historian, independent researcher and architect, currently working in the business-development sector of a leading German architectural firm. His research focuses on the work of the architect and planner Constantinos A. Doxiadis and the development of Ekistics, the "science of human settlements." His aim is to examine the redefinition of urban planning and architecture in the light of major socio-spatial transformations and against the background of the opposing but interacting "processes" that characterized the forging of the post-war world – namely, the drive towards internationalism and the Cold War schism.

Panayotis Tournikiotis, Professor Emeritus at the National Technical University of Athens, taught architectural theory there. He has published critical essays on architecture and the city, covering the modern and contemporary periods, including *The Historiography of Modern Architecture* (MIT Press, 1999), *The Parthenon and Its Impact in Modern Times* (Melissa Books, 1994) and *Le Corbusier's Diagonal* (Ekkremes, 2010). His ongoing research focuses on metropolitan Athens and the intersections of Greek and European architecture, and he is currently President of the European Architectural History Network (EAHN).

Kostas Tsiambaos is an architect and Associate Professor in History and Theory of Architecture at the School of Architecture of the National Technical University in Athens. His research has been published in international journals and edited volumes. His recent books include *From Doxiadis' Theory to Pikionis' Work: Reflections of Antiquity in Modern Architecture* (Routledge, 2018 and 2020). In the fall semester of the academic year 2019–2020, he was a Stanley J. Seeger Visiting Research Fellow at Princeton University. His edited book, *The Architect and the Animal*, is forthcoming from MIT Press.

Mantha Zarmakoupi is an architectural historian and classical archaeologist. She has published widely on Greek and Roman art and architecture – including the monographs *Designing for Luxury on the Bay of Naples (c. 100 BCE–79 CE)* (Oxford University Press, 2014) and *Shaping Roman Landscape* (J. Paul Getty Museum, 2023), the edited volumes *The Villa of the Papyri at Herculaneum* (De Gruyter, 2010), *Looking at the City* (Melissa Books, 2023) and *Hermogenes and Hellenistic–Roman Temple Building* (University of Wisconsin Press, forthcoming) – as well as on the architecture, harbor infrastructure and urban development of late Hellenistic Delos. She also conducts archaeological fieldwork projects in Turkey (Teos) and in Greece (Delos).

Yannis Zavoleas is Associate Professor at the University of Ioannina, Greece and honorary faculty member at the University of New South Wales, Australia. His work introduces interdisciplinary themes from biology, technology, media, the arts and philosophy into architectural discourse. He has awards in the fields of design and writing, and has published widely in books, journals and conference proceedings. He is the author of *Machine and Network as Structural Models in Architecture* (Epikentro, 2023; Futura, 2013); co-author of *Computational Design: From Promise to Practice* (Avedition, 2020); and co-editor of "Patterns and Spatial Organisation: Culture, History & Future Perspectives" (*Nexus Network Journal*, 2021) and *Surface: Digital Materiality and the New Relation between Depth and Surface* (EAAE, 2013).

Bibliography

This bibliography is intended to provide an overview of scholarly sources directly pertinent to Doxiadis and the Delians, as well as some more contextual works that throw light on their wider values, issues and concerns as these have percolated down to the present. It is not exhaustive, however. The endnotes of each chapter contain a wealth of much more specialist scholarly sources – ranging from scientific to literary, philosophical to archival, personal correspondence to formal reports – and often tied to precise geographical regions of inquiry including Africa, Asia, the Middle East and the United States. The reader is invited to follow up with these should they require more detail.

A. Athanassiadis, P. Bouillard, R. Crawford and Ahmed Z. Khan, "Towards a Dynamic Approach to Urban Metabolism," *Journal of Industrial Ecology* 21 (2017), 307–19.

Daniel Barber, *Modern Architecture and Climate: Design before Air Conditioning* (Princeton, NJ: Princeton University Press, 2020), 219–45.

Gwen Bell and Jaqueline Tyrwhitt (eds), *Human Identity in the Urban Environment* (Harmondsworth: Penguin, 1972).

Harrison Blackman, "The Demolition at Porto Rafti: Retracing Doxiadis' Remarkable Life and Contested Legacy," special issue: "Ekistics-Related Research – A Critical Approach to the Ekistics Legacy," *Ekistics and the New Habitat* 82, no. 1 (2022), 91–94.

Kenneth Boulding, "The Economics of the Coming Spaceship Earth," in H. Jarrett (ed.), *Environmental Quality in a Growing Economy* (Baltimore, MD: Johns Hopkins University Press, 1966), 3–14.

Neil Brenner (ed.), *Implosions/Explosions: Towards a Study of Planetary Urbanization* (Berlin: Jovis, 2014).

Ray Bromley, "Towards Global Human Settlements: Constantinos Doxiadis as Entrepreneur, Coalition-Builder and Visionary," in Mercedes Volait and Joe Nasr (eds), *Urbanism: Imported or Exported?* (Hoboken, NJ: John Wiley and Sons, 2003), 316–40.

Markus Daechsel, "Misplaced Ekistics: Islamabad and the Politics of Urban Development in Pakistan," *South Asian History and Culture* 4 (2013), 87–106.
—— *Islamabad and the Politics of International Development in Pakistan* (Cambridge: Cambridge University Press, 2015).

Viviana d'Auria, "From Tropical Transitions to Ekistics Experimentation: Doxiadis Associates in Tema, Ghana," *Positions*, no. 1 (2010), 40–63.
—— "Taming an 'Undisciplined Discipline': Constantinos Doxiadis and the Science of Human Settlements," *OASE* 95 (2016), 8–21.

Filippo De Dominicis, *Il progetto del mondo* (Syracuse: LetteraVentldue, 2020).
—— "To Survey, Control, and Design: Doxiadis and Fathy on Africa's Future and Identity (1959–1963)," in Carlos Nunes Silva (ed.), *Routledge Handbook of Urban Planning in Africa* (New York: Routledge, 2020).
—— "Descriptions of the Inevitable and the Unknown: Constantinos Doxiadis and the Advent of Ecumenopolis, 1960–1961," *Vesper: Journal of Architecture, Arts & Theory* 5 (2021), 196–205.

Philip Deane, *Constantinos Doxiadis: Master Builder for Free Men* (New York: Oceana Publications, 1965).

Constantinos A. Doxiadis, *Architecture in Transition* (London: Hutchinson, 1963).

—— "Islamabad: The Creation of a New Capital," *Town Planning Review* 36, no. 1 (1965), 1–28.
—— *Urban Renewal and the Future of the American City* (Chicago: Public Administration Service, 1966).
—— "The Ancient Greek City, and the City of the Present," in *The Living Heritage of Greek Antiquity* [*L'héritage vivant de l'antiquité grecque*] (The Hague: Mouton, 1967), 192–211.
—— *Between Dystopia and Utopia* (London: Faber and Faber, 1968).
—— *Ekistics: An Introduction to the Science of Human Settlements* (New York: Oxford University Press, 1968).
—— *Architectural Space in Ancient Greece*, trans. Jaqueline Tyrwhitt (Cambridge, MA: MIT Press, 1972).
—— *The Method for the Study of Ancient Greek Settlements* (Athens: Athens Center of Ekistics, 1972).
—— *The Two-Headed Eagle: From the Past to the Future of Human Settlements* (Athens: Lycabettus Press, 1972).
—— *Building Entopia* (New York: Norton, 1975).
—— *Ecology and Ekistics* (London: Paul Elek; Boulder, CO: Westview Press, 1977).

Constantinos A. Doxiadis and Truman Douglass, *The New World of Urban Man* (Philadelphia, PA and Boston, MA: United Church Press, 1965).

Constantinos A. Doxiadis and J. Papaioannou, *Ecumenopolis: The Inevitable City of the Future* (Athens: Athens Center of Ekistics, 1974).

David Ekbladh, *The Great American Mission: Modernization and the Construction of an American World Order* (Princeton, NJ and Oxford: Princeton University Press, 2010).

R. Buckminster Fuller, *Operating Manual for Spaceship Earth* (New York: E. P. Dutton, 1969).

Nils Gilman, *Mandarins of the Future: Modernization Theory in Cold War America* (Baltimore, MD and London: Johns Hopkins University Press, 2006).

Sarah Williams Goldhagen and Réjean Legault (eds), *Anxious Modernisms* (Cambridge, MA and London: MIT Press, 2002).

Thomas Heatherwick, *Humanise: A Maker's Guide to Building Our World* (London: Penguin Random House, 2023).

Carola Hein, "Visionary Plans and Planners, Japanese Traditions and Western Influences," in N. Fieve and P. Waley (eds), *Japanese Capitals in Historical Perspective: Place, Power and Memory in Kyoto, Edo and Tokyo* (Abingdon: Routlege Curzon, 2003), 309–46.

Hilde Heynen and Hubert-Jan Henket (eds), *Back from Utopia: The Challenge of the Modern Movement* (Rotterdam: 010 Publishers, 2002).

Sharmila Jagadisan and Tom Fookes, "Antecedents for the Ekistic Grid and the Anthropocosmos Model: A Critical View of Ekistic Methodology," *Ekistics* 73, no. 436/441 (January/December 2006), 265–76.

Joan Johnson-Freese, *Space as a Strategic Asset* (New York: Columbia University Press, 2007).

Farhan Karim, "Between Self and Citizenship: Doxiadis Associates in Postcolonial Pakistan, 1958–1968," *International Journal of Islamic Architecture* 5, no. 1 (2016), 135–61.

Nikos Katsikis, "Two Approaches to 'World Management': C. A. Doxiadis and R. B. Fuller," in Neil Brenner (ed.), *Implosions – Explosions: Towards a Study of Planetary Urbanization* (Berlin: Jovis, 2017), 480–504.

G. Kazazi and N. Gounari (eds), *Ο Κωνσταντίνος Δοξιάδης και το έργο του, δεύτερος τόμος* [*Constantinos Doxiadis and His Work*, 2 vols.] (Athens: Technical Chamber of Greece, 2009).

Ahmed Z. Khan, "Nature and the City: The Legacy of Doxiadis' Plan for Islamabad," in *Proceedings of the WSSD Workshop on Human Settlements and Environment, Islamabad, December 14–15, 2004* (Islamabad: Ministry of Environment, Government of Pakistan, 2004), 86–98.
—— "Representing the State: Symbolism and Ideology in Doxiadis' Plan for Islamabad," in Mark Swenarton, Igea Troiani and Helena Webster (eds), *The Politics of Making* (London and New York: Routledge, 2007), 61–75.
—— "Constantinos A. Doxiadis' Plan for Islamabad: The Making of a 'City of the Future' 1959–1963," Ph.D. dissertation, KU Leuven, April 2008.
—— "Rethinking Doxiadis' Ekistical Urbanism: Sustainability and Globalization as a Dialectical Framework for Design," *Positions: On Modern Architecture + Urbanism / Histories and Theories* (2010), 6–39.

Rem Koolhaas and Hans Ulrich Obrist, *Project Japan: Metabolism Talks* (Cologne: Taschen, 2011).

Alexandros-Andreas Kyrtsis, *Constantinos A. Doxiadis: Texts, Design Drawings, Settlements* (Athens: Ikaros, 2006).

Ioanna Laliotou, *Ιστορία του μέλλοντος: πως ο εικοστός αιώνας φαντάστηκε έναν 'άλλο κόσμο'* [*History of the Future History: How Did the Twentieth Century Imagine an "Other World"?*] (Athens: Historein, 2015).

Michael. E. Latham, *The Right Kind of Revolution: Modernization, Development and US Foreign Policy from the Cold War to the Present* (Ithaca, NY and London: Cornell University Press, 2010).

Ali Madanipour, "The Limits of Scientific Planning: Doxiadis and the Tehran Action Plan," *Planning Perspectives* 25, no. 4 (2010), 485–504.

Margaret Mead, *Cultural Patterns and Technical Change* (Paris: UNESCO, 1953).

David A. Mindell, *Digital Apollo* (Cambridge, MA: MIT Press, 2008).

Eric Mumford, "CIAM Urbanism after the Athens Charter," *Planning Perspectives* 7 (1992), 391–417.
—— *The CIAM Discourse on Urbanism, 1928–1960* (Cambridge, MA: MIT Press, 2002).

Ijlal Muzaffar, "Boundary Games: Ecochard, Doxiadis, and the Refugee Housing Projects under Military Rule in Pakistan, 1953–1959," in Aggregate Architectural History Collaborative (ed.), *Governing by Design: Architecture, Economy, and Politics in the Twentieth Century* (Pittsburgh, PA: University of Pittsburgh Press, 2012), 142–78.

Inderjeet Parmer, *Foundations of the American Century: The Ford, Carnegie, and Rockefeller Foundations in the Rise of American Power* (New York: Columbia University Press, 2012).

Chaïm Perelman, *The New Rhetoric and the Humanities* (Dordrecht and Boston, MA: D. Reidel Publishing Company, 1979).

Dimitris Philippides, *Κωνσταντίνος Δοξιάδης (1913–1975): Αναφορά στον Ιππόδαμο* [*Constantinos Doxiadis (1913–1975): Reference to Hippodamus*] (Athens: Melissa Books, 2015).

Petros Phokaides, "De-tropicalising Africa: Architecture, Planning, and Climate in the 1950s and the 1960s," *Docomomo Journal* 48, no. 1 (2013), 76–82.
—— "Rural Networks and Planned Communities: Doxiadis Associates' Plans for Rural Settlements in Post-Independence Zambia," *Journal of Architecture* (April 2018), 472–97.

Panayiota Pyla, "Gray-Areas in Green Politics: Reflections on the Modern Environmental Movement," *Thresholds* 14 (Spring 1997), 48–53.
—— "Ekistics, Architecture and Environmental Politics, 1945–1976: A Prehistory of Sustainable Development," Ph.D. dissertation, Massachusetts Institute of Technology, 2002.

—— "Hassan Fathy Revisited: Postwar Discourses on Science, Development and Vernacular Architecture," *Journal of Architectural Education* 3, no. 60 (2007), 28–39.
—— "Back to the Future: Doxiadis's Plans for Baghdad," *Journal of Planning History* 7, no. 1 (2008), 3–19.
—— "Baghdad's Urban Restructuring, 1958: Aesthetics and Politics of Nation Building," in Sandy Isenstadt and Kishwar Rizvi (eds), *Modernism and the Middle East: Architecture and Politics in the Twentieth Century* (Seattle: University of Washington Press, 2008), 97–115.
—— "Counter-Histories of Sustainability," *Volume #18: After Zero* (December 2008), 14–17.
—— "Planetary Home and Garden: Ekistics and Environmental–Developmental Politics," *Grey Room*, no. 36 (Summer 2009), 6–35.
—— "Architects as Development Experts," in Panayiota Pyla (ed.), *Landscapes of Development: The Impact of Modernization Discourses on the Physical Environment of the Eastern Mediterranean* (Cambridge, MA: Harvard University Press, 2013), 6–15.
—— "Gossip on the Doxiadis 'Gossip Square': Unpacking the Histories of an Unglamorous Public Space," *Architectural Histories* 1, no. 1 (December 2013), 1–6.
—— "Delos Symposion: Leaving Earth to Save It," in Giovanna Borasi (ed.), *The Other Architect* (Leipzig and Montreal: Spector Books and Center for Canadian Architecture, 2015), 270–73.
—— "Constantinos A. Doxiadis and His Entopia: Promises of a Moderate Utopia and a Humanized Modernism," *FAM Magazine* 47 (January–March 2019), 96–107.

Panayiota Pyla and Giannis Papadopoulos, "Doxiadis's One Big Pan-Africa," in Benno Albrecht (ed.), *Africa: Big Change, Big Chance* (Bologna: Editrice Compositori, 2014), 67–70.

Jonathan Reynolds, *Maekawa Kunio and the Emergence of Japanese Modernist Architecture* (Berkeley: University of California Press, 2001).

Simon Richards, *Architect Knows Best: Environmental Determinism in Architecture Culture from 1956 to the Present* (London: Ashgate, 2012).
—— "'Halfway between the Electron and the Universe': Doxiadis and the Delos Symposia," in Gerald Adler, Timothy Brittain-Catlin and Gordana Fontana-Giusti (eds), *Scale: Imagination, Perception and Practice in Architecture* (London: Routledge, 2012), 170–81.

Max Risselada and Dirk Van den Heuvel (eds), *Team 10: 1953-1981: In Search of a Utopia of the Present* (Rotterdam: Nai Publishers, 2005).

Hashim Sarkis, "Dances with Margaret Mead: Planning Beirut since 1958," in Peter Rowe and Hashim Sarkis (eds), *Projecting Beirut: Episodes in the Construction and Reconstruction of a Modern City* (New York: Prestel, 1998), 187–201.
—— *Circa 1958: Lebanon in the Pictures and Plans of Constantinos Doxiadis* (Beirut: Dar An-Nahar, 2003).

Hashim Sarkis, Roi Salgueiro Barrio with Gabriel Kozlowski, *The World as an Architectural Project* (Cambridge, MA and London: MIT Press, 2019).

Saboohi Sarshar, "Power and Identity: The Case of Islamabad," *Journal of Urban History* 45, no. 2 (2019 [2017]), 247–64.

Ellen Shoshkes, "East-West: Interactions between the United States and Japan and Their Effect on Utopian Realism," *Journal of Planning History* 3, no. 3 (August 2004), 215–40.
—— "Jaqueline Tyrwhitt: A Founding Mother of Modern Urban Design," *Planning Perspectives* 21, no. 2 (April 2006), 179–97.
—— *Jaqueline Tyrwhitt: A Transnational Life in Urban Planning and Design* (London and New York: Routledge, 2016).
—— "Jaqueline Tyrwhitt Translates Patrick Geddes for Post-World War Two Planning," *Landscape and Urban Planning* 166 (2017), 15–24.

Alison Smithson (ed.), "Team 10 Primer," *Architectural Design* 32, no. 2 (1962), 559–602.

Łukasz Stanek, *Architecture in Global Socialism: Eastern Europe, West Africa, and the Middle East in the Cold War* (Princeton, NJ: Princeton University Press, 2020).

Ioanna Theocharopoulou, *Builders, Housewives and the Construction of Modern Athens* (London: Artifice Books, 2017).

Lefteris Theodosis, "'Containing' Baghdad: Constantinos Doxiadis' Program for a Developing Nation," in P. Azara (ed.), *Ciudad del espejismo: Bagdad, de Wright a Venturi* [*City of Mirages: Baghdad, from Wright to Venturi*] (Barcelona: Universitat Politecnica de Catalunya, Departament de Composicio Arquitectonica, 2008), 167–72.
—— "Previendo el Pasado – El Plan 'Doxiadis' para Detroit y el futuro de la Megalópolis de los Grandes Lagos," in Román Caracciolo, Pablo Elinbaum, Biel Horrach and Mariana Debat (eds), *La metropolis Iberoamericana en sus propios terminos* (Barcelona: RIURB Editores, 2013), 157–79.
—— "Systemic Methods and Large-Scale Models in Ekistics," *Nexus Network Journal* 23 (2020), 171–86.

Ines Tolić, "News from the Modern Front: Constantinos A. Doxiadis's *Ekistics*, the United Nations, and the Post-war Discourse on Housing, Building and Planning," *Planning Perspectives* 37, no. 5 (2022), 973–99.

Panayiotis Tournikiotis, "Η αρχαία και η μοντέρνα πόλη στο έργο του Κωνσταντίνου Δοξιάδη [The Ancient and the Modern City in the Work of Constantinos Doxiadis]," in A. Defner, F. Loikissa, M. Marmaras, S. Tsilenis and V. Chastaoglou (eds), *Η πολεοδομία στην Ελλάδα από το 1949 έως το 1974: Πρακτικά του 2ου Συνεδρίου Εταιρείας Ιστορίας της Πόλης και της Πολεοδομίας* [*Urban Planning in Greece from 1949 to 1979: Proceedings of the 2nd Conference of the Society of the History of the City and Urban Planning*] (Volos: University Press of Thessaly, 2000), 85–98.
—— "Ancient and Modern Cities in the Work of Constantinos Doxiadis," in *The Modern City Facing the Future: Conference Proceedings: Sixth International Docomomo Conference. Brasilia, September 19-22, 2000* (São Carlos: Docomomo International, 2004) 97–112.
—— "Ο Οικισμός 'Άσπρα Σπίτια': Η κληρονομιά του Κ. Α. Δοξιάδη [The Settlement of Aspra Spitia: The Heritage of C. A. Doxiadis]," in G. Kazazi and N. Gounari (eds), *Ο Κωνσταντίνος Δοξιάδης και το έργο του, δεύτερος τόμος* [*Constantinos Doxiadis and His Work*] (Athens: Technical Chamber of Greece, 2009), vol. 2, 209–28.

Arnold J. Toynbee, *Cities on the Move* (New York: Oxford University Press, 1970).

Kostas Tsiambaos, "Isotype Diagrams from Neurath to Doxiadis," *arq: Architectural Research Quarterly* 16, no. 1 (2012), 49–57.
—— *From Doxiadis' Theory to Pikionis' Work: Reflections of Antiquity in Modern Architecture* (Oxford: Routledge, 2018).

Rosemary Wakeman, *Practicing Utopia. An Intellectual History of the New Town Movement* (Chicago: University of Chicago Press, 2016).

Barbara Ward, *Spaceship Earth* (New York: Columbia University Press, 1966).

Mark Wigley, "Network Fever," *Grey Room*, no. 4 (Summer 2001), 82–122.

Mantha Zarmakoupi, "Balancing Acts between Ancient and Modern Cities: The Ancient Greek Cities Project of C. A. Doxiadis," *Architectural Histories* 3, no. 1 (December 2015), 1–22.

—— "Die Hafenstadt Delos," in F. Pirson, S. Ladstätter and T. Schmidt (eds), *Häfen und Hafenstädte im östlichen Mittelmeerraum von der Antike bis in byzantinische Zeit. Aktuelle Entdeckungen und neue Forschungsansätze*, Byzas 14 (Istanbul: Zero Books, 2015), 553–70.

—— "Hellenistic & Roman Delos: The City & Its Emporion," *Archaeological Reports* 61 (2015), 115–32.

—— "Τόπος και εντοπία: τα Συμπόσια της Δήλου [Topos and Entopia: The Symposia of Delos]," in D. I. Kyrtatas, I. Konstantopoulos and C. Boulotis (eds), *Τόπος Τοπίο, Τιμητικός Τόμος για τον Δημήτρη Φιλιππίδη* [*Topos Topio, Honorary Volume for Dimitris Philippides*] (Athens: Melissa Books, 2018), 63–70.

—— "The Urban Development of Late Hellenistic Delos," in Daniel Millette and Samantha Martin-McAuliffe (eds), *Ancient Urban Planning in the Mediterranean: New Research Directions* (London: Ashgate, 2018), 28–49.

—— "Shaping the City of Late Hellenistic Delos," *Journal of Ancient Architecture* 1 (2022), 65–85.

—— "The Blue Marble of Greek Architectural History: Delos and the Delos Symposia," in M. Zarmakoupi (ed.), *Looking at the City: Architectural and Archaeological Perspectives* (Athens: Melissa Books, 2023).

Yannis Zavoleas, *Η Μηχανή και το Δίκτυο ως Δομικά Πρότυπα στην Αρχιτεκτονική* [*Machine and Network as Structural Models in Architecture*] (Athens: Futura, 2013).

Image Credits

Acronyms
CADA = Constantinos A. Doxiadis Archives,
© Constantinos and Emma Doxiadis Foundation.
CDAA = Capital Development Authority Archives, Islamabad.

Cover
CADA, Photographs 34172, photos 566 [back cover] and 766 [front cover]; adapted from CADA, *Ekistics* 20, no. 119 (October 1965), cover [back flap]; Mantha Zarmakoupi, after J.-C. Moretti, L. Fadin, M. Fincker and V. Picard, *L'atlas de Délos, exploration archéologique de Délos* 43 (Athens: École française d'Athènes, 2015), plate 5 [front flap].

Introduction
1 CADA, Photographs 34172, photo 766.
2 CADA, *Ekistics* 16, no. 95 (October 1963), 235.
3 Mantha Zarmakoupi, after J.-C. Moretti, L. Fadin, M. Fincker and V. Picard, *L'atlas de Délos, exploration archéologique de Délos* 43 (Athens: École française d'Athènes, 2015), plate 5.
4 CADA, Photographs 34172, photo 496.
5 CADA, Photographs 34172, photo 566.
6 CADA, Photographs 34204, photo 386.
7 CADA, Photographs 34204, photo 384.
8 CADA, *Ekistics* 32, no. 191 (October 1971).
9 Photo: Mantha Zarmakoupi.

History as a Framework
1 CADA, Photographs 34172, photo 496.
2 CADA, Photographs 31252.
3 CADA, *Ekistics* 16, no. 95 (October 1963).
4 Photo: Mantha Zarmakoupi.
5 CADA, Covers of the twenty-four published volumes of the AGC research project; photo collage by Mantha Zarmakoupi.
6 CADA, *DA Monthly Bulletin*, no. 64 (March 1964).
7 CADA, D-GEN-A 11500/44, File 2701.
8 CADA, Lawrence Halprin, "The Landscape as Matrix: Macro & Micro Infrastructures," Document B, no. 54, July 15, 1971, ATO / ACE AEM 1971, File 2545.
9. CADA, *Ekistics* 34, no. 203 (October 1972), 241–45.
10 © David Rumsey Map Collection.
11–12 CADA, J. Papaioannou, "Outline of Chronology of Sites in the Area of the Tour," Document C, no. 4, July 1, 1970, ATO / ACE AEM 1970, File 2532.

The Past as a Stage Set for C. A. Doxiadis
1 CADA, Photographs 31252.
2 Courtesy of Pikionis family archive, Greece.
3 https://www.ahistoryofgreece.com/biography/kazantzakis.htm.
4 http://alis.reasonablegraph.org/archive/item/2315.
5 el.wikipedia.org/wiki/Κωστής_Μπαστιάς.
6 *Εθνικό Θέατρο: Τα πρώτα χρόνια (1930–1941)* [*National Theater: The Early Years (1930–1941)*] (Athens: ΜΙΕΤ, 2013).
7 https://www.in.gr/2023/11/15/istoriko-arxeio/manolis-triantafyllidis-protypo-zois.

Some Rhetorical Aspects of the Delos Symposia
1 CADA, File 6977; © F.L.C. / 2024, ProLitteris, Zurich.
2 CADA, File 2677.
3–4 CADA, File 6977.
5 CADA, Photographs 31476.
6 Sourced from CADA, File 2677.
7 CADA, File 22831, Folder I.
8 Sourced from CADA, Video 29147.

East–West: The Delos Dialogue with Japanese Urbanism
1 CADA, "Pergamon. Athena Terrasse, in C. A. Doxiadis, *Die Raumgestaltung im griechischen Städtebau*, thesis, Berlin Charlottenburg Technical University, May 1936, fig. 41.
2 CADA, *Ekistics* 12, no. 69 (July 1961), 13.
3 CADA, File 28560.
4 CADA, "Modern Cities: A Jungle of Buildings," *Ekistics* 15 (June 1963), 362.
5 CADA, D-COF 1066, File 26409.
6 CADA, *Ekistics* 25, no. 147 (February 1968), 77.

7 CADA, *Ekistics* 25, no. 150 (May 1968), 291.
8 CADA, *Ekistics* 48, no. 289 (July/August 1981).

Delos and "The Human Factor"
1 CADA, *Ekistics* 19, no. 110 (January 1965), 3.
2 CADA, "The Delians," *Ekistics* 18, no. 107 (October 1964), 251–66, Photographs 31159, photo 3.
3 CADA, Sigfried Giedion, Robert Matthew, Joseph Watterson and H. S. Perloff, "Qualities of Density," *Ekistics* 20, no. 119 (October 1965), 208–13, Photographs 31160, photo 56.
4 CADA, "Urban Life: Its Values and the Problems It Faces," *Ekistics* 22, no. 131 (October 1966), 244–53, diagram 252.
5 CADA, "Points Made in Discussion," *Ekistics* 24, no. 143 (October 1967), 325–30, diagram 325.
6 CADA, C. A. Doxiadis and R. Buckminster Fuller, "Introduction: Report of Delos 7," *Ekistics* 28, no. 167 (October 1969), 215–22, diagram 220.

Ecology, Ekistics and the "Texture of Settlements"
1 CADA, "India. Report and Photographs, Jan–Feb 1954," File 24965, photo 4.19.
2 Photo: © United Nations.
3 CADA, "India. Report and Photographs, Jan-Feb 1954," File 24965, photo I.31.
4–5 CADA, "India. Report and Photographs, Jan-Feb 1954," File 24965, photos 5.11–5.12
6 CADA, "Lebanon, Survey District 2, Akkar Area," R-LB 55, p. 183, File 24906, photo P-LB 58/33.
7 CADA, "Lebanon, Survey District 2, Akkar Area," R-LB 55, p. 169, File 24906, photo P-LB 58/1.
8 CADA, "Lebanon, Survey District 2, Akkar Area," R-LB 55, p. 205, File 24906, photo P-LB 70/36.
9 CADA, "Lebanon, Survey District 1, Tripoli and Surrounding Area," R-LB 17, p. 269, File 24905, photo P-LB 21/32.
10–11 CADA, "Lebanon, Survey District 2, Akkar Area," R-LB 55, p. 115, File 24906, photos P-LB 65/16–17.
12–14 CADA, "Lebanon, Survey District 1, Tripoli and Surrounding Area," R-LB 17, p. 239, File 24905.
15 CADA, "Lebanon, Survey District 2, Akkar Area," R-LB 55, p. 222, File 24906, photo P-LB 71/A; Photo: Panagis Psomopoulos.
16 CADA, "Lebanon Survey District 13, Baalbek Area," R-LB 108, vol. 1, File 24919, photo P-LB 207/12.

Infrastructuring Development
1 CADA, "Dynapolis: The City of the Future," R-GA 185, p. 51, Articles-Papers 2529.
2 CADA, D-COF 5, File 19866.
3 CADA, D-COF 1298, Maps & Drawings 25822.
4 CADA, *DA Monthly Bulletin*, no. 63 (February 1964), File 35409.
5 CADA, R-ERES 6, File 17351.
6 CADA, D-COF 1115, Maps & Drawings 25822.
7 CADA, *DA Monthly Bulletin*, no. 65 (April 1964), File 35409.

Basic Democracy and Doxiadis Associates' School-Reformation Project in East Pakistan
1 CADA, "Pakistan," vol. 4, January–February 1955, DOX-PP 40, p. 69, File 23556.
2–3 CADA, "Pakistan," vol. 3, January 1955, DOX-PP 21, p. 51, File 23555.
4 CADA, "Pakistan," vol. 4, January–February 1955, DOX-PP 40, p. 179, File 23556.
5 CADA, "Pakistan," vol. 128, August 4, 1962, Survey Sheet 71 B and 75 A, DOX-PA 183, pp. 60–61, File 23659.
6 CADA, "Pakistan," vol. 128, August 1, 1962, DOX-PA 184, p. 13, File 23659.
7 CADA, "Pakistan," vol. 128, August 1, 1962, DOX-PA 184, p. 5, File 23659.
8 CADA, "Pakistan," vol. 128, August 1, 1962, DOX-PA 184, p. 3, File 23659.
9 CADA, "Pakistan," vol. 129, August 1, 1962, DOX-PA 185, p. 47, File 23660.
10 CADA, "Pakistan," vol. 129, March 21, 1962, DOX-PA 165, p. 51, File 23660.

Shaping Ekistics
1 CADA, Photographs 30069, photo P-QA 3.18.
2 CADA, C.A. Doxiadis, "No More Regional Planning: A Move towards Regional Development Programs," 1958, File 2509.
3 CADA, booklet issued by the Development Board, Ministry of Development of the Government of Iraq and Doxiadis Associates, File 25320.
4 Doxiadis Associates, *Emergence and Growth of an Urban Region, the Developing Urban Detroit Area*, vol. 3, *A Concept for Future Development* (Detroit, MI: The Detroit Edison Company, 1970), 157, figs. 203–6.
5 J. Palaiokrassas, "C. A. Doxiadis' Way of Working in USA," in Giota Kazazi and N. Gounari (eds), *Ο Κωνσταντίνος Δοξιάδης και το έργο του, δεύτερος τόμος* [*Constantinos Doxiadis and His Work*] (Athens: Technical Chamber of Greece, 2009), vol. 1, 66.
6 CADA, C. A. Doxiadis, *Ekistics: An Introduction to the Science of Human Settlements* (New York: Oxford University Press, 1968), 388, fig. 387.
7 CADA, "USA," vol. 128, DOX-USA-WS 58, p. 79, File 23519.
8 CADA, C. A. Doxiadis, *Architecture in Transition* (New York: Oxford University Press, 1963), 102, fig. 35.
9 CADA, C. A. Doxiadis, *Architecture in Transition* (New York: Oxford University Press, 1963), 109, fig. 40a.
10 CADA, "The Master Plan of Baghdad," *DA Monthly Bulletin* 9 (January 1960).
11 CADA, "Iraq," vol. 88, File 23970, photo P-QA 436.33A.
12–13 Doxiadis Associates, *Emergence and Growth of an Urban Region, the Developing Urban Detroit Area*, vol. 3, *A Concept for Future Development* (Detroit, MI: The Detroit Edison Company, 1970), 305, figs. 337–38.
14 CADA, 1962, DOX-UA 6, p. 191, File 6471.

15 Doxiadis Associates, *Emergence and Growth of an Urban Region, the Developing Urban Detroit Area*, vol. 3, *A Concept for Future Development* (Detroit, MI: The Detroit Edison Company, 1970), 281, fig. 316.

The Visionary in the Marsh
1 CADA, *DA Monthly Bulletin*, no. 51 (January 1963).
2 Photo: Harrison Blackman.
3 CADA, Photographs 32964.
4–5 CADA, *DA Monthly Bulletin*, no. 51 (January 1963).
6 CADA, File 25363.
7 CADA, *DA Monthly Bulletin,* no. 6 (October 1959).

Metacriticisms of Ekistics' Environmental Design
1 CADA, "DA Int. Profile (1972)," File 35840.
2 CADA, Photographs 34200, photo 86.
3 CADA, Photographs 34176, photo 90.
4 CADA, Printed card, File 36434.
5 CADA, Articles–Papers 6378.
6 "Free and Real – The Telaithrion Project," courtesy of Free and Real, https://www.facebook.com/FreeandReal.

Urban Ecosystems and Global Ecological Balance
1 CADA, "Pakistan," vol. 16, DOX-PA 33, p. 7, File 23567.
2 CADA, DOX-PA 168, p. 67, File 36570.
3 CADA, *DA Monthly Bulletin*, no. 64 (1964).
4 CDAA, Socio-economic Survey report, GOP/FCC 1960, p. 2.
5–6 CDAA; Ahmed Z. Khan, "Constantinos A. Doxiadis' Plan for Islamabad: The Making of a 'City of the Future' 1959–1963," Ph.D. dissertation, KU Leuven, April 2008, 63, fig. 4.14.
7 Ahmed Z. Khan, "Constantinos A. Doxiadis' Plan for Islamabad: The Making of a 'City of the Future' 1959–1963," Ph.D. dissertation, KU Leuven, April 2008, 172, fig. 7.34.
8 Ahmed Z. Khan, "Constantinos A. Doxiadis' Plan for Islamabad: The Making of a 'City of the Future' 1959–1963," Ph.D. dissertation, KU Leuven, April 2008, 169, fig. 7.29.
9 CDAA; Ahmed Z. Khan, "Constantinos A. Doxiadis' Plan for Islamabad: The Making of a 'City of the Future' 1959–1963," Ph.D. dissertation, KU Leuven, April 2008, 170, fig. 7.31.
10 Ahmed Z. Khan, "Constantinos A. Doxiadis' Plan for Islamabad: The Making of a 'City of the Future' 1959–1963," Ph.D. dissertation, KU Leuven, April 2008, 173, fig. 7.34a.
11 Sourced from CADA, File 17820; Doxiadis Associates, *Emergence and Growth of an Urban Region, the Developing Urban Detroit Area*, vol. 3, *A Concept for Future Development* (Detroit, MI: The Detroit Edison Company, 1970), 280, fig. 316.
12–14 Ahmed Z. Khan.
15 CADA, C. A. Doxiadis. *Anthropopolis: City for Human Development* (New York: Norton, 1974), 115.
16 CADA, C. A. Doxiadis. *Between Dystopia and Utopia* (London: Faber and Faber, 1966), 80.
17 CADA, C. A. Doxiadis, *Building Entopia* (Athens: Athens Publishing Center, 1975), 234–35, 250–51.
18 Ahmed Z. Khan, based on C. A. Doxiadis, *Action for Human Settlements* (New York: Norton, 1976), 171; C. A. Doxiadis, *Ecology and Ekistics*, edited by Gerald Dix (London: Paul Elek Ltd and Boulder, CO: Westview Press, 1977), 17–37.
19 Ahmed Z. Khan.
20 Ahmed Z. Khan, based on C. A. Doxiadis, *Building Entopia* (Athens: Athens Publishing Center, 1975), 55.

Bio-systemic Thinking for Holistic Design
1–2 CADA, File 17739.
3 CADA, 1961, File 22663.
4 CADA, "The Two Headed-eagle [sic]: From the Past to the Future of Human Settlements," 1972, pp. 50–51.
5 CADA, *Ekistics* 14, no. 84 (1962), 195.
6 CADA, *Ekistics* 29, no. 174 (May 1970), 300.
7 CADA, *Ekistics* 22 (July 1966).
8 CADA, File 17752.

Japanese Delos in 27 Points
1 CADA, *Ekistics* 16, no. 95 (October 1963).
2 Wikimedia Commons.
3 Jean-Luc Godard, *De l'origine du XXIe siècle,* 2000.
4 Udo Kultermann (ed.), *Kenzo Tange* (New York: Praeger, 1970), 266–67.
5 Udo Kultermann (ed.), *Kenzo Tange* (New York: Praeger, 1970), 159.
6 CADA, Alexandros-Andreas Kyrtsis (ed.), *Κωνσταντίνος Α. Δοξιάδης: Κείμενα/Σχέδια/Οικισμοί* [*Constantinos A. Doxiadis: Texts, Design Drawings, Settlements*] (Athens: Ikaros Publishing, 2006), 20.
7 CADA, *Ekistics* 16, no. 95 (October 1963), 226.
8 CADA, *Ekistics* 16, no. 95 (October 1963).
9 Udo Kultermann (ed.), *Kenzo Tange* (New York: Praeger, 1970), 263.
10 Udo Kultermann (ed.), *Kenzo Tange* (New York: Praeger, 1970), 121.
11 Courtesy of Mercedes-Benz Classic.
12 CADA, Alexandros-Andreas Kyrtsis (ed.), *Κωνσταντίνος Α. Δοξιάδης: Κείμενα/Σχέδια/Οικισμοί* [*Constantinos A. Doxiadis: Texts, Design Drawings, Settlements*] (Athens: Ikaros Publishing, 2006), 111.
13 Berlin Academy of the Arts.
14 Ron Herron: © 2024, ProLitteris, Zurich.
15 https://pascalrudelphotography.com/2019/05/17/grece-delos.
16 Udo Kultermann (ed.), *Kenzo Tange* (New York: Praeger, 1970), 121.
17 Udo Kultermann (ed.), *Kenzo Tange* (New York: Praeger, 1970), 275.
18 Udo Kultermann (ed.), *Kenzo Tange* (New York: Praeger, 1970), 280.
19 Udo Kultermann (ed.), *Kenzo Tange* (New York: Praeger, 1970), 287.

20 Tanaka Kakuei, *Building a New Japan* (Tokyo: Simul Press, 1972).
21 Pascal Guyot / AFP / Getty Images.
22 Jean-Luc Godard, *De l'origine du XXIe siècle*, 2000.
23 Utagawa Toyoharu / National Museum of Asian Art, Smithsonian Institution, Freer Collection, Gift of Charles Lang Freer, F1900.113.
24 Rem Koolhaas and Hans Ulrich Obrist, *Project Japan: Metabolism Talks* (Cologne: Taschen, 2011), 524–25. Courtesy of the Institute of Aesthetic Research.
25 Odd Andersen / AFP / Getty Images.
26 Michael Rougier / The LIFE Picture Collection / Shutterstock.
27 Keystone / Hulton Archive / Getty Images.

Doxiadis Associates' Master Plan for Skopje and the Global Ecological Balance

1 CADA, C. A. Doxiadis, *Ekistics: An Introduction to the Science of Human Settlements* (New York: Oxford University Press, 1968), 56, fig. 42.
2 Google Earth: Landsat/Copernicus, © Airbus / © 2024 Maxar Technologies.
3 Google Earth: Landsat/Copernicus, © Airbus / © 2024 Maxar Technologies; drawing: doxiadis+, 2019.
4 CADA, "Outline Plan for the City of Skopje," vol. 1, p. 9, August 14, 1964, DOX-YUG-A 1.
5 CADA, C. A. Doxiadis, "Man's Movement and His Settlements," *Ekistics* 29, no. 174 (1970), p. 317.
6 CADA, "Outline Plan for the City of Skopje," vol. 2, p. 29, August 14, 1964, DOX-YUG-A 1.
7 Google Earth: Landsat/Copernicus, © 2018 DigitalGlobe.
8 Google Earth: Landsat/Copernicus, © 2018 DigitalGlobe; drawing: doxiadis+, 2019.
9 CADA, "Outline Plan for the City of Skopje," vol. 1, p. 17, August 14, 1964, DOX-YUG-A 1.
10 doxiadis+, 2019.
11 doxiadis+, 2019.
12 CADA, "Outline Plan for the City of Skopje," vol. 1, p. 187, August 14, 1964, DOX-YUG-A 1.
13 CADA, "Outline Plan for the City of Skopje," vol. 1, p. 279, August 14, 1964, DOX-YUG-A 1.
14 Google Earth: © 2018 DigitalGlobe.
15 Google Earth: © 2018 DigitalGlobe / © 2018 CNES/Airbus; drawing: doxiadis+, 2019.
16 doxiadis+, 2019.
17–18 Google Earth: © 2018 DigitalGlobe; drawing: doxiadis+, 2019.
19 CADA, C. A. Doxiadis, *Ekistics: An Introduction to the Science of Human Settlements* (New York: Oxford University Press, 1968), 351, fig. 349.
20 Google Earth: © 2024 CNES/Airbus.
21 doxiadis+, 2019.
22 CADA, "Skopje: Master Plan," Slides 10684, no. 1685; CADA. "Outline Plan for the City of Skopje," vol. 1, p. 315, August 14, 1964, DOX-YUG-A 1, DOX-YUG-A 30100/107.
23 CADA, "Outline Plan for the City of Skopje," vol. 2, p. 303, August 14, 1964, DOX-YUG-A 1.
24 CADA, DOX-YUG-S 30302/96.
25 CADA, DOX-YUG-S 30302/97.
26 CADA, "Skopje urban plan: report on transportation," p. 101, September 30, 1965, DOX-YUG-A 5.
27 CADA, "Skopje urban plan: report on infrastructure highway and street system," p. 5, September 30, 1965, DOX-YUG-A 5.
28 doxiadis+, 2019.
29 Google Earth: © 2018 DigitalGlobe / © 2018 CNES/Airbus; drawing: doxiadis+, 2019.
30 Google Earth: Landsat/Copernicus, © 2024 Airbus.
31 CADA, "Outline Plan for the City of Skopje," vol. 2, p. 353, August 14, 1964, DOX-YUG-A 1, DOX-YUG-A 30100/108.

The Three Antiquities of C. A. Doxiadis and the Road to Eutopia

1–7 CADA, File 18469.
8 CADA, C. A. Doxiadis, *Between Dystopia and Utopia* (London: Faber and Faber, 1966).
9 CADA, C. A. Doxiadis, *Between Dystopia and Utopia* (London: Faber and Faber, 1966), 80, fig. 30.
10 CADA.
11 Le Corbusier, *La maison des hommes* (Paris: Plon, 1942), p. 69; © F.L.C. / 2024, ProLitteris, Zurich.
12 CADA, Slides 13646, no. 4649.
13–15 CADA, File 18705.

We have made every effort to identify all relevant rights holders. In those instances where we have not been able to locate and/or notify the rights holder(s), we ask that they contact the author or publisher.

Index

Aalto, Alvar 90, 249
Academy of Neuroscience for Architecture (ANFA) 162
Acropolis (Athens) 59, 74, 115, 130, 467, 469, *470–72*, 475
Activism 149, 378
Aegean Sea 13, 46, 63–64, 99, 107, 480
Africa 9, 25–26, 28, 89, 111, 153, 191–93, 195, 198, 202–5, *210*, 212, 214, 258, 334, *369*
Africa Transport Plan (ATP) 26, 192, 204, 205, *207*, 214
Agriculture 84, 142, 171, 221–22, 224, 242, 252, 254, 324, 347, 349, 354, *355*, 356, 365, 368, 371–72, *375*, 376, 379, *397*, 461
Alexander, Christopher 134, 137
Alpha Mission ΔELOS *35*, 36
American Institute of Architects (AIA) 96, 162
Ancient Greek Cities Project (AGC) 7, 9, 50, 51, *52*, 59, 82, 465, 468, 475–77
Anthropics 152–54
Anthropocene 65, 110
Anthropocene Working Group (AWG) 65
Anthropocentrism 313, 331, 458
Anthropogenic 65
Antiquities 32–33, 183–84, *185*, 465, 468, 480
Antiquity 22, 73–78, 81–83, 85, 415, 467, 468–69, 472, 475, 477–78, 480
Apollo (Greek god) 7, 13, 45–46, *49*, 68, 97, 107–8, 110, 465, 480
Apollo (US space mission) 63–64, 108–9, *109*, 110, 112–13, 157
Archaeology 7, 9, 12–13, 22, 33, 36, 45–46, 58–59, 68, 71, 79, 87, 94, 101, 108, 130, 184, 185, 320, 466, 468, 470, 475–77, 479–80
Architectural Association (AA) 10
Archive of Modern Greek Architecture (ANA) 78
Arendt, Hannah 222
Aristotle 82, 86, 89, 105, 107, 159, *473*
Artificial intelligence 148
Asian Highway 26, 192, 208, 211, *211*
Asian Planning and Architecture Consultants (APAC) 136

Aspra Spitia 56–57, 71, 85, 472
Association for Planning and Regional Reconstruction (APRR) 10
Athens 9–10, 13, 31, 43, 45, *56*, 57, 64, 69, 74, 78, 84, 86–87, 90–91, 96, 105, 113–14, 122–24, 130, 170–71, 179, 186, 198, 202, 219, 246, 279, 285, 292, 379, 395, 465–66, 468–69, *470–72*, 475, 478, 480
Athens Center of Ekistics (ACE) 10, 24, 50, 82–83, 114, 126, *127*, 129, 134, 139, 250, 268, 392, 412, 466
Athens Charter 12, 44, 69, 90, 91, 146, 318, 328, 335, 379, 413
Athens Technological Institute (ATI) 10, 50, 99, 127, *149*, 200, 285, 468
Athens Technological Organization (ATO) 10, 50
Authoritarianism 26, 218–21, 240
Ayub Khan, Muhammad 26, 218, 220–22, 228, 240, 243
Bacon, Edmund N. 28, 38, *45*, 69, 155, 259, 291, 295–97, 304–5, 340, 361
Bacon, Ruth 99
Baghdad 27, 249, 252–54, *253*, 256, 258, 265, 268, *269*, 270, *271–73*, 278–80, 299, 355
Basic Democracy 26, 217, 220–22, 240, 245
Basic Foundation Program (BFP) 254
Bastias, Kostas 73, *83*, 83–84
Behavioral sciences 154
Bellamy, Edward 32, 473
Benello, George 156
Bertalanffy, Ludwig von 395
Biodiversity 31, 349, 355, 374, *375*, 378, 442, 454, 463
Biology 24, 43, 57, 115, 146, 154–55, 194, 251, 273, 320, 331, 339, *358*, 365, 374, *375*, 383, 386, 388–89, 395, 454, 461, 463
Biomimicry 32, 338
Brinkley, David 92, 94
Brohi, A. K. 146, *147*, *149*
Builders 175, *176*, 256, *257*
Building Research Establishment (BRE) 162, 163
Bureaucracy 150, 218, 223, 313, 318, 320, 324, 326, 334
Byzantine 64, 74, 475

498

Capital Development Authority (Pakistan) (CDA) 346, 380
Capitalism 26, 105, 126, 149, 322, 325, 330, 374
Carson, Rachel 439
Cavafy, C. P. 156
Center for International Studies (CIS) 193, 195, 212
Chandigarh 173, 176, 339, 468
Choisy, Auguste 470
Churchill, Henry 297
City of the Future (COF) 13, 58, 114, 198, 201, 202, 208, 209, 268, 279, 306, 342, 345, 372, 428, 440
Civil rights 12, 149
Classicism 12, 83, 86, 148
Clayton, James E. 96-98, 144
Cold War 26, 186, 193, 212, 218-19, 222-23, 251, 275, 278, 325
Communism 26, 186-87, 193, 195, 221, 223, 278, 280
Community 14, 16, 23, 28, 46, 56, 57, 82, 87, 98, 114-15, 120, 124, 126, 137, 143, 149, 150-52, 172, 173, 174, 175, 198, 217, 221, 226, 238, 241-42, 252, 254, 259-60, 266, 268, 270, 272, 278, 280, 283, 289-90, 292, 294-99, 300, 302, 303-5, 323, 328, 344, 358, 359, 360, 392, 415, 430, 432, 468, 471-72, 479
Community planning 11, 149, 152, 164, 259
Computing 10, 27, 30-31, 148, 262, 273, 385-86, 398-99, 402-6
Congrès Internationaux d'Architecture Moderne (CIAM) 10, 12-14, 36, 44-45, 57, 69, 71, 90-91, 104, 117-18, 120, 123, 135, 139, 142, 146, 150, 174, 188, 191, 246, 316, 318, 320, 335, 340, 358, 359, 361, 379, 380, 384, 395, 399, 406, 413, 415, 417, 420, 478
Congress of Cultural Freedom (CCF) 195, 198
Crane, David A. 293, 299
Crane, Jacob L. 38, 69, 173, 178, 186-88, 198, 213, 219, 244, 249, 252, 256, 279, 340
Cybernetics 146, 148, 388
Data 51, 58, 85, 100, 102, 155, 171-72, 178, 180, 182, 188, 228, 230, 232, 237, 243, 246, 255, 280, 344, 383, 388, 390, 391, 392, 396, 398-99, 402, 403-4, 442, 465
Davidoff, Robert 14, 147
Deane, Philip 92, 94, 95, 111, 279
Delos (island) 7, 9, 11, 13, 14, 17, 19, 20, 22-23, 32-33, 35, 36, 38, 44, 45-46, 49, 51, 68, 70, 89, 97, 104-5, 107-8, 113, 153, 465-66, 468, 470, 472, 477, 479, 480
Democracy 14, 26, 118, 195, 217-22, 237, 240, 245, 280, 420, 432-33, 470
Demographics 12, 14, 171, 180, 197, 198, 200-2, 304, 368, 370
Density 23, 74, 130, 211, 272, 274, 319, 327, 330, 333, 356, 358, 369, 373, 375, 376, 411, 424
Despo, Jan 31, 420, 421, 423, 424, 432, 433
Detroit 25, 27, 28, 249, 250, 251, 258-60, 261, 262-63, 263, 265, 272-73, 275, 277, 278-79, 281, 355, 357
Doxiadis Associates (DA) 6, 10-11, 20, 23, 25-32, 43, 56, 73, 79, 85, 89, 91, 96, 99, 102, 104, 122, 147, 159, 172, 178-79, 181, 184-86, 191, 198, 199, 200-4, 206-7, 208, 210-11, 218, 223-24, 228, 230, 237, 243, 250-54, 256, 258-59, 262, 266, 268, 270, 275, 278, 279-83, 285, 288, 289, 292, 293, 298, 299, 300, 302, 303-4, 306, 313, 316, 318, 322, 327, 340, 345, 355, 411, 439-43, 445, 448, 450, 454, 455, 458, 461, 463

Doxiadis Associates Computer Center (DACC) 262, 282
Duhl, Leonard 38, 69, 147
Dynapolis 27, 124, 125, 127, 198, 199, 200-3, 204, 208, 256, 265-68, 267, 270, 272, 275, 276, 278, 329, 360, 389
Dystopia 97, 367, 406, 473-74, 474-75, 478-79
Eastwick 27-28, 258, 272, 278, 283, 285, 287, 288, 289-99, 300, 302, 303-7
Ecological balance 29, 31, 314, 329, 329, 337, 363, 369, 373, 374, 381, 439
Ecology 9, 14, 23, 25, 29-31, 36-37, 57, 119-21, 123, 156, 160, 164, 169-170, 185, 187, 296, 314-16, 322-24, 326, 329, 329, 331, 334, 337, 339, 341-42, 349-50, 354, 355, 359, 363, 365, 366, 368, 369, 371-72, 373, 374, 378-79, 381, 392, 396, 403, 434, 439-42, 450, 454-55, 458, 463
Economic Commission for Asia and the Far East (ECAFE) 208
Economics 7, 27, 63, 74, 81, 119, 126, 129, 157, 162, 169, 174, 187, 191-95, 200-1, 205, 208, 210, 212, 218-23, 230, 237-38, 240, 243, 252, 254, 259-60, 262, 265, 272-73, 278, 282, 292, 296, 313-17, 322-23, 325-26, 331, 343, 347, 358, 361, 362, 370, 390, 392, 394, 428, 441
Ecumenokepos 275, 363, 365-68, 369
Ecumenopolis 27, 64, 104, 114-15, 124, 130, 132, 135, 136, 143, 150, 156, 208, 209-10, 210, 212, 215, 251, 259, 266, 267, 275, 279, 315, 329, 360, 361, 363, 365-68, 369, 370-71, 389, 417, 419, 419-21, 440, 441, 445, 479
Education 7, 10, 26, 27, 50, 62, 97, 108, 126, 142, 149, 155, 161, 169, 189, 183, 187, 189, 194, 201, 217-18, 220-26, 228, 230-31, 237-38, 240-44, 246, 250, 285, 297, 319, 358, 380, 398, 461
Ekistic Grid 143, 145, 163, 360
Ekistics (journal) 11, 12, 21, 24, 36, 38, 47, 59, 68, 82, 120, 121, 124, 125, 126, 129-31, 134, 136, 136-37, 138, 139, 142, 146, 189, 250, 285, 299, 379, 392, 397, 400, 408, 414-15, 415, 417, 423, 468
Ekistics (science) 10, 12, 23-25, 27-29, 33, 44, 50-51, 57, 89, 97, 101, 103-5, 118, 120, 121, 123, 128, 135, 136, 143-44, 147, 154, 169, 170, 172, 178, 184-88, 201, 218, 238, 241, 243, 249-50, 256, 259, 263, 265-66, 268, 272, 275, 278-79, 286, 297, 305, 313-18, 316, 322, 324-26, 334, 340-41, 356, 358, 359, 360, 361-63, 362, 365-68, 371, 380-81, 392-93, 394, 402, 408-9, 415, 415, 423, 440, 440-41, 476
Ekistics Logarithmic Scale (ELS) 361
Ekistics Month 43, 59, 60, 66, 142
Eliot, T. S. 156
Engineering 25, 36, 64, 90, 158, 170, 171, 178-79, 182, 214, 246, 250, 278-80, 285, 289, 335, 356, 361, 392, 441
Entopia 68, 72, 82, 110, 137, 327, 367-68, 371-72, 374, 474-75, 474-75, 479, 479

499

Entrepreneurialism 26, 73, 191, 197–98, 205, 242
Environmental determinism 22
Environmentalism 30, 251, 275, 322–23, 337
Environmental psychology 146
Ethics 154, 157, 159, 161–63, 314, 322–24, 326, 334, *386*
Eutopia 32, 115, 465, 473, 474, 477, 479
Evolution 23, 30, 51, 62, 117–18, 129–31, *132,* 137, *138,* 139, 146–48, 160, 163, 203, 212, 226, 238, 240–41, 261, 268, 270, 279, 341, *358,* 359, *360,* 363, 366–67, 385, 388, 390, 396, 399, 404, 422, 432, 439
Experimental Housing Program (EHP) 253–54
Expert 14, 16–17, 22, 26, 36, 43, 87, 99, 105, *106,* 111, 122, 126, *127,* 148, 154, 155, 157, 171–72, 175, *175,* 178–79, 188, 191–92, 197, 201–2, 219, 221–22, 224–25, 249–52, 258, 268, 213, 316, 318–19, 324–25, 329, 334, 340, 361, 383, 392–93, 398, 405
Extraterrestrial 147
Fahs, Charles Burton 91–92, 110–11
Faraklas, Nikolaos 476
Fathy, Hassan 202–5, *204,* 208, 283, 340
Folk art 78, 187, 226
Food 96–97, 108, 157, 320, 324, 330, 347, 349, 354, 365, 371, 375–76, 380
Ford Foundation 26, 91–92, 111, 114, 129, 130, 186, 195, 200–2, 205–6, 213–14, 218, 222–24, 242, 258–59, 380
Fuller, R. Buckminster 14, 36, 38, 44, 59, *61,* 62–64, *65,* 110, 113, 147–48, 156, 320, 340, 390, 395
Geddes, Patrick 24, 57, 115–18, 121–22, 135, 170, 174, 178, 188, *358,* 359, 361, 388, 439
Genetics 154–55, 157, 319, 340
Geology 65, 108, *358*
Ghana 38, 69, 153, 198, 201, 214, 245, 258
Ghyka, Matila 470, 481
Giedion, Sigfried 14, 38, 69, 90, 104, 119, 120–21, 130, 146, 150, *151,* 319, *319,* 340, 390, 395, 415, 418, 432
Gilpatric, Chadbourne 92
Global 9, 12–14, 16–17, 23–26, 29–30, 36, 89, 109–10, 112–15, 119, 122, 124, 127, 130, *132,* 136–37, 143, 146, 150, 157, 160, 169, 173, 186, 191–97, 200, 208, 212, 222, 246, 251, 258, 265, 275, 314–15, 319, 320, 322, 324–26, 328–31, 337, 340, 361, 365–68, *369,* 370–72, 375–78, 381, 389, 392, 396, 404, 414, 420, 440–41
Global ecological balance (GEB) 29, 31, 337, 341, 363, 365–67, *369,* 371–72, *373,* 374, 376–78, 439
Godard, Jean-Luc 410, *410,* 430, *430,* 433
Gossip square 272, *273*
Gottmann, Jean 14, 44, 114, 127, 130–31, 139, 147, 259, 281, 412, 419, 422
Government 9–10, 12, 27, 84, 111, 121–22, 126, 155, 157, 161, 168, 174, 178, 188, 192, 196, 198, 200, 202, 206, 218–22, 224, 228, 230, 237, 240–41, 243–44, 252, 254, 256, 280, 295, 318–19, 325, 374
Graduate School of Design (GSD) 10, *75,* 118, 120, 122, 174
Graduate School of Ekistics (GSE) 123, 129
Granger, Lester 149–50, *151,* 319
Great Lakes Megalopolis (GLM) 259, 265, 272, 282, 341, 345, 355, 356, *357*

Greece 7, 9, 28, 38, 43, 46, 56, 64, 69, 73, 76, 79, 81, 84, 89, 96, 101, 111, 115–16, 122, 170–72, 178, 181, 186–89, 201, 219, 246, 279, 280, 285, 289, 295, 318, 336, 465–67
Greenhouse gas (emissions) (GHG) 314, *375,* 376
Grid 56, 143, *145,* 163, 231, 266, 267, 270, 275, 330, 349, 350, 352, *352,* 354, 356, 360, 445, 450
Gropius, Walter 57, 90, 249
Group Form 121–24, 129–30, 136
Habitat 50, 57, 71, 120–21, 137, 139, 215, 338, 376, 467, *477, 479*
Halprin, Lawrence 59, *60*
Harmony 23, 51, 68, 112, 115, 194, 203, 221, 259, 266, 275, 326–28, 342, 367–68, *369,* 374, 378, 385, 427, 466–67, 469–70, *472*
Hart, Robert Lamb 160
Harvard Advisory Group (HAG) 196, 198, 219–20, 224
Health 10, 108, 146, 155, 281, 317, 324, 331, 343, 345, 356, *358,* 366, 380, 388, 392, 454
Heatherwick, Thomas 160–61
Hellenism 7, 13, 46, 64, 68, 86, 468
Herrera, Felipe 153
Highway 26, 56, 151, 191, 208, 211, *211,* 260, 278–79, 289, 298, 307, 324, 327, 417, 427, 442, 445, 458
Hippodamus 33, 82
Historicism 14, 150, 359
Human community 82, 268, *360,* 468, 471–72, 479
Human factor 24, 142, 144, 146–48, 150, 153–54, 156–57, 159, 161–63
Humanism 37, 115, 160, 317, 395
Humanitarianism 17, 20, 26, 157, 440
Human nature 16, 24, 25, 37, 143–44, 146–50, 153, 156–57, 159–60, 163–64
Human Sector (HS) 27, 256, 265, 267–68, *269, 276,* 278
Huws-Nagashima, Catharine 130–31, 134, 137, 139, 412, 419, 421
Huxley, Aldous 32, 473
Hydrology 31, 349, 442, 445, *448,* 450–51, *451,* 463
Iatridis, Dimitris 89, 196
Identity 36, 74, 76, 81, 114, 116–19, 134–36, 147, 152, 157, 217, 220, 222, 251, 342, 408, 411, 426
India 11, 38, 69, 89, 120, *173,* 174, *175,* 186–88, 217, 225, 230, 242
Industrialization 57, 137, 187, 195, 219, 221, 281, 325, 327–28, *373,* 392
Industry 36, 63, 136, 148, 164, 187, 205, 219, 231, 243, 252, 262, 265, 287, 298, 329, 354, 356, *358,* 368, 371–72, *373,* 376, 380, 404, 409, 428, *478*
Information Technology 146
Infrastructure 6, 10, 13, 20, 25–28, 31, 38, 56, 59, *60,* 105, 127, 129, 137, 142–43, 150, 159, 171–72, 179–80, 189, 191–92, 197, 202–3, 205, 208, 212, 217–19, 222–24, 230, 240, 249–50, 252, 258, 263, 275, 330, 344, 349–50, 354, *355,* 356, 361, 365, 370, 374, *375,* 389, 442, 458, 461, *462,* 463
Inter-American Development Bank 153
International Federation of Housing and Planning Congress (IFHP) 131

500

Iraq 28, 38, 43, 69, 186–87, 189, 198, 249–52, 254, 256, 258, 268–70, 272, 278–81, 289, 299, 334
Ishikawa, Hideaki 115–16, 118, 121–22, 136
Islamabad 25, 30, 32, *53, 56,* 56–57, 69–70, 87, 198, 201, 258, 267, 341–42, 345–47, *346–48,* 349, *350–52,* 352, 354–55, 362, 380, 450, *453,* 458, 463, 468, 472, 475, 477, 479, *479,* 481
Isomura, Eiichi 38, 69, 114, 121–23, 129–31, 139, 340, 408–9, 412, 414, *414,* 417, 428, 431–32, 434
Isotype 238, 246
Jacobs, Jane 14, 147
Japan Center for Area Development Research (JCADR) 129–31, 134, 136–37
Jiagge, F. K. A. 153
Kalomoiris, Manilos 73, 80, *81*
Kawazoe, Noboru 119
Kazantzakis, Nikos 73, 76–77, *77,* 79, 81, 87
Keller, Suzanne 154–55
Kennedy, John F. 90, 108
Kennedy, Robert 286–87, 299, 305
Kenyatta, Jomo 205, 214
Kepes, György 156
Khartoum 198, 266
Kikutake, Kiyonori 116, 123
Kon, Wajiro 115–16, 129
Korman Corporation 292, 295, 304
Kwinter, Sanford 385–86
La Sarraz Declaration 399, 406
Latin America 153, 225
Lazaridis, Demetrios 476
Lebanon 25, 178–81, *180–84,* 184–89, 258
Le Corbusier 12, 44, 90–91, *93,* 104, 110, 160, 225, 249, 338–39, *418,* 466, 468, 470, 473, *477–79,* 478–79
Liberalism 194, 200
Llewelyn-Davies, Richard 38, 69, 151, 267, 282, 392
Lourie, Reginald 155, 164
Machines 14, 17, 23, 33, 57, 148, 152, 155, 259, 268, 282, 323, 363, 372, *373,* 384, 390, 402, 403, 450
Maekawa, Kunio 117–19, 122, 126, *127*
Maki, Fumihiko 24, 114, 116–19, 121–24, 129–30, 136–37, 139
Maronitis, Demetrios 476
Marshall Plan 193, 195, 250, 281, 295, 318
Massachusetts Institute of Technology (MIT) 122–24, 212, 193
McLuhan, Marshall 14, 36, 38, 44, 69, 98, 112, 146–48, 164, 319, 320, 340, 370, 389, 395, 399
Mead, Margaret 14, 38, 43, 69, 104, 112–13, 140, 144, 146, 149, *151,* 164, 194, 290, 298, 319, *319,* 340
Media 6, 9, 12–14, 22, 36, 104, 112, 146, 149, 157, 320–21, 370
Medicine 154
Mediterranean Metropolis *327,* 327–30
Megalopolis 36, 51, 64, 114, 127, 130–31, 134–37, *136,* 139, 259, 265, 272, 275, 329, 341, 345, 355–56, *357, 360, 400,* 412, *412,* 419, 421–22, 428, 442
Meier, Richard 130–31, 134

Metabolism (Japanese architectural movement) 114–16, 119, 122–24, 131, 134, 376, 417, 424, 426
Metron 231
Meyerson, Martin 122, 129, 412
Migration 157, 215
Militarism 26, 111, 113, 148, 164, 185, 193, 218–19, 221, 280, 329, 334
Mitchell, Robert 151
Modern Architecture Research Group (MARS) 10, 267
Modular 27, 123, *235,* 237, *239,* 244
Moon landing (Apollo 11) 157
More, Thomas 32, 466, 468, 470–75, 479, 481
Mumford, Lewis 174
Nagashima, Koichi 129–30, 134, 136–37, 139
National Housing Program of Iraq (NHPI) 249, 250–52, 254, 256, 258, 265, 279–80
Nationalism 117, 119, 148, 220
National Technical University of Athens 90, 395, 420
National Urban League 149
Natural Resources 157, 191
Nature 16, 23, 35, 29–32, 37, 46, 50–51, 115, 119, 142, 153, 156, *158,* 160, 162, 172, 191, 226, 238, 254, 268, 275, 313–15, 322, 326, 329, 331, 335, 337–46, 349–50, 352, *353,* 354–56, *355, 358,* 359, *360, 362,* 362–63, *364,* 365–68, *369,* 371–72, *373,* 374–79, *375, 377,* 381, 383–86, *384,* 388–89, 392, 395–96, 398, 402, 405, 419, 427, 439–41, *430, 448,* 450, 454, *454, 460,* 461, 463, 474, 476, 478–79, 481
Nature-based solutions (NBS) 30, 337–38, 349, 374, *375,* 378
Nehru, Jawaharlal 174, *175*
Neighborhood 27, 48, 131, *135,* 147, 256, 260, 268, 270, 272, 275, 278–79, 282, 287, 289–90, 294–99, 304–7, 346, 350, *352,* 354, 359, *360,* 389, *433,* 458, 479
Neoliberalism 16
Neolithic 64
Networks 12–13, 17, 22–25, 31–33, 36, 57–58, 68, 71, 98, 115, 117–18, 121, 143, 146, 153, 156, *158,* 184, 188, 192, 196–97, 202, 205–6, *206,* 208, 212, 250, 258–59, 262, 268, 272–73, *277,* 289–90, 298, 305–6, 313, 315, 318–20, 325, 330, 350, 352, 354, *355, 358,* 359, *360, 362,* 367, 372, 374, *375, 377,* 383, *384,* 386, 389, 399, *400,* 402, 404, 413, 417, 445, 448, *450,* 458, 474, 476
Neurath, Otto 237–38, 246
Neuroarchitecture 162
Neuroscience 143, 162
Nielsen, Waldemar 200, 213–14, *319*
Nietzsche, Friedrich 77, 87
Nkrumah, Kwame 204, 215
Nomadism 147, 252
Nostalgia 86
Nudge theory 161
Nuri Pasha al-Said 249
Olynthus 57, 480
Otaka, Masato 116, 122–24
Ottoman 22, 64, 74, 78, 189
Owen, David 38, 69, 340, 390

501

Pakistan 26–29, 43, 56, 69, 89, *149*, 186–87, 196, 198, 217–24, 226, *227*, 228, *229*, 231, *232*, 237–38, 240–44, 258, 267, 289, 342, 346, 380
Pan-Africanism 202, 205
Panopticon 23, 99
Papanek, Gustav 219
Pask, Gordon 388
Pediatrics 151, 155
Perelman, Chaïm 97, 109
Pergamon 121, 469, *469*
Perović, Miloš 104
Personality disorders 157
Philadelphia 25, 27–28, 155, 258, 278, 287, 289–90, 292–98, 304–6, 363, *400*
Philosophy 16, 22, 24–25, 31, 43, 57, 77, 81–83, 97, 115–17, 120, 142–44, 146, 153, 158, 160, 162, 195, 226, 228, 251, 258, 286, 297, 331, 335, 372, 390, 467, 473
Physiology 155, 157, *358*
Pikionis, Dimitris 73, 76–78, *77*, 80–81, 84–87, 105, 440, 467–68, 481
Piperoglou, John 44, 68–69, 89
Planning (city, town, urban) 6, 7, 9–10, 17, 20, 28–29, 32–33, 43–44, 56, 58–59, 97, 99, 115–16, 120, 126, 143, 155, 172, 250, 258, 279–80, 282, 291, 295–96, 304, 316, 339, 381, 384, 413, 423, 439, 466
Plato 32, 105, 107, 148–50, 158–59, 422, 423, 466, 470, 473–76, 478, 481
Pluralism 328, 388
Popper, Karl 142, 144, 163
Population 9, 27, 32, 57, 84, 108, 143, 147, 157, 169, 197, 208, 211, 220, 222, 241–42, 252–53, 262, 265, 275, 281, 287, 290, 303–4, 306, 330, 334, *358, 360*, 361, 368, 370, 376, 386, *391, 398, 401*, 413–14, 419, 461, 477
Poverty 174, 176, 178, 187, 189, 221, 245, 252, 262, 265, 296, 322, 330, 386
Prehistory 64
Priene *56, 57*, 97, 415, 468, 479–81
Privacy 159
Private space 57, 270, 345, 471
Propinquity 149, 156
Protagoras 81–82
Psychiatry 147, 154, 164
Psychology 12, 16, 22, 24, 99, 112, 134, 143, 146, 149–51, 155–56, 160, 162, 241, 427
Public 73, 78, 87, 94, 103–4, 108, 116, 127, 129, 144, 160, 188, 220–21, 238, 244, 246, 252, 282, 293, 296, 304, 306, *386*
Public housing 280, 287, 295–96
Publicity 17, 92, 98, 104
Public space 57, 137, 259–60, 265, 270, 272, 287, 327, 344, 354, 356, 363, *364*, 431, 465
Racism 27–28, 260, 262, 265, 278, 282, 290, 295–97, 303–4, 306, 328
Reform 110, 146, 148, 161, 192, 222, 224, 241, 244, 246, 345, 393, 441
Region 10, 13, 26–28, 31, 57–58, 114, 117–18, 120, 122–23, 126, 129, 131, 137, 147–48, 153, 173, *175*, 180, 182, 196, 198, 200, 203–5, 212, 226, 231, 240, 250, 252, 254, *255*, 262–63, 265, 268, 272, 275, 279, 282, 296, 325, 340, 346–47, *348*, 355–56, *357, 360*, 361, *362, 369*, 378, 380, 394, 411–12, 417, 442, *444*, 445, *448*, 458, 461
Regionalism 16, 25, 38, 75, 116, 118–19, 122–23, 129, 143, 157, 244, 270, 347
Regional planning 10, 57, 114, 117–18, 120, 122–23, 126, 129, 148, 173, 198, 325, 340, 347, 378
Relativism 146
Religion 171–72, 180, 228, 241, 328, 374
Reynolds Aluminum 303
Rhetoric 14, 17, 20, 22–23, 25–26, 33, 89, 96–97, 102, 105, 107–10, 112–13, 160, 222, 225, 243, 289, 292, 305, 323, 325, 328
Riley, John W. 147
Rockefeller Foundation 91–92, 111, 223, 293
Rossi, Aldo 14
Rowntree, Diana 150–51
Rudolph, Paul 224
Safety 152, 159, 187, 268, 282, 298, 367, 372, 374, 388, 390
Sakellariou, Michael 476
Scale 14, 16, 27, 30, 36, *47*, 50–51, 56–58, 68, 82, 99, 105, 110, 118–20, 123–24, 127, *128*, 129, 134–35, *135*, 143–44, 149–53, 169, 171–72, 191–93, 197, 200, 202–3, 218–19, 237, 250–51, 254, 259–60, 262–63, 266, 268, 270, 272, 275, 278, 282, 287, 296, 297, 299, 303, 305, 315, 320, 327, 329, 340–41, 344–47, 350, *351, 352*, 354–56, *355*, 359, *360*, 361, 366–68, 370–72, 375–78, 383, 389, 392, 396, 402, 409, 419, 428, 440, *453*, 454, 458, 461, 466, 468, 476–77
School of Planning and Research for Regional Development (SPRRD) 10
Scott Brown, Denise 14
Segregation 12, 262, 265, 296, 298, 398, *401*
Sensory experience 58, 115
Sert, Josep Lluís 12, 90, 118, 120–22, 249, 281, 395
Simmel, Georg 152
Skopje 31–32, 130, 411, *411*, 416, *416*, 423–24, *425–26*, 426, 433, 439–42, *443*, 445, *447, 451–52*, 454–55, 458, *460*, 461, *462*, 463
Sociability 94, 149, 225
Society 28, 62, 75–76, 78, 82, 120, 123, 129, 137, *138*, 139, 142, 153, *155*, 157, *158*, 162, 175, 189, 194–95, 220–21, 238, 278, 296, 314–15, 318–19, 324–25, 329, 331, *358*, 359, *360, 362*, 367, 376, *377*, 383, *384*, 385, 388, 403, 408, 414, 417, 470, 474, 476
Socio-ecological systems (SES) 337
Sociology 12, 43, 114–15, 121, 143, 147, 149, 152, 154, 174, 188, 195, 201, 213, 319, 340, 388, 390, 392, *394*, 408
Sofer, Cyril 99, 112
Sophistry 82
Special Program of Action (SPA) 252
Sprawl 97, 263, 272, 275, 283, 327–28, 342, 355, 371
Stalin, Joseph 195
Stangos, Asteris 94, 98, 101–2, 104
Statistics 10–11, 51, 56, 58, 162, 254, *255*, 268, 390, 396, 418

502

Stone, Shepard 92, 111
Style (architectural and urban) 16, 143, 150, 286, 292, 384, 390, 398, 404
Suburbia 28, 151, 260, 275, 287, 289–90, 296–98, *302*
Supreme Command of Allied Powers (SCAP) 117, 121
Survey 27, 116, 131, 170–76, 178–79, 181–82, *184*, 185–88, 189, 203, 218, 225, 228, *232*, 238, 241, 243, 268, 342
Sustainability 6–7, 16, 20, 29–32, 36, 109, 314–15, 321–24, 326, 330–31, 334–35, 337–41, 345, 367, 374–75, *375*, 376–79, *377*, 383–84, 399, 440–41
Tange, Kenzo 14, 24, 114, 117–19, 122–24, *125*, 126–27, 129–31, 134, 139, 340, 409, 411–12, *411–12*, 416–19, 423–24, 426–28, 436
Tavistock Institute 99
Taylor, Frederic Winslow 162, 335
Taylorism 243, 318, 335
Team 10 14, 38
Technology 7, 10, 22, 25, 29, 36, 50, 74, 108, 112, 146–47, 152, 156–57, 163, 175, 187, 193, 196, 198, 212, 218, 220, 259, 314, 317, 326, 329–30, 342, 366–68, 370–71, 375, 376, 390, 392–93, *394*, 395, 399, 402, 417–18, 420, 434, 463
Telecommunications 150
Tema Development Corporation 153
Theater *11*, 14, *15*, 17, *17*, *19–20*, *35*, *44*, 68, 76, 78, 82, 84, *84*, 86–87, 97, 104, 153, 219, 415–16, 472, 479
Therapy 51, 161, 165, 480
Tokyo 24, 111, 114–24, *125*, 126–27, 130, 134, *135–36*, 137, 319, 412, 414, *417*, *423*, 423–24, 428, 435
Tokyo Metropolitan Government (TMG) 121
Tombazis, Alexandros 56, 468, *478–79*, 479, 481
Topography 31, 270, 344, *358*, 442, 445, 463
Townscape 143, 151, 340, 342, 345–46, 367
Toynbee, Arnold 14, *20*, 43, 150–51, 153, 156, 212, 215, 481
Trade 13, 58, 183, 193–95, 211, 329, 368
Tradition 22–23, 27, 32, 73–80, 83, 85–87, 97, 115–19, 121–22, 124, 127, *128*, 134, *135*, 139, 151, 172, 175–76, 183, *183*, 188–89, 194–95, 211, 213, 221, 228, 230–31, 237–38, 256, 267, 270, 278–79, 292, 328, 330, 342, *373*, 403, 431, 450
Transport 25–26, 28, 84, *84*, 98, 127, 129, 131, 150, 172, 191–92, 201, 204–05, *207*, 208, 211–12, 214, 249, 251, 262–63, 266, 272–73, *277*, 279, 281–82, 286, 327, 330, 350, 356, *358*, 365, 368, 370, 376, *394*, 417–18, 423, 428, 466
Travlos, John 476
Triantafyllides, Manolis 73, 85, *85*
Tribal Culture 146
Tugwell, R. G. 147
Typology (architectural and urban) 16, 27, 85, 143, 150, 211, 228, 238, 390, 402, 404, 468
Tyrwhitt, Jaqueline 9–12, 14, 24, 33, 36–37, 44, *45*, 68–69, 89–91, 104, 110, 114, 118–21, *121*, 123–24, *125*, 126–27, *128*, 129–31, 134, *135*, 136–37, 139, 142–44, 151–52, 157, 159, 163, 170, *173*, 173–75, *175–76*, 178, 186–88, 208, 212, 320, 340, 343, 383, 395, 412, 465
United Nations (UN) 10–11, 26, 31, 92, 114, 118, 120–22, 126, 129–30, 137, 173, *173*, 174, *175–76*, 178, 197, 205, 208, 214, 221, 318–19, 324–26, 363, 411, *429*, 441
United Nations Economic Commission for Africa (UNECA) 205, 208
United Nations Educational, Scientific and Cultural Organization (UNESCO) 126, 194, 208
United States Agency for International Development (USAID) 222–23, 225, 242
United States of America 26, 111, 115, 178, 185, 191, 193, 222–23, 244, 258, 280, 285, 287, 290, 305, 422
Universalism 27, 238, 278–79
Urban Detroit Area (UDA) 27, 250, 259, 262–63, 265, 272–73, 275, *277*
Urban ecosystem services (UES) 337–38, 354, 374, 378
Urban environmental quality (UEQ) 340, 342, 345, 354, 366–67
Urban heat island (UHI) 344, 349, *375*, 376
Urbanism 6, 9, 23, 27, 30, 36, 46, 50, 114, 121–22, 126, 129, 131, 136, 139, 144, 147, 279, 305, 318–19, *333*, 337–42, 345, 356, 359, *362*, 367, 371, 374, 378–79, 386, 390, 439, 467
Urbanization 68, 86, 108, 127, 137, 142–43, 203, 212, 251, 256, 258–59, 325, 328, 355, *360*, 365, 368, 370, 376, 389, 392, 419, 422–24, 428, 440–41
Urban sustainability 29–30, 337–38, 341, 374, *375*, 376
Utopia 16, 31–32, 36, 68, 72, 97, 109, 114–18, 120, 124, 127, 139, 142, 152, 186, 189, 367, 378, 466, 468, 470–75, *474–75*, 477–80
Venturi, Robert 14
Vernacular (architecture) 75, 79, 83–85, 87, 143, 176, 202, 272, 278, 317, 330, 338–39, 342, *343*, 345, 375
Ville Radieuse 473, *477–78*, 478, 480
Waddington, Conrad 38, 43, 69, 146, 151, 156, 319, *319*, 340
War 9–10, 23, 26, 31, 57, 62, 73–74, 83–84, 86–87, 102, 105, 111, 115, 117–19, 170–72, 174, 178, 181, 185–89, 193–94, 196, 218–19, 222–23, 246, 250–51, 258, 275, 278, 295–96, 316–18, 325, 338–39, 342, 359, 388, 395, 408, 410, 427, 440
Ward, Barbara 14, 38, 43, 69, 319, 340, 365, 439, 441
Water 163, 169, 180, 272–73, 286, 290, 306, 344, 347, 350, 354, 356, *358*, 365, *369*, 371, *373*, 375–76, 378, 380, 450, 455
Watsuji, Tetsuro 115–17, 119–21, 134, 137, 139
Wellbeing 24, 151, 161–62, 342, 354–55, 372
White flight 262, 265, 275, 296
Wildlife *373*, 392–93
World Design Conference (WoDeCo) 122–23
World Health Organization (WHO) 10, 324
World Human Forum *35*, 36
World Society of Ekistics (WSE) 129–30, 136–37, 408
Wright, Frank Lloyd 249, 289, 338, 473
Yoshizaka, Takamasa 116, 129
Zagorisiou, Marika 79, 82, 189
Zoning 12, 146, *211*, 211–12, 219, 328, 341, 354, 371–72, *373*, 374, 378, 411, 427, 445, 450, 458, 461

**The Delos Symposia
and Doxiadis**

Edited by Mantha Zarmakoupi and Simon Richards
Contributing authors: Tilemachos Andrianopoulos,
Harrison Blackman, Filippo De Dominicis,
Thomas Doxiadis, Farhan Karim, Ahmed Z. Khan,
Dimitris Philippides, Panayiota Pyla, Simon Richards,
Ellen Shoshkes, Ioanna Theocharopoulou, Lefteris
Theodosis, Panayotis Tournikiotis, Kostas Tsiambaos,
Mantha Zarmakoupi, Yannis Zavoleas
Copyediting: Ian McDonald
Proofreading: Jacqueline Harvey, Michael Pilewski
Editorial coordination: Hester van den Bold
Design: Integral Lars Müller / Lars Müller and
Esther Butterworth
Production and typographic editing:
Esther Butterworth
Lithography: Gundula Seraphin,
Bad Münstereifel, Germany
Printing and binding: DZA Druckerei zu Altenburg,
Germany
Paper: 1.13 Munken Lynx, 135 g/m²

© 2025 Lars Müller Publishers and the editors

No part of this book may be used or reproduced
in any form or manner whatsoever without prior written
permission, except in the case of brief quotations
embedded in critical articles and reviews

Lars Müller Publishers
Zurich, Switzerland
www.lars-mueller-publishers.com

ISBN 978-3-03778-762-5

Distributed in North America, Latin America and
the Caribbean by ARTBOOK | D.A.P.
www.artbook.com

Printed in Germany

Co-published with the Evangelos Pistiolis Foundation

Published with the support of the Williams Publication
Fund, Department of the History of Art, University of
Pennsylvania

The research workshops that led to this book were
funded by the Arts and Humanities Research Council,
UK